*The Enlightenment and the Intellectual
Foundations of Modern Culture*

LOUIS DUPRÉ

The Enlightenment and the Intellectual Foundations of Modern Culture

Yale University Press
New Haven &
London

Published with assistance from the foundation established in memory of Philip Hamilton McMillan of the Class of 1894, Yale College.

Set in Sabon type by Keystone Typesetting, Inc.
Printed in the United States of America by Sheridan Books.

Library of Congress Cataloging-in-Publication Data
Dupré, Louis.
The Enlightenment and the intellectual foundations of modern culture /
Louis Dupré.
    p. cm.
Includes bibliographical references and index.
ISBN 0-300-10032-9 (hardcover)
1. Enlightenment. 2. Civilization, Modern. 3. Philosophy and civilization. I. Title.
B802 .D86 2004
190'.9'033 — dc22
2003023865
A catalogue record for this book is available from the British Library.

The paper in this book meets the guidelines for permanence and durability of the Committee on Production Guidelines for Book Longevity of the Council on Library Resources.

10 9 8 7 6 5 4 3 2

To Edith,
after twenty-five years, with gratitude

Contents

Preface

Stunned by the attacks on September 11, 2001, I wondered if there was any purpose in writing about the Enlightenment at a time that so brutally seemed to announce the end of its values and ideals. It later dawned on me that the events of that fatal day might not be unrelated to the subject of my reflections. I do not mean, of course, that Islamic culture is or was "unenlightened." It flourished well before that of the Christian West and for centuries surpassed it. But Islam never had to go through a prolonged period of critically examining the validity of its spiritual vision, as the West did during the eighteenth century. The doubt and anxiety that accompanied the West's reassessment of its past have marked the rest of the modern age. Since then Europe has known its own horrors, causing us to question the adequacy of the Enlightenment's answers as well as the effectiveness of its solutions. But it permanently inured us against one thing: the willingness to accept authority uncritically. The particular merit of the Enlightenment did not consist, as some have claimed, in abolishing moral or religious absolutes. Indeed, the loss of moral absolutes, whether caused by the Enlightenment or not, lies at the root of the inhumanity of the past century. But the need to question has advantageously distinguished our culture from others. Islamic culture has, of course, known its own crises, none more painful and less deserved than the loss of its status in the modern world, yet it was never forced to question its traditional worldview. The

Enlightenment was a Western phenomenon that defined the future of the West. In this book I intend to study its implications.

I owe thanks to many for their assistance with this book. In the first place to Jonathan Brent, editorial director of the Yale University Press, who supported this project from the start, to his assistant, the ever-patient Kate Shepard, and to my uncommonly observant copy editor, Eliza Childs. Cyrus Hamlin, Giuseppe Mazotta, James B. Murphy, Kenneth Schmitz, Edward Stankiewicz, Donald Verene, David Walsh, James Wiseman, and Allen Wood read parts of the text and generously commented on it. To Stefano Penna I owe a particular debt. In addition to the many discussions through which he helped me to refine my ideas, he spent days rescuing the book from an early demise caused by computer problems. Finally, my wife Edith patiently and impatiently suffered with me while I wrote and rewrote one slow chapter after another. Despite urgent work of her own, she prepared the final version of several chapters. To her I dedicate the still imperfect result.

Introduction

This book had its origin in the surprise I experienced many years ago when considering the fundamental change in thinking and valuing that occurred during the period stretching from the second half of the seventeenth century until the end of the eighteenth. Curious to know what the intellectual principles of modern thought were, I made a study of the beginnings of modern culture before turning to the critical epoch that forms the subject of the present book. It soon appeared that no direct causal succession links the humanism of the fifteenth century with the Enlightenment. When Max Weber described modernity as the loss of an unquestioned legitimacy of a divinely instituted order, his definition applies to the Enlightenment and the subsequent centuries, not to the previous period. We ought to avoid the mistake made by Jacob Burckhardt in *The Civilisation of the Renaissance in Italy,* and often repeated in the twentieth century, of interpreting the Renaissance as the first stage of the Enlightenment. It is true, though, that the early period introduced one fundamental characteristic of modern culture, namely, the creative role of the person. Yet that idea did not imply that the mind alone is the source of meaning and value, as Enlightenment thought began to assume. To investigate what is new in the basic concepts of this later period of modernity and to find out how it has affected our own culture has been the purpose of this study.

The Enlightenment enjoys no high regard in our time. Many consider its thinking abstract, its feeling artificial. To its modern critics, the very term evokes form without substance, universality without particularity. They are dismayed by the claim that the Enlightenment, concluding centuries of darkness and superstition, introduced a new age of freedom and progress. The condescending attitude of the "enlightened" toward the rest of our species impresses them as arrogant. Certainly the French philosophes felt little respect for the herd they were so confidently leading to truth. They also tended to exaggerate the significance of their achievements. Baron Grimm, a friend of Diderot who issued a bulletin about cultural life in Paris, cast an ironical eye on the pretenses of his age: "Il me semble que le dix-huitième siècle a surpassé tous les autres dans les éloges qu'il s'est attribué lui-même. . . . Je suis bien éloigné d'imaginer que nous touchons un siècle de la raison."[1]

Rarely did the Enlightenment attain true greatness in the visual arts. Some painters have left us major works. Watteau, Chardin, La Tour, Tiepolo, Reynolds, and Gainesborough immediately come to mind. But the eighteenth century lacked the explosive creativity of the preceding two centuries. This holds true even more for sculpture: we remember most of the works only because of the models they portrayed. The case of literature is more complex. French, English, and German prose attained classic perfection during that period. The works of Hume, Johnson, Fielding, and Gibbon in Britain, of Voltaire, Rousseau, and Fénelon in France, and of Wieland and Lessing in the German lands continue to serve as models of elegant, precise, and powerful expression. But little memorable lyrical poetry appeared between Milton and Wordsworth. Or between Ronsard and Lamartine. Dramas were better performed than ever, particularly in England, which also produced excellent comedies. But few major tragedies were written between Racine and Schiller. Music and architecture enjoyed a glorious season. Yet some of its greatest composers — Handel, Bach, Haydn — still drew their inspiration from the spiritual impetus of an earlier age. Significantly, we refer to eighteenth-century composers as Baroque artists. The splendid architecture of the time also, by large part, continued to build on earlier foundations. In Spain, Bavaria, and Austria, the Baroque style culminated in the eighteenth century, while English and French classicism continued to be inspired by Renaissance principles.

In contrast to the often mediocre quality of its artistic achievements, the Enlightenment displays a veritable passion for ideas. The second half of the seventeenth century and the first one of the eighteenth witnessed the breakthrough of modern science and the establishment of new scientific methods. Newton changed not only our world picture but our very perspective on reality. There is hardly a field in which his influence does not appear. The historical works of Montesquieu, Voltaire, Gibbon, and Herder form the majestic entrance to modern historiography. Equally striking is the sudden emergence of major philosophers: Spinoza, Leibniz, Locke, Berkeley, and Hume. Kant, the most gifted thinker of the period and the one who brought its ideas to a synthesis, largely defined the course of philosophical reflection for the next two centuries. The very contrast between the Enlightenment's stunning accomplishments in history, science, and philosophy and the lesser ones in the fine arts (again, with the exceptions of music and architecture) highlights its intellectual orientation. It was first and foremost a breakthrough in *critical consciousness*. Those who criticize its one-sidedness are unquestionably right. But they ought to remember that they attack the movement with the very weapon forged by the object of their attack: that of critical reflectiveness.

In this book I intend to analyze some of the guiding ideas of the Enlightenment, in particular those that have been instrumental in shaping our own assumptions, attitudes, and values. By tracing them to their origins we may hope to gain some insight into principles we had long taken for granted but have recently come to question. The catastrophic wars fought during the twentieth century, its social upheaval, and the environmental predicaments caused by the very technology responsible for that century's greatest triumphs force us to reexamine its moral foundations. Because of their problematic consequences in our own time, many now reject the assumptions of the Enlightenment. My own assessment will be more favorable and my critique less radical. One severely oversimplifies the nature of eighteenth-century thought in dismissing it as rationalism. The rationalist tendency did indeed exist, but so did others pointing in the opposite direction. One might just as well describe the Enlightenment as an era of sentimentality. In disregarding the variety of these currents we risk projecting our own aspirations and aversions upon a self-made image of the past. To understand our relation to the Enlightenment we must attempt to describe it as it understood itself, even while trying to understand its role in shaping the present.

The starting date of this study, 1648, marked the end of the Thirty Years' War and the beginning of a restructuring of Europe's political powers. The half-century that followed shaped the scientific ideas of the modern age. Thinking became simpler, more rational, and more methodic. Religion and morality continued to be primary concerns, but they became subjected to a critical examination. The year 1789, the end date of this book, witnessed an event that shook the political and cultural foundations of Western Europe. The excesses of the French Revolution introduced a strong reaction against the ideals of the Enlightenment, but it did not bring the movement to an end. On the contrary, the French armies spread its ideas to the more remote parts of Europe. The ideals, however, underwent a mutation.

This book is not intended to be an intellectual history of the Enlightenment. Rather have I attempted to draw an intellectual portrait of a crucial epoch in European history with particular emphasis on the development and interaction of those ideas that most contributed to the formation of our own spiritual identity. This ought to explain why some writers receive more attention than others who were perhaps equally significant yet less representative of the movement or less influential in its effect on the present.

In referring to my sources I have as much as possible quoted from readily available editions. Translations are mine except when explicitly attributed to others.

A number of thinkers have influenced my approach. If I had to mention names, they would be those of Ernst Cassirer, Henry Gouhier, and Hans-Georg Gadamer. They taught me that it is possible to understand how the past shaped the present without being reduced to it.

The Enlightenment and the Intellectual Foundations of Modern Culture

A Definition and a Provisional Justification

In 1783 the writer of the article "Was ist Aufklärung?" (What Is Enlightenment?), published in the *Berlinische Monatschrift,* confessed himself unable to answer the question he had raised.[1] Today it remains as difficult to define the Enlightenment. The uncertainty appears in the conflicting assessments of the movement. The second edition of the *Oxford English Dictionary* describes it as inspired by a "shallow and pretentious intellectualism, unreasonable contempt for tradition and authority." Obviously a definition of this nature is not very helpful for understanding a phenomenon distinct by its complexity. But neither is Kant's famous description of it as "man's release from his self-incurred tutelage"—today mainly used as a butt for attacks on the Enlightenment. Rather than beginning with a definition, I prefer to start my discussion by briefly tracing the movement to its sources. The Enlightenment concluded a search for a new cultural synthesis begun at the end of the Middle Ages when the traditional cosmological, anthropological, and theological one had disintegrated.

European culture rests on a relatively small number of ideas. One of them is the assumption that reality as we observe or experience it does not coincide with the principles that justify it. Plato made this distinction a central thesis of his philosophy: appearances are separate from the ideas that ground and legitimate them. He knew well that the theory would be challenged. Why should *what is* not contain within itself the reason for its being? He himself questioned the theory in the dialogue that ironically bears the name of the great thinker who inspired it — *Parmenides*. Later, his most illustrious disciple so radically criticized Plato's theory of the Ideas that it rarely reappeared in its original form. Yet Aristotle did not question the principle itself. He, no less than Plato, distinguished the reason for a thing's existence from that existence itself. This in fact is why the notion of causality assumed such an importance in his thought. In Enlightenment philosophy that distinction received what may well have been its strongest formulation in the principle of sufficient reason: everything must have a reason why it should be rather than not be. Many consider that the essence of rationalism. But the axiom that the real is rooted in an ideal principle does not imply that the human mind is necessarily capable of justifying it. The latter is a rationalist position that the Greeks never held.

Greek philosophy of the classical age incorporated three areas of reality that modern thought has divided into the separate domains of cosmology, anthropology, and theology. Gods and humans were included in an all-comprehensive nature, the *physis* of the Presocratics, the *cosmos* of Plato and Aristotle. Both gods and cosmos had always existed. Hence, the former did not justify the latter. Neither did Plato's Demiurge explain the existence of the world. The myth of the *Timaeus,* according to which some semidivine being composed the cosmos, does indeed attempt to justify the nature of reality, not, however, through its origin, but through an analysis of its metaphysical components. Aristotle might have called this analysis a search for the formal cause of nature. The Semitic teaching that a God created the world justified the world's existence through a transcendent origin. The Creator of the biblical story belongs to a different realm of reality than creation itself.

Despite this opposition between the Greek and the Hebrew-Christian interpretations, Christians started using Platonic concepts for expressing the intimate union between Creator and creature. In and through the human person all creation participated in the divine realm. The doctrine of the Incarnation, according to which God had become part of the world, seemed to facilitate the union. In fact, a profound opposition separated the two views. In the Greek synthesis, an immanent necessity ruled the cosmos. In the Jewish and Christian traditions, a free act of God stood at the origin of all other reality. Inevitably, the classical-Christian synthesis ran into major difficulties. As nominalist theologians began to attribute the origin of all things to the inscrutable will of God, they abrogated the link of intelligibility that connected the source of reality with its created effect. As a result, by the beginning of the modern age reality had ceased to be intrinsically intelligible and God no longer provided the rational justification of the world. Henceforth meaning was no longer embedded in the nature of things: it had to be imposed by the human mind.

The Second Wave of Modernity

It has been written that modernity has reached us in waves. The first wave arrived in the fifteenth century, as the effect of two causes: the collapse of the intellectual synthesis of ancient and Christian thought and the rise of a new humanism. When Descartes, who died in 1650, succeeded in overcoming the skepticism that had resulted from the nominalist crisis by transferring the source of intelligibility to the mind, he brought the first stage of modernity to a close. In establishing self-consciousness as the one point of absolute certainty from which all other certainties could be deduced, he initiated a new stage in philosophical thought. Its validity seemed confirmed by the success of the mathematical method in the scientific revolution of the seventeenth century. The new trust in the power of human reason was to inspire the culture of the Enlightenment, the second wave of modernity. Still Descartes's restoration of the authority of reason remained incomplete. A lingering nominalism surrounded his notion of truth. (It is by divine decree, he had argued, that mathematical conclusions are true!)

In fact, all subsequent rationalism continued to bear unmistakable traces of nominalist dualism in the way it separated the universal from the particular. The synthesis of the universal and the particular, established by ancient philosophy and surviving until the end of the Middle Ages, had come under severe strain in nominalist philosophy. That strain only increased in rationalist thought. It may seem far-fetched to link modern rationalism to a medieval position with which it had so unambiguously broken. Did the rationalist concept of reason not imply a rejection of nominalist particularism and a return to classical sources? In fact, the rationalist universal differed substantially from the ancient one. For Aristotle as well as for Plato, things owed their identity to a universal form that *included* all particular determinations. The Enlightenment concept of the universal, to the contrary, was a rational a priori void of any particular content, a category of thought imposed upon the real, rather than expressive of it. Its formalist character shows a surprising similarity with the universal names that, in nominalist philosophy, the mind imposes upon reality in order to gain purchase on a chaotic multiplicity.

To be sure, post-Cartesian thought, in which the mind alone establishes truth, differs from nominalist theology in which the will of God does so. But that distinction does not weaken a fundamental relation between the two. Social factors also presented a powerful incentive for stressing the primacy of universal concepts and values over particular differences. Regionalism and sectarianism had turned Europe into a thirty-year bloodbath. The restoration of peace in 1648 required that the destructive forces of political and religious particularism be neutralized. To the "enlightened," the differences that had caused the strife were no more than superstitious quibbles or nationalist prejudices. Did the entire cosmos not obey a single law of reason? Did humans, however different from each other, not share a common nature? Destined to live under the rule of reason, they would never attain this goal, according to Voltaire and Gibbon, unless religious particularism was abolished altogether. The Christian religion that had so bitterly divided Europe had to be subordinated to the rule of universal reason.

The Enlightenment's confidence in the powers of reason, its often-naive optimism, as well as its contempt for tradition were too one-sided to remain unchallenged. The excesses of the French Revolution and the rationalist principles that supported it caused a return of the authority of tradition and a revival of much that rationalism had suppressed. The period that followed the revolution introduced a third wave of modernity. It was at first mostly a reactionary movement, yet in time it developed a new, more comprehensive humanism that reincorporated many of the positions established by the Enlightenment while integrating them within a more complex idea of personhood. In Great Britain and in the German lands the transition was gradual: romantic trends had existed all through the Enlightenment.

I assume that the Enlightenment was indeed a distinct epoch in modern culture. Yet this assumption does not entail that there was no continuity in the flow of modern thought nor that it was a homogeneous movement. The Enlightenment remained a project; it never became a full achievement. It continued to question the past and to anticipate the future, but various groups and individuals held different views concerning past and future. It has become increasingly common to exclude traditionalist thinkers such as Vico, Malebranche, Burke, and Herder from the Enlightenment as if they belonged to what Isaiah Berlin has called the Counter-Enlightenment. Yet these writers were not reactionaries. They held modern, though different views concerning their epoch's relation to past and future, and they may have exercised a deeper influence upon future thought than radical critics like Voltaire or Condorcet did. To be sure, in many ways they disagreed with their more radical contemporaries. But those contemporaries in turn found it necessary to respond to their challenges. This dynamic exchange, rather than the static rationalism with which is often identified, characterizes the Enlightenment. It was essentially a dialectical movement.

Finally, conditions and attitudes differed enormously from one area to another. In Western Europe the Enlightenment was mainly a movement of urban intellectuals; in the American colonies, of landed gentry.[2] Nowhere are these differences more visible than in the field of religion. While in France the battle against "superstition" was reaching its pitch, in Bavaria and Austria the Counter-Reformation and Baroque still flourished. French philosophes mostly rejected Christianity; German thinkers consistently sought a compromise with it. In Britain rationalists and anti-rationalists appear to have lived rather peacefully, though often incommunicatively, side by side.

I have restricted my investigation in this book to the *ideas* of the Enlightenment, leaving their economic, social, and political applications to social historians. The battles over the identity, direction, past, and future of a culture are, Husserl claimed, fought by "men of ideas" — philosophers, scientists, theologians, and intellectual historians. Of course, ideas are never born in a vacuum. In an earlier study (*Marx's Social Critique of Culture*) I attempted to show that they originate in, and remain intimately linked to, the immediate practical concerns of society. Yet the influence moves in both directions. For ideas in turn change the social concerns to which they owe their origin. As one distinguished intellectual historian put it: "Ideas powerfully act upon, often decisively shape, the very culture from which they have emerged."[3] My focus here resembles in this respect the eighteenth century's own. Still, a reflection on the ideas of an epoch raises a philosophical problem. Ideas possess by their very nature a timeless quality. We assume that they will last forever. Yet they are conceived in, and form an integral part of, a particular historical conjunction. How can what is essentially transient and historically conditioned have a permanent significance? All thought, including all philosophy, originates in a particular place at a particular time and reflects the concerns of that time. Nonetheless, philosophers, while expressing those concerns, move beyond these limitations and raise them to a universal level.

In an insightful passage R. G. Collingwood describes the dialectical relation between the historical and the eternal roles of ideas. "In part, the problems of philosophy are unchanging; in part they vary from age to age, according to the special characteristics of human life and thought at the time; and in the best philosophers of every age these two parts are so interwoven that the permanent problems appear *sub specie saeculi,* and the special problems of the age *sub specie aeternitatis.* Whenever human thought has been dominated by some special interest, the most fruitful philosophy of the age has reflected that domination; not passively, by mere submission to its influence, but actively, by making a special attempt to understand it and placing it in the focus of philosophical inquiry."[4] We inevitably think and judge with the categories, schemes, and metaphors of our own time, however critical of them we may be. At the same time we believe that ideas are bound to be permanent.

This confronts us with the question: How can ideas conceived for coping with the problems of one time remain meaningful at a later epoch? If indeed a rigid line divides the necessary and eternal from the historically contingent, as rationalist philosophers assumed, then the particular events, achievements, and ideas of an earlier generation hold little meaning for a later one. But the meaning of an epoch lies not only and not even primarily in the "universal" ideas it produces. The significance of a culture exceeds that of the "eternal" ideas we may extract from it. A philosophical reflection on the past differs in this respect from the way mathematics, logic, or the positive sciences reach their conclusions. Past thinkers showed little concern about the question of how their ideas originated. But a reflection on the meaning of a particular age requires more than lifting certain ideas out of the cultural complex in which they were conceived. Each culture possesses an ideal identity within which these ideas have their place and, as Ernst Cassirer pointed out, the task of the philosophy of culture consists in seeking to understand how the elements that compose it form a system, an organic whole.[5] Cultures, like living beings, possess a unity of their own. This unity enables successive generations to build up a collective identity.[6] Over a period of time the various symbolic processes of science, art, religion, and language coalesce into a comprehensive unity.

Premodern metaphysics had neither a need nor a place for a philosophy of culture. The epochs of history may yield lasting results, but their coming or going belonged to a realm of historical contingency that fell outside a reflection on true reality. In modern philosophy, however, the human subject plays a central part in the constitution of meaning. The fact that this subject exists and thinks in time thereby assumes a philosophical significance. Nor is this significance restricted to the individual consciousness. A philosophical reflection on the temporal nature of the subject must take what Ricoeur calls "the long detour around the *selves'* objective achievements in history" and focus on the symbols human consciousness has left us in its various cultural achievements. Only through history do we acquire a true knowledge of ourselves. "What would we know of love and hate, of moral feelings and in general of all that we call *self,* if they had not been brought to language and articulated by literature?"[7]

The primary function of culture is to provide a society with the norms, values, and means needed for coping with the conditions of its existence. Through their various engagements with nature, humans subdue nature's otherness. The domestication of nature begins when humans start naming things. Yet a culture also aims at a spiritual "surplus" that drives its members beyond the satisfaction of immediate, physical needs. In Georg Simmel's words: "Man, unlike the animals, does not allow himself simply to be absorbed by the naturally given order of the world. Instead he tears himself loose from it. Somehow beneath and above [the accomplishment of ordinary tasks and the pursuit of material interests] there stands the demand that through all of these tasks and pursuit of material interests a transcendent promise should be fulfilled."[8] Culture raises the phenomenally transient to ideal permanence and so establishes a symbolic chain in which each historical period acquires an ideal, lasting significance.[9] Levinas captured this potential of cultural symbols to convey an ideal meaning to the temporal in a lapidary sentence: "La culture c'est le sens venant à l'être." If Being becomes disclosed in time, then the passage of time itself is more than a subjective quality of consciousness: it possesses an ontological significance. This position runs counter to Parmenides' thesis, today publicly abandoned but often still tacitly accepted, that Being *is* and becoming *is not*. It responds affirmatively to the question Heidegger raised at the end of *Being and Time:* "Is there a way which leads from primordial time to the meaning of Being?"[10]

A Provisional Profile

Two qualities are commonly considered characteristic of Enlightenment thought: rationalism and emancipationism. The dual meaning of the term "rationalism" has led to misunderstandings. It refers to a philosophical doctrine that insists on the primacy of a priori concepts in the process of knowledge. As such it is opposed to empiricism according to which the origin of our ideas lies in experience. Historically the former was embodied in the theories of Descartes, Spinoza, Leibniz, and Wolff. Yet those who refer to the Enlightenment as a "rationalist" period usually understand this to include philosophical empiricists as well as rationalists. This use of the term assumes that the human mind is the sole source of truth and hence must reject faith as a possible source of truth. Descartes who is often regarded as the father of the rationalist method in philosophy never subscribed to this second, ideological rationalism. For him, at the ground of reality as well as of truth lies a transcendent cause. Nonetheless, he created the conditions for an ideological rationalism when he transferred the question of truth from its traditional ontological basis (according to which truth resides primarily in the nature of the real) to an epistemic one whereby it becomes the result of a method of thinking.

We all know Kant's description of the Enlightenment as an emancipation of mankind through an unconditional acceptance of the authority of reason.

"Enlightenment is man's release from his self-incurred tutelage. Tutelage is man's inability to make use of his understanding without direction from another. . . . *Sapere aude!* 'Have courage to use your own reason!' That is the motto of enlightenment."[11] Kant here expresses his unambiguous opposition to any unexamined authority. Further in the text he more specifically addresses the conditions needed for educating people toward thinking for themselves. This, he claims, requires "the freedom to make *public use* of one's freedom in every respect" (*Freiheit von seiner Vernunft . . . öffentlichen Gebrauch zu machen*). Concretely this means for the "learned" the right to educate the masses through an uncensored press. The ideal of a full human emancipation through uncensored knowledge had already supported the program of the editors of the *Encyclopédie*. They regarded themselves in the first place as educators. Diderot's description, however self-serving, expressed a keen awareness of the social role of the intellectual: "The magistrate deals out justice; the *philosophe* teaches the magistrate what is just and unjust. The soldier defends his country; the *philosophe* teaches the soldier what his fatherland is. The priest recommends to his people the love and respect of the gods; the *philosophe* teaches the priest what the gods are."[12]

Kant's educational project appears legitimate and, by today's standards, uncontroversial. Yet his definition of enlightenment as the "release from a self-imposed tutelage" contains more than the need to think for oneself, which all educated people do and have always done. It has a polemical edge: many deprive themselves of that right by their willingness to accept uncritically the opinions of political and religious authorities. Kant condemns such a submissive attitude as immature (*Unmündigkeit*) and morally irresponsible. Still one wonders: Could anyone survive without accepting a number of unexamined ideas on the authority of others? Or, for that matter, what gives a decisive authority to the one whom the public considers a *Gelehrter*, a learned person?[13]

In many respects Moses Mendelssohn's earlier, more modest contribution to the German debate on the nature of the Enlightenment proves more helpful than Kant's clarion call. In a few pages Mendelssohn attempted to clarify the meaning of the terms that, by the middle of the eighteenth century, had begun to circulate. He distinguishes *Aufklärung* from *Kultur* and *Bildung*. *Bildung* (in this context: "education") refers to people's response to their vocation as human beings, *Kultur* to the practical agenda for reaching this goal, and *Aufklärung* to the more theoretical program — science and philosophy. Ideally, Bildung includes the other two terms and largely defines their meaning. Language constitutes the link among them. "A language attains enlightenment through the sciences and attains culture through social intercourse, poetry, and eloquence."[14] The German Enlightenment with Lessing, Mendelssohn, and Kant, was more self-consciously reflective than either the French or the British. The French Enlightenment may well have been more influential, both because of the impact of its writings (especially the *Encyclopédie*) in a language common to educated Europeans and because of its radical conclusions. But its simplified concepts and radical break with tradition made it also the more controversial one. In this respect it differed not only from the German but also from the English Enlightenment that proceeded at a gradual pace, without causing an abrupt break with the past.

It should be observed that, beside the diversity of expressions of the Enlightenment in different regions, there was also a considerable difference in the degree to which its principles were accepted. Even those who regarded the mind as constitutive of meaning did not necessarily consider its contribution sufficient. Philosophers like Malebranche, Berkeley, and Leibniz grounded the mind's constituting activity upon a transcendent basis — as Descartes himself had done. For all of them, God remained the ultimate source of truth. Nor were rationalists always consistent. A blind belief in progress often conflicted with their thesis of the unchangeable laws of nature. The inconsistency was particularly striking among such materialists as d'Holbach and La Mettrie. Also, men and women of the Enlightenment did not live more in accordance with the rules of morality and reason than their ancestors. One needs only to remember Saint-Simon's reports on life at the French Court, Rousseau's abandonment of his children, Casanova's memoirs of his philandering, and de Sade's account of his sexual gymnastics. People's everyday lives are rarely ruled by reason, despite their frequent appeals to it. Far less than their predecessors in the seventeenth century did men and women of the Enlightenment period submit their passions, feelings, and emotions to the control of reason. The Enlightenment was not so much an age of reason as an age of self-consciousness. People became more reflective about their feelings, their social positions, their rights and duties, the state of religion, and all that touched them near or far. They also became more critical than any previous generation, and this self-consciously critical mentality induced them to question tradition.

The battle against unexamined tradition has continued ever since Kant's declaration of war against it. A social-economic variant of it appeared in Marx's critique of ideologies. The term "ideology" originated in the eighteenth century, and its meaning initially pointed in an opposite direction. When the French aristocrat Destutt de Tracy first used the word in a paper read at the Institut National des Sciences et des Arts, *idéologie* referred to scientific rather than metaphysical knowledge of human nature. Later he expanded the concept, using it against any kind of social prejudice.[15] Soon the critique turned against ideology itself. Napoleon felt that those social theorists whom he contemptuously called "les idéologues" had been responsible for the French Revolution. With Marx the term came to stand for ideas uncritically accepted by most members of a society, even though they merely reflect the interests of the ruling classes. Ideologies serve to confirm the prejudices and interests of those classes. Later commentators qualified Marx's attack on ideologies. Thus Louis Althusser argued that they consist mainly of the unproven assumptions that form an indispensable part of every social structure, not necessarily one that supports the interests of one class. All groups need to hold on to a number of unproven ideas, myths, or representations to preserve their identity. The task of the social critique consists not in destroying those assumptions but in rendering them conscious.[16]

In our own time the controversy about the Enlightenment's attack on prejudices has resurfaced. In his great work on hermeneutics, *Truth and Method,* H. G. Gadamer argued against the Enlightenment's critique of prejudice. He may appear to repeat Edmund Burke's defense of political prejudice: "Instead of casting away all our old prejudices, we cherish them to a considerable degree, and, to take more shame upon ourselves, we cherish them because they are prejudices."[17] Burke assumed that a healthy community, like any normal organism, needs no external interference to overcome its problems. It is capable of correcting itself. Criticism, Gadamer argues, must be guided by a return to the roots of one's tradition rather than by an alleged rule of absolute "rationality." The rationalist critique of the Enlightenment failed to recognize the unproven assumptions on which it rested.

The limitation of the human mind excludes the possibility that it should ever be free of prejudices. Indeed, prejudices constitute an essential part of human reasoning. The Enlightenment's fight against them stemmed itself from a prejudice and followed the Cartesian methodical rule that no position ought to be considered intellectually "justified" before it was proven. Of course, the mind must remain critically conscious of its unproven assumptions and free itself from demonstrably false prejudices. But the rule that traditional authority must in all instances be submitted to the critique of reason is impossible to maintain and hence unjustified. According to Gadamer, the ongoing dialogue among the members of a society should suffice for eradicating those assumptions that would harm a society's rational development.[18] Others have questioned whether a critique based upon the very principles of the tradition it criticizes can ever be effective. On that ground Jürgen Habermas has defended the critical principles of the Enlightenment. If the movement failed, he maintains, it was not because of them, but because they were abandoned before having had the time to prove their effectiveness. I shall consider his argument in the next section.

Ever since Kant described the Enlightenment as an intellectual and political emancipation, we have come to consider freedom the dominant idea of the age. Of course, the idea of freedom, no less than that of reason, had long been a primary concept in Western thought. But with Kant it acquired a more intellectual content. He regarded no act as truly free unless it was based on reason and promoted the rule of reason. Good and evil depend on the law of reason: they are constituted in and through that law. Moreover, freedom came to be viewed primarily as an emancipation of the *individual*. The emphasis upon individual freedom had been implied in the modern theory of the subject, which assumed that the source of value is the human subject itself.

The anthropocentric orientation of Enlightenment culture also affected aesthetic theories. Since the early Renaissance, Western artists had continued to pay homage to the classical ideal of form. Painters had traditionally interpreted it as consisting in simplicity of composition, harmony of color, and clarity of design. What distinguished the eighteenth century "classicist" style was the rigorously rational, at times geometrical way in which these qualities came to be understood. Even Jacques Louis David, the great classicist painter, has been called "puritanically rational."[19] Compared with the dynamic style of the Baroque, much art of the Enlightenment era impresses us today as static and cold. Artists were torn between two conflicting tendencies. On the one hand, they favored a form *idealized* in accordance with rational norms of simplicity, clarity, and harmony. On the other hand, a rational concern for literal truth required that reality be painted *as it is,* however far removed from that formal ideal. Thus the representation of ordinary life and the expression of passions and emotions, foreign to classical art, entered the art of the Enlightenment.

At the same time and due to the same subjective source that had affected the notion of freedom, aesthetics was developing a far more radical theory, which did not have its full impact upon the creation of works of art until the next century. According to this theory, art, rather than imitating or idealizing a given form, had to be in the first place expressive. The new idea entered gradually and not without a major struggle, as we shall see. Artists and even the more progressive theorists continued to repeat the adage that art had to imitate nature. Yet, eventually "imitation" came to be understood in a manner that had little to do with a realistic or idealized representation of nature, but everything to do with nature as a symbol of the artist's inner self. This interpretation differs substantially from that of ancient and even early modern aesthetics. Whereas both had placed the ideal beyond the mind, advanced Enlightenment aesthetics located it *within* the mind. The expressive theory did not reach full maturity until the era of Romanticism. In this instance also,

Romanticism rather than being a mere reversal of the principles of the Enlightenment fully developed their implications.

The Crisis of the Enlightenment

None of the changes described in the preceding profile warrant speaking of the Enlightenment as a cultural crisis. Taken singularly the shifts were rarely abrupt or disruptive, but together they fundamentally altered the direction of Western culture and some major thinkers have regarded this change as a crisis. In a lecture delivered in Prague, entitled "The Crisis of the European People" (1935), Edmund Husserl argued that modern rationalism had moved away from the Greek idea of reason and deviated from Europe's spiritual destiny. According to the founder of phenomenological philosophy, the rationalism of the Enlightenment transformed the Greek concept of reason that had ruled European thought since its beginning. A narrowly objectist idea of reason had deflected Western culture from its original development "in the direction of an ideal image of life and of being, moving toward an eternal pole."[20] Husserl's diagnosis is all the more remarkable in that his own philosophical goal had been to reform philosophy into a "rigorous science."[21] Now he dismissed the modern objectivism implied in that project as a betrayal of the principle of rationality to which it continued to appeal.

While Husserl referred to an intellectual crisis caused by the slide into objectivism, Hegel in a well-known passage of the *Phenomenology of Spirit* had described the Enlightenment as a general cultural crisis. Significantly, in doing so he attributed to a particular historical period the full responsibility for a change in the ideal development of mind. All through the *Phenomenology* he inserts cryptic allusions to historical figures and events, such as ancient skepticism, the coming of Christ, monastic life, the French Revolution, and Napoleon. The Enlightenment Hegel mentions by name, as if it were a historical interruption in an ideal process. That particular event raised consciousness to the universality of reason, enabling it to view reality as expressive of itself.[22]

Not before reality appears as the objective expression of mind, does civilization become *culture* — a Western concept with a uniquely spiritual connotation. Those intent on attaining culture must abandon their natural, self-centered attitude and assume a universal, spiritual one. This change requires effort and denial. Hegel therefore referred to culture as an *alienation* from one's natural self. Beyond this subjective alienation required by the process of education, there is also an objective one inherent in the nature of culture itself. It directly corresponds to what others have called the "crisis" of the Enlightenment. Having intended to build a culture expressive of, and appropriate to, reason, the builders of the Enlightenment had to confront the melancholy fact that culture leads a life of its own, escapes control, and fails to correspond to their intentions. This estrangement has caused a rupture within the modern consciousness. Two tendencies emerge. One uninhibitedly criticizes any content in which the mind does not fully recognize itself; the other, solicitous to avoid reducing mental life to a mere critique without content, projects its essential content into an otherworldly realm where it will be safe from the assaults of critical insight. Hegel refers to this latter attitude as *faith*. Enlightenment for him consists neither in the critical rationalism of pure insight nor in the conservative one of faith, but in a constant struggle between the two.

This esoteric account of the Enlightenment contains two important ideas. One, the very notion of culture belongs to a particular stage of Western consciousness — one that, as Freud was later to confirm in *Civilization* [a more accurate translation would be *Culture*] *and Its Discontents,* imposes severe demands upon the natural consciousness and may degenerate into antinatural perversions. The second idea directly bears upon the concept of the Enlightenment as a cultural crisis. The view of culture as the mind's "own" expression inevitably leads to a split (*entfremdet* [alienated]) consciousness. On the one hand, the mind knows culture to be an expression of itself. On the other hand, once it is objectively established, it begins to lead a life of its own with many restrictions and limitations that make it increasingly difficult for people to recognize it as a self-expression. That sense of alienation from the traditional culture reached a critical point during the Enlightenment.

In addition, Hegel first grasped a crucial feature of the Enlightenment that had been ignored by his predecessors and was often neglected by his followers, namely, that it was essentially a *dialectical* movement. At no point did that movement ever develop into a simple rationalism or an unambiguous anti-rationalism. Without the simultaneous presence of, and the productive struggle between the two currents, it remains unintelligible how the Enlightenment could ever have resulted in Romanticism. In all chapters of this book, therefore, I have given attention to anti-rationalist thinkers (often misnamed "Counter-Enlightenment" thinkers), such as Herder, Shaftesbury, Rousseau, and Fénelon.

This dialectical principle also explains the considerable part religion, the main target of the critique, occupies in this work. Both the critique and the resistance to it have been responsible for the way the Enlightenment has reached us. Even such spiritual movements as Quietism and Pietism that never came to grips with the rationalist critique but instead took refuge in a secluded interiority at a safe distance from the intellectual currents of the time, played a significant role within the culture of the Enlightenment. They initiated a search for interiority that corresponded to the Enlightenment's drive toward self-understanding. For that reason, I have included a chapter on those spiritual movements at the end of this book. The effect of the Enlightenment in the succeeding periods can be understood only if both currents, the rationalist and the anti-rationalist, combine their influence.

Still this dialectical quality of the Enlightenment should not be interpreted as if it were already a synthesis *in nucleo*. The Enlightenment remains a period of tension, opposition, and strife. The two currents never came to peace with one another. They were united only in combat. This appears most clearly in the area of religion, perhaps the only one to which the term "crisis" properly applies. In fact, Paul Hazard in his classic *La crise de la conscience européenne* (published the same year [1935] as Husserl's lecture) held the abandonment of the transcendent source of meaning responsible for a crisis in the European consciousness.[23] Two contemporary scholars of the Enlightenment, Peter Gay (in *The Enlightenment*) and Michael Buckley (in *At the Origins of Modern Atheism*) have in different ways confirmed the dramatic effect of this shift.[24] I also believe that the most drastic transformation of the Enlightenment took place in the religious consciousness. Still, this change occurred over an extensive period of time. People in Scotland, the Low Countries, Rhineland, Austria, Italy, or Spain (to mention only Western Europe) did not think of themselves or their religion as being "in crisis." Even in France whose intellectuals spearheaded the secular revolution, the great majority of the population continued to live unaware of the disturbing questions that had been raised about their traditional beliefs and practices. Not until a long-smoldering resentment against ecclesiastical privileges and against a higher clergy closely linked to an oppressive political regime burst into revolutionary flames can one speak of a religious "crisis" among the general population. In Britain religious decline may have been even more gradual. The constant denominational changes, the unpopular Puritan revolution, and after the Restoration, the constant tensions between the established Church and the nonconformists slowly eroded faith and spread skepticism.

Christianity, for centuries the core of European culture, had left a tradition of values on which even secular intellectuals remained dependent long after having abandoned their faith. Most professed a belief in God even while adhering to a philosophy that emptied the idea of God of its traditional content. They continued to regard the idea as indispensable for morality, though morality had largely ceased to rely on it. Voltaire and Rousseau displayed an uncommon proselytic zeal for their deist faith and an aggressive hostility toward any kind of atheism. But this pragmatic use of the idea of God as foundational principle of the cosmos and as the basis of ethics had too little coherence to resist further deconstruction. Beginning with Hume and Diderot the suspicion grew that neither the origin and preservation of the cosmos nor the sanctioning of morality might require a personal God.

No part of Enlightenment thought has deservedly met with more criticism than the absence of genuine *otherness,* related to a lack of internal differentiation within the rationalist universals. For ancient and for most medieval thinkers, reason had involved a dialectical relation between the universal and the particular. In his later dialogues Plato became intensely aware of the complexity of this relation. In deducing the primary categories of thought he considered it of primary importance that the universal should contain the particular *within* itself. Hence to prevent the concept of *Being,* the most universal of all, from excluding particularization—as had occurred in Parmenides' philosophy—he distinguished in it the categories of *motion* and *rest.* Next, he protected them from collapsing into one another and into *Being* by adding *otherness* and *sameness* (the principle of identity) (*Sophist,* 254D–255E). Identity comes from the universal form, yet it cannot exist without being related to an *other.* Hence otherness, though opposed to identity, is nonetheless intrinsically linked to it.[25] It is by its own intrinsic momentum, then, that the universal moves toward particularization, not by being "applied" to particular instances. Universals convert particular perceptions into ideal structures. Yet if these structures be conceived as independent of the concrete particularity in which they originated, they become permanently removed from the real. Often rationalists treated universals as categories of the mind that remain on the ideal level of mathematics, paralleling the real without ever meeting it.

Spinoza understood the inappropriateness of such a procedure. He considered philosophical definition adequate only if it included not merely the universal idea of an object but also the conditions of its particular existence. So did Leibniz. Most thinkers of the Enlightenment appear to have conceived of universals as patterns of meaning either abstracted from (in empiricist philosophy) or imposed upon reality (in rationalist thought). This accounts for the neat, homogeneous picture they drew of a reality undisturbed by the confusing, disorderly array of the concrete. Plato had shown how a recognition of otherness will move knowledge beyond the static identity of pure universals to the particularity of concrete existence.

The preceding reflections may seem exceedingly speculative until one realizes the consequences the imposition of abstract universals had upon practical life. We know the excesses to which the rift between the universal and the particular led during and after the French Revolution. Even the idea of a universal humanity, unless it allows for a diversity of traditions, inevitably results in political repression. I hope to show the presence and influence of those abstractions in philosophical texts, practical attitudes, literary works, and artistic criticism.

I must postpone a critical assessment of Enlightenment culture to the conclusion of this book, but not without at least raising the fundamental question which so much preoccupies us today: Is the Enlightenment project still valid? Habermas, in his *Philosophical Discourse of Modernity,* claims that its movement toward human emancipation was diverted from its critical course. New oppressive modes of thought, pseudo-religions he calls them, gradually reoccupied the place from which the Enlightenment had evicted the old religion. Thus he turns Hegel's critique of the Enlightenment against Hegel's own theory of the Absolute Spirit. This all-including pseudo-religious category allowed no outside criticism because there was no "outside." In its frozen system of reality the call to emancipation was lost altogether. Habermas therefrom concludes that the valid program of the Enlightenment had been prematurely abandoned.

In contrast to this conclusion, I believe that the problems of the Enlightenment are due not to a subsequent deviation from the original plan, but rather to an inadequate conception of that plan, which later thinkers attempted to remedy. The principle of rationality that lies at the core of the Enlightenment project was undoubtedly legitimate. Its origin goes back to the Greek beginnings of Western thought. The Enlightenment, much to its credit, attempted to restore that principle to its full force. Yet by making reason an exclusive construction of the mind, it fundamentally transformed its nature. The Greeks had conceived of reason as an ordering principle inherent in reality. The mind possesses the unique ability to understand its inner structure and consciously to pursue its immanent designs. Modern thinkers, however, reversed the relation and submitted all reality to the structures of the mind. They imposed the rules of the one science that the mind could indeed claim full authorship of and which depended on no external content, namely, mathematics. The mind thereby acquired an unprecedented control over nature, yet it ceased to be an integral part of it.

The transformation did not occur all at once. The culture of the Renaissance had fully asserted the mind's creative role in the constitution of meaning, yet the mind itself had remained part of a single, hierarchical order of reality that depended upon a transcendent source of power. We find a remnant of this dual creativity in Descartes's epistemology, where the mind alone constitutes meaning yet truth ultimately depends upon the will of God. The Enlightenment drew far more extensive conclusions from the modern premises. Its thinkers detached the subjective principle from the given order. At first this was a purely methodical issue: for all we know, meaning originates in the subject. Of other sources we remain scientifically ignorant and hence they ought not be introduced into the process of knowledge. Later some denied the very existence of an order that apparently contributes nothing to our knowledge of the world. The Frankfurt philosopher Max Horkheimer considered the disconnection of the link with a transcendent source a crucial moment in the new conception of reason: "The divorce of reason from religion marked a further step in the weakening of its objective aspect and a higher degree of formalization, as became manifest during the period of the Enlightenment. The neutralization of religion . . . contradicted its total claim that it incorporates objective truth, and emasculated it."[26] What first was neutralized ended up being discarded from the concept of reason.

Two consequences followed from the transformation of reason. One, the subject, now sole source of meaning, lost all objective content of its own and became a mere instrument for endowing an equally empty nature with a rational structure. Two, since reality thereby lost the inherent intelligibility it had possessed for the ancients and the Schoolmen, the nature of *theoria* fundamentally changed. Thinking ceased to consist of perceiving the nature of the real. It came to consist of forcing reality to answer the subject's question or, as Kant put it in his famous comparison, of compelling a witness to respond to the judge's inquiry. Contemplation, for the Greeks the highest end of life, became an instrument in the hands of, and for the benefit of, an all-powerful subject. This explains the utilitarian streak of the Enlightenment. Reason ceases to be an ultimate good. Henceforth it functions in a system where everything has become both end and means. It has ceased to be an ultimate goal. Yet, as we saw, that was only one current in the dialectic of the Enlightenment. A countermovement, intent on saving the traditional content of reason paralleled this functionalism. It rarely spoke with the eloquence and confidence of the rationalist voice. Moreover, it fell back upon a tradition that was under fire and whose advocates seldom possessed the critical weapons needed to defend it. Nonetheless, those who so lacked the critical power of the Enlightenment may in the end have achieved much toward broadening the Enlightenment's concept of reason. They helped to restore the spiritual content of that subject which had come to occupy a central place in the modern concept of reason. During the time of the Enlightenment the two remained mostly opposed. Yet they were to become, at least in part, reconciled during the subsequent Romantic era.

2

A Different Cosmos

During the Enlightenment the concept of power that had dominated ancient and medieval physics underwent a profound transformation. Previously thought to derive from a source beyond the physical world, it came to be viewed as immanent in that world and eventually as coinciding with the very nature of bodiliness. Aristotle's theory that all motion originated from an unmoved mover had continued to influence Scholastic theories throughout the Middle Ages. For Jewish, Muslim, and Christian thinkers, the impact of divine power went beyond motion and extended to the very existence of finite beings. According to the doctrine of creation, the dependence of nature on God was intrinsic and total. The defining quality of finite being was absolute contingency. Scholasticism supported this claim of contingency with Aristotle's principle of generation and corruption. All that has a beginning must come to an end, and for Jewish, Christian, and most Muslim thinkers, the universe did have a beginning. A contingent thing's existence is not justified by the nature of its being, nor does that nature ensure its continued existence in the future.

Late medieval thought strengthened this creaturely contingency by undermining the certainty, rooted in the idea of divine wisdom, that beings would continue to be and to act in accordance with invariable laws. When nominalist theology shifted the emphasis from God's wisdom to God's absolute power, everything became dependent on an inscrutable divine decision. Creation itself became a discontinuous act to be renewed at each moment of a creature's existence. Thus, the doctrine of divine preservation implied in the act of creation now became one of constant re-creation. Much of this nominalism survives in Descartes. He strongly asserted the dependence of each being on a constantly renewed creation. Other tendencies in Descartes's philosophy, however, qualify this voluntarist notion of contingency, among them a confidence that the divinely instituted laws of nature follow an invariable mathematical pattern.

For Spinoza, contingency did not exist. Within the one, all-inclusive substance, nothing is contingent because nothing depends on another substance. Finite modes share the necessity of the infinite substance. No external influx of power is needed: the drive to be (*conatus essendi*) coincides with the very nature of a thing. "Everything, insofar as it is in itself, endeavors to persist in its own being" and that endeavor is "nothing but its actual essence" (*Ethica*, bk. III, 6 and 7). Once a being exists, it will continue to do so until destroyed by a cause outside itself (III, 4). The power to continue one's being requires no divine intervention: it is inherent in the nature of being itself. Spinoza's substance acts as a center of power, but the effect of that power remains *within* the cause.[1] The notion that the substance is a center of power became one of the leading ideas of the Enlightenment. We shall encounter it in many forms.

Mechanism: The Newtonian Revolution

British scientists remained to a great extent faithful to the principles established by Francis Bacon, according to which science is essentially practiced by means of induction based on observation and ought to yield practical results. Newton himself shared this practical orientation. Michael J. Petry has called him "the most distinguished proponent of the idea that nature was to be mastered in the practical interests of man through the application of the Baconian inductive method."[2] Nor did Newton assume that the course of nature necessarily and in all respects follows mathematical laws. His diffidence with respect to an absolute mathematical a priori may be traced to the nominalist belief that God's absolute power overrules the normal, "ordained" exercise of that power and may, at least in principle, interrupt it at any time. The contingency of nature implies the possibility of exceptions in the normal order. Indeed, for nominalist thinkers, though less for Newton, exceptions constituted an integral part of the normal.[3] Our experience that nature follows a rational course does not allow us to consider that an a priori, necessary principle. Modesty as well as intellectual probity requires the mind to test its calculations by actual observation. If in the end Newton's method in physics won out over Descartes's, it was at least in part due to his refusal to take the mathematical nature of the universe for granted. Therein lies, I think, the primary meaning of his famous declaration "Hypotheses non fingo." He did in fact construe hypotheses but avoided doing so independently of observation.

At the same time Newton's investigations moved him in a direction that eventually undermined the traditional idea that motion results from a constantly infused divine power. Motion and rest have an equal status: a body does not change from motion to rest or from rest to motion unless an external force impels it to do so. Hence if we assume it to be originally *moving,* no additional input of power is needed to keep it in motion, though motion may decrease under the impact of external resistance. This principle of *inertia* obviously contradicts the Scholastic theory, according to which motion had to be constantly induced by a transcendent source. It rather corresponds to Spinoza's axiom that a thing perseveres in being until a cause outside itself forces it to change. The fourth definition of book I of Newton's *Principia mathematica* reads: "Perseverat enim corpus in statu omni novo per suam vim inertiae" (A body maintains every new state it acquires by its force of *inertia*). So, not motion was to be explained, but the change from one state to another.

No less significant was the fundamental change the new philosophy introduced in the notion of causality. In classical and Scholastic philosophy the term "cause" had referred to various modes of dependence of one being upon another — one of which was that of extrinsic, efficient causality. More intimate forms of causality had been the *formal* one whereby a being participates in that on which it depends, and the *final* one that directs it toward a goal. Descartes and all mechanistic philosophers who came after him had conceived of nature as essentially static and affected only by the so-called efficient causality that induces motion from without. Mechanistic philosophers considered any appeal to final causes pure speculation, an undesirable intrusion in a self-contained structure. Newton himself avoided using teleological arguments, not in the first place because they interfered with mathematical deduction, but because they escaped observation.

Yet another change ought to be mentioned: The concept of *matter,* even as that of nature, had received a meaning that differed from the one it had in Aristotle and the Scholastics. For them, it had been a metaphysical principle. Giordano Bruno had first described it as the very essence of physical nature and its immanent center of power. Like Descartes, Newton defines matter as extension. Yet he adds other, empirically observed qualities to it: impenetrability, hardness, and mobility (rather than motion).[4] In addition, he distinguishes extension from space. Attraction, though a universal quality of our world system, may not be an "essential" attribute of matter. Our knowledge of the universe is insufficient to justify the claim that matter possesses this quality in all possible universes. Most significant, Newton defined the qualities of matter as *vires* (forces), a term that implies a dynamic quality. Even inertia, which, according to the third definition of the *Principia*, "differs nothing from the inactivity of mass" since it merely conserves the existing motion, is more than passive extension: it actively resists any force pressing against it. "It is impulse, insofar as the body, by not easily giving way to the impressed force of another, endeavors to change the state of that other."[5] But there is more. If the mechanical system contained only reactive forces, motion would soon become exhausted. In the *Opticks* Newton states: "By this principle [the *vis inertiae*] alone there never could have been any motion in the world. Some other principle was necessary for putting bodies into motion, and now they are in motion, some other principle is necessary for conserving the motion."[6] Motion decreases and must be recharged from sources other than the reactive forces of matter.

Among the forces that actively cause change (rather than resist change), he mentions (in the fifth definition) percussion, pressure, and centrifugal force. Gravity belongs to this kind of force: in our universe it is the force that draws all bodies "toward a point as to a center." The passive forces of resistance and preservation that, for the Cartesians, constituted the whole of mechanics, cannot explain this force. One might even wonder whether the concept of gravity is still compatible with the mechanical principles formulated by Descartes since it operates in spaces empty of resisting matter where no direct contact between bodies occurs. How could there be mechanical action at a distance? How could a wholly active force be an essential quality of inert matter?[7] Newton himself continued to hesitate about the place of gravity within a mechanical system.[8]

In the seventeenth and early eighteenth century all philosophers still assumed that active power must come from God. So did Newton. But his method forbade him to introduce metaphysical speculations about a transcendent cause. Only at the end of the *Principia*, after his system of mechanics had been proven, does he mention divine causality. At that point he even refers to a "spiritual" presence in matter. Immediately following his declaration in the *General Scholium* that he was unable to derive the cause of gravity from the phenomena themselves and yet unwilling to frame "hypotheses" (i.e., positions not established by induction from observations), he asserts: "Now we might add something concerning a certain more subtle spirit which pervades and lies hid in all gross bodies; by the force and action of which spirit the particles of bodies attract one another at near distances and cohere, if contiguous; and electric bodies operate to greater distances, as well repelling as attracting the neighboring corpuscles." This notion of a spiritual force, working at a distance and immanent in matter without coinciding with it, suggests the influence of alchemical and Neoplatonic sources. Newton, who had studied both with considerable interest, accepted the idea of spirit residing *within* matter rather than being exclusively above or outside it, as the Cartesians held.[9] Later the idea of an active force immanent in matter contributed to the formation of a concept of evolutionary, creative matter by Diderot, d'Holbach, and other materialists.

Newton's admission of active forces, such as gravity, enabled him to move beyond the mechanistic conception of matter as being totally passive. In fact, his notion of forces of resistance had already extended mechanical thought beyond Cartesian limits. It supported the idea of self-preservation as an essential drive of all being — comparable to Spinoza's *conatus essendi*. The presence of an active force in matter had the potential to bridge the gap that separated the totally passive nature of matter from the active nature of mind in the Cartesian system. At the time of Newton's writing Leibniz was laying the groundwork for such a bridge by defining substance itself as a center of force, thereby asserting the dynamic quality of all nature.

Newton's concepts of absolute time and space also move beyond a narrowly mechanistic theory. Absolute time and space are not derived from experience. They are in fact metaphysical concepts. In the *Scholium* that follows the definitions of book I, Newton justifies their admission as being necessary for the idea of absolute motion, that is, motion not as measured by the distance from one point in space to another but as related to space as such. Even a body at rest moves with the earth on which it rests. The mathematical concept of "true or absolute motion" presupposes an absolute space and an absolute time. "Entire and absolute motions can be no otherwise determined than by immovable places. . . . Now no other places are immovable but those that, from infinity to infinity, do all retain the same given position one to another."[10] One wonders, however, how an absolute space, which provides no points of reference whatever, can be truly helpful in the calculation of "true or absolute motion." Similarly, what could the concept of absolute time, that is, pure duration unrelated to any actual motion, contribute to the understanding of actual motion?[11] The concepts of absolute space and time would have been less controversial if they had merely served as mathematical, ideal assumptions. But Newton insisted that they are real as well as ideal. On what grounds did he base this claim, for they remain inaccessible to experience? Their reality status appears to follow from the very argument that led him to introduce the notions of absolute time and space in the first place. If motion presupposes space, absolute motion requires the existence of absolute space. In the transmission of motion from its source to any given object, this particular motion presupposes a more comprehensive motion, which in turn presupposes a more comprehensive space. They again presuppose a more comprehensive motion and space, and so on to infinity. Kant, who criticizes this argument, agrees that the idea of an absolute space that synthesizes all relative spaces within a single unit may be essential to mathematical physics, yet he considers its reality both unnecessary and unjustified.[12]

The *General Scholium* at the end of book III conveys a theological meaning to the metaphysical concepts of infinite time and space. In the preceding argument Newton had claimed to be incapable of justifying the cause of gravity within a closed mechanical system. At the conclusion of his work he attributes it to a source that lies outside the mechanical order. "This is certain, that it must proceed from a cause that penetrates to the very centres of sun and planets, without suffering the least diminution of its force" (*General Scholium*, p. 446). He also concludes that other mechanically unexplainable facts, such as the "diversity of natural things which we find suited to different times and places," could not result from "a blind metaphysical necessity which is certainly the same always and everywhere" but must be the work of an infinite, perfect mind and will (ibid.). Yet the transition from an infinite Creator to a finite universe requires a being that mediates between the infinite and the finite. At the same time, Newton assumes that God is directly present to creation: only a substantially present force can be causally effective in a mechanistic system. He attempts to overcome the apparent discrepancy by postulating that God's primary expression must be infinite, as God himself is, yet able to mediate with a finite creation. Only an absolute space and an absolute time, he thinks, would make it possible for God to be present in all places at all times. "He endures forever and is everywhere present; and by existing always and everywhere, he constitutes duration and space" (p. 445). In Query 28 of the *Opticks* Newton writes: "And these things rightly dispatched, does it not appear from Phaenomena that there is a Being incorporeal, living, intelligent, omnipresent, who in infinite Space, as it were in her Sensory, sees the things themselves intimately, and perceives them and comprehends them wholly by their immediate presence to himself."[13]

The question of absolute space and time had a long history. Aristotle had attacked the idea of a void existing beyond the cosmos: neither place nor void could exist outside the heavens.[14] Nor did he believe the cosmos to be infinite in space and time. Yet the Stoics held that an infinite void was needed to include an infinite cosmos. Aquinas in this dispute sided with Aristotle. Nominalist philosophers (specially Thomas Bradwardine), judging that a space restricted to the cosmos itself would unduly limit God's creative power to this universe (excluding a greater or a smaller one), had concluded that only an infinite space would allow God's omnipotence to create a universe of any size He pleased.[15] This void, infinite as God himself, was a purely negative space that shared none of the qualities of experienced space. One might possibly interpret it as the emptiness within God, a precondition for the possibility of creating otherness within the divine fullness.

Newton's conception of absolute space and time appears to have been influenced by some of these earlier discussions. Specifically the Cambridge theologian Henry More, whom Newton admired, may have inspired the concept of an extended void-space. More had argued that extension itself could not exist without the substratum of an infinite, incorporeal space. This spiritual space constituted both the medium within which God creates and, for nature, the condition of its being and operating. For Newton also, God had to be present everywhere: within and outside creation. Was this outside "void" a real, three-dimensional space as we normally conceive ours to be? Clarke appears to have understood Newton as affirming that it was, if I read his assertion correctly: "By void space, we never mean space void of everything, but void of body only."[16]

One may find Newton's argument very "hypothetical" indeed! But we should remember that it appears in the concluding *General Scholium* of the *Principia*, where, at last, he feels free to express his deeply held conviction without being constrained by the self-imposed restrictions of mechanical physics. His theological speculation merely provides additional support for the idea of absolute space and time established by his physical theory. Bishop Berkeley was to object: either that infinite time-space is God, or it must be a reality beside God that nevertheless possesses divine attributes since it is eternal, infinite, immutable, and uncreated.[17] But Newton's absolute time and space merely constitute an empty infinity *within* which God creates. They do not "precede" God's creative act yet accompany it. Newton calls it the divine *sensorium* in analogy with the sensory apparatus in and through which a remote object becomes present in perception. Theologians considered the name not wholly appropriate, since, unlike sense perception, divine knowledge does not depend on a pre-existing object. For God, knowing an object consists of creating and sustaining it.

It appears, then, that serious tensions lurk at the heart of Newton's theory. One was between the nominalist and the Platonic elements of his theory. All power comes from God. Yet in the nominalist version, divine power does not become immanently present as it does in Neoplatonic thought but is imposed from without. God's causality is total yet remains external. Divine power, rather than consisting in the divine presence within the world, becomes *mediated* through the laws of nature. Mechanism functions as a closed system impervious to any influence from outside, even though all that occurs within it results from a transcendent source of motion. In the Neoplatonic version, the effect participates in the divine cause. Moreover it is endowed with a divine teleology that enables the higher spheres to communicate power to the lower ones. Mechanical philosophy replaced the classical and medieval teleological order by a nonhierarchical world of nature.[18]

Newton's philosophical adversaries objected to the absence of meaning or purpose in a cosmos that had no higher end than remaining in motion. The American theologian Jonathan Edwards uses the favorite mechanistic comparison of the world to a gigantic clockwork against him. If the only purpose of the clock is to have parts that assist one another in their motions, the clock itself is worthless. Similarly, if the world has no higher end than to allow its parts to support one another, the world as a whole serves no purpose. "It is nonsense to say of a machine whose highest end is to have one part move another, for the whole is useless."[19] Neither does a consistent mechanical theory have room for freedom — which Newton never questioned. Materialists attempted to rid the mechanical system of its inconsistencies by eliminating any extrinsic source of power and conceiving of it as an autodynamic, self-generating system of reality.

Mechanism had begun as a scientific theory. It soon became a controlling concept for the interpretation of all reality, including life and, with some, of the mind itself. Thus it developed into a worldview, an ambitious attempt to capture all reality within a comprehensive, undifferentiated system ruled by identical laws. This worldview implied an all-encompassing determinism that threatened the very possibility of freedom.[20] It assumed that the mind, being the single source of meaning, is able to capture all reality within a single vision. That assumption, as Heidegger has shown in an essay bearing the same name, belongs exclusively to the modern age. Descartes and Newton, who had restricted mechanism to a scientific interpretation of the physical universe, were, of course, not determinists. But for materialists, nature was a single, homogeneous system that tolerated no exceptions. The naturalism underlying this concept was to survive long after the mechanistic theory had been abandoned. Romantic opponents of Enlightenment culture rejected the mechanist worldview (none more vehemently than Blake). But many retained its subjacent naturalism, including the idea that humanity becomes crushed by nature. Individuals may resist, but in the end nature smothers their futile efforts.

The introduction of mathematical physics drastically changed the knowledge of nature. Instead of conforming the mind to a pre-existing reality, it defined the mind's ideal relation to that reality. In Newton's time mechanistic thought had already begun to penetrate popular culture in England and France. Poets hesitated whether they ought to welcome it. Some considered it the ultimate key to the universe. In "A View of Death, or The Soul's Departure from the World," the poet John Reynolds (1666–1727) looks forward to death when the scientific mysteries of the universe will be fully revealed and the mind will understand that Newton's attraction is God's love operating in matter! Others distrusted the ambitious science. Thus Matthew Prior (1664–1726), in his lengthy poem "Salomon," wonders:

> Can thought beyond the bounds of matter climb?
> Or who shall tell me what is space or time?
> In vain we lift up our presumptuous eyes
> To what our Maker to their ken denies.[21]

From Mechanism to Materialism

Two diverging theories claimed Newton's authority. One used his mechanistic principles as foundation for a philosophical determinism. The other developed the concept of active forces into an organic theory of nature. Eventually the two converged in a dynamic materialism. Newton's definition of inertia as the force that keeps a body in its present state, "whether it be of rest, or of moving uniformly forward in a straight line" (Third Definition), disposed of the traditional belief that rest is a body's natural state while motion must be externally induced. If one assumes that the universe never had a beginning (a position which even Aquinas considered not refutable on rational grounds) and has always been in a state of motion, no external cause is needed to justify the beginning of motion. For eighteenth-century materialists, this proved to be a sufficient ground for overturning the millennia old adage, *Quidquid movetur ab alio movetur* (Whatever moves must be moved by another), on which Scholastics had based one of their arguments for the existence of God. Combining a dynamic concept of matter with an organic concept of nature, materialists attributed to matter a developmental power that accounted for the emergence of plants, animals, and even humans. But even those dynamic materialists never abandoned one of the basic principles of the mechanistic system itself. They denied that even organic nature required the kind of teleology which nonmaterialists like Buffon and Leibniz granted her. To them, nature was a dynamic force, but a blind one, not directed toward any particular goal.

All materialists, dynamic as well as mechanistic ones, agreed that reality was homogeneous and to be explained through material forces alone. The physician Julien Offray de La Mettrie in his two books, *Histoire naturelle de l'âme* (1745) (which led to his banishment from France) and *L'homme machine* (1748) (which earned him a second exile, this time from Holland), attempted to achieve a more consistent mechanism than either Descartes or Newton had conceived. He reduced Descartes's two kinds of substances, body and mind, to one material substance and thus overcame the previously unexplainable cooperation of two heterogeneous functions that produced a single effect. According to La Mettrie, nothing prevents matter from exercising the functions commonly attributed to the mind. "Man is a machine and in the whole universe there is but a simple substance variously modified."[22] In his theory of the body, Descartes had already conceded half the mechanistic thesis. Had he not declared animals to be no more than material substances? But the distinction between humans and animals consisted merely in a higher complexity of motion. Animals also feel and remember. They even possess some primitive moral sense. The dog shows shame or remorse after having broken rules it was trained to observe. It is sad when its master leaves and happy when he returns. The lack of instincts made language a necessity for humans, which their physiology allowed them to develop. Without speech they would have remained below the level of apes. Psychic capacities depend entirely on anatomical and physiological endowments. Thinking, willing, and feeling consist of motions of the brain: "L'âme n'est qu'un principe de mouvement ou une partie matérielle du cerveau."

La Mettrie astutely perceived that the deists' concern was not with the existence of God as such, but with their need of a transcendent support for physics and morality. A consistently materialist theory rendered that support superfluous. He grounded his materialism in a sensationalist theory of knowledge. Knowledge originates in sensations that follow mechanistic principles. Hobbes had earlier defined them as endeavors inward followed by endeavors outward. "All mutation or alteration is motion or endeavour (and endeavour also is motion) in the internal parts of the thing that is altered."[23] Thus the sensation of seeing, for instance, is nothing but a motion first produced in the eye, thence transmitted to the optic nerve, and from the nerve to the brain.[24] The higher functions of thinking, remembering, and judging are developed from primitive forms of imagining — which itself is no more than structured motion. "Pourquoi diviser le principe sensitif qui pense dans l'homme?" Why indeed, if one regards all questions concerning the distinction between "sensing" and "thinking" (which merely demands *plus de génie*) as meaningless.

Diderot's more dynamic materialism succeeded far better in synthesizing mechanism with organic being. To La Mettrie's "dead" mechanism he opposed a concept of matter that possessed creative powers capable of exceeding the purely mechanical. He saw those forces at work in the generative process. New life results from the union of sperm and ovum, neither one of which, he thought, has a life of its own. In his early *Philosophical Thoughts* (1746) he had still held that generative creativity was restricted to the species and that it required a transcendent design. Later he interpreted the emergence of different species as a result of matter's evolutionary powers. He recognized essential differences between the degrees of being but still traced them to a common source, namely, a developing universe that attains order by chance and perfection by excluding defective forms.

Trembley's stunning discovery of the minuscule hydra (*chlorohydra viridissima*) that acted both as plant and as animal had suggested that the boundaries around species might not be as rigorous as had previously been assumed. Different thinkers drew different conclusions from this discovery. Leibniz had welcomed it as a resounding confirmation of his principle of perfection, according to which nature had to be without gaps between species. For Diderot, it meant that the restrictions philosophy had formerly imposed on the creative forces of matter had completely broken down. The entire order of nature might be no more than the random outcome of the powers of motion. Still, there remained the question of the beginning. What started the process? Diderot gradually came to regard the very assumption of a beginning as a scientifically unnecessary postulate derived from creationist theology. Why should we postulate a beginning and extrapolate the source of nature's creative power outside nature? In his *Letter on the Blind for Those Who See* (1749) Diderot showed how the need for a cause beyond nature ceases to be compelling when we abstract from the overwhelming but deceptive impression of *designed* order and beauty. That impression stems entirely from our own aesthetic vision. If we suspend that subjective sense, the issue boils down to a logical question: Does the order of nature indeed require a divine designer?

The *Letter* contains a pseudo-historical account of the death of a Cambridge professor of mathematics, the blind Nicholas Saunderson. A minister called to his bedside attempts to awaken the patient's faith by evoking the marvelous order in the universe. Saunderson admits the existence of order but questions whether it conveys any insight about its origin. "I cannot see anything. Yet I am admitting that there is a wonderful order in the universe, though I hope that you will require no more of me. I am yielding to you on the present state of the universe so that you will permit me, in return, to think as I please about its former and first state, in regard to which you are no less blind than I."[25] Not being confused by the multiplicity of sights, the blind, according to Diderot's Saunderson, are more capable of abstract thinking and less inclined to introduce an unnecessary cause. At the same time their own bodily defect renders them more aware of nature's imperfection and less given to assume the need of a perfect designer. The order of the universe, he suggests, may be the effect of a struggle among incompatible forces. Ill-formed creatures were, for the most part, eliminated by their deficient ability to adjust to their environment. Still some survive, as Saunderson's blindness testifies. He comments: "I conjecture that in the beginning, when fermenting matter was hatching out the universe, men such as myself were quite common. . . . And why should I not assert what I believe about animals to be true of worlds also? How many maimed and botched worlds have melted away, reformed themselves, and are perhaps dispersing again at any given moment, far away in space."[26]

To the paradox of a divine designer creating an imperfect world Diderot opposes the hypothesis of the ancient atomists that in millions of years matter has, by mere chance, organized itself into a more or less orderly cosmos, as Lucretius had claimed:

> Surely the atoms never began by forming
> a conscious pact, a treaty with each other,
> where they should stay apart, where come together.
> More likely, being so many, in many ways
> harassed and driven through the universe
> from an infinity of time, by trying
> all kinds of motion, every combination,
> They came at last into such disposition
> as now establishes the sum of things.[27]

Descartes himself had conceived of matter as moving, and Newton's principle of inertia had abrogated the natural priority of rest over motion. If matter had always existed and always moved, some elements would in time combine with others, and these islands of order would be able to resist the destructive forces of the original chaos. To Diderot, such a scenario appeared far more probable than that of an all-wise, omnipotent God creating a chaos out of which a never perfect universe was to develop. Diderot dearly paid for placing his irreverent opinions in Saunderson's pious mouth: he was imprisoned for a while and permanently banned from membership in the Royal Society. But, undeterred by censorship, he proceeded to answer the questions he had raised in his aphoristic *Thoughts on the Interpretation of Nature.*

This time the biologist Maupertuis served as mouthpiece for Diderot's opinions. Why, he wondered, do we fear to attribute to the material universe as a whole the perceptive qualities we observe in all animals? If we overcome this irrational aversion, we may find nature itself capable of introducing the modifications we now ascribe to the Creator. Nothing prevents the sum of all molecules to be to some extent "endowed with the powers of thought and feeling."[28] "If faith did not teach us that animals sprang from the hands of their Creator just as we know them, . . . might the philosopher not suspect, having given himself up entirely to his own conjectures, that the particular elements needed to constitute animal life had existed from all eternity, scattered and mixed with the whole mass of matter; that these elements happening to come together, had combined because it was possible for them to do so?"[29]

It had long been assumed that all organic beings were built in accordance with a common form and function. The idea of a form that, in a variety of ways, strives toward perfect expression prepared the acceptance of a natural evolution from a single primitive one to a multiplicity of developed forms. The prototypical form had to be conceived as a living force. "When we see the successive metamorphoses of the prototype's outward appearance, whatever it may have been in the first place, bring one kingdom gradually and imperceptibly nearer to another kingdom and people the boundaries of those two kingdoms . . . with uncertain, ambiguous beings stripped to a great degree of the forms, the qualities, and the functions of the one and taking on the forms, qualities, and functions of the other, is it not difficult to resist the belief that there was never more than one first being, a prototype of all other beings?"[30] The purpose of Diderot's rudimentary hypothesis of a spontaneous evolution of the species was inspired by philosophical reasons rather than derived from scientific observations. He merely wanted to show that the creative power might well reside *within* the universe — like a divine world soul — rather than above it.

Still the origin of mental life posed special problems. In three dialogical essays, "Conversation with d'Alembert," "D'Alembert's Dream," and "Conclusion of the Conversation" (written in 1769 but not published during his lifetime), Diderot moves from a theory of universal motion to one of universal sensation. The difference between dead matter and sensitive matter is one of degree, not of presence or absence. In nonorganic matter sensation remains an inanimate force, but it becomes animated in plants and animals. That it can pass from one state to another, Diderot presumed to be established by the transformation of inanimate into living matter in metabolic and genetic processes. "Do you see this egg? With this you can topple every theological theory, every church or temple in the world. What is it, this egg, before the seed is introduced into it? An insentient mass. And after the seed has been introduced into it? What is it then? An insentient mass. For what is the seed itself other than a crude and animate fluid? How is this mass to make the transition to a different structure, to sentience, to life? Through heat. And what will produce that heat in it? Motion."[31]

To derive consciousness from this sensing matter Diderot had to overcome the basic Cartesian distinction between *res extensa* and *res cogitans*. Crucial for this transition was the role of memory—the power to hold on to a past sensation. Diderot simply postulated it through an analogy of covibrating chords that allow a sensing organism to retain past sounds and to recombine them with present ones. At no point does this process move beyond matter. Nor does it require any divine intervention for the creation of a "soul." Diderot's idea of a natural evolution was based on a hunch that acquired traits are inheritable, which Lamarck soon afterward developed into a scientific theory. "Imagine a long succession of generations born without arms; imagine their continued efforts and you will slowly see the two ends of this pair of pincers grow longer, longer still, cross over at the back, grow forward again, perhaps develop fingers at their ends, and create arms and hands once more."[32] With this argument Diderot thinks he has accomplished his goal of uniting the mechanistic theories of Descartes and Newton with a sensationalism derived from Locke and thus of having eliminated the separation between material and mental principles of reality.

Diderot's friend and coeditor of the *Encyclopédie*, d'Alembert, resisted such hazardous generalizations. Like Newton, he opposed metaphysical speculation. He even refused to define the primary properties of matter; he was interested only in how they functioned. "The purpose of philosophy is not to become lost in the universal properties of being and of substance, in useless questions about abstract concepts, in arbitrary divisions and eternal nomenclatures: it is the science either of facts or of chimeras."[33] By means of definitions philosophers merely generalize particular phenomena in order thereby to make them appear universal and necessary. In fact, the complexity of nature defies comprehensive description.[34] The creation of abstract universals obstructs rather than favors the possibility of subsuming experience under mathematical laws. D'Alembert, an eminent mathematician, abstained from construing general philosophical theories on the basis of particular phenomena.

Observation never results in apodictic truth, but if duly repeated and formulated into law, it asymptotically approaches mathematical certainty.[35] In the end the very possibility of a universal science of "nature" can be no more than a postulate. Cassirer confirms d'Alembert's doubts: "Where is the guarantee, the decisive proof, that at least this general system of phenomena is completely self-contained, homogeneous, and uniform?"[36] More orthodox mechanists were not happy with d'Alembert's methodic asceticism. In his funeral oration for d'Alembert, Condorcet regretted that the great mathematician had pushed the demands of mathematical rigor too far. "He may have imposed too narrow limitations upon the human mind. Too accustomed to truths demonstrated and formed by simple, precisely defined ideas, he may have been insufficiently aware of truths of a different order that have more complex ideas as their object, for the discussion of which we may even need to articulate definitions and, so to speak, new ideas, because the words employed in these sciences taken from ordinary language and used in common parlance have only vague and indeterminate meanings."[37]

Paul-Henri Dietrich d'Holbach's *Système de la nature* (1771) stayed closer to Diderot's views, except for its peremptory dogmatism. In this work, published anonymously, the German baron, who in Paris kept an open house for scientists, philosophes, and radical thinkers, construed a coherent materialist system of the universe and of all it contains. Matter is an all-comprehensive, eternal substance that, with the sole support of motion, accounts for the entire scale of the real—from mineral to mind. The author combines a naive reductionism and a simplistic determinism with an impressive erudition and an occasionally incisive critique of established positions. He lacks any *esprit de finesse,* but his passionate eloquence against "superstition" carries the weary reader along through a dense brush of learning and bias. Single-mindedly intent on proving the truth of atheistic naturalism, he borrows from any source likely to provide ammunition for his unholy war. Empedocles, Epicurus, and Lucretius appear side by side with Descartes and Newton, whose theories he thoroughly distorts. "Descartes asked but matter and motion: diversity of matter sufficed for him; variety of motion was the consequence of its existence, of its essence, of its properties."[38] As matter moves, it determines bodies in different modes of being and they result in different modes of action. D'Holbach claims to follow the "rules" of the *Principia,* but his own theory of creative vital forces moves far beyond what Newton's principles allow. In fact, he superimposes Leibniz's dynamic theory of substance upon Newton's mechanism. He also appeals to Leibniz's identity of indiscernibles—two individuals even of the same species can never possess identical qualities—in order to show the infinite fertility of a nature, which he defines as bound by rigorous, mechanistic determinism (I, 9, 60).

Nature is "the great whole that results from the assemblage of motions which the universe offers to our view" (I, 1, 15). Endowed with the attributes of a transcendent principle, d'Holbach's Nature is eternal, comprehensive, organizing, and the sole source of motion. Typical of the baron's breezy way of marching through an argument are his far-reaching equations. Attraction and repulsion are identified with Empedocles' love and hatred (I, 4, 29–32). Physical motion rules the internal functions of willing and thinking. Intelligence results from a particular combination of matter that produces unique modes of action, called "reflection" and "decision." Everything happens necessarily and forms part of an uninterrupted chain of cause and effect. "Chance" and "freedom" merely describe series of events where we fail to perceive the causal link. D'Holbach ascribes unlimited powers to nature. It suffices to consider matter to be animated by motion, rather than dead and inert, to understand the entire order of nature as self-produced (I, 5, 38).

A secret theology has wormed its way into his deterministic system. Nature becomes personified, endowed with divine attributes, and invested with a capacity to act in view of self-chosen ends. "It is part of her [Nature's] plan, that certain portions of the earth shall bring forth delicious fruits, whilst others shall only furnish brambles and noxious vegetables: she has been willing that some societies should produce wise men and great heroes, that others should only give birth to contemptible men" (I, 12, 113). But Nature is indifferent to human life, d'Holbach had asserted in a lyrical passage reminiscent of that earlier rhapsodist of an all-inclusive nature, Giordano Bruno. "Suns encrust themselves and are extinguished; planets perish and disperse themselves in the vast plains of air; other suns are kindled; new planets form themselves, either to make revolutions round these suns, or to describe new routes; and man, an infinitely small portion of the globe, which is itself but an imperceptible point in the immensity of space, believes it is for himself this universe is made" (I, 6, 46).[39] Despite the apparent indifference to human life of d'Holbach's matter, the emergence of forms of being follows a strict hierarchy from the inert to the intelligent, as if mental life were its anticipated goal.

Is matter able to produce new species and to make old ones disappear? D'Holbach does not doubt it. Only the shortness of human life prevents us from seeing species emerging or vanishing. An organic nature constantly transforms itself into ever more complex forms of life, in accordance with climatic and geographical conditions (I, 6, 44). "Everything seems to authorize the conjecture that the human species is a production peculiar to our sphere, in the position in which it is found: that, when this position may happen to change, the human species will, of consequence, either be changed, or will be obliged to disappear" (I, 6, 45). This admission of a possible extinction of the human race is exceptional in d'Holbach's system. Most of the time his concept of nature was inspired by an eighteenth-century belief in progress rather than by biological evidence. Not the struggle for survival nor "mutational" accidents determine the process, but Nature's teleological orientation toward the highest form of life. Once civilization appears it becomes a powerful instrument for the preservation and improvement of the human species.

For all their learning and passion, d'Holbach's tomes failed to impress his fellow philosophes. In his *Correspondance littéraire* about cultural developments in France, the sarcastic Grimm writes: "I find no other danger in them than that of boredom: all of it becomes exceedingly repetitious. The earth keeps on turning and the impact of the most daring opinions equals zero." Grimm's remark cautions us not to exaggerate the esteem d'Holbach enjoyed even in the minds of his enlightened contemporaries. The baron's goal was not scientific but ideological: to justify materialism and theories of progress by sweeping but unproven statements about physics and biology. D'Holbach's originality consisted in popularizing the scientific conclusions of arguments presented by others and in transforming them, well beyond what their scientific support warranted, into tools for a social program. His work may have enjoyed little authority among scientists and even among philosophers, but it effectively served a social project.

His materialism prematurely brought to completion what by its very nature must remain an asymptotic process. The project of scientific research never ends since the gap between thinking and reality never closes. The idea of progress is inherent in the scientific enterprise itself.[40] Although we assume that science comes ever closer to its ideal, it will never succeed in fully justifying why the world continues to appear different from what our accumulated knowledge proves it to be. The materialist resolves this permanent tension between subject and object by simply assuming that subjectivity itself is a mode of the known or knowable object. Once this thesis is accepted the possibility of an exhaustive knowledge is in principle attained. Further progress then consists merely in filling in the details.

The Organic View of Nature

BUFFON

By the middle of the eighteenth century even such loyal apostles of mechanism as d'Alembert, Diderot, and La Mettrie had begun to attribute forces to nature that exceeded Descartes's and Newton's concepts of motion. Buffon and Leibniz's organic theories of nature broke away from mechanism altogether. George-Louis Buffon, a noted mathematician and in his early years an orthodox mechanist, attempted to apply Newton's principles to the organic world. But even the introductory *Discours* to the first volume of his enormous *Histoire Naturelle* spells trouble for the theory. To reduce the order of living organisms to a single homogeneous order, he writes, is an exercise that can satisfy only "the mind of those who know nature poorly." The Creator has dispensed "an infinite number of harmonious and contrary combinations, as well as perpetual destructions and renewals."[41] Buffon even objects to his great contemporary Linné's classification into genus, species, and subspecies.

In botany and zoology only empirical observation yields worthwhile results. Amazingly, Buffon still believed that his battle was only with the Cartesian deductive method, not with mechanism itself. Not until the majestic "Vue de la Nature" that introduces volume XII did he become fully aware of his differences with the mechanistic interpretation of nature. Until then he continued to describe zoological developments as the work of Newtonian forces, though he considered them subordinate to the higher purpose of life. "Motion and life are its scope." Life still obeys the laws of attraction and repulsion, but it does so in a manner that renders the force of gravity subservient to its own goal.

As he gradually became aware of the conflict between the mechanistic forces of attraction and repulsion on one side, and the dynamic, teleological thrust of organic life, on the other, Buffon began to separate the living forces from the "dead" ones. Attraction affects all bodies, yet in the organic ones repulsion dominates. Finally, in the general "Vue de la Nature" Buffon abandoned the notion of a homogeneous system of forces altogether. Nature as a self-moving, animated, and animating power resists being constrained within a single system. Although all bodies remain subject to physical laws, the effect of these laws differs from one kind to another. Condillac and d'Alembert, the watchdogs of mechanistic orthodoxy, objected to such an "unscientific" teleology. How could the order of nature be preserved with a number of uncoordinated systems operating at once? Had the artist Buffon gotten the better of the scientist?.[42]

Buffon's synthesis was indeed a work of the imagination. But that may have been its greatest merit. For him, nature itself was a postulate of the imagination, a projected unity that included a constantly expanding and changing content. By abandoning the belief in a homogeneous reality Buffon succeeded in liberating nature from the prison house within which mechanism had locked the endless variety of bodies living and dead. It was indeed an aesthetic intuition that guided Buffon's scientific observation. With his work the idea of harmony, unity in diversity, that had long since made its way into art, poetry, and philosophy entered science. Nature was an organic body composed of different systems that held each other in balance.

A faith in a natural harmony inspires those exquisite reflections that, much to the delight of the reader, Buffon has dispersed at regular (though seldom predictable) intervals over his entire work. One of them, accompanying the description of the ox, presents an opportunity to discuss the ecology of mutual destruction among animals. To survive, animals must eat plants or other animals. But in order to keep the quantity of life constant, nature *comme une mère économe* has fixed the limits of destruction and granted only few animals carnivorous instincts, while outnumbering them with herbivores. Problems begin with the human species. They use their power to domesticate, over-breed, and slaughter animals well beyond their needs. Humans hunt and fish without restriction. "All of nature hardly seems to suffice for their intemperance and the inconstant variety of their appetites. By themselves humans consume and swallow more meat than all animals together devour. They are the great destroyers and move by abuse rather than by necessity."[43]

Buffon frequently insists on the relative insignificance of the human person in the whole of nature, yet in other passages he stresses his transforming power — for good or ill. Without human care nature becomes "hideous and moribund." We alone can render it beautiful and wholesome — by draining marshes and digging canals. "Let us put the torch at this superfluous growth, at these old, half perished forests, and let us destroy with iron what fire did not consume. Instead of rushes and water lilies from which the toad draws its venom[!], we shall see buttercups, clover, sweet and salubrious herbs."[44] Thus the pioneer naturalist returns home from his walk on the wild side to the artificial French garden and its ideal of transforming nature into a work of art. Enlightenment rationalism and emerging romanticism remain locked in an undecided struggle in Buffon's conception of nature.

Even his later study on the formation of the earth, *Les époques de la nature* (1778), by many considered his best, remains ambiguous. After having been separated from the sun, the planet stayed incandescent for 2,936 years(!). Once it had cooled off, water constantly transformed it during the later epochs. The theory may appear fanciful in the light of modern geology, but its significance lies in Buffon's admission of change in an area of nature that even he, in his earlier works, had considered subject only to immutable mechanical laws. He now views the cosmos that mechanists from Galileo to Newton had held to be static as passing through a succession of stages, each of which had its own history in the total harmony of nature.

Surprisingly, Buffon considered presently living species as ancient as nature itself. The geological foundations of nature and the living individuals in it are subject to change, but not the species. Buffon had engaged the young Lamarck (who had published a study on the flora of France) as a travel companion for his son. Yet he would strongly have resisted the theory of evolution that Lamarck later developed. Still, Buffon's own theory called for change on every level. "Nature has passed through different stages; the surface of the earth has taken different forms; the heavens themselves have changed, and all things in the physical universe are, even as those in the moral world, in a continuous movement of successive variations."[45] In addition, the great botanist and zoologist adduces the kind of evidence that was to lead later scientists to an evolutionary theory of nature. He mentions seashells found on mountains, as well as remnants of species that have ceased to exist. Some of those shells reappear in continents now separated from each other. What we today would count as clear signs of genetic mutations remained merely an intriguing phenomenon for one who persisted in his belief that animal species are fixed. Even so, the evidence Buffon produced was sufficient to alarm Newtonians as well as theologians. Voltaire dismissed the seashells on the mountains as remnants of travelers' picnics or as relics of shell-bearing pilgrims crossing the Pyrenees or Alps on their way to Compostella.

A crucial step in overcoming mechanism was the different conception of form that emerged from the new life sciences — biology, botany, and zoology. The issue first came up in a dispute about the nature of organic species. Are natural forms continuous so that any classification, though useful for purposes of investigation, must be artificial? Or are species distinct steps in the hierarchy of nature, as Linné thought? Since Trembley's discovery of the *zoophyte hydra,* the issue of continuity ceased to divide the scientific community. Henceforth it centered on the question of whether in a continuous system forms might be classified as permanent. Ever since Newton's theory of force the idea of form as a dynamic, teleological principle had been working itself to the surface. It definitively broke through in Leibniz's philosophy.

LEIBNIZ

The scientific study of nature presupposes a trust that all the pieces of the puzzle somehow fit together and that the various lines of investigation converge at a center. Around this assumption of a universal harmony Leibniz built an all-inclusive system of reality. But rather than reducing all things to a single substance, as Spinoza had done, he started from an irreducible plurality of substances. Each one, except the simple divine substance, contained a spiritual core, a simple "monad" surrounded by a cluster of subordinate "monads" that made the substance receptive to outside influences. This radical departure from the mechanistic concept of reality remained a mere hypothesis until the mechanistic thesis had, at least in principle, been falsified by the empirical evidence on which it claimed to be based. Buffon and other naturalists of Leibniz's time had begun to show that animals and plants followed other laws than the mechanistic one of action and reaction.

Leibniz's thought, the most comprehensive and one of the most original of the Enlightenment period, requires a more detailed analysis than appears in this chapter. (More will be said about him in a later one.) Here I shall discuss only his remarkable alternative to mechanist philosophy. Crucial thereby was the restoration of the notion of form, once the determining category of Western thought. The philosophies of Descartes, Hobbes, and Locke all had replaced it by the concept of substance.[46] Substance soon became so all-encompassing as to lose its distinct meaning. Descartes had identified the entire physical nature with extended substance, and Spinoza, anxious to eliminate the absolute dualism between extension and thought, equated substance with the totality of the real. Hume subsequently showed how easily one could dispense with such a broad category altogether.

In an article in the *Journal des Savans* (in June 1695) Leibniz justified his reviving what had fallen into such a profound disrepute.

> I realized that it is impossible to find the principles of a *true unity* in matter alone, since everything in it is only a collection or mass of parts to infinity. Now multitude can only get in reality from *true unities* which come from elsewhere and are quite different from points (it is known that the continuum cannot be composed of points). Therefore to find their real unities I was compelled to have recourse to a formal atom, since a material being cannot be both material and perfectly indivisible or endowed with true unity. It was necessary, hence, to recall and, so to speak, rehabilitate the *substantial forms* so decried today, but in a way which would make them intelligible and which would separate the use we should make of them from the abuse that has been made of them.[47]

By interpreting Newton's notion of force in the sense of Aristotle's goal-directed form principle (the *entelecheia*), he hoped to reconcile the mechanistic with the dynamic theories of matter while at the same time relinking the new physics to the ancient metaphysics. "I grant that the consideration of these [substantial] forms is of no service in the details of physics and ought not to be employed in the explanation of particular phenomena."[48] But if Descartes's collapse of all material substances into one and Spinoza's universal monism were to be avoided, the notion of substance had to be defined in a more specific manner than "that which is in itself and is conceived through itself." The universe contains a multiplicity of qualities, some of them conflicting with others. They cannot be attributed to a single substance without logical contradiction. The differentiating note of form would prevent this.

By the same token Leibniz excluded Descartes's equation of material substance with extension. If forces are an essential feature of the mechanic system, material substances had to consist of more than extension, which is not even an objective quality but a concept needed to describe continuity among material substances.[49] The phenomenon of extension, far from defining the essence of material substance, results from the mind's tendency to equate what is merely similar and continuous. Material entities do indeed share a common passive quality. But, as Newton had shown, a mechanistic system also contains active forces. They require the presence of the spiritual principle of form.

Leibniz disagreed with Newton's theory of physics on one fundamental issue. He rejected the notion of absolute space as an abstraction that freezes into a single, static reality the dynamic relations that all coexisting things in the universe entertain with one another. "I hold it [space] to be an *order of coexistences,* as time is an *order of successions.* For space denotes, in terms of possibility, an order of things which exist at the same time, considered as existing together, without inquiring into their particular manner of existing."[50] Newton's absolute space is independent of the objects in it and hence indifferent with respect to the position of the objects. This means that objects could occupy any other position than the one they actually occupy. But then no reason could be given why things are where they actually are, a thesis that directly conflicts with Leibniz's principle of sufficient reason. "The fiction of a material finite universe, moving forward in an infinite empty space, cannot be admitted. For, besides that there is no real space out of the material universe, such an action would be *without* any design in it."[51] A spatial vacuum exists neither outside the universe nor inside it. The concept of *space* refers to the phenomenal order of coexistence in which objects are related to one another. Leibniz excluded the very possibility of a void surrounding the universe by assuming that it is infinite. ("It does not appear reasonable that the material universe should be finite.")[52]

Time also refers to a relation, rather than to an independent being as it did for Newton.[53] Since time is no more than the appearing order of succession, Leibniz needs no idea of an absolute infinite time surrounding the duration of the cosmos. A substance may last eternally but there is no such *thing* as an eternal duration.[54] Nor could the world have been created "sooner" or "later": time originates with the world, being nothing but the order in which existing realities relate to one another. A time before the world would be "a thing absolute, independent of God; whereas time must coexist with creatures, and is only conceived by the *order* and *quantity* of their changes."[55] Moreover, the idea that God would create the world at a particular segment of an absolute time conflicts with the principle of sufficient reason: Why at this moment rather than at another when in an infinite empty time no moment would have an ontological priority over any other?

Surprisingly, Leibniz holds that duration, in contrast to extension, must have a beginning. "If it is the nature of things in the whole, to grow uniformly in perfection, the universe of creatures must have had a beginning. And therefore, there will be reasons to limit the duration of things, even though there were none to limit their extension."[56] Yet the fact that time has a beginning does not prevent it from stretching out indefinitely into the future. Leibniz's position may have been inspired by a theological concern that if the world had always existed, the divine act of creation would have been jeopardized. But does creation imply more than an absolute dependence of all finite being upon an absolute being? What then is time for Leibniz? An ideal concept resulting not from a single perception but from "a train of perceptions [that] awakens in us the idea of duration."[57] The synthetic concepts of time and space possess an *ideal* truth, though not a real one: they condition our ability to perceive phenomena in an orderly, connected series.

On one other critical issue Leibniz disagrees with Newton, namely, the need for God's occasional interventions to redress the small deviations from the regular concentric orbits the planets describe. In the *Opticks* Newton had written: " 'Tis not possible it should have been caused by blind fate, that the planets all move with one familiar direction in concentric orbs; excepting only some very small irregularities, which may have arisen from the mutual actions of the planets and comets one upon another; and which 'tis probable will in length of time increase be anew put in order by its Author."[58] Leibniz objected to such shoddy workmanship that required the Creator "to wind up his watch from time to time."[59] If the order can be repaired, what prevented God from making it perfect from the start? Does the principle of perfection not require that everything made by a perfect Creator must be as perfect as it can possibly be? This principle of perfection, as all Leibniz's principles, follows from the comprehensive rule of sufficient reason.

That principle most radically formulates the rationalist assumption that the real must be rational in all respects. All that exists or occurs must be justified by a reason for its particular existence or occurrence. That principle also implies that substances must be continuous with one another. Gaps or abrupt transitions in the line of being cannot be rationally justified. It further requires that each substance qualitatively differ from all others, since the existence of a substance that is in no way distinct from another would have no reason for existing. It suffices not for a substance to occupy a quantitatively different position, or to have a different "weight." If simple substances were without differentiating qualities, reality would be totally homogeneous.

The *Monadology,* Leibniz's last major writing, may be read as his final response to mechanistic philosophy. For Leibniz, as for all rationalists, the ultimate condition of rationality is simplicity. Thought operates on the basis of a small number of principles and this implies, according to them, that the real itself may be broken down into simple elements.[60] Leibniz called simple substances *monads* rather than *atoms,* because physical atoms remain subject to division.[61] "Physical points are indivisible only in appearance; mathematical points are indivisible only in appearance; mathematical points are exact, but they are only modalities; only metaphysical or substantial points (constituted by *forms* or souls) are exact and real."[62] Each substance, then, even the complex physical one is built around a simple spiritual core. Contrary to the materialist notion of atoms, these spiritual monads are not moved by external forces but exclusively by their own internal teleology.

Each monad expresses a unique perspective on the totality of the real. All complement one another and, indirectly, influence each other by their greater or smaller power of expression.[63] "Activity belongs to the essence of substance in general."[64] In a letter to the Dutch philosopher De Volder, Leibniz writes: "I believe that our thought of [material] substance is perfectly satisfied in the *conception of force* and not in that of extension. Besides, there should be no need to seek any other explanation for the conception of power or force than that it is the attitude from which change follows and its subject is substance itself."[65] In describing the material substance as an expressive force directed by an inner teleology, Leibniz contradicts mechanism on the most fundamental level. The dynamic qualities that mechanism had reserved to God and humans, he predicated of all substances: "Substance is a being capable of action."[66]

Leibniz even attributes perception, though not apperception (i.e., fully conscious perception) to all beings. The principle of perfection excludes a sudden break between the organic and the inorganic, the mental and the corporeal. Perception is an expressive act and because each substance, even the lowest in the hierarchy of being, is a center of expressive power, each substance must be perceptive. Each reflects in its own way the state of all others with which it is united in a universal harmony.

In declaring power to be the essence of substance — not the kind of causally induced power of mechanistic philosophy but *spontaneous power* that originates within the substance — Leibniz laid a new foundation for the harmony between mind and body. All physical reality is ontologically linked to a spiritual core; in the case of humans, the mind is the spiritual core of the body.

Conclusion: Kant's Internalization of Nature

In Kant's thought empiricist and rationalist theories converged. From the former he retained that only empirical knowledge can convey reliable information about nature; from the latter, that knowledge to be scientific (and hence universal) had to be rooted in a priori principles to become necessary. A mere description of nature as the sum of empirical observations was inadequate for scientific as well as for philosophical purposes. In the *Prolegomena to Any Future Metaphysics* (1783), Kant replaces the traditional description of nature as "the totality of all objects of experience" by "the existence of things so far as it is determined according to universal laws."[67] These laws are more than generalized observations: they consist of the mind's own rules of experience. "We must not seek the universal laws of nature in nature by means of experience, but conversely must seek nature, as to its universal conformity to law, in the conditions of the possibility of experience, which lie in our sensibility and in our understanding" (*Gesammelte Schriften*, IV, § 36, p. 319; Ellington, p. 61). Kant distinguishes these pure and universal laws from the empirical laws of nature known through *particular* observations. The "pure" laws, inherent in the knowing subject, prescribe the general conditions of space and time within which the experience of nature occurs. Kant thereby justified what had remained implicit in modern physical theories since Descartes and Newton, namely, that our knowledge of the world clarifies our relation to the world rather than defining the nature of the world.

His subjective interpretation of space and time laid this contested issue to rest, at least for a while. In his *Dissertation* of 1770, he had rejected the earlier theories of space and time, Newton's as well as Leibniz's. From Newton's concept of absolute space and time he nevertheless retained the idea that the very possibility of conceiving nature depends on an a priori intuition of space and time. But what Newton had called God's *sensorium* Kant reinterpreted as the subjective conditions that enable the mind to *think* the world. Leibniz's conception of space and time as a priori concepts of coexistence and succession would seem to come closer to Kant's own idea. In fact, it became the main target of his attack. Space and time, he objected, are not concepts: they are intuitions of the senses and hence they are not universal as concepts are, but singular. In his judgment Leibniz failed to distinguish the a priori of reason from the a priori conditions of sense perception.[68]

For Kant, the intuition of time, prior to any actual experience, establishes the subjective requirements for coordinating all sense data. Similarly, space is neither abstracted from external sensations nor constituted by the mind but an a priori form of sensibility that, without any content of its own, links the successive perceptions together. To perceive reality as a coherent whole requires that things be situated within a single frame of space and time.

In the *Metaphysical Foundations of Natural Science* (1786), Kant adds a new element to his theory. He shows how a priori principles of judgment determine the laws of mechanical physics. Obviously, the philosopher does not "deduce" the laws of physics from metaphysical premises: they have to be established by methodic observation. Yet reflecting on those laws the philosopher understands how each of them presupposes definite a priori structures of knowledge. The physicist need not know those structures, yet they form the foundation of his science and give its laws their apodictic quality. "A rational doctrine of nature, then, deserves the name natural science only when the natural laws that underlie it are cognized a priori and are not mere laws of experience."[69] In the *Metaphysical Foundations of Natural Science* (1786), Kant reformulates the fundamental concept of matter. At the ground of it lies the a priori intuition of space. Matter is pure or "absolute" space to the extent that it forms the basis of motion (*Gesammelte Schriften,* IV, p. 480; Ellington, p. 18).

Still the a priori intuition of space in no way grounds our understanding of the dynamics of nature. The concept of force, on which the physical law of action and reaction rests, requires a different philosophical justification. If matter were wholly impenetrable, no motion would occur at all. On the other side, if matter offered no resistance to external pressure, it would become totally diffused — and, again, no motion would be possible. Matter, then, must consist of forces that render it intrinsically active, that is, both penetrable and resistant. This a priori quality of matter is, according to Kant, the foundation of physical dynamics. One may question whether these allegedly a priori principles philosophically justify the physical concept of force; indeed, whether they add anything to a mere description.

Kant's intention leaves no doubt. He is waging a battle with what he considers to be the philosophical assumptions of Newton's *Principia,* specifically the notions of absolute space and absolute time. Those notions may be needed as ideal hypotheses for rendering an ever-shifting relative motion measurable, but they are unfit to serve as foundational concepts of physics. "Absolute space is, then, necessary not as a concept of an actual object but as an idea that is to serve as a rule for considering all motion therein only as relative" (*Gesammelte Schriften,* IV, p. 560; Ellington, p. 127). At this point the purpose of his sharp critique of Newton's assumptions becomes clear. If absolute space and time were indeed the objective foundations of physical reality, Kant's claim of having accomplished a "Copernican revolution" in reversing the relation between the knowing subject and nature would become meaningless. In fact, his victory over the objectivist philosophy of nature proved decisive at least in one respect: no major thinker after him continued to speak or write of nature as of a reality wholly independent of the perceiver. The process of knowing plays a crucial role in constituting the object of that knowledge.

By the end of the eighteenth century the revolution begun by Copernicus and Galileo was reaching completion. Not only was the universe larger — infinitely so — than previous generations had thought, but it also had become self-empowered. Nor did it appear to be there for our benefit: we and our planet formed only one minuscule part of it, among billions of others. The very notion that this planet might have a purpose had become questionable. Nonetheless, as Pascal had stated, the mind infinitely surpasses a universe that does not know itself. Kant's philosophy supported and strengthened this awareness of the mind's unique place in the order of reality. Not only does the mind know the universe; its knowledge constitutes it as ideal entity.

The change in the cosmological outlook caused both a feeling of disorientation and a new sense of freedom. Many felt lost in a universe that had ceased to provide a firm dwelling place. At the same time, others welcomed the liberation from a prefixed order that restricted all thinking and acting by clearly defined limits of space and time. Henceforth the mind itself was to determine the coordinates of its position. For the first time people, no longer confined to this earth, started speculating about a plurality of worlds. Other planets might be inhabited. Eventually this new worldview was to affect all other aspects of life — the person's view of himself or herself, the nature of religion, ethics, and aesthetics.

3

A New Sense of Selfhood

The success of the physical and mathematical sciences inspired a demand for a science of human nature. Not only would a systematic knowledge of the person round out the circle of sciences, but, as Hume understood it, such a knowledge would place all other sciences on a secure basis. "It is evident that all the sciences have a relation, greater or less, to human nature; and that, however wide any of them may seem to run from it, they still return by one passage or another. Here then is the only expedient, from which we can hope for success in our philosophical researches to leave the tedious lingering method, which we have hitherto followed and instead of taking now and then a castle or village on the frontier, to march directly up to the capital or center of those sciences, to human nature itself; which being once masters of, we may everywhere else hope for an easy victory."[1]

The science of the person was to provide the foundation for all others. Even Kant, so scrupulous about separating the principles of knowledge from the particulars of human nature, in a later writing declared the philosophical understanding of man the key to all philosophy. In the *Critique of Pure Reason* he had raised three questions: "What can I know? What ought I do? What may I hope?"[2] The three *Critiques* were to answer them. In the *Logik* he adds a fourth question: *Was ist der Mensch?* (What is the human person?) His answer states what had been one of the implicit assumptions of modern thought: "In the end one might count all this [the content of the triple *Critique*] to be anthropology, because the first three questions all relate to the last one."[3] Thus philosophy rested on anthropology. But this knowledge of the self differed from the one to which the oracle of Delphi had summoned Socrates, namely, to understand his place in the whole of reality. For the moderns, the self *defines* that reality, rather than being defined by it.

The Modern Predicament: The Self, Subject or Substance?

From the beginning a basic ambiguity had adhered to the science of the self. The object of the investigation was at the same time the investigating subject. The self was both knowing *subject* and the *substance* to be known. The terms "subject" and "substance" were both translations of the same Greek term, *hypokeimenon*, the permanent base that supports the transient qualities of a being. Descartes uses the term "subject" rarely and never in the pregnant sense here described. The term "substance," originally no more than the permanent core that supports (*sub-stat*) all qualities of a being, had gradually come to refer to that being itself.[4] Early Scholasticism had referred to God, the soul, and the world, as substances. Descartes continued to apply that term to the conscious self (*res cogitans*), but because for him consciousness functions as the source of meaning of all substances, that denomination created a major problem. How can what constitutes meaning be, at the same time, a substance endowed with a meaning content of its own? How can there be an *objective* science of what is supposed to be the source of all objective meaning?[5]

The problem continues to haunt contemporary thought. Michel Foucault referred to it as the paradox of a "being such that knowledge will be attained in him of what renders all knowledge possible."[6] Paul Ricoeur has rephrased the two functions of the self while attempting to avoid the dualism involved in the terminology of subject and substance. He distinguishes the two modes of self-description by the Latin terms *ipse* (the meaning-giving function of the self) and *idem* (the quality whereby a self remains the same substance).[7] The self is both. Yet referring to it through either of those designations singularly is inadequate. If the self is defined only through its sameness (*idem*), it becomes quantitatively distinct from other objective entities, but nothing indicates its qualitative uniqueness. *Sameness* defines the self through bodiliness, which distinguishes it from any other substance but neglects its main quality, namely, to be the source of meaning and acting. The problem is equally serious, however, if I describe the self as a pure *ipse* or subject, the unique and unshareable center of consciousness. It allows no space for genuine otherness, beside that of its own bodiliness. Nor does such a disincarnated self-consciousness possess a particular content to define its spiritual identity.

The problem of the self as subject and/or substance determined much of the theoretical discussion of personhood during the Enlightenment. Rationalist philosophers defined the self mainly as source of meaning, as Descartes had done. But Descartes had described the person as consisting of two substances, mind and body, and had thereby also occasioned a different, indeed an opposite trend. Materialists found in his philosophy some support for overcoming the spiritual dualism inherent in his view of the person. Had he himself not classified animal life as *res extensa,* that is, as part of a mechanistic universe? Extending this view to all living beings, they converted the French philosopher's position into a materialist one, the one he had most strongly attempted to avoid.

Kant brought this discussion to a head and resolved the ambiguity by distinguishing between the two aspects of the self: the transcendental subject or *ego* that constitutes all objective knowledge and, on the other side, the self that is aware of itself as an independent entity (a substance) but of which I have no objective knowledge. "I do not know myself through being conscious of myself as thinking." The *I* is not an object of thought, but a function of thinking. "In all our thought the *I* is the subject, in which thoughts inhere only as determinations; and this *I* cannot be employed as the determination of another thing. Everyone must, therefore, necessarily regard himself as substance, and thought as [consisting] only [in] accidents of his being, determinations of his state. But what use am I to make of this concept of a substance?"[8] Even introspection does not attain the core of selfhood. Our view of ourselves as well as the words in which we express it depend on cultural presuppositions transmitted through language. The child assumes this tradition when it learns how to speak, before even knowing the meaning of the words. To Kant, the issue was of crucial moral significance. As free beings humans are accountable for their actions. Yet as parts of an objective system they are subject to determinations over which they have no control (*KRV,* 448–49; B 476–77). How can the self be free in such a system?

In my opinion, Leibniz came closest to resolving the dilemma of the self as subject and the self as substance, though he did not directly discuss the issue. For him, there were neither pure subjects nor pure substances. *Each* substantial entity is a center of power that consists of a cluster of simple units (monads) acting together under the direction of one leading monad. In the case of the human self, the soul fulfills this leading function. The subordinate monads of the body stand in a subservient but not entirely passive position to the soul's active power. Without body, the mind would not be able to function; without mind, the body would remain a random coalition of unorganized units. The cooperation of mind and body, then, required a different causal relation than that of the efficient causality that science had come to accept and which had resulted in either dualism (as it did in Descartes) or in materialism (as in d'Holbach). For Leibniz, their relation is determined by an inner teleology whereby the mind functions as the body's final cause. Mind and body operate in unison as a single center of power. Leibniz accepts Spinoza's principle that "the essence of the soul is to represent bodies," but he adds that the soul is more than the idea of the body. The body changes; the soul functions as the active principle, the *entelechy,* that determines the body's changes without changing itself.

In British philosophy the search for a coherent theory of selfhood took a very different form. Rather than speculating about what the self was in itself, empiricist thinkers analyzed how and what it *experiences.* They shied away from metaphysical concepts and instead attempted to describe, as accurately as possible, the total array of experience, passions and emotions as well as understanding. John Locke began by bracketing the question of the *substantial self* (referring to it as a *je ne sais quoi* principle of unity), and David Hume ended up denying its existence as an independent "thinking thing" distinct from its thought content. In Hume's words: "The mind is a kind of theatre where several perceptions successively make their appearance; pass, repass, glide away, and mingle in an infinite variety of postures and situations. There is properly no *simplicity* in it at one time, nor *identity* in different."[9] In addition, empiricist philosophers did not restrict introspection to a reflection on the process of thinking, as rationalists had mainly done. With equal interest they observed those emotional and sentimental states in which consciousness appears to coincide with itself rather than being outwardly directed as in intentional knowledge. I am what I *feel* myself to be.

Locke seldom ventured beyond the purely cognitive experience. His *Essay Concerning Human Understanding,* as the title indicates, professes to be no more than an inquiry concerning the modes of knowledge. But a full description of the ways of knowing ought to include all functions of consciousness. The *Essay* is in this regard rather disappointing. Locke disposes of the passions in one short chapter (*Essay,* II, 20). What prevented him from fully exploring the perspectives he had opened was, in the first place, his narrow conception of self-knowledge. If knowledge is a matter of sensation and reflection, the mind is left little creative originality. Leslie Stephen's unfriendly and ultimately unfair assessment of Locke's work contains some truth in its final clause: "Locke was a thoroughly modest, prosaic, tentative, and sometimes clumsy writer, who raises great questions without solving them or fully seeing *the conse-quences of his own position*" (my emphasis).[10] In this case, he failed to grasp the great possibilities his own method had released.

Because of the absence of any ontology of the mind, Locke's theory of experience proved acceptable to idealists like Berkeley as well as to French materialists. Berkeley, faithful to the empirical method, equated mind with the act of thinking. "Whoever shall go about to divide in his thought or abstract the existence of a spirit from its *cogitation* will, I believe, find it no easy task."[11] Yet in order to preserve the continuity of the self, the restriction of selfhood to conscious experiences forced him to the paradoxical conclusion that thinking is never interrupted: "The soul always thinks."[12] If reality consists of a succession of experiences, however, why should we assume those experiences to be linked by a permanent subject? In the end Berkeley's theology of the soul interfered with the empiricist principle he had adopted.[13]

No such religious restraints obstructed Hume in carrying the empiricist program to its ultimate conclusions. He most consistently applied the empirical method to the entire field of experience and thereby opened the road to introspective psychology. In his *Treatise of Human Nature* he grants almost as much space to a discussion of the passions (which, for him, include feelings as well as emotions) as to that of the understanding. Gifted with a rich imagination and a refined perceptiveness, he described emotions, feelings, and passions with accomplished literary skill. Hume wrote marvelous essays on the psychology of feelings and emotions, on aesthetics, and on the secret drives of human conduct. In his *History of England* he put his understanding of the "passions" to the test in scrutinizing the hidden motives and irrational behavior of political figures.

Yet while thus opening untapped sources of experience, Hume's radical empiricism led him to deconstruct not only the substantiality but even the identity of the self. He reduces the reality of the self to its various functions and dismisses any idea of substance, subject, or any other ontological principle. The fact that impressions follow a coherent order need not imply that they are supported by a single sustaining subject. "The true idea of the human mind is to consider it as a system of different perceptions of different existences which are linked together by a relation of cause and effect, and mutually produce, destroy, influence, and modify each other."[14] Yet Hume fails to account for the continuity among these impressions. The continuous transition from one to another presupposes a *retention* that enables one impression to endure while the next is already occurring, as well as a memory capable of recalling past impressions after a prolonged intermission of time. These are hard to conceive independently of a permanent subject. Hume admits that the *awareness* of a single continuous existence accompanies our perceptions, but he considers that no sufficient reason for implying the actual existence of a substantial self, of which we possess no separate impression (*Treatise,* I, 2, 6; also I, 4, 5).

Imperceptibly, Hume's theory of knowledge has turned into a theory of reality, a crypto-metaphysics. As one commentator observed: "The *Treatise* can no longer be considered an epistemological work, but must be regarded as a statement of ontology."[15] It is indeed ontological insofar as it deals with the *being* of appearances, but burdened as it is with the problems of modern epistemology, that being itself turns out to be no more than a mere phenomenon. In one sense, Hume's theory appears to mark the complete victory of the self as subject over the self as substance, with which it had still entertained an uneasy alliance in Descartes and even in Locke. Hume's consistent phenomenalism deprives personhood of substantial consistency. Selfhood is no more than an epiphenomenon of experience. Yet Hume was forced to continue using the very terminology of the philosophy he was destroying. No other language was available but the substantial one that he himself had undermined. Thus, he still spoke of "perceptions" even though there was no percipient left. It has been said rightly that his rejection of the self amounts to "the rejection of solipsism through solipsism."[16]

Few accepted Hume's position. Morality required someone who could be held accountable, and Hume himself soon became aware that his solution left no place for a responsible self. In an appendix to the separately published third part of the *Treatise on Human Nature* he admitted that the description of a self that is neither substantial nor necessarily continuous did not satisfy him. Indeed, he declared himself incapable of explaining the inner sense of unity that accompanies our perceptions except by reintroducing the very kind of substantial selfhood that his theory had concluded to be unprovable. Avoiding Cartesian dualism between body and mind, Hume, with most other empiricists, derived all ideas directly or indirectly from sensation as the single root of experience. In fact, his theory severed the self as moral agent from the self as epiphenomenon of experience. Not before the nineteenth century, and then only in rare instances, did thinkers question the need for a substantial agent responsible for his deeds.[17] Some postmodern writers who refer to the "person" as a fiction of recent origin, in their own way confirm the loss of the self implicit in Hume's theory.

French materialists took the opposite position: they asserted the substantiality of the self and reduced the self as subject to it. On the basis of Condillac's *Traité des sensations* (1754), they concluded that neither a subject nor an immaterial substance was needed to explain all aspects of mental life. In his book the French abbé had argued that sensation, from which all ideas were derived, was a purely physiological process. Dispensing with the qualifying paraphrases of his predecessors, Baron d'Holbach bluntly declared: "Man is a being purely physical. His visible actions as well as the invisible motion interiorly excited by his will or his thoughts, are equally the natural effects, the necessary consequences, of his peculiar mechanism, and the impulse he receives from those beings by whom he is surrounded."[18]

The writers of the *Encyclopédie,* like Hume, intended to construe a science of man. Yet the existing sciences were all of physical substances. Condillac's sensationalist epistemology enabled them to include the realm of consciousness within the physical sciences and thereby to overcome the disturbing gap between mind and matter. Humans are subject to the same laws as other animals and, indeed, as the entire physical universe. Descartes himself had described animals as part of the *res extensa,* the world of physical mechanism. When the physiologist Robert Whytt in 1751 showed that movement in animals and humans could be generated by stimulating the spinal cord, many materialists considered one of the final objections against the homogeneity of the organic and the psychic removed.[19] All materialists recognized that mechanical laws assumed a more complex form in beings who *consciously* reacted to motion, but for most of them, the greater complexity did not basically change the pattern of motion. Does not the mechanical system of a clock produce intelligible results by motion alone, La Mettrie wondered. "The soul is but a principle of motion or a material and sensible part of the brain which may be regarded as the mainspring of the entire machine having a visible influence on all its parts."[20]

Diderot, though he himself had once compared the person to *une horloge ambulante* (a walking clockwork), considered the sensationalist theory insufficient for explaining the birth of consciousness. Condillac had assumed that memory was the essential link between sensations and consciousness. But how did memory itself emerge from sensations? What causes them to be retained after they have ceased to be actually present? Attempting to answer the question on physiological grounds, Diderot, rather gratuitously, claimed that the organs of perception continue to "vibrate" long after the stimulus has desisted. They retain a past sensation while a new one is already entering the nervous system. Even as the vibration of one string of a musical instrument makes all others vibrate, the memory of an impression summons up a second, those two a third, those three together a fourth, and so on.[21] The real question, however, how the mind "stores" these impressions, remains unanswered. Diderot remained faithful to the materialist creed. The laws that determine the physical universe also govern the self. Passions may give us the impression that we act autonomously when we are in fact motivated by them. The feeling of self-determination rests on an illusion. There are no holes in the web of physical determinism. Desire of pleasure and aversion of pain unfailingly carry out the dictates of the biological instinct for survival. In his *Généalogie des passions* Helvetius added to this instinct a drive for power: each living being desires not only to be, but to be powerful and thereby to enhance its chances for survival.

French materialists attempted to overcome Cartesian dualism by reducing mind to the bodily substance. Others followed the opposite road. The French zoologist Buffon held that the human body, contrived to serve as the mind's instrument, substantially differs from animal bodiliness. A famous description in his *Histoire Naturelle* presents human anatomy as reflecting a higher, nonmaterial principle. "He stands erect, his attitude exudes command; his head lifted up to heaven presents an august face imprinted with the mark of his dignity; the soul's image appears in his physiognomy; the excellence of his nature penetrates his material organs and animates his traits with a divine fire; his majestic posture, his firm and daring gait announce his nobility and rank; the earth he only touches by his most remote extremities; he only views her from afar seemingly holding her in low esteem; his arms are not given him as pillars of support for the mass of his body."[22] Still, in that same work Buffon describes animal bodies as purely mechanical, as Descartes thought them to be. His theory overcomes materialist reductionism, but not Cartesian dualism.

That dualism excluded any possibility of human evolution from a lower species. Buffon was familiar with a number of phenomena by which later writers were to support the transformation of species. He acknowledged a continuous ascending order among the animal species. But to him, the gap between these species and human nature appeared so deep as to render a leap from one to the other utterly impossible. "If the person belonged to the animal order, there would in nature exist a number of beings less perfect than humans yet more perfect than animals through which one would gradually, by almost imperceptible shifts, descend from man to ape. But they do not exist. We pass abruptly from the thinking being to the material one, from intellectual power to mechanical force, from order and design to blind motion, from reflection to appetite." Buffon does not even see an analogy between animal and human species. Humans are simply not in the same class as animals. He continues to view the animals, which he so knowledgeably describes, as Descartes had seen them—as *automata*.

In his later work Buffon yielded somewhat to the pressure of progress in the zoological science to which he himself had much contributed. He ended up admitting the existence of sensitivity, memory, and even dreams in animals. But the line that divides them from humans remains as rigidly drawn as before.

Herder, who started the hierarchy from animal to human from below rather than from above (as Buffon had done), defended a teleological move toward humanity. The ascending order of animals gradually prepared a finely tuned instrument for exercising mental functions. Yet neither Herder nor Leibniz, who had formulated the principle of continuity, were ready to embrace any form of biological evolution. Kant, in his review of books one to five of Herder's *Ideas for a Philosophy of History,* severely criticized even the alleged analogy between the organic structures of animals and those of humans.

This investigation of the ambiguity concerning the self as subject and/or as substance may seem a rather arcane philosophical problem, distant from common human concerns. Writers of memoirs and autobiographies, poets, and novelists focused their attention on the immediate states of consciousness that convey a different, more intimate awareness of selfhood. Nonetheless, on a more fundamental level, we detect a common concern. Both philosophy and literature display an awakened subjectivity. However different his moral outlook, La Rochefoucauld in his *Maxims* insists as much on pure intentions as Kant in his *Critique of Practical Reason;* Abbé Prévost's novels of irresistible passions find a justification in Hume's treatment of the same subject; Shaftesbury's discussion of feelings and intuitions echoes Pascal's knowledge of the heart. We now turn to those more immediate forms of self-awareness.

Passions, Feelings, and Emotions

We still to refer to the eighteenth century as the Age of Reason, yet a comparison of its views on reason, passions, and feelings with those current in the preceding century shows that the epithet more properly applies to the earlier period. Despite the persistence and development of rationalist trends, the Enlightenment could more accurately be described as an age of *self-consciousness*. The loss of the person's central position in the post-Galilean universe initiated a reflective mood. Lost in a planet of one of the innumerable solar systems, humans could no longer reasonably assume that the universe existed for their benefit or that they constituted its ultimate raison d'être. This insight released two seemingly opposite but actually concurring reactions. The first one was pointedly expressed in Hume's statement quoted at the beginning of this chapter in which he urges his contemporaries, now that admirable inroads have been made in the domain of the natural sciences, to focus on the human source of this knowledge. However minute a place the person may occupy in the general scheme of things, the human mind has nonetheless brought the entire universe into scientific subjugation. Hence the self presented a new, even more important field for scientific conquests. The other reaction consisted in a withdrawal from the natural world in order to reflect on the interior life where all that really mattered to the person remained greatly unexplored. This inward move was supported by the spiritual trends of the time.

The interest in self-knowledge that suddenly increased during the late seventeenth century would be hard to imagine without the practice of daily self-examination such as that recommended in Catholic spirituality (that of the Jesuits as well as of the Jansenists). Pietists and Puritans also felt the need to scrutinize their inner attitude and to search for signs of election. This unintermittent self-reflection has left its mark on spiritual as well as profane literature in Great Britain and, even more, in New England.[23] I shall analyze some of the sources of spiritual life in the Enlightenment in the final chapter, but here I must at least mention such remarkable works of introspective piety as Fénélon's letters of spiritual guidance, Jonathan Edwards's treatise on *Religious Affections,* and William Law's *The Spirit of Love.* As a French historian of ideas aptly put it: "Pietism is an intermediate phase in the process of a human consciousness on its way toward emancipation. The God of Pietism is the God who hides in the secret of the hearts."[24]

Among the secular sources of the trend toward introspection, Shaftesbury may well be the first name to mention. Convinced that there is more to selfhood than Descartes's and Locke's "punctual" self-consciousness, he dismissed the central *cogito ergo sum* as being no more than an analytic statement (*there is thinking*) that provides no information about the content of the self whose existence it asserts. He anticipated Hume's suspicion that one cannot even derive the existence of a single thinking substance from the *cogito.* Descartes's substantial identity is no more than an unproven supposition. Memory was supposed to link my experience of myself in the past to my present self-consciousness. But Descartes himself had admitted that memory may be deceptive. Indeed, Shaftesbury observed, the self I remember never coincides with the self I really was and even less with the self I am now. "Consciousness may as well be false as real in respect to what is past."[25] Shaftesbury himself never explains what he considers to be the content of the mind, but he emphatically denies that it consists in the capacity to generate clear and distinct ideas. Instead he seeks that content at the deeper, more obscure level of consciousness to which we refer as *feeling.* Self-knowledge, for Shaftesbury, consists first and foremost in an awareness of one's feelings. Others followed him in this direction. Rousseau argued that not reason, but the deeper, more diffuse self-awareness attained in feeling forms the core of mind. At the beginning of the *Confessions* he raises the question, "Qui suis-je?" and answers, "Je sens mon coeur." A far cry from *Cogito ergo sum!* The popular playwright Nivelle de la Chaussée made the difference explicit in one of his dramas: "Plus je sens vivement, plus je sens que je suis." (The more acutely I feel, the more I feel that I am.)[26]

A third factor that affected the emotional climate of the eighteenth century was the nature and sudden success of the novel. It began in France. Originally a tale of adventure — either heroic or picaresque — the novel had in the seventeenth century taken an introspective turn. It became a reflection on the complex interaction of feelings, passions, and emotions in love. Mme. de La Fayette's *La princesse de Clèves* (published in 1678) set the tone for much of the subsequent narrative literature, not only in France but also in England. In this psychological novel few events occur. The story follows its course from private feeling to emotional struggle and moral victory. Having fallen in love with a man who loves her, the princess remains faithful to her husband, even after his death. Richardson's novels *Pamela* and *Clarissa* were soon to refine, if not to surpass, La Fayette's exquisite analysis of feelings. Those romances explored a more intimate layer of consciousness. Characteristic of the shifting interest was a change in the meaning of such terms as *sensibilité* and *sensibility*. Originally *sensible,* in French as well as in English, had referred to intellectual perceptiveness: the ability to sense or to reflect. By the eighteenth century it had become a substantive and acquired a strongly emotional connotation. It then came to mean, as the Oxford Dictionary explains, a power or faculty of feeling and, more specifically, a capacity for refined emotions, as Jane Austen's distinction between *sense* and *sensibility* shows. Such terms as "sensitive" and "thoughtful" likewise broadened their original, purely cognitive meaning.[27]

Philosophy had paid little attention to the emotional side of the self. Of course, Descartes's *Treatise on the Passions of the Soul* (1649) as well as Spinoza's quite different treatment of the same subject had appeared in the seventeenth century. But passions are not feelings. Moreover, with regard to the passions a change in attitude was taking place at the end of the century. Descartes had still unhesitatingly declared that no soul, however weak, is incapable of gaining total control over its passions.[28] Such had essentially been the Stoic position. Passions, though necessary, are to be subdued by reason. Descartes had somewhat qualified the negative Stoic judgment. In his theory passions fulfill a vital function; they assist the will in executing what reason commands. Still, passions originate in the body and disturb mental life until reason gains full control over them.[29] Spinoza also considered passions indispensable, but they need to be converted into active powers.[30]

Corneille's dramas reflect both these positive and negative traits. In the *Examen* that prefaces *Le Cid* Corneille writes: "The high virtue in a nature sensitive to these passions, which she subjugates without weakening them, and to which she leaves their full force in order to triumph over them even more gloriously, has something more touching, more noble, and more attractive than the mediocre goodness, capable of weakness, indeed of crime, to which our Ancients were constrained to limit even the most perfect character of those kings and princes whom they made their heroes."[31] Passions, then, were at once a challenge to moral excellence and a means to attain it. So philosophers gradually started abandoning the negative, Stoic assessment of the passions that had dominated ethical theories since the Renaissance. Typical for the changing attitude was the title of the first chapter of Jean-François Senault's treatise on the use of passions, *Apologie pour les passions contre les Stoiques* (1672). Without passion humans possess no strong motive for acting: some jolt of emotion needs to shake their indolence.

Few questioned that life had to be lived in accordance with reason, but the assumption that this meant a life free of passion and emotion ceased to be part of that rule. Emblematic for the new mentality was Addison's play *Cato* (1713), which, unlike Seneca's stern tragedy, presents the Roman hero as torn between feelings for his family and his patriotic duty.[32] Samuel Johnson (in *Rasselas,* chap. 18) and Henry Fielding (in *Joseph Andrews*) criticized Stoic indifference as unnatural and even perverse in the face of human suffering. In his portrait of the man of virtue, ironically entitled "The Stoic," David Hume has scant praise for the ancient ideal that lacks "the charm of the social affections." In fact Hume's Stoic, who combines "the softest benevolence with the most undaunted resolution," stands closer to the early romantic sensitivity than to ancient *apatheia*.[33]

Gradually passions came to be regarded as the stronger and often the only impulse to action. No one understood the independent and sometimes irresistible power of passions better than the French novelist who went under the name Abbé Prévost, one among several English and French writers whom Shaftesbury directly or (as in this case) indirectly inspired. In his best-known story, *Manon Lescaut,* he describes how a young man's irrational passion for a faithless woman drives him to his doom. Prévost passes no moral judgment on his conduct. He simply presents emotions as more powerful drives of human behavior than rational judgment or moral precept. The turbulences of emotional life show how the self, far from being the serene kingdom of reason or the undisturbed center of Stoic equanimity, is a snake pit of uncontrollable passions jostling for supremacy. Still, despite their often disastrous effects, Prévost has no doubt that emotions constitute the richness of inner life. "Most people are aware only of the five or six passions within which their lives are spent and to which all their affections are reduced. Take away love and hatred, pleasure and pain, hope and fear, and nothing remains. But persons of noble character may be moved in a thousand different ways."[34] Nor were men and women of the time bashful in expressing their emotions. In *Mémoires et avantures d'un homme de qualité,* a multivolume *roman fleuve,* Prévost's hero exclaims: "If tears and sighs cannot carry the name of pleasures, it is nevertheless true that they contain an infinite sweetness for a mortally afflicted person. All the moments I gave to my grief were so dear to me that, in order to prolong them, I hardly took any sleep."[35] In fact, it took far less than "mortal affliction" to make the hero shed sweet tears. In the "age of reason," weeping belonged to the *bon ton,* for men as much as for women. Even hard-headed cynics like Voltaire cried at the slightest occasion; no less than his notoriously tearsome opponent, Rousseau, who proudly confesses: "Peu d'hommes ont autant gémi que moi, peu ont autant versé de pleurs dans leur vie."[36]

Herbert Richardson, Prévost's model, discovered that no literary form was more appropriate for the unrestrained expression and analysis of feelings and emotions than the letter. The epistolary form of his novels allowed his effusive heroines to express the whole gamut of feelings—love, aversion, ambivalence—as they attempt to sort out their emotional confusion. Richardson knew how to extend the chain of reflection indefinitely. Beside gushing their own feelings out to parents and friends, Pamela and Clarissa report stories and opinions imparted to them concerning the feelings of thrice removed acquaintances. These reports in turn invite searches for hidden intentions, new expectations, and so on. Each event prismatically breaks open into a fan of feelings and emotions. In fact, events merely provide occasions for feelings. Although the young women (and perhaps their author as well) remain blissfully ignorant of the measure to which their most private feelings reflect the moral and social codes and prejudices of their time, the letters nevertheless remain marvelous exercises in introspection. For Richardson, truth lies within ourselves, in our feelings and emotions.

Yet such romantic explorations of the emotional content of selfhood, however favorably contrasting with the sterility of the rationalist analyses, suffer from a poverty of their own. They detach feelings and emotions from the complexity of the psychic life, secluding them within a separate "sphere" that lacks structure and unity. The sentimental self is no more than a succession of floating moods, barely united by loose associations. In the end the preromantic novel of the eighteenth century may reveal less about the nature of personhood than such sturdier predecessors as *Don Quixote* and *Gargantua.* Where the main content of consciousness consists of feelings, actions that give direction to life lose their supremacy.

Less self-conscious but often more revealing was the real correspondence among members of the upper classes in France during the late seventeenth century. Madame de Sévigné raised this naive form of introspection to classic elegance in the almost daily warm and witty letters she exchanged with her daughter. In gossipy, occasionally catty, yet always fascinating reflections on the events around the Sun King's Court, the marquise discloses as much about her own feelings as about the objects of her ironical observation. Her elegantly phrased sentences move with the flow of private thoughts, emotions, and feelings rather than following the lines of logic and consistency. Other letter writers reveal an unexpected side of themselves. Voltaire, the confident author of sarcastic epigrams, cold dramas, and critical barbs against all people other than himself, exhibits a quite different persona in his letters. In some of them, we encounter a witty, warm-blooded yet vulnerable man, devoted to his Jesuit masters, loving of his friends, and fearful of his enemies (especially Rousseau). One may wonder, however, whether such epistolary self-disclosure may not be an easy means to hide or idealize one's true feelings. The suspicion is particularly strong in such a Protean figure as Voltaire. Dr. Johnson suspected that the personal tone of the letter as well as the writer's relation to his correspondent may tempt the writer to express rarely felt affections as if they were habitual ones. "There is indeed no transaction which offers stronger temptations to fallacy and sophistication than epistolary intercourse. In the eagerness of conversation the first emotions of the mind often burst out before they are considered; in the tumult of business interest and passion have their genuine effect; but a friendly letter is a calm and deliberate performance in the cool of leisure, in its stillness of solitude, and surely no man sits down to depreciate by design his own character."[37]

The knowledge of human nature was pursued on the generic no less than on the personal level. In France, a new literary genre of aphoristic observations on the mostly negative, common traits of human nature gained instant popularity. Among the numerous *moralistes,* as its authors were called, we remember mainly La Rochefoucauld, La Bruyère, and Vauvenargues. In his *Maximes,* the acidic Duke François de La Rochefoucauld (1613–80) dispenses searing observations on human vice and virtue, love and hatred, glory and envy, but even more on the petty motives that mostly inspire one as well as the other. Not a word about himself, his contemporaries, or the social conditions of his time. From the perspective of this seventeenth-century aristocrat's eagle's eye, "humanity" appears to consist of exchangeable persons, timeless *types.*

As the old nobility was slowly yielding its rule to the *noblesse de robe,* reflections became more personal. In his *Caractères* (1645–96), La Bruyère revived the psychological typology that Theophrastus, Aristotle's successor, had written to complement his moral theory. But the French *moraliste* turned the Greek philosopher's gallery of ethical "types" into a series of portraits. His universal "characters" display individual features. They bear no names, but behind the sharply drawn models one senses the presence of contemporary faces. "The whole supremacy of La Bruyère's art, Lytton Strachey writes, consists in that absolute precision, that complete finish, that perfect proportion, which gives his *Characters* the quality of a De Hoogh, and his aphorisms the brilliant hardness of a Greek gem."[38] Indirectly, *La Bruyère* criticized the social and political environment of his models. He foresaw the collapse of a society in which peasants were living on "black bread, water, and roots." "Once the people start moving, one no longer knows how peace can return."

With the Marquis de Vauvenargues (1715–47) the tone becomes moralistic, occasionally sentimental, the language larded with such programmatic terms as *raison, liberté, nature*. The young Vauvenargues, an unusually generous person himself, introduced a note of *suspicion* that was to sound ever more loudly in the later period of the Enlightenment. Whereas La Rochefoucauld had explored the universal qualities (especially the bad ones) of human nature, and La Bruyère its social conditionedness, Vauvenargues preromantically focused on the disproportion between human aspirations and their chances of being fulfilled. The *moraliste* reflections, though derived from introspection as much as from observation, lacked the personal touch of memoirs and auto-biographies. The quintessential portraitist of character was the duc de Saint-Simon (1675–1755).

Opinionated in the extreme, incapable of doubting his own prejudices, ferocious in his hostility, and always on the barricades, he succeeded, despite his vices, or possibly because of them, in capturing the irreducible singularity of his subjects. For the jaundiced duke, no types exist, only individuals. In his mind, he alone possesses the insight to perceive the hidden motives behind people's actions and the courage to confront them with his superior knowledge. The expression, "I looked him straight in the eyes" constantly returns in his *Memoirs*. He regards himself as the absolute witness, to whom nothing escapes and who is endowed with an infallible judgment. Though himself uninterruptedly implicated in intrigues, he reserves his sharpest barbs for other intriguants. Watchdog of the old aristocratic order, he is merciless for those who ascend the social ladder without having ancient "blood." His resentment goes in the first place to Madame de Maintenon, the king's morganatic wife, who, like an evil stepmother, has wormed herself into an undeserved proximity to the king. Saint-Simon's attitude to Louis XIV reflects the kind of ambiguity a son feels for a father: he hates his autocratic authority, yet he feels filial devotion and, above all, a protective hatred for all intruders into his privileged intimacy. His portrait of Madame de Maintenon, as well as those of General Vendôme, of finance minister Pontchartrain, and of the duc de Noailles, are classics of vituperative literature. Yet he was hardly less severe for other aristocrats whom he considered degenerate members of his own class. In the first place, Monsieur, the king's lascivious brother, and even more Monsieur's granddaughter, whose marriage the duke himself had helped to arrange and who turned out to be "a fat, nasty, self-indulgent drunk." His white-hot, unmitigated hatred for those traitors of their class knows no limit. Some have interpreted the scarcity of his loves and the multitude of the hatreds as projecting the ambivalence that marked the early relation with his parents.[39]

His rare admirations remain rarely unmixed. While praising his gentle father figure, the duc de Beauvilliers, and his friend, the equally high-minded duc de Chevreuse, both of whom Saint-Simon genuinely loved, he refers to the latter as a naive optimist, more given to talk than action, and to the pious Beauvilliers as being "narrow" in his principles. Nor does the spiteful duke relent after the death of his victims. His necrology of one Madame d'Hendicourt begins with the words: "The court was delivered from a *familiar* [i.e., an informer] by the death of Mme. d'Hendicourt. . . . She had grown old and hideously ugly, but in her time no one was more agreeable or better informed, more cheerful, witty, and unaffectedly diverting. On the other hand, there was no one more gratuitously, continually and intentionally malicious, and therefore more dangerous, on account of her familiarity with the king and Mme. de Maintenon. Thus everyone, favorites, nobles, officers of State, ministers, members of the royal family, even the bastards, bent the knee to that old bitch, who enjoyed doing harm and never had the faintest wish to oblige. With her passing [Mme. de Maintenon] the king lost a great source of amusement, but society at whose expense this was provided was immensely relieved, for she was a heartless creature."[40]

British character portraits (except for an occasional distychon by Pope) rarely approach the vitriolic acidity of Saint-Simon's portrayals. Addison's "Observations" in *The Spectator* and Samuel Johnson's sketches in *The Rambler* and *The Adventurer* were kinder but less probing. Yet they resembled the duke's characters at least in the respect that they depicted concrete individuals, not universal types, and also, particularly in Johnson's case, that they resisted any kind of social change. Carlyle has, not unfairly, called him the last Englishman who, with strong voice and wholly believing heart, preached the virtue of standing still, tenaciously clinging to "decaying materials for want of anything better."[41] Regarding human nature as unchanged and unchangeable, Johnson attributed the problems of his time to a tampering with the eternal social and religious foundations of human nature. His melancholy disposition gave the doctor a keen eye for other people's foibles. His sketches, intended as universal moral lessons, bear the signs of personal spleen and mostly lack psychological depth. Only in his biographical explorations in the *Lives of the Poets* does he, with one stroke, attain unscaled critical and psychological heights.

Biographies have been written since Greek antiquity. But over the centuries their purposes have changed. Ancient ones, such as Plutarch's *Vitae* or Tacitus's *Life of Germanicus,* mostly pictured their subjects as models to imitate or to avoid. Medieval hagiographies served an additional purpose, for next to being *exempla,* they responded to the believers' need for the mediation of saints no less than to their obligation to imitate them. Even the best, such as Gregory's *Life of Saint Benedict,* follow universal models of heroic virtue. Except for the "miracles," they reveal so few personal traits as to be interchangeable. This pattern prevailed in the early modern lives of political heroes. Eighteenth-century biographers, however, by and large abandoned the ideal of a model for imitation. Instead, they showed the historical or cultural significance of their subject — good or bad. Such was certainly Samuel Johnson's primary motive for writing his *Lives of the Poets.* His essays penetratingly explore the psychic makeup of his subjects in order to discover the deeper meaning behind the poems, the hidden drives that attracted the author to one topic rather than another as well as to a particular way of treating it. Johnson introduced what later became a substantial part of literary criticism. His *Life of Pope* ranks in this respect as a masterpiece. While admiring Pope's genius with words, he mercilessly exposes the deviousness, vanity, and morbid sensitivity of his character, as well as the complexity of his relation with others. "He [Pope] frequently professes contempt of the world. . . . These were dispositions apparently counterfeited. How could he despise those whom he lived by pleasing and on whose approbation his esteem of himself was superstructured? — His scorn of Great is repeated too often to be real: no man thinks much of that which he despises. — In the Letters both of Swift and Pope there appears such narrowness of mind as makes them insensible of any excellence that has not some affinity with their own."[42]

Johnson's own hagiographic biographer was right: the man possessed a peculiar art of drawing characters "as rare as good portrait painting."[43] But Boswell himself surpassed his model in scrutinizing its own particularities. The slavish disciple obsessively wrote down every word, every deed, whether significant or trivial. Then he worshipfully arranged his master's *logia* in a loosely chronological order, faithfully reporting the sparkles of Johnson's vigorous mind as well as his equally vigorous prejudices, all in the same respectful monotone. In this relentless pursuit of a total portrait of an individual with all his quirks and mannerisms lies, in spite of its author's common intellect, the lasting fascination of Boswell's *Life of Johnson.* It soon surpassed the popularity of its subject's own writings. Carlyle was enthralled by it. "In worth as a book we have rated it beyond any other product of the eighteenth century: all J's own writings, laborious and in their kind genuine above most, stand on a quite inferior level to it; already, indeed, they are becoming obsolete for this generation; and for some future generation may be valuable chiefly as prolegomena and expository scholia to this Johnsoniad of Boswell."[44] Macaulay, another countryman of Boswell, writing forty years after the appearance of his famous work when Romanticism had fully conquered the minds for the primacy of the individual, attributed the quality of the *Life* to the average mind of a biographer who, not knowing the difference between the significant and the insignificant, left us a "complete" picture of its subject. "Many of the greatest men that ever lived have written biography. Boswell was one of the smallest men that ever lived; and he has beaten them all. Others attained literary eminence in spite of their weaknesses. Boswell attained it by reason of his weakness. If he had not been a great fool, he would never have been a great writer."[45]

Boswell's devotion to his subject did not produce a hagiography. Repeatedly we hear him chiding his hero for not abiding by his own moral principles. Boswell's Johnson is not a universal model but a unique individual: a man of slovenly appearance with a rolling gait, extremely industrious yet at times immovably sluggish, a methodical scholar yet uncommonly irregular in his habits, benevolent and generous yet a harsh critic of others — an irreducible original. Boswell's biography of the man who so solidly belongs to the Enlightenment announces the quest of the individual so single-mindedly pursued by Rousseau and the Romantics. The eighteenth-century biographical portrait, even when totally particular and no model of perfection, still invites the reader to *compare* the subject with him or herself. Though the person whose story is told may surpass the reader in some respects, he or she appears quite ordinary in other respects. The relation between the self and the other has changed in modern biography. One might say that the subject is there not to be admired but to justify the reader's own existence.

We notice an analogous but even more pronounced egocentric trend in the autobiography. Earlier autobiographies had described the self in its relation to others. Augustine's had entirely consisted of a dialogue with God and Teresa of Avila's *Life* of her relations with superiors and fellow sisters. Yet during the Enlightenment the relation with others ceased to be a dialogue and instead displayed the controlling presence of the author. Modern autobiographies became increasingly self-centered and self-conscious. The certainty of self-consciousness that since Descartes had become the foundation of truth here becomes the ground of the indubitable truth about oneself. As each person possesses a strictly private, incommunicable awareness of him or herself, so each must find his or her own way to truth. Descartes had stressed the auto-biographical nature of his search, describing it in the *Discourse on Method* as "a fable in which amongst certain things which may be imitated, there are possibly others also which it would not be right to follow." The truth based on self-consciousness is universal, yet the road to it, the *methodos,* differs from one person to another. Hence the personal, almost chatty tone of his story: "From my childhood I lived in a world of books. I had been in one of the most celebrated schools in Europe. . . . I was in Germany, where I had gone because of the wars which are still not ended. . . . I remained all day alone in a warm room."[46]

Most revealing of the link between personal and universal truth is *The Life of Giambattista Vico Written by Himself* (1730). For Vico, the universal is not merely the outcome of an autobiographical process. It permeates that process itself. He considered truth to be intrinsically historical and the story of the self to form an integral segment of that universal history. Yet, his notion of univer-sality was not an abstract idea, but a concrete universal that incorporated the particularity of his life. Vico tells his story from that historical perspective. The solemn tone of the first paragraph — "G.V. was born in Naples in the year 1670 of upright parents who left a good name after them"[47] — in which he reports on the characters of his parents and on the events of his early youth, leaves no doubt that he regarded himself as a link in the chain of history moving toward a providential destiny. Each event of his life takes its place within an ideal totality.[48]

Vico, a teacher of rhetoric himself, may have been inspired by the panegyric exercises of Petrarch, Cardano, and other humanists. Yet his work sprung pri-marily from a philosophical ambition to show, on the small scale of his own life, the universal significance of even the most contingent events. He regarded history (including his own) as a theodicy that justified the ways of Providence in guiding the entire human race toward its natural destiny. His autobiography forms part of this sweeping motion of history. Vico's *Life* complements *The New Science* (*La scienza nuova,* 1744) insofar as universal history proceeds through personal decisions toward self-chosen ends. Giuseppe Mazzotta is right: "The *New Science* [of history] is the real subject matter of the text: it is at the same time, a symbolic event which, in retrospect, gives coherence, direction, and intelligibility to the apparent roundness of Vico's intellectual quest."[49]

Public figures often feel urged to write an autobiography in order to set the record straight by describing how they reached the decisions of which out-siders only know the results. For Vico, the public effects form part of a prede-termined, providential plan, yet the individual's decisions make the execution of that plan possible. These decisions, though free, were influenced by circumstances over which the person exercised no control. As a child Vico fell from a ladder and nearly died. This incident caused him to grow up, he claims, "with a melancholy and irritable temperament such as belongs to men of ingenuity and depth."[50] This particular disposition enabled him freely to take decisions that were to move history toward the fulfillment of the providential plan.

By writing an autobiography a person of some repute attempts to fill the gap between the intentions of his deeds, known only to himself, and their actual effects known to others. The writer thereby hopes to overcome the discrepancy discussed at the beginning of this chapter, between the self as *subject* and the self as *substance*. Such an effort never fully succeeds. The reader will continue to distinguish the author's words from his unrevealed intentions. The author himself experiences an inevitable discrepancy. Even Augustine mentions the difficulty. He considered self-knowledge in this life impossible: we are incapable of gaining definitive insight into ourselves as long as we have to do so within the distention of time. Rousseau attributed the main obstacle to authentic self-description not to the limits of introspection, but to the insurmountable misunderstanding by others. For him, the crucial distinction is no longer the one between private intentions and public actions, but between the subject of both intentions and actions on one side and, on the other, the objective, universal norms by which others judge one. He regarded a perfect self-identity not only possible but in his *Confessions* actually realized.[51]

By portraying himself as faithfully as possible, with his qualities as well as his defects, Rousseau attempts (without much hope of ultimate success) to render himself as transparent to others as he is to himself. He wants to be seen as an individual, distinct from any other individual and not to be judged by objective standards. "I am made unlike anyone I have ever met; I will even venture to say that I am like no one in the whole world. I may be no better but at least I am different."[52] He recognizes no predecessors and, he claims, will have no imitators. He neither justifies nor excuses his obsessions and manias, his irresponsible attitude, and his objectionable conduct. His uniqueness dispenses him from the need to justify his actions. With disarming openness (though not always with full objectivity) he discloses his embarrassing traits: his sexual obsessiveness, his habit of giving his children up for adoption as soon as they are born. Far from feeling humbled by this baring of his questionable behavior, he appears to think that his sincerity renders him immune to criticism and he criticizes those whom he suspects of being less candid.[53] Contrary to earlier autobiographies, the *Confessions* were not intended to justify its author but to exhibit his uniqueness. Such at least was his stated intention. But it did not stop him, especially in the second part, from settling accounts with his enemies — Voltaire, Diderot, Grimm, d'Holbach, Hume, all of whom feared his searing attacks.

Despite his moral duplicity, Rousseau displays an unprecedented insight and honesty in reporting the hidden, often unflattering complexity of his motives. The account he gives of the theft of a silver ribbon that he had committed and of which he accused a young fellow servant may serve as an example. In scrutinizing the motives for a deed he considered "*affreux*" even at the time he committed it, he concludes: "Never was deliberate wickedness further from my intention than at that cruel moment. When I accused that poor girl, it is strange but true that my friendship for her was the cause" (*Confessions,* bk. II, O.C., I, 86; Cohen, p. 88). Indeed, he suggests that he stole the ribbon in order to give it to her as a present. When the theft was detected, however, he accused her, the person closest to him. She was promptly dismissed. In his last work, the *Rêveries d'un promeneur solitaire,* he returns to this shameful episode, the guilt of which continued to haunt him all his life.

Obviously the center of selfhood has been replaced! Not Descartes's substantial *res cogitans* nor Hume's loosely coherent stream of perceptions are the subject of the *Confessions*. Rousseau regards all that as still objective. He aims at reaching the subjective core of feeling from which all specific acts of consciousness, ideas, passions, and emotions, emerge. His description owes more to the sentimental novels of his time than to philosophy. The first paragraphs remind us of the initial sentence of Abbé Prévost's *Mémoires d'un homme de qualité* (1728–31): "This story will be read if anyone finds it worth reading. I have written down my misfortunes only for my own satisfaction. I shall be content if as the fruit of my work I draw some tranquillity during the moments I shall spend writing it." Novels starting with this kind of confessional exordium had become common. The hero, reminiscing upon the events of his life, confesses his errors and weaknesses, "mes désordres et mes plus honteuses faiblesses" as the love-struck hero of *Manon Lescaut* puts it.[54] Rousseau had read Prévost as well as Richardson and a great many less illustrious writers of romances. He converted his autobiography into a romance of feelings.

In the *Confessions* Rousseau remembers expressions, gestures, and words too elusive to be fully captured at the moment of their appearance: the look of a stranger, the fleeting change in a familiar face, the unexpected move. Rousseau himself draws attention to the "secondary," reflective bent of his mind. "I can only see in retrospect (*Je ne vois bien que ce que je me rappelle*). It is only in my memories that my mind can work. I have neither feeling nor understanding for anything that is said or done or that happens before my eyes. . . . But afterwards it all comes back to me, I remember the place and the time, the tone of voice and look, the gesture and vibration; nothing escapes me" (bk. III,

O.C., I, 114–15; Cohen, p. 114). Only when interiorized in memory do past experiences disclose their significance. He may have been mistaken in their interpretation, he admits, or he may inaccurately have recalled them. What counts for him are the feelings connected with the facts *as he remembers them.* "I have only one faithful guide on which I can count; the succession of feelings which have marked the development of my being, and thereby recall the events that have acted upon it as cause or effect. . . . I may omit or transpose facts, or make mistakes in dates; but I cannot go wrong about what I have felt, or what my feelings led me to do; and these are the chief subjects of my story." (*Confessions,* bk. VII, O.C., I, 278; Cohen, p. 262). Of course, one may be very wrong about the feelings one remembers: they are often no more than the ones present at the time of writing. In reflecting on past feelings one never merely recalls them. A feeling remembered may over time have increased or decreased in intensity, or even have changed its quality altogether. To remember one's feelings, then, is more than a reproductive act: it consists essentially in producing new feelings on the basis of old memories and thereby recreating the past.[55]

If feelings constitute the core of selfhood, as Rousseau thinks, the self never *is,* but continuously *becomes* and redefines itself. In remembering past feelings, however inaccurately, we link the past more solidly to the present than in recalling emotionally indifferent past events. We know that memory may distort or fully contradict the facts. Yet we do not distrust our past feelings because we experience them as an uninterrupted bond with our past. In feelings, the self appears, so to speak, as extended in time. To remember them is to link the time of their original experience to an indefinite future. Feelings remembered carry with them an unmistakable sense of self-recognition: I cannot doubt that I am the same person I was when I felt that way. In a masterly way Rousseau evokes this sense of self-identity through the recollection of past feelings.

A perceptive and knowledgeable student of his work, the Swiss psychiatrist Jean Starobinski has shown how Rousseau's autobiographical writing was born out of a desire to become fully "transparent," to others as well as to himself.[56] In his final *Les rêveries du promeneur solitaire,* Starobinski argues, the great writer at last recognized that the ultimate goal of his relentless introspection proved unattainable: no one ever becomes fully transparent not even to himself. In feeling one experiences oneself as *continuous* with oneself from one time to another. But full transparency would require a *coincidence* with one's past.[57] A self distended in time, never reaches complete reunion with itself, as Augustine had known. My past remains irretrievably separated from my present. The possibility of becoming transparent to others remains even further out of reach. I may communicate my feelings to others. But such a communication can never be more than indirect.

Rousseau hoped to awaken in his readers a desire to scrutinize their own inner life and so to understand themselves.[58] To do so effectively required a language of utmost precision and simplicity that would draw all attention to the message, none to the expression. France's foremost critic of the past century, Charles Augustin Sainte-Beuve, attributed most of Rousseau's enormous influence to his spare, lucid style. "The writer who brought about the greatest single change in the French language since Pascal and who ushered in, linguistically speaking, the nineteenth century, is Rousseau. . . . The day he bared himself wholly to himself, the century recognized in him the writer most capable of giving expression to the unformed ideas which had been agitating it, the writer best able to state them with originality, vigor, and impassioned logic."[59] Jean Paul in *Titan,* Benjamin Constant in *Adolphe,* Goethe in *Wilhelm Meister* and in *Dichtung und Wahrheit,* as well as countless romantic writers were to follow Rousseau in their search for the soul.

New Perspectives on Language

The intense interest in language that emerged in the eighteenth century shed new light on the problems of selfhood caused by the modern turn to the subject and the subsequent search for its place in the objective order of things. It proved impossible to give an adequate account of speech within the perimeters of a subject-object opposition. That speech was a given of human nature, evolved from animal expressiveness as French sensationalists claimed, was the first theory to be refuted. Yet the idealist position, according to which speech was a necessary part of the mind's expressive power independent of social environment and physiological structures, proved equally untenable. Further reflection on the nature of language showed how a dichotomous concept of selfhood (such as we encountered in the first section of this chapter) proved to be not only in principle but also in practice untenable. Language depends on an intimate cooperation between the subjective and objective aspects of selfhood, which excludes any description of it in terms of only one or the other. In speech, human expressiveness shows its unique creativity. Still, even that creative power remains dependent on such elementary objective data as physiological disposition, social conditions, and the existence of natural sounds — such as the cries of animals, the songs of birds, and the rustling of wind and rain.

As theories of human nature gradually changed from static to dynamic, problems of expression assumed an increasing significance. Linguistic studies thereby moved to the center of cultural interest. In less than a century the Enlightenment succeeded in developing a complex theory of language. Locke defined the critical question: How does language relate to meaning? The relation between word and reality had remained relatively stable until the late Middle Ages. Augustine had described the word as *simillimum rei notae* (most similar to the thing known). That this similarity did not mean a "copy" appears from the clause he adds: *et imago eius* (and its image).[60] The image nature of language had theological roots. In the doctrine of the Trinity, the Word (*Logos, Verbum*) was the *image* of the Father. Similarly, the human mind is an image of the archetypal divine Word, and human words imitate God's expression. Yet only the *verbum internum*, that is, the mind, could be called a true image of the Word; not the *verbum externum*, the actual word we utter. Augustine thereby resumes a distinction, first made by Stoic philosophers and taken over by Neoplatonists, between the *logos endiathetos* (the inner word) and the *logos prosforikos* (the uttered word). In Augustine's view, only the revealed words of the Bible participate directly in the eternal Word. Ordinary words merely function as arbitrary instruments of the mind's *verbum internum*. As such they are mere signs, not images.[61] Aquinas and the many Scholastics who followed him conceived of the link between inner word and verbal expression as being more intimate. Inner knowledge does not reach completion until it is uttered in language. For Aquinas, truth requires verbal expression.

Those speculations lost much of their power in the nominalist theory of language at the end of the Middle Ages, which stressed the simple fact that words, whether spoken or written, are arbitrary signs that present no guarantee of truth but often lead the mind into error. They do so specifically in suggesting the real or ideal existence of universals. Yet nominalism played a significant role in the rise of modern theories of language by stressing its creative power. At the beginning of the modern epoch, then, three different conceptions of language competed with one another: the Neoplatonic tradition stressed the image quality of the spoken or written word; the nominalist tradition wherein words serve as signs; and the Aristotelian tradition, continued by the Thomists, adopted an intermediate position.

The nominalist theory may have inspired Descartes's idea of a *mathesis universalis*, a system modeled after mathematics that would integrate all knowledge within a universal system of signs. He assumed that as mathematical units are interrelated, so all segments of knowledge may be linked with one another if we refer to them by mathematical signs. The creation of such a comprehensive sign language presuppposes that we are able to break knowledge down into simple elements. But neither science nor philosophy had sufficiently advanced to make a comprehensive analysis of knowledge possible. Leibniz, who had worked on a similar project, concluded that this difficulty was not prohibitive. If one started by attributing a characteristic number to each segment of knowledge, the system did not have to wait until all essential information on a given subject was available to complete the analysis. In fact, combinations of existing numbers would lead to new discoveries. The universal language would serve as a grid that could be filled in as science progressed and that would itself advance this progress.[62] Leibniz's metaphysics supported the possibility of such a universal language. As all things coming from the hands of a perfect Creator must be compatible and continuous with one another, a universal symbolism, a *characteristica universalis* had to be possible. The search for an ideal language that would overcome the ambivalence and confusion of common speech was yet another version of the age-old quest of the original, Adamic language wherein words had exactly corresponded to things.

Meanwhile, a less ambitious search for the common structure of ordinary speech was being pursued in linguistic studies proper. In their *Grammaire générale et raisonnée* (1660), grammarians of Port-Royal tried to compose a grammatical structure that would fit all languages. Those efforts, however flawed, nevertheless marked a significant step toward a symbolic conception of language. In assuming that concepts (expressed in language) and things are naturally related, the authors of the *Grammaire* do not imply that concepts bear a similarity to things, but rather that they render things *present*. In the *Logique* of Port-Royal that appeared two years later, they insisted that these representations constitute reality *as we know it*. "We possess no knowledge of what exists outside us, except through the intermediacy of the ideas that are in us."[63] Yet ideas become manageable and effective only as they are translated into words.

The preceding theories are all based on the assumption that thought precedes speech and that words bring preformed ideas to expression. They do not account for the fact that those allegedly private thoughts themselves owe their origin to verbal discourse. Not before Herder and Hamann in the second half of the eighteenth century does the notion that language conditions thinking as much as thinking conditions language make its appearance. Enlightenment thinkers reached that insight after a number of discussions concerning the relation between writing and speech, the symbolic nature of words, the relation between proposition and meaning, and, above all, the origin of language. To these we now turn.

The story begins with Locke's treatment of the relation between thought and language in the third book of the *Essay Concerning Human Understanding*

(1690). There he raises the fundamental question: How do words mean? That question has continued to engage philosophical thought ever since. Locke still assumed that ideas, derived from primary impressions, originate independently of language. Words come in at a later stage as signs of ideas that allow the mind to order, arrange, and express them. Their role, though indispensable to maintain thought, remains instrumental. People use words "either to record their own thoughts for the assistance of their own memory; or, as it were, to bring out their ideas, and lay them before the view of others" (*Essay*, III, 2, 2). Yet words, being merely signs, rarely convey the full meaning of ideas, all the less so since their common use inevitably lacks precision. This renders the presumed correspondence between ideas and words increasingly problematic. All the more so since one person's understanding of a word's meaning may vary from another's. Still, the private character of impressions and the imprecise use of the terms do not imprison each speaker within a private language. Language pre-exists *my speaking* of it. It already possesses a structure that a child learns together with the ability to speak. This guarantees at least a practical agreement on the meaning of words.

For Locke, a verbal sign refers to an idea as if the two followed a common order of signification. In fact, the structure of language essentially differs from that of ideas. Words do not signify *directly* as Locke assumes. Grammar, syntax, and semantics vary from one language to another. Berkeley quite appropriately criticized Locke's theory of signification. When Locke writes: "Words become general by being made the signs of general ideas," Berkeley replies that a word becomes general by being made the sign "not of an abstract general idea, but of several particular ideas." He illustrates this by the function of a line in a geometrical theorem. "As that *particular* line becomes general by being made a sign, so the *name* 'line,' which taken absolutely is particular, by being a sign is made general."[64] One may object to Berkeley's nominalist thesis that general ideas are no more than particular ideas with a general sign coefficient attached to them. But he is undoubtedly right in denying a direct relation between language and ideas, as if one were a copy of the other. Locke's and Berkeley's lasting credit in the modern study of language consists in having established, albeit in an overly simplified way, the essential link between language and ideas. Correct thinking is bound to linguistic conditions and errors in thinking may be rooted in the improper use of language.[65]

Locke's onetime pupil, Anthony Ashley Cooper, the third earl of Shaftesbury, though not primarily concerned with the problems of language, nonetheless contributed a notion that proved to be of some consequence for the future of linguistics, namely, that of *dynamic form*. All forms of expression, as appears in the arts, rather than being mere means to retain or to record ideas derived from preverbal impressions, are themselves *form-giving acts*. Language, the primary expression, "does not copy ideas: it structures them."[66] Shaftesbury's nephew James Harris developed this insight into a comprehensive linguistic theory. The title of his once famous *Hermes or a Philosophical Inquiry Concerning Universal Grammar* (1751) may have been inspired by the *Grammaire Générale* of Port-Royal, which assumes that the basic structure of grammar is universal.[67] But Harris's theory of spiritual form, inspired by his theory of art, moves well beyond the rationalist universalism of the French.

Harris developed the first fully symbolic theory of language. Speech can never *imitate* ideas, since it relies exclusively on sound. How could sound imitate color? Moreover, the complexity of ideas excludes any one-to-one correspondence between words and ideas.[68] Harris holds on to the theory that words express pre-existing ideas, but he abandons the empiricist basis on which Locke had established that theory. General ideas, for him, are not abstracted from sense impressions. They are *intelligible forms*. This appears obvious enough in the case of arts or crafts where the mind's design precedes any sensible realization. Nor do the words in which we express those ideal forms imitate them; they *symbolize* them in independent intelligible structures (p. 335). Harris incorporates his theory of ideal archetypes within Shaftesbury's notion of the special genius proper to each individual or nation. The way a nation conceives ideas determines its use of language. "These particular Ideas become the Genius of their Language, since the *Symbol* must, of course, correspond to its *Archetype*" (p. 407). The language of the Romans, who excelled in politics and legislation, reflects juridical precision but lacks speculative genius. With the more philosophical Greeks, the opposite occurred. About the English language, which combines French with German idioms, Harris observes: "What we want in elegance, we gain in copiousness"(p. 409).

In France the discussion of language took on an explicitly comparative direction. How is speech related to other forms of expression? How does one language differ from another? Diderot who rarely developed a comprehensive theory on anything, but who sparked light on many things, developed a brilliant intuition concerning the nature of language in his *Lettre sur les sourds muets*.[69] Different modes of expression, he argues, are irreducible to one another. A common characteristic of all modes of them, whether in words or in gestures, consists in their being *discursive*, that is, moving in time. Words are spoken, written, or read in a certain order; gestures follow a different succession. The order of succession depends on the purpose and means by which we express ourselves. The sign language of the deaf mute follows a wholly different sequence than the words of a speaker or of a writer. Even a person of normal hearing uses gestures that are neither synchronic nor harmonious with the words they accompany. Diderot discovered this through his strange habit of stopping his ears in the theater while attending a play he knew well. He observed that few actors succeed in bringing gesture and mime to the same expressive pitch as the words they pronounce.

Nor does the sequence of verbal expression correspond to the logic of ideas, as Abbé Batteux had maintained when defending the Latin syntax as the most logical and hence the normative one. Diderot considers the logical order of speaking and writing highly artificial. The natural sequence of words rarely coincides with the logic of ideas. In sign language, the oldest form of communication, the first gesture articulates the principal idea, while subsequent gestures follow according to their relation to that primary one. In a logical structure all parts are presented at once, as in a painting. Language, however, has to break up into temporal segments what to the mind appears simultaneous. This may require an inversion of the logical order of words. Only the "natural" sequence effectively conveys ideas, emotions, and feelings in the order in which they impress us. Even the most theoretical discourse requires varying accents and degrees of intensity and rarely submits to any kind of a priori definable order.

In an article originally written for the *Encyclopédie* and posthumously published as a short book, Rousseau agrees with Diderot that originally humans did not express their meanings in words but in gestures. Yet he considers the impulse to speak wholly natural, as it is necessary to satisfy other human needs than those of the body. "If the only needs we ever experienced were physical, we should most likely never have been able to speak; we would fully express our meanings by the language of gesture alone."[70] What urges humans to speak is the moral impulse to express strong emotions like love, fear, and hatred. The most ancient words were emotional cries. Most important, Rousseau denied the assumed priority of ideas with respect to language, a priority that all British writers, including James Harris, had steadfastly maintained. In fact, we speak not to express previously conceived, articulated ideas: language serves as the indispensable means for articulating ideas. Before they acquired speech, humans had no ideas to express! In his early *Discourse on the Origin of Inequality* Rousseau had argued, against the philosophes, that language could not possibly owe its origin to human inventiveness. To invent requires ideas, and ideas require language.

Still, though natural, speech is not an instinct, such as birds have for nesting or ants and bees for communicating. Precisely the virtual absence of instincts and the urge of a limitless *perfectibilité* forced humans to speak. The most specifically human trait is the ability to speak, both in gestures and in words.

With Rousseau, then, the problem of language shifts from one of origins and communicative needs, to one of progress and culture. Primitive human expressions consisted of vital cries, onomatopoeic more than articulate, sung rather than spoken. As humanization progressed, those animal sounds became transformed into fully articulate ones that enabled people to communicate beyond the limits of their immediate families. This progression marks the beginning of organized society. "The earth nourishes men; but when their initial needs have dispersed them, other needs arise which reunite them, and it is only then that they speak, and that they have an incentive to speak" (p. 39). In the pastoral stage, especially in mild climates, passion and feeling, more than utility, stimulate the development of language. In harsher climates, where the need to work is more urgent, linguistic development tends to follow a more utilitarian lead. Hence, Rousseau notes, the languages of the north became more articulate and those of the south more melodious.

Far less natural was the invention of writing. Practical needs alone were responsible for it, especially the need to establish commercial relations with distant partners. Writing removes language farthest from its original expressiveness. Letters substitute for the direct presence of the speaking person. Still, the language of passion or of feeling, even when written, conveys some sense of physical presence, as if speech had never totally yielded to writing. Poetry also, in prosody and rhythm, has preserved some of the directness of sound. Poems were meant to be sung or recited. One who only reads them loses much of their musical impact: the prosody of written verse is only a poor substitute for the more complex intonations of singing or reciting. What originally had been different sounds, writing reduces to weaker or stronger emphasis. For Rousseau, the transition from speech to writing indicates an increasing alienation from a natural state of being. Language itself, even the most primitive, already causes a rupture in the original state of oneness with nature. To one who speaks, life has left the immediate *now*. Discourse, as the term suggests, extends consciousness across time: it presupposes foresight and remembrance. Speech defers meaning to the very end of a phrase and often its full meaning does not appear before the end of a discourse.

What feelings and emotions lose in directness by being spoken, they gain in intensity. "As you watch the afflicted person, you are not likely to weep. But give him time to tell you what he feels and soon you will burst into tears. It is solely in this way that the scenes of a tragedy produce their effects" (p. 8). On the negative side, the separation from immediacy renders language manipulative. In his *Discourse on the Origin of Inequality* Rousseau considers the acquisition of language the principal cause of social corruption. The more it becomes refined, the more means it acquires for being deceitful. Why, then, one wonders, did Rousseau become a writer? In Jean Starobinski's interpretation, writing for Rousseau was a means of last resort: the only way of communication his alleged accusers left him to clear his name. He counted on posterity to avenge him, and in order to reach later generations he *had* to write. "The act of writing becomes a happy one for Rousseau only when he ceases to address it to an outsider."[71] Not before his final *Rêveries d'un promeneur solitaire* did Rousseau at last write for himself. His message to others had been delivered. His book to himself became his most honest one.

Inherited and enriched from one generation to another, language shapes the identity of a people no less than that of an individual. This idea became central to Herder's theory. He may have read some allusions to it in Rousseau, though probably not in the posthumously published essay. In Herder's *Essay on the Origin of Language* (1772), the various strands of Enlightenment linguistics coalesced into a coherent whole. From the start he opposes the thesis that language naturally develops from cry to speech: "While still an animal, man already has language."[72] Speech may have started as a cry of passion. But that cry was from the beginning articulate, and its passion is still audible in the rhetoric of even the most theoretical discourse. Like Rousseau, Herder rejected Condillac's theory, popular among the philosophes, that language is the outcome of an evolved animal instinct. But Rousseau had failed to draw the conclusion that therefore it had to be invented. Necessity drove humans to seek this essential means of survival. Animals need no more than the minimal expressiveness required for communication among members of the same species. Humans would be unable to survive without an extensive range of expressiveness present from the beginning. Nothing, then, would be more erroneous than to regard speech and reason as a "stepped-up potentiation of animal forces" (p. 109).

Herder attempts to stay a middle course between Condillac's evolutionary naturalism, on one side, and Süssmilch's theory (1766) that language is a divine gift to humanity, on the other. "With our course set for [the truth], we perceive to the right and the left why no animal can invent language, why no God need invent language, and why man, as man, can and must invent language" (p. 127). A full development of the human ability to speak requires from the beginning a different organization of *all* bodily powers, not just a particular physiological disposition of throat and mouth. In addition it needs a human environment: children that grow up wild do not learn how to speak. But that is not to say, as Rousseau wrote in the *Discourse on Inequality*, that speech is only potentially present. It belongs to the fundamental structure of being human. Humans have to invent language and to learn how to speak, but that ability to invent and to learn is "as natural to them as being human" (p. 112).

The basic question is not: How do humans form sounds? They collected their first vocabulary from the sounds of the world — the cry of animals, the noise of thunder, the rustling of leaves in the wind. But: "Whence comes to man the art of changing into sound what is not sound?" (p. 138). Primitive human sounds articulate only undifferentiated feelings. In that archaic *sensus communis* the awareness dawns that some things *look* the way others *sound*. Herder all too briefly justifies the human ability to express an unlimited variety of meanings through sound by arguing that all perceptions merge in feeling, hence that all forms of perception are related, and that one may be used in lieu of another. But the more fundamental question remains: What enables the mind to transfer meaning to sound? How does a distinct meaning emerge from an indistinct pool of meaningfulness? Despite this and other obscurities that cloud his theory, Herder discovered what had escaped his predecessors (even Rousseau), namely, that language, rather than bringing pre-existing meanings to expression, *creates* meaning.

Herder's friend, the cryptic Johann Georg Hamann, took Herder to task for not having recognized that speech is not "natural," as if humans had from the beginning an aptitude for creating it. That aptitude requires that someone first address them. This, according to Hamann, God did in revelation.[73] Humans are able to speak and to read in response to God's revelation in nature and Scripture and thus to decipher the mystery of reality (III, 301–3). With this far-fetched thesis about the divine origin of language, Hamann attempted to justify the metaphorical capacity required for the creation of language, which Herder had simply taken for granted. Moreover, the idea that all languages came from the same source shows an awareness of the common structure that underlies their irreducible diversity. Precisely this synthesis of universality and diversity makes translation possible. George Steiner has rightly observed: "To translate is to descend beneath the exterior disparities of two languages in order to bring into vital play their analogous and, at the final depths, common principles of being."[74]

Conclusion

Thinkers of the Enlightenment spent considerable, though mostly unsuccessful, efforts on closing the gap between the self as subject of meaning and the self as substantial reality, which the preceding period had opened. Some did so by placing all the weight on the subject; not only empiricist philosophers like Berkeley, but also preromantic writers like Rousseau and some novelists. On the opposite side stood those who viewed the self as a substance among other substances, though most endeavored to preserve its

spiritual identity. Both sides experienced major difficulty in giving that substance or subject a content of its own.

Both sides also found it hard to preserve genuine *otherness*. A self reduced
to a meaning-giving function—a mere subject—loses its personal identity
and, as a result, is no longer able to recognize the identity of the other. Ever
since Descartes, the problem of solipsism has haunted the subjective conception of the self. Where reality becomes a function of the subject, the real ceases
to be truly distinct from the self. Likewise, if the self is merely a substance,
albeit it a distinct one, it becomes absorbed within an objective totality that
admits no real otherness. For Descartes, any substance that was not a subject
became an undifferentiated part of a *res extensa*. The preceding analysis has
shown how difficult it was to preserve both aspects at once and even, for those
who succeeded in doing so, to adequately integrate them with each other.

My conclusion concerning the absence of fully recognized otherness may
appear to conflict with the well-known fact that the Enlightenment was a time
of unrestricted exploration of ethnic differences, varying customs, and alternative moral systems. Indeed, the *experience* of otherness was abundantly
present, but the ability to recognize and to justify it was missing. Cultural
differences came to be interpreted against the horizon of a universal reason
originating in the mind. As a dialectical tension with the *other* constitutes an
essential part of selfhood, a weakening of the sense of otherness creates a
major problem for self-understanding. The introspective literature of the time,
which resisted the trend to conceive of the self as either subject or substance,
gave the self a content that was more than functional and more than objective.
I have mentioned the fictional, the autobiographical, the aphoristic writings of
the *moralistes*. The practice of religious introspection also reasserted the self
as a spiritual center in its own right. Above all, the new theories of language
extricated selfhood from the narrow limits Descartes, Locke, and their followers had set to it. Reflection on speech laid the ground for a new concept of
intersubjectivity that was to reach maturity in the next two centuries. Dialogue requires that in some way one abandons one's own position to enter
into that of the other.[75] The more I give myself to the other, the better I know
myself and the more I acquire a unique identity.

In the next chapter I shall consider concepts of art that paralleled the later
theories of language in resisting the sharp subject-object division characteristic
of modern philosophical anthropology. Ideas of beauty and harmony do not
allow themselves to be explained in either of those terms, even though aesthetic theories kept hesitating between the two, leaning at first more to the
objective and later to the subjective side. The division has continued to determine the modern idea of selfhood, resulting either in a naturalist or in an

idealist conception of the person. The two tendencies were to remain locked in combat all through the nineteenth century. The consequences of this internal division have been severe. In chapter 5 we shall see how the moral crisis of the Enlightenment was directly linked to it. In our own time some have started speaking of "the death of man," a forceful expression of the predicament that persists in affecting not only anthropology but also the entire compass of theoretical and practical thought.

4

Toward a New Conception of Art

Artistically the Enlightenment may not compare favorably with the Renaissance or Baroque periods, but the aesthetic criticism of the eighteenth century surpassed that of the two earlier periods and provided most of the categories used in the two centuries that followed. One of its major achievements was to raise the idea of beauty to the level of truth. It accomplished this in three stages: at the beginning the imitation theory prevailed, next the expressive theory, and at the end the symbolic theory made a tentative entrance. Each of these movements made a definitive contribution to the modern conception of art and literature. A first wave of poets and critics continued to defend the ancient theory that art imitates nature. Originally artists, particularly early novelists, tended to interpret this rule quite literally. Others held that artistic truth consisted in imitating the *ideal* rather than the reality of nature. For many, particularly in France, that meant adhering to the formal standards of harmony, unity, and proportion allegedly derived from ancient models. Shaftesbury considered the observation of such formal rules necessary but insufficient. For him, the imitation of nature consists in the first place in following nature's creativity rather than its accomplishments. Partly inspired by Shaftesbury, such critics as Diderot and Lessing came to conceive of art as being primarily expressive rather than imitative. They thereby gave the idea of aesthetic truth a distinct, irreducible identity. Finally, with the notion of aesthetic symbolism, Baumgarten and Kant raised the idea to the level of truth as symbolic disclosure, which is where it remains today.

Art as Truth: From Boileau to Shaftesbury

At the beginning of the seventeenth century a concern for truthfulness began to dominate aesthetics. Yet truth could be attained in different ways. Plato had described art as an imitation of nature. But since nature itself was no more than an imitation of the true, ideal reality, he considered it a lesser, derivative mode of truth. Aware of his criticism, later Platonists, from Plotinus to Michelangelo, concluded that art ought to imitate nature's ideal form. Hence art had to correct nature whenever it fell short of ideal perfection. The truth of art, then, consisted less in resemblance than in ideal abstraction, not in nature but in "nature beautified."

Boileau, the despotic arbiter of literary taste in France, decreed: "Rien n'est beau que le vrai, le vrai seul est aimable. Il doit régner partout, et même dans la fable" (*L'art poétique*). Literary truth, for him, consisted in verisimilitude of content, harmony of form, and strict observation of the rules of style appropriate to each genre. Pope, one of the few followers of the French rubric in England, echoed, "Those rules of old discovered, not derived / Are Nature still, but Nature methodiz'd" (*Essay on Criticism,* vv. 88–89). Classicist writers and artists appealed to Greek aesthetics. Yet instead of pursuing the Greek *idea* of perfection, as Renaissance artists had attempted to do, they were too often satisfied with observing formal rules they claimed to draw from ancient art and letters. Aesthetic truth thereby became restricted to what could be justified by well-established principles. In France, these principles, conscientiously followed and, in literature, enforced by the high authority of the royal Académie, produced an orderly art of little originality but considerable polish. Nor was this literature deprived of feeling. In fact, it became increasingly sentimental. But feelings themselves were not allowed to stray into irrationality or violence. They had their place in the harmoniously regulated universe of art. Poets and artists constantly appealed to classical sources. But they thoroughly domesticated the ancient models, gentrifying primitive Greek myths and ascribing Stoic and Christian virtues to wild ancient heroes. A rather instructive example of this appears in the libretto of Glück's opera *Orphée*. In the myth, Orpheus retrieves his beloved Euridice from the underworld, violates the prohibition not to look back, and loses her forever. This unhappy ending seemed unacceptable to the eighteenth-century sense of justice. So the artist has "Amour" restore the lovers to one another!

The question of truth assumed a crucial importance in biblical poems. In

Paradise Lost (1667) Milton attempted to preserve its veracity by maintaining the division between celestial and terrestrial space of the ancient cosmology, and by presenting the confrontation with the rebellious angels as a regular modern war on a battlefield. In fact, however, his literalism jeopardized the credibility of his poem. After Galileo, the division of the cosmos into a heaven above and an earth below, which had so effectively supported Dante's vision, lost its meaning in a universe of which all parts obey the same mathematical laws. Milton tries to save the image of two parallel realms by means of a theological analogy: "measuring things in heaven by things on earth" (VI, 893). But in a modern cosmology such an analogy had to exclude literal similarity. Milton's insistent realism resulted in a succession of absurdities. Even dim-witted terrestrials would know better than to wage an unwinnable "war" against the Almighty or to aim darts at immortal spirits. To render his vision of fighting angels at least minimally credible, the poet endowed the celestial rebels with bodies capable of physical pain. The faithful angels appear exempt from this encumbrance. The description of a heavenly battle fought with chariots, swords, and gunpowder has a comical rather than tragic effect. Milton gains little by committing himself neither to a geocentric nor to a heliocentric view. ("Whether heaven move or earth imports not" [VIII, 70–71]). The problem was not whether the sun or the earth was the "center" to the world" (VIII, 122–23), but whether the universe could still be conceived as consisting of two separate parts. The main difficulty stems from introducing a literal understanding of the Bible into a modern epic at the time when the biblical cosmology had simply ceased to exist. The nineteenth-century critic Hyppolite Taine wondered: "What a heaven God runs! . . . We have orders of the day, a hierarchy, exact submission, extra duties, disputes, regulated ceremonials, prostrations, etiquette, furbished arms, arsenals, depots of chariots and ammunition. Was it worthwhile leaving earth to find in heaven carriage-works, buildings, artillery, a manual of tactics, the art of salutations, and the Almanac of Gotha? Are these the things which 'eye hath not seen, nor ear heard, nor hath entered into the heart to conceive?' "[1]

Nor could the problems of literalism be solved by keeping the celestial figures away from time and space, as Klopstock attempted to do in his *Messias*. His strategy merely resulted in a bloodless, abstract poem, far inferior to Milton's masterwork. An epic requires characters of flesh and blood in a concrete, identifiable setting. Apart from the incongruities I have mentioned, the literalism of *Paradise Lost* also weakened the heroic quality indispensable in an epic poem. Louis Martz appropriately calls it an "anti-heroic epic."[2] Rather than imitating Homer's grand style or even Virgil's pathetic one, Milton, he claims, displays a surprising affinity with Ovid's ironic *Metamorphoses*.[3]

Milton may originally have been allured by the drama of the human race in its battle with evil (as some of the most beautiful passages suggest), yet the Bible's report of a prehistorical lapse from a state of happy innocence to one of guilt and pain induced him to move the action from earth to heaven. Thus the key figure of the heavenly "preface" to the story, Lucifer, came to replace Adam as central figure of the poem.

Paradise Lost illustrates the tension between realism and truth in the particular instance of the religious epic. Yet even when no biblical literalism was involved, the question of truth assumed a new importance in the fictional narrative to which the French referred as "roman" and the English as "romance." The learned Pierre Daniel Huet, later to become bishop of Avranches, in one of the earliest treatises on the subject, *De l'Origine des Romans* (1670), distinguishes novels from historical accounts as "fictional stories of amorous adventures, written in prose for the pleasure and instruction of the reader." The term *instruction* alerts the reader that he regards the roman as more than mere entertainment. Works of history, he clarifies, are for the most part true, whereas romans are fictional, yet they contain some truth. Indeed, the term "roman" originally referring to the language of Romanized Gallia (as opposed to Roman Latin), eventually became the name of historical reports written in that Vulgar Latin. As they began to be put in poetic form (for instance, in the *chansons de geste* surrounding Charlemagne's battle with the Muslims), more and more fictional elements entered the story until only a vague historical frame remained. In the sixteenth and seventeenth centuries, novels assumed the fictional form Huet describes. In the process, however, they developed a new kind of truth. Well-composed novels, Huet maintained, made their readers aware of the richness and complexity of emotions and moral inclinations. Thus their historical falsehood was in fact what Augustine called a "significant falsehood," a figure of truth, like the parables in the Gospel narratives.

English writers proved marvelously equipped for successfully practicing the new literary genre. Instructed by French models, they no longer felt compelled to weave their stories around historical events or ancient legends. Neither did they, as French writers tended to do in the rationalist climate that had followed Cartesian philosophy, feel obliged to express universal truths. *Moll Flanders* and *Robinson Crusoe, Pamela* and *Clarissa, Tom Jones* and *Joseph Andrews,* with their particular characters and individual personalities, stand at the opposite side of the universal types that filled the French tragedies and novels of the classic century.[4] Individuals and events, not types and ideas, define British narrative prose. Nowhere had the nominalist stress on the particular in contrast to classical universalism been more visible than in the eighteenth-century English novel.

The search for veracity assumed several forms — Fielding differs both in style and intent from Defoe and Richardson — but all of them firmly believed that their stories had to reflect reality as it appears. Daniel Defoe came closest to interpreting this demand of veracity in a literalist sense. He thereby responded to the expectation of ordinary readers of his time who, familiar only with the Bible, had to assume that any report about a contemporary figure had to be "true" if its author was an honest man. Otherwise, why would it be in print?[5] Thus Defoe presented his famous *Journal of the Plague Year* (1722) as an anonymous eyewitness's account of the bubonic plague in 1665 (when the author himself was only five years old). It was in fact a unique mixture of journalistic reporting complete with casualty figures, medical observations, investigations of the causes of the disease, and an imaginative reconstruction of the total collapse of civilized life as a result of the plague. *Robinson Crusoe* and *Moll Flanders* also appeared as autobiographical writings. Defoe's success in presenting his work as historically truthful backfired. Readers charged the author with deceit when they learned that Robinson Crusoe had been a figment of the author's imagination. He responded by showing how seriously concerned he had been about the veracity of his imaginary reconstructions, as he had already suggested in the preface to his early *The Storm*. Eventually he seized upon the idea of *moral* truth, and in the preface to the third volume of *Robinson Crusoe,* he compares the truth of his work to the allegorical one of the popular *Pilgrim's Progress.*

In his masterpiece *Moll Flanders* (1722) Defoe pursues a more fundamental truth, namely, the difference between moral appearance and reality. In the guise of an edifying tale of sin and repentance Defoe ironically contrasts Moll Flanders's moral posturing with her venal conduct. Repentance comes to her only when one of her questionable enterprises fails, as when her partner in adultery suddenly calls the affair off. The novelist doubles the irony by taking his distance from the narrator as well as from the characters of the story, thereby erasing whatever moral import it might have possessed. Some readers still persisted in considering *Moll Flanders* a moral tale; others dismissed it as an immoral book. Of course, it is neither, nowhere less so than in the preface where Defoe expresses his "moral" intentions: "Throughout the infinite variety of this book, this fundamental [to expose vice] is most strictly adhered to; there is not a wicked action in any part of it but is first or last rendered unhappy and unfortunate; there is not a superlative villain brought upon the stage but either he is brought to an unhappy end, or brought to be a penitent; there is not an ill thing mentioned but it is condemned, even in the relation, nor a virtuous, just thing but it carries its praise along with it." In view of this noble goal the author recommends his book, from every part of which "some just and religious inference is drawn by which the reader will have something of instruction." As Ian Watt wittily puts it: "The spiritual dimension is presented as a series of somewhat inexplicable religious breakdowns in the psychic mechanism, breakdowns, however, which do not permanently impair her healthy immorality."[6]

For Richardson, literary truth consisted in a faithful analysis of the feelings and attitudes of his characters. His novels betray the influence of Marivaux's masterly analysis of feelings and emotions in *La vie de Marianne*. Richardson improved the genre by writing his novels in epistolary form. This procedure enabled him to present the same events from various perspectives, as they were reflected in different minds. It allowed the reader to learn the characters' dispositions toward each other. Richardson handled this new stylistic device with such perfect competence that it became popular all over Europe. Yet Fielding questioned the truth of the noble feelings Richardson's heroines so edifyingly expressed in their letters. In *Joseph Andrews* he lampoons the prudish Pamela as a pioneer capitalist, a middle-class entrepreneur of virtue who used her chastity "as a commodity to be vended for the purpose of getting on."[7] Fielding himself was a moralist of a different kind. His target was hypocrisy and moral pretense. The picaresque Tom Jones parodies a code of sexual conduct universally professed yet rarely practiced. Fielding considered his works morally more truthful than Richardson's because he exposed the unsupported moral pretenses of his contemporaries. He even claimed "historical" truth for his stories. In *Tom Jones* (bk. IX, chap. 7) he insists that they "have sufficient title to the name of history," contrary to the romances of sentimental scribblers. His novels derive their historical authority not from actual events but from a study of the "book of nature." He claims to have acquired his skills through a direct acquaintance with the kind of people he writes about and through insight in their characters. This places Fielding's history more on the side of "natural history" than of that of chronicles of past events.

In some eighteenth-century writers the irony with which they exposed the hero's false claims ended up undermining the novel's own internal credibility. In two experimental stories of the time the authors deconstruct the authority of the narrator, the critical voice that gave the ironical novel a semblance of truth. The author thereby abandons the role of moral critic to question the validity of the novel itself. In Sterne's *Tristram Shandy* (1760), the constant digressions of this "autobiography" that ends at the narrator's conception destroy whatever coherent meaning was still holding the novel together. The paradox that accounts for the enduring charm of this "autobiography" lies in the role of a self that is always intruding yet nowhere to be found. In a more studied, less spontaneous way, Diderot imitates Sterne's irony in *Jacques le fataliste* (1772 and 1778, published posthumously) while also borrowing from *Don Quixote* and Le Sage's picaresque novel *Gil Blas*. In this masterpiece of quick wit, sharp insight, and biting sarcasm, the secondary quality of the story itself becomes yet a further subject of irony. By drawing attention to the narrator's "plagiarism" the author destroys the last feature of the novel that had survived Sterne's onslaught, namely, its originality. Only the author's *persona* remains: he no longer identifies with his work since he does not even claim to be its creator.

This double irony proves to be a dubious weapon of moral criticism. In the novel's most remembered episode the hostess of the inn where Jacques and his master have spent the night tells the story of one Madame La Pommeraye's revenge on a sleazy marquis who, after having seduced her, continues to appeal to her for favors and financial support with no intention of marrying her. She arranges for him to fall in love with a beautiful younger woman who, however, insists on marriage as a condition for erotic intimacy. The marquis reluctantly submits. On the day of the wedding the vindicated lady informs the marquis that he has just espoused a prostitute. At that point the novelist, who until then had been a silent companion, interrupts Jacques's and his master's protest against what they consider an unwarranted cruelty, to proclaim that any man who seduces and abandons an honest woman ought to be condemned "to the courtesans." The author thereby breaks the spell of irony, yet without benefit to the moral lesson he now wants to teach. The ironic tone, sustained throughout a narrative, has deprived him of his moral authority. If the novelist effectively wants to criticize the morals of his time, he ought to keep his irony within the story, as Defoe and Fielding did, or otherwise tell his story straight, as the realist novelists of the nineteenth century did or as the sentimental novelists of the eighteenth century tried to do.

No writer of the Enlightenment grasped the full complexity of aesthetic truth better than the German poet and novelist Christoph Martin Wieland (1733–1813). He tackled it first in the original preface to *Agathon* (1766), the Enlightenment novel par excellence. In the second edition (1772) he added an essay, "The Historical in Agathon." The question of truth keeps returning throughout the long narrative and induces the author to make substantial changes from the first to the third edition. It tells the story of the adventures and moral trials of a young Athenian whose name appears among Plato's friends in the dialogue *Protagoras*. Attempting to justify the historical veracity of his novel, Wieland claims that the hero of Euripides' tragedy *Ion* (who, like Agathon, grew up in the temple of Delphi), as well as Plato's character in the dialogue of the same name, stood model for his hero. In the novel the young

Agathon, on his way to a promising political career in Athens, is captured by pirates and sold to the sophist Hippias. In order to break the idealistic young slave's resistance to his own hedonist philosophy Hippias introduces him to the beautiful hetaera Danae. Agathon becomes her lover, but he eventually grows tired of his lascivious life with her and flees to Dionysus's Court in Syracuse, which he hopes to reform in accordance with philosophical rule. With no more success than Plato himself, he barely escapes execution and takes refuge with the philosophical ruler of Tarentum—Archytas. All the names appearing in this story (except for Danae's) belong to well-known historical figures. This "probable" composition of an educated Athenian of the fourth century prefigures what a gifted young man of the Enlightenment age—such as Wieland himself—experienced in the process of growing up. Presenting his entire story as *Geschichte* (a term that means "history" as well as "story"), the author, citing ancient sources, vouches for the accuracy of the historical figures and their theories as they appear in his novel. (He devotes an entire book to a careful analysis of Hippias's philosophy.) He justifies his romantic reconstruction by the fact that all historical reflection requires imagination no less than factual knowledge.[8] To be morally significant and to possess a universal meaning history needs to be reimagined. A mere chronicle of facts carries no universal truth. Still, the imagination does not enjoy the same liberty in a historical study that it enjoys in a historical novel where Wieland allows it to add nonhistorical characters.

On the other hand, Wieland is particularly concerned to be psychologically true. He constantly cautions the reader that, however credible his characters appear, neither their words nor their thoughts about themselves ought to be taken at face value. In addition, Agathon changes as he grows older and the author is anxious to stress the distance between present and past in a developing person. Wieland concludes the final edition (1798) of his work with a chapter on the wisdom of Archytas, who taught that the ultimate truth is interior and cannot be adequately communicated. "It may well be that in the visible world most of it is deceptive and all is merely appearance. But is there not in our inner being an invisible world the limits of which no moral treatise has explored?" (bk. XVI, chap. 3). Perhaps more explicitly than any other work of the time *Agathon* raises the question: How can a narrative be fictional and nevertheless be true? Wieland took the hardest case—a historical novel, taking place in a distant past, that at the same time was meant to be modern, autobiographical *Bildungsroman*. As a contemporary critic, Christian von Blankenburg, noted, the author thereby conveyed yet another truth through fiction, namely, that the customs and traditions of a particular society shape the ideas of those who live in it.[9]

In the visual arts the concern with veracity led mostly to formalist conclusions. The question of whether art, to be truthful, should represent objects as they are or as they ideally ought to be was almost always answered in favor of the ideal. The Greek and Roman statues discovered in the excavations of Pompei (1748) and Herculaneum (1738), as well as Johann Joachim Winckelmann's interpretations of Greek sculpture and architecture spread the notion that ancient art favored idealized models of reality. Especially French classicism imitated the simple lines, perfect proportions, and harmonious compositions of the Greeks. But somehow its cold, well-drawn forms remained far removed from the ancient models that inspired them. Even Jacques-Louis David, who in his paintings applied the classicist principles with more genius than others, always appears disengaged from his heroic subjects. Classicist art, despite its formal perfection, appears to have replaced concrete flesh and blood by universal rules of reason. Winckelmann himself had explicitly warned against this way of interpreting and imitating the ancient models. Classical motifs had, of course, been common since the Renaissance. But before the eighteenth century their influence had been restricted to the presence of ancient columns or temples in painting. The two great painters of the French seventeenth century, Nicholas Poussin (1594–1656) and Claude Lorrain (1600–1682), had also found inspiration in ancient landscapes and classical myths. But their bucolic Arcadias with Roman ruins had never degenerated into the formalist "truthfulness" characteristic of the later classicist style.

Even some contemporaries of the classicists felt the artificiality of the rationalist canon and pursued a different kind of artistic veracity. Jean-Baptiste Chardin (1699–1779), the loving observer of ordinary objects and domestic intimacy, succeeds in directly conveying the touch of velvet, the shine of polished brass, the smell of freshly baked bread instead of concerning himself with geometrical compositions or ancient heroes. Antoine Watteau's (1684–1721) canvases evoke the secret hidden at the heart of what we thought we knew. The enigmatic beauty of his *Embarkment for Cythara*—a classical theme treated in a nonclassical way—approaches the viewer from a timeless dreamland. It answers none of our questions. Why are the pilgrims, frozen in the imperturbable peace of an immobile *fête galante*, on their way to Aphrodite's sacred island? He sublimates everything into aesthetic mystery. His Pierrots stare at us from a distant world, very alive yet unresponsive to our scrutiny.

Neither does the term "classicist" apply to Giambattista Tiepolo's exuberant apotheoses. His radiating hues and rapturous motions defy the subdued colors and static harmonies of the neoclassicists. The four panels of the encounter of Rinaldo, the hero of Tasso's *Gerusalemme liberata*, with the enchantress Armida, in their striking contrasts of bright and pale tints, assume the viewer into an unearthly sphere closer to the Baroque sources that inspired it than to classicist patterns. In England Gainsborough's and Reynolds's idealized portraits do indeed display a pure though by no means static classicism. But next to them we find Hogarth's satirical scenes and the many landscapes inspired by Poussin, Claude, and the dramatic Salvator Rosa, far removed from French classicism.

The art of the eighteenth century continued to maintain strong ties with the Baroque. Not only is the Baroque not forgotten — indeed, it culminates in the architecture and sculpture of southeastern Europe, and, even after having lost its spiritual content, the Rococo style preserved much of its form. Yet the history of art never parallels that of philosophy. What Arnold Hauser asserted in general about periodization in art holds particularly true for the eighteenth century: "One ought, really, never to speak of a uniform 'style of the time' dominating a whole period, since there are at any given moment as many different styles as there are artistically productive social groups."[10] Indeed, the term "classic" itself soon lost much of its reference to ancient art and literature. It began to be predicated of any work of art that by its power and formal perfection set a model for later generations.[11]

The distinction between art and ideas finds a strong confirmation in the difference between theories about art and what poets and artists were actually doing. For d'Alembert, a typical representative of Enlightenment rationalism, art hardly differs from science, and even less from craft. In his "Preliminary Discourse" to the *Encyclopédie,* he divided the "sciences" according to the faculties most active in them: memory, reason, imagination. Imagination included mechanical as well as fine arts. Both are practical ways of knowing, but they rest on a system of "positive and invariable rules" as much as theoretical sciences do. The sole merit of these rationalist speculations was that they restored the element of truth in art. Seventeenth-century critics had fundamentally distrusted the imagination, and Samuel Johnson still described it as "a licentious and vagrant faculty, unsusceptible of limitations, and impatient of restraint."[12] D'Alembert's attribution, then, of some mode of truth to art was not insignificant. Yet obviously art is not "science": the aesthetic symbolization entirely differs from the scientific one.[13] Indeed, if art is primarily imitation, as d'Alembert still continued to hold, then its truth must consist exclusively in a correspondence between an idea and a thing, and that may reasonably evoke some comparison with science, as it did in Plato. But at no time did its aesthetic quality primarily reside in the correctness of the representation. Rather does the artist aim at transforming an ordinary reality into a symbol that discloses a previously unknown aspect of reality.

Rationalist critics recognized only two forms of truth: *correspondence* between idea and reality, and *coherence* among the parts and the whole. They never mention the most essential quality of aesthetic truth, namely, the *disclosure* of a new aspect of reality. This began to change with the writings of Anthony Ashley Cooper, earl of Shaftesbury, one of the most original and influential writers of the early eighteenth century. His ideas, elegantly expressed in allusive rather than assertive phrases, paved the road toward a new aesthetic theory. He had been inspired by Platonism, but also by Leibniz's idea of moral harmony and by his former tutor John Locke's empiricism. The latter's influence accounts for the subjective perspective he imposed upon a basically Platonic theory of beauty. The harmonious proportions of nature become truly beautiful only when viewed as symbolic of the mind's own inner harmony. "Nothing affects the heart like that which is purely from itself, and of its own nature; such as the beauty of sentiments, the grace of actions, the turn of characters and the proportion and features of the human mind."[14] Only a subjective "sense of beauty," analogous to the bodily senses, enables us to perceive the proportion between physical and mental harmony. How powerful a role this subjective element played in his aesthetics appears in the following passage, in which he describes the male perception of female beauty: "We should find perhaps that what we most admired, even in the turn of outward features, was only a mysterious expression, and a kind of shadow of something inward in the temper; and that when we were struck with a majestic air, a sprightly look, an Amazon bold grace, or a contrary soft and gentle one, 'twas chiefly the *fancy* of these characters or qualities which wrought on us: our imagination being busied in forming beauteous shapes and images of this rational kind, which entertained the mind and held it in admiration."[15]

Applying this subjective factor to artistic creation, Shaftesbury warns the artist against copying nature. "A painter, if he has any genius, understands the truth and unity of design; and knows he is even then unnatural when he follows Nature too closely and strictly copies life."[16] The work of art originates in an inner vision of harmony between mind and nature. The artist becomes "a second Maker, a just Prometheus under Jove."[17] Only in the mind does nature attain aesthetic truth. "All beauty is truth," Shaftesbury writes. Not the truth of faithful description, which is the lower kind based on observation of a given form, but the unique truth attained by the mind's power to create forms of spiritual harmony. "The beautifying, not the beautified, is the really beautiful."[18] "The beautiful, the fair, the comely, were never in the matter, but in the art and design; never in the body itself but in the form or forming power."[19] The ability to create beauty requires the existence of moral harmony in the artist's mind. To be a great poet one must first be a good man. Lack of moral sensitivity weakens the sense of beauty: aesthetic perception is directly conditioned by moral harmony. Shaftesbury united ethics to aesthetics. "Arts and virtues are 'mutually friends' — and thus the science of virtuous and that of virtue itself become, in a manner, one and the same."[20] Harmony and proportion, the foundations of art, form also the ground of morals. Moral refinement, no less than aesthetic taste, requires education.

Shaftesbury's ideas, however influential, did not survive in their original form. His followers transformed his spiritual empiricism into a sensational one. For Shaftesbury, the subjective experience merely *discloses* the spiritual form in which beauty resides. For Francis Hutcheson, who claims to apply Shaftesbury's principles, beauty consists primarily in a subjective experience.[21] He does distinguish the ideas from the experience of pleasure they cause: "the ideas of beauty and harmony, like other sensible ideas, are *necessarily* pleasant to us" (I, 3). But in his empiricist epistemology, ideas themselves have a subjective origin: they are reflections of sensations. He admits that the perception of beauty reveals qualities inherent in the thing perceived rather than mere sensations of the perceiving mind (I, 16). But the question remains whether it is the perception that causes objects to be beautiful or the qualities of the perceived object. Hutcheson compares the inner sense of beauty to the senses of hearing and seeing, "because of its affinity to the other senses" (I, 13). He never intended to identify beauty with pleasure. Indeed, he emphasizes the objective qualities of the form required for inducing aesthetic pleasure, such as uniformity in variety, proportionality, pictorial harmony. Yet those qualities merely "occasion" aesthetic pleasure. The theory of beauty is thereby bound to become subjective. Hume, drawing the conclusion from these principles, collapsed the idea of beauty with the pleasure it causes. "Pleasure and pain . . . are not only necessary attendants of beauty and deformity, but constitute their very essence."[22]

Still, Hutcheson was a perceptive observer who followed his observations wherever they might lead. Thus he radically reinterpreted the mimetic theory of art. Art ought to imitate nature, but unless the mind idealizes nature, the artist will not be able to answer Plato's critical question: Why should the artist attempt to copy poorly what nature has done well? In Hutcheson's view, the artist ought to imitate a natural model in such a way that it becomes a symbol of a spiritual ideal. As Shaftesbury had suggested, in the aesthetic intuition the mind becomes aware of the affinity between its own inner life and the outer world. There exists a concordance between the mind's disposition and "natural, inanimate objects." "Thus a tempest at sea is often an emblem of wrath; a plant or tree drooping under the rain of a person in sorrow — in short, everything in nature, by our strange inclination to resemblance, shall be brought to represent other things, even the most remote, especially the passions and circumstances of human nature in which we are more nearly concerned" (IV, 4). Despite his associationist terminology — "inclination to resemblance" — Hutcheson is already preparing the turn from imitation to expression. For him, the model the artist imitates needs not be beautiful. The deformities of an aging face or the monotony of a barren landscape become "beautiful" once the artist or the viewer shows their congruence with a mental state and thereby evokes the harmony that unites the order of nature with that of the mind. Indeed, that inner harmony becomes more apparent when the model is *not* physically perfect because the feeling of tension awakens the mind to the deeper harmony between inner and outer reality. Too facile a concordance fails to alert the mind to its own part in the aesthetic creation.

The Extension of the Aesthetic Field: From Imitation to Expression

DIDEROT

The conflicts among different views concerning the relation between beauty and truth made the eighteenth-century discussion of "aesthetics" very lively. Most instructive in this regard are the constant changes in Diderot's intellectual development. As a young man he published an essay on art that later appeared in the first volume of the *Encyclopédie*. In it his position hardly differs from d'Alembert's. "If the object leads to action, we give the name of 'art' to the compendium of rules governing its use and to their technical order. If the object is merely contemplated under different aspects, the compendium and technical order of the observations concerning their object are called science."[23] The description exposes the utilitarian outlook of the *Encyclopédie* team. But by the second volume of the *Encyclopédie*, in an article later published separately as *Traité du beau*, Diderot had abandoned this conglomeration of arts with crafts. He understood that the prospect of uniting all the mind's activities within a single comprehensive system (the original purpose of the *Encyclopédie*) had become impossible. Instead he now attempted to integrate Augustine's objective definition of beauty with Hutcheson's subjective one. He concluded that the subjective "sense of beauty" failed to account for the qualities inherent in the beautiful object and that beauty was based on the objective qualities of order, proportion, and relation in the object. "I term 'beautiful,' independently of my existence everything that *contains the power* of awakening the notion of relation in my mind; and I term 'beautiful' in direct relation to myself everything that does awaken that notion."[24] Diderot thus appears to leave the subjective element of pleasure out of the description.

But then he proceeds to qualify the objectivity of the beautiful so much as to virtually undo it altogether. The ideas of proportion and of all other "objective" characteristics do not exist before we perceive them, he claims. In themselves they "are nothing but abstractions made by our minds" (*Oeuvres*, IV, 98; *Diderot's Selected Writings*, p. 52). Moreover, those ideas depend on cultural conditions. What the French consider beautiful, others may not. Diderot enumerates no less than twelve varying factors that influence aesthetic judgments — some of them no more than local and national conventions. Still, he concludes, "despite all these causes of diversity in our judgment, there is no reason at all to think that *real beauty*, which consists in the perception of relations, is a creation of fantasy" (*Oeuvres*, IV, 111–12; *Diderot's Selected Writings*, p. 59). Within a given culture educated persons agree on the fact that some relations induce aesthetic pleasure while others do not. This claim falls far short of the thesis of objective beauty Diderot claimed to advocate. He uncomfortably moves between the traditional objective concept of beauty and the newer, subjective one. Much of the inconsistency in the essay is due to his ambivalent attitude toward Shaftesbury and Hutcheson, both of whom influenced him more than he was willing to concede. He meant to show that objective qualities and subjective sense together constitute the aesthetic experience, but he did not succeed in integrating the two.

In the simultaneously published *Letter on the Deaf and Dumb* (1751) he approached the subject from a different angle and accomplished a veritable breakthrough in aesthetic theory. This short essay was written as a letter addressed to Abbé Charles Batteux, author of *The Fine Arts Reduced to a Single Principle* (1746). According to Batteux, art imitates nature, though not nature as we actually find it "but as it can be and as it may be conceived by the mind."[25] The French critic attempted to maintain the principle of imitation while at the same time avoiding Plato's objection: How could there be any merit in imitating what is imperfect in itself? Moreover, art being a work of the mind ought to reflect the universality of the mind's concepts, whereas the observation of nature yields no more than singular impressions. The relation between the universal and the particular in aesthetic perception had also preoccupied Batteux's contemporary Johann Joachim Winckelmann. For the great German classicist, the surpassing quality of Greek art had consisted in its power to express a universal truth in a particular representation. By idealizing an aesthetic object the mind raises that particular, imperfect object to universal perfection. Thus the late classical statue of Antinous, besides showing a resemblance to Emperor Hadrian's friend, stands as a universal icon of male beauty, such as nature never attains in any single individual. Even more, in the transcendent beauty of Leochares' Apollo Belvedere (in the Vatican collection),

Winckelmann perceived how much the artist might enable nature to surpass itself and become divine. Hence, he concluded, the artist ought not to imitate nature directly, but only the standards of artistic representation the Greeks have left us. The Greeks discovered the forms ("the correctness of the contours" Winckelmann calls it) through which the human figure may attain universal beauty.[26] Nature as we actually observe it never reaches perfection. The often-cited two qualities by which the art historian described Greek art — *edle Einfalt und stille Grösze* (noble simplicity and silent grandeur) — both refer to the *mind*.

Batteux did not know Winckelmann's essay that appeared nine years after his own, but the classical ideal dominated the entire epoch and he pays homage to it in his own notion of the *belle nature*. Unlike Winckelmann, however, he proved incapable of properly integrating this universal ideal with the imitation theory, as Diderot was to remind him again and again. Diderot ironically requested that in the next edition of his study the abbé add a chapter on what he means by "beautiful nature," "for I know there are people who agree with me that without [it] your treatise lacks a foundation" (*Oeuvres,* IV, 43; *Diderot's Selected Writings,* pp. 38–39). Yet Diderot himself failed to bring the imitation theory into accord with the ideal nature of art. Tzvetan Todorov has shown the remarkable inconsistency of both Batteux and his critic. "If imitation were the only law of art, it ought to bring about the disappearance of art: the latter would differ in no way from 'imitated' nature. For art to endure, the imitation must be imperfect."[27] Neither Batteux nor Diderot shows how an imperfect imitation may be beautiful!

But more important for the future of aesthetics was the groundwork Diderot laid for a theory of symbolic expression. Whereas his *Treatise on Beauty* had still remained within the ambit of the old dispute whether beauty lies in the thing or in the eye of the beholder, he now approached the subject from a different angle. An attentive reading of the *Letter*'s untidy jumble of linguistics, rhetoric, and aesthetics shows those various elements linked by an analogy of expression. Art is not primarily imitative but expressive and emblematic. In poetry, the immediate subject of the dispute with Batteux, both qualities appear in the inversion of the logical construction of sentences typical of rational discourse. The succession of words in ancient languages, such as Greek and Hebrew, does not follow the logical syntax but the order in which impressions affect the speaker's mind. The poetic syntax symbolically suggests the order of impression. The diachronic character of all speech forces us to break language down into segments. Scientific and ordinary modern languages (certainly modern French) reorganize those segments into a logical order. This order no longer reflects the original impact of the impressions.

Poetry alone overcomes this discursive quality by symbolizing the mind's impressions in the order of the words. It *represents* things as soon as it says them, and it *presents* them as symbolic expressions of the mind. This emblematic character of poetic language appears not only in the order of the words but also in their sounds and in the rhythm of their conjunction. A poem is "a fabric of hieroglyphs," "a forest of symbols" (*Lettre sur les sourds muets,* in *Oeuvres,* IV, 34).

Connected with this thesis on linguistic symbolization Diderot advances another, even more fundamental one, on the analogy and irreducibility of all modes of aesthetic expression. Visual images may be aesthetically as expressive as poetry, yet, contrary to the title of Batteux's treatise, they cannot be reduced to "a single principle." Each mode of expression is different. No mode of aesthetic symbolization can be directly transposed into another. Virgil's graphic description of Neptune who, disturbed by the sudden storm at the beginning of the *Aeneid* (I, 124–27), raises his head above the waters would merely look ludicrous in a painting. Diderot's thesis anticipates Lessing's concerning the irreducible contrast between Virgil's poetic description of Laocoön and the Belvedere's Hellenistic sculpture, which we shall discuss later. Diderot's argument has not been lost on contemporary psychologists who came to oppose the method of teaching the deaf-mute a surrogate form of speech (such as lip-reading) rather than educating them in the different, more appropriate visual sign language.

Despite these irreducible differences, a definite analogy unites the various modes of aesthetic expression. The analogy consists not in a similarity of the aesthetic objects but in a comparable pattern of symbolization. Diderot supports his view of functional analogy by referring to the newly invented light-organ that projects beams of color corresponding to musical tones. A deaf-mute, he claims, could come to understand indirectly what speech is like by observing the organist's finger movements as they become instantly translated into light. Indeed, a person of normal hearing has occasion to observe a similar analogy among different forms of expression. When walking through an art gallery, Diderot writes, he feels like a deaf-mute: the paintings speak a silent language; one that essentially differs from spoken language in that each canvas displays the whole scene at once rather than unfolding it in temporal succession, as language does.[28]

For all his objections to the imitation theory, Diderot continued to maintain that in some way art imitates nature. Through a detailed study of actual paintings in France, Holland, and Germany, as well as through his reading of Christian Ludwig von Hagedorn's *Betrachtungen über die Malerei,* Diderot gradually acquired a new respect for realistic representation. Where nature serves a symbolic function, its excesses and deformities may as much stand model to the artist, as harmony and balance. The first sentence of the *Essais sur la peinture* (1766), in which he synthesized this fresh experience, sounds like a manifesto: "La nature ne fait rien d'incorrect. Toute forme, belle et laide, a sa cause." Diderot commends Chardin's everyday realism as an *imitation très fidèle de la nature*, "the very substance of the objects, the air and the light you take at the point of your brush and apply to the canvas" (*Salons* [1763], in *Oeuvres*, IV, 265). In the *Essais* he applies the same rule to the portrait: to qualify as a work of art a portrait must present more than a flattering resemblance. It must dare to reveal what age or smallpox has done to a face. It must reflect individuality rather than a universal type or a moral virtue. Artistic conventions hold no authority against nature's primeval power (*Essais*, in *Oeuvres*, IV, 467–69). Passions and feelings, wild nature and monsters, deserve to be represented as well as rational harmony, among things. "The arts of imitation need something savage, crude, striking, and enormous" (*Essais*, in *Oeuvres*, IV, 498).

We are a long way from *la belle nature!* But have we returned to the literalist theory of imitation? I think not, because what the artist imitates is not in the first place the object as simply perceived but as perceived through an emotional prism. The symbolic function of the model is "purely ideal and not borrowed from any particular image of nature" (*Salons* [1767], in *Oeuvres*, IV, 524). Art that focuses entirely on rendering an accurate perception of nature leaves out most of nature's spiritual meaning. Instead, the artist ought to represent nature as reflected in *les grands enthousiasmes de la vie*. Diderot developed this insight in a series of critical reviews, written for Grimm's *Correspondance littéraire* on the yearly art exhibitions at the Louvre and later published as *Salons* (*Oeuvres*, IV, 193–1005). His theory of expression called for a more radical transformation of the aesthetic object than the one art critics of his time called *la belle nature*. He refers to La Tour's portraits that seem "made of flesh and blood," not in the first place because they resemble the facial features of their models, but because they capture their spiritual identity. He "idealizes" nature by internalizing natural forms. Nature remains the only model available to the artist but he must present it as reflected in ideas, feelings, and memories. Nature as imitated by the artist always symbolizes an inner state of mind. Diderot accepted the empiricist principle that all knowledge is derived from sense impressions, but for him, the imagination transforms those impressions into symbols of inner life. This internalization of the impressions justifies Arthur Wilson's paradoxical interpretation of Diderot's aesthetics: "When Diderot used the word 'imitation' as he did frequently in all his aesthetic writings, it was in the sense more readily conveyed to twentieth century students by the word 'expression.' The scrupulous imitation of nature that he called for is accomplished by expressing her."[29] The ideal model is not derived from nature: it resides in the artist's soul. Herbert Dieckmann, another perceptive interpreter of Diderot, arrived at a similar conclusion: "To the question of imitation he substitutes that of expression or, more correctly, of the relation between 'thought' or the artist's internal state and his expression in the work."[30]

Still, Diderot's position is not free of ambiguity. Yes, he constantly reminds his readers that copying nature has no aesthetic merit. Yes, the inspiration for painting or sculpturing a particular scene or a particular face must entirely come from within and thus be expressive of an inner state. Yet his sensational-ist theory of knowledge often stands in the way of his theory of expression. The rules of painting described in the *Essais sur la peinture* all insist on a realistic rendition of things as they appear. Feelings may be conveyed only through the choice of the physical subject — not by a transformation of the forms of appearance. Diderot even objects to disharmonious expressions of passion. Regardless of the subject, the artist must observe the traditional con-ventions of harmony. Obviously the French critic's attempt to avoid subjectiv-ism as well as naturalism did not always succeed.

The narrowness of his aesthetic ideal also imposes strict moral norms upon artistic expression. The author of the lascivious *Family Jewels* as well as of a number of risqué stories turns surprisingly moralistic in his art criticism. Throughout the *Essais sur la peinture* he insists that the moral quality of a work of art forms an essential part of its aesthetic merit. "To render virtue lovable, vice odious, and to expose the ridiculous — that is the project of each honest man who picks up the pen, the brush, or the chisel" (*Essais,* in *Oeuvres,* IV, 501). Linking the beautiful to the good and the true, he adds to the ancient definition of beauty as *splendor veritatis,* the splendor of goodness. "The true, the good, and the beautiful stay close to each other. If we add to one of the two former qualities a rare, brilliant condition, the true will be beautiful and the good will be beautiful" (*Essais,* in *Oeuvres,* IV, 513). Diderot despises Boucher for being "licentious" and neglects Watteau for being frivolous while he praises the often-sentimental Greuze for the moral nobility of his work (*Es-sais,* in *Oeuvres,* IV, 500). With Diderot, nothing is ever simple, however. His moral high-mindedness was balanced by a sensuous temperament as well as by an ingrained skepticism concerning all values, including the ones he so zealously defended. His own descriptions of Boucher's canvases are more erotic than the works themselves!

His art criticism reveals as much, if not more, about his own feelings, moral principles, and prejudices as about the paintings he discusses. Madame

Necker, charmed by his subjective approach, praised Diderot's art reviews because she "liked painting only in poetry." Others, like Barbey d'Aurevilly, could hardly contain their irritation about the critic's continuous intrusions. "In his novels as in his other works, he never forgets himself, himself and his sermonizing. . . . The painter breaks through the painting to stick his head out of a hole in the canvas to make sure that everyone sees him well and always understands him well."[31] The charge is all too true, yet vanity may not have been the sole reason for Diderot's pertinacious presence. He felt so driven by the importance of his literary mission that, indeed, he rarely dropped the preaching tone. Art, for him, formed part of a comprehensive project to improve the condition of the human race.

LESSING

It is hard to find two men who occupied more similar positions in the aesthetic life of the eighteenth century than Lessing and Diderot. As art critics and playwrights, both strongly influenced the ideas of their time. Both expressed themselves in an easy, conversational style. Lessing admired Diderot's dramas and aesthetic theories and Diderot admired Lessing's. Yet each one succeeded in preserving his own literary identity. Diderot was light-hearted, sensitive, and folksy with a touch of vulgarity; Lessing more focused, serious-minded, capable of irony and sarcasm, but hardly ever indulging in levity. The expressive theory intimated in Diderot's *Letter on the Deaf-Mute* Lessing elaborated into a full-fledged philosophy.

His views on aesthetics are spread out over his Hamburg theater reviews (*Hamburgische Dramaturgie*) and a long essay in which he compares poetry with the plastic arts (*Laocoön*). I shall discuss Lessing's dramatic work in an appendix to chapter 5. His essay *Laocoön* (1766) introduces a category that brought the centuries-old debate about the comparative merit of poetry and of the visual arts to a close.[32] Beauty, Lessing concludes, is the defining characteristic of the visual arts, expressiveness that of poetry. Lessing illustrates the distinction by comparing a passage from a literary work with a recently discovered Hellenistic sculpture that represented the same subject. Virgil's *Aeneid* (II, 199–224) describes how the Trojan priest Laocoön, together with his two sons, is killed by two gigantic serpents Minerva has summoned from the sea. Johann Winckelmann had previously compared the two works of art (*Thoughts on the Imitation of Greek Works of Painting and Sculpture*, 1755). In his view, the statue bears the composed artistic expression of the classical period, whereas Virgil's poem displays the uninhibited emotion characteristic of the later, Roman age. Lessing accepted Winckelmann's surprising interpretation of the sculpture as "composed" and of the poem as "emotional," but he rejected Winckelmann's explanation of the difference. In his judgment, the emotional treatment of Virgil's poem has nothing to do with its presumed later age, but with the specific nature of literature. Even Greek poetry of the classical age had been capable of violent expression, as Sophocles' *Philoctetes* shows. But, he argued, neither Greek nor Roman taste tolerated emotional distortion in statuary.

The comparison between the two artistic genres presented a unique occasion for testing Horace's oft-quoted and mostly misinterpreted *ut pictura poesis* (a poem must be like a picture). Lessing conjectured that Virgil's poem had preceded the statue in time and hence ought not be read as a description of an existing work of art.[33] On a more substantial level, he argued that, since poetry develops in time while pictorial art remains fixed in space, the passing emotional images of poetry have a slighter impact than a picture frozen in immobility. In a statue emotional tension lastingly distorts the subject's features and thus conflicts with the aesthetic harmony required in a work of art. Traditionally beauty has been considered the dominant category of visual art. But if beauty were the principal quality of poetry (as the later interpretation of *ut pictura poesis* suggested), then none but the pictorial passages of a poem would possess aesthetic merit, while physically or morally disturbing scenes and portraits would detract from its aesthetic value. Homer's description of the ugly Thersites (*Iliad*, II) as well as Shakespeare's portrait of Richard III proves that the opposite occurs. Restricting the aesthetic to the beautiful submits poetry to an inappropriate norm.

Lessing obviously overstates his thesis: a poem must also be beautiful, and visual art may be strongly expressive, as the Laocoön statue, contrary to Winckelmann's and Lessing's assessment of it, shows. In fact, Lessing himself refers to contemporary theorists who argued that even in the plastic arts expressiveness had become the primary law. "Truth and expression (they claim) are art's first law and as nature herself is ever ready to sacrifice beauty for the sake of higher aims, so must the artist subordinate it to his general purpose and pursue it no further than truth and expression permit" (chap. III, p. 19). Lessing suspended judgment on this opinion until, after having completed the twenty-fifth chapter of his book, he read Winckelmann's *History of Ancient Art* (1768). It fully persuaded him that the visual arts also might be expressive. By that time he already had reached the conclusion that poetry, besides being expressive, can and must also be beautiful, though its means for being so differed from those of the visual arts. Poetry moves in time and is able to describe things in motion; visual arts are static. With this distinction Lessing exposed a more subtle difference than the one between beauty and expressiveness. The purely spatial nature of painting and sculpture reveals all features at once, while the dynamic, temporal one of poetry develops images in the order in which they appear. He cites Homer's description of Achilles' shield in which the poet focuses on the process of forging it, rather than on the finished product. The principal merit of Lessing's theory consists in having enlarged the aesthetic canon with an essential category, that of expressiveness.

REYNOLDS

In his annual discourses to the Royal Academy in London, its founder, Joshua Reynolds, recorded the successive phases and transitions of his and his contemporaries' assessments of the meaning and quality of painting in the preceding two centuries. As the works of Michelangelo, Raphael, Claude Lorrain, and Salvator Rosa passed his review from year to year, no study reflects more accurately the changing taste of the eighteenth century, especially (but not exclusively) in Britain, than the collected *Discourses*. Reynolds's aesthetic eclecticism as well as his constant experimentation with different styles predisposed him to be receptive to any new current. His early concept of artistic beauty may be traced back to Shaftesbury's Platonic notion of an ideal nature. "Instead of endeavoring to amuse mankind with the minute neatness of his imitations, he [the painter] must endeavor to improve them by the grandeur of his ideas. . . . All the arts receive their perfection from an ideal beauty, superior to what is to be found in individual nature."[34] Like Shaftesbury, Reynolds links the beautiful to the good (IX, 142). Together they constitute the *true*. It is in fact the search for truth that directs the search for beauty and goodness. Moral virtue, he claims, serves as an indispensable condition for a proper assessment of aesthetic quality. "It has been often observed that the good and virtuous man alone can acquire this true and just relish even of works of art" (VII, 109). On the other side, any aesthetic imperfection, anything that is too particular or deformed or deviating from the common form, falls short of a true representation of nature and is therefore related to a moral mistake. The sculpture of classical Greece, which captured this ideal form, ought to serve as a model (III, 27). Shaftesbury himself might have written this.

Yet once Reynolds starts discussing actual paintings, his high moral ideal often takes second place to the traditional, formalist norms of harmony, balance, and so on. According to idealist principles, Michelangelo ought tot be a greater painter than Raphael: he takes "a firm hold and entire possession of the mind as to make us desire nothing else" (V, 63). Nevertheless, Reynolds concludes, Raphael deserves the palm. Why? Because his work burns with "a more pure, regular, and chaste flame" (V, 63). Over the years the author gradually shifted his preference and, in the conclusion of his final discourse, completely reversed his position: "I should desire that the last words which I should pronounce in this Academy, and from this place, might be the name of — Michael Angelo" (XV, 242). Through the preceding years, however, Reynolds continuously wavered between Neoplatonic idealism, scholastic formalism, and preromantic expressiveness. This explains why he looked down upon the realist art of the Flemish and Dutch masters, who "depart from the great purposes of painting, catching at applause by inferior qualities" (IV, 45). Rubens's work in particular, with its fleshy bodies, comes in for criticism. But a year later he changes his judgment to one of admiration for the perfect harmony of Rubens's composition and color (V, 66). In his early years he considered landscapes subject for a lesser genius, unless they serve as background to a historical scene or at least allude to such a scene. Obviously Reynolds had not yet discovered the sublime in nature, which he was to praise so highly in his later discourses.[35]

What must have puzzled even his contemporaries was Reynolds's low opinion of the great Venetians, especially Veronese and Tintoretto. Though they perfectly accomplished what they attempted to achieve, their ideal, in his opinion, was still too pedestrian to rank them with the "noble schools" (V, 45). Their splendor of style, so pleasing "to the eye or sense," their dramatic alternation of light and shade, their brilliant colors dazzle more than they reflect "the ideal beauty of form" (IV, 49). Yet even while he was writing those controversial judgments, some doubt began to invade Reynolds's idealism, and later, in the same fourth discourse, he praised the "senatorial dignity" of the school. "The Venetian is indeed the most splendid of the schools of elegance; and it is not without reason, that the best performances in this lower school are valued higher than the second-rate performances of those above them: for every picture has value when it has a decided character, and is excellent in its kind" (IV, 50). Faint praise for great masters! But enough to show how opposing principles were combating each other in Reynolds's mind. Particularly revealing in this respect is his assessment of Salvator Rosa, the seventeenth-century Neapolitan painter of dark, dramatic landscapes and seascapes. He had anticipated much of what Reynolds himself longed to paint but what his own aesthetic formalism never allowed him to do. "He gives us a peculiar cast of nature, which though void of all grace, elegance, and simplicity, though it has nothing of that elevation and dignity which belongs to the grand style, yet, has that sort of dignity which belongs to savage and uncultivated nature" (V, 65). Rosa and a few artists like him form the link between the classical ideal of moral greatness and the preromantic one of emotional expressiveness. The tension he felt in the great Baroque works of art led Reynolds to reconceive the notion of genius that played such an important part in late eighteenth-century aesthetics.

Although in the earlier discourses artistic genius had included formal harmony in color and composition as well as moral grandeur, in the later ones it tends to move beyond harmony. (I write, "tends to" because nothing is ever definitive for this versatile critic!) "Genius is supposed to be a power of producing excellencies, which are out of the rules of art; a power which no precepts can teach, and which no industry can acquire" (VI, 74). "Genius," then, refers to the capacity to achieve a qualitative leap in aesthetic excellence that cannot be justified by established rules or conventional ideals. It still follows rules, both formal and moral, but they are rules of its own making (V, 76). As such it surpasses both conventional moral ideals and classicist harmony. But it reconciles them on a higher level. In this new conception of genius the expressive concept of art definitively breaks through. The aesthetic weight shifts altogether from the imitation of external nature to "the nature and internal fabric and organization of the human mind and imagination" (VII, 99). Nature remains the fountain of all forms, but she reveals her inner secret only to the mind and hand of the artistic genius. "Thus the highest beauty of form must be taken from nature; but it is an art of long deduction and great experience, to know how to find it" (VI, 80). Copying nature's appearances is no art, but merely "a scanty entertainment for the imagination" (VII, 102).

With his reinterpretation of the concept of taste Reynolds completes his move toward an expressive theory of aesthetics. Taste, according to him, consists not in sensitiveness to the formal qualities of a work of art (harmony, composition, etc.), but in some of that ability to partake of nature's creativity, which characterizes the artist of genius. "Genius and taste, in their common acceptation, appear to be very nearly related; the difference lies only in this, that genius has super-added to it a habit of power of execution; or we may say, that taste, when this power is added changes its name, and is called genius" (VII, 96). Still Reynolds never became an unbridled romantic. Even artistic genius must obey certain established rules, without which nothing would be left but "caprice and casualty" (VII, 99). But these rules differ from the guidelines of academic training. Unfortunately Sir Joshua remains exceedingly vague in defining them. The principles of orderly composition, harmony of light and shade, and a happy blending of colors are too general to function in this capacity.

Reynolds's theory suffers from a discrepancy between the sensationalist theory of knowledge, to which he persistently turns for philosophical support, and a concept of aesthetic truth that in fact has its base in the creative imagination. Thus, after having asserted that the criterion of beauty resides not in the external form of things but in the mind and the imagination, he immediately hastens back to Lockean orthodoxy in denying the imagination any creative power. "The imagination is incapable of producing any thing originally of itself, and can only vary and combine those ideas with which it is furnished by means of the senses" (VII, 107). Inconsistencies of this nature show the eclectic as well as the transitional character of Reynolds's work. Over the years he borrowed from various aesthetic theories, without fully embracing any single one. In the earlier discourses he increasingly stressed the subjective and "moral" factor. Not until he expressed his unambiguous preference of Michelangelo in the final discourse did he definitively embrace the principles of a new era in aesthetics. With Kant the expressive theory of art at last received its theoretical justification.

On the Way to a Symbolic Theory of Art

THE CONCEPT OF TASTE AND THE BIRTH OF AESTHETICS: FROM SHAFTESBURY TO BAUMGARTEN

The term "taste" current in the vocabulary of eighteenth-century aesthetics varied in meaning from one author to another. For Boileau and Fontenelle, it had consisted in a capacity of judging art in accordance with right reason, that is, with objective principles of harmony, verisimilitude, and insight. A famous article ("Goût") in the *Encyclopédie,* begun by Montesquieu and completed by Voltaire with an appendix by d'Alembert, wavers between an objective, rational, and a mildly subjective interpretation. Voltaire argued that taste requires more than an acquaintance with the principles of harmony: "One must feel beauty and be moved by it." But aesthetic sensitivity needs to be educated. A genuine judgment of taste must be able to claim the consensus of all educated persons. Voltaire still assumed that the foundation of beauty lies in the things themselves.

For Montesquieu, however, taste had consisted in the pleasure one takes in an object without regard to its use. "When we find pleasure in something that is useful for us, we say that it is *good;* when we find pleasure in seeing it, without discerning for the moment any utility in it, we call it *beautiful.*"[36] Not a word about the objective qualities of the beautiful here! "Perfection in the art consists in presenting objects to us in such a way that they cause us as much pleasure as possible" ("Goût," p. 343). Montesquieu admits that the work of art must meet certain objective conditions, but he explains them as derived from primary sense impressions. Thus the pleasure we find in symmetry would derive from the fact that symmetry is "useful to the soul and able to further its functions" ("Goût," p. 349). This concept of taste, based mostly on beauty's objective effects, opened up a space for perceptions, feelings, and emotions — those subjective elements that Boileau's theory of *le vrai seul* had not been able to accommodate. But how could aesthetic pleasure preserve that universality which art critics claimed for taste? In an appendix to the *Encyclopédie* article, d'Alembert tried to resolve that problem, arguing that the "true philosopher" knows how to distinguish the universal element in taste from the conventional one and thus to determine which pleasures are genuine and which are "illusory pleasures" ("Goût," p. 366). The term "illusory" reveals the bad conscience of the rationalist who, afraid of the anarchy of pleasure, withdraws by objective qualification much of what he had granted to subjective feeling.

In Britain the concept of taste had similarly wavered between an objective and a subjective meaning. Shaftesbury, who with Addison made the word fashionable, used it in defense of objective norms that he felt were threatened by the subjective relativism of Locke's epistemology. Far from being at the mercy of arbitrary feelings, taste for him consisted in the awareness of the objective harmony that unites the physical cosmos with human feelings and emotions.[37] Shaftesbury vaguely intuited what was to become the fundamental principle of Kant's theory of the beautiful, namely, that the aesthetic experience originates in the primary awareness of harmony between the faculties of the mind and the represented object. For the British critic also, the disinterested attitude necessary for aesthetic taste demands a detachment that does not come naturally but must be learned. In addition, taste requires a sense of moral grandeur and even a feeling of tension between the self and its surroundings. Only the awareness of an unresolved contrast induces the mind to search for that deeper harmony which causes the properly aesthetic pleasure. The contemplation of uncultivated nature may arouse or heighten that tension. "Even the rude rocks, the mossy caverns, the irregular unwrought grottos and broken falls of waters, with all the horrid graces of the wilderness itself, as representing Nature more, will be the more engaging, and appear with a magnificence beyond the formal mockery of princely gardens."[38]

With Hume the pendulum swung in the opposite direction and the notion of taste became wholly subjective. According to his early *Treatise on Human Nature* (1738), the aesthetic experience depends on "such an order and construction of parts, as either by the primary constitution of our nature, by custom, or by caprice, is fitted to give a pleasure and satisfaction to the soul."[39] In a later essay, "Of the Standard of Taste" (1757), he moderates that subjectivism somewhat by referring to the "general rules of beauty." But the rules themselves are drawn from "the observation of what pleases or displeases."[40] To speak of "real" beauty is as fruitless as "to pretend to ascertain the real sweet or real bitter." Nonetheless, Hume considers the judgment of taste universal. But he ascribes this quality to the similarity of the subjective processes of thinking and feeling, which vary little from one person to another. Hence the paradox that, though judgments of taste are in principle universal, only few people are endowed with enough aesthetic sensitivity properly to evaluate a work of art.

Neither French nor British critics had succeeded in satisfactorily incorporating their analyses of the aesthetic experience within a general theory of knowledge. To do so was Kant's project in *The Critique of Judgment*. He thereby relied heavily on the work of Alexander Baumgarten, the philosopher who had first used the term "aesthetics" for referring to the science of the beautiful. In his *Aesthetica* (1750), the rationalist Baumgarten intended to complete Wolff's theory of knowledge that had included little about sense perception and imagination, though both play an essential part in the epistemic process. Together they constitute what Baumgarten calls the "aesthetic" knowledge, the *perfectio cognitionis sensitivae*.[41] This knowledge lacks the objective quality of conceptual cognition, but in the intuition of harmony it grasps the unity in the multiplicity of phenomena that, according to Wolff, was a distinctive quality of truth. In contrast to reason, however, the aesthetic intuition never moves beyond perceiving the harmony between the universal and the particular. It experiences this harmony but is incapable of rationally justifying it. The aesthetic judgment, then, can claim no objectivity. Still the fact that most educated people agree on the principles of art indicates that the aesthetic experience occurs in accordance with certain rational norms.

On its own level art aims at attaining what constitutes the objective of reason, namely, subsuming diversity under unity, particularity under universality. Though not rational in itself, the aesthetic judgment is nonetheless analogous to the rational one (§ 42). Baumgarten grounds the analogy between logical truth and aesthetic perception on the rationalist assumption that the actual world as perceived by senses and imagination must in all respects correspond to the laws of the mind. Aesthetic perception, in an obscure yet intuitive awareness of the logical harmony of the world, presents what *ought to be* (in the rational order of things). Baumgarten's *Aesthetica* overcomes narrow rationalism and inconsistent subjectivism by granting aesthetics an indispensable place in the realm of truth. In his earlier *Reflections on Poetry* (1735), where the term "aesthetica" first appears, he had argued that a good poem must be like the world: the whole ought to be harmonious and the parts well ordered. Yet the poem need not refer to the real world: it constitutes a virtual world of its own, independent of any external reality.

The problems inherent in such a comparison appeared soon enough. Despite his sympathy for Baumgarten's aesthetic conception, Kant noted that a work of art can never be entirely "pure" or self-sufficient. Aesthetic forms always refer to a world beyond the work of art. This is particularly the case with poetry. Words continue to bear the mark of their original destination: to articulate our life world. A poem's meaning, then, moves inevitably beyond the virtual aesthetic reality that it construes. Still Baumgarten's aestheticism proved to possess a durable staying power. Even in the early part of the twentieth century some art critics still restricted a poem's significance to a self-contained meaning. In isolating the poem from the "real" world the German philosopher did away with the imitation theory, which, despite many modifications and reinterpretations, had remained dominant among critics. But he did so at the expense of art's ontological significance.[42]

THE KANTIAN REVOLUTION: INTUITION AND GENIUS

For Kant, as for Baumgarten, the judgment of taste belonged in the realm of truth. Art and beauty present *ideas* that, because of their rich emotional content, cannot be conceptualized. At the beginning of his "Analytic of the Beautiful," the first part of the *Critique of Judgment*,[43] Kant explains how the aesthetic judgment differs from the objective, cognitive one "In order to discern whether or not something is beautiful we do not relate the representation through reason to the object for knowledge. Rather, we relate it through the imagination (perhaps in conjunction with reason) to the subject and its feeling of pleasure or displeasure" (*KUK*, § 1; *AB*, pp. 3–4). In objective knowledge the imagination serves a purely instrumental function: it unifies the multiple data that enter consciousness through the senses into a single representation. In the process of thinking the mind is hardly aware of this operation. But if the mind, instead of moving directly to full objectification, lingers at this intermediate stage of the imagination a different, nonconceptual representation emerges. This intermediate level, according to Kant, is the birthplace of aesthetics. The representations constituted at this level hold the middle between objective concepts and sense perceptions, but they also cause a pleasurable feeling of harmony between the mind and its representations. With respect to them the mind has not yet achieved that intellectual distance essential to objective cognition. They remain, so to speak, inherent in the mind itself, in such a way that the mind can freely play with this product of its creative imagination without being tied by the fixed rules of objective reality.

Kant insists that the concomitant feeling of pleasure does not constitute the essence of the aesthetic experience. It merely follows the judgment of taste. Analogous to the cognitive judgment and in contrast to feelings of pleasure, the aesthetic judgment is universally valid, even though it lacks the irrefutability of logical propositions or scientific conclusions. "There can be no objective rule of taste which determines by concepts whether an object is beautiful. For all judgments from this source [i.e., taste] are aesthetic, that is to say, their determining ground is the subject's feeling and not any concept of an object. Any effort to search for a principle of taste that would furnish the universal criterion of the beautiful in terms of definite concepts is bound to be sterile, for what is sought is impossible and self-contradictory" (*KUK,* § 17; *AB,* p. 39). Nonetheless, someone who judges with taste may assume his feeling to be universally communicable without having to prove it by logical arguments.

Kant's theory is not subjectivist in the way Hume's notion of aesthetic pleasure is. Yet the question remains: Which objective, universal criteria justify the mind in considering an object beautiful, since the aesthetic experience consists entirely in the mind's subjective response to it? Without some such criteria it becomes impossible to distinguish a genuine work of art from a flawed one or even from an ordinary object. Kant therefore was forced to present certain specific qualities that distinguish representations capable of inducing aesthetic experiences from others. One of them was that of *ideal form.* This criterion differs from the *belle nature* of the French and English writers, which had been purely objective. For Kant, the aesthetic potential of an object depends on the spiritual power the artist has been able to invest in it, not on pre-established objective characteristics. A withered tree or a dying animal was not botanically or zoologically ideal, but Ruysdael and Rembrandt repeatedly made it into an ideal expression of a state of mind. Kant complicates matters by adding the condition that the ideal form excludes serious deviations from a general type. This criterion of a fixed ideal form appears to conflict with the subjective nature of his aesthetics.

More consistent with his theory and far more important for the modern theory of aesthetics was Kant's insight that the aesthetic representation functions as a *symbol* of the mind. In the *Prolegomena to Any Future Metaphysics* Kant had described symbols as representations that refer to ideas to which no direct sensuous intuition corresponds, such as the idea of God. Those representations then substitute for sense intuitions of the actual object. They do so on the ground of "a similarity of relations between two quite different things."[44] Aesthetic representations fulfill a similar function. They symbolize ideas too rich in content and too indeterminate in form to be adequately expressed in concepts. The mind thereby gains some insight in ideas it cannot prove to be true or even conceptually articulate. The restrictions inherent in Kant's epistemology prevent him from calling them "true." But when he introduced the well-established notions of genius and of the sublime into his aesthetic theory he opened the door to a more fully symbolic understanding of those ideas.

No term had become more popular in eighteenth-century criticism than that of "genius." Much of this popularity may be traced — again — to Shaftesbury who used it sparingly but appears nevertheless most responsible for its modern usage. The origins of the term go back to the Latin *ingenium:* what is innate or belongs to a person's nature or inborn talent (Herder applied the term to what distinguishes one nation from another) and the related term *genius* (the protective spirit of a person or place). But, the ancients had no single term for the *concept* of artistic genius. They somehow indirectly referred to it, as when Plato in the *Ion* described it as a kind of divine madness that takes uncontrollable possession of the poet, or when Roman rhetoricians claimed that rules do not make art *(Poeta nascitur, orator fit)*. In the eighteenth century the term often served as counterpart to the observation of rules in aesthetic creation. Great artists are rarely aware of rules and often violate them. In Shaftesbury's Neoplatonic interpretation, genius consists primarily in the artistic power of expression. The artistic genius re-creates the inner form of things and thereby imitates nature in its spontaneous creativity.[45] Joseph Addison also stressed the difference between the traditional concept of art as imitation of nature and the modern one according to which it imitates nature's creative power and thereby adds to nature.[46]

Ever since Shaftesbury, the concepts of genius and of taste had been related. Taste consists in the ability to experience beauty, but genius alone creates beauty. Still, taste must guide genius to the right project and assist in achieving it. The article "Génie" in the *Encyclopédie,* attributed to Saint-Lambert but thoroughly rewritten by Diderot, opposes genius to taste. Genius is all natural, taste merely the result of "study and time." Shakespeare may occasionally lack taste, but he possesses genius. Similarly a thinker of genius may at times neglect the rules of logic (the "taste" of reason), but he introduces new ideas. "There are few errors in Locke and too few truths in Lord Shaftesbury. Yet the former is no more than a comprehensive, penetrating, and just mind, while the latter is a genius of first order; Locke saw, Shaftesbury created, built, edified."[47] Pope also, in the preface to his translation of Homer's *Iliad,* identified genius with an extended comprehensiveness of the imagination." But it was the Scottish philosopher Alexander Gerard's *Essay on Taste* (1759) followed by his *Essay on Genius* (1774) that mostly influenced Kant's notion of genius. Gerard considered inventiveness the primary quality of the imagination.[48] The artist invents associations rather than finding them: he "calls in from all quarters the ideas that are necessary for executing his designs."[49]

In his *Anthropology* (1798) Kant praises Gerard for having perceived the creative power of the productive imagination, which had played such an important part in *The Third Critique.* There he had described genius as "the innate mental disposition (*ingenium*) through which nature gives the rule to art" (*KUK*, § 46; Bernard, p. 150). Yet Kant adds a surprising specification: works of genius become models, "not to be copied but to be imitated" (*KUK*, § 47; Bernard, p. 152). Genius, then, though itself above the rules, sets up rules for others to follow. This paradoxical conclusion (Does genius not exclude imitation?) makes sense only if we remember that for Kant, even the artist of genius must be directed by taste, even though he may take some liberties with established rules. "Taste, like judgment in general, is the discipline (or train-ing) of genius. It severely clips its wings, and makes it cultured and polished. But, at the same time, it gives guidance, as to where and how far it may extend itself if it is to remain purposive" (*KUK*, § 50; Bernard, p. 163). Kant's notion of genius creates the conditions for genuine aesthetic truth. The great artist raises art beyond subjective experience to where it becomes symbolic of great ideas. Kant here approaches a fully symbolic theory of art.[50] But in the end he fails to overcome the subjective interpretation of aesthetics. When he describes genius as "the innate mental disposition through which *nature* gives rule to art," one may wonder whether "nature" means more than the fundamental structure of the mind itself.

THE SUBLIME AND THE BEAUTIFUL

The three most common categories of eighteenth-century aesthetics — taste, genius, and the sublime — complement one another. A particularly close relation links genius to the sublime. In the sublimity of nature and morality, genius finds its inspiration. Many critics of the Enlightenment therefore re-garded sublimity in a work of art the mark of genius. The term "sublime" entered aesthetic theory through the Latin translation of a Greek treatise on "high style" in rhetoric. Its third-century anonymous author (Longinus [?]) located the sources of the sublime style in the soul's "invincible love for all that is great and more divine than ourselves," which induces it to cross "the bound-aries of the surrounding world."[51] Rediscovered in the sixteenth century, the tract was translated into Latin in 1572 and became popular through Boileau's French translation (1674). In the notes he added, Boileau extended the cate-gory of the sublime beyond rhetoric and applied it to consciousness itself. Great *thinking* was more sublime than great *style*. Moreover, the French critic traced the origin of both meanings to an objective quality in nature itself: the sublimity of nature evokes great thoughts, strong emotions, and noble expressions.

In England the idea first received a more specifically aesthetic content. Ac-cording to Samuel E. Monk's classic treatise on the subject, "the sublime tended to become the all-inclusive category for those objects and these emotions which the strict neo-classic doctrine could not admit as beautiful, but which English-men were traditionally and constitutionally [!] ready to accept as of aesthetic value."[52] For Shaftesbury, as for Addison and Burke, the consciousness of the sublime stems from the tension between the soul and the surrounding nature. Thus, wild and savage nature arouses the soul to strong emotions and mag-nanimous feelings. Joseph Addison argues (in twelve issues of *The Spectator*) that the sight of vast expanses in nature makes the mind aware of its own boundlessness. "A spacious horizon is an image of liberty, where the eye has room to range abroad, to expatiate at large in the immensity of its views."[53] Yet it was the young Edmund Burke in his *Philosophical Enquiry into the Origin of Our Ideas of the Sublime and the Beautiful* (1756) (begun and virtually com-pleted when he was still an undergraduate at Trinity College) who defined the sublime's distinct character by separating it from the beautiful. A representa-tion that causes emotions of terror or of grandeur has little in common with the beautiful, though it still falls within the aesthetic range.

Remembering Lessing's discussion of the expressive character of literature (in *Laocoön*), one would expect the sublime to be primarily a poetic category. Poetry alone was fit to express strong emotions. Yet by the end of the eigh-teenth century many felt that the grandeur and terror of nature could be more forcefully presented in painting than in words. No poetic description would equal a pictorial representation of the awe-inspiring power of nature. But to achieve the full emotional effect of this power, painters ought not to be satis-fied with a faithful representation of scenery; they had to intensify certain aspects and exclude others until their picture of nature reflected the soul's inner landscape. Salvator Rosa was considered a master of this pictorial ex-pressionism. British painters, influenced by him, amplified the power of nature by the "architectural sublime" of solitary buildings, Gothic cathedrals, and, above all, ruins of abbeys and castles. A landscape could hardly be sublime without some reference to history: a dilapidated remnant of the past, an allu-sion to an ancient battle or hero. In the end, it was not nature itself, but nature as related to the soul that interested them. Such romantic canvases as Joseph Turner's *Hannibal Crossing the Alps* and John Martin's *Deluge* triptych show dwarflike humans struggling with the titanic powers of nature. The pursuit of the sublime formed a natural transition between the art of the Enlightenment and that of Romanticism.[54] The morally sublime came to consist in actions undertaken with strong passion and carried through with extraordinary cour-age, even if they conflicted with accepted moral norms. Great crimes may require as much moral energy as deeds of heroic virtue.[55]

Here also Kant provided the definitive expression. In his early *Observations on the Feeling of the Beautiful and Sublime* (1763),[56] Kant had followed Burke in attributing the distinction between the beautiful and the sublime to different mental states. But while Burke links the sublime primarily to emotions of terror, Kant associates it mostly with moral feelings. For him, courage, honesty, universal affection, and, in general, "true virtue," more than ragged mountain peaks, raging storms, and visions of Milton's infernal kingdom, evoke sublime feelings. In Kant's moral writings, the *Groundwork for the Metaphysics of Morals* (1785) and the *Critique of Practical Reason* (1788), he attributes the sublime to the moral will. It consists primarily in an attitude rather than a feeling, though the moral attitude itself produces sublime feelings.[57] In the lengthy and profound "Analytic of the Sublime" that appears in the later *Critique of Judgment* (1790), Kant also refers to nature as sublime but always in connection with the person's unique dignity, which surpasses the majesty of nature. There also he compares the beautiful with the sublime, as Addison and Burke had done. But he traces the difference to his own distinction between understanding and reason. The beautiful symbolizes an indefinite *concept* of the understanding; the sublime an indefinite *idea* of reason. The former does so by means of finite forms; the latter through the absence of form.

In beauty, imagination and intellect attain a state of balance. In the sublime, the imagination strains this balance to a point where it threatens to disrupt the aesthetic harmony altogether. This tension between idea and representation produces the experience of the sublime. While the imagination enjoys free play in the experience of the beautiful, in that of the sublime the idea does "violence to the imagination" through a vision that both attracts and repels (*KUK*, § 23; Bernard, pp. 82–84). No image, no aspect of nature is sublime in itself: it only becomes so when the mind recognizes the disproportion between idea and representation. In various ways artists and poets evoke this excess of mind over nature, of idea over image. They may do so by giving their subject proportions that exceed the capacity of the imagination and thereby suggest the *idea* of the infinite (ibid., § 25–26), or by painting or describing scenes of overwhelming power (threatening rocks, volcanoes, waterfalls) that oppress the imagination yet make the mind aware of its superiority over nature (*KUK*, § 28; Bernard, pp. 99–101). Or they may depict desolate spaces that awaken the soul to its own boundlessness. All such images drive the mind into itself. For Kant, the sublime remains essentially a subjective experience.[58]

The experience of the sublime conveys an awareness of the "unconditional" that lies at the root of the moral act. "In fact, a feeling of the sublime in nature cannot well be thought without combining therewith a mental disposition which is akin to the moral" (*KUK*, § 29; Bernard, p. 109). Still, the feeling of the sublime intrinsically differs from the moral consciousness, which requires a definite idea of the good: it merely establishes an *analogy*. Kant had drawn attention to this analogy when he compared the sublimity of the starry sky with that of the moral law. For him, strong affections remain merely "sentimental" as long as they lack a moral orientation (*KUK*, § 29; Bernard, p. 114). Feelings and emotions remain, by their very nature, private and subjective. Yet as they form part of an aesthetic judgment they command a universal assent. According to Kant, they could not do so without being linked to some a priori principle. In the case of the sublime that principle consists in their reference, direct or indirect, to a moral absolute (*KUK*, § 29; Bernard, pp. 119–20). Kant's analogy between the moral and the aesthetic consciousness indicates the extent to which by the end of the eighteenth century the idea of freedom had come to dominate the entire spiritual life of the period.

Kant's theory marks a major step forward in the direction of a symbolic interpretation of aesthetics. In the *Critique of Pure Reason* he had defined a symbol as an empirical intuition that assists the mind in representing an idea that eludes the mind's comprehension. In the *Critique of Judgment* he considers all aesthetic representations to be symbolic. All present images of ideas that cannot be articulated in concepts (*KUK*, § 59; Bernard, p. 197). In the ordinary aesthetic representation the analogy between intuition and idea remains vague. The symbolic character appears more directly in the sublime where the ideal content dominates the entire representation. Still, even in the case of the sublime, it falls short of being fully symbolic. Essential to a full symbol is that the image *participate* in the truth to which it analogously refers. This, in Kant's judgment, the aesthetic feeling never achieves: it remains an external illustration of the idea, albeit particularly in the case of the sublime, a necessary one. A fully symbolic interpretation of art would require a more intimate unity between image and idea than Kant's aesthetics was able to grant.

Where Kant failed, Goethe, largely on Kantian grounds, succeeded. A discussion of his aesthetic theory falls beyond the limits of this study, yet a short reference to his work may suggest how thoroughly Kant's thought had prepared the terrain. The German poet united image and idea *within* the aesthetic intuition. At first he saw this unity realized only in the human form. Echoing Winckelmann's rule, "The highest subject of art for the thoughtful person is the human form," the young Goethe wrote, "The highest purpose of art is to show the human form, as sensuously significant as possible."[59] Later he extended the aesthetic synthesis from human nature to all of nature, thereby uniting the two teleological models that Kant's *Critique of Judgment* had still kept separate: the teleology of nature and that of art. The work of art presents a sensuous image with a spiritual meaning comparable to the immanent teleology of organic nature. Eventually Goethe came to consider art the *expression* of nature itself. Reviewing his poetic development, he writes in *Dichtung und Wahrheit:* "I had reached the point where I came to regard the poetic talent that inhabits me entirely as the voice of nature."[60] Here the teleology of nature and the harmony of art stem from a single source. "The highest works of art are also the highest works of nature as articulated by the human [mind] in accordance with true and natural laws."[61] In these words, written after conversations with the poet Karl-Philipp Moritz, Goethe appears to embrace a Platonic ideal of beauty. Yet he steadfastly denied any separation between the universal idea and the particular image. The image represents the entire universal type. "The particular is always subject to the universal; the universal must always suit the particular."[62] Rendering the universal concrete, raising the particular to universal significance, seeing the eternal in the transient — that is for Goethe the goal of artistic genius. In that also consists the essence of the aesthetic symbol. "Symbolism transforms appearance into idea, idea into image, in such a manner that the idea remains infinitely active and yet unattainable in the image."[63]

I conclude. The eighteenth century raised beauty to an idea of truth. Starting from an objectivist conception in which artistic truth consisted in an imitation of reality, aesthetics soon adopted such subjective experiences as aesthetic pleasure and taste as expressions of an inner truth. Concepts like *genius* and *sublime* that had emerged like wild shoots initially resisted assimilation. Once they became integrated with the traditional objective and subjective interpretations, they played an essential part in moving aesthetic theory in a symbolic direction. Kant who, in this domain also, brought together what an entire century had collected, in the end proved incapable of tying all the elements together. The next generation with the symbolic philosophies of Goethe, Schelling, and Hegel completed what he had prepared.

5

The Moral Crisis

In chapter 1, I expressed reservations about applying the term "crisis" with its modern negative meaning to eighteenth-century culture as a whole. The questioning of the traditional foundations of morality, however, definitely caused a crisis. In France, libertinism flourished among the rich and the educated. During the reign of Louis XIV much of the Court was thoroughly corrupt — from the king's own brother down. Corruption increased during the regency period and the reign of Louis XV. England also passed through a period of moral decline. The axiomatic beliefs that had supported traditional moral principles had become dubious. In the wake of the scientific revolution, philosophers started developing a theory of the person modeled after the science of nature. David Hume, who did this most consistently, understood that in a purely empirical science of the person the concept of obligation became problematic. Science justifies what *is*. But it cannot make rules of what *ought to be*.[1] The term "law" changed its meaning from being absolutely normative, as it had been in moral discourse, to descriptive, referring to what always occurs or what by a necessity inherent in the nature of things must occur. Naturalists like La Mettrie and d'Holbach interpreted the general law of survival that governs the entire animal world as the supreme rule of human conduct. Few embraced this extreme naturalism, but many accepted the underlying principle that no moral absolutes exist.

The ensuing moral predicament was unprecedented. Socrates, Plato, and Aristotle, as well as the Hebrew prophets and Christian theologians, had felt the need to justify the rules by which they lived or ought to live. But they had felt no need to question the foundations of those rules. Ethical principles had changed little in more than a millennium. After Europeans ceased to agree on the foundations of ethical life, however, a number of different systems sprang up. Within the century that began with the publication of Spinoza's *Ethics* (1678) and concluded with that of Kant's *Critique of Practical Reason* (1788), ethical thought gave birth to most of the theories that continue to influence our thinking today. In the following pages I shall consider the three major schools: the rationalist one, the theory of moral sense and its slide into utilitarianism, and the new interpretation of the moral law.

Rationalism and Its Deconstruction

SPINOZA AND MODERN RATIONALISM

Benedict Spinoza (1632–77), the greatest moral thinker in the rationalist tradition, accomplished the singular feat of construing an ethical theory without admitting freedom of choice. According to the Dutch philosopher, freedom and necessity coincide in the one substance of which all things form part. Being all-inclusive this self-contained substance has no end beyond itself, nor can it be compelled or attracted by anything outside itself. Everything in the substance occurs necessarily. That necessity extends to the finite modes of this one divine substance—body and mind. Spinoza wrote his *Ethica* as a guide that would lead from the bondage of ignorance to the liberating insight that all external causes are in fact modes of a divine self-determination. What most people regard as evil is no less "necessary" than what they consider to be good. In one case, they oppose forces that they fail to understand. In the other, they accept forces that appear to support them but remain equally unintelligible. True freedom consists in the insight that both are necessary and in a full understanding and acceptance of divine causality in oneself. Many never start the arduous process to true freedom, and few ever complete it.

In contrast to other rationalist philosophies, in Spinoza's ethics emotions and pleasure play an essential role in the attainment of virtue and the ascent to freedom. Since body and mind are united in the one substance, Spinoza firmly rejects not only any contempt for the body but even any dualism of mind and body as if they were two different substances. His ethical ideal includes the well-being of the body: that of the mind depends as much on it as the body's well-being depends on the mind. Emotions thereby attain a crucial significance.

They determine the body's relation to the mind. "By emotion I mean the modifications of the body whereby the active power of the body is increased or diminished, aided or constrained, and also the ideas of such modifications."[2] Emotions belong to a still "confused" stage of consciousness. Yet some increase the body's power while others weaken it. "If we can be the adequate cause of any of these modifications, I then call the emotion an activity, otherwise I call it passion, or state wherein the mind is passive" (ibid.). All emotions, even the active ones, remain in some way passive insofar as they do not originate in the mind. The so-called passions are entirely induced by external causes and not, or not adequately, controlled by the mind.[3]

Although they belong to a lower level of mental life, emotions are indispensable. Only persons endowed with a rich emotional life reach moral greatness. The potential for intellectual awareness (and hence for moral progress) depends on the body's ability to be emotionally affected. The emotions link the body to the mind. Without understanding their role we are unable to guide them and we remain entirely at the mercy of destructive passions, such as envy, hatred, and strife (*E*, IV, 37N). Reflection alone allows us to integrate our desires with each other and to direct them toward a universal well-being (*E*, V, 4N). Spinoza's ambiguous claim that all actions determined by (passive) emotions (provided they are not intrinsically evil) may also be determined by reason without emotion (*E*, IV, 59), may appear to render emotions altogether dispensable. Yet he is not denying the necessity of emotions; he is merely asserting that what emotions induced by external causes accomplish may also be accomplished by emotions induced by reason alone. The more morally mature a person is, the more the mind controls the emotional power that, in the immature one, the body passively undergoes. In understanding its emotions the mind converts passions into actions. That conversion is not a purely intellectual or voluntary process. It requires recognizing an emotion *as emotion* and treating it as such. Moral insight alone "cannot check [i.e., restrain] any emotion by virtue of being true, but only insofar as it is considered as an emotion. One emotion can only be controlled or destroyed by another emotion contrary thereto" (*E*, IV, 14). Knowledge itself must become "emotional" in order to be effective.

On the other side, those who fail to understand their emotions remain in the state of bondage analyzed in the fourth book of *Ethics*. "Human infirmity in moderating and checking the emotions I name bondage: for when a man is prey to his emotions, he is not his own master, but lies at the mercy of fortune" (*E*, IV, preface). Spinoza recognizes the difficulty of the road to freedom. Passions may never be so completely subdued as to leave the mind undisturbed. He therefore offers some rules for gaining gradual control over one's emotions. "The best we can do so long as we do not possess a perfect knowledge of our emotions, is to frame a system of right conduct, or fixed practical precepts, to convert it to memory, and to apply it forthwith to the particular circumstances which now and again meet us in life, so that our imagination may become fully imbued therewith, and that it may be always ready to our hand" (E, V, 10, note). This advice, somewhat reminiscent of Ignatius of Loyola's *Spiritual Exercises,* should prepare the moral novice for withstanding the assault of uncontrollable passions, especially the more vehement ones of love and hatred (E, IV, 45N; E, IV, 32, appendix).

For Spinoza, the essence of any being lies in its ability to preserve itself. "The endeavor with which everything endeavors to persist in its own being, is nothing but the actual essence of the thing in question" (E, III, 7). Pleasure increases the body's *conatus essendi,* its basic drive to be, and thereby promotes the person's well-being. "The greater the pleasure wherewith we are affected, the greater the perfection whereto we pass; in other words, the more must we necessarily partake of the divine nature." (E, IV, 45) Yet if pleasure is sought for its own sake, it stymies the mind's active power and hinders its capacity for action. Hence it benefits only when attained in conjunction with reason. For Spinoza, asceticism is not a moral ideal, as it was for the Stoics. "It is the part of a wise man, I say, both to refresh and to recreate himself in moderation with sweet food and drink as also with scents and the amenity of green plants with adornments, music, and the exertion of games, and with other recreations of this sort such as anyone can do without any injury to others" (E, IV, 45). Insofar as it promotes the body's active power to be (E, III, 41), pleasure is good, but since it often derives from one part of the body rather than from the whole, it is a poor guide toward the good life (E, IV, 60). Only pleasure induced by the person's total well-being may count as unqualifiedly good and is worth pursuing. The morally mature person, then, is both desirous and suspicious of pleasure.

Finding the right balance requires what Spinoza calls virtue, understood in the ancient Roman sense of *virtus* (power). "By virtue and power I mean the same thing" (E, IV, def. 8), namely, the power to increase the active potential of one's *entire* nature and thereby also the pleasure that accompanies such an increase. Virtue, then, is both an end in itself and a means to happiness (*felicitas*) and fulfillment. The more a person endeavors to seek what is useful to him, the more virtuous he becomes (E, IV, 20), because the more he approaches the maximal power of being. Yet "virtue is [also] to be desired for its own sake" (E, IV, 18 *scholium*): through its practice humans participate in blessedness itself, that is, in the knowledge of God (E, IV, 28). Here and throughout book V, "Of Human Freedom," Spinoza appears to shift the goal of ethics from the attainment of freedom through insight to the *amor Dei intellectualis,* the intellectual love of God. Whereas the idea of freedom was self-contained and included both pleasure and emotions, here he seems to identify freedom with understanding. In fact, the two descriptions remain coherent. The intellectual quality of Spinoza's ethics, in the last book as well as in the earlier ones, was never detached from bodily satisfaction and affective fulfillment. A freedom that consists in total self-knowledge implies recognizing oneself as part of a totality and that totality is God. If the happy life is the life stimulated by the highest emotions and yielding the highest pleasure, then the one that pursues the most comprehensive knowledge and the most inclusive love is the happiest. To know and to love God enables the mind to view itself and all things *sub specie aeternitatis (E,* V, 36).

Spinoza has often been described as a rationalist thinker, and it is true that he was influenced by Descartes's thought, as were all rationalists. But his ethical system shows none of the one-sidedness of rationalism. It features hedonistic and even utilitarian qualities that distinguish it from rationalist ethics. Indeed, his position displays a moral realism seldom encountered since Aristotle. His method of overcoming the disruptive power of emotions by insight, a central theme of his thought, anticipates a basic principle of modern psychotherapy. At the same time, his conception of the blessed life aims higher than any other modern system of ethics. None surpassed and only Kant equated the scope of Spinoza's moral vision. Two factors contributed to its enduring appeal. First, he never prescribed what he felt not capable of practicing himself. Bertrand Russell once wrote that Spinoza was the one philosopher who lived entirely by the rules of his own teaching. Second, his ethics, beyond being a theory of human conduct, enabled humans to find meaning in their lives by recognizing themselves as part of a meaningful totality.

THE DECONSTRUCTION OF RATIONALIST ETHICS IN EMPIRICIST PHILOSOPHY

John Locke, the father of British empiricism, assumed a considerable part of Descartes's rationalism, but he consistently Descartes's theory of innate ideas. He did so with particular assertiveness when it came to moral ideas. Locke admits that humans are born with a desire for happiness and an aversion to misery.[4] But such a desire can hardly function as an adequate moral principle. Indeed, inclinations to happiness are so far from being innate impulses to virtue that "if they were left to their full swing, they would carry men to the overturning of all morality" (*Essay,* II, 20, 2). Nonetheless, Locke succeeds in including that desire in his moral system by declaring happiness a reward God attaches to the observation of the natural law. Insofar as true happiness is inextricably linked to that law, the pursuit of happiness becomes a moral principle. This divinely instituted link allows us to consider as good what is apt to produce pleasure, but it fails to explain at which point the inclination to happiness attains the "full swing" that would overturn all morality. He avoids a flat hedonism by restricting "true happiness" to those pleasures that are conducive to the perfection of one's intellectual nature (II, 21, 51). Still, the law of nature so considered ultimately depends upon a statutory divine decree. "He [God] has a right to do it (to promulgate law); we are his creatures. He has goodness and wisdom to direct our actions to that which is best; and He has power to enforce it by rewards and punishments, of infinite weight and duration, in another life" (II, 28, 8). Thus what began as a theory of experience ends in a voluntarist notion of divine law. With Locke, the battle between a nominalist and a rationalist conception of morality enters a decisive phase. He still attempts to combine the empiricist principle (the experience of pleasure or pain) with the positive will of God. Later empiricists more consistently replaced this a priori, authoritative principle by conclusions drawn from experience alone. Their position led to two quite different ethical theories. One based morality on the unique intuition of a moral sense. The other, appealing to a less specific kind of experience responded to the practical question: What kinds of actions contribute most to general well-being? It laid the groundwork for a utilitarian ethics.

In France also, a radical shift away from the rationalist theories of seventeenth-century ethics occurred. The idea of nature, which in the earlier theories had functioned as the moral norm, ceased to be defined by reason alone. For Voltaire, Diderot, and Rousseau, living in accordance with nature no longer meant having one's life ruled by the law of reason. In several of his stories, especially in *L'ingénu,* Voltaire suggested that moral standards vary from place to place. He agreed with Locke that the ideas of good and evil were not "innate." Each individual has to discover them for himself. Yet all end up with more or less similar conclusions. As he wrote to the future King Frederick II of Prussia, "No one is born with the idea that it is necessary to be just, but God has so formed the organs of man that all at a certain age agree to this truth."[5] Customs and laws differ, but all peoples agree on some essential principles of conduct.

According to Diderot, human nature and its basic needs stand at the origin of the universally accepted distinction between good and evil. But from this fact moralists have mistakenly concluded that the idea of nature contains unchangeable, universal principles of moral law. Rather than adjusting the principles of conduct to the demands of life at a particular place and time, they have deduced "universal" principles from Western customs that may appear most unnatural to members of a different society. In his *Supplément* to the French explorer Bougainville's famous report of his journey to Tahiti, Diderot compares what the West regards as universal principles of morality with the very different moral ideas of "primitives." Their lifestyle may seem less "rational" to us, but it certainly is more "natural" and often more generous. Diderot graphically illustrates this point in his fictional additions to the official report. In a "Conversation Between the Chaplain and Orou," a Tahitian host offers his wife and three daughters for the nightly comfort of the chaplain of Bougainville's shipwrecked boat. When the chaplain declines an offer so much in conflict with the principles of his religion, Orou replies, "I do not know what this thing is that you call religion, but I can think only ill of what prevents tasting an innocent pleasure to which nature, our sovereign mistress, invites us all, namely, to bring to existence a being similar to ourselves."[6]

At first Orou appears to advocate little more than a hedonistic naturalism, but the perspective changes when he informs his guest that the island is badly underpopulated. In such circumstances sexual abstinence is harmful to society, though it would be justified if overpopulation demanded a restrictive policy. The indigenous custom, ruled by the demand of nature, issues a more flexible imperative. Each member of a society ought to serve the common good by all necessary means. Nor must the physical expression of love and affection be restricted to the purpose of procreation.[7] Every society possesses its own norms derived from what human nature requires in accordance with the conditions of its physical and social environment.

How harmful it is to impose standards appropriate to one society upon another appears in an old man's farewell speech to the Frenchmen when they finally leave the island. He accuses them of having corrupted the very people who had so generously rescued and sheltered them. Orou's story had contained only half the message: "Let us imitate the chaplain: religious celibate (*moine*) in France, savage in Tahiti."[8] The old man adds the other half. "We are innocent, we are happy, and you can only destroy that happiness. We follow the pure instinct of nature, and you have tried to erase its impress from our souls. Here everything belongs to everyone, and you have preached us this distinction you make between yours and mine."[9] It is the obsession with property, according to Diderot, that lies at the root of sexual repression. Since men came to regard their wives as legal property, they started claiming exclusive sexual rights over them. This has resulted in unhappy marriages and, for women who break the code, in social ostracism. The male, being the owner, has never felt restricted by the monogamous marriage contract, and applying a double standard of conduct, he has jeopardized the very institution that sexual exclusiveness was intended to protect. Even those who abide by the rule suffer from the indissolubility of marriage. Emotions are by nature inconstant: feelings of love inevitably wither and die. Why, then, impose restrictions that so obviously conflict with human inclinations? And why judge so severely a person who follows the natural emotion of the moment when swearing eternal love to someone, but whom the same nature later allows to fall in love with others? Still, not even the primitive "state of nature" is free of crime, as the narrator at the end of the *Supplément* concedes. Nor does Diderot seek to return to a state of nature. He primarily wants to expose the duplicity of the moral standards of his time and to advocate more flexible norms. Yet in the process he radically changes the content of nature from what it had been in the natural law tradition. How could nature be morally normative while functioning as an empirical concept of infinitely stretchable norms?

The problem of freedom presented an even more serious objection to traditional moral principles. The difficulty is illustrated in the picaresque novel *Jacques le fataliste*. Diderot's real difficulty with free will, which he carefully avoided confessing, stemmed from his materialist worldview. Only once, in a letter to a contributor to the *Encyclopédie,* does he openly admit it. "Look at the matter closely and you will see that the word 'liberty' is devoid of meaning. There are not, and cannot be, free beings. We are merely what is consonant with the general order, with our organization, education, and the whole chain of events."[10] Few of Diderot's contemporaries shared his radical views. Montesquieu and Voltaire certainly did not. Even Diderot's friend and collaborator on the *Encyclopédie,* d'Alembert, insisted that morality required observing the universal law of reason, the demands of which are as exacting as those of a divinely sanctioned code of morality.[11]

In his final work on ethics, *Essai sur les règnes de Claude et de Néron* (1782), Diderot returned to a Stoic-rationalist position. Originally intended as an introduction to a new translation of Seneca's writings, the work had continued to grow into a shapeless mass of philosophical remarks on Seneca, caustic observations on moral and political conditions of his time, and a settlement of scores with former but still potentially dangerous adversaries. One may wonder why Diderot in this rambling commentary wanted to return to a Stoically inspired morality that he had so severely attacked in his annotated translation of Shaftesbury's *Essay on Merit and Virtue*. Particularly at a time when the Stoic norm of reason had lost much of its moral appeal. He probably wanted to protect the positions established by the philosophes (morality based on reason alone) against those who had deserted the cause and whose critique could hurt it. In particular, he feared that Rousseau's expected assault on them in the forthcoming second part of the *Confessions* might further jeopardize a secular morality that had already been discredited by La Mettrie's immoralist *Anti-Sénèque*.

On a more fundamental level, he regarded Seneca's secular "Stoicism" useful in his effort to emancipate ethics from religion. "Stoicism is nothing but a treatise of freedom taken in its fullest sense. If this doctrine, which has so much in common with religious cults, had spread as fast as the other superstitions, the earth would long have been cleared of slaves and tyrants" (II, § 68). To render his model effective Diderot first had to restore Seneca's moral authority. In his youth he had accused the Roman philosopher of cynical collaboration with Nero. Now he argued that Seneca's conniving attitude had in fact protected the city against some of the emperor's worst excesses. This defense of moral "flexibility" justified the philosophe's own political compromises. Diderot never achieved a moral synthesis: his rejection of moral absolutes prevented him from doing so. Yet at least Diderot kept searching! His friend, Baron d'Holbach, never appears to have experienced any doubts about freedom or other moral issues. "Morals is the science of the relations that subsist between the minds, the wills, and the actions of men, in the same manner that geometry is the science of the relations that are found between bodies."[12] Motives of action that determine with the same inevitability as physical laws, are, in fact, no more than physiological causes internalized through education. "Good" education fills the young with notions conducive to virtue, that is, contributing to the welfare of society.

Moral Sense and Moral Feelings

SHAFTESBURY'S MORAL SENSE

While the debate around the universal norms of reason enlivened the conversation in Parisian salons, a different, more intuitive approach to morality had begun to conquer parts of the thinking public in England. The third earl of Shaftesbury initiated it. Shaftesbury has often been called a moral relativist because, so the objection goes, he transferred the source of moral judgment from reason to "natural affections." In fact, he never abandoned the rule of reason yet asserted that the mind discovers the norms of reason not by deduction, but by moral intuition. An intuition of the ideally good and beautiful, being a primary experience of reason itself, surpasses any intellectual argument. He attacked Locke's moral theory for its lack of a rational foundation, accusing him of basing his moral norms on such problematic grounds as "mode and custom" or, at other moments, on the inscrutable will of God. The critique was somewhat unfair. For Locke, the divine law was indeed supreme, but that law had been "promulgated by the light of nature" and hence was by no means arbitrary or lacking in intellectual foundation. As for "mode and custom," Locke had stated that opinion and reputation do act as some kind of law by which most people abide, either because they fear to damage their reputation or they hope to enhance it. But he had never claimed this criterion to be adequate. He only asserted its currency "whether those rules were true or false."[13]

More important than the correctness of his critique, however, is Shaftesbury's genuine concern for a foundation of moral norms on the rational order of reality. The mind has a direct intuition of the universal harmony of all things. Partaking itself in this harmony the mind naturally apprehends what is morally good as well as what is aesthetically beautiful. The good and the beautiful are but different aspects of the same harmony. We perceive both by direct experience. That experience, unlike Locke's, is not derived from sensations but from the mind's connatural presence to an ideal reality. Even as for the Stoics and for Spinoza, nature, the all-inclusive order that includes all things and renders them interdependent, served for Shaftesbury as supreme norm of ethics. Moral duties are defined by a person's place within this orderly universe. The mind's moral sense, the "inward eye," directly apprehends the moral quality of any act. This apprehension does not require a comprehensive understanding of nature (*The Moralists,* II, 4, in *Characteristics,* ed. M. Robertson, II, 60–84).

Shaftesbury's principal objection against Locke was that he, for the lack of aesthetic sensitivity, had been incapable of perceiving the universal harmony that is the essence of moral virtue. "Had Mr. Locke been a *virtuoso,* he would not have philosophized thus. For harmony is the beauty, the accord and proposition of sounds; and harmony is harmony by *nature,* let particular errors be ever so bad, or let men judge ever so ill of music. . . . The same is true in the case of virtue and honesty; the *honestum* and the *decorum* in society, for which you, my friend, can never lose your relish."[14] Shaftesbury attributed his deceased mentor's lack of sensitivity to an inadequate knowledge of classical philosophy.[15] Shaftesbury refused to develop his moral thoughts into a system. "The most ingenious way of becoming foolish is by a system," he wrote in "Advice to an Author" (pt. 3 in *Characteristics,* I, 189). His essays on morality, *An Inquiry Concerning Virtue or Merit* (1699) and *The Moralists* (1709), contain no methodical analysis of the moral act of the kind in which Kant was to excel; they are inspired but rambling discussions on the human place within a panentheistic universe.

Shaftesbury's theory of moral intuition restored a facet of ancient ethics that had become lost in voluntarism (for which the moral norm is God's will), as well as in rationalism (which deduces its norms exclusively from reason). In his interpretation, the ethics of Plato and Aristotle centered on ideas of harmony, order, and beauty. The ancient ideal consisted more in gaining the right insight and then doing the right, or even the elegant thing than in obeying some kind of higher command (though that became an important element in the Stoa). Moral reason, immanent in the nature of things, included not only what logic dictated, but also what convention and common sense suggested. To a significant extent it was, as the term *kalokagathon* suggests, a matter of *taste,* that is, of aesthetic discernment between the noble act and the vulgar or villainous one.

"Natural affections" link human beings to one another. They direct the moral sense. The term "affections" apparently required no definition in eighteenth-century British thought. But its vagueness has created numerous problems of interpretation for us. Shaftesbury uses it to refer to an entire range of desires, impulses, feelings, emotions, fundamental dispositions, and occasionally even passions.[16] Natural affections guide the mind toward acts of benevolence, the moral goal of life. Benevolence requires not that we sacrifice our self-interest, for that also forms an essential segment of the well-being of the whole. Yet contrary to what Mandeville and Adam Smith were later to claim, the pursuit of self-interest alone will never result in a state of universal harmony. Only social affections do so. Humans must actively seek the good by *deliberately* following the course of their natural affections. In his early writings, Shaftesbury adopted an austere, Stoic attitude toward passions. "In a higher relation, nothing can be more distant than this; nothing more inconsistent with that true affection, which in a mind soundly rational is, as it were, in the place of all."[17] Later he came to regard passions as indispensable for converting moral affections into action.

With the theory of moral affections Shaftesbury opened what Charles Taylor has called a new ethical space that allows the *good* to appear within human subjectivity.[18] Without them morality turns negative, "confrontational" as Iris Murdoch calls it, a constant struggle with one's inclinations. Attaining an *inner* harmony with all of nature neither needs nor tolerates obedience as primary motive. Those who practice virtue because of a divine command he calls "nominal moralists" (*The Moralists,* II, 2; *Characteristics,* II, 46–47). In this battle against moral nominalism he followed the Cambridge Platonists. These theologians, fellows of Calvinist Emmanuel College, considered moral principles to be grounded in "immutable reason" rather than in the sovereign will of God. Shaftesbury knew them well: he had published the sermons of Benjamin Whichcote, one of the founders of the movement. According to

Ralph Cudworth (1617–87), the most learned of the group, ethical principles inhere in the nature of things. "Though the will and power of God have an absolute, infinite and unlimited command upon the existence of all created things to make them to be or not to be at pleasure; yet when things exist, they are what they are, this or that, absolutely or relatively, not by will or arbitrary command, but by the necessity of their own nature."[19] No positive command of God can render human acts good or evil. Cudworth takes position not only against fellow Puritans, but also against Descartes who had claimed that all order, law, and reason depended upon God.

Anticipating Kant, Shaftesbury places the entire moral weight on the *intention*. Moral goodness is not inherent in the objective deed, but in the deed as intended by the agent. To be virtuous, then, an act must be so intended. Yet the intention remains attached to the objective meaning of the act. The moral intention therefore requires that we know the objective nature of the act. The moral sense *discovers* its objective goodness; it does not "constitute" it. The objective quality of Shaftesbury's moral theory appears in the fact that a misjudgment, for which the agent bears only a slight responsibility, is nevertheless a moral wrong. Even if our moral assessment is warped "through superstition or ill custom . . . this is not, nor ever can be, virtue of any kind or in any sense, but must remain still horrid depravity" (*Virtue and Merit,* bk. I, pt. 2, 3; *Characteristics,* I, 255).

Still, Shaftesbury's position remains elusive. The danger of subjectivism is never remote, as the subsequent history of moral feelings confirms. Only the strong Platonic strain in his thought prevented him from ever fully admitting it. Nor were his efforts to expand his idea of moral harmony into a cosmic theory altogether successful. He claims that the entire animal kingdom moves beyond individual well-being: each species of animals contributes to the well-being of some other (bk. I, *Characteristics,* I, 245). The benefit appears far from mutual, however. The spider needs the fly, Shaftesbury argues. But does the fly need the spider? Voltaire certainly saw no evidence that the ecological balance resulted from altruistic feelings. "Flies are born to be devoured by spiders, which are in turn devoured by swallows, and swallows by shrikes, and shrikes by eagles, and eagles are born to be killed by men, who in turn live to kill each other and to be consumed by worms, or by devils at least in thousand cases to one." The dependence of all creatures upon each other suggests indeed a coherence of nature, yet not necessarily a peaceful one.[20]

A theory of morality conceived as an attitude of universal benevolence may easily lead to a utilitarian ethics. It actually did so, indeed, in Shaftesbury's most devoted yet least faithful follower, Francis Hutcheson. He equated universal benevolence with directing one's actions toward the greatest possible benefit for the greatest number of people. For Shaftesbury, the good had been intrinsically valuable, independently of the consequences. A deed is good to the extent that the agent sincerely *intends* to further the harmonious integration of the whole, not to the extent that it actually benefits others, although such benefits should normally follow from it. Nowhere did he consider the utilitarian calculation of pleasures and pains, used as norm by Hutcheson and later by Bentham, a sufficient or adequate ethical criterion.[21] In this respect Shaftesbury stands closer to Kant than to Hutcheson or to any empiricist philosopher. In shifting the moral emphasis from what we ought to do, because God or reason prescribes it, to what it is sensible and orderly to do, Shaftesbury accomplished a revolution in ethical theory. He revived the ideal of *kalokagathia* and restored the ancient link between morality and aesthetics.

ROUSSEAU'S MORAL SENTIMENTALISM

With Rousseau, feelings assumed an even more crucial role in moral life. As he tells it in the *Confessions,* both his father's lessons and his youthful readings in Plutarch had taught him to subdue his passions and to lead a simple life of self-sufficiency. The second part of that instruction Rousseau never forgot. In his early, prize-winning *Discourse on the Sciences and Arts* (1750), Rousseau still defended a Stoic conception of the moral law. But in his second major essay, *Discourse on the Origin of Inequality* (1755), Rousseau identified feelings as the root of morality. He takes issue with Hobbes's position that the state of nature is amoral, neither good nor evil, devoid of virtue as well as of vice. Nor was it the drive of self-preservation that compelled humans to enter society, but rather a natural feeling of compassion that, prior to reflection, moves them to care for the whole species and often that of other species as well. Compassion naturally spawns those social virtues that Hobbes denied. "What is generosity, clemency, or humanity, but compassion applied to the weak, to the guilty, or to mankind in general? Even benevolence and friendship are, if we judge rightly, only the effects of compassion."[22]

To develop this affective source of all morality must be the primary purpose of the child's moral education. That education, described in book IV of *Emile,* begins relatively late. The child must be given the time to develop its natural faculties before it is able to be morally educated. But moral development, in Rousseau's theory, is a natural process. Guidance may be needed to protect the child against ignorance, but force must never be used against allegedly evil tendencies. Unless education deforms their natural inclinations, humans spontaneously develop into moral beings. Rousseau left no doubt about his primary assumption. The first sentence of *Emile* reads: "Tout est bien, sortant des mains de l'Auteur des choses; tout dégénère dans les mains de l'homme" (All is good as it leaves the hands of the Creator; all degenerates as it enters the hands of man). He pointedly ruled out the concept of original sin: "Il n'y a point de perversité originelle dans le coeur humain" (There is no original perversity in the human heart). We know the vehement reaction this statement provoked. The archbishop of Paris condemned the book; the Sorbonne ordered it to be burned. Even in England it caused shock waves. It occasioned the famous outburst of Dr. Johnson noted by Boswell: "Rousseau, Sir, is a very bad man. I would sooner sign a sentence for his transportation than that of any felon who has gone from the Old Bailey there many years. Yes, I would like to have him work in the plantations."[23]

It was not only the radical break with a Christian tradition distrustful of the "state of nature" that Archbishop Christophe de Beaumont and Dr. Johnson feared, but, even more, the collapse of the entire social system that had been built on it. In Rousseau's view, if people can be good at all, they must be so from the beginning. Goodness must be in the heart before it can be achieved by the will. That natural goodness includes human passions, which serve as indispensable means for self-preservation. They must be guided, not suppressed. All originate in the healthy *amour de soi,* a drive to protect one's existence. Still, self-love easily degenerates into selfish love (*amour propre*), an unnatural desire of superfluous possessions and of power over others. Once the child enters adolescence it begins to compare its condition with that of others and tries to subjugate their desires to its own. While natural self-love (*amour de soi*) naturally grows into a love of others, selfish love excludes others. All passions develop from these original, inclusive or exclusive attitudes: the kind and affectionate passions from the former, the destructive ones from the latter. To raise a child to virtue it suffices to preserve and develop its original self-love.

With Shaftesbury, Rousseau assumed the presence of a cosmic harmony that gently guides inanimate as well as animate creatures toward their natural goal. Unlike the English thinker, however, Rousseau concluded that living in accordance with nature required a separation from a corrupt society, either by returning to a pastoral lifestyle (as the lovers in *Julie* did) or by restoring society to a state of integrity that would no longer be subject to property relations and a state of virtual slavery (as Rousseau outlined in the *Discourse on Inequality* and *The Social Contract*). In his novel *Julie, ou la nouvelle Héloïse,* Rousseau shows how his moral ideals may be realized even before a new society has been built. The two lovers, Julie and Saint-Preux, slowly and painfully rise above a conventional morality of precepts and obligations toward the natural "law of the heart." In book III Julie, torn between the duty to obey her father and her love for Saint-Preux, exclaims: "Nature, oh sweet nature! Resume all your rights. I forswear the barbaric virtues that crush you.

Are the inclinations you have given me less trustworthy than a reason that has so often led me astray? . . . Duty, honor, virtue, all that means nothing any more to me — I have made up my mind: I shall distress none of those I love."[24] With this she marries the man her father has chosen for her, not out of "duty" but out of filial piety, yet she informs her husband that she loves another man. He responds with equal generosity by inviting Saint-Preux to share their household.

Julie vows herself to a life of marital chastity. Unlike Diderot's heroes, she does not place her feelings above the rules of marriage. She, as well as her husband and her lover, purify their love from the exclusiveness inherent in erotic possession.[25] For them, morality consists in recapturing their aboriginal innocence by listening to the voice of nature in their hearts. Shaftesbury's theory of *moral sense* may have influenced Rousseau. Yet for the British Platonist, feelings point beyond themselves, toward an ideal of goodness. Rousseau felt no sympathy for Platonic speculations on the good. In his optimistic conception of human nature, private morality involved little more than total authenticity. He considered universal moral norms always insufficient and occasionally detrimental for leading a moral life. One cannot ignore the most intimate part of one's nature, revealed in one's feelings, without being unfaithful to oneself. Here began what in our time was to become an ethics of authenticity.[26] In fact, feelings are not as deeply rooted in human nature, as Rousseau believed them to be. They are too dependent on mood and occasion to serve as reliable moral principles.

Rousseau encapsulated his subjective morality in the ideal of the *beautiful soul* (*la belle âme*), popular during the Enlightenment. For some writers, such as Christoph Martin Wieland, the term preserved some Platonic and Christian connotations; for Rousseau it functioned as the secular counterpart of grace.[27] Julie, who incarnates the ideal, declares that the only man she could ever love would have to be a beautiful soul: a person uncommonly rich in feeling (*Julie*, bk. I, L60 and bk. II, L2). Comparing the beautiful soul to Kant's moral ideal of duty, Schiller was to write: "In the beautiful soul not the individual acts are properly moral, but the entire disposition is."[28] Having reached a state of total simplicity and of unrestricted communication with others, the beautiful soul restores the pristine "transparence" of human nature.

The ideal of utter sincerity also inspired Rousseau's controversial writings against modern culture in general and against the theater in particular. The theater, consummate product of an artificial civilization, conflicts with the natural life of virtue. His caustic *Lettre sur les spectacles* (1758) unpleasantly shocked the editors of the *Encyclopédie* with whom he had collaborated. It was in fact a direct attack upon their work. Under the word "Genève," d'Alembert had supported the building of a theater in the Calvinist city, contending that the pastors would not object because most of them were in fact freethinking deists. Rousseau protested. The theater ought to be banned from modern life altogether: it corrupts more than it instructs. If virtue requires controlling one's passions, how could a dramatic display of passions not be harmful to public morality? To arouse the passions on the stage can only increase moral turmoil. Nor does the theatrical presentation of virtue compensate for this negative influence. Heroic virtue seen on the stage merely overwhelms. It does not incite to imitation. Moved to tears by the display of high virtue, the spectator applauds himself *"de sa belle âme"* but never intends to follow the ideal examples displayed on the stage.

The problem with Rousseau's code of authenticity is, of course, that it contains no objective moral norms, as appears in Rousseau's own conduct. Questioned by an aristocratic lady about having abandoned his four children, he laid the blame for whatever "objective" evil might have occurred at her own doorstep: the rich were responsible for the "crimes" of the poor.[29] Similarly, in the first book of the *Confessions* Rousseau justifies the constant larcenies of his early years as a means to avoid the "dishonorable mediation" of money. He feels that his confession in some way justifies his past. In "confessing" the deeds as well as his often questionable motivations, he considers himself purified from the only genuine evil, namely, insincerity with oneself and with others.

In a famous passage in the *Phenomenology of Mind,* Hegel criticizes "the beautiful soul" as an immature stage in the development of conscience wherein, after much doubt and insecurity, the romantic consciousness becomes *certain* of itself, convinced that the ground of morality lies within itself.[30] This certainty, however, is no more than an enhanced sense of selfhood that lacks any substance and, as Hegel was to put it, "dissolves as a shapeless vapor into thin air." The beautiful soul in fact refuses to assume moral responsibility for the consequences of her actions, even while appealing to the "law of conscience." If protracted, this immature attitude undermines the very ground of morality.

THE MOVE TOWARD UTILITARIANISM: HUTCHESON, MANDEVILLE, AND HUME

No one absorbed Shaftesbury's ideas more devotedly than the Scottish thinker Francis Hutcheson. Yet a spiritual gulf separates his *Inquiry Concerning Moral Good and Evil* from the *Characteristics.* Shaftesbury, the aristocratic virtuoso, had rarely been concerned about the coherence of his theory or about its practical application. Hutcheson attempted to translate his vision into a detailed, systematic treatise. The difference between the two authors goes beyond style: it affects the very essence of their thought. At times Hutcheson does little more than add much-needed clarifications to the Englishman's ambiguous ethics of intention. Thus he correctly specifies that actions inspired by self-interest but "not wanting in benevolence" may still be virtuous.[31] But more often Hutcheson writes from a different perspective. He lacks Shaftesbury's magnanimous vision and reduces the ethics of benevolence to the outcome of a moral computation. Measuring goodness by effectiveness, he takes Shaftesbury's ideals down to the bottom line of an account sheet.

To calculate virtue by a direct relation to the amount of good produced and an inverse one to the agent's ability to achieve it (in Hutcheson's formula $B = M/A$) (*Inquiry*, III, 11) turns Shaftesbury's ethics into a simple consequentialism. To be sure, in any moral theory, the intention must take the foreseeable consequences of the act into account. But Hutcheson's assumption that we can *measure* the goodness of an act by its material consequences introduces a purely empirical factor that in fact deprives morality of any a priori norm, as Hume was to point out. For Shaftesbury, goodness and happiness had been *intrinsic* to virtue rather than dependent on its consequences. His moral theory ruled out a definition of goodness through consequences, even though a more precise definition of his principle of benevolence would have forced him to take a more serious account of the implications of the benevolent attitude.

When Shaftesbury equated moral virtue with the benevolent intention, he left the objective nature of the act inadequately determined. But he certainly would not have measured virtue by its material consequences. For him, the highest perfection was a virtuous life, and true benevolence consisted in creating adequate conditions for *the practice of virtue,* both for oneself and for others. Hutcheson's interpretation transformed Shaftesbury's concept of moral perfection through virtue into pursuing the advancement of material well-being. Like Locke, Hutcheson wedged a divine ordinance between the virtuous act and its favorable consequences. Virtue *leads* to happiness because God so decided; it is not intrinsically conducive to it. On the other hand, Hutcheson's principle of universal benevolence demands that the virtuous person create social conditions promoting actual public happiness. Since effective benevolence includes benevolence to oneself and hence also the need to create conditions for one's own material well-being, his position causes a conflict between the pure intention of virtue and the self-interest involved in the efforts to attain happiness for oneself as well as for others. In his mature *System of Moral Philosophy* (1755), Hutcheson admits that whenever a conflict arises between one's own interest and that of others, most people prefer the former.[32]

Bernard Mandeville, the sharpest critic of Shaftesbury and Hutcheson, was well aware of the difference between the two moral systems, both of which he firmly rejected. In the first part of his *Fable of the Bees* he primarily attacks Shaftesbury; in the second (published years later), Hutcheson. But tracing Hutcheson's errors back to their source he concludes that second part with the following damning praise of the master: "[Shaftesbury] was a man of erudition and a very polite writer; he has displayed a copious imagination and a fine turn of thinking, in courtly language and nervous expressions. But as, on the one hand it must be confessed that his sentiments on liberty and harmony are noble and sublime, so, on the other, it cannot be denied that the ideas he had formed of the goodness and excelling of our nature, were as romantic and chimerical as they are beautiful and amiable."[33] He peremptorily dismisses Shaftesbury's assumption that human beings are born with affection for each other: "His notions, I confess, are generous and refined: they are a high compliment to humankind. What a pity it is they are not true" (*Fable,* I, 323–24). No one could ever meet Shaftesbury's moral standards. That only altruistic acts deserve to be called virtuous appears preposterous to Mandeville. What would virtue require from a poor woman ready to put out her six-year-old son as apprentice to a chimney sweep? Though she could never pay to have her own chimney cleaned, her concern for the public good of having fewer chimney fires and uncontaminated broth morally urges her to give up offspring and estate in order to assist in preventing the damage caused by soot. "Free from selfishness, [she] sacrifices her only son to the most wretched employment for the public welfare" (*Fable,* II, 44).

Society could not survive with such perfect members! What would happen to the economy without the vices of luxury and ostentation? "Superfluous knickknacks and elaborate trifles invented to gratify either a needless curiosity or else wantonness and folly" sustain the craftsman who produces them. In the first part of the *Fable* Mandeville had, in a well-known satire, called private vices, such as prostitution, public benefits. Did he merely want to show the absurdity of unmitigated altruism? Or did he intend to expose the hypocritical inconsistency between the eighteenth-century goals of national wealth and power, ruthlessly pursued at home and abroad, and the universally professed code of moral altruism. In Mandeville's jaundiced view, altruistic virtue requires a person, "*contrary to the impulse of nature,* to endeavour the benefit of others" (*Fable,* I, 48–49). Of course, Mandeville misinterpreted Shaftesbury as well as Hutcheson. The absence of altruistic motives does not necessarily vitiate an act. A person may still be virtuous without acting with a purely unselfish intention. Hutcheson himself had already obviated Mandeville's critique when he distinguished "formal" from "material" goodness. A generally benevolent intention renders any act morally good, as long as the nature of the act itself does not conflict with an altruistic attitude. A few spiritual writers, including William Law, one of Mandeville's most incisive critics, appear to have held that any intrusion of self-interest jeopardizes the purity of the moral intention.[34] This may have been a spiritual ideal, but it never was a moral imperative.

According to Mandeville's critique, self-love rooted in the instinct of self-preservation excludes love of others. For Shaftesbury, one had implied the other. In the second part of the *Fable* Mandeville specified that the instinct of self-preservation always compels the individual to place his own interests above those of others. Even social acts are inspired by our need of others: we seek their approval or their future assistance for improving our own condition. Competitive and endowed with unlimited appetites, humans are prepared to sacrifice private satisfaction to the good of the community only when they realize that survival depends on social strength. Pride alone induces the best ones to serve the community at the risk of life or personal possessions, while shame restrains the less ambitious from blatantly acting against the public good. Honor and shame, then, the more effective social virtues, are mostly "counterfeited" passions (*Fable,* II, 100). Mandeville preceded Adam Smith in assuming that the pursuit of private profits would benefit the common good. Yet far from running parallel with the practice of altruistic love, this pursuit is in fact incompatible with it. Moral altruism and benevolent intentions would not be conducive toward achieving the kind of prosperity Hutcheson had expected from them. Economic success requires a different code of behavior, one far removed from the Christian ideal of love and its deist derivative of benevolence.

Thus Mandeville severed the artificial link that most British moralists of the eighteenth century maintained between moral idealism and practical hedonism. According to Locke, God's will constituted that link; for Hutcheson and implicitly for Shaftesbury, the essential harmony of nature united altruism with self-love. Private and public happiness had been the end, and moral restraint the means. Mandeville fully accepted the end but cynically denounced the means as hypocritical and ineffective.[35] He raised the fundamental question about utilitarian ethics even before the theory had been adequately formulated: How could traditional morality survive the conception of human nature that lies at the ground of economic utilitarianism? The benevolent, virtuous agent will in the end prove less "beneficial" than one who pursues private interests even at the expense of others. Of course, the utilitarian principles of morality cannot so easily be disposed of as Mandeville thinks. No one had ever seriously maintained that the norms of morality are the most effective ways to attain economic prosperity. Shaftesbury and Hutcheson claimed only that self-interest was not incompatible with altruism. To establish the limits of their parallelism required a more comprehensive vision of society as well as a firmer grasp of the implications of utilitarian theory than either of them had. Bentham was the first to grasp the implications of both. I shall discuss his theory in the next chapter.

Although David Hume possessed neither Spinoza's nor Kant's originality, his influence on the development of ethical thought may have exceeded theirs. His particular strength lay in the critical acumen with which he analyzed the implications and deficiencies of the theories of his time. Besides, Hume was a master of phenomenological description. The pages he wrote on sympathy, on moral intention, and on justice remain a permanent part of our cultural patrimony. His careful analyses as well as his elegant portrayals of moral attitudes have made him a classic in literature as well as in philosophy. At the outset of his discussion of ethics in the *Treatise of Human Nature* (1739) (bk. III), he boldly declares that reason does not directly influence actions and affections. Reason establishes relations between ideas, as it does in philosophy, and between ideas and facts, as it does in historical and empirical sciences. Yet the distinction between good and evil is neither a relation nor a matter of fact. The moral *ought* does not belong to the domain of reason. The only "facts" morality knows are feelings of approbation or disapprobation. Here we might wonder: Why only those feelings and not the awareness of a moral obligation which appears to be a no less obvious fact than approval or disapproval? Did Hume want to avoid any factor that might appear to render morality dependent on a religious concept?[36] Kant considered the moral imperative a primary fact, or as he called it, "the sole fact of pure reason," even though his position was no less secular than Hume's.

All here depends on how Hume understands moral approbation or disapprobation. In the *Treatise* he explains them as the arousal of pleasure that the mind experiences in the presence of certain acts and of pain in the presence of others. Those feelings belong to the calmer modes of love and hatred the mind experiences with respect to the consequences that certain acts are likely to entail. What evokes moral approbation or disapprobation stems from a natural sense of sympathy, the key concept of Hume's theory. "It appears that sympathy is a very powerful principle in human nature, that it has a great influence on our taste of beauty, and that it produces our sentiment of morals in all the artificial virtues. From thence we may presume, that it also gives rise to many of the other virtues; and that qualities acquire our approbation, because of their tendency to the good of mankind."[37] Much of Hume's ethics rests on this remarkable statement. He distinguishes artificial virtues from natural ones, according to their origin in a *natural* or an *artificial* sense of morality. The former is direct and instinctive. The latter "arises from circumstances and necessity of mankind" (*Treatise*, II, 2, 1, p. 477).

Hume devotes the entire second part of the *Treatise* to the (artificial) virtue of justice. The sense of justice is not a "natural" feeling, he claims, because it depends on the particular structure of a society as well as on the education of its members. Communities that have no developed institutions of private property possess no sense of justice as we do. Ours is formed by a desire to live in the kind of social structure that allows us to possess things not only commonly but also individually. The reasons usually invoked in support of a natural sense of justice, such as regard for the public interest, universal benevolence, and so on, are inadequate. Hume explicitly denies the existence of an inborn instinct of benevolence toward *all* human beings. But if the sense of justice is artificially induced by education and convention (III, 2, 1, p. 483), does it still deserve to be called a moral sense? Is it not the conclusion of an argument rather than an immediate awareness? Not according to Hume. For what excites universal benevolence is not reason, but a feeling of *sympathy* evoked by an awareness of the similarity of human feelings of affection. Sympathy arouses interest in the good of mankind as a whole (III, 3, 1, p. 584). Yet sympathy is no virtue: it only enables us to *feel* what others feel (III, 3, 2, p. 593).

In the *Inquiry Concerning the Principles of Morals* (1752), Hume spends much effort in showing how the artificial *virtue* of justice extends to all an attitude of benevolence that *naturally* embraces only the few whom we know. Only after having been so universally extended can the moral sense of benevolence induce us to support the interests of the larger community, even in instances where they conflict with our immediate *natural* feelings of benevolence. Such a generalization requires the intervention of reason. But the moral determination itself is not derived from reason. "Though reason when fully assisted and improved, be sufficient to interest us in the pernicious or useful tendency of qualities and actions, it is not alone sufficient to produce any moral blame or approbation. — It is requisite a *sentiment* should here display itself in order to give a preference to the useful above the pernicious tendencies."[38] A deed beneficial to our immediate acquaintances yields moral pleasure. The feeling of sympathy extends that pleasure beyond that narrow circle to humanity as a whole. That pleasure "is the *sole* source of that high regard paid to justice, fidelity, honor, allegiance, and chastity" (*Inquiry*, V, 57).

Although the notion of utility occupies a central place in Hume's moral theory, he did not claim that utility is the only principle that determines the morality of an act. In the *Inquiry* (VII), he declares such virtues as cheerfulness, dignity, and tranquility exempt from the rule of utility. Even benevolence, which lies at the root of all useful virtues, cannot always be measured by social benefits. "As a certain proof that the whole merit of benevolence is not derived from its usefulness, we may observe, that in a kind way of blame, we say 'a person is *too good*,' when he exceeds his part in society and carries his attention to others beyond the proper bounds" (*Inquiry,* VII, 81). Nor is the ultimate end of "useful" virtues happiness, that is, a subjective state of peace and pleasure, as later utilitarians maintained, but the more objective *eudaemonia,* which Hume tends to call *humanity.* For him, the theory of moral sense balanced and qualified utilitarianism. For Jeremy Bentham (1748–1832), the moral sense theory was the chief rival of utilitarianism. To introduce feelings in a moral system that rests on calculating reason can only confuse the issue. Bentham's utilitarianism restores the primacy of reason, which Hume had dislodged from morality. Reason alone can decide what are the most effective principles for establishing a state of universal well-being.

The nature of utilitarian morality remains strictly hypothetical: *If* one desires a particular kind of society, certain rules have proven to be effective in obtaining it. Even a rational utilitarianism could not close Hume's unbridgeable chasm between *is* and *ought.* If the motive of action is no more than a natural propensity, either immediate or artificially induced, the term "moral obligation" appears to be out of place. Nonetheless, Hume himself continues to speak of "a sense of obligation." Without the higher authority of a moral law or a divine order, the expression is hard to support.[39] As long as the moralist refuses to set up an idea of goodness that requires more than what we ordinarily do, he is unable to provide us with a moral *ideal* that we *ought* to pursue. Charles Taylor, in the excellent pages he has devoted to the subject, rightly argues that utilitarians are debarred by their ontology from formulating their own moral sources.[40]

Kant's Critical Theory of Morals

In Germany the ideals of the Enlightenment found their strongest supporter in Kant. From the beginning of his philosophical life until the end, he defended reason against arbitrary authority and intellectual obscurantism. The nontechnical writings of his later period, from the 1784 essay "What Is Enlightenment?" to the 1798 "Strife of the Faculties," directly or indirectly advocated the rule of freedom and the emancipation of the individual. Yet not until his last great work, *Religion Within the Limits of Reason Alone* (1794), did he disclose the assumptions implied by his concept of Enlightenment. In contrast to Rousseau, Kant did not believe human nature to be intrinsically good. We all enter the world with an inborn disposition toward evil, the "radical innate evil in human nature" that invalidates the optimistic myth of the noble savage.[41] Even the well-disposed person is inclined toward evil.

The *Critique of Practical Reason* combined with *Foundations of the Metaphysics of Morals* contain a synthesis as well as a fundamental critique of all ethical theories of the age. Regrettably we mostly remember the critique, forgetting that it was probably the synthetic quality of Kant's work that left the strongest mark on moral philosophy. Kant so severely criticized the theories of his time more because of the moral climate that had produced them than because of their flaws. Those who equated the moral disposition with benevolence of feelings or a utilitarian calculus had, in his view, eroded the seriousness of the ethical demand. Goethe praised his great contemporary for having brought ethics back "from the effeminacy in which we were wallowing."[42] In his youth Kant had greeted the theory of moral feelings as a liberation from the rationalism of his own philosophical education. In the early "Investigation about the Evidence of Natural Theology and Morality" (1764), he praised the theory that advocates *experiencing* (*zu empfinden*) the good, rather than knowing it, and in his lectures of 1765–66 he still referred to the theory of moral sense as "a beautiful discovery of our age."[43] Shaftesbury, Hutcheson, and Smith had brought much-needed psychological insight to the study of ethics, but they had left Hume's question unanswered: What allowed the mind to consider a psychic state or inclination morally imperative?

KANT'S CRITIQUE OF EARLIER THEORIES

The epistemic distinction between sense experience and rational knowledge that Kant made in the *Inaugural Dissertation* (1770) also separated his early from his critical theory of morality. No sensuous inclination could morally legitimate a human act. Conduct becomes ethical only to the extent that it follows the dictates of reason. Kant's rationalist teachers had made similar claims. But what distinguished Kant's principle was the exclusiveness of reason's authority: only norms that were totally universal could qualify as moral. Shaftesbury and Rousseau, whom he had admired in the past, at once lost their moral authority. He now lumped them together with Epicurus as supporters of hedonism. The joy induced by moral feelings was, in Kant's eyes, hardly distinct from any other form of pleasure. Feelings as well as desires, happiness no less than pleasure, all rely on the sensuous part of our nature and are therefore declared unfit to serve as ethical criteria. Later he abandoned this crude identification of moral feelings with sensuous pleasure. But he never wavered in his resistance to admitting feelings as legitimate moral determinants. In his mature *Critique of Practical Reason* (1788), he still attacks the moral sense theory as "a desire for one's own happiness."[44] Unfairly so.

Hutcheson had already pointed out that private pleasure plays no determining role in feelings of benevolence. If it did, benevolence would cease to be unselfish. But to Kant, the distinction between genuinely altruistic and self-oriented feelings remained insignificant in light of the more fundamental question: Can *feelings* ever function as legitimate moral determinants? He excluded them one and all.

Even Aristotle's concept of *eudaemonia,* rather than being a truly universal idea, was in his esteem no more than an empirically generalized concept of "happiness." Kant knew, of course, that happiness, particularly the ancient *eudaemonia,* consists in a state of *well-being* rather than of *well-feeling,* the outcome of a number of factors including insight, skills, prudential judgment, even health and possessions. Yet in his view, even the noblest kind of happiness was unfit to serve as moral ideal (*C.Pr.R.,* 23; Ak, V, 24). In addition, all these factors depend on external circumstances over which the will has no control. What renders humans happy is highly contingent, differs from one time and place to another, and varies from one individual to the next. Kant, of course, does not deny that humans ought to promote the well-being of all. Yet happiness, that of others no more than one's own, ought not to serve as a motive for doing so.

In this concept of morality as obedience to the command of reason, the idea of the *good* loses the moral primacy it had enjoyed since Socrates and from which even the notion of *duty* had been derived. For Kant, the process ran in the opposite direction: the idea of the good does not serve as foundation of the moral law, but the law defines what is good and evil (*C.Pr.R.,* 65; Ak, V, 62–63) To derive the moral law from the idea of the *good* subordinates what ought to be a rational a priori to empirical concepts, whether they be happiness, human perfection, moral feeling, or even the will of God. In all these cases the source of morality lies outside the rational will. To deduce what is primary from a previously "given" principle constitutes for Kant the essence of moral heteronomy. Obviously, Kant does not question the moral nature of the idea of the good — to do one's duty *is* a good — but he denies that the idea of the good is the primary moral category. In the *Critique of Pure Reason* Kant still had sought support for his position in Plato because the Greek philosopher had grounded all moral rules in a priori ideas. "It is, however, in regard to the principles of morality, legislation, and religion, where the experience, in this case the *good,* is itself made possible only by the ideas . . . that Plato's teaching exhibits its quite peculiar merits."[45] In the *Critique of Practical Reason* he no longer makes this claim.

The pursuit of human perfection remains, also for Kant, the essence of virtue, but that perfection itself needs to be measured by a norm that surpasses experience. Reason alone defines moral perfection, and it does so by imposing absolute obligations. Its categorical imperative directs us to ends that are unqualifiedly good, that is, chosen by the rational will on the sole ground of their conformity to reason. All other goods, the ancient ideal of *eudaemonia* as well as the modern one of happiness, are conditional ends. Nothing but the rational will is capable of converting conditional ends into unconditional goods. Even the concept of virtue that had occupied such a prominent place in Greek and Scholastic ethics must be subordinated to the pure law of reason. In Kant's view, the ancient ideal of virtue lost much of its moral dignity when modern interpretations of it substituted empirical norms to the earlier a priori idea. The primacy of the subject as source of meaning and value, characteristic of modern thought, far from securing the rational a priori required by moral-ity, presented in fact a formidable challenge to it. In all his writings Kant attempted to disencumber the subjective principle of modern thought from its subjectivist interpretations.

But Kant's alternative presented problems of its own. A first one appears in the very title of the *Critique of Practical Reason*. In what sense can reason be "practical"? At the end of the *Critique of Pure Reason*, Kant explains that reason has two functions: to justify the order of actual appearances, but also, beyond the actual phenomena, to establish what it requires for reality to be rational and how to make the rational real. About the second task Kant writes: "Reason does not here follow the order of things as they present themselves in appearance, but frames for itself with perfect spontaneity an order of its own according to ideas to which it adapts the empirical conditions, and according to which it declares actions to be necessary even though they have never taken place and perhaps never will take place. And at the same time reason also presupposes that it can have causality in regard to all these actions, since otherwise no empirical effects could be expected from its ideas."[46]

This remarkable passage implies that an inner necessity drives reason to become practical and to dictate, as far as it lies within its power, the course reality ought to follow. Freedom, then, the power to transform the contingent into the rational order, is in Kant's theory, the other side of reason. Nor is this transformation left to the choice of rational beings. It is an obligation, an *ought*. "*Ought* expresses a kind of necessity and of connection with grounds which is found nowhere else in the whole of nature."[47] Self-determining rea-son surpasses the given order of the physical universe. "Reason demands that it determine *itself* in *praxis* and impose its own rationality upon the real" (*C.Pr.R.,* 45; Ak, V, 43). In his later *Religion Within the Limits of Reason Alone* (1794), Kant stresses that the potential to act rationally belongs to human nature from the beginning, but to convert that potential into actuality requires a deliberate effort. "From the fact that a being has reason it by no means follows that this reason, by the mere representing of the fitness of its maxims to be laid down as universal laws, is thereby rendered capable of determining the will unconditionally, so as to be 'practical' of itself."[48]

Once reason has become practical, it wields a causal power that competes with, and is conditioned by, the causality of nature. In the first *Critique* Kant had allowed for this possibility. Yet reason's *actual* effectiveness could be established only on the basis of *a fact* within the existing order. Kant discovers that fact in the mind's experience of the unconditional dictate of the moral law itself. The categorical "Thou shalt" summons reason to move beyond the given, causal order of nature. The imperative proves, according to Kant, that the experience of freedom we all have is not an illusion. The unconditional obligation to enact the law of reason in the physical world implies that rational beings have the capacity to do so. Yet one may wonder whether reason can ever issue an unconditional imperative. Reason may inform us about a moral course of action. Thinking may even condition us against perpetrating evil, as Socrates suggested when he identified virtue with knowledge. And it is certainly true that thinking alone enables the mind to reach a right judgment about good and evil. A disposition toward absolute evil requires a willful suspension of thinking, Hannah Arendt argued in *Eichmann in Jerusalem*. But the formulation of the moral imperative has a transcendent quality, which Kantian morality cannot justify on the basis of reason alone.

Not only the form of Kant's imperative raises problems; its content does so as well. "Act as if the maxim of your action were to become through your will a universal law of nature" requires that any action be such that, when universalized, it promotes the rational order. But does this principle provide an adequate moral criterion? A moral system that uses such a purely formal standard faces the dilemma: If given a determinate content, the rule can never be fully universalized (each case has an unrepeatable uniqueness), but without a concrete content it cannot be applied. In answer to this objection, Kantians have argued that the moral principle refers to the act in its full complexity, including its concrete content and foreseeable consequences. Only the *actual* consequences fall entirely outside the moral domain. As John Silber put it: "Our calculation of duty is not to rest on empirical prognostication of the consequences of our actions. But we are required to consider what are the *willed* consequences of our action by projecting in imagination the sort of world that would come into existence were the maxim of our act to become a universal law of nature."[49] Moral reason demands not that the choice be made in a vacuum, but that the decision be based on rational rather than empirical considerations. This is undoubtedly true. The question is, however, whether the act when taken in its full complexity is still fit to be subjected to the principle of generalization, *as Kant understood it*. It is by no means clear how an act that is determined by particular and always unique circumstances could ever be fully universalized.

Any action may be universalized, as long as the person who considers it morally right is convinced that the same action would be right for others acting in the same conditions The difficulty is, however, as Peter Winch in *Ethics and Action* argues, that each person enters adulthood with at least the outline of a moral code that he or she rarely has cause to question and that code may lead him or her to universalize a particular choice in a manner that differs from that of persons living by another moral code.[50] The formalist nature of Kant's rule appears in the fact that he excludes alternatives by the law of contradiction. Going against the rule is logically inconsistent, he argues. But does a thief really "contradict" himself when he steals? Hegel, as Hume had done before him, wondered whether any action ever *contradicts* reason. Does a thief implicitly assert the existence of private ownership, while explicitly denying it through his action? Does he do more than taking advantage of the fact that others assert the validity of that law?[51] Property is not a universal condition of rationality, but a practical rule for social living arranged differently in different societies. Whoever breaks that arrangement may deny its legitimacy. Or he may consider the prevailing laws of property unfair, as Proudhon did when he declared, "La propriété c'est le vol." Their denial, then, implies no contradiction.

There are, however, alternative interpretations for understanding the term "contradiction." According to the British Kant scholar H. J. Paton, a moral contradiction occurs when an action goes against its natural purpose, that is, when it disrupts the systemic harmony of purposes in human nature. Any such action might be considered *teleologically* contradictory. But the person who so acts may thereby express that he or she regards such a teleology as nonexistent or as carrying no moral weight. A second alternative to the logical interpretation would be to regard it as a "practical contradiction": the immoral act, if universalized, would turn the internal teleology of acting against itself.[52] It may well be that this is what Kant had in mind. The sinner *needs* the very system he or she violates in order to obtain the effects that the act intends. But is it contradictory to deflect an act from its ordinary purpose toward one that it does not normally pursue?

KANT'S SYNTHESIS OF EARLIER THEORIES

From the preceding it should appear how concerned Kant is to avoid making the concepts of good and evil dependent on empirical elements. But then, in the remarkable third chapter of the *Critique of Practical Reason*, where he discusses the incentives of pure practical reason, his argument takes a surprising turn. Even though the law of reason ought to be the only incentive of moral action, the nature of the will is such that it operates through impulses and inclinations. The unconditional acceptance of the moral law affects these inclinations. Thus the moral incentive converts the "natural" inclination to selfishness into one of rational self-love (*C.Pr.R.*, 75; Ak, V, 73). By the same token, the moral law, being an object of respect, excites a feeling of respect for law (*C.Pr.R.*, 76; Ak, V, 73). Kant regards this feeling, produced "solely by reason" (*C.Pr.R.*, 79; Ak, V, 76), indispensable for the efficacy of the moral law.

We may remember the passage in which he links duty to the experience of the sublime. "Duty! Thou sublime and mighty name that dost embrace nothing charming or insinuating but requirest submission and yet seekest not to move the will by threatening aught that would arouse natural aversion or terror, but only holdest forth a law which of itself finds entrance into the mind and yet gains reluctant reverence" (*C.Pr.R.*, 89; Ak, V, 86). This rare lyrical expectoration echoes Rousseau's Vicaire Savoyard: "Conscience! Conscience! Instinct divin, immortelle et céleste voix."[53] Kant here attributes to the moral law the very quality which he, in the third *Critique,* associates with the infinite vastness of the cosmos (*C.Pr.R.*, 166; Ak, V, 162). The passage suggests that feelings may act as emotional incentives for living by the principles of the moral law. It also shows how the doctrine of the third *Critique* complements that of the second: the rational motivation of freedom here assumes an aesthetic quality.[54] Freedom introduces a teleology that science cannot prove to exist in the physical world, but which is symbolized in the aesthetic harmony between the mind and the aesthetic object.

Nor was the moral significance of feelings a transient thought of Kant's middle period. In "The Metaphysical Principles of Virtue," the principal part of the late *Metaphysics of Morals* (1797), Kant assigns a critical role to the development of feelings of sympathy for the natural world as well as for one's fellow humans. The pleasure derived from disinterested love for nature (rocks, plants, animals), though not intrinsically moral in itself, does much "to promote a state of sensibility favorable to morals."[55] In the same vein, Kant declares the propensity wantonly to destroy inanimate beings and, even more, animate ones indicative of a deficient moral sensitivity. Empathy with others— feeling pleasure in their joy, sadness in their pain—deserves to be fostered as being conducive to an attitude of universal benevolence. Kant even claims that without moral feeling a person is "morally dead." Yet he stops short of declaring "moral" feelings a duty: "There can be no duty to have a moral feeling or to acquire it" (*Virtue,* Intro., 58; Ak, VI, 399). But without feelings of benevolence the world would "lack a great moral ornament" (*Virtue,* § 35, 123; Ak, VI, 458). Indeed, the third form of the categorical imperative as stated in the "Metaphysical Principles of Virtue" actually appears to equate feelings of benevolence with respect for the moral law. "Respect for the law, which in its subjective aspect is referred to as moral feeling, is one and the same with the consciousness of one's duty. Therefore, showing respect for man insofar as he is a moral being . . . is also a duty which others have to him" (*Virtue,* § 35, 123; Ak, VI, 458). At the very least, moral feelings appear indispensable for attaining the moral ideal.

In the *Critique of Judgment* Kant laid the foundation for the link between aesthetic feelings and moral sense. Here the argument follows the opposite direction from the one it had hesitantly taken in the third part of the *Critique of Practical Reason* and the one it was to take resolutely in "The Metaphysical Principles of Virtue." In both these writings, feelings formed a part (albeit a nonessential one) of the moral ideal; here the moral ideal itself is declared necessary for the development of aesthetic sensitivity. Kant regards the fostering of moral feelings everywhere "the propaedeutic for the founding of taste."[56] Thus he describes the experience of the sublime as consisting in the mind's awareness of its moral superiority when confronted with the immensity or the horror of nature (*C.J.,* § 28). The enormous power or solitude of nature drives the mind back into itself forcing it to confront its own solitary greatness. In evoking this feeling of transcendence the sublime symbolizes the moral attitude. Indeed, for Kant the moral element, more than the stormy or grandiose landscape or seascape, constitutes the defining quality of the sublime. "A feeling for the sublime in nature cannot well be thought without combining therewith a mental disposition akin to the moral" (*C.J.,* § 29). The powerful, dialectical harmony between the two infinities — that of nature and of the moral law — distinguishes Kant's moral theory of art from the moralistic one of Diderot and other French art critics.

The discussion of the teleology of nature in the *Critique of Judgment* establishes an even more fundamental link with morality. The teleological and the aesthetic judgment share a common principle. Yet, while the aesthetic judgment originates in a feeling of subjective purposiveness, specifically in an awareness of the harmony between the appearing form and the subject's perceptive powers, the so-called teleological judgment stems from an undeniable impression of objective purposiveness in nature: all phenomena appear to form part of an integrated system. Without assuming that they do, science would not be possible. Yet no scientific statement could ever define the purpose of this teleological system itself. Even if science were to confirm the existence of such a system, it still does not answer the question: What, if any, is the purpose of the whole? Without an unconditioned end, present only in a being that never serves as mere *means,* the decisive element needed to consider creation meaningful as a whole would be missing. The moral theory provides that missing part of the system by showing that the person as moral subject is always an end in itself. He or she alone conveys a purpose to the whole of nature and enables us to regard it as a hierarchical system of final causes (*C.J., § 86*). Cosmic teleology, then, attains its end in the moral agent.

The moral consciousness in turn postulates the teleology of the physical world. In discussing the "postulates" of practical reason, Kant shows that in the end all things must support the moral agent. Here he reintroduces those empirical elements that he had previously excluded as motivations for the moral act. The very teleology of the empirical world order (required by science) to remain consistent must, in one way or another, provide the empirical benefits, which the moral agent may not claim for him or herself. On the basis of this cosmic teleology Kant postulates empirical well-being as a necessary complement to the theory of virtue. This allows him to add to the "highest" good (*bonum supremum*), which consists in the pursuit of virtue for its own sake, the "perfect" good (*bonum consummatum*), in which virtue is rewarded by actual happiness. Though happiness, if taken as a primary *incentive,* spoils the moral purity of the virtuous act, for nature to withhold happiness from those who practice virtue would ruin the universal harmony of which the human person forms the center and purpose. "[Happiness] rests on the harmony of nature with [a rational being's] entire end and with the essential determining ground of his will" (*C.Pr.R.,* 129; Ak, V, 124).

As we know, however, virtue does not necessarily yield happiness, nor is happiness the privilege of the virtuous. All we may claim, then, is that the *order of reason* (a teleological consideration) *entitles* virtue to happiness. Kant first attempted to bridge the gap between virtue which makes me *worthy* of happiness and actual happiness by means of a feeling of contentment that, though not happiness itself, at least is an "analogue" of it (*C.Pr.R.,* 123; Ak, V, 119). But then he realized that the austere satisfaction of having accomplished one's duty falls short of virtue's rightful desert. Kant therefore attempts to reunite virtue with happiness in a more substantial way by postulating an omnipotent Creator, source of the moral as well as of the natural order, who is able to rejoin what in this life must remain asunder (*C.Pr.R.,* 129; Ak, V, 125). In an afterlife at last the Creator will grant virtue the happiness it did not obtain in the present life. One may question whether such a posthumous reward, when the cosmic order no longer exists, adequately shows the alleged orientation of that order toward the human person.

PROSPECTS OF KANT'S ETHICAL THEORY:
THE IDEAL OF HUMANITY

One of the formulations of the categorical imperative that appears in the *Foundations of the Metaphysics of Morals* goes as follows: "Act so that you treat humanity in your own person as well as in that of another, always also as an end and never as a means only" (*Foundations,* 54; Ak, IV, 429).[57] The assumption underlying this imperative is that only a being "whose existence in itself has absolute worth" could be an unconditional end and, as such, be the object of a categorical imperative (*Foundations,* 52; Ak, IX, 428). Kant here equates rationality, the determining principle of ethics, with *humanity,* thereby giving the moral law a "material" content. I write this not to reopen the question whether Kant indirectly smuggled an empirical content into his formal law. We know that he did. But the particular nature of this content as here formulated points in a different direction from the one he followed elsewhere in his ethical theory. In the later writings he increasingly regarded the attainment of true humanity the goal of all ethical endeavor.

Does the term "humanity" *(Humanität)* merely refer to any being endowed with reason who therefore is entitled to be treated as an end? If so, practical reason does no more than applying a conclusion of theoretical reason. Undoubtedly, this consideration must have been present to Kant's mind, and it may well have been the primary one. But Kant's use of the term "person" in the second form of the categorical imperative appears to support a richer interpretation. To be a person implies more than belonging to a class of rational beings: it suggests a being-with-other persons, an encounter of individuals. Some find here at least the suggestion of a personalist ethics. In the *Foundations of the Metaphysics of Morals* (*Foundations,* 66; Ak, IV, 401, 440) Kant had argued that persons are entitled to *respect (Achtung)* and that respect requires reciprocity. I must recognize the other as a *self,* if I am to respect him or her. Yet in this earlier work Kant restricts this respect to a respect for the law: "All respect for a person is only respect for the law . . . of which the person provides an example." The later concept of humanity is no longer tied to the formal one of legality.

The work that inspired Kant to conceive of *Humanität* as a moral end was Herder's *Ideas for a Philosophy of the History of Mankind* (1784). We saw that, according to the *Critique of Judgment,* nature's ultimate purpose consists in preparing the conditions for the possibility of a moral life. That purpose, however, differs from nature's more immediate goal: the satisfaction of natural desires and instincts. (*Der erste Zweck der Natur würde die Glückseligkeit, der Zweite die Kultur des Menschen sein* [*C.J.*, § 83].) The life of reason frequently demands that we forego the satisfaction of natural desires. Obviously, many humans do not pursue this higher goal of reason. They rarely behave rationally, collectively no more than individually. The question, then, how the human race might finally attain a mature humanity came to assume an increasing significance in Kant's thought. In his "Idea for a Universal History" (1784), he set up as the proper task of culture the raising of humans to full *Humanität*.

With age Kant grew more pessimistic about the human race's chances of ever attaining that ideal. He increasingly stressed the fundamental flaw in the human disposition with respect to its rational end. He also ceased to consider the difference between the sensuous and the rational parts of our nature sufficient for explaining the human inclination to evil. Evil appears as an unexplainable fact. That fact, however, renders the ascent from animality to morality and rationality an arduous, endless struggle of which the eventual success remains far from assured. In "An Old Question Raised Again: Is the Human Race Constantly Progressing?" (the second part of "The Strife of the Faculties" [1798]), Kant still professes a belief in the possibility of reaching a rational humanity, but he suggests that the adversaries of the humanitarian ideal appear to have the stronger voice: "Bustling folly is the character of our species: people hastily set off on the path of the good, but do not persevere steadfastly upon it; indeed, in order to avoid being bound to a single goal, even if only for the sake of variety, they reverse the plan of progress, build in order to demolish, and impose upon themselves the hopeless effort of rolling the stone of Sisyphus uphill in order to let it roll back down again."[58]

The fundamental discrepancy between the call to humanity and our imperfect response to it leads Kant to raise the question again: Can we still confidently assert that human beings in their actual behavior will ever achieve the kind of rationality which alone renders them absolute ends? He modified the claim from *actual* achievement to the *capacity* of choosing rational ends. Even if a person behaves irrationally or is mentally deficient, we owe it to the human race as a whole to honor that *capacity*. It may be impossible to recognize a person who acts irrationally as an end, but respect for the capacity of reason, in however minimal degree present, forbids us to treat him or her as a means. Moreover, since humanity is a process as well as a state, morality demands more than respect for humans in their present condition. It requires that we actively pursue the ideal of a *full* humanity. As historical beings we must assume the moral task of raising culture unto a process of humanization. We are morally bound to promote progress in culture by creating conditions favorable to the attainment of a full humanity. Kant does not imply that the state of culture "conditions" moral behavior. At best a morally more advanced state of culture may facilitate "a disposition toward goodness," but the actual achievement of moral goodness remains each individual's private responsibility. Hence virtue consists not only in a person's conformity to reason but also in his or her contribution to the future moral condition of the human race.

This cultural ingredient in the categorical imperative inspired Fichte's philosophy of freedom as well as Hegel's theory of culture. I do not believe, however, that it quite overcame the one-sidedness of Kant's system of ethics. To do so, it would have had to satisfy the demands of human nature in its entirety, including its desire for harmony and serenity. Kant's theory seems in this regard more restrictive than the theory of moral sense. Even during his lifetime, Schiller (in *On Grace and Dignity* [*Ueber Anmut und Würde*, 1793]) had objected to a theory of the "good" life that praised the dignity of the moral law at the expense of moral grace. Kant apparently saw the point. In a long footnote in *Religion Within the Limits of Reason Alone* he answered: "I freely grant that by very reason of the dignity of the *idea of duty* I am unable to associate *grace* with it. For the idea of duty involves absolute necessity, to which grace stands in direct contradiction. The majesty of the moral law . . . awakens a *sense of the sublimity* of our own destiny which enraptures us more than any beauty" (*Religion*, 19; Ak, VI, 23). Perhaps one might claim that fulfilling one's duty finds its perfection in "grace." Yet the fact remains that, after all due qualifications, Kant's *moral object* is, as Bernard Williams describes it, "a rational agent and no more" and the self of the moral agency "a noumenal self, outside time and causality" (Williams, p. 64).

An equally serious problem lies in the ambiguity of a morality of intention. Even before Kant wrote his moral system, Abbé Prévost had exposed how good intentions often hide selfish motives. In his *Histoire d'une Grecque moderne* (1740), a French diplomat bitterly reminisces about his successful attempt to liberate a young woman from a Turkish serail. He had educated her and treated her like a daughter. Having fallen in love with his ward, he had hoped that a long courtship and an uninterrupted stream of benefits would induce her to return his love and to grant him freely the favors that the Pasha had extorted from her by force. Instead, she used the very freedom he had given her to refuse him. The moral interest of the novel lies in the narrator's gradual awakening to the ambivalence of his own motives. He at last discovers the secret desire that had driven him to secure Théophé's freedom. Prévost's work anticipated what Sartre later called *la mauvaise foi* (bad faith) — the very attitude the narrator had most studiously attempted to avoid (*J'étais de si bonne foi . . .*). Théophé's rescuer also understands that the ambivalence of his virtuous intention had frustrated the end that he had secretly pursued. "Is it not miserable that I, enslaved to the pleasures of the senses, have undertaken to render a girl (kept in a serail) chaste and virtuous! Alas, I have been well punished for it!"

Both the narrowly deontological and the ambiguously intentional character of Kantian ethics have their ground in its subjective character. In contrast to the traditional priority of the good, for Kant, freedom, the rational will, determines the morality of the act. To be sure, this freedom, far from being a subjective inclination, is reason itself in its practical aspect. Nonetheless, Kant's reason differs from Plato's and Aristotle's: it is not *given* but constituted by the subject. Kant's transcendental subject, of course, surpasses the scope of the individual mind. Reason, for him, is not a psychological concept. But since the principles of practical reason are to be *applied* by intellectually limited and psychologically complex individuals, subject to passions and emotions that inevitably obscure their judgment, the decisions made are rarely perfect. That Kant himself was aware of those restrictions appears in the sharp distinctions he drew between the intention of the agent and the nature of the act, as well as between the internal order of morality and the external one of legality. As long as the subject, even a transcendental subject, is solely responsible for the meaning and content of the moral act, the danger of subjectivism can never be exorcised.

Conclusion

Philosophers of the Enlightenment attempted to resolve the moral crisis of their time by redefining the very notion of ethics. Yet they rarely succeeded in combining the two conditions that render a moral theory both universally normative and specifically concrete. Rationalists stressed universal norms while neglecting either concrete application or particular fulfillment. Empiricists focused on particular experiences, such as individual moral sense, private satisfaction, or public benefit, but failed to link them to the universal element of obligation. This discrepancy reflects the general disjunction between the universal and the particular characteristic of Enlightenment thought. In the ethics of Aristotle and medieval Scholastics, the universal had mostly, though not exclusively, stressed the deontological moment. But that universality included particular, personal satisfaction. Aristotle derived his entire ethics from the teleology of nature. Later theories followed him in this respect but increasingly formulated the synthesis in terms of the Stoic concept of natural law, to which Jews, Christians, and Muslims added the idea of a transcendent sanction. Toward the end of the Middle Ages, Scholastics so exclusively emphasized this transcendent element that the earlier synthesis collapsed. Ethics came to consist primarily in obedience to a transcendently imposed law, whereby human fulfillment became in fact a secondary, extrinsic end. For Locke and some of his followers explicitly, for others (including Descartes) implicitly, obedience to God's law is "rewarded" by happiness. But obligation and well-being had ceased to be intrinsically linked. The two appeared to become reunited in modern thought when the subject, the source of meaning, also became the source of value. But now a different problem arose. If the ethical obligation rested on a rational a priori, it remained purely formal. On the other side, if ethics was conceived on the basis of experience (as in the moral sense theory or in utilitarianism) it could not function as an absolute obligation.

Another problem with the modern principles of ethics follows from the fact that the subject as only source of value allows no room for genuine otherness. It reduces the other to an extension of itself. Contemporary authors have drawn attention to the moral solipsism of the modern theory of the subject. In it, according to Foucault, "man's other must become the same in himself."[59] Even Kant's theory of obligation, so absolute in its demand to treat the person never only as a means, deals with the other only as a universal, not as an individual person with particular needs and a unique identity. Treated as member of a universal class the individual naturally puts up what Emmanuel Levinas has called an "ethical resistance."[60]

Appendix: Moral Changes Reflected in Enlightenment Drama

By the end of the seventeenth century, the drama in France had shifted from a conflict between moral ideals and passions (as it had been for Corneille) to a conflict between opposing passions. Heroic virtue scores no victories in Racine's moral crises. The destructive power of their passions predestines his characters to moral failure and unredeemable misery. But in this failure lies a moral lesson. Unaided human nature is defenseless against its own destructive passions. Racine returns the drama to its religious origins. Ancient fate now assumes the forbidding face of a Jansenist God. In his splendid study on Pascal and Racine, *Le Dieu caché,* Lucien Goldmann defined the dramatic agon as taking place between religiously sustained virtue and a hostile, secular world.[61] This interpretation still remains too much within Corneille's moral compass. In Racine's plays the fundamental opposition is between a horizontal level of human striving and a vertical one of divine election or rejection. The transcendent dimension of the conflict, caused by what George Steiner has called "the intolerable burden of God's presence," conveys to Racine's plays an unprecedented dramatic tension.[62] Confrontations and revelations occur against the background of this inscrutable presence, never perceived but constantly felt.

At the end, the ruling passion moves the hero or heroine with inescapable force toward destruction. Phèdre, Athalie, Néron are no longer able to resist their fall: God has abandoned them to their passions. The significance of the catastrophe surpasses the human motives that led to it. In that ultimate crisis, Nero reveals the extent of his inborn corruptness, which previously had remained hidden to all but his mother. At the decisive moment, Titus and Berenice finally decide to obey a destiny that had been decreed from all eternity: he to be Roman emperor, she to abandon him, without their passion being resolved. In the final act Phèdre openly surrenders to the destructive passion for her stepson that has been consuming her. Reason and will are powerless against the fate of strong passions: a higher power leads men and women to their doom. Andromaque, at the end of the play that bears her name, understands that a transcendent force has guided her tragic fate.

> Yes, heaven, I praise thy high tenacity,
> Upon my punishment relentless bent,
> Thou'st made me drink the dregs of chastisement.[63]

Eighteenth-century "classicists" resumed ancient plots—as Voltaire did in *Oedipe,* Addison in *Cato,* Gottsched in *Dying Cato*—but their work lacked the superhuman dimension that had given Greek tragedy its dramatic power. Ancient drama had been rooted in the belief that human acts possess an inherent, prereflective meaning. Born in ritual it stripped the elementary deed bare to its primeval significance. The modern principle of subjectivity required conscious motivations: meaning had to be *given* by the playwright. Thus the drama became a moralistic *projection* rather than a ritual of ideal deeds. It dispensed moral lessons, but the source of moral inspiration had dried up. The theater rarely attained moral greatness. Plays had to end happily: virtue had to be "rewarded." Enlightenment plays lacked not only the depth of the Greek classics, but also that of the early moderns, Shakespeare, Corneille, and Racine. Playwrights pretended to continue the classical tradition; in fact, they eviscerated the ancient drama. In *The Lying Lover,* Richard Steele resumed the theme of Corneille's *Le menteur*—itself harking back to Terence. The preface justifies its different ending: the liar suddenly repents, "perhaps an injury to the rules of comedy, but . . . a justice to those of morality." In his dedication of *The Tender Husband,* Steele discloses his intention to avoid "every thing that might look ill-natured, immoral, or prejudicial to what the better part of mankind hold sacred and honourable." Leslie Stephen blamed the century's complacent, passionless mode of living for this moralist mediocrity. "The society to which Addison and his fellows belonged was a society of good, commonplace, sensible people, who were fighting each other by pamphlets instead of swords; who played a game in which they staked not life and death, but a comfortable competency . . . and who had a hearty contempt for romantic extravagance. A society in which common sense is regarded as the cardinal intellectual virtue does not naturally suggest the great tragic themes."[64]

One of the few who, in my opinion, recaptured some of the existential depth of the ancient tragedy and succeeded in reconciling it with a modern sensibility was Vittorio Alfieri. As he resumed the classical themes in such dramas as *Polinice* and *Antigone,* he preserved the full impact of superhuman forces upon human freedom. Emotions and feelings are anchored within an ancient sense of fate. His dramas, written with a romantic ardor for freedom and a hatred of tyrants, do more than transfer modern aspirations to ancient plots: they remain faithful to the spirit of the Greek tragedy. Antigone in caring for her deceased brother displays modern feelings of sisterly love and moral independence, yet her ultimate motive remains the eternal law of the family.

French tragedies of the time suffered from an even greater decline than the British. Baron Grimm attributed the departure of moral greatness to an exhaustion of the traditional themes. "Tous les ressorts de notre système dramatique semblent usés après deux ou trois mille pièces jetées pour ainsi dire dans le même moule."[65] In fact, the decline resulted less from repetition than from a loss of heroic inspiration. The combination of preachy seriousness and sentimental happiness created a new genre that mixed the qualities of tragedy with the happy ending of comedy. The derogatory name *comédie larmoyante* fully captures the genre's ambivalence, though not its underlying moralism.[66] Diderot, always anxious to improve human nature, considered it a most effective means for propagating those moral principles that would assist the middle class in its social rise. "How much it would benefit humanity if all the imitative arts agreed on this common objective: to make people love virtue and hate vice!"[67] His two dramas, *Le Fils Naturel* and *Le Père de Famille,* have deservedly vanished from the repertoire. Nor do we readily understand how they could ever have entertained a contemporary audience. Lessing had them performed in his theater in Hamburg, though he himself wrote much better plays.

An unfriendly critic (Palissot) wrote about the less unsuccessful first one: "Ce qui est bon n'est pas nouveau; ce qui est nouveau n'est pas bon." The charge of a lack of originality hit Diderot at a particularly vulnerable spot because he had borrowed the entire plot from Goldoni and was accused of plagiarism. Diderot equates morality with the promotion of a more equitable social order. "Virtue" had to serve as the great social equalizer. In *Le père de famille,* a later, less-than-mediocre play, Diderot more directly but not less cautiously criticizes the barrier between social classes. In it an aristocratic young man wants to marry a poor commoner. The playwright considered such a *mésalliance* still too shocking for his audience. So, at the end his poor heroine turns out to be a long-lost noble relative. The compromise, as much as the play itself, illustrates the total absence of moral scope in this moralistic theater. Dialogues are trimmed to social lectures, uttered by cardboard models of virtue and vice.

Why did Diderot, otherwise such a witty writer, want to spread his moral gospel by means of such dull dramas? Some of his contemporaries must have raised that question. To defend his idea of the theater, he wrote some *Entretiens,* the quality of which far exceeds that of the plays. In one of them we read: "The theatrical scene is the only place where the tears of the virtuous become mixed with those of the evil. Here the evil person allows himself to be aroused against the injustices he himself has committed; here he feels pity for unhappiness which he himself has occasioned; here he becomes angry with men of his own kind."[68] These words at least recognize the existence of a serious inner struggle — which his plays fail to display.

Moralizing theater may refine feelings, but it never plumbs the depths of existence, as Greek or Shakespearean drama had done. Through fear and compassion, ancient and early modern tragedies awakened the spectator to a different state of moral awareness. The ideals of the bourgeois drama barely grazed the surface of moral life: their models of benevolence and honesty were weak attempts to reconcile moral ideals with questionable social conditions, easy targets for parody.

Bourgeois drama fared better in Germany. Lessing, though an admirer of Diderot's aesthetic theory and director of his plays, was nevertheless conscious of the Frenchman's unfortunate tendency to display universal representatives of virtues and vices rather than individual characters. Anxious to avoid Diderot's abstraction, Lessing delivered his message in a far more dramatic form. His *Minna von Barnhelm* takes place during the Seven Years' War that had just ended. The plot — a Prussian major falls in love with a Saxon girl, a political enemy — contains a symbolic plea for reconciliation among Germans and, beyond that, for a union of all German-speaking people. In other plays, especially in his powerful *Emilia Galotti* (1772), Lessing attempted to arouse his German contemporaries from their feudal slumber. Since the new bourgeois class, whose spokesman he wanted to be, was barely emerging in Germany, he placed his characters either in a society where customs were still more feudal, as he did in *Emilia Galotti*'s Italy, or in one that was more advanced, as in *Miss Sara Sampson*'s England. Lessing was not inclined to please his audience with a happy ending. In *Emilia Galotti,* the prince, who abducted Emilia on her wedding day and was responsible for the murder of her spouse and her own death, remains unpunished. Such a harshly realistic conclusion conveyed a far stronger message about the abuses of the ancien régime than Diderot's edifying comedies.

Still, Lessing's tragedies (with the exception of *Nathan der Weise*) remained moralistic, and the young Schiller castigated him for it in "The Theatre Stage as a Moral Institution" (1784). In Schiller's view, the playwright had to confront his audience with the fundamental dilemmas of human existence. He ought to present models, not sermons. Dramatic heroes had to show how to suffer, how to struggle with destiny, and how to choose between opposite duties. Above all, they ought to assume full responsibility for their destiny. Whether the behavior of the characters on the stage corresponds to conventional moral norms matters not. Schiller did not expect that the tragic ending of his robber hero, Karl Moor, would make the streets safer. But the aim of the stage is not to achieve "moral improvements" but to fathom the human condition. Goethe's and Schiller's outlaws, Goetz von Berlichingen and Karl Moor, rejected by society, incarnated a new ideal of freedom and authenticity to be developed in the romantic theater.

Ironically, the Enlightenment comedy, so often censured for its frivolousness , may have had a greater moral impact than the moralistic bourgeois drama, particularly in Britain. The discrepancy between the moral standards by which people pretended to rule their conduct and their actual behavior provided a particularly appropriate target in a society where appearances had become socially more important than reality. Comedies that punctured the balloon filled with the hot air of moral respectability offered a welcome relief from empty moral pretenses. No one had exposed the hypocrisy of late seventeenth-century Parisian life with more wit than Molière. His lighthearted lampoons of moral posturing probe social conflicts more deeply than the pseudo-heroic theater of the eighteenth century. His comedy *Le Misanthrope,* a more serious moral drama than most tragedies of the time, presents the sad fate of the person who pursues perfection but merely succeeds in attracting ridicule. Molière expresses so much sympathy for his hapless anti-hero that his play could have passed for a tragedy had he not presented Alceste as rigid as he was virtuous. With bemused interest, but not without compassion, the spectator watches a man in his effort to do "the right thing" stubbornly plot his own undoing. Rousseau denounced Molière's parody of virtue as immoral. But he missed the play's moral critique of the spiritual poverty of his age. Molière denounces the falsity of *Tartuffe*'s self-serving piety, the false prudery of *Les précieuses ridicules,* and the pretentious airs of *Le bourgeois gentilhomme.*

In the eighteenth century it is to England that we must turn to assess the moral significance of the comedy. The development of the British comedy of manners, so splendidly begun by Ben Johnson, was cut short by Cromwell's revolution. Restoration comedies, rather than resuming the Renaissance tradition, explosively released the pent-up aversion to Puritan moralism. Pretending to be critical of the licentious manners of a hypocritical society, they displayed more sympathy for the vices they decried than for the virtues they praised. In William Wycherley's lascivious *The Country Wife* (1675) and William Congreve's cynical *The Way of the World* (1700), the wicked do indeed get punished in the end, but one can hardly claim that virtue triumphs. Of their moral pretenses Macaulay wrote: "The heroes and heroines have a moral code of their own, an exceedingly bad one." After Jeremy Collier's indictment of the raunchy Restoration comedy in *A Short View of the Immorality and Profaneness of the English Stage,* the theater became more "respectable," but the insipid "moral" plays that followed lowered dramatic standards.

Two masters of plot and language, Oliver Goldsmith and Richard Sheridan, restored the vitality of the comedy of manners. In his *Essay on the Theatre,* Goldsmith called the sentimental comedy that had come to dominate the British stage "a false tragedy," unworthy of the name "comedy." But the moralistic expectations were deeply ingrained in the critics, as appears in Horace Walpole's assessment of Goldsmith's comical masterpiece *She Stoops to Conquer:* "the lowest of farces that tends to no moral, no edification at all." Only Sheridan's *School for Scandal,* first performed at Drury Lane in 1777, persuaded everyone, including Walpole, that "a marvelous resurrection of the stage" had begun. The British repertoire of the late eighteenth century still parodied hypocrisy and duplicity, but with their characters serving as vehicles for plot and witty dialogue, they were less comedies of manners than early versions of a theater of the absurd.

I conclude these remarks on the moral import of eighteenth-century drama with a note about satire. Since its ancient origins, satirical poetry has pretended to serve a moral purpose. Particularly in the eighteenth century it claimed this high moral ground for its attacks, even when they were only intended to settle personal accounts. Edward Young cautiously concluded about the satire's moral effectiveness: "It is much to be feared, that misconduct will never be chased out of the world, by satire; all therefore that is to be said for it, is that misconduct will *certainly* never be chased out of the world by satire, if no satires were written."[69] Satire measures its victims against established norms either by absurdly inflating their qualities or by deflating their pretenses. Unlike common irony, satire is, as Northrop Frye suggested, a "militant irony."[70]

While common irony runs the risk of weakening the seriousness of its moral criticism (as we saw in the case of the ironical novel), satire tends to overshoot the moral goal and to be *too* critical to be morally constructive. In the eighteenth century, personal attacks often became so harsh as to diminish both the aesthetic and the moral quality of writing. In many of Pope's epigrams, directed at any person he happened to dislike, one looks in vain for a moral purpose or, in many instances, for common decency.

No writer handled the powerful weapon of sarcasm more destructively than Jonathan Swift. His moral indignation takes satire well beyond aesthetic moderation. In his notorious "A Modest Proposal," Swift takes his critique of the British government's exploitative attitude toward the Irish population to its extreme conclusion. Why should the British table not take advantage of the tender meat of newborn Irish children instead of letting their unnecessary bodies go to waste in famine? No less sardonic are the final scenes of Gulliver's voyage to the Houyhnhnms, in which the merciless Dean Swift appears to release an unadulterated hatred of the human race. Upon leaving the peaceful kingdom of the horses, Gulliver exclaims: "By copulating with one of the Yahoo species (the human race) I had become a parent of more." The loving embrace of his wife as well as the smell of his children repels him. A letter to Pope (September 9, 1725) discloses that these feelings were more than literary fiction: "I have ever hated all nations, professions and communities. . . . But principally I hate that animal called man, although I heartily love John, Peter, Thomas, and so forth." Swift's inner demons transform the targets of his critique into objects of disgust. He himself describes satire as "a sort of Glass wherein Beholders do generally discover everybody's Face but their Own." But when satire is as ferociously administered as it was in some of Swift's most violent pieces, beholders are not likely to discover any face in it but the cruel satirist's own. Taken to an extreme, satire turns against itself and loses its effectiveness as a moral weapon.

6

The Origin of Modern Social Theories

The Enlightenment may have made its most lasting impact on the way we live and think today through its social theory. Our institutions and laws, our conception of the state, and our political sensitivity all stem from Enlightenment ideas. This, of course, is particularly true in the United States, where the founding fathers transformed those ideas into an unsurpassed system of balanced government. Remarkably enough, at the center of these ideas stands the age-old concept of natural law. Much of the Enlightenment's innovation in political theory may be traced to a change in the interpretation of that concept. Originally it had a descriptive as well as a prescriptive meaning: it referred to the universal order of nature, to the way things are in their communality and in their particularity. This comprehensive order had a normative quality as well. Freedom ought to conform to nature as all other things do. Yet this ideal aspect was never separated from the real one described in the theory of natural law.

The voluntarist philosophies of the late Middle Ages shifted the emphasis from the intrinsic rationality of natural law to the decision of the lawmaker. The obligation of the law thereby gained ascendancy over its being an expression of a universal order of reason. By the eighteenth century, the prescriptive element had become relatively independent from the descriptive one. This may seem surprising. Was the rationalist conception of the natural law not a pure, perhaps too pure, philosophical description of social reality? In fact, it is not descriptive at all; its abstract universals take no account of particular historical realities. In fact, many Enlightenment theorists attempted to disguise a radical project of social reform under the appearance of an impartial speculation on human nature. Ignoring all factual information about the origin, development, and particular conditions of civil societies, such political thinkers as Rousseau decreed what they ought to be. But others, such as Montesquieu, avoided those speculative abstractions and instead investigated the origins and development of civil law and social institutions. Montesquieu mentions natural laws, but he defines them as "the necessary relations arising from the nature of things," thus taking us back to the descriptive concept of law. All positive laws, according to him, are but human attempts to adapt the law of nature to the physical and moral conditions of a particular area and tradition. Practical conclusions ought to be based on historical evidence, not on abstract speculation. At the end of the century, the pioneers of the new science of economics also broke with the prescriptive concept of natural law. For the early economists, specifically for the French Physiocrats and for Adam Smith, the laws of economics were the empirical laws of nature, not a priori moral or political dictates.

The Recasting of Natural Law and the Origin of Natural Rights

That a universal law rules relations among nations as well among individuals was not a new idea. It was the founding principle of Stoic ethics and had been suggested by Plato and Aristotle. Aristotle anticipated a crucial feature of the natural law when he distinguished a law that applies everywhere from statutory laws that differ from one constitution to another. "By the two kinds of law I mean particular law and universal law. Particular law is that which each community lays down and applies to its own members: this is partly written and partly unwritten. Universal law is the law of nature. For there really is, as everyone to some extent divines, a natural justice and injustice that is binding on all men, even on those who have no association or covenant with each other" (*Rhetorica*, 1373b). Elsewhere he adds that every form of legislation requires deliberation, a function of practical reason (*Eth. Nic.*, 1141b–1142b), and that "there is but one [law] which is everywhere *by nature* the best" (*Eth. Nic.*, 1135a). Thus Aristotle relates law to reason and reason to nature.[1] Still, the theory of natural law did not reach its definitive form before Stoicism, because neither Plato nor Aristotle held that all humans shared the same nature and were therefore entitled to equal rights. Free men differed essentially from slaves, men from women, Greeks from barbarians. The Stoics first clearly stated that all humans equally partake of a common nature, and on the basis of that assumption they conceived of human nature as a universal rule of conduct. Living well meant living *convenienter naturae* (Cicero, *De finibus*, III, 73), and that, for humans, meant living in accordance with reason. The same law of reason manifest in the human mind underlies the order of nature. Reason converts nature's *order of rightness (ius naturale)* into a *morally normative order* (the *lex naturae*).[2]

For the Romans, the *lex naturae* possessed no juridical authority except when no civil law on the subject existed. Their jurisprudence accepted as "law" only a stipulated ordinance issued by a civil authority entitled to do so. Neither did positive laws derive their juridical authority from the natural law. As A. P. d'Entrèves pointed out in his classic text on natural law: "Nowhere, in fact, do we find in the *Corpus Juris* an assertion of the superiority of natural to positive law, in the sense that in a case of conflict, the one should overrule the other. . . . We must indeed divest ourselves, in order to understand the Roman conception of natural law, not only of the modern conception of natural rights, *but of the subordination of positive to natural law* with which later ages have made us familiar."[3]

How, then, did natural law eventually acquire its sovereign authority over civil law? The natural law had always had some moral authority insofar as nature itself always possessed a somewhat sacred character, either because it was divine or because it was derived from a transcendent source. Thus Cicero writes: "True law is right reason in agreement with Nature; it is of universal application, unchanging and everlasting; it summons to duty by its commands, and deters from wrong-doing by its prohibitions; . . . one eternal and unchangeable law will be valid for all nations and for all times, and there will be one master and one ruler, that is, God over us all, for He is the author of this law, its promulgator and its enforcing judge."[4] Still, as I have noted, this high moral authority did not give the natural law direct juridical power.

The Christian tradition adopted much of the Stoic doctrine. Natural law reflects the rational order of the universe, an order that itself was grounded in the *lex aeterna* of God's government On the basis of this concept of eternal law, Aquinas developed a comprehensive theory of law in the *Summa Theologiae* (arts. 90–96 of pt. I–II). "The world is ruled by divine providence — the whole community of the universe is governed by the divine reason. Therefore the very notion of the government of things residing in God as in the ruler of the universe, has the nature of a law" (*S. Th.*, I–II, q.91 a.1).[5] St. Thomas traces the authority of all positive law to the natural law. "Every human law has just so much of the nature of law as it is derived from the law of nature" (*S.*

Th. I–II, q.95 a.2). A statutory law is mostly a "determination" of the natural law. For Aquinas, the primary concern of law (natural or positive) is not the good of the individual, but the common good. The social order has a priority over the individual and the first task of law is to secure peace on the basis of distributive justice. (*S. Th.,* I–II, q.90 a.2).

The guiding idea of the concept of natural law, namely, that all humans share a common nature, lost much of its significance in late medieval nominalist thought. Instead, the prescriptive element that had been present from the beginning, the will of God, became prominent, and natural law derived its authority from a divine decree. In fact, the legal character of any law (natural as well as positive) resides exclusively in the decision of the lawgiver. According to the nominalist Marsilius of Padua (1340–96), God has restricted his direct jurisdiction to the natural law, while entrusting positive legislation to the human community. Still, no human law can contradict divine law without losing its authority. Thomists and nominalists disagreed on the source of the natural law. Did it originate in God's wisdom or in God's will? In the latter case, favored by nominalists, the natural law attained a quasi-legal character. Both parties continued to agree that reason was the source of our *knowledge* of the natural law.

The Reformation strengthened the voluntarist interpretation, while the concept of nature (tainted by sin) lost much of its former significance. For Calvinists, not nature but the will of God became the determining factor of the moral law. In reaction against this position, naturalist thinkers revived the original Stoic conception of natural law. In fact, the ancient Stoic theory had not been religiously neutral: a divine Logos filled all of nature and thus endowed nature's law with a divine authority. But this religious meaning, already weak in the Renaissance interpretation of Stoic morality, had almost entirely vanished by the eighteenth century.

It was John Locke who introduced the notion of natural law to the Enlightenment as a rational ground of moral and legal obligations as well as of juridical rights. Yet unlike the Stoics, the Roman jurists, and most medieval Scholastics, he stressed its juridical authority. The natural law, as he described it in the *Second Treatise of Civil Government,* initiated in fact a theory that neither Stoic philosophers nor Roman jurists nor medieval Schoolmen would have recognized. Although for all of them, the natural law had been the law of a rational world order inherent in nature, for Locke, it had been the conclusion of a divine decision. Still, the English philosopher stressed the "natural" character of the law and even admitted an historical "state of nature" in which that law would be the only norm. All the while he insisted firmly on this natural law's legally binding authority.[6] "The state of nature has a law of nature to govern it, which obliges every one, and reason, which is that law, teaches all mankind, who will but consult it, that being all equal and independent, no one ought to harm another in his life, health, liberty, or possessions."[7]

Some passages in the *Second Treatise on Civil Government* leave the impression that natural law rules archaic society and that civil law belongs to a later stage. " 'Tis plain the world never was, nor never will be, without numbers of men in that state — I moreover affirm, that all men are naturally in that state, and remain so, till by their own consents they make themselves members of some politic society" (II, 14, 15). Locke here asserts (1) that the state of nature is an actual, historical state in which some people still continue living today; and (2) that the natural law ruling that state continues to be the supreme law, the norm of all positive laws in civil society. Other passages suggest that the state of nature was the pristine condition of the human race before it was corrupted by the fall. Since the fall occurred at the beginning, it appears to be a theological assumption rather than an historical condition. John Dunn describes it as that original state of innocence: "The state of nature is a topic for theological reflection, not for anthropological research."[8]

But more often Locke refers to this state of nature as if it were an enduring, rather than a prehistorical or prelapsarian one. Every sovereign remains permanently in the state of nature with respect to every other sovereign. It is the natural law itself that drives humans to leave the state of nature and to enter civil society. The transition, though achieved through a free contract, is nonetheless dictated by and needed for, the full application of the natural law. For that application requires the presence of social conditions that are not available in the state of nature.[9] The principles of natural law are insufficient to settle even elementary disputes concerning ownership. The need for their interpretation through civil laws excludes the permanence of a state without public arbitration. When Locke, then, declares that some civilizations remain in the state of nature today, as he does in the passage quoted above, he implies that, though subject to the law of nature, they lack the benefit of a civil society needed for fully observing that law. The claim that Locke simply juxtaposes two states, one of which is natural (the state of nature) while the other results from a "free" decision (civil society), misses the essential meaning of the state of nature, which, for Locke, serves as a *foundation* for the political state.[10] Locke's concept of a natural law as source of political authority opposes both Filmer's divine right of kings (the target of Locke's first *Treatise*) and Hobbes's lawless state of nature.

One of the most significant changes in modern social theory concerns the notion of natural rights. The notion of individual rights inherent in the person did not exist before the twelfth century. What did exist was an objective order of lawfulness (*jus*) that allowed those who lived under the law to actively pursue whatever did not conflict with the law. The idea of subjective rights, that is, rights independent of that objective condition, was foreign to Roman as well as to Christian legislators. It has long been assumed that the concept of individual rights emerged in the fourteenth century dispute between Pope John XXII and the Franciscans on the question of evangelical poverty. Could the Franciscans legitimately claim to have the *use* of things necessary to life without *possessing* them? The pope denied it: each person has an inalienable natural right to possess. Many, including myself, used to interpret this episode as the birth of the idea of natural rights. In his recent *The Idea of Natural Rights,* the eminent historian of medieval law, Brian Tierney, has proven that the notion of individual rights originated some two centuries earlier and had originally nothing to do with the nominalist philosophy to which it has so often been attributed. In fact, Ockham's own formulation of it remained entirely within the objective Thomist theory of natural law.[11]

The twelfth-century commentators on Gratianus's *Decretum* (c. 1140) — an accumulation of the recovered Roman law and of various, not always consistent canons of Church law — first conceived of *right* as a *subjective power* inherent in humans. This subjective interpretation of rights survived into the modern age, mostly, as Tierney shows, through the intermediary of the Spanish Scholastics of the sixteenth century. Ockham, long considered the father of the idea of subjective rights, did in fact no more than repeat the earlier arguments based upon the law of reason, which Aquinas and other Dominicans had formulated well before him. For those Scholastics, *jus* had continued to define, as it had for the Romans, the legal condition of the social state of rightness (the sphere of the *justum*).[12] St. Thomas's description of *jus* as "what is fair" still remains in line with the idea of a legal order that *makes* right.[13] That order links the individual to a number of social bodies, such as guild, principality, kingdom, or empire, through which rights and duties reached the individual.

The nascent national state gradually absorbed most functions of the intermediate multiple bodies, thereby equalizing all citizens in principle yet isolating them in practice. The states granted them political rights but severed the links with the intermediate social entities that integrated the person within a *community* of right. Princes legitimated their authority in a different way than the vassals of the feudal society had done. The source of authority within the states was neither the emperor nor the pope who represented a universal order, but the particular will of the sovereign. By the same token the rights derived from this particular source were restricted to a limited territory and to particular groups (e.g., Catholics or Protestants). Eventually members of groups that did not share the rights other groups enjoyed within the state (especially religious rights) began to appeal to a doctrine of "universal human rights." The source of rights became thereby transferred from the community to the individual. What began with particular claims made by religious dissenters in sixteenth-century France and England resulted in the eighteenth-century declaration of universal human rights. Alasdair MacIntyre describes the outcome as follows: "The degree to which a particular individual identifies him or herself with the life of the community in which he or she lives is always, on the modern view, conditional. For it is only if, and insofar as, the community satisfies the conditions prescribed by each particular individual's view of rights, that that individual has good reason so to identify."[14] Not the community but an individualized conception of natural law grants each individual equal rights.

The notion of the person as source of individual rights independently of the social order to which he or she belongs was not entirely new. It had its roots in the participation in a superior order that transcended the earthly community and bestowed a unique dignity upon the individual as *imago Dei*. It granted the person who belonged to it the right and duty to resist any power that opposed that order. Conflicts between the Roman Empire and groups of Jews and Christians had occurred all through the first three centuries of the common era. During the Reformation many appealed to those early precedents. Yet there was a difference. At that earlier time rights had reached the individual via a *sacred community*. To some extent this was still the case with such early religious dissenters as the Anabaptists and Calvin himself who always stressed the priority of the sacred community even in dealing with the secular state. But later dissenters (Protestants in France, Catholics and Calvinists in England) usually appealed to individual rights grounded in the natural law. At any rate, by the eighteenth century the supernatural notion of the person had become totally secularized, and human rights were claimed on the basis of an abstract theory of natural law. Those rights isolated persons from such concrete social structures as the community in which they lived, the trade or profession they practiced, the religion to which they belonged. Indeed, they "universalized human solitude."[15]

Two philosophers perceived the social danger of such unmediated appeals to rights. They did not deny individual rights but showed how any effective exercise of them required them to be mediated by the community. In *Leviathan,* Hobbes defined natural right as "the liberty each man hath, to use his own power, as he will himself, for the preservation of his own nature; that is to say, of his own life."[16] In a prepolitical condition, if such a condition exists, each person has indeed a right to everything. But as that right is constantly threatened, no one possesses the power to enforce it. Hence *real* rights come with laws passed and enforced by civil society. Spinoza's theory in the *Tractatus Politicus* (1670) resembles Hobbes's. He defines the right of a nature as coextensive with the power of that nature: "Each natural thing has by nature as much right as it possesses power to exist and to operate — as this power of each natural being is none other than God's own power, which is absolutely free."[17] An individual's rights, then, are equivalent to his power to protect them. In the state of nature, however, where even the weakest person can kill the strongest, no single person is able to protect his rights.[18] Therefore, Spinoza concludes, no person in the state of nature possesses any real rights, but only the illusion of rights.

Although both these theories reject the traditional concept of natural law, their conclusions stand in fact closer to it than those of Locke and the eighteenth-century theorists of rights. Independent of civil society no real natural rights exist. For Locke, on the contrary, the existence of individual rights precedes that of the community, which previously had been considered the concrete source of right. In the original, allegedly prepolitical state of nature, the person already possesses all fundamental rights needed for the preservation and free development of human life. Locke follows Hobbes in describing self-preservation as the fundamental natural right. Though he restricts that right far more than Hobbes did, for whom it was a right to "everything," he nevertheless extends it well beyond mere self-preservation. For him, some form of property is essential to the fullness of life, since property enables the person to extend his power. "Every man has a *property* in his own *person.* . . . The *labor* of his body and the *work* of his hands, we may say, are properly his" (V, § 27). But the institution of property is a historical concept that assumes various forms in different societies. Marx who, like Locke, describes property as "a human being's relation to his natural conditions of production as belonging to him . . . which only form, so to speak, his extended body" agrees with the British theorist that the early forms of appropriation occurred as preconditions of labor.[19] The point is important, for if the natural law attaches property rights to labor, as Locke claims, rather than leaving them to the consensus of society (as Grotius and Pufendorf still had claimed), the concept of *natural* rights becomes not only detached from the community but also stretched to indefinable limits.

If already the state of nature grants such extensive rights, the need to move to a civil state becomes much weaker. For Hobbes, that move had been dictated by the very need to survive. Locke, however, is forced to raise the question: "If man in the state of nature be so free as has been said; if he be absolute lord of his own person and possessions; equal to the greatest and subject to nobody, why will he part with his freedom?" (IX, § 123). His answer that the possibility of enjoying native rights is uncertain, because many are "no strict observers of equity and justice," exposes, once again, the tension between Locke's two different conceptions of the state of nature. Was it a nonhistorical, permanent state or a primitive historical condition that in the end may not differ too much from Hobbes's pessimistic position? In either case the transition to the civic state occurs in order to *preserve* the original condition of natural law: it insures that those who fail to respect the rights of others be restrained. Civil society, then, protects existing rights; it does not establish them. The *Treatise* puts it bluntly: "The great and chief end therefore of men's unity into commonwealths, and putting themselves under government, is the preservation of their property" (IX, § 124).

In the original state of nature, Locke assumed that its members cooperated with one another. They even had a right to defend life, liberty, and property by punishing trespassers (II, § 9). But how can there be a *right* to punish, defined as "lawfully do harm to another," prior to rules to apply it? That crime ought to be punished, all agree; but it becomes a right only within a community that has legally established the conditions for doing so. Comparing Locke's position to Kant's, one commentator writes: "Locke's claim is that we have a natural right to punish and that we move to civil government in order to punish more efficiently — Kant's claim, on the other hand, is that we have a natural *need* to punish but no natural right."[20]

Far from considering the political community the source of rights, Locke argues that to join it individuals must give up some of their natural rights in order to hold the fundamental ones more safely. Individuals are fully endowed with rights before the political community is established. The role of the civil state becomes thereby reduced to what Otto Gierke calls "an insurance company" for the protection of property and liberty.[21] Ironically, to protect those very interests other eighteenth-century liberals, Hume, Smith, and Bentham, opposed a theory of natural rights. In their view, it might lead to social instability and obstruct material progress.[22] Inspired by communitarian considerations, Edmund Burke also rejected those abstract individual rights. He denied the legitimacy of the French Revolution because, he claimed, it was based on nothing but the "abstraction" of human rights, an unreal "metaphysic" concocted by men of letters and philosophers.[23]

The thesis of natural rights responded to economic and political conditions that prevailed during the later seventeenth century. The concept of individual human rights detached the person from the restrictive ties to the state and thus benefited the economic expansion that had just begun. While Britain, having introduced a constitutional government based on the theory of natural rights, entered a prolonged period of prosperity that eventually made her the economic ruler of the world, France stagnated socially and economically before erupting in a series of violent political revolutions that were to last more than half a century. At the same time we wonder whether the economic success of a social system that one-sidedly favors the individual over the community justifies the theory as it was formulated in the eighteenth century. How little protection it offered against the pauperization of large parts of the population became obvious in the early stages of industrial capitalism. Since then, however, most Western societies have reincorporated the theory of rights within some *order* of right, rather than linking it to a vague notion of human nature. Nor is the artificial distinction between a state of nature ruled by natural rights and a social or political state ruled by positive laws still needed to legitimate the foundations of the just society. That distinction served a purpose during the Enlightenment as it drew attention to the neglected place of the *individual* in the absolutist structure of the national state. Today the concept of a state of nature in which humans have rights independently of any communitarian structure would only perpetuate the social abuses caused by an individualist theory of society.

The Social Contract

The theory of social contract was less a scientific interpretation of political facts than an ideology for change. As formulated in the late seventeenth and eighteenth centuries, it had little basis in history. Its meaning differed substantially from a notion that bore the same name in the sixteenth century. According to the earlier theory, human beings lived in structured societies from the beginning and needed no contract to do so. The contract concerned merely the particular form of government they wished to adopt. Thus according to Francisco Suarez, the chief political theorist among sixteenth-century Scholastics, humans constituted a *unified* group — *corpus quoddam mysticum* — when they adopted or rejected a particular political system. Hugo Grotius had projected the idea of a prepolitical condition as a working hypothesis for the purpose of extending to international law the legal principles valid within a nation. But he did not question the thesis that humans have always lived in structured societies any more than the Scholastics did.

For Locke and his followers in Britain and later in France and Germany, the idea of a social contract had to serve a different purpose, namely, to justify the modern state. According to them, the natural law, conceived as a historical process, drove humans from a prepolitical to a political state. They thereby assumed (1) that the civil state constitutes an advanced "stage in the evolution of natural law itself . . . added to [that of] the pure natural law,"[24] and (2) that the human race consists of discrete individuals able to form a society only by explicit consent. The social contract was the only legitimate means to move from one state to another.[25] A free decision of individual wills thereby became the only legitimate foundation of society. Nonetheless, contrary to Hobbes, Locke regarded the state of nature as a genuinely social state. He rarely speaks of a social "contract" but instead prefers the term "compact," with its connotation of communitarian trust. Nor does he distinguish two stages in the transition from the state of nature to that of civil society: first, a *social* contract to introduce social cohesion among individuals and next a *political* contract to constitute political sovereignty. Even as Hobbes before him and Rousseau after him, Locke assumed that humans become social by their own free will. The problematic thesis that humans transform themselves from sociable into social beings follows from the modern principle that persons *choose* their own way of being. If they live in society, it must be because they decided to do so. The social contract seals that decision and converts the mass into a coherent body.

Humans are by nature sociable. This induces them, Locke argues, by formal agreement to enter into a politically structured society. Those who do so freely submit "to the determination of the majority" (VIII, § 97) and convey a limited mandate to a governmental power that executes the decisions that their legislating representatives have made into law. The genius of Locke's theory lay not so much in the division of powers as in the way he balanced them against each other, nowhere more so than in the relation between the power of the executive and the legislative. The executive convokes and supervises the legislative but obeys its decisions and remains subordinate to it. Yet as circumstances change and no written law keeps pace with historical vicissitudes, the legislative must leave some discretionary power to the executive — which Locke calls the "prerogative" (XIV, § 159–60). It even allows the government sometimes to act "against the direct letter of the law" (XIV, § 164).

Locke influenced all political philosophers in France during the eighteenth century, yet not all accepted his version of a social contract. Montesquieu rejected it. According to him, there could only be a political contract. In the *Lettres persanes* he writes: "I have never heard people speaking of public right without starting with a careful research about the origin of society — which I consider ridiculous. In fact they are linked to each other from birth. A son is born near his father, and he stays there. That is society and the cause of society."[26] For Rousseau, on the contrary, the idea of a social contract forms the centerpiece of his political philosophy: it makes a political contract superfluous. Yet he does not derive it from the theory of natural law as Locke had done. His argument rests primarily on historical grounds. All rights and obligations of modern society are to be initiated by an explicit agreement. In *Julie,* Rousseau had presented a romantic model of a natural society. In his political writings, the *Discourse on the Origins of Inequality* and *The Social Contract,* he showed how modern society precludes the kind of natural community that people once enjoyed in "the state of nature." The current political system needed drastically to be reformed. Yet whatever changes it required, they would not aim at restoring the state of nature but at removing society as far from its original state as possible.

In his early *Discourse on Inequality* (1755), Rousseau assumed that the original condition of the human race was one of equality. Since no private property divided people, their earliest state was not one of war, as Hobbes had assumed. But neither was it fully social. Savages are neither social nor antisocial. They are "sociables en puissance" as Rousseau was to describe them in *Emile.* Still some social bond must have existed among them. Otherwise humans would never have learned how to speak. Yet in that primitive state humans had no defined obligations to one another. They were "neither good nor bad, virtuous or vicious."[27] Upon entering the pastoral stage humans became more fully social. Still, they continued to live on a footing of equality and their societies needed no formal contracts. With the invention of metallurgy and agriculture, however, production began to exceed immediate needs and private property emerged. With it came strife, social chaos, and the kind of war that Hobbes had attributed to the entire state of nature.

The passage on private property that introduces the second part of Rousseau's *Discourse on the Origin of Inequality* has become famous. "The first man who having enclosed a piece of ground, bethought himself of saying *This is mine,* and found people simple enough to believe him, was the real founder of civil society. From how many crimes, wars, and murder, how many horrors and misfortunes might not any one have saved mankind, by pulling up the stakes, or filling up the ditch, and crying to his fellows, 'Beware of listening to this imposter.' "[28] Rousseau, then, regards as the source of all evil what Locke had considered the beginning of the humanization process. The laws and institutions of the existing political states legitimate this condition of social injustice. As political powers grow stronger, inequality spreads from the economic to all social levels until society becomes divided into a class of masters and one of slaves. Such inequality prepares a radical social revolution.

In the *Social Contract* (1762) Rousseau shows that modern civil society needs a contract to survive. Yet it fundamentally differs from Locke's in two respects.

1. The very possibility of a *contract,* for him, presupposes a state of equality,

a condition that does not exist wherever private property has already established an unequal distribution of power. By recognizing property as a natural right that precedes the contract, Locke's contract legalized an existing inequality and thereby perpetuated it. No free person would ever sign a contract whereby he loses everything and gains nothing! "Such an act of surrender is illegitimate, null, and void by the mere fact that he who makes it is not in his right mind." Much less can one assume that a whole people have lost their senses.[29] Rousseau derived his argument from *L'esprit des lois*. In bk. XV, chap. 2, Montesquieu argues that a contract whereby one party loses its freedom is by its very nature invalid. Nor is it legally enforceable. No man can sell himself or his children in slavery. Civil law cannot forbid a slave from fleeing from his master, since slavery has deprived him or her of the equality of rights on which civil society rests.[30] Locke himself presents some version of this argument, though he supports it on different, religious grounds. "A man, not having the power of his own life, cannot, by compact or his own consent, enslave himself to anyone, nor put himself under the absolute, arbitrary power of another to take away his life when he pleases" (IV, § 23). Yet, Locke did not consider an unequal distribution of property sufficient to invalidate a social contract. Quite the contrary, the social contract's main purpose is to *protect* existing property rights. Indeed, it is hard to see what Rousseau himself understands by contractual equality. He does not require that private property be abolished: "I do not mean that power and wealth must be absolutely the same for all, but only that power should need no sanction of violence but be exercised solely by virtue of rank and legality" (*SC*, II, 1). In his *Discourse on Political Economy* he argues only for a rough equality of private holdings.

2. The transition to a legitimate civil society should not imply any sacrifice of freedom. No one can by contract alienate even part of his freedom. To do so would deprive the person of the full moral responsibility required for a legal contract. Even if an individual were able to sacrifice part of his or her freedom, such a contract would not be binding on his or her descendants. "They are born free, their liberty belongs to them, and no one but themselves has a right to dispose of it" (*SC*, I, 4). Nor does the original state of nature form an adequate basis for social rights (as Locke believed), since rights require a degree of reflection not yet present in a state ruled by instinct rather than by reason. "Rousseau distinguishes the primitive natural right antecedent to reason from the natural right established by reason."[31] Only if the natural law is recognized as the law of reason, does it establish a ground for social rights.

People will not cross the chasm that divides the civil from the natural state until "the obstacles to continuing in the state of Nature were stronger than the forces which each individual could employ to the end of continuing it" (*SC*, I,

6). Once made, however, the social contract transforms the person "into part of something greater than himself" (*SC*, II, 7). He receives new powers and rights but must surrender all personal control over them. Is Rousseau not contradicting the very condition he set up for a contract to be valid? How can a person surrender what is by nature inalienable? On one side, he opposes Hobbes's thesis that in the state of nature might is right and that, upon entering civil society, a person surrenders his natural rights (*SC*, I, 3). On the other side, he argues that once the social contract is in place, there occurs "a complete alienation by each associate member of the community of all his rights" (*SC*, I, 6). Civil liberty becomes "curtailed by the general will" (*SC*, I, 8). Rousseau justifies this apparent loss by claiming that the social contract does not abolish natural rights, but *transforms* them and thereby secures a safer possession of them. Here also lies the ground for Rousseau's recognizing only a social contract and not a second, political one, contrary to Samuel Pufendorf, the weightiest German political thinker of that time, who held that a pact of social equality, granting all members of society the same rights and obligations, must precede a political pact by which they transfer political power to chosen leaders. Rousseau firmly rejects such a political contract: the institution of a government requires no contract at all, since the citizens release no power. "To argue that the sovereign [that is, the citizens all made equal by the social contract] can impose a superior upon himself is absurd and contradictory" (*SC*, II, 16). Government remains a function of the people. Those charged with executive powers are functionaries, not masters, who apply the laws made by the people.

We now turn to what undoubtedly is the linchpin in Rousseau's political theory — the conception of the *general will* (*la volonté générale*). Marsilius of Padua (1280–1343), writing centuries earlier, mentions the common will of the citizens as the source of all secular authority. "Their minds are reciprocally stimulated to consider that truth at which not one of them could arrive apart or separately from the others."[32] Rousseau first used the term *volonté générale* in an article, "Economie politique," published in volume V of the *Encyclopédie* (in 1755). In this essay, sometimes called the *Third Discourse,* he follows Locke's ideas and terminology. He even claims that the purpose of the social compact is to secure the peaceful possession of property, thereby squarely contradicting the central thesis of the *Discourse on Inequality,* published the same year.[33] In spite of this individualistic tendency, he claims that the general will overrules all particular pursuits of private interests. It is the source of social virtue and constitutes the body politic as a moral being (*A Discourrse in Political Economy in the Social Contract and Discourses,* pp. 253, 264). In *The Social Contract,* the general will assumes an even more autocratic character. It brooks no dissent. Since not *all* particular wills spontaneously agree with the general will, the state must educate its citizens and, if necessary, compel them "to be free" (*SC*, III, 15).

Rousseau optimistically hoped to prevent abuses by a strict political control of education and religion. As early as the *Discourse on Political Economy* he wrote: "If children are brought up in common in the bosom of equality; if they are imbued with the laws of the state and the precepts of the general will ... we cannot doubt that they will nothing contrary to the will of society" (p. 269). According to *The Social Contract,* this concept of public education was to become law. It remained, of course, far removed from the precepts given in *Emile,* Rousseau's guide on education, published the same year. Yet the two concepts were not wholly incompatible. *Emile* contains the rules for educating a child in the imperfect society in which we now live, whereas the education to citizenship presented in *The Social Contract* aims at the ideal state.[34]

A constant subject of controversy has been Rousseau's conception of the state's relation to religion. As a powerful body, the Church might easily stir up resistance to political decisions. Rousseau therefore requires that the state strictly control religion. In addition, all citizens must swear allegiance to a "civil religion" established for the sole purpose of fostering good citizenship.[35] "Though it has no power to compel anyone to believe, it can banish from the State all who fail to do so" (*SC*, IV, 8).[36]

The social contract conveys all power to the body politic and deprives the existing intermediate bodies of authority. Absolute sovereignty can be neither delegated nor mediated: Rousseau replaces the entire hierarchy of economic, cultural, and religious associations by a unitary state. As Hegel was to point out in his *Philosophy of Right* (1820), this suppression of "civil society" (*Bürgerliche Gesellschaft*) abolished any possibility of mediating particular interests with the common good and thereby prepared major conflicts.[37] Rousseau assumed that those semi-independent corporations increased social inequality. Little did he foresee that allowing the state to absorb their role would weaken its economic effectiveness while deepening economic disparity. He had no notion of the dynamic potential of a free market economy. He conceived of wealth as a constant factor, so that one person's increase of it would entail another's equal decrease. Still, the principles of modern economy had been clearly spelled out by the French economist Quesnay in the very volume of the *Encyclopédie* in which his own *Discours* appeared.[38]

Rousseau's theory inspired the principles of the French Revolution as well as those of every totalitarian regime in the West. Parties of the extreme right no less than of the extreme left have found their dogmas in *The Social Contract*. It influenced the fascist theory of the strong state as well as the communist dogma that after a period of political dictatorship, society would no longer need a political state. The surprising fact that both egalitarian and totalitarian regimes have been inspired by Rousseau's political doctrine is due to the fundamental ambiguity that lies at its root. A state based on a contract among all members is in principle egalitarian. Yet since no principle of universal order restricts its authority, that authority inevitably becomes totalitarian.[39] With the hindsight of history one may find it hard to disagree with Ernest Barker's melancholy conclusion: "There is no comfort for the Center in all the shot fabric of Rousseau's book. That is why it is natural and even permissible to prefer the hodden gray of Locke's cloth to the brilliant but parti-colored silk of Rousseau."[40]

The Legal Foundations of Society: Universal Principles and Historical Traditions

Charles-Louis de Secondat, baron de Montesquieu, collaborated on the *Encyclopédie* and strongly supported constitutional reform. Yet his historical studies on the origin and development of legal institutions in France had taught him the limits of change that a political tradition allowed. Although on religious issues he was a rationalist, on political ones he often assumes an antirationalist position. Compared to the political writings of Locke and Rousseau, Montesquieu's monumental *De l'esprit des lois* (1748), despite its comprehensive title, appears far less ambitious. It contains no a priori principles of legislation that may be universally applied. Nor do his conclusions present a universal system of government. The author may have begun his historical investigation with an eye on constitutional reform in France. Yet contrary to his younger contemporary Jean-Jacques Rousseau, the president of the Academy of Bordeaux was no revolutionary. Aware that history and geography impose severe limits on the possibility of change, he understood that no radically new society could replace the complex social fabric it had taken centuries to weave. The origin as well as the development of the main political systems — monarchy, aristocracy, and democracy — depend in each instance on specific historical and physical conditions. In the preface the author states: "I write not to censure anything established in any country whatsoever. Every nation will here find the reasons on which its maxims are founded; and this will be the natural inference, that to propose alterations belongs only to those who are so happy as to be born with a genius capable of penetrating the entire constitution of a state."[41] Montesquieu's declaration of neutrality is somewhat disingenuous: he *does* want change, but no revolution.

The secret of a country's past lies buried in customs, laws, and legal institutions., and these also set limits to its future. (The Italian jurist Gravina had already shown not only that laws determine the course of history, but that history determines the development of the laws.)[42] Nor did the author of *The Spirit of Laws* share the assumption of constant historical progress held by so many of his contemporaries. No political system is perfect and all are bound to decline. Neither do ascent and decline follow a uniform pattern, as they do in Vico's cyclical view of history. Montesquieu's theory, less sweeping, stays closer to empirically proven facts. A nation's success or failure depends on historical circumstances over which it has only limited control. In an early essay, "Observations on Nature" (1721), Montesquieu had praised Descartes's system for dispensing with any idea of divine intervention in nature beyond the general movement of matter.[43] His own conception of history followed an analogous principle. The course of history follows from inherent causes, some of them physical and some moral. They alone determine the fate of a political system: they raise it, preserve it, and destroy it. God has left the human world as well as the natural one to its own inner dynamics.

Events, singularly considered, may seem contingent. But viewed in their historical context they all have causes, albeit often remote ones. "If the fortune of a battle, that is, a particular cause, has ruined a State, a general cause was always responsible for the fact that this State had to be ruined by a single battle."[44] Montesquieu stresses the historical uniqueness of each political society. All undergo external influences, but each one absorbs them in its own way. Visigothic and Lombardic societies both were subject to Germanic law and both underwent the influence of Roman law, yet they assimilated that influence in wholly different ways and thereby gave birth to distinct forms of Frankish legislation (bk. XXXVIII).

Nothing is more instructive of Montesquieu's method than the historical monographs on Roman laws of succession (XXVII), on French civil law (XXVIII), and on Frankish feudal law (XXX, XXXI, XXXVIII) that appear in the final part of *The Spirit of Laws*. Together with book XI on British and Roman law, they constitute a remarkable contribution to legal history. Here especially the great historian deserves the praise the French critic Sainte-Beuve, who credited him with the gravity of Titus Livy, the expressiveness of Sallust, and the imaginative power of Tacitus. The essay on the Roman laws of succession (XXVII), a pioneering study of a development the sources of which lay hidden in obscure antiquity, continues to rank among the classics on the development of Roman law. It establishes the principles and limits of eminent domain in republican Rome, where the common good took absolute priority over any private claims. Later writers judged Montesquieu to have been insufficiently critical of his sources. Perhaps, but at least he overcame the anachronistic prejudices common to his contemporaries. In *The Spirit of Laws* he expresses his constant concern "not to modernize all the ancient ages" (XXX, 14).

These historical essays possess great merit in their own right, though they often fit but awkwardly within the whole. Several of them were written long before the final composition of the book. Thus, the long sixth chapter of book XI on the British constitution was written before 1743 (and most of it before 1738) in the form of a report on his 1731–34 visit to England. Another essay, "Considération sur les richesses de l' Espagne," written in the 1720s, appears integrally as chapter 22 of book XXI. Two historical investigations in particular played a central role in the establishment of Montesquieu's method. The impact of Frankish legal institution on French law (bk. XXXVIII) proved to be important for discovering the roots of the French civil tradition and hence for defining the possibilities of reform. The other, a description of the British political system, served as a realistic model for the distribution of political powers.

The influence of Frankish feudal institutions on French law had long been a controversial subject in France. Two opposite interpretations existed. In his *Histoire de l'ancien gouvernement de la France* (posthumously published in 1727), Henri de Boulainvilliers had argued that French institutions plunged their roots in Frankish feudal law that allowed the free men of the tribe to elect or depose their chieftains. This "natural right" of the aristocracy had fallen into desuetude when tribal leadership became hereditary. According to Boulainvilliers, the development toward a monarchy had deflected French history from its traditional course. Early Frankish power had rested with the nobility and it ought to have stayed there. Another text disputed this claim of the aristocracy. Abbé Jean-Baptiste Dubos, in his *Histoire critique de l'établissement de la monarchie française dans les Gaules* (1734), had defended the thesis that the French state had a monarchic origin. The Franks, when entering Gaul at the invitation of the Roman authorities, did, in fact, inherit the imperial rights. Charlemagne's consecration in 800 merely confirmed that inherited sovereignty. Montesquieu adopted the former position, claiming that French institutions were basically of Frankish origin, but he allowed for a strong Roman influence in diverse regions of France. In *The Spirit of Laws* he reported the results of these historical investigations and drew some general conclusions from them concerning the founding principles of civil societies and the means to preserve them.

Faithfulness to tradition is an indispensable condition for preserving a state from major harm, but it is not sufficient to secure its survival. Tradition merely sets the limits within which the state's well-being must be sought. But its actual well-being depends in the first place on the harmony among the functions through which it exercises its powers: the powers to make laws, to execute them, and to interpret them as well as to deal with those who break them. These functions ought to be exercised by separate bodies, each one of which needs to possess sufficient authority to keep the others in balance. In book XI, Montesquieu describes a model of what he regards as the most successful distribution of powers, namely, the British political system. England was a monarchy, but a similar balance might be obtained in an aristocratic or a democratic government. Nor did Montesquieu unqualifiedly admire the political attitude of the English. His critique of them in book XIX, 27 is quite harsh.[45] In his view, England achieved its exemplary balance as much by its weaknesses as by its strengths. The peculiar defects of the English people assisted them in restoring the balance of power which a monarchy tends to disturb. A king tends to weaken or, as in France, to abolish the intermediary bodies indispensable for a balance of powers (VIII, 6). Yet in a nation that lacks the virtue needed for supporting a strong monarchical state, the crown is too weak to encroach upon intermediary bodies. The strength of a monarchy rests on a *sense of honor* among citizens who consider it the highest reward to be honored by the king. Montesquieu claims about the English of his time that they were too much concerned about their material interests to be bothered about honor.

But this mundane attitude itself stems from the very liberty they had enjoyed for a long time and indicates that political powers in England had somehow always had been more in balance than they were in France. A free state allows its citizens to pursue their own interests, and thus "this nation, which liberty and the laws render easy, has become a trading people" (XIX, 27). Liberty, however, is effect as well as cause. Precisely because the English, according to Montesquieu, have an extreme passion for independence, they succeeded in building a political system that guaranteed the highest political liberty. *Independence* (the desire to do as one pleases) and *liberty* (the power to do what one *ought* to do) are by no means identical: the former is a vice, the latter a state of perfection (XI, 31). Yet the former has brought the English to such a heightened "love of liberty" that they are willing to suffer any hardship, pay any taxes, fight any war to preserve their liberty (XIX, 27).

How does Montesquieu, who repeatedly stresses the historical uniqueness of each nation's political institutions, succeed in formulating universal rules? In fact, he does start from one general assumption. The primary laws, he argues, are the laws of nature, "the necessary relations arising from the nature of things" (I, 1). That these relations follow a rational order requires no proof, he argues, since this world and its inhabitants have been created by an obviously intelligent Being and must therefore be intrinsically rational. Through positive laws humans attempt to adapt the laws of nature to the physical and moral conditions of their geographical area and historical tradition (I, 3). As I have pointed out, Montesquieu here returns to a descriptive concept of nature, such as the physical sciences adopt when they refer to the laws of nature. Nonetheless, he starts his investigation with the foundation of a universal, a priori principle, namely, that intelligent beings in establishing their social institutions are guided, or at least ought to be guided, by reason (I, 1). The natural law, then, demands of humans that they organize their political life in a rational way. Institutions that conflict with reason ought to be changed or abolished altogether. I suppose Montesquieu would justify this rule on the ground that not doing so would eventually lead to their destruction. He devotes much of book XXVI to a discussion of laws invalidated by the fact that they conflict with this basic rationality.

At the same time, he describes history as a continuous, causally determined chain, in which past traditions continue to define present political needs. At times the reformist and the historical strands in Montesquieu's theory appear to conflict with one another. The laws and institutions of a nation's past form a powerful counterweight to the moral force of the natural law. To bypass tradition, except when it directly conflicts with essential principles of natural law, is ineffective as well as politically hazardous. Montesquieu illustrates this point by the strange ways in which Czar Peter the Great attempted to modernize his subjects, obliging them to cut off their beards and to shorten their clothes (XIX, 14). From the successes and failures of Western societies in adapting their laws to their ancient traditions he also draws some general conclusions. But these are descriptive universals, not a priori precepts for any society.

The discussion of the moral attitudes required for the survival of political systems often exceeds the descriptive method that Montesquieu usually follows. All legitimate constitutions need some form of political virtue to succeed. None more so than the democratic state. It demands devotion to the republic, love of equality, and sobriety of living (V, 3). An aristocratic government requires an attitude of moderation. Modesty and simplicity are called "la vertu dans l'aristocracie" (V, 8). Similarly, honor, characteristic of the monarchy, must include a code of moral conduct as well as a hierarchical court system. Only despotism requires no virtue to survive: fear suffices. Essential in all systems is a general respect for the laws of the land.

Still, moral attitudes alone do not suffice for preserving a civil society. Legislation must remain in tune with the specific demands of each form of government. Inappropriate institutional changes will ruin any political system, no matter how moral its leading class may be. An aristocratic government becomes corrupted once the nobles grow arrogant, but no less so when their power becomes hereditary, for inherited power undermines the spirit of an aristocratic constitution (VIII, 5). A monarchy violates its principles when it sets out to conquer territories that lie beyond a nation's natural boundaries. A democracy can be preserved only as long as citizens actively participate in political life. In addition, the balance among the classes must be maintained. The demise of the Roman republic shows how a democracy disturbs this balance by seeking indiscriminate equality (*Le peuple pour établir la démocratie choqua les principes mêmes de la démocratie* [XI, 16]). Or when one social class obtains privileges denied to other classes, as when the representatives of the plebeians, the tribunes, were given the right to veto legislation or to elicit plebiscites, while neither the senate nor the magistrates possessed the power to overrule the people's veto right (XI, 6). Similarly, when the populist Gracchi succeeded in having judicial power transferred from the senatorial to the mercantile, equestrian order, their action, rather than mediating between patricians and plebeians, turned that power over to the most selfish class, which used it for its own profit. "Attempting to protect the freedom of the citizen [the plebeians] struck at that of the constitution; but the former perished with the latter" (XI, 18).

In the second part of *The Spirit of Laws* (bks. XIV–XVIII), Montesquieu abruptly changes the tenor of his argument by introducing the controversial thesis that political systems, as well as the attitudes that support them, are conditioned by climate, geography, air. At times his position comes close to physical determinism, as when it links slavery and servile attitudes to indolence induced by a hot climate. Where climate discourages labor, Montesquieu claims, humans must be forced to work. He qualifies this statement, however, by insisting that good laws are capable of overcoming all negative environmental conditions, and that bad laws, more than a hot climate, induce indolence. "Possibly there is not that climate upon earth where the most laborious services might not with proper encouragement be performed by free men. Bad laws having made lazy men, they have been reduced to slavery because of their laziness" (XV, 8). The purpose of good laws is precisely to overcome the negative impact of the climate.

Still, all other conditions being equal, inhabitants of hot regions, being less motivated to cooperate actively toward establishing a political order, are more likely to fall under the sway of a despotic authority. Thus Montesquieu attributes the political geography of Asia to its continental climate. In Asia, unlike in Europe, hot zones are directly adjacent to cold ones, he argues. As a result the brave races of the cold regions could easily conquer their indolent neighbors. This gave rise to the enormous empires of the East. In Europe, on the contrary, the inhabitants of moderate climates live next to nations with almost similar climates. Thus they keep each other in balance (XVII, 3–4). In this, the shortest part of Montesquieu's work, the careful analyses of Roman and Germanic laws have made room for sweeping generalizations rarely supported by accurate information. The weight of *The Spirit of Laws* does not rest on this crude sociologism, though unfortunately it is the part mostly remembered today.

Later, Montesquieu strongly qualifies the geographic thesis. Physical causality is always mediated by "moral attitudes." For instance, the nature of commerce depends on the geographical conditions in which trading nations find themselves: they evidently differ in an island such as Great Britain from those prevailing in the landlocked nations of Central Asia. While the former require sea trade, the latter must follow caravan routes. Yet the decisive factor is how effectively a nation knows how to exploit its physical conditions. Most important, Montesquieu here establishes a link between the nature of laws and what he calls the *spirit* of the nation. The very title of book XIX suggests a close dependence of one on the other: "Of laws in relation to the *principles which form the general spirit,* morals and customs of a nation" (my emphasis). Unfortunately, the lengthy argument through which the author intends to prove his thesis may count as one of the most disorderly in a work notorious for the looseness of its composition. He ominously announces at the beginning: "I shall be obliged to wander to the right and to the left that I may investigate and discover the truth" (XIX, 1). After reading the many pages devoted to Chinese customs, Spanish character, Russian beards, and Athenian wits, no reader will doubt the truth of this prediction. The coherence of *The Spirit of Laws* also suffers from Montesquieu's mode of composing. He rarely completes an argument. The French literary historian Gustave Lanson aptly described it: "His reflection is not a continuous act, but a series of isolated acts, each of which begins and determines a separate effort between two pauses."[46]

Nevertheless, three conclusions emerge with sufficient clarity. (1) Each nation possesses a spirit of its own formed by climate, customs, religion, and moral and legal tradition. (2) "The legislature must follow this spirit when it is not contrary to the principles of government" (XIX, 5). (3) The legal principles, once established through the customs of a tribe or the foundational laws of a republic, influence the character, customs, and spirit of the people. In this same book XIX, Montesquieu ranks conditioning factors in a hierarchy that begins with the physical ones. As the social factors grow stronger, mainly under the impact of religion, morality, and law, the impact of the physical ones grows weaker. Good laws build nations by bringing customs, traditions, climatic and geographical conditions into harmonious coordination.

In his intellectual biography, Robert Shackleton describes how Montesquieu views the educational task of the legislator: "[He] must shift the emphasis, within the framework of the *esprit général,* from physical factors to moral factors. He must rely less than his predecessors on climate, and more on manners, morals, laws, religion, and the appeal to past usage."[47] The possibility of establishing good laws decreases when a nation attaches a disproportionate weight to custom and tradition, as Montesquieu thought to be the case in China, or when moral norms are inappropriate to custom and climate, as they were in Sparta. Only a balanced combination of customs, morals, and laws allows a nation to attain political maturity. Viewed from this perspective, the chapters on climate and soil lose much of their significance.

Historians have objected to the abstractness of Montesquieu's concept of law and to the sweeping conclusions he draws from single instances. Rightly so. But his insight that laws must be studied within the wider context of the history of a nation and that the laws themselves play a determining role in shaping that history has proven to be enduring. The discussion of the development of civil law in the territory of France (bk. XXVIII) sets a model for a new mode of history writing: laws and institutions are active agents of history as well as reflections of the history of a nation.[48] Others had written histories of legal institutions: Montesquieu had learned much from Jean Domat's *Les lois civiles dans leur ordre naturel* (1689) and from Gian Vincenzo Gravina's *Origines juris civilis* (1717). Yet his own work surpassed these specialized studies in assessing the relation between the laws and their historical context.

Montesquieu never fully clarified the relation between the universal principles of natural law that he assumed lay at the root of legislation and the particularity of laws conditioned by the historically developed *esprit d'une nation.* How seriously do legislators aspire to fulfill the natural law, which is supposed to direct their work? Natural law and historical necessity stand side by side. The idea of natural law, though conceived much more concretely by Montesquieu than by the natural law philosophers, remains abstract in *The Spirit of Laws* and history appears to have no part in it. Even this outstanding historian of law had not entirely overcome the antihistorical bias of rationalist thought. The discrepancy between the universal and the particular discloses, once again, the dualism that, since its Cartesian beginnings, had inhered to rationalist thought. A comparison between Montesquieu's *esprit de la nation* and Herder's *Volksgeist* reveals the dualistic character of the French concept. As we shall see in the next chapter, for the German thinker, the spirit of a nation integrates the historical uniqueness of a people with the destiny of other, equally unique nations within the universality of a common humanity (*Humanität*).

Similarly, that universal humanity functioned as the all-inclusive, meaning-giving idea of the particular national identities.

The Social-Economic versus the Political: The Triumph of the Particular

In the *Second Treatise on Civil Government* John Locke described property as an essential condition for preserving life and liberty (VIII, § 87). In that same text appears the influential idea of labor as constituting the original title to property. Work alone allows the individual to lay private claims to what by nature belongs to all (V, § 27–28). In his theory a new social category comes to existence: economic value. " 'Tis labor indeed that puts the difference of value on everything" (V, § 40). The rise of capitalism in the fifteenth century and particularly the adoption of mercantilist policies by the governments of Spain and France in the next two centuries had brought economics to the center of social life. The governments of those countries had equated national wealth with a favorable balance of trade. The inflation caused by Spain's massive import of gold from the American colonies had caused that country to go bankrupt. Before the middle of the eighteenth century, France, more diversified in its trade yet impoverished by the wasteful policies of Louis XIV, came close to the same fate. Faced with this impending disaster, a group of French intellectuals led by the royal physician François Quesnay (1694–1774) and finance minister Anne-Robert-Jacques Turgot (1727–81), concluded that national wealth consisted not in hoarding gold or silver but in agricultural production. In their view, agricultural labor alone brings more goods into the world than it expends. The Physiocrats, as they were called, favored free markets and capital accumulation. Attempting to convert the ideals of the Enlightenment into attainable goals, they perceived their efforts as serving the cause of freedom and progress. To succeed in this, however, the egalitarian dreams expressed by writers on economics in the *Encyclopédie* (first of all, Rousseau's) had to be abandoned.

During a year spent in France, Adam Smith, the Scottish author of *The Theory of Moral Sentiments,* acquainted himself with these new theories, to which he never ceased to acknowledge his debt. But Locke's universal theory of labor convinced him that the Physiocrats' theory erred in restricting economic value to agricultural labor. *All* productive labor creates value. Locke had identified labor as the original title to ownership. Smith declared labor the source of value itself and thereby emancipated economic value from what Marx was to call the "fetishism of commodities." Economic value, which earlier writers had regarded as a function of use, Smith declared to be a value in its own right, essentially different from "use value." The value of labor in a capitalist economy is not to be determined by the use of its product. Economic or exchange value must be computed according to the difference between what the producer invests in labor and the instruments of labor on one side, and the price received for the product on the other. From this difference Ricardo, the most original of Smith's followers, developed the concept of "surplus value." Marx took this a further step, attributing "surplus value" entirely to "surplus labor," that is, labor for which the worker has not been compensated. His move was highly questionable but reveals an ambiguity in Smith's concept of value.

In 1776 appeared Smith's *An Inquiry into the Nature and Causes of the Wealth of Nations,* the founding treatise of classical political economy. It detached economics from its earlier link with the state. Of course, by increasing the wealth of individuals, economic exchange raises the nation's cumulative wealth. But free exchange cannot be restricted to one nation. Indeed, from an economic perspective the state mainly serves as a means. Exchange takes place among individuals or among particular groups. If, as Locke and Smith assumed, the function of the political state consists primarily in the protection of property and property relations, the political order becomes in fact reduced to a social umbrella over interindividual relations. Where economic well-being of its citizens becomes the principal aim of the state, the relation between politics and economy becomes inverted from its original position. What formerly functioned as an indispensable support of political life now subordinates the state to international economic activity. In Rousseau's *Social Contract* the state had absorbed all social spheres within itself, including the economic one. In Smith's *Wealth of Nations* the state became a particular segment of civil society, namely, the one that legalized and protected property relations.

Smith's economic theory did not directly conflict with his earlier moral ideal. Indeed, his economic argument owed a great deal to the moral principles he had developed in his *Theory of Moral Sentiments*. Francis Hutcheson had taught him that universal benevolence harmonized private with public interests. Nor need this benevolence be intentional. Those who merely seek their own interests are often "led by an invisible hand . . . without knowing it, without intending it, to advance the interest of society." Still, the "invisible hand" of *The Wealth of Nations* was no call to virtue, but rather an assumption that the uninhibited pursuit of personal gain contributes most to the common good. In economics, the need for benevolent intentions ceases to exist altogether. Where public wealth is the goal and exchange the means, self-interest is the only effective motive. We know the famous lines: "It is not from the benevolence of the butcher, the brewer, or the baker that we expect our dinner, but from their regard to their own interest. We address ourselves, not to their humanity but to their self-love, and never talk to them of our own necessities but of their advantages."[49] To be economically credible the virtue of benevolence demands an active pursuit of economic success. Smith had dimly foreseen this conclusion in his *Moral Sentiments:* "In the middling and inferior stations of life, the road to virtue and that to fortune . . . are happily in most cases very nearly the same."[50] What had been a concession in Smith's moral philosophy became a law in his economic theory.

The moral justification of selfishness had been the sarcastic theme of Mandeville's *The Fable of the Bees,* a book universally censured yet commonly believed. After having piously criticized it, Smith had to admit that the cynical author had a point; "How destructive soever this system may appear, it could never have imposed upon so great a number of persons, had it not in some respects bordered on the truth."[51] Smith even appeared willing to accept the darker consequences of Mandeville's principle as inevitable. The author of *The Fable* had predicted that the building up of capital required an amount of labor that workers would be reluctant to perform except under the pressure of survival. Employers should not take away that pressure. "It is wisdom to relieve [poverty], but folly to cure."[52] The abolition of child labor and of illiteracy ought not to be recommended, the cynic Mandeville declared, since it would leave much needed tedious work undone. The kindly Adam Smith never stated those brutal conclusions, but the premises of his argument left little room for alternatives.[53]

Unlike Mandeville, however, Smith felt a genuine concern for the fate of the workers and anxiously stressed the moral importance of such virtues as honesty in business transactions, prompt payment of wages, and a general attitude of benevolence that went beyond minimally securing the worker's survival. That kind of benevolence was likely to be rewarded by more goodwill on their part and a greater fitness for accomplishing their tasks. Still, the principles of an unrestricted market economy could not but render their lot very harsh, especially during the early period of industrial capitalism when accumulation of capital was largely to be earned at their expense. Smith followed his teacher Hutcheson in measuring moral benevolence by utilitarian principles, whereby the most "useful" actions deserve to be ranked as the most benevolent. If an undistracted pursuit of self-interest turns out to be profitable to the community as a whole, no moral argument should prevent manufacturers from following what Smith considered an unavoidable law of economic activity.

Adam Smith's economic theory emancipated the principle of utility from the moral philosophy that had given birth to it, even though it seemed to extend its application. Jeremy Bentham followed his mentor in the assumption that moral laws and economic principles run parallel. Yet he did not believe, as Smith did, that social harmony automatically resulted from a providentially pre-established order. For him, such a harmony had to be established by a deliberate effort of the legislator. Laws had to be drafted in a way that allowed individuals as well as society to attain the purpose of moral and of political life, namely, the maximum of pleasure and the minimum of pain. For this purpose the economic principle of laissez-faire did not suffice. By means of a system of punishments, the state had to force everyone to act in accordance with the principle of public utility. Political legislation was to promote public morality as well as economic progress. In fact, however, its subordination to social-economic interests definitively detached politics from ethics of which, according to the ancients, it had been the summit. In Jeremy Bentham's *Introduction to the Principles of Morals and Legislation,* the moral principle of utility could be consistently maintained only if defined by the material welfare of the whole community.[54]

Bentham himself never wavered in his conviction that the utilitarian principle could serve both as a moral rule for the individual and as a foundation of public policy. He opposed his utilitarianism to two rival theories that had dominated the moral discussion in Britain: the theory of natural law and the ethics of "moral sense" presented by Shaftesbury, Hutcheson, and Hume. The former lacks *specific* norms of action; the latter fails to justify why one's subjective feelings should be considered objectively valid principles. Still, for achieving an identity of private and public interests, Bentham eventually saw himself forced to reintroduce the need for a feeling of benevolence in human beings. The satisfaction of this feeling proved indispensable for supporting his axiom that most people would comply with the law even when their private interests appeared to suffer by it. To be sure, penal laws were needed to compel those who resisted the common good. But those laws would not suffice for creating social harmony unless the conditions for such harmony already existed. How else could one expect most people to observe laws that conflicted with their private interests, at times when they could reasonably anticipate to suffer no ill consequences from not observing them? Bentham treats private ethics as *conditioned* by general welfare, though he often derives the link between the two from feelings of benevolence or sympathy.[55]

This utilitarianism raises the question whether maximizing public happiness and minimizing public pain suffices as a basis for social policy. Few earlier theorists would have thought so. To the extent that politics is intrinsically linked to ethics, it must be guided by an idea of perfection that always exceeds, and often conflicts with, the presence of pleasure and the absence of pain.

Legislators must be educators, at least in this minimal sense that they ought to promote the intellectual, spiritual, and artistic well-being of the citizens. Making the means available for obtaining what the majority of people consider "happiness" could hardly serve as standard for public policy. To abolish all restrictions and taxes on alcoholic beverages in a country where alcoholism is rampant does little for the welfare of the citizens, though it may correspond to the desires of most. Nor should the government put public treasures (works of art or historical monuments) up for sale in a manner that depletes the cultural patrimony, even if many might prefer this to paying taxes for their maintenance. Bentham was not unacquainted with those objections. His main purpose, however, was not to construe a comprehensive political theory, but merely to establish a foundation for a theory of penal law that would prevent individuals from obstructing the common good. Moreover, to attain at least the general goal of his ethical system, a maximum of happiness and a minimum of pain, Bentham regarded the building of a strong economic foundation a necessary condition.

In the theories of Smith and Bentham it became obvious that the advent of industrial capitalism had effected a shift in the hierarchy of social values. Economic concerns came to dominate the entire social structure. Unquestionably, political economy creates the material conditions required for social coexistence on a large scale. But in the late eighteenth century the means tended to replace the end. In Greek and Roman antiquity economics had remained subordinate to politics. Even in early capitalist societies where the economic sector had assumed a crucial significance, as in the gold economy of sixteenth-century Spain and the mercantilist one of seventeenth-century France, the state had initiated, directed, and benefited from economic activity. Eighteenth-century British theories inverted the relation between economics and politics, rendering the latter subservient to the interests of the former. When industrial capitalism put these principles into practice they caused a social crisis that has continued until our own time. The domination of the political by the economic marked a fundamental reversal in our political tradition. Hannah Arendt once observed that neither the Greeks nor the Romans would have recognized the term "political economy," since politics dealt with the *res publica* and economy with the maintenance of one's private estate (*oikos*).

The writings of Edmund Burke (1729–97) appear to return to the older tradition. For him, the state was neither a product of reason nor an instrument for the promotion of economic interests but a partnership in virtue. Its concrete form and needs had been shaped by a history that, though it had not followed logical lines of development, had nonetheless resulted in the benevolent social system. Burke strongly opposed Rousseau's principles not because he rejected the concepts of natural law or natural rights, but because he considered Rousseau's rationalist formulation of rights abstract, arbitrary, and dangerous. During his long career the Irish politician supported four revolutions: the British of 1688 (in retrospect), the American (1776), that of the Indians against the East India Company (1788), and the one that led to the emancipation of Catholics in Ireland (1797). But he thoroughly repudiated the French Revolution and accurately predicted the horror of the *Terreur*. This apparent inconsistency suggests that his critique was not inspired by a conservative bent of mind but that a fundamental principle was at stake. He objected to the assumption that a political system ought to follow a priori rationalist norms identical in all places at all times. Not an abstract formulation of the natural law, but the historically *interpreted* principles of natural law ought to direct the order of society.[56] The natural law contains no blueprint for political institutions. The communal wisdom of history has incorporated that law in social customs, institutions, and civil laws.

Rousseau and most of the philosophes regarded it as their task to emancipate the whole political system from its past tradition and to bring it in conformity with reason. Montesquieu alone understood that institutions vary according to a country's historical development. But Montesquieu no more approved of the current political condition than the other philosophes did. Burke, on the contrary, regarded any radical interference with the historical tradition with great suspicion. The unpredictable and often irrational course of history realizes, in often unintelligible but nevertheless effective ways, a universal and, indeed, sacred order. Not all that occurs in history is in harmony with that order. But the longstanding tradition of a peaceful nation presents the only guidelines its citizens possess, at least until a major historical upheaval leaves them no choice but to break with part of that tradition.

Burke supports his position by the very principle that had been the main target of the Enlightenment's attacks, namely, *prejudice*. "Instead of casting away all our old prejudices, we cherish them to a very considerable degree, and, to take more shame to ourselves, we cherish them because they are prejudices; and the longer they have lasted and the more generally they have prevailed, the more we cherish them."[57] Burke's prejudices are not personal biases, nor are they irrational. They consist, in fact, in the unquestioning acceptance of time-honored institutions by the citizens of an orderly nation. The French revolutionaries intended to replace these assumptions by abstract, untested theories. "[Jacobinism] is the attempt . . . to eradicate prejudice out of the minds of men, for the purpose of putting all power and authority into the hands of persons capable of occasionally enlightening the minds of the people."[58] Those who deduce the principles of society from abstract reason start from a belief that humans are naturally reasonable and good. In fact, they are neither. Civilized life follows not the rigid rule of abstract reason, but the impulse of organic growth. Burke favorably compares what he regards as the spontaneous development of the British Constitution with the simplistic political philosophy of Rousseau and the revolutionaries.[59]

Even the idea of a common human nature appeared to Burke an inadequate basis for a political theory. The alleged natural equality of all persons, which, according to the philosophes, ought to serve as guiding principle of the political constitution, is a "monstrous fiction, which, by inspiring false ideas and vain expectations into men destined to travel in the obscure walk of laborious life, serves only to aggravate and embitter that real inequality, which it never can remove" (*Reflections*, p. 49). Nor was there ever a "state of nature" in which humans obeyed only the natural law. The so-called state of nature as well as the subsequent social contract are no more than metaphors of the human development toward more complex social structures. Not just once, but several times, did those developments require a new "political contract" to reformulate the basic principles of life in a community, especially after unpredictable events like migrations, revolutions, and military invasions. Those contracts remain in force only as long as citizens consider them appropriate to their social needs.

For Rousseau, natural rights existed before the social contract. For Burke, rights remain abstract principles until defined and granted by the established political community. He does not dispute the legitimacy of attempts to establish an order of right. But such an order must remain an ineffective ideal until it can be inserted into a nation's historical tradition. Still, Burke admitted, above the course of history stands the *law of nature*. This law overrules all existing institutions that seriously violate it. Thus he considered the revolution of 1688 fully legitimate. In fact, he denied that it was a "revolution" in the sense of a radical break with the nation's political tradition. James II was expected to impose a state religion that conflicted with the beliefs of the majority of the British people. Such an act would go against what Burke considered the respect a sovereign owed to the consciences of his subjects.

Here, however, a problem occurs. If natural rights are not a priori definable, how do we know when the government seriously violates them? Burke's answer is vague: "The rights of men are in a sort of *middle,* incapable of definition, but not impossible to be discerned" (*Reflections*, p. 75). The natural law sets a process in motion that is not completed until it becomes politically concrete in the course of which "potential" rights turn into real rights. Its outcome is unpredictable. Not only do institutions and laws change: the prin-

ciples of right themselves develop. They do not become normative independently of the concrete historical institutions to which we apply them.

Nor does a political contract abrogate the existing rights of associations
established for the attainment of religious, economic, or cultural ends. Most
significant, Burke restored the idea of civil society to its original comprehensive meaning. For Rousseau, the state was to absorb all other social bodies. In
the opposite direction, some economists tended to lower the principal function of the state to the protection of property. Burke rejected both positions.
Against Rousseau he argued that it was the task of the state to integrate the
rights and functions of existing associations within a coherent social totality.
With equal determination he repudiated the social-economic version of the
social contract. "The State ought not to be considered as nothing better than a
partnership agreement in a trade of pepper and coffee, calico or tobacco, or
some other such low concern, to be taken up for a little temporary interest,
and to be dissolved by the fancy of the parties. . . . It is a partnership in all
science; a partnership in all art; a partnership in every virtue, and in all perfection" (*Reflections*, p. 110). For Burke, all social structures — the cultural, economic, and religious as well as the political — form part of one comprehensive
civil society. They constitute a hierarchical order of which the parts are harmoniously integrated with one another and mediate one another within the encompassing synthesis of the state (*Reflections*, pp. 222, 100).

He dismisses as pure fiction any theory of a social contract conceived as a
free decision taken in a political vacuum. In reality, each social agreement
occurs within an already established social order as "a clause in the great
primeval contract of eternal society" (ibid.). It rarely requires a formal agreement. Humans are essentially "civil" as soon as they live in groups, that is,
from the beginning. They may change their social arrangements. But at no
time did a historical gap separate a presocial from a social state or a precivil
from a civil one. Disaster threatens the state that refuses to recognize existing
social institutions and cultural distinctions. The French revolutionary government, inspired by Rousseau's principles, abolished regional and corporate
differences and concentrated all power in the central authority of the state. It
broke up naturally grown regional identities and replaced historical districts
by artificial ones (provinces, arrondissements, cantons). The revolutionary
bureaucracy treated France the way the Romans treated a colony. "It boasted
that the geometrical policy has been adopted, that all local ideas should be
sunk, and that the people should no longer be Gascons, Picards, Bretons,
Normans, but Frenchmen, with one country, one heart, and one assembly. But
instead of being all Frenchmen, the greater likelihood is, that the inhabitants
of that region will shortly have no country. No man was ever attached by a

sense of pride, partiality, or real affection to a description of square measurement" (*Reflections*, p. 213).

Burke's critique was not inspired by nostalgia of the past, but by a new, organic-historical idea of the state that in many respects corresponded to the one Herder was developing at the same time in Germany. Unlike Herder, however, Burke failed to realize the historical necessity of a rupture with a past protected by a tenacious power structure such as ruled eighteenth-century France. He rejected the legitimacy of a revolution of which he only saw the excesses while legitimating four others in the name of natural rights. Yet without some a priori concept of human rights (which he rejects in his *Reflections*), no political revolution can ever be legitimated. Burke's theory remains ambiguous. At times he comes close to equating the law of nature with the course of history. At other times he regards that law as the moving power of history that stirs a people to revolution when fundamental principles of its legitimate tradition are at risk, as was the case in 1688. It is hard to see by which norm he distinguishes the English from the French revolution. Were the anticipated abuses of the Stuart monarchy in 1688 worse than the actual ones of the ancien régime in 1789 France?

Among Burke's many critics we best remember Thomas Paine of *Common Sense* (1776) fame. Paine lived in France through the revolution, was imprisoned during the *Terreur,* banished from England, and after his return to America in 1802 ostracized as a freethinker. In 1791 he published *The Rights of Man,* a direct attack on Burke's thesis and an apologia of the French Revolution. He immediately saw the weak spot in Burke's argument. The 1688 Parliament that expelled James II changed the conditions of British government for all posterity: no Catholic would ever be allowed to occupy the British throne. Yet no law is eternal: it remains valid only until the sovereign authority of the people repeals it. "When man ceases to be, his power and his wants cease with him."[60] Soon Paine abandons the historical discussion and takes the high ground of eternal principles "engraved in the heart of every citizen." The French Revolution, contrary to the British one, he claims, is all about those principles. Human rights are grounded in a more ancient tradition than the short political one to which Burke appeals. Indeed, historical tradition, an untidy mixture of usurpation and legitimacy, establishes nothing by itself. "It is authority against authority all the way, till we come to the divine origin of the rights of man, at the Creation" (*Rights,* pt. I, p. 303). Civil rights are legitimate only to the extent that they are derived from natural rights or are needed to secure them.

Paine praises Adam Smith's "political wisdom" for heeding what he regards to be the primary task of government, the protection of property and property exchange. How decisive a role economic considerations played in Paine's conception of natural rights became fully evident in the second part of *The Rights of Man*, written a few months later. Whereas in the first part the state had still been the protector of natural rights, in the second one it served merely as an instrument of economic utility. "Government is nothing more than a national association; and the object of this association is the good of all, as well individually as collectively. Every man wishes to pursue his occupation, and enjoy the fruit of his labors, and the produce of his property, in peace and safety, and with the least possible expense. When these things are accomplished, all the objects for which government ought to be established are answered" (*Rights*, pt. II, p. 434). In this utilitarian concept of rights, the notion of natural law, which in Locke's *Treatise* still had functioned as the foundation of rights, became an unnecessary addition. The defenders of natural rights gradually abandoned grounding them on natural law and, instead, treated them as self-evident and requiring no ulterior justification.

Conclusion

The eighteenth century decisively transformed political thought by granting the idea of individual freedom a primary position in its theories. In doing so it restored the ancient bond between ethics and politics, which had been jeopardized by such early modern writers as Machiavelli and Hobbes. Yet the reunion remained precarious and by the end of the century was threatened from two sides. Restricting the moral aspect of freedom to the internal moral intention, Kant relegated politics to an external, legal order. On the opposite side, Smith and his followers placed all the emphasis on the economic aspect of political institutions and paid little attention to the ethics of public policy. Both legalism and economism continued to affect politics all trough the nineteenth and the twentieth centuries. One hears echoes of Kantian dualism in the commonly used excuse for immoral conduct that no positive law was broken or that crimes were actually performed in obedience to legitimate authorities. On the other hand, the acceptance of economic interest as the supreme rule of politics has resulted in social inequality or in violent reactions against it.

The social concept that underwent the most substantial changes in the eighteenth century may well have been that of *civil society*. As we have seen, the term "civil society" originally had a more comprehensive meaning than that of politics in the narrow, modern sense. It included the entire public realm. Adam Ferguson still preserved this meaning in his famous *Essay on the History of Civil Society* (1767). Political institutions presented only one branch of civil society. In the eighteenth century, however, politics (in the narrow sense) *either* absorbed all other forms of the social order *or* became so heavily influenced by particular interests that public policy functioned mainly as an organizational structure for protecting those interests. In both cases the traditional distinction between politics and other social spheres vanished. The former presented, of course, Rousseau's position; the latter that of the British economists Smith and Stewart, though already Locke's *Second Treatise on Civil Government* with its emphasis on the protection of private property leaned in that direction. Communitarian thinkers in our time are, once again stressing the importance of the intermediate groups as buffers between *étatisme* and laissez-faire policy. Social relations on that intermediate level define our concrete social identity. Without them political life remains abstract and may easily degenerate into some form of tyranny or totalitarianism. "We cannot regard ourselves as independent in this way without great cost to those loyalties and convictions whose moral force consists partly in the fact that living by them is inseparable from understanding ourselves as the particular persons we are."[61]

One cannot claim that the Enlightenment achieved a satisfactory synthesis between the universal and the particular aspects of political life. Rationalist theories favored the universal; empirical theories, especially economic ones, the particular. At the same time, eighteenth-century social universalism, whether it be the a priori, philosophical version implied in the modern concepts of natural law and human rights, or the empirical one assumed by international economic traffic, moved beyond the supremacy of the state as social body and prepared the globalist thought of the late twentieth century.

The New Science of History

The writing of history has always been inspired by the belief that the knowledge of the past sheds light on the present. Yet the nature of this knowledge has varied from one period to another. Ancient writers, both classical and biblical, assumed that the essential patterns of life remained identical and therefore that history provided lasting models for instruction and imitation. Hence the search for historical prototypes of current customs and institutions. Legendary founders of cities, ancestors of existing professions, prehistorical legislators, and establishers of rituals were believed to grant them legitimacy. This belief in tradition persisted among Christians, even though the coming of Christ divided their time into two distinct periods. The basic relation between past and present remained constant, except for the unique event of the Incarnation that had set a new beginning and a new end to history.[1]

The scientific revolution of the seventeenth century undermined this stable concept of time. The abrupt change it caused in the modern worldview suggested that time was pregnant with novelty and directed toward the future rather than repeating the past. The new orientation was supported by a philosophy that viewed the person as the source of meaning and value and hence capable of changing the course of history. The modern conception of history resulted in two quite different attitudes toward the past. Some, beginning with Descartes and all those primarily interested in the scientific achievements of their age, felt that the study of the past could contribute little to the scientific enterprise. For others, however, a more accurate knowledge of the past formed an integral part of that comprehensive renewal of knowledge introduced by the scientific revolution. Thus, David Hume regarded the study of history as essential to the study of human nature, the basis of all scientific knowledge. Some historians, such as Montesquieu, Voltaire, and Gibbon, were convinced that a solid acquaintance with the past was to vindicate the changes of the present.

Although the idea of change played a crucial role for all, it did not necessarily imply that history followed a progressive line. None of the major historians assumed this. Those who did, such as Turgot and Condorcet, were philosophers of history rather than historians. Vico proposed a cyclical theory of history in which civilizations move from growth to decline, only to be followed by others that go through a similar cycle. Still, even for Vico, each new stage of a civilization preserves enough of the previous ones to raise its achievements to a higher level and also to lower declines to greater depth. At the end of the Enlightenment epoch, Herder formulated yet a new theory of progress. Each nation, while following its own organic development, brings the human race closer to its ultimate destiny — the fullness of humanity. This organic view of history, however, implied no continuous progress from one civilization to another. Each one must be judged on its own terms.

Meanwhile some earlier approaches continued to exist. The religious notion of history as disposition of God's Providence had survived through the seventeenth century: Bossuet gave it one of its final expressions. In his *Discours sur l'histoire universelle* (1681), epochs follow each other as stages of a divine plan, of which the earlier prepare the later. Ancient Rome had to fall in order to make room for the spiritual realm it had helped to establish and of which Rome remained the center. Since the nations beyond the traditional borders of Western civilization fell outside Christendom, Bossuet gave them even less attention than Augustine had done more than a millennium before him. The American Puritan Jonathan Edwards pursued a comparable theological interpretation in his *History of the Work of Redemption* (1774). For the New England divine also, history remained entirely a supernatural drama, though one moving in a direction opposite to that of Bossuet's ecclesiastical triumphalism. It told the story of the anti-Christ who had been at work since Constantine, allowing only for a short interstice of genuine Christianity during the early Reformation.

Aside from Edwards's odd exception and a few minor ones like him, the view of history as a story of the *magnalia Dei* was clearly on the decline. Yet one aspect of this providential concept of history deeply influenced secular history, even though it ended up attacking the idea of providence. Enlightenment historians continued to see regional history as part of a *historia universalis*. The Göttingen professor Johann Christoph Gatterer wrote: "Properly speaking there is only one history — the one that includes all peoples, and that is the true and authentic universal history."[2] All human histories are intertwined and none is isolated. While for Gatterer, this had been an a priori philosophical principle, for others, it became a battle cry against the narrowly Western and Christian conception of history that had guided Bossuet's work. Voltaire in his *Essai sur les moeurs* (1756) (in English often referred to as *Essay on General History*) concluded that the idea of a Providence that promoted only Christian interests ignored the Chinese and Arabs.

But the Enlightenment notion of universal history suffered from similar problems. All too often historians, especially those of the Göttingen School, subjected or sacrificed concrete facts to an abstract, universal idea. Even Gibbon's "causes," Vico's "cycles," or Montesquieu's laws were harnessed to such universalizing theses.[3] Although those historians understood that the parts of the story had to be interpreted through the whole, they often failed to observe that the whole must be understood through the parts. A proper balance appears only at the end of the Enlightenment in Johann Gottfried Herder's theory of history.

The great historians of the Enlightenment, all magnificent writers, still fully adhered to the narrative conception of history. Once they started telling their tales, they felt little hampered by the general ideas that may have inspired them in the first place. Nor did they much reflect on the critical questions that were to become so important at a later period concerning the nature and validity of the general principles on which causal deductions in history depend.[4]

History as Truth: Giambattista Vico

Vico's presence in this story requires some justification. He firmly belongs to what Isaiah Berlin has called the anti-Enlightenment. Working and thinking within the older Italian rhetorical tradition, he appears to be more a late humanist than an early Enlightenment thinker. He had so little in common with the great historians of the eighteenth century that they would have found it hard to understand his position had they read him. Few would have considered a theory of history based on legendary sources, literalist readings of the biblical creation story, speculative interpretations of ancient myths, and fantastic etymologies worth refuting. Even today a first encounter with *The New Science* is disconcerting. Croce himself, who was greatly responsible for its rediscovery in the past century, called it an alternation of light and darkness, truth and error.[5] Nonetheless, *The New Science* now ranks among the period's most lasting contributions to a philosophy of history.

Vico understood the significance of the issues raised by Enlightenment thought and he shared Descartes's epistemological concerns. Yet he saw the unsatisfactory conclusions to which a rationalist philosophy would lead. He accepted the modern axiom that truth originates in the mind. Yet he denied that the mind operates exclusively by rational categories. For him, truth is not primarily to be attained through a deduction process patterned on the model of mathematical reasoning, but through reflection on what humans have actually *done* in history. Despite their erratic behavior, history follows a regular, recurrent pattern. A true science of history, then, must be more than a chronicle of facts and events. It must account for these returning movements and include a justification of their implied universal cycles. Unlike the universals of rationalist philosophy, however, the historical ones are based on observation. In his cyclical theory of history Vico attempted to fill the gap that separated universalist rationalism from historical empiricism. As we shall see, he lacked the conceptual apparatus for succeeding in what he intended to do, but he anticipated in many respects what Herder and Kant were to accomplish at the end of the Enlightenment period.

Like Descartes, Vico links the question of truth to the subjective principle of certainty. For Descartes, truth and certainty coincide in the self's awareness of itself, yet he had not succeeded in extending this coincidence beyond the point where the mind is certain of its own existence. Vico claimed to have found a more inclusive source of certainty in the mind's awareness of what it has *made* — the *verum factum*. He may have read in Hobbes's *Leviathan:* "If one wants to know something, he must constitute it himself." Yet his support for it came mainly from the humanist conception of rhetoric. The rhetorician's truth is not given: he must shape it himself. In this *poiesis* (the substantive of *poiein*, to make), *making* and *certainty* are indissolubly united. To be sure, Descartes also had relied on the certainty of mathematics, where the mind deals with its own construction and hence cannot be wrong. Vico accepted the certainty of mathematics and even pretended that his own science followed a geometrical method.[6] Still, he considered mathematics of little use in establishing a true knowledge of the real world. That, he claims, may be obtained only by imitating God's mode of knowing, namely, by creating another reality.[7] Mathematics is but "an imaginary [universe] of lines and numbers that accomplishes in abstraction what God accomplishes in reality in the universe." Vico failed to see the crucial function of mathematics for understanding the physical world: for him, nature is too far removed from the mind to yield certain knowledge of any kind. Rather than pursuing the abstract certainty of mathematics, the mind should turn to the study of culture, its own creation through the centuries.

The choice may seem puzzling. What guarantees the mind certainty in the extremely vague and often inaccurate knowledge it has of human achievements in a prehistorical era? Lessing was to draw the opposite conclusion: no knowledge is less certain than the historical one; between present and past yawns an unbridgeable chasm. Historical facts are, by their very nature, excluded from the indubitable truths of reason. Vico, however, considers indubitability too narrow a criterion for truth. Even for momentous decisions of practical life we rely on *certainties* that no one would consider "indubitable."[8] Of many things we are certain on the authority of others. Our certainty may be misplaced, and *The New Science* is meant to serve as a critique of beliefs too readily accepted as certain. Nonetheless, the first step on the way to truth consists not in doubting but in *trusting* our beliefs. Concretely this implies accepting the principles one's community considers self-evident.

The Roman concept of *sensus communis,* well known to Vico through his studies of rhetoric and Roman law, justified the authority of those beliefs that theory alone cannot prove but that are indispensable for practical life. Vico's rejection of the need for indubitable foundations places him, together with Pascal, at the head of a line of critics of Descartes that stretches all the way to the present. Modern epistemology, in his view, arbitrarily dismisses millennia of conscious life as if they were no more than a prolonged state of error and ignorance. Yet to those early, prerational ages the human race owes all that made modern reflection possible: language, religion, and civilization. Still, as Croce observed and others have confirmed, on the crucial issue, the turn to the subject, Vico himself remains solidly within the modern tradition. "He also entered the subjectivism of modern philosophy inaugurated by Descartes and, in this very general sense, he himself may be called a Cartesian."[9] But Vico fundamentally disagreed with Descartes's formalist study of method independently of content. For him, as later for Hegel, method can be defined only in union with content.

On what ground, then, does Vico hope to gain truth from a turn to an uncertain past? He appeals to the Ionian notion of *physis,* according to which a thing's nature lies in its origin. An echo of this axiom still appears in Aristotle's assumption that the *nature* of an organic being resides in an initial principle that determines its entire development.[10] Vico applies this to the "unfolding" of history. "The nature of *things* is nothing but their coming into being at certain times and in certain guises. Whenever the time and guise are thus and so, such and not otherwise are the things themselves" (147).[11] But the authority of that ancient principle is of dubious value when applied to historical origins. Aristotle had referred to the nature of organic beings when claiming that their beginning defines their further development. The Neapolitan thinker stretches the principle well beyond that organic meaning in equating truth with the development of mental life through the centuries. For him, truth consists in the history of its development.

Aside from a theoretical problem, Vico here also confronts the practical one—how we are to know the origin of a mental life that lies hidden in a preliterary past. If the beginning of humanity remains veiled in darkness, how can it serve as a source of truth? Vico himself compares the search to a "dense night through a wild sea, surrounded by so many rocks of difficulties."[12] Nonetheless he believes that a philological study of ancient texts discloses not merely the language and history of historical times, but that of the prehistorical ones as well. Early poets, such as Homer, record not only the achievements of the "age of the heroes," but their writings also reflect even older preliterary traditions. Combined with the most archaic legal texts, their poems contain the story of the transition from an almost bestial to a human existence.

Although philology is needed for uncovering the past, it never yields the definitive truth that philosophy requires. Historical information about past beliefs and institutions contains by itself no philosophical truth at all. Yet philosophy cannot attain its own truth without knowing the *facta* that philology and history provide. To convert the historical *certum* into a permanent *verum*, philosophy must critically reflect on what history, linguistics, literature and law present. Only a critical reflection on the facts of history may validate the *verum factum* principle.

In addition to philology, Christians possess the revealed story of the beginnings of the human race. Interpreting Genesis literally, he attempts to harmonize the time after the expulsion from Eden with the primitive first age of secular history. Cain is reported to have "wandered the earth" as a fugitive. With him the corruption of the human race began. According to *The New Science*, the story of Homer's cyclopic giants corresponds to the biblical report that the sons of God "married the daughters of men" and produced "the heroes whose fame has come down to us from long ago" (Genesis 6:4). After Noah, sacred history definitively separates from the "history of the nations." Since a common Providence rules both, a new sacred history, more comprehensive than the biblical one, commences. From this point on, Vico only writes about the latter.

Vico regards the primitive inhabitants of the earth far removed from the bucolic idylls popular among his contemporaries. Rather than noble savages they were speechless brutes, *bestioni tutti stupore e ferocia,* who lived not in peace and harmony but in a state of violence and superstition. Vico calls their epoch the age of the gods, not because of their piety but because, ignorant of natural causality, they regarded all forces as divine. Their views of the transcendent were entirely inspired by fear. The religion of the Gentiles (contrary to revealed religion) was born from primitive terror for the unknown. Still these superstitious beliefs restrained the primeval fierceness of the tribes and instilled in them a respect for authority (916). All law was divine and all government theocratic (922, 925). Even the first hieroglyphic script was held to be sacred (929, 933). Through this archaic religion, especially through the "theological poets," civilizing forces slowly conquered the chaotic ones. By naming the divine forces active in nature and in social institutions — marriage, death, family life — the primitive tribes acquired some control over them and became capable of courting the gods' favors. Indeed, the primitive religion of fear was more fundamental to the development of the human race than the establishment of "the true faith" in Israel.

Civilized life began when the "god-fearing giants" started burying their dead rather than allowing them to decompose in the fields. Eventually males and females came to stay with the same mate rather than having casual sexual encounters. Thus they formed family groups and thereby decreased the amount of violence in settling disputes. The civilized subjected or killed the uncivilized, and the weak took refuge with the strong. Vico refers to this stage as the age of the heroes. It featured the beginning of settled life, the establishment of primitive law, and the creation of mythological poetry. It was the period of the Trojan War, of the first Greek colonies, of the foundations of Alba Longa and Rome.

As families expanded under authority of the fathers, a "barbaric aristocracy" emerged. In an earlier work on Roman law, *De universi iuris uno principio et fine uno* (1720), Vico had described the legal development of other societies on the pattern of Rome. In *The New Science* he continues to do so. The need to cope with the harsh conditions of a primitive society, he claims, forced people to rediscover the natural law, preserved in the Law of Moses, but in barbaric times lost among the *gentes*. During this entire period morality was primitive, authority absolute, imagination the dominant mental faculty. Even law was articulated in poetic form (170). During the next stage, the age of the humans, the power of the imagination declines: thinking becomes rational and loses its mythical quality. Law, now grounded on rational principles, rules society.

The poets and legislators of the heroic age were the first makers of that spiritual *factum* on which truth is based. Their metaphoric speech assumed different objects under a single expression, thus preparing abstract universal concepts. In his concept of "the imaginative universal" (*universale fantastico* or *genus fantastico* [809]) that preceded rational universals (460), Vico captured the essence of metaphorical thought that raises consciousness beyond the singularity of sense perception. Vico's *imaginative universals* may be viewed as "ideal portraits" that point the way toward universality and, as such, open the road to rational knowledge.[13] Since truth includes the road to truth as well as its final conceptualization, he claims these metaphorical universals to be true in their own right.

In Vico's theory all truth is historical. Even self-knowledge remains inaccessible to direct intuition; it can be obtained only through an autobiographical narrative. This narrative character of truth has its first expression in the myth, the extended metaphor. Originally the myth had a practical function: to enable primitive humans to cope with the primeval fear of the unknown. But it also contains a lasting truth insofar as it complements the insufficiency of rational discourse in dealing with those all-encompassing existential issues that analytic reason is unable to handle. As the roots of words have remained metaphorical, they preserve the memory of their mythical origins.

In his reflection on the "barbaric" stage of the mind's odyssey toward truth, Vico deliberately retains some of the mythical idiom in which primitive generations conducted their quest for truth. Thus in book II of *The New Science* he describes the birth of morality in the imagery of Greek and Roman mythology. "The giants, enchained under the mountains by the frightful religion of the thunderbolts, learned to check their bestial habit of wandering wild through the great forest of the earth, and acquired the contrary custom of remaining hidden and settled in their fields. Hence they later became the founders of the nations and the lords of the first commonwealths" (504). This kind of metaphorical language, so far removed from that of eighteenth-century philosophy, induced many to dismiss *The New Science* as being a remnant of an uncritical past.

Yet, as Vico's critical discussions of myth and legend (for instance, concerning Aeneas's coming to Italy [770–73]) indicate, he was by no means a "naive" thinker, but one fully aware of the difference between myth and science. He knew Bacon's *Novum Organum* to which the title of his own *The New Science* alludes. He was also acquainted with the discoveries made by Copernicus, Kepler, and Galileo, to which he refers in *De nostri temporis studiorum ratione*. But, as Giuseppe Mazzotta has shown, he felt that another form of knowledge about the natural world had been missing: the hermeneutical retrieval of ancient wisdom through the study of language and myth. As long as we restrict the study of nature to the methods of Galilean and Cartesian physics, we fail to see why and how the mind became intellectually involved with nature in the first place.[14] This "poetic wisdom," the knowledge of what the mind has "made" over the centuries, stands at the origin of the scientific study of nature.

Nor has science swept it aside (149–50). The truth of the myth is eternal: the historian's task consists in rescuing it from forgetfulness. The recovery relies much on etymological analysis, as the roots of words still bear the traces of ancient myths. Vico's entire new science consists, in fact, of what he calls Roman jurisprudence: "a science of interpretation" (999).

In the third book, "Discovery of the True Homer," Vico demonstrates how keenly he was aware of the difference between mythical thinking and critical historiography. He raises what was later called the "Homeric question" concerning the authorship as well as the historical quality of *Iliad* and *Odyssey*. He rejects the historical character of both epics and even the existence of Homer as a single person. Yet he argues that the poetic wisdom of the ancients provides indispensable material to the science of history. The poets, he claims, were "the first historians of the nations" (820). The events reported in the ancient poems may not be historically reliable. But the philological study of the language in which they were written, the institutions they describe, and the links with contemporary monuments or texts enable the historian to establish the nature of the culture they reflect. Philology itself forms part of history: in disclosing the meaning of time-bound works, it "reveals the pastness of the past."[15]

Moreover, the narrative form of the myth preserved in the ancient poems testifies to the early presence of a belief, essential to historiography, that events constitute a coherent story. It affirmatively answers Hayden White's fundamental question concerning the meaningfulness of history: "Does the world really present itself to perception in the form of well-made stories, with central subjects, proper beginnings, middles, and ends, and a coherence that permits us to see 'the end' in every beginning?"[16] When in *The New Science* Vico refers to the myth as a "true narration," he means more than that the narrative form was once a necessary stage of the process of truth. That narrative form continues to be the only appropriate one for the writing of history. The truth about historical beings can be told only as a story that unfolds and moves to an end.

In the course of discussing his method Vico declares: "Our science . . . comes to describe an ideal eternal history traversed in time by the history of every nation in its rise, development, maturity, and fall" (349). That statement of purpose returns several times in *The New Science* (e.g., 145, 245, 294, 393). But a philosophy of history — for that is what Vico is after — requires more than incorporating history within a general theory of truth. It needs a guiding concept of the nature of history, justified by a philosophical argument and supported by empirical evidence. Has Vico provided that? His assumption that history *must* move through cycles of ascent and decline is neither an a priori principle of reason nor a conclusion based on empirical observation. Even if Vico had analyzed a great number of civilizations (as Toynbee later attempted to do) rather than only the development of Greek and Roman institutions, he still would not have established a sufficient empirical support for his claim that history always follows an identical pattern. In fact, Vico merely subsumes particular events, laws, and cultural achievements under a universal, "ideal" concept that he expects to transform their significance from contingent to necessary. His insistence on the autonomous development of each nation even seems to preclude a universal pattern. How could one draw a meaningful general conclusion from the course of history when each and every nation develops and declines in a unique way?

In fact, Vico's method relies neither on logical principles alone nor on empirical investigations, but, in the manner of the ancient myth, subsumes the particular under the universal in the form of a idealized narrative. He does so even in his *Autobiography* where he tells the story of his life in the light of an ideal necessity.[17] In order to fit the pattern he did not just "make" the facts of his life, he also in part "made them up" (e.g, the erroneous date of his birth) and composed them into a self-made, "poetic" order. Historians remain justifiably wary of such generalizations. Yet his theory deserves to be remembered for other, more significant reasons. Surprisingly for a "cyclical" thinker, Vico considered the course of each civilization relatively independent of that of any other. *The New Science* thereby breaks with the ancient and medieval view of history as *magistra vitae,* which assumes that the past does not essentially differ from the present. For him, no two historical constellations are alike. Certainly, earlier institutions may survive from one civilization to the next. All through the early Middle Ages much of the Roman Empire survived and as late as the fourteenth century France revived Roman law. But in these renewals or revivals, ancient laws and institutions assume a different function in a new context.

Vico spends considerable time and effort disproving the legend, commonly accepted since Titus Livy, that the Roman Law of the Twelve Tables had been "imported" from Athens for the purpose of reconciling patricians and plebeians. He shows that a delegation of Romans to Athens was at that time historically impossible. To him, the question was important. It proved that civilizations do not directly communicate in reaching vital decisions concerning their institutions. The thesis is dubious, but later scholarship proved him right on the facts. He also used the story against his own contemporaries who regarded the Law of the Twelve Tables as the birth date of Roman democracy. He considered it a mean-spirited document that ungenerously conceded as little to the plebeian majority as the social tension of the moment allowed (109–10). Those who convey democratic meanings to such terms as "liberty" and "people" are mistaken: the Roman republic recognized only a small minority as full citizens. Legislation was entirely inspired by patrician interests that conflicted with those of other classes.[18]

Since both the age of the gods and the barbaric age of the heroes prepare the third, human age, in which people are "intelligent and hence modest, benign and reasonable" (918), one might think that the movement of history follows a progressive course. But with the human age also comes the decline of a civilization. Reason loses contact with its own past and an abstract rationalism announces the return of a new barbaric age — the *barbarie di reflessione*. The "barbarism of reflection" starts at the high point of the age of reason, a time of unparalleled progress and enlightenment. A civilized nation begins to decline when it falls "into the custom of each man thinking only of his own private interests" (1106). Such a selfish attitude inevitably leads to cultural disintegration. "As the popular states became corrupt, so also did the philosophies. They descend to scepticism" (1102). To Vico, the political corruption of his contemporaries, the loss of faith, and the philosophies of self-interest introduced by Machiavelli and Hobbes displayed the same symptoms of cultural decline that announced the end of earlier periods, specifically that of the Roman Empire. The description of the barbarism of reflection bears a remarkable similarity to some contemporary criticism of modern culture, specifically that of the Frankfurt philosophers Horkheimer and Adorno.[19] In their *Dialectic of the Enlightenment* they criticized modern thought for having lost the immediate contact with things. Our present functionalism, they claimed, has resulted in a diminished sense of reality and a warped hierarchy of values.[20] Vico also regarded abstract universalization as a means for gaining control over the natural world: it reduced reason to functional universals more appropriate for controlling reality than for understanding it.

The final part of *The New Science* deals with the return of the cycle — the *ricorso*. Essential is that the *ricorso* initiates no mere *repetition* of the previous cycle. Vico mentions only a "correspondence" between cycles (1048). He never accepted the Stoic theory of an eternal return of the same. Thus the first "barbaric" age was a unique, never to be repeated, event. The barbarism of the early Middle Ages that followed in the wake of the Germanic invasions was of a wholly different nature. Roman civilization collapsed, but life did not return to its original, primitive state. It retained the cultural acquisitions of the previous epoch: language, religious institutions, and ordinary rules of living. The barbaric corruption of his own age repeated neither the first nor the second

barbaric age of the West. An overall progressive movement, then, overdeter-
mines the cyclical theory and excludes predictions of the future. The cyclical
pattern remains constant, but both the rhythm of succession and the quality of
the periods differ from one to another.[21]

Does Vico's cyclical theory in the end not destroy itself? Decline continues
only as long as people remain ignorant of its causes and therefore fail to make
the necessary changes. Would the cycle not come to an end if Vico's diagnosis
of the causes of decline came to be accepted and acted upon? Vico himself in
the so-called *Pratica* of *The New Science* (drafted for incorporation in the
third edition but never actually inserted) states that his work was an effort
"toward delaying if not preventing the ruin of nations in decay" (1405). All a
civilization needs to overcome corruption are visionary leaders and effective
institutions capable of teaching and implementing principles such as the rule
of Providence, the moderation of passions, and the belief in immortality. If the
wise and strong, "the form and mind of this world of nations," prevail, disaster may be avoided (1410). Why did Vico not include the *Pratica* in the third
edition? Did he in the end despair of the efficacy of human intervention? Or
did he, more likely, feel that introducing the idea of an alternative would
require a substantial recasting of *The New Science,* a task he, having come to
the end of his life, felt no longer capable of undertaking? If humans, fore-
warned about the road to decline, would be able to avoid it, Vico's theory
would become restricted to an interpretation of *past* history. Such an interpretation would conflict with the concluding paragraph of book V, according
to which the cyclical theory is all-comprehensive and valid in all possible
worlds. "There will then be fully unfolded before us not the particular history
in time of the laws and deeds of the Romans or the Greeks but . . . the ideal
history of the eternal laws which are instanced by the deeds of all nations in
their rise, progress, maturity, decadence and dissolution [and which would be
so instanced] even if . . . there were infinite worlds being born from time to
time throughout eternity" (1096). Vico abhors physical determinism. Yet the
short conclusive section on Providence that follows the quoted text arouses
the suspicion that he may have held a theological determinism.

Disputes have raged about the significance of the idea of Providence in *The
New Science* since its rediscovery in the twentieth century. Some dismiss it as
an umbrella to shield Vico from censorship. Others understand it as referring
to the unchangeable course of history, indispensable for his theory, but regard
the religious term "Providence" misleading. Such was the view of the two great
scholars responsible for the Vico revival, Benedetto Croce and Giovanni Gentile. Still others consider it part of the traditional Catholic view of history,
which Vico, a sincere believer, accepted without granting it a major role in the

development of his theory. None of these interpretations seems adequate. Rightly or wrongly, Vico thought that without the idea of Providence his theory would lack the "ideal, eternal" quality he intended to give it. In the first book, he introduces Providence as one of the three principles on which the new science is based (360). Vico distrusted mathematical-type deductions from rational principles. Yet no more than Bacon did he consider an empirical description of institutions and events sufficient for a universal theory of history.[22] The idea of Providence for him functioned as the indispensable link between his universal thesis and the limited empirical evidence that supported it. In addition, the idea of an all-encompassing guidance was needed to unite the various autonomous cultures into a coherent totality if his theory of history was to be universal at all.

Indeed, the idea of Providence, much like Hegel's Spirit, is so overarching that no argument can prove it. It presented itself quite naturally to Vico as it had been a standard part of Christian as well as of Stoic and Platonic philosophies. The question remains, however, whether the idea retained its traditional religious quality in the process of being transferred into a philosophy of history. In Vico's account, Christianity, though dividing history into two parts and initiating a new cycle, plays no major role in the development of the cycles themselves: none in the ones that precede it and no obvious one in the succession of those that follow it. This in itself does not argue against a religious interpretation of the idea. Vico's conception of Providence may have been "deist," not in the sense of excluding revelation, but in the sense that Christian revelation should not occupy the centre in an account of history that started long before the coming of Christ. In this universal, but not specifically Christian sense, *The New Science* may indeed be called "a rational civil theology of divine providence" (342), that is, a comprehensive vision of God's working in the "world of nations in all the extent of its places, times, and varieties" (345). The final sentence of *The New Science* confirms this religious intentionality: "This science carries inseparably with it the study of piety, and that he who is not pious cannot be truly wise" (1112).

But if there should be no question about Vico's religious intention, there remains considerable doubt whether a notion of Providence understood in a religious sense is compatible with his conception of history. That conception presupposes a total immanence of God in history. In and through human decisions Providence realizes its designs, often against the purposes of human agents. Beyond human acts and intentions, a higher power accomplishes a grander design on the realization of which all peoples unwittingly cooperate.[23] Precisely this total immanence of God in history made Gentile conclude that Vico's Providence meant no more than the development of history toward increasing rationality.[24] In Vico's mind, however, Providence aims at a goal that exceeds human consciousness qualitatively, not merely in scope. In a polemical passage Vico defends the religious nature of reason in history. He appeals to the Roman jurisconsults and the common belief that the natural law was instituted by God (633). How could all nations have agreed on moral norms without transcendent guidance (145)? Yet in fact they do agree on basic moral principles as soon as they become civilized, without having been influenced by one another. Each nation follows the same order of development and arrives at the same conclusions on the basis of the same principles (344).

Vico also detects the hand of Providence in accomplishments of the human race, achieved without any awareness of the higher goal of civilized life yet uniquely effective toward furthering it. Humans are too short-sighted to pursue more than fragmentary, particular objectives, They fail to recognize that they form part of a more comprehensive reality. If the cosmic order requires a transcendent origin, as people generally assumed at the end of the seventeenth century, the establishment of a civil order that renders limited, selfish endeavors subservient to the complex harmony of a social totality did so even more. Vico concludes: "This axiom proves that there is divine providence and further that it is a divine legislative mind" (133). But does it? Does the difference between the historical effects of human actions and the intentions that inspired them require a divine Providence for these effects to be beneficial? Of course, they do if one assumes that the eventual outcome is the best possible and that none but a divine power could have made it so. But that is precisely the question. Is it necessary to regard as teleologically directed, actions to which there might have been alternatives, different but no less beneficial in their effects? On what grounds do we consider the present ones the best? Vico leaves all these questions unanswered.

It may well be, however, that he was attempting to establish a different, more fundamental principle. At one point he attacks the "inexorable chain of cause and effect" of Stoic philosophy (342). Vico's qualm is not with causality as such, but with the modern reduction of all causality to the efficient one. For Plato and Aristotle, final and efficient causality had always been combined. They regarded even natural processes as inherently teleological. The end of a natural process was not merely its terminus, but also its goal. In modern thought, teleology came to be the exclusive quality of conscious acts, while efficient causality became the ruling category for interpreting the physical world. This freed scientific investigation from earlier, anthropomorphic interpretations of nature. Yet eventually it led to a tendency to apply it to *all* processes — even historical ones.[25] Vico criticized Hobbes, Spinoza, and Machiavelli for their denial of final causes. He intended to avoid determinism as well as chaos by assuming a divine guidance directing the human pursuit of limited ideals. At the same time he considered human freedom, however limited and selfish, indispensable for realizing this divine teleology. Providence does not determine human actions; it merely subordinates them to a more comprehensive purpose.

What, then, is God's providential plan of history, according to Vico? Obviously not to realize the philosophes' ideal of unlimited progress. Progress in Vico's view exists only in the limited sense that each decline results in a less complete loss of civil life. Though that may result in cultural improvement, it certainly does not raise moral standards. The *barbarie di reflessione* is morally inferior to the primitive state of the barbaric ages. But what good could be achieved by a succession of *corsi* and *ricorsi* in which all that rises is bound to fall? Surprisingly, Vico sees in the endless repetition of cyclical patterns a divine disposition. "Since these institutions have been established by divine Providence, the course of the institutions of the nations had to be, must now be, and will have to be such as our science demonstrates, even if infinite worlds were born from time to time through eternity, which is certainly not the case" (348). Vico thereby grounds his historical pessimism on a theological foundation. But the term Providence here loses its traditional meaning. The absence of an ultimate, all-inclusive common destiny that defines the nature of history through a transhistorical end of the human race distinguishes Vico's notion of Providence from the theological one. As the frontispiece of *The New Science* suggests, only God's light enables us to understand the course of history. He describes the purpose of his work as being "a civil theology of divine providence" (2). But since he never justifies the designs of Providence in history, his theory of Providence brings him close to a blind theological determinism that sheds little light on the course of history.

Two tendencies compete in Vico's work. On one side, he wants to establish a new concept of truth by means of a historical, empirical method. On the other side, he imposes his cyclical theory upon slim historical evidence. His discussion of dubious documents concerning the prehistorical age is more inspired by the demands of his theory than by hard evidence. With precocious insight he observed that the Homeric writings, documents of Greece's barbaric age, reflected a culture that long preceded the time of their writing. But all too often he fills the enormous gaps in our knowledge of that age by pure speculation. Only in his discussions of Roman law and institutions does he attain the methodical rigor of the slightly younger Montesquieu. Yet Vico attempted to answer a different, more general question that he was one of the first to raise: Is it possible to find a universal pattern in historical processes that by nature are always particular and never identical? Ancient historians may have *assumed* that such a pattern existed, but if it did, it was restricted to the civilized era. Christian apologists extended the historically "meaningful period" to the beginning of the human race. But they restricted their perspective to a narrowly conceived salvation history. Vico abandoned that Christian universalism. The idea of Providence allowed him to integrate the particularity of the nations within a fully comprehensive theory of history.

History as Progress: The Philosophes

The idea of historical progress, popular in the eighteenth century, implied that history moves from a less perfect state to a more perfect one. Those who supported it rarely defined in what precisely that greater perfection consisted. They agreed that society was gradually becoming liberated from intolerance, superstition, political lawlessness, and juridical arbitrariness. Their ideal also included the uninhibited development of science, as well as the attainment of a maximum of personal liberty compatible with living in an orderly society. Yet what was the immediate goal of this process of liberation? Was the process finite or would it indefinitely expand? The philosophes seldom raised and never answered those questions, preoccupied as they were with the need for immediate improvement. Because of the unlimited ambition of their project, their theories of progress have been called secularized eschatologies.[26] But, as Hans Blumenberg shows, a closer look reveals a fundamental difference: "An eschatology speaks of an event breaking into history, an event that transcends and is heterogeneous to it, while the idea of progress moves . . . toward a future that is immanent in history."[27] In the secular theory the impulse toward progress comes entirely from within. The idea of Providence, central in the eschatological view of history, vanishes, even if the name remains. The human race creates its own destiny.

Some notion of historical progress existed even in antiquity.[28] Hesiod, Aeschylus, and Protagoras linked it to the myth of Prometheus who brought practical knowledge to the human race. Yet all versions of the story caution that practical knowledge without wisdom and virtue leads to disaster. Moreover, the ancient idea of progress applied only to the past without moving beyond the present whereas that of the eighteenth century stretched toward an indefinite future. The real predecessor of the modern theory of progress is Francis Bacon. As he articulates it in the *Instauratio Magna* (1620), history moves toward an unlimited expansion of science. One of his followers, Joseph Glanvill, adopted the chancellor's motto, *plus ultra,* in the title of a work that fully anticipated the eighteenth century's expectation of a glorious scientific future.

Infinite progress was indeed inherent in the modern concept of science. It required constant correction, but it also promised ever-expanding horizons of knowledge. The ancient notion of truth, valid until the fourteenth century, had held no such promises. It had a definitive, pre-established character. Each thinker might be able to express it more adequately and would thereby give a later generation some advantage over an earlier one. But truth itself did not advance. The increase of empirical and practical knowledge of nature did not add to truth in the strict sense. In the modern concept of science, truth became an ongoing process. It never fully existed and its results had to be constantly emended. Nor would that process ever come to an end. Though its general objectives remained roughly the same, subject, method, and content had to be newly discovered at each epoch. Truth, then, consisted in a *relation* to an ever to be redefined object. As Hannah Arendt put it: "[Truth] was transformed or, rather, broken down into a string of verities, each one in its time claiming general validity even though the very continuity of the research implied something more provisional."[29] Though science, by its very nature, had to remain provisional, it made the same kind of definitive claims that once had been made for the unchanging idea of truth.

In France the early discussion of progress had a more literary character. It sparked a revival of the famous quarrel of the ancients and the moderns.[30] But the content of the *Querelle* had changed since the sixteenth century. The issue was no longer the use of the vernacular language — that question had long been decided — nor even the comparative merits of modern writers. At stake was imitation versus innovation. The French critic Saint-Evremond put the issue succinctly even before it became polemical: "If Homer had lived today, he would have composed admirable poems in harmony with the century in which he wrote. Our poets today compose bad ones imitating the Ancients and led by rules that have become obsolete, on subjects that time has long disposed of."[31]

With Voltaire and Diderot, however, and mainly under English influence, the discussion moved to the domain of science and later to that of morals and politics. The *Encyclopédie* served as the main organ for spreading the gospel of science and political reform, but also, according to d'Alembert, for recording mankind's difficult ascent to truth in the face of prejudice.[32] The idea of progress in the *Encyclopédie* had a strongly utilitarian slant. Diderot wanted to restore the "mechanical arts" to the place of honor they deserved as being the most useful to the human race. Prejudice against them, he wrote, "has filled the cities with useless spectators and with proud men engaged in idle speculation, and the countryside with petty tyrants who are ignorant, lazy, and disdainful."[33] The editors showed the seriousness of their practical interest in the magnificent engravings of technical instruments that accompanied the text. In the course of time the *Encyclopédie* became itself a historical document, especially in those parts that were least intended to be so, namely, the articles on science, which Diderot assumed to contain definitive information. Despite his optimistic expectations of science and technique for the future benefit of the race, Diderot remained sensitive to the incurable moral deficiency of the human race.[34]

As some philosophes moved toward materialism, human history became part of the biologically and chemically determined *histoire naturelle*. At times this reductionism assumed comical proportions. D'Holbach attributes the spread of Islam to Mahomet's physiology. "What was the matter from the combination of which resulted a crafty, ambitious, enthusiastic, and eloquent man; in short, a personage competent to improve on his fellow creatures, and competent of making them concur in his views? They were the insensible particles of his blood, the imperceptible texture of his fibres, the salts, more or less acrid, that stimulated his nerves, the proportion of igneous fluid that circulated in his system."[35] Similar, though less picturesque passages could be culled from the works of La Mettrie. Amazingly, those determinists stood in the front line of the advocates of "progress," convinced that their work would advance it.

No more than Montesquieu or the British historians of the eighteenth century did Voltaire believe that scientific progress or the overcoming of prejudice alone would ever result in a reasonably moral or enlightened society. Calling history a "ramas de crimes, de follies, et de malheurs," he certainly harbored no illusions about the chances of a definitive improvement of human nature. His pessimism increased with the years. At age seventy-nine he called the world a chaos of absurdity and horrors (letter to d'Alembert, July 6, 1773). Nonetheless, he believed to the end that it was the philosopher's task to continue working for the *possibility* of a more open society by fighting intolerance, war, and nationalism. Sages like himself could "lead" the educated: the masses "are not worth instructing."[36] In this educational project, history was to serve as a weapon against the enemies of progress. He used it most effectively in his *Essai sur les moeurs* (1756; final edition 1769).[37] Prodded by his hostess at Cirey, the Marquise de Châtelet, who found the Christian perspective of Bossuet's *Discours sur l'histoire universelle* too narrow, Voltaire went to work on a more inclusive secular interpretation of history.

Humans, he argued, are subject to the laws of physical causality even as the rest of nature.[38] But a different law determines the life of the spirit. Since the mind retains what it has learned, it is capable of some improvement from one generation to the next. Thus it may slowly overcome prejudice and irrationality. Historiography should in the first place record that process. In the "Avant-propos" to the *Essai,* Voltaire states his intention to shift the emphasis from a chronicle of battles and natural events to the history of ideas: how they developed or what prevented them from doing so. "As much as we ought to know the great deeds of sovereigns who made their peoples better and happier, as much may we ignore the run of the mill kind of kings—they only burden our memory" (*Essai,* Avant-Propos, p. 195). The principal subject of history, then, must be the gradual enlightenment of the human race.

We know virtually nothing about the earliest period. We do know, however, that by the time the Hebrews began to record their past, several ancient civilizations in the Near East had flourished: the Chaldean, Phoenician, Egyptian. Voltaire commences his lengthy *Discours préliminaire* with their story. A comparison of these early civilizations puts both the morality and the reliability of the biblical accounts severely to the test. With biting wit he exposes the inconsistencies and impossibilities of the Pentateuch, but, above all, the conquest of Canaan. Why would God have chosen to establish his kingdom on earth through a succession of murders, betrayals, and crimes? In his report on the diaspora, Voltaire fully exposes his *animus* against Jews as well as Christians who accepted them as their models. "If one simply follows the historical thread of this small Jewish nation one sees that it could have no other ending. She prides herself on having moved out of Egypt like a gang of thieves taking along all that they had borrowed from the Egyptians. She boasts of the fact that she has never spared old age, sex, or infancy in the villages and towns she was able to conquer. Always superstitious, always desirous of other people's good, always barbaric, crawling in misery and insolent in prosperity: that is what they were in the eyes of Greeks and Romans capable of reading their books. But to Christians enlightened by faith, they were our forerunners, those who prepared the way, the heralds of Providence" (*Essai,* sec. XVII, p. 151).

Next, Voltaire measures the morals of the Christian West by those of the older Far Eastern cultures. In contrast to forever-warring Christians, Indians consistently practice a universal charity toward all living beings. Christianity was born among ignorants and developed amidst barbarians; China never passed through a stage of barbarism and was from the beginning ruled by sages rather than priests (*Essai,* chap. XI, p. 304). After having been persecuted for undermining the Roman religion that supported the empire, Christians, having gained political power, did the same to the pagans from whom they had previously requested tolerance. They basely conformed their faith to the opportunist policies of thoroughly immoral "Christian" emperors or kings, such as Constantine, Clovis, or Charlemagne—all of them murderers. Voltaire concludes his survey: "The Church must surely be divine, since seventeen centuries of roguery and imbecility were not capable of destroying it" (*Essai,* chap. IX, p. 295). The *Essai* inflated the ideological bias of the French Enlightenment to epic proportions. History here serves the nonhistorical purpose of judging the past by the present, the present by the past, and of criticizing both by the prospects of the future. Later generations have not taken kindly to the "history" of the *Essai.* Yet in two other works Voltaire's universalism played a more constructive role.

In *L'Histoire de Charles XII, Roi de Suède,* Voltaire expanded the narrow limits that had restricted French historiography within the western part of Europe and confined its perspective on other nations to their relations with France. Focusing on the northern and eastern borders of the subcontinent, Voltaire extended the geographical precincts of European history.[39] In *Charles XII* he tells the fascinating story of the young king of Sweden who, during much of his short life, was engaged in a struggle with Czar Peter I for the supremacy of northeastern Europe. The work owed its success as much to its literary as to its historical qualities. The portraits of the two antagonists are painted with psychological perceptiveness, and the dramatic description of the final battle of Pultawa bears comparison with Tolstoy's famous one of the Russian disaster in Borodino.

In *Le Siècle de Louis XIV* (1751), his historical masterwork, Voltaire seeks a different kind of universality by broadening the scope of the historical object rather than by extending its geographical limits. To be truly universal, history must report the story of a civilization rather than political and military exploits. In a letter to the president of the parliament of Paris (whose permission he needed to publish his work) Voltaire wrote: "I have passed lightly over war details which, in their own time, cause so much misery and draw so much attention, while a century later they only bore us" (letter to Hénault, January 28, 1752). As early as 1738, Voltaire had started preparing this work, which he described as an account of "the most glorious century of the human spirit" (letter to Abbé Dubos, October 30, 1738). In it the author displays an encompassing intellectual grasp as well as a rare aesthetic sensitivity. In *Le Siècle de Louis XIV,* Voltaire succeeded in combining ideas and events, poetry and politics, into a complex picture of seventeenth-century culture.

Two conflicting tendencies in the historiography of the French Enlightenment appear together in Voltaire's work. On one side, the idea of progress is always, at least implicitly, present: a new age has dawned for the human race. On the other side, the rationalism of the French Enlightenment assumed that human nature remains basically unchanged and is therefore incapable of serious progress. Philosophes who came after Voltaire appear to have abandoned the idea of an unchanging nature altogether. Turgot and Condorcet stressed the infinite perfectibility of human nature.

At the incredible age of twenty-three the theology student Anne-Robert-Jacques Turgot delivered the customary "Discours" at the opening and the closing days of the academic season at the Sorbonne—July 3 and December 11, 1750. The first is a eulogy on the benefits the Christian faith has brought to humanity; the second surveys the progress accomplished by the human race since its beginning. During that same productive year Turgot also wrote extensive précis for two related discourses on the idea of progress. The young author displayed a respect for tradition and a modesty in his claims most uncommon among the enlightened French. History, in Turgot's view, moves slowly toward greater perfection, though not in all respects. Knowledge and technique advance steadily; arts and morality do not.

Turgot sensed that even this qualified idea of progress required some justification. Compared to nature's invariable rhythm, human history presents a confused spectacle. Empires, raised on each other's ruins, follow in rapid succession. "Like ebb and tide, power moves from one nation to another, and, in the same nation, from princes to masses and from masses to princes."[40] The very remnants of our ancient civilization lie buried under the hooves of barbarians invading from the north and Muslims from the east. The endless repetition of short ascents and long declines hardly suggests progress. Turgot wonders: "Do men rise only in order to fall?" (II Discourse, p. 606). Nonetheless, he perceives modest signs of progress. After centuries of barbarism, Christianity succeeded in restoring some of the classical culture and in reestablishing a common language. Eventually commerce was revived and the nations of the West became reunited to one another.

In the extensive précis for a "Discours" on universal history, Turgot anticipates Comte's three stages of progress. At first humans regarded all natural phenomena as effects of supernatural causes. In the next, "philosophical" stage, they explain the world by means of abstract notions—"essences," "faculties"—thereby replacing the old mysteries by new ones. Finally, the discovery of the mechanical interaction of bodies introduces the scientific stage of truth. At this point the process of civilization gains so much strength as to make its achievements irreversible. "Enfin toutes les ombres sont dissipées. Quelle lumière brille de toutes parts! Quelle foule de grands hommes dans tous les genres. Quelle perfection de la raison" (II Discourse, p. 160). But, Turgot qualifies, scientific and technical progress does not necessarily improve the human condition. Technical advances, for instance, have little to do with refinement of aesthetic taste. To the contrary, people all too easily confuse the difficult with the beautiful ("Discours sur l'histoire universelle," p. 657). Gothic buildings, "in the worst possible taste"(!), require great technical skills (ibid., p. 666). Nor does morality follow the ascending line of science: moral perfection may precede the scientific age and decline may occur during it. Still, scientific-technical progress establishes a cultural continuity without which neither morality nor the arts could survive.

Not coincidentally Turgot's planned "Discours sur l'histoire universelle" bore the same title as Bossuet's famous work on the theology of history. It did, in fact, undermine the bishop's thesis without appearing to do so.[41] Turgot also claims to detect the guidance of divine Providence in the course of history. But whereas in Bossuet's theory, evil had formed no part of a divine plan (though God could convert it into an instrument of grace), in Turgot's "Discours," Providence, through human vice as well as through virtue, promotes the goals of the Enlightenment. Thus ambition, indispensable for the building of nations, has contributed "to the plan of Providence, the progress of Enlightenment, and the increase of human happiness" ("Discours," p. 632). Even violent passions play an essential role in the providential design. As in Vico's *New Science,* Providence combines the various actions pursued for selfish ends into a single power for progress. But in Vico's cyclical theory, actions perpetrated for selfish purposes may cause a civilization's decline and never *directly* promote its good except after a divine "rearrangement." For Turgot, the line to progress is a direct one: selfish deeds are no obstacles but inevitably lead to progress.

In spite of the eminent role he attributes to religion, Turgot's theory in fact prepares the secularist theories of progress that ran from Condorcet to Comte and from Comte to Marx. They all assume that truth, happiness, and freedom are to be realized only in the final period of history and that earlier generations prepare the perfection of the later ones. In the original religious view of history, all generations are equal, earlier ones being no more "instrumental" to the attainment of the end than later ones are identified with its fulfillment. As we shall see, Herder's theory of history remained closer to the original when he attributed to all civilizations an equal part in the building of humanity but rejected the idea that one civilization's goal consisted in furthering the interests of another. Turgot's position remains ambiguous. In his first "Discours," he implied that religion conveys equal meaning to all human life, but in the précis, religion itself serves as an instrument for achieving secular progress.

No such ambiguity clouds the Marquis de Condorcet's *Esquisse historique des progrès de l'esprit humain* (1795), an aggressively antireligious tract written in support of the ideals of the French Revolution while its author was hiding from the *Terreur* (1793–94). Condorcet had collaborated with Turgot during Turgot's tenure as finance minister to Louis XVI and had written a hagiographic biography of his deceased friend. He fully adopted Turgot's early thesis: scientific and technical progress was inevitable and irreversible. The marquis carefully purged the concept of historical progress of any religious traces his master had left on it in his early "Discours." Indeed, he hypostasized progress itself into some kind of secular deity. Traditional religion, even reduced to a deist belief in God, had no other merit than that of having awakened humans from their somnolent state through the superstitious terrors it evoked. At last, with the French Revolution, the decisive epoch of freedom had broken through. Like some of the accused in Stalinist trials, Condorcet continued to sing the praises of a regime that was preparing to execute him.[42]

He devoted the discussion of the final stage of history to a projection of indefinite progress based on three conditions. Condorcet regards it as certain that they will be met, even though they depend on future human decisions. First, cultures must be homogenized (on the model of the French republic) and a universal language ought to be created of simple and precise propositions.[43] A second condition requires that all citizens within the same nation have equal rights. Science and technical innovation do little to advance society unless its members are economically able to acquire the new inventions and are socially prepared to use them.[44] Condorcet proposes that all protectionist policies (such as France had known through most of the eighteenth century) be abolished and that commerce and industry be allowed to follow their natural course. In addition, Condorcet supported mandatory education. Where all enjoy equal opportunities, social and economic inequality would soon disappear.

The third condition is not a condition at all but a wild leap into utopia. "The perfectibility of the person is indefinite," he claims (p. 371, also p. 260). The progress of reason will transform human nature, not only intellectually but also morally. For Condorcet, the Socratic principle that virtue is knowledge, is axiomatic. It suffices that people understand human nature, its potential, and its goals to become moral. Even arts and letters will improve from one generation to the next. Corneille had already surpassed the Greek tragedians and Molière the ancient writers of comedy, while contemporary French painting, in Condorcet's questionable judgment, had much improved upon the unprecedented Italian art of the previous century (pp. 214, 305, 306). As diet, medicine, working conditions improve, the human life span will become unlimited (p. 374). Most promising of all: these marvelous physical, intellectual, and moral qualities will be inherited by future generations. A remarkably sanguine view for a man expecting execution!

Will these prophecies be fulfilled only *if humanity chooses* to follow the rules, or will they be realized *regardless* of choice? Condorcet forecast that history itself would convert the forces opposed to social equality into supportive ones. Progressive and obstructionist forces remain inextricably intertwined. History consists in a struggle of these two opposite principles.[45] Progress results from the struggle itself. Setbacks, delays, and reactions play an indispensable role in the dialectic of progress. Nonetheless, the course of progress may be accelerated or slowed down by human choices. Yet with undaunted optimism Condorcet expected that an effective social organization would eventually compel people to embrace principles that so obviously benefited their future happiness.

Condorcet's social-economic project brings to the surface what had remained hidden in all preceding theories of progress, namely, that the ideal of the good life had ceased to refer to what is good in itself. It now came to be defined by what previously had belonged to the sphere of means, namely, an increased access to material benefits and social services. Nor does the useful merely serve as a substitute for an ideal of the good on the nature of which members of a pluralist society have become unable to agree. For Condorcet, the useful *is* the good. To the question, then, "What is the end of progress?" he would have answered that it was progress itself. When suddenly the French Revolution made the changes possible that had been most needed — religious and political freedom — Condorcet made those intermediate goals into unqualified ends.[46] For Condorcet, the political and social emancipation would convert human nature into what it had never been before. He set a precedent for the twentieth-century gigantic projects of human engineering with their devastating effects.

Gibbon: History as a Moral Saga

In his majestic *Decline and Fall of the Roman Empire* (1776) Edward Gibbon reunited historical narrative, conceived in accordance with the ancient rhetorical tradition, with modern philological and archaeological research, two strands that had been separated since the Renaissance. His recombination of them enabled him to write a history richer in texture than that of any modern historian of Roman antiquity. Gibbon possessed a, for his time, stunning knowledge of the ancient sources and, aided by the French Jansenist Lenain de Tillemont's reputed *Histoire des Empereurs* (published posthumously in 1732), knew how to assess their reliability. At the same time, an uncanny ability to enter the emotional reality of the past enabled him to convey what it felt like to be part of a decaying empire. It allowed him to understand the minds of Rome's enemies as well as those of the Romans. Among the former he counted in the first place the Church, which, in his view, hastened the empire's decline. Gibbon took the theological disputes of the time very seriously and spent more effort analyzing them than he did on most military expeditions. Moreover, he understood that culture is never the achievement of a single nation, but that it results from an interaction among nations.[47] All of these qualities enabled him to convey a uniquely dramatic power to his history of an empire that, by the weight of inner as well as external causes, moved to a tragic end.

Gibbon's approach has been described as "empirical" and in his *Autobiography* he reports that he had indeed been influenced by Locke's philosophy.[48] Yet "conclusions" are more than the outcome of an empirical investigation. Gibbon rejects any kind of historical determinism, whether theological (as Vico did) or physical (as some French materialists did). Climate and geography, so heavily emphasized in the second part of Montesquieu's *The Spirit of Laws*, play only a minor role in his work. For him, history remains essentially a human process in which moral factors play the leading part. Only after the publication of part 1 (chaps. 1–16) did the English historian fully realize the importance of economics in a people's ability to turn physical conditions to political advantage. Later chapters betray the influence of Adam Smith's *Wealth of Nations*, which had appeared in the same year (1776) as the first part of *The Decline and Fall*. Gibbon's claim that as a society begins to produce more durable goods than the needs of the community requires, it increases its wealth "by the division of labor and the facility of exchange" might have been lifted out of Smith's classic.

Still, the moving causes of history remain moral. Nowhere does this appear more clearly than in the discussion of Christianity. In Gibbon's assessment, the rise of Christianity and the alleged changes it wrought in the moral attitude of the Romans weighed more heavily than any institutional reforms at the end of the republic. Unlike Vico and Montesquieu, he did not attribute the decline of the empire to the democratization of an originally aristocratic constitution. He admits that democracy opened the gates to demagogy and eventually led to an absolute monarchy. But the struggles between plebeians and patricians were not fatal to the life of the republic: they resulted in a "firm and equal balance of the constitution" (chap. 38, "General Observations," p. 630 [b]). Nor was the rise of the principate in itself a source of decline. Gibbon estimates that the second century was the happiest period in all of human history.

Many have read the controversial chapters 15–16 as basically repeating the arguments of fourth- and fifth-century pagans who blamed the Church for the disasters that were destroying their civilization. But this oversimplifies his position. In Gibbon's mind, the Church indeed bore major responsibility for *accelerating* a fatal decline. But the polemical chapters about the rise of

Christianity bear no direct relation to that decline, since it had been well on its way before the Christian faith became a major power. The Church accelerated it by draining much-needed energies away from the moral remnant of the state. She bore responsibility not so much for what she did as for what she failed to do, namely, to lend moral support to the state when it was sorely needed. Instead of coming to the rescue of an empire struggling for survival, the Church consumed whatever moral forces were left for furthering her own sectarian goals. "The last remains of the military spirit were buried in the cloister; . . . and the soldiers' pay was lavished on the useless multitudes of both sexes who could only plead the merits of abstinence and chastity" (chap. 38, p. 631 [b]). Gibbon repeats Rousseau's argument that the Christian emphasis on such otherworldly virtues as humility, obedience, and resignation weakened the moral fiber needed to resist the invasions of Goths, Vandals, Huns, and Franks. The Church's universalism failed to foster the patriotic attitudes indispensable for national solidarity. Gibbon never claims that, without the rise of Christianity, Rome could have survived. What he does assert is that only the moral force of the Church might have restored the empire's strength and conceivably halted the decline. On the other side, he credits the Church with civilizing the barbarians and thereby with having "cemented the union of the Christian republic" with similar morals and a common jurisprudence (chap. 8, p. 601 [b]).[49]

How, then, did the empire start to decline? Gibbon postpones discussing this question until the "General Observations" of chapter 38. He initiates his argument with an axiom partially borrowed from Montesquieu: "Honor, as well as virtue, was the principle of the republic" (chap. 38, p. 630 [a]). But its meaning differs from that of *The Spirit of Laws:* not just *virtue,* essential to the life of a republic, but also *honor,* Montesquieu's principle of the monarchy, are needed. While the transition from a democratic form of government to a principate played no essential role, the absence of virtue and honor to sustain it did. Contrary to Voltaire (*Essai sur les moeurs*) and an *Encyclopédie* article, "Empire Romain," written by Louis de Jaucourt, Gibbon maintains that the transfer of the seat of government to Constantinople was in itself no more than an administrative division of powers, not an abandonment of the West to the barbarians. It became disastrous only when competition and betrayal made the administrative separation a moral division and a religious schism.

Once Rome began to expand its territories beyond the Italian peninsula, her armies had to recruit soldiers who had never seen the city and were not attached to the empire. Mercenaries are notoriously unreliable. They follow their leaders but have no stake in preserving the state. Moreover, if political oppositions, inevitable within a state, carry over to the armed forces, they are likely to turn into civil wars, as the struggles between the armies of Marius and Sulla, Pompeius and Caesar in the final years of the republic had shown. Behind those particular causes stands the general one: the immense size of the empire. "The decline of Rome was the natural and inevitable effect of immoderate greatness. Prosperity ripened the principle of decay; the causes of destruction multiplied with the extent of the conquest; and as soon as time or accident had removed the artificial supports, the stupendous fabric yielded to the pressure of its own weight. The story of its ruin is simple and obvious and instead of inquiring why the Roman Empire was destroyed, we should rather be surprised that it had existed so long" (chap. 38, p. 63 [a]).

When a state expands beyond its natural borders it becomes vulnerable both to attacks from without and from within. Huge empires die from a loss of patriotic motivation among its nationally diverse inhabitants. No strong sense of citizenship is to be expected from those who lost their independence to a superstate. Thus the empire becomes dependent on citizens it cannot trust. In addition, the subjugation of many nations exposes its territory to threats that can hardly be foreseen. How could the Romans suspect that the peace of Italy was to be shaken by revolutions in distant China? Yet the Chinese annals may well contain "the secret and remote causes of the fall of the Roman Empire" (chap. 30, p. 483 [b]). Fleeing the marauding armies of Kublai Khan in their territory near the Caspian Sea, the Huns moved west toward Hungary and pressured the Gothic tribes who occupied that area into crossing the *limes* of the Danube. Even today Western empires ought not to feel confident that barbarians will never threaten them again. The power of independent "barbarians" may appear to have contracted too much to be a cause for apprehension among civilized nations. "Yet," Gibbon cautions, "this apparent security should not tempt us to forget that new enemies and unknown dangers may *possibly* arise from some obscure people, scarcely visible in the map of the world. The Arabs or Saracens, who spread their conquests from India to Spain, had languished in poverty and contempt till Mahomet breathed into those savage bodies the soul of enthusiasm" (chap. 38, p. 632 [b]).

Gibbon's ominous prediction that appears to have acquired a new probability in our own day returns the argument to his main thesis: the sources of historical ascent and decline are *moral*. Yet the "morality" of *Decline and Fall* differs from what we ordinarily consider "virtuous" behavior. It includes fearless courage, ruthless ambition, and political guile. Only nations endowed with those primitive qualities, rejected as vices by the morally refined, will conquer the earth. "The warlike states of Antiquity, Greece, Macedonia, and Rome, educated a race of soldiers; exercised their bodies, disciplined their courage, multiplied their forces by regular evolutions. . . . But this superiority insensibly declined with their laws and manners" (chap. 38, p. 633 [a]). Unless the peaceful learn to resist the violent with their own weapons, the barbarians will overrun them.

Despite this defense of Machiavellian *virtù,* Gibbon often appeals to a more traditional morality when his conquerors exceed the limits of what conventional standards of behavior tolerate. Indeed, it is by its moral vision, however ambiguous, that *The Decline and Fall* continues to fascinate the modern reader. We feel irresistibly drawn in by the epic conflict between the good and the bad, the generous and the selfish, the refined and the barbaric. But even more by the melancholy feeling of the transience of all human affairs, the very experience that stood at the origin of Gibbon's great work. In his memoirs he recalls the occasion: "It was at Rome on the 15th of October 1764, as I sat musing amidst the ruins of the Capitol, while the barefooted friars were singing Vespers in the Temple of Jupiter [then, as now, the church of Santa Maria in Aracoeli] that the idea of writing the decline and fall of the city first started to my mind." Gibbon views the past as irretrievably lost: heroism and cowardice, vice and virtue, in the end will leave nothing but ruins. This pervasive feeling of permanent loss has always conveyed a romantic attraction to *The Decline and Fall.*

In the concluding chapter 71, he once again contemplates the ruins, not *in propria persona,* but through the eyes of the fifteenth-century humanist Poggio. "The place and the object gave ample scope for moralizing on the vicissitudes of fortune, which spares neither man nor the proudest of his works, which buries empires and cities in a common grave; and it was agreed that, in proportion to her former greatness, the fall of Rome was the more awful and deplorable" (chap. 71, p. 590). What for Poggio had been a reflection on the eternal law of events, however, has in the British historian awakened a sorrowful sense of never-to-return pastness. Nor does the story of the past contain any providential design for future generations. The few times Gibbon mentions Providence, he does so in an ironic way, as when four thousand veterans unexpectedly land in the port of Ravenna and liberate the weak and incompetent emperor Honorius from an imminent invasion by the Goths. "But there *is* a Providence (such at least was the opinion of the historian Procopius) that watches over innocence and folly, and the pretensions of Honorius to its peculiar care cannot reasonably be disputed" (chap. 31, p. 508 [a]). Or again, when Augustine justifies the ways of Providence in the destruction of Rome by citing the respect the invading Goths paid to the sacred vessels (chap. 31, p. 509 [b]).

In contrast to ancient historians, Gibbon no longer turns to the past for exemplars. Even for Machiavelli, history had still served as *magistra* for our conduct in the present. The later historian paints his memorable characters, men like Marcus Aurelius, Athanasius, Alaric, Attila, or women like Theodora and Placidia in colors that make them appear very remote from our time. Precisely thereby do they hold a deeper fascination for us than examples of imitable virtue or avoidable vice might ever do. They present the more sweeping moral story of the infinite, ever changing variety of human nature. Like the aphorisms of the French *moralistes, Decline and Fall* gives insight through the observation of a human nature that, for all its universality, remains forever unpredictable.

The very title of *Decline and Fall* reveals Gibbon's historical position. The view of late antiquity as moving toward a "fall" was far from generally accepted before his work appeared and has become almost universally rejected by historians of our own time. In a recent lecture at the American Academy Professor Glen Bowersock pointed out how the obsession with "the fall of Rome" dates mainly from the publication of Gibbon's work. "This means that the reflections of a Montesquieu or even a Vico . . . do not represent what we have in mind when we speak of the fall. For Montesquieu, decadence and decline were deduced from the study of ancient literary texts, as were the shifting *corsi* and *ricorsi* of Giambattista Vico. For Gibbon, the primary inspiration was his own personal experience of ancient ruins in Italy, and especially in Rome. It was a very different experience from Poggio's."[50]

Did the empire ever actually "fall"? Concerning the end of the Eastern Empire there can be no doubt: in 1453 the Ottoman forces conquered Constantinople and absorbed the Byzantine Empire within their own. But the Western case appears far more complex. One might, indeed, claim with some justification that in 476 the Western Empire expired, since the title of "emperor" was lost when the barbarian Odoacer pensioned the young emperor Romulus Augustus off to Lucullus's villa on Capo Miseno. But ought the conquest by an unassimilated barbarian and the loss of the imperial title be called "the fall of the empire?" Odoacer was not the first "barbarian" sovereign of Rome, though he was the first who had no Roman citizenship. Nor did any abrupt change of civilization or even of juridical administration occur. Historians of the early Middle Ages feel less inclined to place the end of the Western Empire in 476. Henri Pirenne argues that the end did not come until the Islam definitively divided East from West. Peter Brown rejects the notion of a "fall" altogether and prefers to speak of a cultural transformation.

Gibbon continues the history of the Western Empire beyond "the fall." In 800 when the Eastern Empire still had a legitimate emperor with legal jurisdiction over East and West (the Roman senate had returned the title of imperial authority to Constantinople), Pope Leo III, acting as self-proclaimed heir of the entire empire, crowned Charlemagne as universal emperor. The legitimacy of this act was anything but certain, as the later need for a forged *donatio Constantini* proved. Yet when the Eastern Empire collapsed in 1453 the crowning might appear to have received some posthumous legitimation from the fact that no other title stood in its way. Assuming a minimal continuity of a title that persisted all through Christian civilization, one might even claim that the Holy Roman Empire continued until Napoleon formally abolished it. Even after that, some sizable part of it was resurrected at the Council of Vienna as the Austro-Hungarian Empire, which survived until 1917.

If the Western Empire, then, never really "fell," the Eastern one never seriously "declined" before its abrupt ending in 1453. The period of its greatest weakness, under the successors of Theodosius, Arcadius, and Theodosius II, preceded the very strong reign of Justinian and his powerful successors. Not only did Constantinople not collapse under the barbarian assaults of the fifth century, but its armies managed to reconquer Africa, and parts of Italy and Spain. Admittedly, compared to the earlier republic or even the early empire, the later empire may be said to have in some way "declined." But few historians agree on the nature and causes of this downward slide. Was it moral, social, political, economic decay, or all of these together, and if so, in which order? What, then, do the terms "decline" and "fall" stand for? They served Gibbon's purpose of telling a moral tale. Without a definite conclusion prepared by a preceding decline, the story would have lacked the coherence required by a moral saga. To meet this purpose, however, it needed not be coherent in all its particulars. The chapters 30–40 on the Gothic invasions show how loosely particular episodes of *Decline and Fall* were strung together. They are well-told stories, complete within their own right and in a general way contributing to the "decline" of the whole. But they leave the chronological order of events to the reader's industry and imagination.

For Gibbon, as for many historians of ancient Rome, a decisive political event occurred when the first Gothic tribes, pressed by migrating Huns, crossed the Danube. The invasions led to an ever-growing "barbarization." But would Rome have suffered any ill effects from it if the city had not expanded into an empire? Or if it had not changed its political system from aristocratic to democratic and then monarchic? Economic changes also played a major role, especially after the third century, and caused the cities, the source of a higher economy, to become deserted.[51] But what in this complex web of factors was cause and what effect? It is hard to disagree with the conclusion of resigned ignorance expressed by J. B. Bury, the excellent editor of Gibbon's work: "The gradual collapse of the Roman power in this section of the Empire was the consequence of a series of contingent events. No general causes can be assigned that made it inevitable."[52] Gibbon's great work, then, is not merely history; it is also rhetoric. Indeed, to a major extent it owes its popular success as a work of history to its rhetorical qualities.

This should not surprise us. Throughout Greek and Roman antiquity the writing of history had been an exercise in rhetoric. Composing the speeches of political and military heroes formed an essential part of the historian's craft, and much of the quality of his work was judged by his ability for posthumous speech writing. Gibbon, of course, endeavors to set himself apart from this kind of rhetorical inventiveness. Yet he continues to abide by what Isocrates called the "hegemony" of the *logos*, the rhetorical approach to his subject. A work of history had to excel by literary qualities as well as by historical exactitude. That Gibbon did succeed is attested even by such an unfriendly witness as Samuel Coleridge who calls him "our most eloquent historian."[53] Above all, Gibbon was a master of the sweeping moral tale in which virtue and vice, insight and insipience, become repaid in equal measure by success or failure in the outcome of events. In *The Decline and Fall* narrative history scores a total victory over the chronicle. The chronicle lacks a plot: it misses the symbolization indispensable for transforming mere facts into carriers of a human, spiritual meaning. Gibbon, like Hume in large parts of the *History of England* and like Voltaire in *Charles XII*, gives the events an enduring significance and their connection a literary composition. The grand scheme of the eighteenth-century storytellers moves them toward a dramatic ending. History here appears as essentially a result of human designs, and historiography as a product of the imagination as well as of knowledge and insight. Gibbon achieves this effect by pursuing a single theme throughout his work, but also in part by weaving events around a few major characters, such as Alaric, Genseric, Theodoric, Justinian, or Julian, even if such a condensation requires sacrificing the historical importance of others to the dramatic impact of the whole.[54]

Ever since its appearance, readers have praised the dignified style of *Decline and Fall*, worthy of the grandeur of its subject. This acclaim has profited from the fact that few have read the entire work. To those who have, the majestic periods and the cascading adjectives tend to lose some of their initial impressiveness once it appears that they are often unrelated to the nature of the subject. It has been said that Gibbon imitates Cicero; if this is true, he appears to have modeled his style only on Cicero's perorations. As Gilbert Highet wrote, *The Decline and Fall* is a perpetual peroration. Some find his prose condescending and self-congratulatory. I disagree, but I can hardly deny that occasionally Gibbon's grand style serves as a screen behind which the author hides a lack of precise information or even an inability to reach an adequate interpretation of the events. The solemn phrases inspire confidence that the writer remains in full control of the subject and that whatever may be missing is the subject's own fault. At times the reader suspects that, for Gibbon, the ultimate meaning of history lies in his writing it.

Yet another rhetorical quality distinguishes the writing of *The Decline and Fall*, a quality that Plato critically referred to as the art of making the weaker argument appear the stronger. Certainly, Gibbon never allowed rhetorical sophistry to jeopardize his historical credibility. But he does have axes to grind and grinds them with a vengeance. The famous diatribe on the rise of Christianity in chapters 15–16 fits but oddly in the general argument. Similarly, the lengthy discussion of the Islam serves more than an exclusively historical purpose: it does double duty as an object lesson in religious "fanaticism," the problem of Christianity writ large. Beyond these particular objectives lies the general one of Gibbon's story: to convince the reader of the central message of the Enlightenment, *sapere aude*. He never loses sight of the fundamental function of his eloquent narrative: to persuade his contemporaries to cast an critical glance at a past that hitherto had remained clouded in prejudice and "superstition." While uncovering the truth about late antiquity, Gibbon intends to spread the modern message of the reign of reason and of the universality of the human race. Other eighteenth-century writers — Vico, Voltaire, Turgot — had laid out the principles of a secular history of humankind. Gibbon actually showed in the one concrete instance of the Roman Empire how the fate of all human beings is interrelated and codetermined in places and by peoples far removed from the precincts of their own nation. Huge empires, such as the Assyrian, Babylonian, Persian, Hellenistic ones and the Roman, have played a role in making people aware of their solidarity with others.

Yet Gibbon did not present the global character of those empires as models for the future. Political structures of this magnitude, especially when inhabited by heterogeneous populations, are bound to collapse. Instead, he proposes the model of a loose union of small, independent nations that entertain an uninterrupted cultural exchange with one another. Such was ancient Greece; such were the socially advanced states of Europe at his time. "In all the pursuits of active and speculative life, the emulation of states and individuals is the most powerful spring of the efforts and improvements of mankind. The cities of ancient Greece were cast in the happy mixture of union and independence, which is repeated on a larger scale, but in a looser form, by the nations of modern Europe: the union of language, religion, and manners, which renders them the spectators and judges of each other's merit: the independence of government and interest, which asserts their separate freedom, and excites them to strive for pre-eminence in the career of glory. The situation of the Romans was less favorable" (chap. 53, p. 327 [b]).

This passage discloses the dual objective of Gibbon's work: one, to promote a cultural union through education and liberation from prejudice; the other, to caution against enforced political and cultural uniformity. Gibbon did not possess Montesquieu's acute perceptiveness for the sense of historical identity that a nation derives from its institutions and laws. Yet his study of Rome's expansion and decline had convinced him that oversized, politically centralized states end in ruin. At the same time, his lengthy exposure to what he regards as a millennium of "decline" discouraged him from nurturing any but the most cautious optimism for the future. Yes, he believed in the possibility of moral and cultural progress, and he was convinced that the advances in science and technology would prevent the West from relapsing into full barbarism. But his overall view of human behavior remained quite different from that of most philosophes. Where they held great expectations about the future of mankind, Gibbon remained skeptical to the end. A profound relativist, he was one of the first "historicists" of the modern age.[55]

Particular History, Universal Humanity: Herder and Kant

Herder presented the most serious challenge to the theories of the Enlightenment. In all three his studies on history, *Another Philosophy of History Concerning the Development of Mankind* (*Auch eine Philosophie der Geschichte zur Bildung der Menschheit* [1774]), *Reflections on the Philosophy of the History of Mankind* (*Ideen zur Philosophie der Geschichte der Menschheit* [1784–91]) (his only properly historical work), and *Letters for the Advancement of Humanity* (*Briefe zur Beförderung der Humanität* [1793–97]), he attacks the philosophes, though in the later works less so than in the earlier ones.[56] In the early *Another Philosophy* he rejects the Enlightenment idea of historical progress altogether. In the *Reflections* he admits the possibility of moral progress but denies that it coincides with the advance of "reason." In the *Letters* he hesitantly accepts the philosophes' theories of freedom and equality as he saw them realized in the French Revolution. Throughout these shifts Herder's position remained consistently anti-rationalist. The light of reason does not warm the soul, he often repeats. "In our century we have, alas, so much light" (*In unserem Jahrhundert ist leider so viel Licht*) (*Another Philosophy*, in *Werke*, V, 524). "While light has been endlessly exalted, the drive and passion to live have become disproportionately weakened. Ideas of universal love for humanity, peoples, enemies, have increased, but warmth in the natural affections toward fathers, mothers, brothers, and friends has infinitely decreased" (ibid., p. 538). The Enlightenment has replaced ancient prejudice by the more harmful prejudice of reason. Great art and poetry would not have existed without a commitment to ideas and values we now call "prejudices," while the unprejudiced age of reason can claim few memorable achievements. Richness of experience has yielded to poverty of abstraction (*Another Philosophy*, in *Werke*, V, 543–544).

Yet far more significant than Herder's critique of the Enlightenment was his success in synthesizing its leading ideas and in overcoming their one-sidedness. He balanced the universal ideal of *humanity* with the irreducible particularity of each nation, the idea of organic growth with that of causal determinism, the divine guidance of history with the uninhibited autonomy of human efforts. Each culture forms an independent, organic entity and each people is animated by its own spirit — the *Volksgeist* — and "each functions as means and end at once" (ibid., p. 527). Nor does the purpose of earlier civilizations consist in preparing the later ones, as Turgot or Condorcet claimed. History has known good and bad times, periods of beauty and of ugliness. But the better ones are not necessarily the later ones, though later epochs profit from the lessons of the past. The philosophes proclaim their own age the goal of all previous history: "We are the healers, the saviors, the enlightened ones: the times of the mad fever are gone" (ibid., p. 556). Herder insists: no individual exists "for the sake of another or of posterity" (*Ideen*, bk. XV, chap. 5, in *Werke*, XIV, 246; *Reflections*, p. 113). Each nation expresses a different mode of living, based on different standards of perfection. Isaiah Berlin called Herder the first cultural pluralist of the West. He was indeed the first major thinker to maintain that the values of different cultures are irreducible to a common denominator. Yet in the end the term "pluralism" fails to do justice to Herder's thought, since the irreducible cultural variety forms part of an all-integrating unity.[57]

Neither ought the historian assume that a final causality determines the succession of events. If the physical sciences have reaped no benefit from the concept of final causes, how much less will history do so "with its endlessly complicated machinery of causes that mutually act upon each other" (*Ideen*, bk. XIV, chap. 6, in *Werke*, XIV, 202; *Reflections*, pp. 266–67). Human affairs form only an infinitesimal link in the chain of nature. Seeing no more than our own contribution to the whole, we imagine that we must be the centerpiece of creation. Yet human history forms only a small part of natural history and historians ought to follow the same empirical method that has proven so successful in the natural sciences. Herder's lengthy treatise on world history begins with a startling sentence: *Unsre Erde ist ein Stern unter Sternen* (Our earth is a star among stars), followed by a discussion of the earth's geological formation (*Ideen*, bk. I, chap. 1, in *Werke*, XIII, 13; *Reflections*, pp. 13–46). Human history takes its place within this cosmic process. Still, despite his opposition to teleological speculations, Herder remained unwavering in his conviction that history follows a *meaningful* course. Its completion is both an ideal and a reality in progress. Only when all civilizations have run their course will the human race have completed its task of achieving a comprehensive moral community. Meanwhile, the moral ideal of *Humanität* summons each individual and each nation to follow his or her own vocation in the process of history. *Humanität*, then, remains a very elusive concept. It is at once a norm of action, an ideal of moral development, a construction of historical perspective, and a world-historical process.[58] Some individuals and even some nations have left universal models of perfection. Such were the aesthetic ideal of humanity realized in classical Greece and the moral one preached by Christ. Yet all civilizations, however imperfect, have their place in a process that irresistibly moves toward a universal, moral community.

Since this process is a necessary one, Herder feels justified in calling *Humanität* a *reality*, albeit one in progress. He supports the necessity of its realization by a surprising principle: "Whatever can take place among mankind, within the sphere of given circumstances of time, place, and nation, actually does take place" (*Ideen*, bk. XIII, chap. 7, in *Werke*, XIV, 144; *Reflections*, p. 213). If this means that over an endless stretch of time anything that can take place must take place, the principle does not apply to history, because we have no assurance that time extends into an infinite future, and even if it did, the conditions of the process change from moment to moment in an irreversible succession. But Herder appears to have had something else in mind. The "necessity" he writes about is a conditional one: given a certain situation and the link that connects cause and effect in natural history, it follows that, if history is indeed a natural process, certain events are bound to occur. "The whole history of mankind is a pure natural history of human powers, actions, and propensities, modified by time and place" (*Ideen*, bk. XIII, chap. 7, in *Werke*, XIV, 145; *Reflections*, p. 214). One may, of course, question whether the view that human affairs are no more than a link in the chain of nature is compatible with the freedom he praises in his *Letters for the Advancement of Humanity* as the main accomplishment of the modern age.

Matters become even more complicated when Herder attributes this determinism to a providential disposition. His interpretation of Providence differs, however, from Turgot's. To conceive of history as a progressive development guided by God's hand (as the French thinker did) conflicts with the most elementary observation of the crimes and disasters that terrorize the world.

Such a "progressive" view of Providence stems from the same overblown opinion of one's own epoch that gave birth to the secular philosophies of progress. Herder denies that God furthers the fortunes of one nation or of one epoch at the expense of others. In his conception, humanity forms part of a divine plan that includes all of nature and conveys meaning to all times. God realizes his comprehensive design through the same natural appetites that drive individuals and nations to irrational, violent behavior as well as to virtue and culture. Even after they discover the wisdom of reason and order, humans continue to oscillate between chaos and rule. The eternal law of nature points toward balance, but human nature, torn by conflicting powers, "vibrates between extremes . . . till [it] reaches the temperate mean" (*Ideen,* bk. XV, chap. 5, in *Werke,* XIV, 246; *Reflections,* p. 114). Through the unhappy consequences of mindless deeds, nations like individuals eventually learn to observe the laws of reason. "To all these disorders Providence has applied no other remedy than what she administers to individuals; namely, that each fault should be followed by a corresponding evil, and every act of indolence, folly, malice, rashness, and injustice by its own punishment" (*Ideen,* bk. XV, chap. 5, in *Werke,* XIV, 247–48; *Reflections,* p. 115). So, in the end, all enter into God's design. That design aims at the good of *all* nature and in humans, at the fullest realization of their humanity.

Within this "natural" course of history, Herder admits only one direct divine intervention. In the person of Jesus appears a moral ideal of perfection, which the human race will not attain until its final stage. "The most genuine humanity is contained in the few discourses of [Jesus] that are preserved: humanity he displayed in his life and confirmed by his death: and the favorite name, by which he chose to distinguish himself was that of the son of man" (*Ideen,* bk. XVII, intro., in *Werke,* XIV, 290; *Reflections,* p. 269). That divine model, however, lost much of its power in the very Church founded to keep it alive. Nevertheless, the Church, in linking all peoples by a spiritual bond, formed an inclusive European culture. "Christianity has knotted a tie among the peoples as the conquests of Alexander, the Romans, and the Huns had never succeeded in doing. It was intended to be a bond of peace, however often it became a cause of strife and disputes. In the hands of Providence it also became a bond of *culture,* of a common culture among the nations" (*Letters,* Collection V, # 1, in *Werke,* XVII, 301). Even the papal "despotism" of the Middle Ages, harshly criticized in *Ideen,* XIX, had an unintended beneficial effect. "The pressure of the Romish hierarchy was perhaps a necessary yoke, an indispensable bridle for the rude nations of the Middle Ages. Without it Europe had probably been the prey of despots, a theatre of eternal discord, or even a Mungal [Mongol] wilderness. Thus as a counterpoise it merits praise" (*Ideen,* bk. XX, chap. 6, in *Werke,* XIV, 492; *Reflections,* p. 397).

Herder never discusses how much any given civilization realized the ideal of humanity. His critique of the Roman and the medieval Christian one appears severe for one who believed that each civilization contributes an essential part to the whole. In the *Ideen,* he thoroughly demolishes the neoclassical ideal of the Roman republic as a moral model. The genius of the Romans, idealized in European schoolbooks, was not *humanitas* (even though they invented the term), he claims, but an extraordinary ability for military conquest. "By degrees Rome drained, enervated, and depopularized Italy," so that barbarians were needed to repopulate it again (*Ideen,* bk. XIV, chap. 3, in *Werke,* XIV, 171; *Reflections,* p. 238). Having first subjugated Italy Rome attacked Carthage, transforming a flourishing North African civilization into a cultural desert. Roman civilization, undeniably, transmitted Greek culture to the West and even produced a few original creations of its own. But were Virgil's *Aeneid* and Horace's *Epistles* worth "the rivers of blood"? (*Ideen,* bk. XIV, chap. 6, in *Werke,* XIV, 201; *Reflections,* p. 265). Does Rome deserve credit even for having "preserved" Greek culture? Its intent was to conquer and, having little culture of its own, it took from others what it had been incapable of creating itself. "The Romans were destroyers, and in their turn destroyed: but destroyers are no preservers of the world. They irritated all nations, till at length they became their prey; and Providence performed no miracle on their behalf" (ibid., p. 267). Nor ought Christians look at Roman expansionism as a providential means for spreading their faith. "It would be derogatory to divine Providence to suppose that, for her noblest work, the propagation of truth and virtue, she could employ no other instrument, than the tyrannical and bloody hands of the Romans" (ibid., p. 266).

Nonetheless Herder himself considers the empire a step toward a global community. Its very collapse made a fresh beginning possible. Vigorous Gothic and Germanic tribes reoccupied the enormous territory and infused the exhausted empire with new, vital forces. Earlier Herder had written: "Whoever observes the condition of the Roman lands (they made up the entire civilized world at the time!) in the final centuries will marvel and wonder at the ways of Providence's work in having prepared such a peculiar replacement of human forces" (*Another Philosophy,* in *Werke,* V, 514). Rome's fall negatively created the conditions of moral renewal of which she herself was incapable. Moreover, the city left the barbarian invaders a common language and political structures.

Herder's discussion of medieval Christianity displays a similar ambiguity toward a culture that fell short of its ideal vocation yet unwittingly moved history closer to its final ideal. Surprisingly, after his early defense of the Middle Ages as a period of experience and dynamic vitality (*Another Philosophy,* in *Werke,* V, 524–26), and the later one of Christian culture as indispensable for the unification of Europe (bk. XIX of *Ideen*), he thoroughly denounced the enslavement of the European nations by papal and ecclesiastical despotism. What had Christ's humanitarian message accomplished, if it led only to a moral condition inferior to that of pagan society? Here as in other instances Herder distinguished the moral quality of a particular epoch from its part in the realization of the universal goal of history. Medieval Christianity failed in the former, yet it strongly contributed to the latter.

The discrepancy between the fundamental principles lying at the ground of Christian culture and the highly imperfect history of that culture raises a more comprehensive question about the role of religion in attaining the ideal of *Humanität*. For Herder, religion forms the core of that universal ideal. Yet religions have also been responsible for the divisions among nations and have constituted the most serious obstacle to the formation of a universal human community. Herder rejects Rousseau's solution of the problem, namely, the creation of a universal civil religion. The Lutheran minister knew too much about the nature of faith to adopt such an artificial stratagem. Religion is by its very nature *specific* and ought to be so, if it is to be practiced at all. He only demanded that this practice not conflict with the universal ideal of *humanitas*. Herder distinguishes particular doctrines from the universal principles that support them. All ought to cultivate the principles and respect the doctrine. This synthesis of religious particularity and universality does not imply that he considers all doctrines equal. The fundamental principles of Christianity, for him, incarnate the very ideal of *Humanität,* but he disdains the conflicting interpretations the Christian Churches have given of Jesus' message.

One might wonder how civilizations so basically opposed to one another in their moral ideals as the Greek, the Roman, and the medieval, not to mention the Far Eastern ones, could ever constitute a harmonious whole. His belief in a final concordance of irreducibly diverse civilizations was, in fact, inspired by an aesthetic notion of harmony, rather than by the moral one he proclaimed. In art and poetry, oppositions, however strong, may complement one another in a way they cannot do in a moral system. Influenced by Winckelmann and Goethe, Herder increasingly came to use the harmonious form of Greek art and poetry as a model for his cultural ideal of *Humanität*. Classical sculpture and architecture presented the "epitome of all that is sensible on earth" (*Letters,* in *Werke,* XVII, 343). The pages he devoted to Greek art and poetry and to their role in the new German educational ideal substantially contributed to a Greek renaissance in Germany, the romantic counterpart of the Enlightenment's Latin classicism in France.

The advent of the French Revolution, which he greeted as a major victory of the human spirit, may have convinced Herder that his own theory implied a more rectilinear idea of progress than he had previously admitted. He discontinued work on the *Ideen,* for which he had planned five more books, and in his next *Letters for the Advancement of Humanity* (1793–97), he changed his assessment of the Enlightenment and its idea of progress. The breakthrough of freedom in this one revolutionary event suddenly appeared to shorten the road to the realization of his moral ideal in an irreversible move toward freedom. The sympathy with which other nations had greeted the revolution suggested that a morally united community of the peoples of Europe was about to be born. Yet in a second collection of *Letters* (1793), written at the time of the *Terreur* in Paris, Herder wondered whether his idea of a definitive moral progress of the human race had been more than a utopian aspiration (*Letters,* Collection II, # 24, in *Werke,* XVII, 113). He concludes this *Letter* on an uncharacteristically skeptic note: "Allow me with Lessing to consider the entire dream of the increasing perfection of our race to be a salutary deceit. Humans have to aim at something higher, if they do not want to sink lower" (ibid., p. 114). At least the illusion of *perfectibility* preserves people from morally degenerating.

Soon, however, Herder reasserts his belief in the possibility of a truly human community. Yet more than before, he stresses that moral improvement ought to accompany cultural progress in the complex combination of cultural refinement and moral growth, to which he refers by the word *Bildung.* This defining term of Germany's new humanism combined the pursuit of a cultural-aesthetic ideal with the moral one of noble conduct. It included, next to a schooling in the classical *studia humaniora,* a moral training in the virtues of moderation, equanimity, and kindness, inspired by the Roman ideal of *humanitas* and the Christian one of brotherly love. Herder considered such a program necessary to avert the dangerously competitive drive that continued to estrange peoples from one another. Having witnessed ever more nations drawn into international conflicts, he darkly prophesied: "A conflict of all nations of the earth might well be imagined. In fact, the ground for that has already been established" (*Letters,* Collection II, # 16, in *Werke,* XVII, 118). Despite those somber forebodings, Herder preserved his faith in the possibility of achieving a universal peace. Humans enter the world with a predisposition toward full *humanity* (*Letters,* Collection III, # 27, in *Werke,* XVII, 138).

Herder's idea of the end of history remains purely hypothetical. Will the human race ever realize the *moral* ideal of *Humanität?* Even if rational beings learn from their mistakes, as he claims, we may wonder whether they ever learn enough to live up to that ideal. People tend to invent new vices even as they develop new virtues. Despite the utopianism inherent in Herder's thought, the remarkable balance between universality and particularity in his theory of history strongly influenced the views of the romantic era. The sweeping conclusion of a recent commentator may not be exaggerated. "No one in our tradition has thought more radically about the need to accomplish a mediation between the particular and the universal, pluralism and monism, just as no one else has produced such a startlingly ambitious attempt to do so."[59]

Herder saw his ideal incarnated in Kant, the "teacher of *Humanität.*" What impressed the former disciple most in his master was that in his personal life Kant abided by the strict moral code he advocated in his philosophy. After much hesitation, Kant adopted his disciple's moral ideal. He provided the concept of *Humanität* with a more solid moral foundation in the second form of the categorical imperative: Treat persons as ends, never merely as means. Still Kant's primarily moral meaning was more restricted than Herder's, for whom the idea of a fully humanitarian development consisted in an uninhibited, open communication among nations in which the cultural as well as the moral potential of the human race would be fully realized.

Kant's initial reaction to *Ideas Toward a Philosophy of the History of the Human Race* (1784) had been quite critical. He had frowned upon Herder's analogy between the growth of an organic being and the cultural development of human beings. "There is not the least resemblance between the gradient progression in the same man who is ever ascending to a more perfect structure in another life and the ladder which one may conceive among completely different types and individuals in the realm of nature."[60] Nonetheless, shortly thereafter Kant himself began to write of *Humanität* as the moral destination of the human race. In his "Conjectural Beginning of Human History" (1786), he traces the development of the human species from an animal state to one of genuine humanity. The current condition of Europeans, compared to that of primitives, warrants at least a "responsible conjecture" that humans have made some progress since the beginning of the race ("Conjectural Beginning" in *Kant on History,* p. 59; *Schriften,* VII, 114). But not all in the area where it matters most. Earlier Kant had written: "To a degree we are, through art and science, *cultured.* We are *civilized* — perhaps too much for our own good — in all sorts of social graces and decorum. But to consider ourselves as having reached *morality* — for that much is lacking. The ideal of morality belongs to culture; its use for some simulacrum of morality in the love of honor and outward decorum constitutes mere civilization" ("Idea for a Universal History" in *Kant on History*, p. 21; *Schriften*, VII, 26).

In his famous essay on the Enlightenment, Kant admitted that culture had taken the road toward irreversible progress. Once reason has become enlightened and freedom emancipated, no political or religious authority is capable of halting humanity on its course to full enlightenment.[61] Still, the removal of the obstacles does not imply that we have *actually* become enlightened. We do not yet live in an enlightened age, Kant insists, but we do live in age of enlightenment. Moral progress has not kept pace with the intellectual advances of the modern age. Yet without moral improvement we have not moved closer to the ideal of *Humanität*.

Finally, in one of his last writings, "An Old Question Raised Again: Is the Human Race Constantly Progressing?" (1798), Kant conceded that we have actually achieved moral progress. Yet he still refused to embrace the optimistic thesis of the French philosophes that humanity constantly advances. Even if we have progressed, what assures us that we shall continue to do so in the future? At the same time, Kant dismisses the hypothesis that history moves back and forth between good and evil. Though logically irrefutable, that position must be rejected on moral grounds. A constant alternation of good and evil, he argues, rules out what the moral imperative demands, namely, that moral life follow an ascending line in the human species as well as in the individual.

Kant never abandoned his position that a morality exclusively determined by the intention cannot be objectively measured. But at least we are able to ascertain whether prevailing conditions favor or obstruct the practice of morality. By that measure, changes that promote the attainment of a higher level of freedom must be considered signs of moral progress. The French Revolution was, in this respect, an irreversible breakthrough toward freedom. The disinterested sympathy that its contemporaries showed for it indicated that it met with universal approval. Kant's surprising opinion was by no means shared in countries where the revolutionary armies had wrought havoc and violated the sovereignty of the nation. Nonetheless, he confidently declared: "Now I claim to be able to predict to the human race even without prophetic insight — according to the aspects and omens of our day, the attainment of this goal."[62]

At the conclusion of the war between the French Republic and the League of European Monarchies, Kant had even expressed his belief that a universal peace among European nations was possible and likely to be concluded. In his early "Conjectural Beginning" he had considered war indispensable for the development of culture. At a time of conflict a nation rallies all its powers, becomes inventive in its attempt to outwit the adversary, and produces at maximum capacity. In the essay "Toward Perpetual Peace: A Philosophical Project" (1795), he argued that in an advanced civilization this brutal means of self-assertion turns against itself.[63] The nation's resources, instead of being used for the benefit of the citizens, are squandered on the conduct of war. Freedom becomes restricted and moral values jeopardized. Indeed, an advanced culture requires peace for its survival.

For the maintenance of peace Kant recommended establishing a court of international law to enforce the observance of the moral law in international relations. Kant's theory of a purely internal morality has frequently been held responsible for moral indifference with respect to public policy, as if in legal matters obedience to the legal authority of one's own nation were the only moral requirement (a principle still invoked by a number of Nazi war criminals). The treatise on peace shows that, far from consenting to such a moral duplicity, he vigorously strove to abolish it. As long as policy has not made public life conformable to the moral law, the age of reason has not truly begun. To be sure, Kant never ceased to stress that no political institutions can achieve the moral end of history. The moral struggle begins with each person anew and will not be concluded before the end of time. But part of each individual's moral obligation consists in improving the conditions favorable to the development of humankind's moral capacities.

8

The Religious Crisis

The impact of the Enlightenment was undoubtedly felt most deeply in the area of religion, either as loss or as liberation. It was particularly severe in France and in England, where for a long time skeptical philosophies had undermined the foundations of Christian beliefs. By the end of the eighteenth century, the French masses, pressed by economic hardship, felt abandoned by a Church closely linked to a political regime indifferent to their suffering. In England, after two centuries of religious turmoil, the willingness of the Church to adapt its doctrine to the will of the sovereign had drained common people of any expectation of receiving teaching in the body that had traditionally dispensed it. Still, much piety, even mystical fervor, remained. Yet when compared to the Baroque, the last season of religious exuberance that preceded it, the age looks bleak. Science was flourishing; philosophy was reaching one of its greatest periods. But as life was losing its mystery, many, even among the pioneers of the intellectual revolution, felt that it was losing its depth.

To define the causes of the transformation is both easy and difficult. Easy because they appear so obvious. Difficult because after analyzing the "causes," the strength of their impact upon Western consciousness continues to escape us. What follows, then, is not so much an explanation as a description. In past centuries religion had been the integrating factor of Western culture; in the eighteenth century it was forced to the sidelines. Christianity had once formed the core of Western culture: the Church ruled intellectual life, directed the universities, set the norms of moral conduct. For a long period she had also controlled the political structures. But since the struggle between pope and emperor and the rise of national states in the fourteenth century, political power had gradually slipped from her hands. The loss of Christian unity during the Reformation confronted political leaders with a new problem. Should they accept the division among their subjects and embrace a policy of religious toleration, or should they attempt to enforce religious homogeneity? We know that at first they tried the harsher method, causing a general con- flagration of Western Europe that lasted almost a century and concluded in the shaky compromise of the 1648 Peace of Westphalia. In the second half of the seventeenth century, dissenting minorities, particularly in England and France, insisted on their right to practice religion in accordance with their conscience. To recognize that right required an unprecedented separation between Church and state. This privatization of faith aroused protest from the established Churches since it deprived them of the right to implement their principles in public policy and to conform society to their theological norms. As the Churches never reached an agreement on mutual recognition, the very princi- ple of tolerance became a hotly contested issue. All of this led to a great deal of confusion among the faithful.

A more immediate cause was undoubtedly a new image of the cosmos, which was strongly at variance with the one presupposed by Christian theol- ogy. The conflict first appeared in the interpretation of Scripture. The primary problem was no longer the formal one it had been for Galileo and his contem- poraries: How can we reconcile the letter of the Bible with the new scientific theories? The text itself had become unintelligible. Its language suddenly ap- peared utterly incongruous with the scientific worldview. Its symbols had lost their transparency.[1] In the second half of the seventeenth century, Bible schol- ars initiated a long overdue historical critique of the ancient text. Their conclu- sions soon became a powerful argument against a Church that had built her doctrines on what now seemed to be an untrustworthy foundation.

Not only the discrepancy between the new cosmology and the text of the Bible, but the very notion of divine causality had become questionable. When efficient causality, conceived on the model used in modern science, came to define the relation between Creator and creature, the more intimate depen- dence implied by the traditional doctrine, was lost. Creation so conceived opened the door to a number of alternative interpretations. As Hume showed, a purely efficient cause of nature need neither be divine nor personal. The three factors, then, that most contributed to the religious crisis of the Enlightenment among intellectuals were biblical criticism, scientific rationalism, and the unresolved division of the religious communities.

Biblical Criticism

Early humanists and reformers had launched a concerted effort to rescue the literal meaning of Scripture from the figurative ones that had freely flourished since Augustine. This new literalism had raised the expectation that the narratives of the Bible were historically accurate. But further philological study had evoked serious questions about this assumed accuracy. Allegedly historical accounts, especially those of the first chapters of Genesis, came to vary ever more widely from the historical, geological, and physical discoveries modern science was making at an accelerated pace. By the middle of the eighteenth century the entire sacred history began to look like one comprehensive exception to all we know both of the physical world and of human history. The six days of creation, the strange longevity of the patriarchs (Mathusela lived a record 969 years—figures hard to contest as not literally "intended." Why otherwise would they be so precise?), the Flood that covered the whole earth, yet of which other nations knew nothing—these were all questions that urgently required an answer.[2]

The most drastic among the solutions proposed for saving the meaning of the sacred text was the theory of a double historical truth, proposed by the famous inventor of the Pre-Adamites, Isaac de la Peyrère. In his *Theological System upon the Presupposition That Men Were Before Adam* (1656), he postulated two creations: one of Adam at the beginning of Jewish history, and an earlier one that gave birth to all other nations. Thus with one stroke he reduced the whole history of the Bible to a local phenomenon. Amazingly, even such scientists and scholars as Pascal and Arnauld continued to insist on a literal interpretation. The exegetical problems created by philology touched off a crisis when it appeared that no adequate answers compatible with traditional Christian doctrine were forthcoming. In his *Tractatus Theologico-Politicus* (1670), Spinoza proposed a radically different method of interpreting the Bible. Catholic and Protestant theologians unanimously rejected it, though eventually many ended up applying it themselves. In the course of the discussion it appeared that the questions raised by biblical hermeneutics required a more fundamental philosophical reflection on the status of a historical religion than either philology or history could provide.

Many exegetes had been conscious of a distinction between the *meaning* and the *accuracy* of the biblical narratives. For centuries commentators had been questioning Moses' alleged authorship of the entire Pentateuch (which includes a description of his death). But it was Spinoza who drove a decisive wedge between the meaning of biblical writings and their historical reliability. Supported by a solid knowledge of the Hebrew language (he had published a Hebrew grammar) and a lifelong study of Scripture, he proposed a new, subjective principle of exegesis, namely, the intention of the author. This, of course, had been virtually absent from the ancient belief that the author served as a mere mouthpiece of divine communications. Spinoza's method consisted in interpreting Scripture by principles present in Scripture itself. A correct understanding of the text will disclose what the author had in mind. To acquire it, readers had to acquaint themselves with the particular idiom of the Hebrew language and the historical circumstances of the time when a text was written in order to establish the author's intention. Only in this way would they be able to establish the meaning of the text. "We are at work not on the *truth* of passages, but solely on their *meaning*."[3]

Traditionally, the historical events reported in the text had formed part of the eternal truth of revelation and hence that report had to be free of factual errors. To this tradition Spinoza opposed that the allegedly historical parts of the Bible were narratives, told in various degrees of accuracy, by means of which the ancient writers attempted to convey a timeless truth. These historical reports possess neither the universality nor the certainty that true knowledge of God requires. "The truth of a historical narrative, however assured, cannot give us the knowledge nor consequently the love of God, for love of God springs from knowledge of Him, and knowledge of Him should be derived from general ideas, in themselves certain and known, so that the truth of a historical narrative is very far from being requisite for our attaining our highest good" (*TTP*, III, 61; Elwes, 61). Thus, Spinoza cut the Gordian knot that had linked biblical realism to historical inerrancy. For him, the Bible moved on two planes. On one, Mosaic Law and the Hebrew prophets prepared the still primitive Hebrew tribes for their historical mission. On the other, they laid the groundwork for a religion of universal truth that required neither historical miracles nor legal institutions. Israel's historical mission was completed, according to Spinoza, when its religion ceased to be linked to its particular history and became universal in the person of Jesus. "Christ was sent to teach not only the Jews but the whole human race, and therefore it was not enough that his mind should be accommodated to the opinions of the Jews alone, but also to the opinion and fundamental teaching common to the whole human race — in other words, to ideas universal and true" (*TTP*, 64; Elwes, 64). Though Christ enjoyed a direct insight in God's nature, he nevertheless had to express this to others through parables, miracles, and doctrines adapted to "the ignorance and obstinacy of the people" (ibid.). Whereas biblical realism had formerly depended on a correct reporting of facts, in Spinoza's interpretation it consisted in a correct conveyance of the writer's *intention* in reporting alleged facts.[4]

The *Tractatus Theologico-Politicus* leaves many questions unanswered. How does the historical role of the prophets and the coming of Christ relate to the impersonal, unchangeable God of Spinoza's *Ethics?* Some interpreters have read the text as a cryptogram decipherable only to the learned but hiding its pantheistic content under theological terminology.[5] Others (including myself) read the *Tractatus* as a philosophical reflection on a way of salvation that runs parallel with that of philosophy without ever coinciding with it.[6] While philosophy pursues truth in a purely theoretical way, revelation requires in the first place obedience to practical precepts, though they are built on theoretical "foundations." "Philosophy has no end in view save truth; faith . . . looks for nothing but obedience and piety. Again, philosophy is based on axioms which must be sought from nature alone: faith is based on history and language and must be sought for only in Scripture and revelation" (*TTP,* 179; Elwes, 189).

Philosophy and faith rest on a common foundation: the mind's participation in the nature of God (*TTP,* 15; Elwes, 14). Since this participation constitutes the very essence of the mind, Spinoza considers all knowledge of God natural. But reason alone is unable to justify the salvific character of obedience to God. "The power of reason does not extend so far as to determine for us that men may be blessed through simple obedience, without understanding" (*TTP,* 184; Elwes, 194). Revelation, therefore, must complement rational reflection. Scripture itself, however, assumes some philosophical principles that are indispensable for understanding its precepts. Among them: the existence of God as one, omnipresent, all-powerful, benevolent to those who worship him in justice and charity, and forgiving the sins of those who repent (*TTP,* 103, 77–78; Elwes, 104, 187). Genuine faith never conflicts with those philosophical presuppositions, "the fundamental dogmas of the whole of Scripture" (*TTP,* 177; Elwes, 186). Indeed, the "dogmas" of faith *materially* coincide with the fundamentals of speculative knowledge, though *formally* they differ from them, as they have not been deduced by reason but passively accepted from revelation. Theological faith is incapable of rationally justifying its own foundations. Yet the *practical* attitude of faith carries its own authority, protected by the theoretical foundations of biblical religion.

True faith, then, remains free of "superstition," that is, of any belief that conflicts with the laws of nature established by reason. For Spinoza that means that the "miracles" reported in the Bible must have been natural events. Whether one considers them so or regards them as miraculous "signs" matters little, since faith is not about truth but about obedience. "Everyone is free to think on the subject as he likes, according as he thinks it best for himself and most likely to conduce to the worship of God and to single-hearted religion" (*TTP*, 96; Elwes, 97). Nor ought the discrepancies among various parts of the Bible disturb the faithful. Given the fact that all sources of revelation are "natural" and, indeed, that "man himself is the main source of revelation," errors are unavoidable. Such errors do not affect the principles that lie at the ground of the practical goals of religion — justice and charity. In reading Scripture we must seek what is most universal and what the prophets unanimously commend as most conducive to a good life. "Quod universalissimum . . . et quod tanquam aeterna et omnibus mortalibus utilissima doctrina ab omnibus Prophetis commendatur" (*TTP*, 102; Elwes, 104). Those principles parallel the principles of reason. Both lead to the same religion, the *amor Dei intellec-tualis*. But philosophy recognizes no authority but that of reason.

This clear picture becomes murkier if one attempts to incorporate the various remarks that Spinoza occasionally inserts in his argument. At one point in the *Tractatus*, the parallel lines of philosophy and revelation appear to meet, namely, in the person of Christ.[7] Spinoza attributes to Christ an intuitive knowledge of God that surpasses both rational cognition and faith (*TTP*, 21; Elwes, 18). "Inasmuch as God revealed Himself to Christ's mind immediately, and not as to the prophets through words and symbols, we must needs suppose that Christ perceived truly what was revealed, in other words, He understood it, for a matter is understood when it is perceived simply by the mind without words or symbols" (*TTP*, 64; Elwes, 64). The basic content of Christ's insight could be transmitted to his followers because of its extreme simplicity: Love (one) God and love your neighbor (*TTP*, 156; Elwes, 162).

Once revealed this universal message required no external authority. Christian faith thereby ceased to be a "particular" religion, resting on one person's authority. Indeed, further theoretical or practical specification of it betray the original message. All who adhere to the religious precept of love receive their religion through Christ, though not necessarily through the Christian Church. "Paul concludes that since God is the God of all nations, that is, is equally gracious to all, and since all men equally live under the law and under sin, so also to all nations did God send this Christ, to free all men equally from the bondage of the law" (*TTP*, 54; Elwes, 53). The message of Christ is intrinsically universal and all who honor God by practicing justice and charity possess the spirit of Christ.[8]

But Christ's message must be distinguished from New Testament *Scripture*. The apostles derived their insight from Christ, but being incapable of fully assimilating it, their interpretation of the message was limited by their imperfect understanding of it. They tended to understand that message as a new "law," and thus again reduced it to a *particular* revelation, albeit one addressed to all peoples. In defending the universal quality of the Christian faith, Spinoza by no means intended to equate it with philosophy. Indeed, he criticizes the early Christian writers' attempt to express Christian doctrine in philosophical arguments. In so doing they distorted what was essentially a simple, moral religion and set off an endless succession of schisms and heresies that turned the message of charity into an acrimonious debate. "I have often wondered that persons who make a boast of professing the Christian religion, namely, love, joy, peace, temperance, and charity to all men, should quarrel with such rancorous animosity, and display daily towards one another such bitter hatred, that this, rather than the virtues they claim, is the readiest criterion of their faith" (*TTP*, 8; Elwes, 6).

Still, in the end a problem remains. If Christian doctrine is to fulfill more than an educational heuristic function for the sole purpose of reaching practical conclusions that reason could have reached by itself, does revelation not become superfluous once the mind attains the level of reason? Is the true follower of Christ, then, not the one who abandons the exclusive claims of a particular religious community, its specific rituals, and even the significance of its founder? Spinoza neither draws this conclusion nor explains how he can avoid it. He denies that the cognitive content of the Christian faith carries any salvational meaning in itself. Yet the *obedience* required by faith does require some cognitive content.[9] "Faith consists in a knowledge of God without which obedience to Him would be impossible" (*TTP,* 175; Elwes, 184). For that purpose religious doctrines need not be philosophically true: it suffices that they *introduce* the believer to the truth that is written in the human heart (*TTP,* 158; Elwes, 165).

Richard Simon's monumental *Histoire Critique du Vieux Testament* (1678, partial publication in Paris; 1685, full publication in Rotterdam) shows an extensive, though unrecognized, debt to the *Tractatus.* This radical revision of the study of the Old Testament by an Oratorian priest caused far fewer reverberations in France than Spinoza's work had done in Holland. In a mostly Catholic country, doctrinal authority remained exclusively with the Church and a reinterpretation of the Old Testament seemed less alarming as long as that final authority was recognized. In fact, Simon's thesis that the entire Old Testament was the outcome of a tradition and must be read in the light of that tradition, displayed some affinity with the Catholic principle that tradition was the ultimate authority in biblical interpretation. Yet Bishop Bossuet, who had vainly attempted to draw the author into his own camp, perceived a fundamental difference between the two positions: the tradition from which

Scripture derives its authority according to Simon differed from the tradition on which the Church grounded its own authority for defining the meaning of Scripture. The Protestant philologist Ezechiel Spanheim put his finger on the ambiguity: Which tradition was at stake? The one that gave rise to the sacred texts? Or the one of the Church that sanctions them? Obviously, for Simon the ultimate interpretive authority belonged to the tradition discovered by the historical critique. It was a "tradition" that undermined the Protestant authority of Scripture as well as the Catholic one of tradition.[10] The texts of the Old Testament stem from an earlier, oral or written, tradition, he argued, which alone must decide their meaning.

The impact of Spinoza's *Tractatus* appears everywhere. Still Simon's work substantially differed from it. In his opinion, the *Tractatus* failed to address one of the basic questions of historical criticism: What motivated an author to write a particular text in given historical circumstances? Simon pays a great deal of attention to the historical conditions that led to the sacred author's expression, but he neglects what later generations have come to regard as essential in that expression. In his exegesis, the reception of a text and its later interpretation play hardly any role. "Tradition," for him, referred exclusively to the historical formation of a text. Hermeneutics has no part in his method. Yet to explain the Old Testament within a Christian context, as Simon attempted to do, without taking account of the Church's reading of it over the centuries makes little sense. For Catholics, Orthodox, and Anglicans, as well as for most Protestants, the spiritual interpretation of the Old Testament had been essential for their own Christian self-understanding.

Simon's historical reading of the Bible played right into the deist idea that a revelation addressed to one particular people at one particular time that claimed to contain the definitive truth concerning the human condition for all times loses its credibility at a later period. Scripture crudely stated for one people what enlightened reason was capable of formulating more accurately for all. *Either* revelation is intrinsically universal *or* it lacks universal authority. These ancient texts, written at different epochs, and referring to historical events of their own time, could not be read as if they were pointing forward to Jesus of Nazareth without granting a religious authority to their later interpretation. To these textual problems eighteenth-century deists added the overriding objection that the miracles alleged to support the message were themselves to be excluded a priori as conflicting with the natural laws of the universe. At this point biblical interpretation turns into *critique* of the Bible.[11] In contrast to the more radical British and French critics, the German ones alone continued to attribute a providential function to the historical form and context in the transmission of an *eternal* message.[12] According to Lessing, the function of these historical Scriptures was to educate the human race toward understand-ing the universal truth of religion.

Gotthold Ephraim Lessing (1729–81), mainly remembered for his aesthetic theory and dramatic work, did not begin to publish theological writings until his later years. Yet originally his studies had been in theology and at heart he had remained a theologian. Shortly after he was appointed librarian of the duke of Brunswick's Wolfenbüttel library (1769), he started publishing *Beiträge* from the duke's collection. The first one set the tone for all the follow-ing. It contained a typically ambiguous defense of Leibniz's essay on the eter-nal punishment of hell. Neither he nor Leibniz believed in those punishments, but as he wrote to his freethinking brother Karl, who had been taken aback by Gotthold's apparent return to orthodoxy: "I only prefer the old orthodox theology (at bottom, tolerant) to the new (at bottom, intolerant) because the former is in manifest conflict with human reason, whereas the latter might easily take one in. I make agreement with my obvious enemies in order to be able to be better on guard against my secret adversaries."[13] Even before com-ing to Wolfenbüttel, Lessing had become a deist. In an early fragment post-humously published by his brother, he called the "positive" religion of revela-tion a popularized version of natural religion. No particular faith enjoys an absolute priority over others. "All positive and revealed religions are equally true and equally false." But the one that contains the fewest additions to natural religion is, relatively speaking, the best."[14] That, he specifies in a later annotation, is the Islam, because "almost all in Mahomet's doctrine amounts to natural religion."[15]

With his publication of the so-called Reimarus fragments he engaged in a series of exegetical discussions. Hermann Samuel Reimarus was an Orientalist who at his death left a bulky manuscript (*Apology for Rational Worshippers of God*) that, via his daughter, came into Lessing's hands. Lessing published six anonymous fragments in the *Beiträge*. As these philosophical and histor-ical investigations of biblical issues appeared, they became increasingly critical of the official Christian interpretation. Lessing accompanied them by his own "counterpropositions," pretending to defend orthodoxy but in fact adding fuel to Reimarus's flames either by ill-directed criticism or by absurdly ortho-dox refutations. When attacked, he justified his publication by declaring the fragments harmless to ordinary Christians. Theologians may be confused, but the believer "*feels* [the Christian faith] to be true and in it he *feels* blessed" (my emphasis). Reimarus's critique, he argued, concerned the Bible, not religion. "The letter is not the spirit, and the Bible is not religion." Religion existed before the Bible, and Christianity before the Gospels. Even if the entire New Testament were lost, Christian faith would survive. Moreover, "religion is not true because the evangelists and apostles taught it, but they taught it because it is true."[16]

Lessing carefully selected the fragments for the purpose of divulging his own views on biblical revelation. The first one was an attack on the critique of reason in the pulpit. It enabled Lessing to defend the idea that reason has the final say concerning what is revealed and what is not. "Whether there can and must be a revelation and which one among the many that claim to be so is probably the true one, only reason can discern" (L-M, XII, 432). To Reimarus's objection that a scriptural revelation would remain inaccessible to most people, since they live at places and times different from those of the historical revelation, Lessing responds that such a limitation is indeed inherent in the nature of a historical revelation and concludes therefore that scriptural revelation cannot be necessary to salvation. He distinguishes "revelation" from the "books of revelation." The former is available to all through natural reason. The latter are merely a means to awaken reason. The problem with Reimarus, Lessing now ironically observes, is that he interprets the symbols of the Bible as if they contained the true substance of Christianity, but neither the doctrine of Christ nor that of the Church equates the letter with the spirit. We recognize yet another version of the distinction between factual truth and meaning.

What, then, is letter and what is spirit? The need for a distinction appears in Reimarus's argument that six hundred thousand Hebrews with women and children could not have crossed the "sea" in one night, as Exodus reports. Lessing "criticizes" Reimarus by driving the improbability up to absurdity. If God could miraculously open the sea for the Hebrews, why could God not miraculously accelerate the speed of those who passed through it? Does Exodus 19:4 not teach that God carried Israel on "eagle's wings"? In a more serious vein he argues that much in the Old Testament conflicts with essential principles of Christian doctrine, such as the denial of life after death (in *Kohelet* and repeatedly in the Book of Psalms) or the admission that other gods exist. Abandoning all irony, Lessing then outlines the principles of an evolutionary theory of religion. The Bible describes the various stages through which humans gradually attain a metaphysical notion of God. To regard the primitive texts of the early stage as still authoritative for interpreting the later ones excludes such a development, in addition to attributing to God all the vices of jealousy, anger, and vindictiveness, which later "revealed" texts so obviously deny.

Shortly after having written this Counterproposition Lessing developed it into a now famous essay on religious evolution: "The Education of the Human Race" (1780) (only the first part of it appeared in the *Beiträge*). Positive religions are stepping stones to a mature consciousness of God: "Why are we not more willing to see in all positive religions simply the process by which alone human understanding in every place can develop and must still further develop, instead of either ridiculing or becoming angry with them?" (L-M, XIII, 415; Chadwick, p. 82). In principle, then, revelation may contain nothing that humans could not have learned by themselves. But first they must be educated! The Jewish people performed this educational task for the entire human race (§ 18). That essential doctrines are absent from the Bible in no way diminishes the religious significance of the biblical initiation process. The role of Christ marked a wholly new stage in this process as he was the first reliable teacher of life after death (§ 58). Lessing claims that the ancient teachers of immortality merely "speculated" on the subject without realizing its practical consequences (§ 60) (a highly implausible interpretation of Plato).

The evolutionary notion of truth allowed Lessing to defend specifically Christian doctrines, such as that of the Trinity, as being *intrinsically* rational. God's self-expression presupposes a divine self-reflection, the image of which must itself be divine (§ 73).[17] But the significance of this Christian mystery as of all others, he confirms, is instrumental: it serves to develop "revealed truths into truths of reason" (§ 76). The "errors" of Scripture trouble him less than Reimarus and his deist colleagues, who criticized Christianity for being a corruption of the original natural religion, as Lessing himself had done in his early "On the Origin of Revealed Religion." The truth of religion, he now asserts, does not lie in the past but in the future, and Christianity alone shows the way to that future.

Lessing is fighting on two fronts. Against the orthodox he argues that religious truth is universal and independent of any historical revelation. Against the rationalists he maintains that a historical revelation was indispensable for discovering this truth. In both cases he opposes a dynamic, evolutionary concept of religious truth to a static one. "Education gives man nothing which he could not also get from within himself. In the same way, too, revelation gives nothing to the human race which human reason could not arrive at on its own; only it has given, and still gives to it, the most important of these things sooner" (§ 4).

Lessing assumes a similar, intermediate position in his comments on the fifth fragment that dealt with Christ's resurrection. From the discrepancies in the Gospel reports, Reimarus had concluded that the event never occurred. Lessing challenges this conclusion. He distinguishes the alleged witnesses of the Resurrection from the evangelists who wrote about it. Both may have been mistaken, which, of course, would have been more serious in the former case than in the latter. Yet even conflicting reports given by eyewitnesses do not necessarily discredit their authority, as long as all agree on the event itself: their perception of it may have been inaccurate or they may have remembered it incorrectly. As for the writers, they can only report how they understood the witnesses. In a later reply to an orthodox attack, Lessing adds that a description of the same event often varies from one historian to another, without discrediting either. "Yet if we treat Livy and Dionysius and Polybius and Tacitus generously enough not to place them on the rack for each syllable, why then not also Matthew and Mark and Luke and John?" (L-M, XIII, 26.) Over the years Lessing had spent much effort on a critical comparison of the four Gospels, treating them as historical documents independently of their religious significance. He now uses his considerable biblical erudition first to argue the "thesis" that contradictions do occur in the Resurrection reports without necessarily jeopardizing the truth of the Resurrection story, and next the "hypothesis" that there may actually not be any contradictions at all (except in minor details). Through the proofs of his "hypothesis" Lessing hoped to convince the orthodox of his good faith, but by accepting it, they would be forced to admit his "thesis" that there might be errors in the Bible.

In fact, Lessing's position is far more radical than his distinction between the essential message of revelation and the accidental errors of Scripture suggests. Once the mind attains the level of reason, historical reports are not only useless; they positively conflict with the conclusions of reason. Or so he argued in "On the Proof of the Spirit and the Power" (1777). This short essay has become so well known that entire phrases in it have entered the vocabulary of modern theology and even of common intellectual discourse. In it Lessing presents two theses. First, the historian ought to be skeptical with regard to past reports of miracles, if they are not confirmed by the occurrence of similar events in our own time. "Miracles, which I see with my own eyes, and which I have the opportunity to verify for myself, are one thing; miracles of which I know only from history that others say that they have seen them and verified them, are another" (L-M, XIII, 3; Chadwick, p. 51). Next, he moves to the more general thesis that *no* historical report, however reliable, could ever prove a metaphysical truth. Such a truth can be derived only from the unchangeable rules of reason. "What does it mean to accept an historical proposition as true? . . . Does it mean anything other than this: to accept that there is no objection to be brought against it? . . . If on historical grounds I have no objection to the statement that this Christ himself raised to life a dead man; must I therefore accept it as true that God has a Son who is of the same essence as himself?" (L-M, XIII, 6; Chadwick, pp. 53–54). As is not uncommon with Lessing, his argument remains slippery, constantly shifting from one thesis to another. At times he wonders why we should accept as true what is insufficiently established; at other times he questions how even historically reliable narratives could result in existential conclusions. The second thesis follows from Leibniz's sharp division between truths of reason and truths of fact: the former are universal and necessary, the latter particular and contingent. Lessing excludes the particular from the field of universal truth altogether: between the two yawns an "ugly, broad ditch." With this conclusion he has in fact invalidated the original distinction between accidental errors and essential truth: even accurate historical reports are inadequate for the function they are intended to fulfill in the Scripture, namely, to change the reader's entire intellectual orientation.

Not all detected Lessing's strategy in publishing the Reimarus fragments and his Counterpropositions. One who did, though, was the Hamburg Pastor, Johann Melchior Goeze. He accused the polemicist of having no other intention but to undermine the orthodox Christian faith. Lessing answered Goeze's charge in ten axioms ("Axioms, If There Are Any in Such Matters") (1778) (L-M, XIII, 107–40).[18] His primary intention in the polemics with Goeze was to show that the Christian religion, if studied in its original sources, might be reduced to a religion of reason. The historical elements in the New Testament (as in the entire Bible) form no part of the message; they were needed to transmit its message to the uneducated readers of an earlier epoch. Lessing restates his distinction between the essential and nonessential elements in Scripture. Historical reports are not essential. While conceding that not every word of Scripture is of equal moment, Goeze contends that the text cannot be so neatly divided into essential and nonessential sections. The nonessential forms an inseparable part of the biblical content. Modern generations may regard as insignificant what to earlier ones appeared crucially important (e.g., whether the "miracles" in the Bible are of divine origin or must be attributed to natural causes). Unless the whole Bible is divinely inspired, no particular parts can be considered to be so.

Goeze possessed a keen sense for the literary continuity of a biblical text. But he naively concluded that if all was inspired, nothing could be erroneous, even though he himself had admitted that the critical quality of even the more recent historical books of Scripture falls far short of modern norms. For him, the question came down to: If God has revealed himself in Scripture, how could the Bible be erroneous? Did Lessing imagine that the Christian religion could exist if the Bible had long been lost or had never been written? In his brief "Necessary Answer to a Very Unnecessary Question" (1778) (L-M, XIII, 331–36; Chadwick, pp. 62–64), Lessing pointed out that the earliest

confessions of faith preceded the New Testament writings. Were those believers who lived and died before the New Testament not Christians? Once
writings began to circulate, they selected into a canon those that seemed to
agree with a previously existing rule of faith. What Scripture contains in addition to this *regula fidei* was, according to the spirit of the first four centuries,
not necessary for salvation. In a First Sequel (*Erste Folge*) Lessing denies
Goeze's claim that "all Christians" accept the Bible as sole doctrinal ground of
the Christian religion. For Catholics, the Bible is subject to the authority of the
Church.[19] Indeed, the first major heresy, Arianism, stemmed from an exclusive
reliance on the text of the Synoptic Gospels, read independently of the
Church's later tradition.

While the anti-Goeze controversy was in full swing Lessing published one
more Reimarus fragment: the last, the longest, and the most radical, "On the
Intentions of Jesus and His Disciples." In it, Reimarus maintained that Jesus
taught or believed none of the central dogmas concerning his own divinity, the
dogma of the Trinity, the abolition of Jewish law and ceremonial. Instead he
preached a "rational, practical religion" based on universal values and certainly not intended to be a new, particular religion. His version of the Kingdom of God included, however, an apocalyptic liberation of Israel from Roman occupation. His disciples changed this message into one of redemptive
sacrifice, bodily resurrection, and divinization. The publication of this large
fragment and its Counterproposition made it evident to all readers that what
separated Lessing from Reimarus were details, with one major exception:
Lessing regarded Christianity not as a degeneration of natural or rational
religion, but as a necessary preparation of it. In the *Axioms* against Goeze
Lessing had persistently argued that scriptural traditions are to be interpreted
through an *inner truth* rather than the inner truth through Scripture.

Lessing here radicalizes a position implied in a principle of the Reformation:
the Holy Spirit conveys the inner truth *at the occasion of* the personal reading
and interpretation of Scripture. But Lessing moves far beyond Luther's principle, detaching Christian faith from its scriptural moorings altogether. The
questions he raises exceed the fields of philology and history. Does religion
consist *entirely* of an inner attitude? If so, can it be subject to any external
authority? What is the significance of the historical elements that have played
such an important part in Judaism and Christianity? Those questions require
philosophical answers. The philosophy of religion of Lessing's time, however,
dealt only with such metaphysical problems as the existence and attributes of
God, the justification of the created world, and the immortality of the soul.
The specific questions he raised had to wait for Kant and his successors.

Deism, the Substitute Religion

I doubt whether any factor has contributed more to the rise of deism and, indeed, of atheism in the modern age than the exclusive use of a narrowly defined concept of efficient causality for describing the relation between creation and Creator. This interpretation reduces the intimate union between the divine Cause and its creation to the extrinsic one between two separate entities. To be sure, some facet of what Aristotle calls an "efficient causality" had always formed part of the Judeo-Christian idea of the relation between God and creation. But in the past it had never been thought to constitute the entire relation, nor had it been conceived in the narrow terms of the scientific concept of causality. Seventeenth-century thinkers, following the systems of Descartes and Newton, replaced traditional ways of symbolizing the relation between the finite and its transcendent source by a type of causality conceived on a mechanistic model. God became, once again, a remote Prime Mover responsible for the motion of the universe. Deism was the inevitable outcome of this distant relation to God. Atheism was to follow as soon as the need for an external source of mechanical motion ceased to exist.

In his *Discourse Concerning the Being and Attributes of God* (1704–5), Samuel Clarke distinguished four kinds of deists: (1) those who believe in the existence of an eternal, intelligent being that created a certain quantity of matter and motion without concerning itself with its development or government; (2) those who believe in the Providence of God but not in divinely sanctioned moral obligations; (3) those who believe in God's moral commands but not in immortality; (4) those who believe in Providence, moral obligations, and immortality, but not in revelation. The last ones, he claims, are "the only true deists."[20] Most eighteenth-century deists belonged in the fourth class. They believed that the Creator of the universe, known by the light of reason, rewards good and punishes evil in this life as well as in the next.

Originally, deism had not excluded revelation. Fausto Sozzini (1539–1604), to whom friends and foes used to trace the deist lineage, accepted the truth of biblical revelation, the divinity of Christ (though conceived in a functional rather than a personal way), and the Resurrection. Even the more radical John Toland (*Christianity Not Mysterious* [1696]) and Matthew Tindal (*Christianity as Old as Creation* [1730]) professed, albeit with dubious sincerity, a belief in a revelation that their theories, however, showed to be superfluous. Both of them drew their conclusions from Christian authors: Tindal from Clarke who unambiguously accepted both the idea and the content of revelation; Toland from Locke, who in *On the Reasonableness of Christianity*

(1695) firmly declared that those who understood him to claim anything more than that the content of the Christian revelation agrees with the laws of reason and can be justified by it misunderstood him.[21]

English deism drew heavily upon Stoic philosophy and more particularly upon Roman writers who had developed that philosophy into a monotheist, natural theology. Augustine had found in Cicero and Varrho an arsenal of arguments against polytheism and atheism. Later writers mined Cicero's *De natura deorum* to establish what reason alone was able to ascertain about the nature of God. Contrary to this earlier Christian use, seventeenth-century writers had begun to use Stoic sources for the foundation of a natural theology that took the place of revealed religion. Peter Gay describes the shift: "It seems as though Stoicism was detaching itself from Christianity only to be reabsorbed into the great philosophical reappraisal of the seventeenth century. . . . Whenever men are told to live according to nature, to acquire knowledge by discovering universal truths and the natural laws by which the physical and the moral world are governed — whenever we encounter such ideas, we are witnessing Stoicism lending strategic support to the campaign for the independence of philosophy."[22]

Stoic support for the religious meaning of nature lost much of its credit after Mandeville's ironic assault upon its two principal qualities, the order of nature and the providential subordination of all creatures to the good of the human race. Mandeville anticipated Darwin's thesis, that the apparent order of nature might merely be the outcome of a destructive struggle in which only those fit enough to survive a hostile environment had been able to attain a modus vivendi with others. The idea of a providential guidance of nature for the benefit of humans flies in the face of experience. The human species almost succumbed in its early struggles with other animals. "To ascribe all this to Providence, otherwise than that nothing is done without the divine permission, seems inconsistent with the ideas we have of a perfectly good and merciful Being. It is possible that all poisonous animals may have something in them that is beneficial to men. . . . But when I look upon the vast variety of ravenous and blood-thirsty creatures, that are not only superior to us in strength, but likewise visibly armed by nature, as it were on purpose for our destruction; when, I say, I look upon those, I can find out no use for them, unless it be to punish us."[23] To be sure, the outcome of the struggle with those animals may still be favorable to the human race, and indeed to all of nature. Our species would have overstocked the earth and "we could not have had that variety of living creatures there is now" (*Fable*, II, p. 253). But balance and variety have resulted from killing, not from kindness.

Eventually Stoic philosophy became a weapon in the battle for atheism, as it did in Diderot's moral writings. The development is not too surprising. When nature serves as the only ground on which the idea of God rests, it may easily turn into a substitute for God, or, as in Spinoza's case, become equated with God. But this development was by no means necessary. There had always existed a more intrinsically religious view of nature as that through which God becomes manifest to reason. The Cambridge Platonists continued to look at nature from this perspective. For Nathaniel Culverwell, the light of reason, "the candle of the Lord" (Proverbs 20:27), is none other than the light of nature itself as it dwells within the human mind.[24] Benjamin Whichcote developed this view of nature into a full-fledged natural theology that remained well within the boundaries of Christian orthodoxy.

Eighteenth-century poetry reflects the impact deism was having on the intellectual climate in England. John Dryden's *Religio Laici* (1682), written against an emerging deism, nonetheless expresses a need to come to terms with it. Reason cannot serve as the foundation of faith; nevertheless faith must justify itself in the face of reason. Dryden raises all the disquieting questions that evoked the deist answer. "How can revealed religion alone be salvational when most people never heard of it? Of all objections this indeed is chief to startle reason, stagger frail belief" (*Religio Laici,* 184). Where is the meaning to be found in the often corrupt and unintelligible text that has reached us? Newton's cosmology, originally received as a glorification of God's immensity, now began to stir up disturbing doubts. Where was Providence in this cosmic clockwork? How could an unmoved and immovable Creator care for the minute inhabitants of this tiny planet? The powerful religious inspiration of the metaphysical poets had dried up. Pope adopted Voltaire as his model, "at once a freethinker and a lover of quiet; no bigot but yet no heretic."[25] He defended his own deist *Essay on Man* as an attack upon atheism, but the underlying thesis appears to be that all religions are in their core identical. Toward the end of his life, however, he appears to have abandoned all deist sympathies. His final work, the *Dunciad* (1742–43), contains a firm rejection of the deist idea of a God "wrapt up in self, a God without a thought, regardless of our merit or default" (bk. IV, vv. 485–86).[27]

Other poets of the period profess a more sentimental deism. James Thomson, author of the much-celebrated *The Seasons,* presents a prime example. God, to him, appears only in the beauty of nature and in human happiness. His smiling God has been called the last glimpse of the Cheshire cat, of which all "has faded away except the cosmic grin."[28] Thomson and some of his preromantic contemporaries appear to have been inspired by a sentimental deism with vaguely pantheist connotations. But it is also possible to view their religious feeling as rooted in the experience of the inner light that, according to

Puritan doctrine, accompanies conversion.[29] In that case their position is more closely related to Jonathan Edwards's religious affections than to Shaftesbury's Stoicism. It remains true, however, that the internalization of religion played a part in the development toward deism (as we noticed in Lessing's controversy with Goeze). In that sense at least H. N. Fairchild's judgment about the sentimental religious poet stands: "His sense of a divinity within him being far stronger than his sense of a divinity above and beyond him, he emphasizes the immanence of God so much more strongly than His transcendence that the distinctions between *God and man* are blurred. Nature then becomes divine."[30]

Turning now to the contemporary philosophical sources of modern deism, the first point to mention is that the principles of modern epistemology had made it hard to avoid the deist position altogether. If the mind is the only source of meaning, how can it admit as true what is derived from a different source? In the fourth book of the *Essay Concerning Human Understanding* (beginning with chapter 14), Locke outlines the rules for dealing with this question.[31] He admits that a responsible assent ought to be proportionate to the degree of probability of its object and hence that the mind must "not entertain any proposition with greater assurance than the proofs it is built upon will warrant" (*Essay,* IV, 19, § 1). The assent the believer gives to religious dogmas obviously surpasses the evidence needed to justify his acceptance of them. Yet, Locke claims, the importance of the object of faith strengthens its probability and thus supplies what it lacks in evidence.[32] The adequacy of this argument, remindful of Pascal's wager, may be doubted. Yet Locke wisely avoids justifying the religious trust in revelation on purely rational grounds. Rather than risking to add grist to the deist mill, he plays the powers of reason down.[33]

Revelation, then, serves as an indispensable complement to reason, not only for assisting those who lack the time or mental capacity to follow complex philosophical arguments, but also for enriching the meager religious content of philosophical theology. The mind welcomes the assistance of revelation, but reason does not abandon it right to be the ultimate norm. Revelation must be reasonable. Miracles may confirm the credibility of the Christian message (*Reasonableness* [# 227]), but its reasonableness primarily rests on internal grounds. Not only does no part of the Gospel conflict with the laws of reason, but also its inner coherence strongly suggests its overall conformity to reason. Does Locke mean that no part of it directly conflicts with reason? Or does he hold that the *entire* content of revelation is in principle accessible to reason alone? The ambiguity of Locke's expression is probably the main reason why deists often supported their theories by appealing to his work.

When a Calvinist divine accused Locke of Socinianism,[34] Locke pointed out that his position, contrary to Socinius's, was entirely based on Scripture and not on independent reason. Further controversy followed, and Locke in *A Second Vindication of the Reasonableness of Christianity* explicitly and, I think, sincerely declared that he wrote his treatise for the benefit of "those who thought that there was no need of revelation at all" or of those who considered the articles for salvation incompatible with their way of reasoning — the two objections "which were with most assurance made by deists against Christianity but against Christianity misunderstood."[35] To the bishop of Worcester he wrote: "The reason of believing any article of the Christian faith . . . to me and upon my grounds, is its being a part of divine revelation" (*Works,* IV, 303). In light of those declarations it appears astonishing that Locke's treatise became a rallying text for early deists. John Toland in *Christianity Not Mysterious,* published a year after *The Reasonableness,* was the first to amplify what he considered Locke's unstated implications. If Christianity was indeed reasonable and intelligible, it contained not only nothing contrary to reason but neither anything above reason. Though Locke publicly expressed his disagreement, deist interpretations of his work continued to appear.

Matthew Tindal in *Christianity as Old as the Creation* (1730) started from a principle similar to Locke's. "In all cases where I am capable of understanding a proposition, 'tis Reason must inform me, whether 'tis certain, probable, or uncertain."[36] This statement may be understood as saying merely that the test of truth lies entirely within reason and in that case it does not substantially differ from Locke's thesis. But it may also mean that the human mind cannot admit any proposition as true that lies in part beyond the grasp of reason. This is, in fact, how most of Tindal's contemporaries did understand its meaning.[37]

Part of the confusion may have stemmed from the ambiguity inherent in the modern use of the term "rationality." The older interpretation had not excluded a reality that transcends reason, provided it did not conflict with reason. The ancient or medieval philosopher encountered the idea of God as a given at the root of the rationalization process itself, previous to any argument.[38] Aquinas, to take one illustrious example, held that all philosophy leads to the necessary acceptance of a transcendent principle. But the specification of this principle to what Christians, Jews, and Muslims recognized and adored as God came from a "revelation" that might be justified by reason (as being free of contradictions) but did not originate in reason.[39]

Modern rationalism restricted the rational to that of which the mind is the sole ground and hence which it is able to prove. For the deists, this paradoxically included the content of the allegedly "transcendent." They claimed to derive God's existence as well as his "natural" and "moral" attributes from a religiously neutral idea of nature. Nowhere does the inversion of the argument appear more clearly than in Hume's *Dialogue on Natural Religion*. Cleanthes, the advocate of a deist natural theology, argues that we must model the idea of God on the basis of our conception of the world. Carl Becker notes the shift: "Cleanthes does not conclude that the world must be rational because God is eternal reason; he concludes that God must be an engineer because nature is a machine."[40] The idea of God thereby comes to depend directly on a particular representation of the world. Despite these claims of pure rationality, the deist idea of God itself displayed enough vestigial Christian traits to leave no doubt about its origin. More than a deduction, as it pretended to be, it was a rationalist abstraction of a specifically Christian idea, an undocumented survivor of the rejected revelation. "I know of no greater tribute ever paid to the God of Christianity," Etienne Gilson quipped, "than His survival in this idea, maintained against Christianity itself and on the strength of pure natural reason."[41]

The fact that ethics, for the deists, constituted virtually the entire content of religion, also contributed to the rationalist interpretation of Locke's philosophy. Had not Locke himself claimed that the mind might, at least in principle, independently reach the ethical precepts taught by Scripture? For the deists, God had scarcely any function left but that of sanctioning morality. As Voltaire had written with characteristic assurance: "I understand by natural religion the principles of morals common to the human race."[42] D'Alembert was even more explicit: "One would do a great service to mankind if one could make men forget the dogmas; if one would simply preach them a God who rewards and punishes and who frowns on superstition, who detests intolerance and expects no other cult of man than mutual love and support."[43] Thus a religious *ethos* superseded altogether the religious *pathos*.[44]

Deism stemmed from practical concerns as much as from theoretical discussions. Its advocates hoped that if the idea of God were detached from the various interpretations of a divine revelation, the religious conflicts that had torn Europe apart would end. John Locke, illegitimately adopted by the deists as father of their philosophy, acquired a more legitimate reputation as the first major proponent of religious tolerance. He grew more tolerant over the years but never went beyond the limits of Christian faith. In 1660–61 he still maintained that an edict of toleration would return England to the political turmoil from which the Restoration had just rescued it. He supported the status quo by arguing that the matters that divided Christians were not in the gospel and hence might be regarded as indifferent. In "An Essay Concerning Toleration" (1667) Locke reversed his position. For the state to support the religious supremacy of the Anglican Church seemed not only unfair in view of that Church's self-serving use of its power, but even more, because the things Locke had previously called "indifferent" appeared by no means "indifferent" to believers, some of whom were prepared to die for them. Hence toleration seemed to be the only effective way to avoid future civil war, regardless of the objective merit of each party's claim to truth. Finally, in a definitive "Letter Concerning Toleration" (1685), written during his exile in Holland, Locke pleaded for an equal treatment of all Christian denominations as being the only practical and conscientious solution.[45] Even if civil authorities succeeded in pressing citizens into conformity, they would merely force them to violate their conscience. Neither civil nor religious good could ever come from such a policy. Locke's argument rests on the sharply drawn distinction between a civil jurisdiction that is not responsible for the "care of souls" and an ecclesiastical one that wields religious authority over its voluntary members but has no right to interfere in civic matters. The magistrate should neither impose nor forbid any form of worship nor attempt to impose any article of faith. Locke desired to make a clean break with the theocratic tradition that had ruled the West after the civil functions of the collapsing Roman Empire had fallen to the Church.[46]

Shaftesbury converted Locke's mainly practical principles of religious tolerance into theoretical ones: they became the cornerstone of his deist philosophy.[47] Religious intolerance assumes that God reserves salvation to a single religious body. But why should salvation depend on the place where one is born? "He who is now an orthodox Christian would have been infallibly as true a Mussulman, or as errant a heretic, had his birth happened in another place?"[48] All religions ought to be subjected to rational inquiry, which is possible only "where comparison is allowed, examination permitted and a sincere toleration established.

What distinguishes Shaftesbury from most other deists is that, for him, religion is more than a matter of reason. It draws its inspiration from affections that raise the soul to magnanimity, love, and spiritual greatness by elevating the mind to the source of all reality (Miscell., IV, 2, in *Characteristics,* II, 294). His concept of religious feeling avoids the dominant rationalist reductionism and anticipates Schleiermacher's romantic theory of religion. British deists had persistently avoided an open break with Christianity. The debate on tolerance had originally remained separate from the theoretical discussion that led to deism. Only in Shaftesbury did the two issues merge.

In France, the repressive religious policy of Louis XIV's later years, supported by the bishops and the censorious Sorbonne faculty of theology, stifled critical discussion of Catholic doctrine as well as of the political hegemony of the Church. When the king revoked the Toleration Edict of Nantes in 1685, thereby depriving French Huguenots of political rights, tolerance became a primary concern. It soon came to be the moving power of a sharply polemical deism. During the early period Pierre Bayle (1647–1706), a Huguenot refugee who had settled in Rotterdam, became its influential spokesman. His *Dictionnaire historique et critique* (1697), probably the most extravagant glossary ever written, contains no entries on many topics of primary significance and a great number on very obscure ones. Moreover, the titles of the ones included rarely correspond to the content of the articles. The only thing that is predictable in this strange book is that on any given issue, the author will present unpredictable views. In some entries, he questions the foundations of central Christian dogmas, while in others he severely censures those who question them (e.g., Spinoza) or defends the Catholic position against the Reformed one. He remains a mysterious figure. Was he a Protestant Christian, as he claimed to be and as his faithful attendance at the Calvinist Church seemed to confirm? Or was he a Pyrrhonist skeptic sensible enough not to practice what he preached? Or merely a critical historian, as Dr. Johnson thought? Whatever the answer, Bayle had more than the religious controversies in France on his mind. Repeatedly he appeals to an innate, moral law that unites all humans beyond religious differences. In his article "Epicure" he attacks the deist equation of religion with morality, claiming that atheists may be as moral as believers. By the same token he deprived religion of the only content deists had left it.

Montesquieu's attitude is far more typical of the way religious tolerance was linked to deism in France. He defended it by dismissing what he considered nonessential differences in religion (which included most Christian dogmas) as cultural differences. In his *Lettres persanes* (1721) he denies that religious pluralism leads to intolerance. "I concede that history is filled with religious wars. But note well: not the multiplicity of religions has caused these wars, but the spirit of intolerance that animated the one that considered itself to be dominant" (Letter 85). In support of this religious pluralism Montesquieu refers to Cicero's monotheist interpretation of Roman polytheism. Active in the manifold works of nature and in a variety of cultures, God receives many names. For the Romans, Venus represents his generative power, Minerva his wisdom, Neptune the force of the ocean, and so on. "From this belief originated the [Roman] spirit of tolerance and kindness that reigned in the pagan world. People felt no need to persecute and attack each other: all religions, all theologies were equally good. Heresies, religious wars, and disputes were unknown."[49] From the point of view of this "natural" monotheism, all religions, whether polytheist or "revealed," must be regarded as no more than contingent attempts to give a concrete form to what is in essence the religion of reason. Any particular claims, then, must remain subordinate to this universal religion.

With Voltaire the scene changes. He introduced British deism into France. He lived long, wrote much, and participated in virtually every controversy of the eighteenth century. He meant different things to different people: a mortal enemy of the French Church yet a lifelong friend of his Jesuit teachers, a major star in the literature of the eighteenth century but also a popularizer of Newtonian physics, besides being France's foremost historian. In almost all his works he wrote about, and mostly against, the Christian religion, particularly in its Catholic form. The subject obsessed him, yet his attitude toward Christianity is far from unambiguous. It varies from venomous hostility to skeptical deism, to polemical zeal against atheism, even to intermittent returns to the rites of the Church (particularly when he felt his life to be in danger). His (a)religious gospel lies spread out over all his writings, but most directly in the *Lettres philosophiques* (1734), *Traité de métaphysique* (1734), *Essai sur les moeurs* (1756), *Traité sur la tolérance* (1763), *Dictionnaire philosophique* (1764), *L'Ancien Testament: L'Examen important de Milord Bolingbroke* (1767), and, most aggressively, in hundreds of letters. The two earlier works, reflecting impressions of his prolonged stay in England, are more philosophical than the later ones that mostly deal with biblical and historical criticism. In the *Lettres philosophiques* he compares the experience of living in pluralist England with the intellectually restrictive conditions of life in France. The lesson he learned from British tolerance is that the many sects keep each other in balance. "If there were one religion in England, one might fear despotism; if there were two, they would be at each other's throats; but there are so many of them and so they all live in peaceful happiness" (*Lettres philosophiques*, Letter 6).

Some time after his return from England, while he was living at Madame de Châtelet's ruinous castle in Cirey, Voltaire summarized the philosophy he had gathered from his exposure to British ideas. The resulting *Traité de métaphysique* remained locked in his hostess's drawer for many years: she deemed it far too dangerous for publication. It introduced a number of theses that were to remain definitive in Voltaire's thought. The existence of God he considered certain, not so much on logical grounds as because of the absurdity of its denial. How could nature follow mathematical laws without a divine mind to define and establish them? Though we ignore the nature of this divine legislator, we must assume that God interferes neither with his own laws nor with the course of history. Hence, miracles must be considered impossible and any assumption of a special Providence beyond the act of creation is to be ruled out. Two theses separate Voltaire's position from that of other deists: the immortality of the soul and the divine sanction of morality. In the thirteenth Letter Voltaire had written that we could not possibly prove the immortality of the soul, since we do not know what the soul really is. "[But] the common good demands that we believe the soul to be immortal and faith orders us to do so. We need no more: the issue is decided" (Letter 13). In the *Traité de métaphysique* he is less assertive. Since matter is not incompatible with consciousness (as he had learned from Locke) and material beings are essentially corruptible, no philosophical necessity supports the existence of an immortal soul — indeed, probability is against it. Nor does morality depend on it. Sanctions in an afterlife have rarely restrained criminals. Still, God remains the foundation of morality as the legislator who issues the principles of natural law. Later Voltaire returned to the common deist thesis that God must reward the good and punish the evil ones in a future life.

Deism, for Voltaire, meant more than the independence of natural religion with respect to revealed faith: the former excludes the latter as a rival faith. Biblical criticism and Church history were more congenial to his literary talent than philosophy. They also proved to be more effective weapons against a Church still bound by the principle of inerrancy and by a literal interpretation of Scripture. Particularly in the first part of the *Essai sur les moeurs* and in a critique of the Old Testament that he attributed to Bolingbroke, he aimed his sarcasm at every vulnerable spot in the harness of traditional exegesis. One of them was the originality of the biblical accounts, at the time considered to be crucial to their revealed character. The Christian "fulfillments" of Hebrew prophecies he dismissed as ridiculously farfetched. The canonic Gospels were forged after the fall of Jerusalem in order to appear miraculously predicting the destruction of the Temple, while they were in fact written after the temple had been destroyed.[50]

Like Lessing, Voltaire challenged the reliability of historical reports written in a remote past. "That which regards history gives birth to a thousand disputes."[51] But most problematic of all to him was the very notion of a particular revelation addressed to some and denied to others. "If God had wished to make his cult known to me, it would be because this cult was necessary to our species. If it were necessary he would have bestowed it on all alike, just as He has given everyone two eyes and a mouth. . . . The principles of universal reason are common to all civilized peoples, all recognize a God; they can then flatter themselves that such knowledge is truth. Yet each of them has a different religion."[52] The *Essai sur les moeurs,* from which this quotation is taken, may well count as the most massive assault on the Church's history ever written. Combined with the historical fragments on the ancient Church found in chapters 20–38 of *An Important Study by Lord Bolingbroke,* it covers the entire history of Catholic Christianity.

However unreliable this biased and polemical work is, one cannot read it without being impressed by the author's stunning erudition, not only with regard to the history of the Church but also to that of other religions. He devotes much of the book-length "Introduction" of the *Essai* (which he had published separately) to a comparison of Catholicism with other faiths. Not surprisingly, in Voltaire's report all turn out to be more tolerant and more moral. Voltaire found his own idea of natural religion formulated in a document allegedly issued by Zaleucus, a legendary legislator of the South Italian (Greek) city of Locri. According to Zaleucus, every citizen must accept the existence of God. No dogmas or ceremonies are needed, but all must please God by virtuous conduct (*Essai sur les moeurs,* p. 95). Only some Asian religions approach this rational ideal. China adores a Supreme Being, "without superstition or fanaticism (p. 237). The Persian Zend-Vesta contains all that is commendable in Christianity, though Jews and Christians fail to recognize its originality (p. 248). Only one faith is, in Voltaire's eyes, worse than the Christian and greatly responsible for Christian vices and superstitions: the exclusive, tribal religion of Israel. The biblical story of Joshua burning cities, murdering women and children, and shamefully executing thirty-one "kings" in the conquest of Canaan provokes the following outburst: "Compared to the children of Israel, the Hurons, the Canadians, and the Iroquois have been humanitarian philosophers; and it is in favor of these monsters that the sun and the moon were made to stand still at full noon (Joshua 10:11–13)! And why? To give them time to pursue and massacre the poor Amorites already crushed by a rain of stones that God threw upon them from on high" (*Bolingbroke,* chap. 7, p. 112).[53]

In his old age, Voltaire tended to recycle his biased stories under the guise of history. In the late *Letters of Amabed* (1769) he trots them out again.[54] What disturbs him most in Christianity is the discrepancy between Jesus' moral message and the Church's transformation of it into a concoction of false prophecies, fantastic doctrines, and fraudulent miracles. Once that Church gained control over the Roman Empire, she discarded the principles of tolerance she had previously invoked on her own behalf and became engaged in a ruthless drive for power. The *Essai sur les moeurs* is a Church history in reverse: an ecclesiastic *chronique scandaleuse,* erudite but wholly untrustworthy.

But it is in Voltaire's letters that the full complexity of his attitude toward religion appears. Depending on the correspondent and also his own mood, he writes about Christianity with some respect and even affection, or with white-hot hatred. Letters addressed to d'Alembert were mostly conspiratorial and vitriolic. Destroying the Church appears a Catonic obsession. "To my last breath I shall repeat my *caeterum censeo: Ecrasez l'infâme*. It is a major battle, a battle of all thinking beings against the non-thinking beings" (October 20, 1761; also January 1, 1764, and June 26, 1766). These letters reflect a pent-up rage that a few years later exploded in a general rebellion against the Church's dominance in France. Amazingly, Voltaire wrote these letters from his little castle in Ferney where he had a chapel built for religious services and where his friend, Père Adam, regularly came to say a Mass piously attended by his host.

In his later years he began to feel more concern about the progress of atheism than about a Church that was obviously in retreat. In a story of that period, *L'histoire de Jenni* (1775) (in English translated as *The Sage and the Atheist*), Voltaire passionately defends the existence of a benevolent Deity. God's existence needs no metaphysical proof: it clearly appears in the order of nature and the goodness of creation. Most surprisingly, in "The Sage and the Atheist" Voltaire replaces reason by feeling as the primary ground for a belief in God. His hard-nosed rationalism here appears to melt into the kind of sentimentalism that he had so often ridiculed in Rousseau. But, in his defensive attitude with regard to religion as well as in his offensive, Voltaire's conception of it is always one-dimensional and flat, forcefully suppressing any sense of mystery.

Shaftesbury had already protested that religion is not, or is not primarily, a matter of reason but of the heart. We experience it in feeling and we respond to it through feelings ("The Moralists," II, 3, in *Characteristics*, II, 55). Yet the advocate of the gospel of feeling we remember today is Rousseau. In the fourth book of *Emile,* the famous *vicaire savoyard* initiates his young pupil into the rudiments of natural religion. With the philosophes, the priest assumes that true religion consists in obeying the moral law. But for Rousseau, the divine law may be perceived only through *feeling*. Reason merely teaches that the maker of the universe must be powerful, just, and good. In feeling, God reveals himself directly to the heart. "All that I feel to be right is right; whatever I feel to be wrong is wrong: conscience is the ablest of casuists, and it is only when we are trafficking with her that we have recourse to the subtleties of logic."[55] For the education of Sophie, Emile's female counterpart, Rousseau even more firmly opposes a discussion of religious doctrines. "Forget those mysterious dogmas which for us are words without ideas, all those bizarre doctrines the idle study of which takes the place of virtue in those committed to them whom they make insane rather than good. Children ought to be kept within the narrow circle of dogmas related to morality" (*Emile,* bk. V, p. 729). Until they reach the age of reason, children will accept whatever their elders tell them, mostly by example. When the time comes when they are able to judge for themselves, they are to be given an inflexible rule for separating truth from prejudice: *le sentiment intérieur* (*Emile,* bk. V). In *Julie,* Rousseau's idea of religious feeling receives a somewhat more specific content. Approaching the end of her life, Julie is overtaken by a strong longing for God. This longing, she hopes, will be fulfilled in the union with God after death. In this book, where Rousseau links ethical disposition to mystical aspirations, appears the famous sentence, whose meaning Marx, and particularly Lenin, strongly distorted: "La dévotion est un opium pour l'âme."[56]

How surprising, then, to find a man of such delicate religious sensitivity to be the author of the chapter on "civil religion" that concludes *The Social Contract*. This totally pragmatic theology serves a purely political goal: to remedy the loss of spiritual unity in the state. Ancient religion coincided with the life of tribe or nation. The problem began when Jesus severed the internal, spiritual kingdom from the external realm of politics. It became acute when Christians (especially Catholics) subordinated their political allegiance to their obedience to a religious leader, thus dividing loyalties that should have stayed united. Christianity created a further political problem by promoting virtues opposed to the ones needed for building a strong state. "Christianity preaches only servitude and dependence. Its spirit is so favorable to tyranny, and the latter always draws its profits from that fact."[57] Rousseau's critique of the virtues of Christianity, anticipated in Bayle's *Pensées sur la comète* and in Voltaire's *Essai sur les moeurs,* also became a dominant factor in Gibbon's *Decline and Fall of the Roman Empire*. To counteract the nefarious influence of a religion of meekness Rousseau suggests that the state impose a civil religion that inspires virtues needed for a strong republic. Its doctrine should not exceed the fundamental articles of natural religion: an acceptance of God as creator and governor of the universe, who rewards good and punishes evil after death. The state ought not to interfere with the citizens' private beliefs but exact strict conformity to the official cult and adherence to its principles. He refers to the Roman Empire as a model for his distinction between public and private religion. But the example of China that had recently become known through missionary letters and travelers' reports may have influenced him as well.[58]

Even those who opposed Rousseau's principles felt the need for some religious bond among the citizens. Edmund Burke attributed a comparable role to the established Church of England. It had to function as a general religion of the citizens without, however, excluding private beliefs.[59] The doctrinal content imposed by this established Church would amount to little more than what Rousseau's civil religion required. Yet Burke's model differs in one significant respect: he assumed that the general principles of the Church of England remained in basic agreement with the private beliefs of the citizens. The assumption was questionable since that Church was in open conflict with the "dissidents" and was bound to discriminate against them. The founders of the American republic, though strictly opposed to any form of established

Church, likewise considered the profession of some religious principles neces-sary for the spiritual unity of the new nation. The original Puritan Covenant theology of the New Israel, tempered by the founders' deist convictions, for a long time forged a powerful bond among American citizens and even today conveys some religious appearance to public life.[60] American civil religion, however, is neither established nor imposed. Nor does it claim to be a com-plete religion in its own right. It *invites* the kind of specific content that only a more personal faith provides, without compelling the citizens to seek it or even to accept its own vague principles. Contrary to Rousseau's separate civil reli-gion, the nondenominational creed of America relies for its concrete content on the actual religious beliefs of its citizens. The experience of Gulf War II shows, however, that at critical moments a conflict may arise between the two. Although most of the mainstream Churches strongly declared against the war, the majority of the people sided with the president's crusade against "the forces of evil," and they did so with all the fervor of a religious patriotism.

Atheism

The term "atheism" has rarely preserved the same meaning for a long time. Socrates was condemned for one kind of atheism and Epicurus was accused of another. Both of them believed in gods and today we regard neither as an atheist. Spinoza, that most religious thinker, was considered an atheist because he changed the relation between divine immanence and transcen-dence, though he continued to maintain a distinction between the two. In the eighteenth century, critics became less inclined to brand as atheist anyone who was not an orthodox Christian or Jew. Yet new candidates for the title ap-peared. In the preface to his long poem, *Creation . . . Demonstrating the Existence and Providence of God* (1702), Richard Blackmore states that two sorts of men have rightly been called atheists: "those who frankly and in plain terms have denied the being of a God; and those who though they asserted his being, denied those attributes and perfections, which the idea of a God in-cludes." On those grounds, he ranks deists under the second head, because their God is totally "unconcerned about the direction and government of the world." Now it may have been the case, as Addison suggests in *The Spectator* (March 10, 1711), that some atheists "retired into deism" when their position became socially hazardous. But most deists firmly believed in their distant God.

Deism did indeed pave the road to atheism by undermining the traditional basis of religious faith. Yet that road was long and far from straight. During the eighteenth century few followed it to the end. (Diderot was one of those few.)[61] Even disaffected deists rarely turned atheist: they mostly became agnostics. Early mechanistic philosophy had concluded the existence of God on the basis of the need for a first principle of motion. But the moment it appeared doubtful that motion required a transcendent cause, the argument collapsed and, with it, the logical necessity of the idea of God. The rationalist proofs on which deists had built their case depended entirely on the concept of efficient causality. Hume rightly wondered why a *God* should be needed for mundane tasks that might be performed by physical causes. Or as Diderot put it: Why should we attribute to an unknown power *outside* matter what a more dynamic concept of matter could do itself? Modern agnosticism and atheism were always, directly or indirectly, linked to the idea that efficient causality alone defines the relation between Creator and creation.

Descartes had considered God's creative act indispensable for bringing the physical mechanism of the world into being as well as for setting it in motion. Nor did he restrict God's creative impact to a one-time communication of power, as is often claimed. He insisted that creation is a never-ending process without which the cosmos would immediately return to nothingness. Nonetheless, the fact that he identified the act of creation with one of efficient causality, as that causality was understood in mechanical physics, made the need for a Creator dependent on his theory of motion. When Newton's principle of inertia abrogated the assumption that rest had a natural priority over motion, a theory of creation conceived in terms of motion became extremely vulnerable. It sufficed to abandon the unproven hypothesis that the universe must have had a beginning for the need of a transcendent cause of motion to disappear. The cosmos might have moved from all eternity. This argument took Diderot from deism to atheism.

The reduction of creation to an act of efficient causality led to even greater problems in the moral area. From Newton's exclusion of "chance" in the physical world, it was easy to conclude a universal determinism. This caused serious problems for the deist conception of God in which the existence of a moral law had remained deism's chief defense against naturalism. Indeed, deism had virtually identified religion with a transcendent promulgation and sanction of moral rules. The conflict between human freedom and divine foreknowledge, already a subject of intense controversy during the sixteenth- and early seventeenth-century disputes on predestination, became even more heated as creation became defined exclusively in terms of efficient causality. Freedom understood as the power of self-determined action was incompatible with a closed system of physical causality. Even Kant found no way out of that dilemma. He merely placed freedom and physical determinism on two different levels of meaning and excluded from the moral act any causal dependence on God. Two central ideas of modern thought, that of freedom as self-constituting and that of causality as a closed system, though conflicting with one another, conspired in creating a kind of religious predicament out of which atheism was born.

Agnosticism has been called an atheism that ignores itself. The agnostic acts as if God did not exist, though he may feel incapable of proving it or may not find it worth his while to do so. About the "agnostic" David Hume, however, one can hardly claim that he ignored where his arguments led. Still, being consistently skeptical he did not believe that the absence of proofs for God's existence and the inadequacy of the foundations of revelation sufficed to justify an atheist conclusion. There always remained the remote possibility that at some point a new, hitherto unknown argument might come up. To assess Hume's position requires that we consider *all* his writings on the subject: not only the *Dialogues on Natural Religion* (basically completed in 1761, published in 1779), but also sections X and XI of the *Enquiry Concerning Human Understanding* (1748) on miracles and on immortality, and the *Natural History of Religion* (1757). Taken separately, each one leaves room for some form of religion. Together they preclude the justification of any religious faith.

In the *Dialogues* Hume criticizes the rational arguments for the existence of a God conceived on the monotheist model: omnipotent, omniscient, and benevolent. Philo, the skeptical character, claims to be satisfied by the evidence in favor of some transcendent "Designer," but the proofs for a wise and good God leave him unconvinced. His critique may be read as primarily an attack on deism. The idea of a Creator who cannot be proven to be benevolent is inadequate for supporting the deist thesis that God rewards virtue — the main support of morality. Faith, on the other side, requires no positive proof of this goodness, as long as no proof excludes it. In his *Enquiry Concerning Human Understanding,* however, Hume had already argued that the one support faith claims to possess, namely, that of miracles, so totally conflicts with all laws of empirical probability and even with the idea of a consistent divine lawgiver that they deserve no credence whatever. The critique of immortality in section XI of that same book (and repeated in an independent essay), though not decisive, also went to the heart of the deist position. Hume's claim, then, that "our most holy religion is founded on faith, not on reason" can only be understood in an ironical sense.

After all rational arguments have been refuted, one might still claim that religion is primarily a feeling or emotion, as Shaftesbury and Rousseau had argued. Hume's own theory of moral feelings might have seemed to favor that approach, all the more so since religious feelings were generally thought to have a positive influence on human behavior. The *Natural History of Religion* closed that door. It presented religion as derived from fear, one of the most primitive emotions, and one that has consistently had a nefarious impact on human conduct. Despite this comprehensive critique of religious belief, Hume never formally ruled out the logical possibility that a good God may indeed be proven to exist and even that the Christian faith may be right. Nothing, however, justifies that belief and everything argues against it. Let us look at the details.

In the *Dialogues,* Philo prefaces his attacks by stating that the existence of an intelligent designer is not at issue. "The question can never be concerning the *being* but only the *nature* of the Deity. The former truth, as you well observe, is unquestionable and self-evident."[62] That this truth is, in fact, far from self-evident appears in part VII where Philo questions whether order requires indeed a designer. But for the time being, Hume is willing to grant the existence of a transcendent cause and to listen to the empirical arguments, popular at the time, in favor of a perfect, wise, and benevolent nature. Cleanthes, who advocates empirical, rather than rational arguments, presents an impressive analogy in support of divine causality. How could this world not be the creation of a wise designer? If we heard a voice in the sky addressing us in intelligible language could we escape concluding that it belonged to an intelligent being? Could the books in the library have been written by any but intelligent authors? "Could you possibly open one of them and doubt that its cause bore the strongest analogy to mind and intelligence?" (III, 24). But, then, nature does not show the coherence of a book nor does it contain such an obvious sign of transcendence as a voice calling from the sky. That leaves open a number of nontheistic candidates to account for the existence of an incomprehensible universe.

In the central dialogues (IV–V–VI) Philo proceeds to attack the foundations of the argument from analogy. He questions (in part IV) how much insight can be gained about the mysterious origin of this world by ascribing it to a source beyond the sphere of reliable knowledge. Even if we admit the causal dependence of this universe upon an unknown transcendent source, we are not justified in attributing more qualities to this cause than are needed to achieve the known effect. How, then, could we justifiably infer the existence of an infinite, single, and perfect being from our knowledge of a finite, complex world of doubtful perfection? Much here depends on how we conceive of the universe as a whole. Is it a machine? How intelligent an engineer does it take to construe it? Or is the world an animated being? Why should its cause, then, be more than an impersonal animating principle, such as Plato's world soul (VI)? Nor can we exclude the possibility that the world had no beginning and required no designer at all. Why would the chaos of formless but constantly agitated matter, after myriads of alterations, destructions, transpositions, not reach a point of stability from which order spontaneously emerges? "The universe may for many ages have followed a continued succession of chaos and disorder. But is it not possible that it may settle at last, so that as not to lose its motion and active force . . . , yet as to preserve a uniformity of appearance, amidst the continual motion and fluctuation of its parts?" (VIII, 51).

This very hypothesis led Diderot and his follower d'Holbach straight to a materialist worldview. We need not conceive of matter as inert and moved only by external forces. What prevents it from being endowed with active powers of its own? Today Ilya Prigogine's theory of self-organizing matter, according to which natural systems spontaneously develop coherent patterns, renders Philo's theory less far-fetched than it appeared to his partners in the dialogue.[63] Hume does not deny that the presence of order requires an explanation, but he questions whether we ought to seek that explanation *outside*, rather than *within*, the universe. To postulate an outside coordinator before considering the possibility of an order spontaneously emerging within the universe is yet another form of a misplaced analogy between the universe and a man-made object.[64]

Since the popular arguments of analogy have all suffered shipwreck in the course of being transferred from the finite to the infinite, Demea, the rationalist, at last invokes the traditional a priori argument: "Whatever exists must have a cause or reason of its existence, it being absolutely impossible for anything to produce itself or be the cause of its own existence" (IX, 54). Cleanthes turns the full force of Hume's empiricism against this thesis. Before Kant, he detects an ontological fallacy underneath the age-old cosmological argument. "There is an evident absurdity in pretending to demonstrate a matter of fact, or to prove it by any arguments *a priori*. Nothing that is distinctly conceivable implies a contradiction. Whatever we conceive as existent, we can also conceive as non-existent. There is no being, therefore, whose non-existence implies a contradiction" (IX, 55). Hence the concept of "necessary existence" on which the argument depends turns out to be meaningless.

The brunt of the attack on natural theology (found in parts X and XI of the *Dialogues*) is directed at the assumption that the transcendent cause of the universe must be benevolent. That a transcendent cause exists, Philo had conceded in the beginning (though his subsequent critique had weakened that concession into extinction), but as long as we have not proven the first cause to be benevolent to its creatures, the argument has not established the existence of a Christian or even of a deist God. To succeed in this task, the argument must reconcile the idea of a benevolent Creator with the existence of much physical and moral evil in the world. Philo, again in the front line, does not claim that evil excludes the existence of a benevolent Deity, but that the evidence for proving that existence remains inadequate as long as the deist has not shown the inevitability of evil in a finite world. At this point the principle of analogy encounters its strongest challenge. When Cleanthes, its protagonist, tries to meet it by the arguments borrowed from a partly Stoic, partly Leibnizian theodicy, Philo points out that showing the compatibility of a good God with the presence of evil in creation is one thing; proving the existence of such a God on the basis of the available evidence is another. Theodicy presupposes the existence of God and needs to prove only a *possible* compatibility, while an argument for the existence of God possesses no probative force unless it previously establishes that the two must be compatible. Philo finds both positions, Demea's rationalist one that insists on the inevitability of evil in a finite universe, and Cleanthes' empirical one that modifies the idea of God's omnipotence, unsatisfactory. The presence of so much apparently remediable evil fatally weakens the case in favor of the goodness of an even less than omnipotent Creator. A capacity for pain may be needed for survival in nature as ruled by its existing laws. But why the pain caused by incurable diseases or natural disasters? Freedom includes the potential to commit evil. But why should that potential in some individuals be so slanted toward actually committing evil, when a more harmonious psychic disposition would have avoided much human misery.

The final dialogue seems to throw all the acquired positions into disarray. Philo commences by professing his "deep sense of religion" and his "profound adoration" of God (XII, 77), even defending the analogy of nature he had so effectively attacked. "That the works of nature bear a great analogy to the productions of art is evident; and according to all the rules of good reasoning, we ought to infer, if we argue at all concerning them, that their causes have a proportional analogy" (XII, 79). Yet in these few words of approval Philo has shifted the ground of the discussion of analogy. Proportional differences among the effects indicate that the causes also are proportionally different. Surreptitiously Philo has transformed the direct analogy of proportion into the much looser one of proportionality (a/b = c/d), thereby widening the differential gap between the areas of comparison to a point where the argument loses its force. "No man can deny the analogies between the effects: to restrain ourselves from inquiring concerning the causes is scarcely possible. From this inquiry the legitimate conclusion is that the causes have also an analogy: and if we are not contented with calling the first and supreme cause a *God* or *Deity,* but desire to vary the expression, what can we call Him but *Mind* and *Thought,* to which he is justly supposed to bear a considerable resemblance?" (XII, 80). But nothing in the argument requires that we restrict this cause to a personal God: a pantheistic or materialist interpretation will work just as well once the analogy directly ceases to refer to the same principal analogate. To one who believes in God, such reasoning may be sufficient; to one who intends to prove the existence of God, it is not conclusive.

Philo declares his strong support of "the philosophical and rational kind" of religion (XII, 83) and his firm rejection of "vulgar superstitions" (XII, 82)—which in fact includes any sort of positive faith. Where does this leave us? All philosophical attempts, both a priori and a posteriori, to justify a rational (deist) religion, have been refuted. Nonetheless Philo declares that rational religion deserves to survive! The dialogue concludes with Philo's pious profession that he accepts all the arguments he had previously refuted. Hume confirms the ambiguity of his conclusion in a footnote attributed to the author himself (XII, 81–82) that refers to the differences among those positions as a matter of "habit, caprice, or inclination."[65] In one final blast of irony, Philo, the critic both of the arguments and of "superstitious religion" concludes: "A person seasoned with a just sense of the imperfections of natural reason, will fly to revealed truth with the greatest avidity. . . . To be a philosophical skeptic is, in a man of letters, the first and most essential step towards being a sound, believing Christian" (XII, 89).

If Philo seems to leave room for a religion based on revelation (provided its tenets do not run counter to reason), section X of the *Enquiry* had effectively closed that avenue by rendering the miracles and prophecies, from which revealed faith claims to draw its credibility, themselves incredible. For someone to believe in miracles requires itself a miracle.[66] The report of a miracle, especially one that has reached us from a remote time, ought to be admitted only if falsehood of the testimony on which it rests would be even more miraculous than the fact itself. For Hume, this practically eliminates any ground for belief in miracles. How then do we explain the persistent belief in them? Hume, this time without irony, attributes it to a "passion of surprise and wonder" which tends to cast aside the common rules of evidence, particularly if that passion is excited within a religious context. Wonders continue to appear today "among ignorant and barbarous nations," and they are reported to have occurred before Christianity and outside the world of the Old Testament. "What have we to oppose to such a cloud of witnesses, but the absolute impossibility of the events which they relate?" (*Enquiry,* X, 100).

One might be surprised to see Hume become such an ardent advocate of the immutability of the laws of nature, of which he had so effectively undermined the a priori necessity in the same *Enquiry*. By the purely descriptive meaning he has given of the "laws of nature" no event, however exceptional, could ever be considered to conflict with these laws. Moreover, the "laws of nature" never formed an essential factor in the religious understanding of the miracle. The New Testament merely refers to *signs (semeia)*, abnormal events that occur within a well-defined religious context and therefrom derive a specific meaning. The text never claims that those signs violated "laws of nature." More to the point is Hume's assertion that "a miracle can never be proved so as to be the foundation of a system of religion." Indeed, miracles receive their specific meaning within an already established religious setting. They may *confirm,* but they do not *prove.* Outside that context they are merely unexplained events, possibly of psychic or psychosomatic origin. Miracles prove nothing as long as the particular religion that they are supposed to support has not clarified what to expect and what not to expect.[67]

The last refuge of faith, popular in England in Hume's time, was that religion consisted of a distinct feeling that supports moral attitudes. In *The Natural History of Religion* (1757) Hume denies both that religious feelings are distinct from other emotions and that they exercise a positive influence upon morality. The very title of the work is revealing. Rather than being a feeling of transcendent origin as deists like Rousseau considered it, Hume claimed that the allegedly religious feeling was not even an original instinct, but one derived from other emotions, primarily from fear. If religion had been a primary impression it would have been universally present and not subject to basic changes.[68] "Some nations have been discovered, who entertained no sentiments of religion, if travelers and historians may be credited; and no two nations, and scarce any two men, have ever agreed precisely in the same sentiments. It would appear, therefore, that this preconception springs not from an original instinct or primary impression of nature."[69]

The "natural" quality of religion, then, carries no assurance of its truth or moral rectitude. Indeed, the emotion of fear tends to distort one's judgment by phantoms of the imagination. "Agitated by hopes and fears —, especially the latter, men scrutinize, with a trembling curiosity, the course of future causes and examine the various and contrary events of human life" (II, 28). There they claim to detect "the first obscure traces of divinity." Hume also takes issue with the assumption that religion began as a primitive monotheism: its origins are radically polytheistic. Only later does some form of monotheism emerge, and then not under the influence of increased insight but rather from equally "irrational and superstitious principles." Because a particular nation worshiped one god or goddess more than others, it gradually came to regard him or her as wielding supreme authority over all others by being more powerful (VI, 42). The idea of a single God creating the entire universe and supervising all its operations could not have occurred to minds incapable of comprehending the cosmos as one coherent system subject to invariable laws. The monotheism of popular religion continues to remain unsettled: believers still flock to innumerable sanctuaries, invoke various saints for various purposes, and regard extraordinary events far more significant than the principles of monotheist theology. Polytheism and popular theism, though resulting in different social structures, share a common irrationality.[70]

Nor do such superstitions, whether polytheist or theist, foster moral progress. At the most primitive stage gods or spirits are devoid of moral qualities. Yet even when religion culturally matures, the object of worship does not become more moral. "As men farther exalt their idea of their divinity, it is their notion of the god's power and knowledge, not of his goodness, which is improved" (XIII, 67). Indeed, efforts to raise the level of moral obligations often end up having the opposite effect: they become a religious substitute for morality. The faithful regard the attendance at sermons intended to inculcate a moral attitude an easy means to acquit themselves of their moral obligations. No bond joins virtuous conduct to religious belief. Quite the opposite, religious fanaticism has been responsible for the most heinous crimes. Any but the "religion of reason" sets morality back.

Hume's *Natural History of Religion* presented a more damaging attack on religion than the *Dialogues,* whose publication he prudently postponed. That the early work received no stronger negative critique was due to the fact that he attacked only the religion of the masses while excepting that of the educated. Taken together with the *Enquiry* and the *Dialogues,* however, the moral critique of the *Natural History* precluded a rational justification of any form of religion: philosophical, revealed, and sentimental. In fact, Hume's writings on religion undermined the case of deism as much as that of religion proper. Deism had attempted to rescue the ideas of creation, of immortality, and of the transcendent source of the moral law from their irrational context in popular religion. Hume intended to show that those ideas were as far from being rational as the popular superstitions. The idea of a transcendent Creator was justified neither by logic nor by experience; the idea of life after death conflicts with all we know about human nature; faith, even rational faith, far from being indispensable to morality obstructs moral progress. Deism ceased to be a viable substitute for revealed religion. Still, Hume never professed himself to be an atheist. Rather than "opposing one species of superstition to another," he declared himself "to make [his] escape into the calm, though obscure regions of philosophy."

Having closed off all ways to prove God's existence, Hume claimed, albeit with more irony than conviction, to leave open the way to faith. French materialists such as La Mettrie, Diderot, and d'Holbach, were explicitly and, in d'Holbach's case, aggressively atheistic. They replaced Descartes's metaphysical dualism of mind and body by a single material substance capable of both mental and corporeal functions. Condillac's sensationalist theory of perception provided the physiological support needed for this transformation. In chapter 2 I have sketched Diderot's philosophical development toward such a dynamic materialism. His evolutionary concept of matter had rendered the idea of God superfluous.[71] D'Holbach wrote later and fully profited from Diderot's ideas on the subject. To him, atheism was a logical conclusion as well as a practical imperative for the intellectual and moral liberation of the human race.[72] His *Système de la Nature* (1770) remained the most elaborate *summa* of atheism until the Soviet encyclopedias of the twentieth century. The author must have spent years collecting the information with which he packed his pages. Did he write it all himself? Rumors persist that Diderot had a hand in it (especially in the footnotes). They knew each other well, and it may have been Diderot who converted d'Holbach to atheism. The German baron certainly borrowed Diderot's dynamic concept of matter. But his *Système* lacks Diderot's sharp wit and irony. It is not a subtle book. Arthur M. Wilson in his biography of Diderot aptly compares the two philosophes: "Diderot's doctrine is much more elusive, ambiguous, and therefore closer to life than d'Holbach's. Diderot's philosophy, hard to be sure of, has a great deal of poetic insight, and should properly be called godless rather than atheistic."[73]

The basic principle of d'Holbach's philosophy was the dynamic, creative nature of matter. If matter is dynamic and eternal, as he assumes it is, it requires no explanation as to how the causal process got started or why external causes must be ruled out. Motion and the heat it produces suffice to explain all changes and modifications. Motion, the source of diversity, also functions as the bond of unity: it relates the whole to the parts and the parts to the whole. Religious believers look upon nature "as a heap of dead, inert, formless matter, which has not within itself the power of producing any of the great effects from which emanates . . . *the order of the universe*" (I, 5, p. 38). Nor does d'Holbach equate his materialism with a "blind" physical determinism. The idea that letters thrown down at random could ever produce the *Iliad*, he considered as absurd as Voltaire did. Works of the mind cannot be explained directly through material causes, but mind itself results from such causes.

Having established matter as the single source of reality, d'Holbach predicates the traditional attributes of God to an all-inclusive, creative matter. True, matter is not "intelligent" as God is alleged to be, but "intelligence" is merely "a personification of an abstract quality" of matter as a dynamic source of power. By not attributing the creative process to a source beyond nature, he avoided the contradictions he thought to be inherent in the idea of a wise and good Creator. Nature, indifferent to what humans call good or evil, merely follows her necessary course. Evil becomes an insoluble problem only when a personal God is considered responsible for all that occurs in the world.

How could a good God have created a world "groaning under such a multitude of calamities" (II, 1, p. 193)? The more theologians attempt to extricate themselves from this difficulty by assuming a balance of justice and mercy, the more they expose the inconsistency of their concepts. Where is "mercy"? On what ground do they call "just" a Creator so cruel to the works of his hand? The allegedly merciful and compassionate God condemns fragile beings to endless torments "for transitory offenses, for false reasonings, for involuntary errors, for necessary passions, which depend on the temperament this God has given them" (II, 1, p. 197). If God owes nothing to his creatures and is not bound by either justice or goodness, why should they owe God anything? How can they worship a Deity so deprived of all respect for what humans regard as the laws of nature and of reason? Even the idea of a historical revelation conflicts with the notion of a good God because it leaves uncountable humans unacquainted with truths deemed essential to their salvation. All believers and most deists postulate an afterlife to compensate for the evils the good have suffered in this life. But why should a future state, of which we know nothing, have to compensate for the happiness God has denied us in this life? How does one reconcile such a painful and unnecessary detour with the idea of an omnipotent, benevolent God? All these absurdities vanish, according to the *Système*, if we stop projecting our own optimistic or jaundiced moods onto the universe. Deists are no less superstitious than believers. Both start from the contradictory principle that an immaterial God is able to create a material world and yet cannot prevent evil from occurring in it. "As soon as they suppose such a God, they can believe anything" (II, 5, p. 259).

D'Holbach also sketches a natural history of religion. Since the dawn of consciousness humans have never ceased to acknowledge a causal principle beyond the creative power of nature. Religious apologists consider the universality of this belief in God a proof of God's existence (II, 4, p. 205). What all humans believe, they argue, cannot be false. In fact, the universality of religion is due to a tendency inherent in human nature to "anthropomorphize" its projections. "Man has never been able to prevent himself from drawing together from his own particular nature the qualities he has assigned to the being who governs the universe" (II, 1, p. 191).

Despite its flat-footed, question-begging materialism, *The System of Nature* remains a disturbing book for believers. Obviously theology had not kept pace with scientific revolutions in astronomy, geology, and biology. D'Holbach's often casually formulated objections hide serious questions concerning fundamental concepts in Western religion. At the heart of them lie the problematic notion of a creation exclusively conceived in terms of efficient causality, of a heavily anthropomorphic idea of God, and often of the absence of a genuine autonomy of finite beings (and hence the inevitability of suffering and evil). The assault on these inconsistencies by which theologians and philosophers have all too often supported their religious beliefs retain much of their strength, even after we have dismissed d'Holbach's nonsequiturs and simplistic conclusions.

Surprisingly few readers of the Enlightenment surrendered to d'Holbach's logic. Unbelievers no less than believers felt that he left out an essential element. He simply assumes that the *real* coincides with the *objective*, allowing no mode of being other than a homogeneous naturalism. Eighteenth-century attempts at closing the gap between subject and object, opened during the previous century, often ended up reducing one to the other. No one did so more radically than d'Holbach. In his system the source of meaning becomes itself an objective entity. The "inner" becomes an integral part of the "outer." As he states at the beginning of his book: "The distinction which has been so often made between the *physical* and the *moral* man is evidently an abuse of terms. Man is a being purely physical" (I, 1, p. 11). The *System* admits as truth only what is accessible to the methods of the positive sciences. The objectivism heralded by d'Holbach came to play a major part in the scientific philosophy of the nineteenth century. Those who have read Edward Wilson's *Consilience* would hesitate to declare it extinct today.

Despite its unambiguous hostility to religion, eighteenth-century atheism displays an affinity with its enemy that makes one suspect the presence of a hidden dialectic between the two. That doctrinal atheism differs from today's secularism, which is less concerned with opposing religion than with filling the cultural vacuum left by its disappearance. Pierre Bayle, the author of the historical and critical *Dictionnaire*, intimates that atheism may not be as far apart from religion as its defenders think. In a famous article titled "Pauliciens" (Remarque I), he makes the charge, surprising for a confessing member of the French Reformed Church, that Calvin's doctrine of predestination entails consequences that would be fatal to the idea of God if consistently thought through. But then follows the interesting conclusion: lack of logical consistency alone does not determine the religious or nonreligious quality of a theological doctrine.[74] Indeed, all radical monotheism has an atheistic streak in it: the fight against idols will never be complete as long as any positive determination remains. On the other hand, all doctrinal atheism has a religious origina: it needs a God to deny.

In his *Phenomenology of Spirit* (VI, A), Hegel first drew attention to the dialectical nature of the Enlightenment's critique of religion. He explained it as resulting from an opposition between the *act* of thinking and its *content*. In the crisis of the eighteenth century, the rationalist mind ended up disowning the traditional representations of faith as being no more than idealized projections of the present world unto an otherworldly realm of fantasy. In so criticizing religion as an illusory mode of thought, however, the rationalist mind deprived thought of its most fundamental content. Threatened by the assault of reason, faith withdrew into a sphere impervious to the control of reason. Thus faith and reason, both indispensable to thought, became separated. One preserved the content of thought but lost the rigorous method of reason; the other preserved the formal method of reasoning but lost the content. They continue to communicate, however, in a dialectical opposition. The atheist critique forces the believer to recognize that there is no transcendent "object." On the other side, faith shows the emptiness of content in purely critical thought.

Nineteenth-century atheists and agnostics still remained aware of the ties that continued to link their thought to the religion they once had embraced. Thus Ernest Renan wrote: "I feel that my life is governed by a faith that I no longer possess. Faith has this peculiar quality that, after it has disappeared, it continues to work." A similar feeling inspired much of Leslie Stephen's *Agnostic Apology*. Long before his contemporaries, Nietzsche understood the depth of the crisis caused by this rupture in the Western mind. He realized how the death of God had changed the very nature of our culture.[75]

In our own time, when atheism has mostly turned into secularism, it has loosened its ties with religion. Secular men and women have ceased to define themselves in the antireligious terms that still imply a dialectical dependence on faith. They no longer describe themselves as "atheists," a name derived from an attitude with which they have broken.[76] With the change has disappeared much of the polemical attitude. But so has the former dialectical relation to religion. Today modes of "low" transcendence are often filling the place previously occupied by the high transcendence of God. Primary among them may well be the aesthetic experience. Like religion, that experience integrates the various aspects of our world within a single coherent vision that radiates with a glow of transcendence. The aesthetic transcendence, like the religious one, opens a new, symbolic dimension in the real. Beauty, even as religion, albeit only for a moment, *justifies* the world. "After one has abandoned a belief in God," Wallace Stevens wrote, "poetry is that essence which takes its place as life's redemption."[77] Whether that suffices for rendering existence meaningful is a question I do not have to answer in this book.

9

The Faith of the Philosophers

In this chapter I shall discuss the main philosophical responses to the challenges to religion described in the preceding one. Some philosophers, such as Leibniz and Clarke, responded from within the rationalist tradition. Others, among them Malebranche, Berkeley, and Jacobi, considered philosophical rationalism the very source of the religious crisis and repudiated it altogether. The first group attempted to revive philosophical theology, a branch of metaphysics that had existed since the early Stoics and that aimed at establishing the existence and nature of God. The Arabs, in their commentaries on the works of Aristotle, revived it as a rational foundation for revealed religion. When Western theologians of the twelfth and thirteenth centuries became acquainted with these commentaries, they adopted some form of it as a preparation to the traditional course of studies in scriptural theology.[1] Thomas Aquinas integrated this new discipline with the traditional one of theology. The nominalist theologians of the fifteenth century did not favor this kind of philosophical theology based on a priori principles. Yet they continued to assert the need for some natural justification of faith. Some then started exploring the signs of God's presence in nature. The Catalan theologian Raymond of Sabunde called his *Theologia naturalis* (first printed edition in 1487), an unsystematic collection of random observations and ideas remembered only for Montaigne's critique of it, the *prima scientia*.[2] We have seen in the previous chapter how thoroughly Hume destroyed those efforts.

The Rationalists

With the concept of rationality introduced by Descartes the kind of integration between reason and faith achieved by St. Thomas was no longer possible. If reason was essentially a quality of mind, revelation from a transcendent source as well as the faith based on it belonged to a different order. The two might peacefully coexist and possibly support each other. But henceforth theology and philosophy ought to remain separate. Descartes and major thinkers of the rationalist school, such as Leibniz, Clarke, and Wolff, tried to show the convergence of reason with faith. A critical role thereby played the so-called arguments for the existence of God. In exposing the weakness of those arguments, Kant proved that even the alleged parallelism between reason and revelation rested on questionable grounds. The arguments assumed a pre-existing intellectual intuition of the idea of God. In fact, reason does not possess such an intuition. It borrows the idea of God from sources different from itself — revelation, attempts to explain experiences of unknown origin, traditions based on either or both. All reason might do for religion is, after a critical reflection on religious phenomena and sacred texs, discern their rationality and explore how religious doctrines could be interpreted in conformity with the rules of reason as eighteenth-century philosophy understood them. Its contribution consisted not so much in support as in understanding a field that did not belong to its own domain. Religion was thereby removed to the sidelines of philosophy, as object of a subordinate branch — the philosophy of religion.

The deists broke with traditional theology. They either took no account of it or they reinterpreted it as essentially coinciding with philosophical theology. The philosophers presented in the first part of this chapter followed a middle course. They accepted revelation though they did not allow it to interfere with their philosophical speculation. At first sight they seem to have taken their philosophical arguments from Scholastic sources. Yet the Scholastic five "ways" (*viae*) leading to the existence of God had not been purely rational arguments. At the beginning of the *Summa Theologiae* (I, 8) Aquinas declares that reason does not prove the principles of faith: those principles are derived from revelation. Without revelation, philosophy would be incapable of proving the object of faith.[3] Contrary to that position, deists started their argument from nature conceived as independent of God; next, they attempted to show that this nature required the existence of God. Needless to say, such a doubtful project rarely met with success.[4] Leibniz and Clarke, the two thinkers here considered, took a different approach. They considered revelation an indispensable source of knowledge of God, complementary to philosophical insight but not reducible to it. Their work, even as that of the deists, mainly covered three subjects: the existence of God, the attributes of God, and the justification of evil and suffering in a world created by God.

LEIBNIZ AND GOD'S JUSTIFICATION

Leibniz, the most systematic thinker of the Enlightenment, never composed a system. He treated the weightiest philosophical questions in letters and short essays. Though mostly remembered for his *Théodicée* (the only book published during his lifetime), he packed more substance in his short pieces on the existence and nature of God than in that lengthy, rambling essay. Leibniz was a rationalist in the philosophical sense (not in the religious one). This created considerable problems for his project in philosophical theology, since strict rationalism demands that all multiplicity must be reducible to a single principle. In fact, Leibniz himself compared his method to the attribution of many predicates to the single subject of a proposition. According to Bertrand Russell, it was only by logical inconsistency that Leibniz escaped Spinoza's metaphysical monism.[5] However one judges this claim, the German philosopher keenly perceived the threat of monism and assiduously tried to avoid it.

Could the rationalist principle be reconciled with the kind of ontological pluralism required by a theistic worldview? How do finite beings succeed in remaining distinct and relatively independent substances despite their total dependence on the principle in which they have their justification? Leibniz attempted to preserve both the unity of the system and the plurality of finite substances by conceiving of them as intrinsically linked to a single all-inclusive principle exclusive of any extrinsic dependence upon other finite substances. God, the one, absolute principle explicates itself in an infinity of substantial units, each of which presents a particular, finite perspective of the absolute on which it intrinsically depends. "God preserves [the creatures] and can produce them continually by a kind of emanation just as we produce our thoughts."[6] In and through this absolute principle each substance communicates with all other substances. "A particular substance never acts upon another particular substance nor is it acted upon" (*Discourse on Metaphysics,* # 14).

To maintain the substantial independence of finite beings, their causal dependence on the Creator could not be restricted to one of efficient causality, as was usually done in the eighteenth century. If finite things were linked to the Creator as to an efficient cause only, the relation would remain purely external and their existence would not be justified through an ultimate, absolute principle, as the rationalist method required. They then would owe their entire being to the blind will of God and have no intrinsic reason for their existence.[7] Leibniz therefore reintroduced what the mechanists of his time had most radically excluded from thought, namely, a final causality, as well as the kind of immanent dependence on God asserted by Thomists and by most mystics, whereby God constitutes the very being of his creatures. "I, for my part, hold that far from excluding final causes from the consideration of physics, as Descartes pretends, . . . it is rather by them that all should be determined, since the efficient cause of things is intelligent, having a will and consequently tending toward the Good."[8] Unless all things were directed toward a single purpose, we would no longer be able to account for harmonious "fitting" together in one universe.[9]

God unites all substances in a *meaningful* totality, a universal harmony, without suppressing their identities. Yet God can do so only because He is actively present in each and all as the very source of their being. "It is God alone (from whom all individuals emanate continually . . .) who is the cause of this correspondence in their phenomena."[10] Leibniz's system is rooted in Neoplatonic thought, which starts *from above*, from the first principle itself, rather than from below. Leibniz often refers to Henry More, the Cambridge Platonist, whose dynamic concept of reality driven and unified by a divine spirit inspired his own thought. For that reason, Philip Clayton correctly points out, Leibniz's "arguments" for the existence of God serve a different purpose than Descartes's. They are valid only *within* that system.[11] The system itself is one ontological argument. It needs no others.

This Platonism also explains why the (Platonic) idea of *perfection* dominates all other divine attributes. The *Discourse on Metaphysics* (1686) begins with the words: "The conception of God which is the most common and the most full of meaning is expressed well enough in the words: God is an absolutely perfect being." God's perfection is both ontological and logical. It includes the highest reality and, at the same time, the greatest possible intelligibility. The Platonic view of perfection implies self-communication: *bonum est diffusivum sui* (the good is self-communicating). For Leibniz, this implies that creation, in which God expresses this perfection, must be both necessary and perfect: it could not be other than it is and no other creation could contain a greater amount of reality. "The primitive simple substance must contain in itself eminently the perfections of all the substances which are its effects; thus it will have perfect power, knowledge and will: that is, it will have supreme omnipotence, omniscience, and goodness."[12]

This "necessary perfection" appears to bring Leibniz's theory close to Spinoza's. He himself admits that God creates "by a kind of emanation" (*Discourse on Metaphysics,* # 14). In his notes on Spinoza's *Ethics,* book I, Leibniz accepts definition 7 without objection: "A free thing is that which exists and is determined to action by the necessity of its own nature" (I, 7). Nor does he appear to have any problems with proposition I, 16. "From the necessity of the divine nature must follow an infinite number of things in infinite ways." Still, Leibniz's theory essentially differs from Spinoza's on the issue of necessity and contingency. In the margin of Spinoza's definition of things produced by God: "their essence does not involve existence" (*Ethics,* I, 24), he writes: "From this proposition it follows, contrary to Spinoza's own interpretation, that things are not necessary." The term "necessary" applies to God's creative *act,* but not to the nature of the created universe, which, being totally dependent, is entirely contingent.

Elsewhere he even concludes, somewhat inconsistently, from this absence of intrinsic necessity that all things must have been created by divine choice: "Beings do not emanate from the divine essence: they do not emerge necessarily from it" ("Causa Dei," # 10, in *Schriften,* VI, 440). A divine decision is needed to bring contingent things to existence, since in themselves they might exist or not exist. In the *Theodicy* (1710) he unqualifiedly rejects Spinoza's position: "He teaches that all things exist by the necessity of the Divine nature, *without God making any choice.* We will not waste our time here refuting an opinion so bad, and indeed so inexplicable."[13] An even more baffling declaration appears in an until 1948 unpublished fragment: "And certainly he [God] wills freely, because outside his will no other reason can be given than the will."[14] To Samuel Clarke, who objected to the idea of a necessary creation, Leibniz responded that God's creation implied no logical necessity. A different universe or none at all would involve no contradiction, since there is no necessity on the side of creation.[15] It is not hard to find conflicting tendencies in Leibniz's work, some of which may have been inspired by less than purely theoretical motives. Yet I do not believe that he ever wrote anything that would inevitably result in Spinoza's conclusions.[16] What preserved him from doing so was the Neoplatonic idea of participation that implies a real plurality and a true contingency on the side of creation.[17]

Real problems, however, surround the relation between human freedom and divine foreknowledge. In his *Theodicy* Leibniz considers the two theological positions on foreknowledge and free will current in the early seventeenth century. Bañez asserted that God's foreknowledge also includes God's *foreordinance* of all future free acts (including the evil ones). Molina held that God foresees those acts as mere *possibilities before* he decrees their actual existence (*Theodicy,* # 42). Perceiving the heavily anthropomorphic implications of the before and after in both positions, Leibniz repudiated the disjunction of *either* free will and imperfect divine foreknowledge *or* perfect divine foreknowledge and no real freedom. Instead, he argued that the knowledge of all possible worlds enabled God to know a priori, i.e., independently of actual creation all that was to occur in each of these possible worlds. This comprehensive vision included possible divine decrees as well as possible human actions. Thus he bypassed Molina's highly criticized "middle science" (*scientia media*), without compromising human freedom, as Bañez had done.[18] But in discussing the relation between God's foreknowledge and God's decision, Leibniz himself admits an equally anthropomorphic distinction between God's "will" and God's "intellect."[19] In the *Theodicy* Leibniz uncritically adopts the anthropomorphic terms of his questioners and adversaries. Thus he distinguishes God's *primitive antecedent will* from the *mediate will* and the *final and decisive will* (*Theodicy,* # 119). The idea of a ratiocinating God, first deciding on the principles, next balancing the various possibilities against each other, and finally reaching a wise decision, is so unworthy of a thinker of Leibniz's stature that one cannot but wonder whether he intended it as a popular representation of his own, quite different conception of divine rationality. If so, it betrayed the fundamental principles of his philosophy!

The interminable discussions of free will, divine foreknowledge, and predestination in the early modern age all stemmed from the seventeenth-century notion of God's creative act conceived exclusively in terms of efficient causality. As we saw, Leibniz supported a more intimate form of creaturely dependence. In the *Discourse on Metaphysics* (# 32) he writes: "It appears clearly that all other substances depend on God just as our thoughts emanate from our own substances; that *God is all in all and that he is intimately united to all created things,* in proportion, however, to their perfection; that it is he alone who determines them from without by his influence, and if to act is to determine directly, it may be said in metaphysical language that God alone acts upon me and he alone causes me to do good or ill, other substances contributing only because of his determinations."[20] God here is conceived as an inner presence, a conception closer to Augustine and Malebranche than to Descartes. Unfortunately, Leibniz did not consistently adhere to this more intimate relation between Creator and creation, and he became constricted in the same kind of anthropomorphic distinctions that misguided so much of seventeenth-century theology.

It particularly confused his attempt to justify the existence of evil in a world created by a good God. If God knows that the world He actually chose to create was to contain a great deal of evil, why did He create it? Why not another or none at all? Leibniz answers that a "moral" necessity drives God to create a world that includes a maximum of reality and variety compatible with a minimum of evil. Since moral perfection is an essential attribute of God's nature, no other than the most perfect (or least imperfect) world could have been created. Yet Leibniz gives that principle an unexpected twist when placing it above the need to remove moral evil from the world. "There is no reason to suppose that God, for the sake of some lessening of moral evil, would reverse the whole order of nature. . . . It is certain that God sets greater store by a man than by a lion; nevertheless it can hardly be said with certainty that God prefers a single man in all respects to the whole of lion-kind" (*Theodicy,* # 118). This rationalist rule of perfection, like the Greek Ananke, stands above God. "The eternal verities, objects of his [God's] wisdom, are more inviolable than the Styx" (*Theodicy,* # 121). If Leibniz, instead of subjecting the cosmic order to an ideal law of reason, had given due weight to the intrinsic contingency inherent in the very notion of creation, he could have dispensed with the flawed idea of a "best possible world" altogether. Contingency voids any world, good or bad, of internal necessity. This affects not only its existence, but also its perfection. The very doctrine of creation implies that it is gratuitous, an "unmerited grace."[21] Whether a better world is possible, given the constraining and complex conditions of finitude, seems a meaningless question.

The extraordinary significance the Enlightenment attached to theodicy reveals its moralistic slant. The real must be justified: it must earn our moral approval before being deemed worthy of a divine Creator. Such an anthropomorphic defense of the Creator threatens in fact the very life of religion. "Theodicy, in contrast to the radical critique of religion, regards itself as an intellectual operation that is friendly to religion, Hermann Lübbe writes, nonetheless it is, so to speak, an heretical attempt to dismiss as a mere illusion the condition of what a truly religious attitude requires, namely, a contingency of life that surpasses the meaning of action."[22] Goodness had always been regarded as a primary divine attribute. But after the modern view reduced it to the quality of what a thing is worth to us, considerations of moral rightness came to overrule the intrinsic contingency of all that is finite.

All contingency implies imperfection. But, according to Leibniz, within that restriction the world must still be "the best possible" to be worthy of a perfect Creator. He thereby transforms existential contingency into rational necessity. The real question, however, remains whether the existence of evil does not jeopardize the idea of divine perfection. Hume posed it better than Leibniz: Does the presence of so much suffering and evil not conflict with the idea of a perfect Creator under *any* circumstances? How could the answer be other than affirmative, if the ultimate criterion for justifying the real is taken from the moral scale of values? The answer to the question lies not in Leibniz's *Theodicy*, but in his Neoplatonic idea of the Good as a self-communicating Absolute. If he had remained faithful to this original intuition, the "justification" of the cosmos would have assumed a quite different form — as it had in the Cambridge Platonists Cudworth and More who in other respects influenced him so strongly. Rather than becoming bogged down in divine deliberations "before" the creation of the world, Leibniz then would have referred to the participation of all contingent being in the self-communicating principle of the Good.[23]

Leibniz never accepted the narrowly rationalist position of the deists who restricted the knowledge of God to the conclusions of reason. Revelation extends the range of truth as well as it confirms reason. "The ancient philosophers knew very little of these important truths." (*Discourse on Metaphysics*, # 37). The principle of rationality demands only that the possibility of a revelation be supported by adequate "motives of credibility." In the *Systema Theologicum*, an unpublished text written around 1686, Leibniz defines the relation between reason and revelation as follows: "As right reason is the natural interpreter of God, it is necessary that, before any other interpreters of God be recognized, reason should be able to pronounce upon their authority; but when they have once, so to speak, established their legitimate character, reason itself must henceforward submit to faith."[24] Obviously Leibniz rejected Bayle's strange thesis that the truths of revelation may conflict with the truths of reason. Indeed, to refute that position was one of his main motives for writing the *Theodicy*. The principle of perfection requires both harmony and continuity between all strata of truth, even those that surpass human knowledge. At the end of his late essay on "Principles of Nature and Grace" (1714) he still repeats what he had already asserted in his early *Discourse on Metaphysics*, namely, that the realms of nature and grace meet on the level of *spirit*.[25] A spiritual nature, he argues, *naturally* calls for an intimate relation with God, which the mind is, however, unable to establish itself. The guiding idea of a self-expressive divine goodness that attracts all "spirits" to itself, shows again the Platonic direction of Leibniz's thought.[26]

APOLOGETICS: CLARKE AND BUTLER

Samuel Clarke (1675–1729), Newton's philosophical disciple, advocated a methodically less rigorous parallelism between reason and revelation. He mixes a mechanistic view of creation with teleological speculations that move so far beyond it as to jeopardize the coherence of his theory, and nowhere more so than in his discussion of what determines the order of the universe. Was it God's "arbitrary will" as nominalist theologians claimed, or was it a rule of reason to which the Creator himself owed obedience? Clarke never decided the issue and it led to overt contradictions in his thought. His theory exercised an enormous influence upon his contemporaries. Later generations, having read too many arguments for the existence of God and heard too much about the "rationality" of their faith, brought him in for a severe reassessment. Leslie Stephen condescendingly but not wholly unjustly portrays him as "a man of sufficient intellectual vigour to justify a very high reputation, and [whose] faults are those which are less obvious to the eyes of contemporaries than of posterity, . . . with perspicuity enough to avoid some of the extravagances of the school to which he belonged, but not enough to detect its fundamental fallacies."[27] Stephen pairs Clarke with Tindall. Unquestionably, Clarke accepted much of the deist's thesis that the content of revelation coincides with the principles of reason. But he steadfastly asserted the need for a revelation, though in the light of his theory such a need appears dubious.[28]

Clarke's position on natural theology did not become fully clear until his later epistolary exchange with Leibniz.[29] Like Leibniz, he accepted the principle of sufficient reason. Yet as early as his first letter he interpreted it in a manner that Leibniz found quite puzzling. "This sufficient reason is often the simple or mere will of God" (*L*, III, 7, p. 47). For Clarke, the will of God is the *ultima ratio*. While defending the miracles reported in the Bible, the main target of the deist critique, Clarke had argued that no intrinsic necessity guides "the course of nature," since matter is totally inert. Only "the arbitrary will and pleasure of God exerting itself and acting upon Matter continually" determines all events in nature (*Discourse*, Prop. XIV, 3, p. 223). God's miraculous interventions, though deviating from the regular method of Providence, do not conflict with it.

For Leibniz, such a view meant nothing less than the end of philosophical theology, since it reduced the principle of sufficient reason "to the simple and mere will of God." The notion of sufficient reason thereby loses all philosophical significance: anything is possible for the arbitrary will of God (*L*, III, 7, p. 54, also III, 17, p. 87). Even Clarke's expression "the mere will" conflicts with the very definition of the will as the ability to act on rational grounds. On his side, Clarke felt that Leibniz's interpretation of the principle of sufficient reason left no need for God at all. "The notion of the world's being a great machine, going on without the interposition of God, as a clock continues to go without the assistance of the clock-maker, is the notion of *materialism* and *fate*, and tends to . . . exclude Providence and God's government in reality out of the world" (*L*, I, 4., p. 31). To Clarke, Leibniz's principles of reason stand above God. To Leibniz, Clarke's rationality rests entirely on a divine decision.

Clarke was convinced that he had adequately met the principle of sufficient reason when, in the so-called *Demonstration* of 1704 (later published as the first part of the *Discourse*), he had deduced the existence of God from the rational order of the world. "Whatever exists, has a cause, a reason, a ground of its existence . . . either in the necessity of its own nature, and then it must have been of itself eternal, or in the will of some other being and then that other being must, at least in the order of nature and causality, have existed before it" (I, Prop. I, p. 3). Thus, he concludes, something must have existed from all eternity that is not subject to generation and corruption. One may wonder why Clarke postulates an absolute Being *beyond* the series before having properly excluded the possibility that it lays *within* the series.[30]

In the "synthetic" part of his argument Clarke identifies this independent, necessary being with God. Contrary to rationalist custom, he begins by admitting his total ignorance of divine nature. Yet he feels that at least some of the attributes follow from the proof of God's existence. Thus eternity must be a quality of a Being whose existence does not depend on any external cause (I, Prop. V, p. 39). Moreover, what does not depend on anything cannot be limited by anything; hence it must be infinite in time as well as in space. "The infinity of the self-existent being must be an infinity of *fullness* as well of *immensity*" (I, Prop. VI, p. 42). Clarke appears to be somewhat aware of the problems connected with an infinity defined in terms of space and time because he writes: "As to the particular manner of his being infinite or everywhere present, in opposition to the manner of created things being present in such finite places, this is as impossible for our finite understandings to comprehend or explain as it is for us to form an adequate idea of infinity" (I, Prop. VI, p. 43). But if it is incomprehensible, why attribute it to God?

With the deduction of those divine attributes that identify the self-existent being as a personal God, the argument becomes predictably even more controversial. From the existence of intelligent creatures as well as from the wise design of the universe as a whole, Clarke concludes that the being on which they depend must be intelligent itself. We know what Hume thought of this argument. But then we come to the point where Clarke definitively parts company with Leibniz. God's perfection requires "to do always what is best in the whole" (I, Prop. IX, p. 59). Yet, he adds, nothing should prevent God from acting arbitrarily in matters of indifference. In the end, however, everything appears to become a matter of indifference for God and Clarke's rationalism breaks down altogether. "The nature, indeed, and relations, the proportions and disproportions, the fitnesses and unfitnesses of things is only upon supposition that the things exist and that they exist in such a manner as they at present do. Now that things exist in such a manner as they exist at all, depends entirely upon the arbitrary will and pleasure of God" (II, Prop. II, p. 95).

In the second *Discourse,* which deals with morality and immortality, Clarke expresses his intention to prove the need for revelation. In fact, he assumes that with the principles of morality engraved in human nature one may wonder why mankind still needs a revelation. Why would a revealed system of morality be more necessary than an inspired system of mathematics? Clarke answers that revelation was needed to restore the authority of the natural law after that law had gone into decline (II, Prop. I, p. 90). In his argument for immortality he follows the same line. In the ordinary course of events the observation of the natural law would be enforced by rewards and punishments. Since the order of nature has been perverted, however, rewards and punishments no longer follow virtue or vice in this life. Revelation promises a restoration of the natural order in a future life. Yet Clarke had already proven by Plato's argument of the immateriality of the soul that the existence of a life after death was essential to spiritual beings. He himself proves it and sees it confirmed by the belief of "the most learned and thinking part of mankind" (II, Prop. IV, pp. 14–15). Then, why revelation? Once again he blames human corruption (carelessness, prejudices, passions) for failing to recognize what all are supposed to know. Hence, he concludes, even the most noble ancient thinkers themselves felt the need for a divine revelation. As Socrates confesses in the (inauthentic) Platonic dialogue *Alcibiades:* "It is absolutely necessary that we wait with patience till such time as we can learn certainly how we ought to behave ourselves both towards God and towards men" (II, Prop. VII, p. 157).

This alleged expectation of the ancients at last provides the British apologist with a somewhat more solid ground for distinguishing his natural theology from that of "modern" (as opposed to ancient) deists who claim that philosophy needs no revelation. In fact, he claims, the principles of modern deism are themselves derived from the revelation it rejects. This explains why it succeeds in formulating moral positions more precisely than the wisest men of antiquity did. " 'Tis one thing to see that those rules of life, which are beforehand plainly and particularly laid before us, are perfectly agreeable to reason; and another thing to find out those rules merely by the light of reason, without their having first been otherwise made known" (II, Prop. VII, pp. 162–63). The discomfort he experiences about the similarity of his own moral position to that of the modern deists induces Clarke to accuse them unfairly of lacking a serious regard for morality and of being "atheists at heart." In fact, Clarke has merely set the deist story in a different key — not reason, but the will of God, justifies the natural order. He has thus converted the entire natural order into a super-natural event and undermined the very purpose of philosophical theology.

But the originality of Clarke's work lies elsewhere. At the end of his second series of lectures he compares the prophecies of the Old Testament with events allegedly fulfilling them in the Gospels. The often far-fetched linkage between the two had become a favorite target of deist attacks. By introducing a different notion of "fulfillment," Clarke breaks new ground in exegesis. He increases the challenge by refusing to take this "fulfillment" in a "typical, mystical, allegorical, or enigmatical" sense. He considers it a literal, though "amplified," one (II, Prop. XIV, p. 237). Revelation, he argues, occurred "in different degrees and proportions," starting with a few tribes that "steadfastly adhered to the worship of the God of nature, the one God of the universe" (ibid., p. 238). Since the prophets predicted an everlasting reign of truth and virtue, Clarke feels justified to interpret their prophecies as including more than a political liberation from Assyrians, Egyptians, and Babylonians. The Spirit of God directed them "to be uttered in such words, as may even more properly and more justly be applied to the great event which Providence had in view than to the intermediate event which God designed as only a pledge or earnest of the other" (ibid., p. 254). Taken in their entirety, the prophecies receive their ultimate fulfillment in Christ. He vindicated the "direct" ones by his miracles. To the "indirect" ones, the "types, and figures; and allegorical manners of speaking" (ibid., p. 260) he gave a new meaning. In no way do they prove the truth of Christian doctrine, but they confirm its continuity with the biblical revelation. "The correspondence of types and antitypes, though they are not themselves proper proofs of the truth of a doctrine, [yet they] may be very reasonable confirmations of the foreknowledge of God; of the uniform view of Providence under different dispensations; of the analogy, harmony, and agreement between the Old Testament and the New" (ibid., p. 263). With his method of amplifying the prophetic meaning of the Old Testament, Clarke abandoned rationalist concordism altogether and returned to theology proper. Here the quality of his hermeneutics, though marred by the literalism of his reading, far exceeded that of his "proofs" of the agreement of revealed religion with natural theology. Unfortunately only the latter, in which Clarke so closely approached the deism he set out to combat is mostly remembered today.

Here precisely lies the difference between Bishop Joseph Butler (1692–1752), whom John Henry Newman once called "the greatest name in the Anglican Church,"[31] and Clarke, with whom he seems to have so much in common. Butler's *Analogy of Religion Natural and Revealed* (1736) had an enduring impact upon religious thought in England. Like Clarke's *Discourse,* the *Analogy* was directed against deists yet centered around the same principles that served as foundation to most deist systems of rational religion: the immortality of the soul, the reward of virtue and the punishment of vice, the moral government of the world. In his view, these principles also form the core of revealed religion. Christianity "teaches natural religion in its genuine simplicity."[32] Yet as "an additional dispensation of Providence" it adds some truths inaccessible to natural religion.

But Butler differs from Clarke in his conviction that conclusive proofs in religious matters are impossible. His confidence in reason hardly exceeds that of the skeptical Hume, his younger contemporary. The mind possess no exhaustive knowledge of anything in a constantly changing world. How, then, could it attain a certain knowledge of God? All through the *Analogy* one hears a note of skepticism that is more than theoretical. Butler obviously is acquainted with the intellectual conflicts and existential anxiety of modern life. Like Pascal, he has acutely experienced the sad discords of the universe. Contrary to the deists, this odd apologist confesses that we ignore the nature of this world and, even more, the source from which it emerged. Butler's great work, then, is not a philosophical theology, such as Clarke wrote.

Rather than "proving" the truth of natural or of revealed religion, he shows a parallelism between our observations of nature and the teachings of religion. "If there be an analogy or likeness between that system of things and dispensation of Providence, which experience together with reason informs us of, i.e., the known course of Nature, this is a presumption that they have both the same author and cause" (Intro., 6). As an apologetic argument, this transition from the *like* to the *likely* is weak. But Butler, fully aware of the weakness of the allegedly "strong" arguments of reason, decided not to move beyond experience and this, as David Hume was to show, never yields more than probability. He argues that probability may still result in *practical* certainty. He agrees with Locke that in matters "of great consequence" a person ought to be prepared to admit lower probabilities. The moral element he introduces to justify the transition from probability to the certainty required by faith reminds us of Pascal's waiver: when facing the most momentous consequences one is morally bound to make the safest choice, even though the evidence supporting it is slight.

Butler's notion of analogy differs from that of late Scholastic philosophy, which derived an indirect knowledge of God from a direct knowledge of nature. Such an inference from the manifest to the unmanifest presupposes that the transcendent cause of the universe must in some way be similar to its creation. For Butler, the mind possesses no philosophical knowledge of that cause at all. Nothing is properly *like* God: the one, simple yet infinite source of reality cannot be compared to the multiple, finite creatures. But if no similarity exists between God and nature, no philosophical analogy may be assumed. Revelation alone provides an adequate basis for comparing the manifest with the unmanifest. Butler's analogy moves not from the creature to God, but from God (known through revelation and spiritual experience) to the creature. Only after the mind accepts God's revelation will it be able to discern some *traces* of God's presence in nature. These are signs rather than *images* of God. Precisely because of the dissimilarity between the two terms, the analogical correspondence cannot be more than symbolic. Revelation and religious experience alone are capable of interpreting the world as a symbol of the infinite. Butler's *Analogy,* then, is more a symbolic theology than a treatise of apologetics: it assumes the very principle that apologetics ought to prove, namely, that nature obviously, that is, by clear proofs, refers to a transcendent source.

In the second part of the *Analogy,* Butler applies his theory on the relation between sign and signified to the relation between the New Testament and the Hebrew Bible. He denies that the Old Testament literally predicts the events of Christ's life. Instead he refers to them as "the completion of prophecy," in the sense that if a long series of prophetic sayings applies to later events, one may consider them "intended" (II, 7, 23). Obviously the author of a prophetic text did not intend its later Christian interpretation. But the meaning of a text may be extended beyond the intention of its author—a principle we accept for all significant literary works.

Butler's strategy in his polemics with the deists consists not in attacking the content of their natural theology, but the absence of a valid foundation. The deist argument for a natural analogy between a "creator" and the natural world presupposes what it ought to prove, namely, the nature of a transcendent creator. According to Butler, one must already be a believer to see the analogy. Only after the idea of God has been given and accepted (from divine revelation) is the believer in a position to discern the relation between the two terms. Both in his distrust of purely logical proofs and in his stress on the need for a revelation Butler stands closer to Pascal than to Clarke. His *Analogy* rests on a spiritual vision that unites revealed faith with natural insight.

PHILOSOPHY OF RELIGION: KANT

The birth of the philosophy of religion marked a new stage in the philosophical theology of the Enlightenment. Philosophy of religion differed from natural theology in that it studied the *phenomenon* of religion in itself, independently of the truth of its content and claims. Hume had initiated it in his *Natural History of Religion,* but as we saw in the previous chapter, mainly for critical purposes. His treatment had remained on a general level. Only primitive religion and Christianity had received some particular attention. Philosophical theologians like Leibniz and Clarke had been satisfied to test the Christian faith against the standards of reason. Their religious basis appeared insufficient after a Jewish thinker, Moses Mendelssohn, showed that a very different relation between religion and philosophy was possible. Though Judaism, no more than Christianity, could claim to have added any speculative "truth" to natural theology, Mendelssohn argued, it had accomplished a unique task among religions in preserving the great moral truths of reason throughout the centuries.[33] Mendelssohn's thesis about the role of Judaism drew attention to the philosophical significance of those specifics that distinguish one religion from another. But not before the romantics (especially Schelling) were the differences among particular faiths sufficiently recognized for a genuine *science* of religion to be possible. In his *Religion Within the Limits of Reason Alone* (1793), Kant laid the groundwork for it, though he knew little about other religions. But, unlike other deists, he at least analyzed specific Christian doctrines in detail.

It may appear as if philosophy thereby granted religion a more significant place among its formal objects. In fact, the study of religion as a separate subject — and a marginal one at that — marked a major step in the progressive secularization of Western thought. What previously had belonged to the very core of metaphysics now became relegated to the boundaries of philosophy. In his triple *Critique*, Kant removed philosophical theology from the center of his investigation. The idea of God, though indispensable as a philosophical ideal, remained beyond philosophical "knowledge." Philosophy may justify the use of the notion of causality in the sciences, but that notion cannot be legitimately applied to a transcendent reality. Only a reflection on the moral act postulates the existence of God.

Nonetheless, Kant's interest in religion, rooted in a profound personal concern, had always been intense, and his knowledge of theology exceeded that of most writers of the Enlightenment. Contrary to French deists who dismissed any historical faith, Kant, a deist himself, considered the Christian faith indispensable for leading the human race to what he considered the core of religion, namely, morality. Religion, for him, constitutes an essential stage of the moral consciousness. Nor is *Religion Within the Limits of Reason Alone* the inferior product of an aging mind, as his critics have too often claimed. Indeed, it displays qualities absent from his great trilogy, specifically, a sustained analysis of theological sources. To be sure, in this late work Kant remains no less convinced than in the earlier ones that religion is essentially a moral ideal that grants no rational certainty about the real existence of its content. But at least Kant displays an intimate acquaintance with the doctrinal sources and he makes a serious effort to show how in the case of Christianity doctrine parallels morality.

Both the merits of his analysis and the limits of his interpretation appear in the first book, which is entirely devoted to the dogma of original sin. The whole discussion labors under an unresolved tension. On one side, Kant confirms the Lutheran doctrine that all humans are born corrupt. On the other, he defends a notion of freedom according to which moral evil can result only from a person's free decision. "The source of evil . . . can lie only in a rule made by the will for the use of its freedom."[34] Their sensuous nature entices humans to attitudes and deeds that conflict with their spiritual nature. They prefer ease and prosperity to obedience to the moral law. Through that fundamental option the propensity to evil becomes itself immoral and the source of all subsequent immoral acts. One still wonders how a corruption that begins so early in life can be a free and definitive choice. Kant's puzzling answer does little to solve the problem. He claims that the propensity to evil, though freely acquired, "has not been acquired in time" (Ak, VI, 25; *Religion,* Intro., p. 20). It is a choice that may not be observable even to the person himself (Ak, VI, 20; *Religion,* Intro., p. 16). But how can a human choice not be anchored in time? And why should *all* humans make the wrong choice, even though all possess an inclination toward virtue?

Although Kant's attempt to force his philosophy into the Lutheran theology of sin rarely succeeded and satisfied theologians no more than believers, the tone of the discussion refreshingly differs from that of the deist treatises of the time. Kant harbors no illusions concerning the innocence of primitives, nor concerning the moral superiority of his own age. The primitive state of nature, often praised as morally pure by his contemporaries, exceeds the civilized one in brutal inhumanity. As we become civilized we merely refine expression of our vices. But Kant warns, that refinement does not entail moral improvement. "If we incline to the opinion that human nature can better be known in the civilized state . . . we must listen to a long melancholy litany of indictments against humanity: of secret falsity even in the closest friendship, so that a limit upon trust in the mutual confidences of even the best friends is reckoned a universal maxim of prudence in intercourse; of a propensity to hate him to whom one is indebted, for which a benefactor must always be prepared . . . and of many other vices still concealed under the appearance of virtue, to say nothing of the vices of those who do not conceal them, for we are content to call him good who is bad in a way common to all" (Ak, VI, 33; *Religion,* I, 3, pp. 28–29). This is not the voice of the Enlightenment, but of Paul's Epistle to the Romans: "They are all under sin, there is none righteous, no, not one" (Romans 3:9–10, quoted in *Religion,* I, 3, p. 34).

In the *Critique of Practical Reason* Kant had established the principle of moral autonomy: reason alone must be the source of moral legislation. God merely sanctions morality by balancing, in a future life, the merit of virtue with the happiness it deserves. Now he argues that religion does more! While the *idea* of a consummate good essentially belongs to the moral consciousness, its *reality* does not. The moral postulate that good be rewarded does not insure that virtue will actually be rewarded by happiness. The existence of this ultimate fulfillment of our moral endeavors cannot be deduced from the moral obligation itself (which by its very nature must remain indifferent to practical consequences), though that obligation is a necessary condition for its realization (Ak, VI, 8; *Religion*, Preface, pp. 6–7). Only the religious love of God can assure the believer of the actual realization of the happiness postulated by the moral disposition. The religious promise of realizing what the moral act merely postulates induces Kant to reverse the axiom of his moral philosophy, that religion complements morality. He now claims: "Morality leads to religion" (Ak, VI, 8; *Religion*, Preface, p. 7). The certainty religion conveys about the realization of the moral postulate may, of course, not be more than subjective, since the content of religion itself is a transcendent ideal that cannot be proven to exist.

Kant's exclusive stress on the moral side of religion reflects a Pietist upbringing that favored good works over intellectual insight. It is at odds with "orthodox" Lutheran theology. In a letter written in March 28, 1776, Kant had expressed his impatience with the traditional need of religious worship. "The idea that religion is nothing but a kind of ingratiation and fawning before the Highest Being — is an illusion which, whether based on dogmas or freed from them, makes all moral thinking uncertain and ambiguous."[35] Genuine religion imposes no ritual obligations, no cult, no prayer, no beliefs beyond the acceptance of a Creator and preserver of this world who will reward good and punish evil in an afterlife. It does not exclude revelation, yet neither does revelation add any content to the religion of reason.

Kant describes revealed religion as the larger circle within which the smaller one of the religion of reason appears. The metaphor is misleading, for the inner circle contains not only that minimum of religion, which reason by its natural power may attain: it constitutes the entire essence of it. What lies beyond the small circle possesses no more than an educational value. To require a divine revelation, over and above the self-explanation of reason, amounts to demanding a divine authority beyond the one revealed in the moral obligation itself. Churches ought to teach only what reason could in principle attain through its own insight. Christian doctrines, rightly understood, are *objectively* natural. Only for subjective, educational reasons have they been revealed (Ak, VI, 156; *Religion*, IV, 1, p. 144).

The historical accounts of redemption belong exclusively to what he calls "the ecclesiastical faith." This faith may be justified to the extent that it predisposes the mind "to the unity of the universal church" (Ak, VI, 124; *Religion,* III, 2, p. 115). Its inclusiveness, unrestricted by culture or race, predestined the Christian faith to become a universal faith. Yet when attempting to sever its link with the exclusive religious faith of Israel by means of new rituals, different prescriptions, and historical reinterpretations, the Church betrayed its universal message: she recast Jesus' message into a *particular* faith not essentially different from others, not even from the Jewish faith against which it attempted to define itself. For Kant, no fundamental opposition exists between natural and revealed religion, but only between a religion in which revelation constitutes a necessary addition to its moral content and one in which it does not. He rejects both the supernaturalist view that takes revelation to be intrinsically necessary, and the naturalist one that excludes revelation altogether (Ak, VI, 154–55; *Religion,* IV, 1, p. 143). Still, he considers revelation practically indispensable for awakening the mind to a truth that otherwise would remain dormant.

In the age of reason, Christian revelation serves no other purpose but to transmit the universal message to later generations. Meanwhile the uneducated continue to receive that message in symbolic form. At the center of that symbolic system stands the person of Jesus. Kant limits the historical message of the New Testament to Jesus' preaching, suffering, and death. "With that the public record of his life ends," he concludes (Ak, VI, 128; *Religion,* III, 2, p. 119). But does this truncated account of the Gospel story legitimate Kant's dressing his moral message in the language of a "Christology"? The idea of the Church receives a similar reinterpretation. In one sense Kant considers a Church indispensable. The fight against evil and the promotion of good, the principal objective of Kantian religion, requires the combined efforts of many as well as the social support that only a community can provide. But such an ethical-religious society, unlike a juridical one, possesses no legal authority over its members. The bond among them must, by its very nature, remain internal. Kant refers to the communion of those who share a stable moral disposition as the Church invisible. Its members recognize no authority but that of the One who imposes ethical duties as divine commands. Still, communication among them demands that this Church also assume a visible form in institutions and laws. Unfortunately, the visible Church, especially the Catholic one, is constantly tempted to impose its statutory rules as if they were the laws of the moral kingdom (Ak, VI, 135; *Religion,* III, 2, p. 126 note).

"Mysterious" for Kant is the divine cooperation in the moral act: the act postulates a transcendent support, whereas the agent experiences it as entirely his own. The mystery stems from the fact that freedom is *created* and hence dependent, and yet it remains fully autonomous. Kant concludes that the principle of divine assistance is a postulate of moral striving, but a hazardous idea to guide one's practical life by. The right attitude consists in not counting on God's grace and, even less, attempting to acquire it by prayer or sacraments. The mysterious gap between moral autonomy and dependence on God, essential in Christian doctrine, widens with the so-called vicarious satisfaction. Human efforts alone cannot overcome the propensity to evil once it has taken possession of the human will. "This evil is *radical, . . . inextirpable* by human powers" (Ak, VI, 37; *Religion*, I, 3, p. 32). To purify the moral intention of a corrupt nature, then, requires a moral cleansing that, according to Kant, can be accomplished only through the vicarious satisfaction of one untouched by corruption. But how could such a satisfaction ever be compatible with moral autonomy? No one else can assume responsibility for a free agent's deeds. For Kant, the Redeemer merely symbolizes the good principle that we all carry in ourselves. Conversion, then, means that the sinner assumes his guilt and atones for it as his own redeemer. Such a radical reinterpretation of Christian dogma into a moral precept, in this and in other instances, suggests that at the end of his explanation Kant rejoins the deism he appeared to have abandoned in the beginning. He uses Christian doctrine as a symbolic starting point for philosophical reflection on the moral act.

But what distinguishes him from other deists is that in his theory religion *intrinsically* sanctions morality. The two pillars of his moral system, respect for the moral law and for human beings, possess by their very nature a transcendent dimension. One even might read *Religion Within the Limits of Reason* as a treatise on the moral aspect of religion. As a philosophical interpretation of religion itself, however, Kant's treatise fails to capture the uniqueness of the experience. A few years after the appearance of *Religion* a young German theologian directly attacked the one-sidedness of Kant's position. In his *Discourses on Religion* (1799) Friedrich Schleiermacher argued that religion consists neither in a moral nor in an intellectual act but, as some British poets had suggested, in a feeling. His thesis was, of course, as one-sided as Kant's moral one, and Schleiermacher himself abandoned it in his later works. But it was sufficient to expose the deficiency of Kant's interpretation.

Kant never wrote a theodicy, as Leibniz and Clarke had done. In a short essay, "On the Impossibility of a Philosophical Theodicy," he explains why it would conflict with the principles of his moral philosophy.[36] It assumes that a transcendent God is not beholden to human rules of conduct. Kant curtly dismisses this argument. "An apology in which the justification is worse than the charge requires no refutation." If the Deity shares no moral judgment with us, any attempt at a moral justification of its acts becomes futile. Even the claim that God produces good out of evil raises more questions than it answers. Why would the road to good have to lead through the detour of evil? How could moral evil be a means to good? Similarly, the argument that the laws of nature render suffering unavoidable begs the question. Why should those laws rule the world? The complex and ingenious structure of the cosmos inspires us to admire the creative wisdom (*Kunstweisheit*) of its Maker, while our practical reason leaves no doubt about God's moral wisdom. But the two often seem to clash. The evidence of what divine power accomplishes in creation may suggest what divine morality and wisdom ought to be, but instead of experiencing this wisdom, we see creation subject to a divine will that commands rather than explains. We may only hope that justice will be satisfied. But we do not understand how so much suffering of innocents will ever be vindicated. With Job, Kant definitively closes the subject to philosophical speculation. "Theodicy, as has been shown, presents not so much a task for speculative knowledge as a matter of faith."[37]

These three thinkers — Leibniz, Clarke, and Kant — argued from a Cartesian perspective on reason. Leibniz and especially Clarke did so in order to restore rational credibility to a faith that had suffered from rationalist attacks. They attempted to return the idea of God to the center of rationality. Yet they weakened that argument by detaching reason from what they proclaimed to be its source. Leibniz appears to place reason *above* God when presenting it as ruling and restricting God's choice. With Clarke, the opposite occurs. The principle of rationality itself loses its authority as it becomes overruled by an inscrutable divine will. Perceiving the weakness of those rationalist attempts to justify the idea of God, Kant declared its content to lie entirely beyond the bounds of reason — in the realm of faith. So he shifted the focus back to religion proper, in a way that allowed him to show the moral significance of Christian doctrine without committing philosophy to its claim of absolute truth. Its parallelism with the rules of morality granted it at least a relative one.

But in the process Kant loses sight of all other facets of religion, in particular of its mystical quality. In his critical philosophy Kant exposed the flaws of rationalism. In the *First Critique* Kant had promised to make room for faith. In his *Religion Within the Limits of Reason Alone* he reduced faith to a symbol of the moral attitude. We are not mistaken, then, in regarding Kant, the great slayer of rationalist philosophies, still a reductionist in his interpretation of religion. In this he differed from the philosophers I shall consider in the next section.

The Search for a Religious Philosophy

Three influential thinkers of the Enlightenment period, each in his own way, attempted to restore the idea of an intrinsically religious philosophy and to place it on a new footing. Malebranche, Berkeley, and Jacobi regarded the sharp division between so-called theological issues and philosophical problems proper as inevitably resulting in a nonreligious philosophy. Truth does not allow itself to be so divided. For them, the finite mind had to participate in some way in the divine mind. Malebranche achieved this by denying secondary causality altogether; Berkeley by arguing that the mind receives its ideas directly from God; Jacobi, by absorbing reason into faith. All abandoned the fundamental modern principle that the human mind is the primary source of truth.

MALEBRANCHE'S INTUITIONISM

Historians of philosophy continue to agree that Nicolas Malebranche (1638–1715) was indeed a philosopher, even though his system was inspired by a religious vision and based on theological assumptions. The secular Léon Brunschvicg has called him "the typical and essential representative of a Christian philosophy," while for the religious Henry Gouhier, his work articulated the Augustinian idea of religiously enlightened reason. The genius of Malebranche consists in having understood that modern philosophy could not fulfill the same function for theology that medieval and early modern philosophy had. The Oratorian admired Augustine who had integrated philosophy and theology within a single intellectual synthesis. But that synthesis no longer corresponded to the scientific interpretation of the world. In Descartes's system he thought he had found what he needed: a philosophy that had assimilated the new science yet remained open to an Augustinian vision. Such an interpretation may appear surprising, since Descartes had made it a strict rule of his philosophy to keep it separate from theology, whereas Malebranche considered it his main task to reintegrate the two.

His contemporaries, both in France and in England, respected him, but few were swayed by his argument. Of course, Malebranche's peculiar talent for making intellectual enemies did little to further the acceptance of his doctrine. The publication of the anti-Jansenist *Traité de la Nature et de la Grâce* sparked Arnauld's smoldering hostility into flames never to be extinguished. The Jesuits had considered the brave Oratorian a fellow soldier in the battle against Port Royal until he took a firmly adversarial stand against their position in the controversy concerning the admissibility of ancestor worship for Christian converts in China. A protracted debate concerning pure love took a similarly bad turn. A Benedictine monk appealed to Malebranche's support of Fénelon's thesis, which he thought the Oratorian's theory implied. The appeal unchained four increasingly polemical writings. In the end, even the superior general of the combative mystic's order turned against him. By that time Church authority had long expressed its disapproval by placing most of his works on the Index of Forbidden Books. None of these critiques and controversies seem to have disturbed the pious Oratorian's serenity or deflected him from his course — least of all the judgment of the Roman congregation, which he referred to as an "Italian" problem. He kept on writing and republishing his "forbidden" books with a sacred indifference worthy of the Quietists he so arduously fought.

Today even studies sympathetic to Malebranche's work end on a note of disappointment about what most consider an inappropriate intrusion of theology into philosophy. He failed because he attempted to restore the unity of philosophy and revelation by means of Cartesian principles, whereas precisely those principles had ruptured that unity. Malebranche himself held the Aristotelianism of medieval Christian thinkers chiefly responsible for the secular character of philosophy. Descartes's Christian thought, on the contrary, had provided a solid foundation for modern science as well as a profoundly religious insight. Had not Cardinal Bérulle himself, the founder of the *Oratoire* to which Malebranche belonged, considered young Descartes the bright new hope for returning philosophy to its original Augustinian piety? Bérulle's expectations turned out to be misplaced, but Descartes's thought did indeed possess an Augustinian quality. Nowhere more so than in the idea, central in the third Meditation, that the mind knows the finite only against the backdrop of infinity and hence that an implicit knowledge of God precedes all knowledge of creation. This idea attracted the young Oratorian, who had recently completed his seminary journey through the desert of late Scholasticism, to Cartesian philosophy. Henceforth he regarded it as his vocation to develop a new religious philosophy on Cartesian foundations.

From the Augustinian idea that God is directly present to the mind he drew the conclusion (present also in Descartes) that the soul is closer to God than to its own body. The solemn declaration made at the beginning of his first and greatest work, *De la Recherche de la Vérité (The Search for Truth)* sets the tone and defines the content of the following one thousand pages. "The human mind is by its nature situated, as it were, between its Creator and corporeal creatures, for, according to Saint Augustine, there is nothing but God above it and nothing but bodies below it. But as the mind's position above all material things does not prevent it from being joined to them and even depending in a way on a part of matter, so does the infinite distance between the sovereign Being and the mind of man not prevent it from being immediately joined to it in a very intimate way."[38] The end of creation, Bérulle, Malebranche's spiritual master, had always insisted, is the glory of God: "God can have no other special end for His actions than Himself" (RV III/II, 16, O.C., I, 442; *Phil. Sel.,* p. 43). God would have had no sufficient reason for creating the world if the mind had not been capable of contemplating God in creation. The human mind, then, accomplishes the deepest purpose of creation, namely, to render God present to creation in order that it may be present to God.[39]

Theological speculations of this sort leave no doubt about the radically theocentric direction of the system: the glory of God defines its departure as well as its intended terminus. Philosophy itself forms an integral part of a more comprehensive theory of contemplation. In the controversy with Arnauld, Malebranche insisted that he wrote only for the contemplatively inclined. "I pride myself in speaking only to the *méditatifs.* I want to consult only the interior Master, the eternal Word, and I will happily bear to pass thereby for a visionary, the most ridiculous person who ever lived."[40] Malebranche's style of writing reflects the meditative bent of his mind. He contemplates ideas with reverence as if they were sacred symbols and articulates them in a clear, classic language. No philosopher wrote more elegant French than he did. Victor Delbos, a superior writer himself, described his style as "harmonious, luminous, and deployed with ease, though not incapable of succinctness and pithy formulations."[41]

Malebranche's mystical inspiration does not make his thought anti-rational. Indeed, he embraces a more thorough rationalism than Descartes, whose voluntarism he rejects. To him, God cannot arbitrarily decide that two times two equals four. Truth is rooted in the necessity of God's essence, not in a divine decree (RV, "Eclaircissement" 10, O.C., III, 136; *Phil. Sel.,* p. 66). He intends to bridge the modern gap between reason and faith by treating faith itself as a participation in God's eternal reason. Science and faith are complementary ways leading to the same divine intelligibility. In both cases the mind draws its derived light — its *lumière illuminée* — entirely from God's *lumière illuminante.*[42] Malebranche interpreted Augustine's word literally: *animam humanam non illuminari nisi ab ipsa substantia divina* (the human soul receives no light but from the very substance of God) (RV III/II, 6, O.C., I, 442; *Phil. Sel.,* p. 43). To know is to know ideas *in* God.[43] Contrary to the always shifting human understanding, reason, infinite in content, immutable, and necessary, coincides with God's own substance, for the infinite and universal being coincides with infinite and universal reason. (RV, "Eclaircissement" 10, O.C., III, 130; *Phil. Sel.,* p. 62). Reason is God's self-expression, to which Scripture refers as God's eternal Word. Human knowledge partakes in that divine reason in a twofold way: through the act of knowing *and* through its divine object.

Malebranche excludes all secondary causality from the intellect as well as from the will. Descartes had already deprived inert matter of inherent causal power. Malebranche extends that incapacity to the mind. The mind is no more capable of creating clear and distinct ideas than the body is of self-caused motion. It experiences only shifting "modifications," barely distinct from the body's sensations. (In fact, Malebranche occasionally uses one term for the other.) Ideas, however, are eternal and unchangeable. They are to be infused from a source beyond the mind. The intellect is incapable of forming them (RV III/II, 7, *O.C.*, I, 452; *Phil. Sel.*, p. 47): it can only "feel" its own modifications, even as the body can only "sense" what affects it, without being able to interpret the meaning. The necessary, eternal, immutable quality of ideas distinguishes them from the process of thinking proper, which is subjective and changing. Thus the *idea* of extension, for instance, which Malebranche identifies with bodiliness, has an infinite and necessary quality that surpasses the finite mind. Whatever perception of extended objects I may have is merely a modification of my mind. The idea of extension remains independent of that modification, whether perceived or not perceived.[44] Descartes had argued that there must be at least as much reality in the cause of an idea as in the idea itself and had therefore concluded that the idea of the infinite must come directly from God. Malebranche extended this argument to all ideas. All exceed the power of the mind and, a fortiori, of sense impressions.

Yet in the *Entretiens sur la Métaphysique* he distinguishes the idea of the *absolutely infinite* (which he, like Descartes, equates with God) from the infinity of other ideas. Only the former contains infinite perfections and so far exceeds the power of the mind that the mind possesses no clear and distinct idea of it (*Entretiens* II, *O.C.*, XII, 52; *Phil. Sel.*, p. 161). Other ideas participate in the idea of the infinite, but the absolutely infinite has no archetype. God does not participate in the infinite. God *is* the infinite. Clearly, then, Malebranche introduces a distinction in the idea of the infinite that is absent from Descartes's third Meditation. Also, the relation between ideas and reality differs from Descartes's theory. Descartes had linked ideas to reality by the authority of a veracious God. Malebranche needed no such extrinsic divine support: his epistemology recognizes no transition from ideas to reality, since ideas *are* the true reality. He did not deny the existence of physical reality, but, like Plato, he held that ideas constitute the true intelligible nature of that reality.

But if sense impressions cannot be causes of ideas, what is their function in the process of knowledge? Do they possess no cognitive qualities? We *see* colors, we *hear* sounds — and though they may not have the stability of ideas, their immediate presence is unmistakable. Malebranche does not deny it. But, for him, the "confused" feeling (*sentiment*) of seeing colors is totally distinct from the idea of extension that corresponds to them. He equates sense perceptions with affective states: they are fully conscious, but they owe their origin neither to a causal impact of physical objects, nor even to one initiated by the mind itself. They fulfill an intermediary function in the perception of ideas. Serving as prompters in the process of awareness, they open the mind to the intelligible fullness of ideas (RV, "Eclaircissement" 10, *O.C.*, III, 147; *Phil. Sel.*, p. 71). God alone touches the mind immediately and is the sole cause of these lower stages of consciousness as well as of the higher one through which we perceive ideas proper (ibid., p. 69). Malebranche explicitly rejects even the tenuous link of cooperation between body and soul that Descartes had presented in a succession of tentative hypotheses (animal spirits, pineal gland, etc.) (cf. *Méditations*, I, 9; *O.C.*, X, 13). Instead, he opts for a radical occasionalism: sensations and ideas reach us at the occasion of bodily motions. God alone is the cause of both.

Arnauld, a Cartesian himself as well as a theological follower of St. Augustine, protested that Malebranche's theory had strayed far from the principles of their common master. Descartes had indeed held that the immediate objects of the mind are ideas, but that through them the mind knows the real world.[45] For Malebranche, truth consists not in a *correspondence* of ideas with reality, but in the *coherence* of those ideal relations which, prior to the mind's perception, have existed from all eternity. The very basis of Cartesian certainty — the mind's awareness of its own thought (*cogito*) — is subjective and inadequate to render it immune against doubt. Malebranche anticipated Kant's objection that the indubitable certainty of my existence fails to inform me about the nature of the "I" that exists. The mind's destiny is not to know itself, but to know the truth that is not in the mind (*Méditations*, I, 27; *O.C.*, X, 18). His lengthy response to Arnauld's attack in *Des Vraies et des Fausses Idées* contains an eloquent passage on the mind's ignorance of the self: "I know of it only what an interior and confused feeling, sensibly and not intelligibly, discloses. I am convinced that I am only darkness to myself, that my substance remains by itself unintelligible to me, and that I shall never know who I am until it pleases God to reveal to me the archetype on which I have been modeled."[46] Paradoxically, the mind possesses a far greater clarity about extension, the essence of bodiliness, than it has about itself. Only mathematics and the physical sciences yield certain knowledge. Contrary to Descartes's claim, the mind possesses no clear and distinct idea of itself, though it has an undeniable certainty of its existence. Nor does it have such an idea of God, because the infinite exceeds all ideas (RV III/II, 7, *O.C.,* I, 448–55; *Phil. Sel.,* pp. 46–49). To the Christian Spinozist Mairan he wrote: "Not even the soul has any knowledge of itself; it has only an inward awareness of itself and its modifications. Being finite, it is even less capable of knowing the attributes of infinity."[47]

Malebranche's solution was not without theological difficulties, as the ideas appeared to introduce real distinctions within God. He attempted to avoid this conclusion in a manner somewhat reminiscent of Bonaventure. In God's eternal Word all divine perfections became manifest. Without being really distinct, the divine perfections nevertheless contain the ideal principles of distinct realities. In knowing those ideal archetypes the mind contemplates *the divine essence, but only to the extent that this essence relates to the created world* (RV III/II, 6, *O.C.,* I, 439; *Phil. Sel.,* p. 41). Malebranche denies that God "creates" ideas, as Descartes had implied when claiming that even mathematical truths depend on God's free decision. Ideas *coincide* with God's own nature as it relates to creation: they are uncreated and immutable.[48] Later Malebranche qualified his position, with questionable consistency, when admitting that future events "and several other ideas depend on the will of God and even of the human will, as they are not eternal truths" (*Méditations,* III, 16; *O.C.,* X, 31).

Remarkably, Malebranche combines his religious rationalism with a negative theology that uncompromisingly denies the mind any knowledge of God. We know *in* God, but we do not know God. "There is a difference between seeing the essence of God and seeing the essence of things in God. For though one sees immediately the substance of God when one sees the essence or the ideas of things in God, one sees God exclusively as He relates to the creatures; one sees God's perfections merely insofar as they represent what is other than God" (*Conversations chrétiennes* III, *O.C.,* IV, 63). Again: "When we see, directly and immediately, the ideas, we do not truly see God, the infinitely perfect being, but the essence of the creatures" (ibid., pp. 79–80). Malebranche resisted any kind of anthropomorphic conception of God. Even the traditional reference to God as spirit (based in Scripture) may be inadequate, except in the relative sense that spirit belongs to a higher class of being than body. Who knows if there may not exist a more perfect form of being (RV III/II, 9, *O.C.,* I, 473)? As decisively as Spinoza, Malebranche rejected the distinction between intellect and will in God. It would be wrong then to equate Malebranche's ontologism with an intuitive knowledge *of* God. The intuitive vision of God remains reserved to the saints and to the blessed. God is indeed immediately present to the mind, but the mind does not know God directly. We know God only through revelation and the feeling of attraction that efficacious grace bestows on the elect. Through its natural powers the mind knows the infinite as the implicit presupposition of all finite knowledge. To explicate this implicit presence constitutes "the loftiest and most beautiful proof of God's existence" (RV III/II, 6, *O.C.,* I, 441; *Phil. Sel.,* p. 42). Malebranche had, of course, read this argument in Descartes's third Meditation, but he carried it further by positing that this infinity, as the universal good that fulfills all desires, including the desire to know, also constitutes the mind's ultimate end. God is directly present to the mind as the unity that precedes all multiplicity and as the universal good that makes particular goods desirable.

At an early date some had detected a resemblance between Malebranche's ideas and those of that other unorthodox Cartesian, Spinoza. At the end of his life, he still had to suffer the unwelcome admiration of one Dortous de Mairan, who insisted that the Oratorian's principles basically coincided with those of the Dutch "pantheist." How, Mairan wondered, could Malebranche hope to escape Spinoza's conclusions after having accepted his principles? Specifically, for Malebranche as for Spinoza, all causal power remained within a single substance. God alone is responsible for all physical motion and acts as sole cause of every human feeling and action. But if there is only one cause, there can be only one substance. Malebranche defended his position as well as he could, considering the cards he had dealt himself. The assumption of multiple causes, he claims, derives from an ancient philosophy tainted by polytheism. When thinking of causes, "pagan" philosophers commonly assumed that a divine power inhabits them. In fact, a consistent monotheism should have abandoned this opinion long ago. "Il n'y qu'une vraie cause, parce qu'il n'y a qu'un vrai Dieu . . . toutes les causes naturelles ne sont point de véritables causes, mais seulement des causes occasionnelles" (RV VI/II, 3, *O.C.,* II, 312).

Malebranche's conception of God acting as sole cause undermines the very notion of causality. If, as he asserts, a genuine cause is one of which the mind perceives the effect as necessarily linked to a cause, only the dependence of the creature on the Creator qualifies for it. Anticipating Hume, Malebranche showed that the phenomenon of constant succession was insufficient to justify this necessary link. "Because a ball does not have the power to move itself, they should not judge that a ball in motion is the true and principal cause of the movement of the ball it finds in its path. They can judge only that the collision of the two balls is the occasion for the Author of all motion in matter to carry out the decree of His will, which is the universal cause of all things" (RV III/II, 3, *O.C.,* I, 428; *Phil. Sel.,* p. 35; also RV VI/II, 3, *O.C.,* II, 313; *Phil. Sel.,* p. 94). The first ball may indeed be called the "natural" cause of the second one's motion, but the natural is only an "occasional" cause. Malebranche thus initiated the deconstruction of causality that Hume was to bring to completion.

Can freedom survive a theory of occasional causality? Malebranche firmly believed it can. The will, no less than the intellect, becomes an effective agent only as God directly moves it. God propels the will irresistibly toward the *good* and He constitutes that *universal good* from which all particular goods derive. But the will itself determines to which *particular good* the divine impact will move it. "The will cannot arrest the [divine] impression, but it may direct its impulse in any sense it pleases and thereby *cause* the entire disorder we find in its inclinations and in all the miseries that are the necessary and certain results of sin" (RV I/I, 1, § 2, O.C., I, 46; *Phil. Sel.*, p. 11 [changed]; cf. also "Eclaircissement" 15, O.C., III, 225; *Phil. Sel.*, p. 111). Malebranche distinguishes the *will,* the divinely induced, irresistible yet indeterminate inclination toward the good in general, from *freedom,* i.e., the mind's capacity to direct the divine impulse toward a particular good. To attain a particular good, the mind must choose from a number of options, none of which is absolutely compelling (*TNG*, III, 3, O.C., V, 118–19; *Phil. Sel.*, p. 270).

The more comprehensive the choice, the greater the freedom. The totally free person understands that God is the only true good (*TNG*, III, 8–9, O.C., V, 122; *Phil. Sel.*, pp. 272–73). The more the desire of a particular good excludes others, the less the will is free. Though no particular choice literally compels the mind, passions may almost irresistibly diminish the agent's free choice. Appealing to Augustine's notion of the Fall, Malebranche asserts that no one is wholly free (RV II/I, 7, O.C., I, 248). But can we ever claim to be free? If God causes all movements, not only the ones affecting the physical world, but also the spiritual ones, how can the mind pretend to make free choices? Malebranche never satisfactorily answered the question. Nonetheless he regarded the certainty of freedom as immediate and no less infallible than the mind's awareness of its own existence. Yet no more than the *cogito* can that awareness be translated into a clear and distinct idea. The process by which we convert a motive into a determining choice remains a dark, confused feeling of simultaneously acting and being acted upon. The necessity to preserve the freedom of the will forces Malebranche to restrict his thesis that God is the sole cause to the *real* changes in the world. Decisions are ours, but their real effects depend on the general physical laws by which God rules the universe. The moral quality of an act comes thereby to depend entirely on the intention, not on its effects.[49] Kant was to develop this intentional morality into a coherent theory.

A theological dispute forced Malebranche to qualify his idea of freedom even further. His lifelong antagonist Arnauld had accused him of abandoning Augustine's doctrine when he denied that any external motive or power, including the impulse of God's grace, could compel the soul and eliminate the freedom of choice. Malebranche's position on predestination, in agreement with his theory of free will, had been the opposite of Arnauld's. God saves only by general principles, not by personal election or private grace. Salvation must occur in accordance with divine perfection, "par les voies les plus simples," that is, by universal laws (*TNG*, III, p. 22, O.C., V, 133). Initially Malebranche neither accepted a particular Providence nor did he consider God's prevenient grace irresistible, as Arnauld and other Jansenists did. If God's prevenient grace had forced Adam to pursue the true good, he would never have sinned (*TNG*, III, 25, O.C., V, 135)! Nevertheless, stung by Arnauld's critique, he came to distinguish *la grâce de lumière,* the prevenient grace that enables all humans to recognize their true good, from *la grâce du sentiment,* the grace that attracts them to the godlike life.[50] The grace of light alone leaves the will cold with respect to the good. The grace of feeling, granted to various persons in varying degrees, moves it toward the good and thus directly affects the will (*TNG*, III, p. 18, O.C., V, 131). Salvation then depends on the "saintly concupiscence" that enables the soul to counteract the sinful concupiscence of the Fall. Malebranche's admission of degrees in the efficacy of grace constituted a major concession to Arnauld and implied at least a partial acceptance of the idea of a particular Providence.[51] But the fact that Malebranche allowed the philosophical question of freedom to be determined by a theological controversy of his day shows the fragility of his synthesis of science, philosophy, and theology. His conclusions satisfied neither philosophers nor theologians — whether orthodox, Jansenist, or Quietist.

The link Malebranche forged between creation and general Providence generated even more controversy. God might have created a more perfect world, he claims, but to do so would have required abandoning the law of simplicity, which the nature of divine perfection compels God to observe. The laws of nature, in fact the mechanical laws of motion, thereby come to express the immutable wisdom of God's eternal Word (*TNG*, I, 13–14, O.C., V, 28–29; *Phil. Sel.,* p. 260). God has no choice but to follow his *volontés génerales,* regardless of the particular consequences. Malebranche concedes that these "simple ways" have resulted in an enormous amount of disorder and suffering. Yet from the perspective of the highest order, they proved inevitable. "If God *in equally simple ways* could have created a more perfect world, He would not have established laws resulting in so many monsters. But it would have been unworthy of his wisdom to multiply his decisions [*ses volontés*], merely to prevent particular disorders" (*TNG*, I, 22, O.C., V, 35; *Phil. Sel.,* p. 263 [changed]). This narrows Leibniz's idea of the most perfect world down to the simplest possible one.

Malebranche is willing to carry his conception of divine simplicity to its ultimate consequences. God loves all his works and He wants to save all humans, yet, he claims, God allowed "an infinite number of people to perish during the centuries of error [i.e., the time before Christ]" ("Eclaircissement" 15, O.C., III, 220; *Phil. Sel.*, p. 108). From the fact that God acts through the simplest ways and follows a universal order, our author concludes that God, though granting grace to all, often gives insufficient grace to be effective, which therefore remains useless for the conversion of its recipients (ibid.). The universal order of nature dominates God's creation as the highest law. To avoid subordinating God to the order of nature Malebranche interpreted that order as coinciding with "the relations of perfection among his attributes and among the ideas enclosed in God's substance" (*Entretiens* VIII, O.C., XII, 191). The restriction of divine activity to general laws precludes the possibility of miracles, as Arnauld had been quick to point out. Malebranche attempted to circumvent the problem by compromising. The universal order can be maintained even while exceptions to the laws of nature occur. The admission again forces Malebranche to reintroduce the idea of a *particular* Providence. "I have repeatedly claimed that God always acted by this sort of [particular] will whenever the order required it and often even when the order permitted it, because the immutable order is the inviolable law of the divine decisions [*volontés*]." He had, indeed, asserted in the *Traité de la Nature et de la Grâce* that only the general order of creation fully coincides with God's divine Word and bears no exceptions, while God occasionally dispenses with the laws of nature when the higher order demands it (*TNG*, I, 20, O.C., V, 33; *Phil. Sel.*, p. 262; also, the long "Eclaircissement" 15, later added to the *Recherche de la Vérité*, O.C., III, 223; *Phil. Sel.*, p. 110). By moving the immutability of order to a level above nature, Malebranche may have answered his opponent, but at the price of weakening the concept of *les voies les plus simples* to the point of meaninglessness. The "universal order" now seems to consist of whatever occurs. What does the term "universal law" mean when applied to an "order" which we fail to understand altogether? Moreover, the reference to the laws of nature as *lois arbitraires* jeopardizes his overarching theory that the ideas of general laws participate in God's very nature.

Malebranche must have perceived the difficulty himself for in a later "final" Eclaircissement he interprets miracles as attuned to the general laws of nature. They may be part of a system of laws more comprehensive (but still natural) than the mechanistic laws of motion. Miracles, then, remain exceptional as measured by ordinary events, but they no longer need to conflict with the general laws of nature (known and unknown) as he had claimed before. This meandering argument about the laws of nature has removed the *voies de simplicité* from the area of reason altogether. As a Cartesian philosopher Malebranche conceives of nature entirely in mechanistic concepts. As a religious thinker he wanted to abide by the interpretation of Catholic theology. His rationalism undermines his mysticism and his mysticism corrodes the rationality of his system. Malebranche writes his best pages when discussing *either* science *or* mystical theology without mixing one with the other. He was a respected scientist and an excellent spiritual writer.[52] But his attempt to achieve a synthesis of modern philosophy with theology failed. His mechanistic concept of causality proved wholly inadequate for expressing the relation between Creator and creature: it reduced that relation to one of extrinsic dependence. Malebranche, the mystical thinker, attempted to restore the intimate divine presence excluded by a purely efficient causality by eliminating secondary causality altogether. Finite "causes" were no more than occasions. Yet to escape Spinoza's pantheism, Malebranche had to grant finite substances some independence and even some causal impetus. He did so by converting the entire finite universe into a system of signals that, without any power of its own, conditioned God's exclusive action. He thought he thereby saved creaturely independence as well as divine presence. The discussion of free will has shown that his solution never attained full consistency. The only way the single cause theory could be maintained was by adopting Spinoza's thesis of a single substance. This he found unacceptable. So he adopted a compromise: God remains ontologically distinct from creation but operationally coincides with it.

BERKELEY'S PLATONISM

In Britain the most significant trend in religious philosophy (as distinct from philosophical theology) remained within the empirical tradition. Yet its empiricism fundamentally differed from Locke's. Not sensations lie at the roots of consciousness, but the *experience* of states of mind. This "radical" empiricism had its remote ancestry in Plato's theory of Ideas and its immediate one in Calvin's doctrine of self-knowledge as implying knowledge of God. A group of Anglican divines, fellows of Cambridge's Calvinist Emmanuel College, developed those ideas into the fundamental principles of a new religious philosophy. The fruitfulness of their insights is reflected in the variety of thinkers they influenced. A continuous line stretches from the Cambridge Platonists — Benjamin Whichcote, John Smith, Ralph Cudworth, and Henry More (he of Christ's College) — to bishops Berkeley and Butler and, via the latter, to John Henry Newman. Berkeley followed their Neoplatonic empiricism despite his linguistic nominalism; Butler often appears to walk in Clarke's footsteps, but his basic inspiration is Platonic; Newman combined a Platonic intuitionism with a mild philosophical skepticism.

The Cambridge Platonists wrote against the "atheism" of their age, for which they held Thomas Hobbes mainly responsible. Consciousness, they claimed, did not start from sensations gradually developed into ideas, but from an implicit intuition of God. Cudworth attempted to prove this by investigating the religious ideas of the ancient world. Their rampant polytheism hid, in fact, a belief in one God with many attributes. Descartes's and Hobbes's mechanistic notion of causality had severed modern thought from the richer founts of experience. The original, more comprehensive notion of divine causality had been formal — penetrating the very being of creatures — rather than efficient. The mystically oriented Cambridge divines intended to restore that more intimate causal relation between God and the soul. Berkeley developed this theological empiricism into an idealist philosophy.

A comparison with Malebranche seems inevitable. Both assume that ideas have their origin in God. For Malebranche, they remain in God, even while referring to real objects. For Berkeley, ideas, though immanent in God, receive an independent existence within the human mind. Nor do they refer to extramental objects: they themselves *are* the objects. Ideas, then, have an *ectypal* as well as an *archetypal* existence in God. In the *Philosophical Commentaries* (written 1707–8; published 1871), Berkeley sharply contrasts the independence of the mind's ideas and of the human will with what he takes to be Malebranche's position. "We move our legs ourselves. 'Tis we that will their movement. Herein I differ from Malebranche."[53] They most fundamentally differ, however, on Malebranche's theory of universal, "abstract" ideas, which the bishop contemptuously rejects as "enthusiasm."[54]

As I mentioned, Berkeley, despite his Platonism, persistently held on to a nominalist theory of language. Charles Peirce remarked on this odd combination of Platonic idealism with a theory that had mostly been linked to a sensationalist theory of knowledge: "Berkeley is an admirable illustration of this national (British) character, as well as of that strange union of nominalism with Platonism, which has repeatedly appeared in history, and has been a stumbling block to the historians of philosophy."[55] Berkeley combines the two by declaring words and universal concepts no more than signs of reality; while reality itself is wholly ideal.[56]

Everyone remembers Berkeley's paradoxical principle, *esse est percipi*. If he had limited it to the mere phenomena of cognition, it would be hard to quarrel with. Kant put the same point more clearly but no less radically when he declared *things in themselves* to be unknowable. Yet when Berkeley concluded from the mental character of perception to the nonexistence of the physical, he took, of course, a logical leap. Moreover, he steered the entire discussion in the wrong direction by changing the issue from a distinction between the phenomenal and the real to one between the material and the immaterial. I shall not enter into the epistemological questions discussed in the early *Principles of Human Knowledge* (1710) and the *Three Dialogues* (1713) but restrict my comments to *Alciphron* (1732) and *Siris* (1744), in which Berkeley deals directly with the religious issues that occupy us in this chapter. The elegantly written dialogue *Alciphron* approaches the literary quality of Plato's philosophical dramatizations by presenting real-life persons with particular prejudices, emotions, and temperaments. An easy conversation in the leisurely setting of an English country home drifts toward the problems confronting religion. What in a rationalist, freethinking age could still critically justify a faith in what lies beyond the boundaries of reason? When Alciphron, the agnostic to whom Berkeley refers as the "minute philosopher," claims that no metaphysical argument has ever persuaded him, and that only a direct sensible perception of God's presence would do so ("Nothing so much convinces me of the existence of another person as his speaking to me"), Euphranor, representing Berkeley's position, agrees.[57]

Yet sense perceptions never *represent* reality. Even the perception of a divine voice could not do so. In his early (1709) *Theory of Vision* Berkeley had shown the insufficience of visual perceptions to convey the real distance or size of an object seen. The eye, he claims, perceives nothing but light and colors. From this questionably sensationalistic interpretation of vision he concludes that our perceptions have no direct causal link with the *ideas* of distance, dimension, and figure. They function merely as *signs* of ideas, "not by similitude, nor yet by inference of necessary connection."[58] The indirectness of all perceptions with respect to the reality they signify justifies Euphranor's conclusion that the absence of any single perception (such as that of a voice from the sky) by no means rules out the idea of what is usually signified by it. Yet with respect to the knowledge of God, the subject of the dialogue, there is a further complication, since the human mind possesses no *idea* of God. Its ideas are only of the physical world. What then justifies a belief in a reality of which we have neither a perceptual sign nor an idea?

Berkeley answers that our perceptions may indirectly suggest the idea of a transcendent power. Our perceptions of the world follow a steady pattern of succession. Whenever water reaches a temperature of 100 centigrades, it boils. The fact that it always does so makes it predictable, even though no sense impression of causality links heat to boiling. Only ideas convert the succession into a rule of causality.[59] The constancy and coherence of the world order suggest that a single agent must direct this infinite variety of phenomena. "Will it not then follow, Euphranor asks his freethinking friend, that this vastly great, or infinite power and wisdom must be supposed in one and the same Agent, Spirit, or Mind; and that we have at least as clear, full, and immediate certainty of the being of this infinitely wise and powerful Spirit, as of anyone human soul besides our own?" (*Alciphron,* IV, 5). The "minute" philosopher demurs at this hasty conclusion. But, Euphranor insists, the same evidence with which other signs suggest the existence of a never directly perceived thinking principle, accompanies our idea of the order and harmony of the universe.

Even if we concede this, what entitles us to call this coordinating agent "God"? Once the mind on the basis of its ideas of the world has concluded to the existence of an active agent, a further reflection on the order and harmony of one's ideas as well as of those of other agents induces the *notion* (not the idea!) of a superagent endowed with intellectual powers and free of imperfections.[60] The notion of God, then, according to Berkeley, is the outcome of a mental process that occurs in several stages. It starts with sensible appearances. At the occasion of these appearances the mind receives *ideas* from a philosophically unknown source, which converts the perceived phenomena into *signs* of ideal objects. By means of another set of signs, different from the natural signs of physical phenomena, words, ciphers, and other symbolic characters, the mind establishes relations among these ideas.[61] It thus construes these ideas into a coherent world picture. By a "skillful management of [those] signs" (*Alciphron,* VII, 11), the mind surpasses both the realm of ideas and concludes to the existence of a Being to which no ideas correspond. The notion of God, then, is not deduced from a perception of a regular succession of phenomena, but from the fact that the system of signs itself requires at every moment a coordinating intelligent Agent.

In his last great work, *Siris,* all too often dismissed because of the large part devoted to the cure-all qualities of tar-water, Berkeley describes the nature of this final metaphysical stage of thought: "If proceeding still in his analysis and inquiry, he [the "curious inquirer"] ascends from the sensible into the intellectual world, and beholds things in a new light and a new order, he will then change his system, and perceive that what he took for [physical] substances and causes are but fleeting shadows; that the mind contains all, and is to all created beings the source of unity and identity, harmony and order, existence and stability."[62] The term "mind," in analogy with the Neoplatonic *nous,* stands here for the transcendent Mind, source of the human mind and of all reality. With the Rhineland and Flemish mystics, Berkeley interprets the Platonic principle that "the *nous* is the place of all forms" (*Siris,* # 328) to mean that God, the ideal source of all things, is inmost present to them (# 275). "It is the opinion of Plato and his followers that in the soul of man, prior and superior to intellect, there is somewhat of a higher nature, by virtue of which we are one; and that by means of our one or unit, we are most closely joined to the Deity. And as by our intellect we touch the divine Intellect, even so by our *to hen* or unit, the very flower of our essence, as Proclus expresses it, we touch the first One" (# 345). This is, indeed, the language of Proclus and of Eckhart, not of Locke. Textbooks continue to rank Berkeley with empiricists such as Locke and Hume because for him also all mental activity begins with sense perception. But perception is never a *cause* of ideas—only an occasion. The true reality, for him as for all Platonists, is *ideal*.

Even to classify Berkeley's philosophy as a subjective idealism is inadequate. For reality does not depend only on *my* perception. He clearly affirms that objects continue to exist even when no one perceives them: God perceives them. This reply has been called a betrayal of the principle *esse est percipi* that restricts reality to sense perception. Yet for Berkeley, God's "perception" of things is, in fact, the real source of their being. The term "perception" as applied to God may be clumsy, not to say faulty. Here it merely serves to support the principle, common to religious Platonists, that all reality exists ideally in God. Berkeley draws more radical conclusions from this principle than earlier Christian Platonists had done. In his interpretation, finite reality never leaves this ideal existence in God: it constitutes the very core of its nature.[63] Reality exists only in God and God allows the human mind to observe this intradivine presence by granting it "ideas." If the real were ever to move out of its ideal inexistence in God, creation, according to Berkeley, would become independent of the Creator.

Berkeley's theory of the creature's permanent inexistence in God evoked a suspicion of pantheism. He appears to have foreseen the charge and insists that his view of the divine mind as immanent in creation is no more pantheistic than ancient Egyptian religion or Pythagorean or Neoplatonic thought were (*Siris,* # 300). "Whether the *nous* be abstracted from the sensible world, and considered by itself, as distinct from, and presiding on, the created system; or whether the whole universe, including mind together with the mundane body, is conceived to be God, and the creatures to be partial manifestations of the divine essence; there is no atheism [meaning: pantheism] in either case, whatever misconceptions there may be, so long as mind or intellect is understood to preside over, govern, and conduct, the whole frame of things" (*Siris,* # 326). Above all, Berkeley wanted to avoid a naturalism he considered inevitable if the creature's dependence on God becomes reduced to the extrinsic link of efficient causality. With Christian Platonists, especially Ralph Cudworth (to whom he repeatedly refers), he holds that all things exist in God, which for him means that they only exist as ideas. The bishop thereby reasserted what for Plato and Aristotle had been "formal causality." If philosophy was to avoid skepticism and atheism, in his opinion, it had to admit a more intimate relation between finite reality and its transcendent ground than efficient causality warranted. He attempted to do so by suppressing the concept of matter that, for him, symbolized the separation between Creator and creature, and he justified this radical move on the ground of the ideal nature of the cognitive act. If knowledge was ideal, its object also had to be ideal.

Berkeley went further than other empiricists in claiming that the process of knowledge points beyond the data of perception and even the ideas occasioned by them, toward an ideal absolute. He therefrom illogically and, for his thesis, needlessly, concluded that things possess no physical existence whatever. Instead of supporting his theological purpose this egocentric fallacy undermined it. The real purposes of Berkeley's idealism consisted in showing that the ultimate reality of all things resides in an unknown God, not in an all-comprehensive Spirit who could be grasped by the human mind. He remained essentially a negative theologian in the Platonic-Christian tradition. No analogy, no image, no idea even, links human knowledge directly to God.

Jacobi's Philosophical Faith

I doubt whether the eighteenth century knew a more elusive thinker than Friedrich Heinrich Jacobi (1762–1814). A central figure of the German Enlightenment; personally acquainted with Lessing, Mendelssohn, Wieland, and Kant; sympathetic to Spinoza's and Hume's philosophies, he nevertheless opposed most of what the Enlightenment stood for. Despite his life-long battle against rationalism, he never shook himself free of it. Although constantly at odds with the ideas of the Enlightenment, he did everything he could to play a role in the movement. The impression of intellectual duplicity, created by his ambiguous attitude toward Spinoza, Hume, and Kant, aroused suspicions about his true motives. Jacobi presented himself as a knight of faith, yet Hamann, his companion in arms in the battle against rationalism, kept reminding him that he was a deist like the rest of them. He spent his entire life embroiled in intellectual feuds and polemics and was deeply involved in the two major controversies of his time: the *Pantheismusstreit*, which his report on the late Lessing had stirred up, and the *Atheismusstreit*, in which he took the side of Fichte — whose philosophy he nevertheless firmly rejected.

Jacobi enjoyed a certain literary reputation before he wrote his philosophical essays. Founder of the *Teutscher Merkur* (1773), to be edited by Wieland, he was one of the initiators of the *Sturm und Drang* ("Storm and Stress") movement, in which the young Schiller and Goethe found their voice. A young businessman, mostly self-educated, he came to philosophy through the urgency of his convictions, not because of any academic prospects. Lucien Lévy-Brühl in his insightful account of Jacobi's thought put it well: "He was not a professional philosopher, but became one by vocation."[64] His two novels, *Allwill* (1775–76) and *Woldemar* (1777), written in the epistolary tradition of Richardson and Rousseau, mainly served as vehicles for his ideas. (A malignant critic claimed that *Woldemar* reads like a review of a novel, rather than a novel.) Goethe saw in *Woldemar* a questioning of the truth of feeling and emotion, the founding thesis of *Sturm und Drang,* and, literally, pilloried the book to a tree. In the earlier novel Jacobi had already opposed the liberated ethics of the "beautiful soul."[65]

Today we look upon him as a transitional figure, but the impact he had on his contemporaries may be compared to Kant's. Whereas Kant completed the Enlightenment, Jacobi paved the way to Romanticism. To be sure, he never approached Kant's intellectual stature. Jacobi was intuitive, brilliant in short treatises, letters, and aphorisms, but incapable of elaborating his insights into a coherent system. But his ideas strike us as fresh and original in a way Wolff's do not, though Wolff was a superior thinker. Jacobi reintroduced the metaphysical question of *being* and *nothingness* at a period when it was submersed by epistemological concerns. With him, the idea of God, once again, stands at the center.

Always mindful of the dramatic gesture, Jacobi leaped onto the philosophical stage with a set of *Letters on the Doctrine of Spinoza* (1785), that immediately captured the attention of Germany's intellectual community. They contained a revealing report on Lessing's secret thought. Moses Mendelssohn, to whom Jacobi addressed them, had always felt close to Lessing and had developed some of his friend's fragmentary ideas into elegantly written, rationalist treatises. Mendelssohn enjoyed an enormous respect in Germany because of his clear mind and balanced judgment. When learning that he was preparing a book on his deceased friend, Jacobi preceded him by publishing the remarkable conversation he had with Lessing shortly before his death. Jacobi had shown Lessing Goethe's anonymous poem, "Prometheus" — a scathing attack upon the Judaeo-Christian God. Far from being shocked, as Jacobi had expected, Lessing found it excellent and proceeded to reveal his previously hidden thoughts on religion. "The orthodox concepts of the Divinity are no longer for me; I cannot stomach them. *Hen kai pan!* (One and all). I know of nothing else." When Jacobi suggested that he then was likely to agree with Spinoza, Lessing answered: "If I have to name myself after anyone, I know of nobody else."[66]

The letter accomplished two things: it deprived German deists, including Mendelssohn, of the founding father of their philosophy, and it showed that Jacobi knew Lessing's intellectual position better than the man who claimed to have been his intimate. Jacobi further argued that Spinoza's philosophy was incompatible with Mendelssohn's deism, and that it was the only consistent form of rationalism. He supported his argument by displaying such a thorough acquaintance with Spinoza's thought that the astonished Mendelssohn wondered whether Jacobi himself might perhaps be a Spinozist. That was exactly the effect Jacobi had intended. He wanted to show that a philosophical theology independent of revelation left no alternative but Spinoza's "pantheism." (Later he was to make a similar claim about Fichte's thought.) In a later letter to Mendelssohn, he gave the reasons why. A finite world could not have come from an infinite Being. Hence the world must have existed from all eternity as an integral segment of the infinite, not as the result of a free creation. Spinozism was plain and simple pantheism and that, Jacobi argued, amounted to *atheism*. The protracted discussion developed into what is now known as the *Pantheismusstreit*. For Jacobi, God had to be a personal individual, opposed to other individuals, a *Thou* confronting my *I*. Any other conception of God resulted in pantheism. Others, such as Herder (in a letter to Jacobi of December 12, 1784) considered such a narrowly defined idea of God anthropomorphic. Behind Jacobi's questionable reasoning, however, lies a legitimate concern that too close an identification of the finite reality and God excludes that *otherness* without which transcendence is not possible.[67]

When the deeply shocked Mendelssohn requested further explanations, Jacobi hastened to comply. While Jacobi had previously argued that rationalist philosophy entailed pantheism and, indeed, atheism, he now added that it also implied fatalism, as had been obvious in the case of Spinoza. Any attempt to compress reality within a system of pure thought renders future events not only in principle predictable but also predetermined in fact. That the theory is false, is proven by the experience humans have of being able to manipulate nature. They are capable of foresight and regret, of anticipating results, and of feeling proud or ashamed of past decisions. Therefore, according to Jacobi, a closed system of reason contradicts our awareness of freedom. Still, Jacobi repeated, he preferred Spinoza's straightforward admission of fatalism to the subterfuges of other rationalists ("Vorrede," in *Werke*, II, 116–17; *Main Phil. Writings*, 586–87).

In the course of their discussion Jacobi had invited Lessing to make a *salto mortale* outside philosophy in order to cross what Lessing had called the "broad, ugly ditch" that separates particular and historical events from the unchanging, permanent principles of metaphysics. In fact, Jacobi had claimed, each system of thought would have to cross the ditch between the universal and the historically particular if it was to be more than an empty abstraction. Philosophy could do so only by moving outside philosophy into the area of faith. Kant reacted sharply against these unphilosophical acrobatics in an essay entitled "What Does It Mean to Orient Oneself in Thought?" ("Was heist sich im Denken orientieren?") (1786).[68] He did not object to the notion of "faith" itself. Indeed, he claimed, the mind can orient itself concerning supersensible objects only by means of a rational faith (*Vernunftglaube*). But such a faith never becomes knowledge: it remains a subjective aspiration. Even the idea of the highest object of faith, that of a supreme being, adds nothing to knowledge if reason cannot demonstrate its rational necessity. To deny reason the capacity to prove so means to reduce belief in God to superstition or *Schwärmerei*. Jacobi's faith was neither religious nor philosophical. In a letter to Herder, Jacobi insisted that "any acceptance of a truth not inferred from principles" with the same certainty as the conclusion of an argument was faith.[69]

In *David Hume on Faith, or Idealism and Realism* (1787), Jacobi took a different approach than in his *Spinoza Letters*. Appealing to Hume's notion of "belief" he reinterpreted his own concept of faith as referring to the kind of immediate evidence that accompanies sense perception. The mind reaches certainty not only through the conclusion of a rational argument, he argued, but also, and primarily, through the immediate evidence of the senses. Obviously, the evidence acquired by sense perception had nothing in common with what Jacobi had called "faith" in his exchange with Lessing. There faith and knowledge had been mutually exclusive; here they became complementary. Stung by Mendelssohn's earlier remark that Christians, when short on arguments, could always count on the escape door of faith, he now insisted that he argued from philosophy to philosophy and remained on the level of a *natural* belief, upon which he, even as Hume, assumed all knowledge to rest. According to Hume, we always assert more than we know. From the primary evidence of sense perception we rush to affirm that reality outside the mind corresponds to our experience. It is in fact the imagination that links the perceived appearances and synthesizes them into complex objects. We trust this transition because we cannot command it at pleasure. But in the end it all remains a matter of belief.

Jacobi accepts Hume's comprehensive notion of belief, yet he rejects his skepticism, which, he claims, stems from Hume's subjective idealism. In the novel *Allwill* this idealism is shown to result in epistemic and moral nihilism. From the fact that we only see *with* our eyes, hear *with* our ears, one of the characters concludes that "we see nothing *but* our own eyes, and hear nothing *except* our own ears," and hence that we see and hear nothing.[70] But a philosophy that ends up with nothing inevitably prohibits any moral commitment, an attitude incarnated by Allwill, a prototype of the "aesthetic" man in Kierkegaard's

Either/Or. Jacobi detected that same nothingness at the core of all purely metaphysical reflection, he later wrote to Fichte.[71] To this nihilist idealism he opposed his own "philosophy of non-knowledge."[72]

Unable to prove that reality corresponds to our ideas, he appeals to immediate experience. The truth of experience allows no doubt. In "perception" (*Empfindung*) the mind cannot question the reality of what it perceives.[73] For Jacobi, this suffices as foundation for a realistic theory of knowledge. "The object contributes just as much to the perception of consciousness as consciousness does to the perception of the object. I experience that I am and that there is something outside me, in one and the same indivisible moment."[74] The certainty that accompanies this encounter possesses an immediacy that neither requires nor admits logical inference. The reality of the object becomes doubtful only when the mind assumes that it is itself the sole source of its ideas. Jacobi supported his realism with the theory of common sense of the Scottish philosopher Thomas Reid. For Reid, as for other empiricist philosophers, knowledge begins with sensation. But *through* sensation the mind directly apprehends reality. In his *Spinoza Letters* Jacobi had conceived of philosophy as a closed rationalist system and the awareness of reality as attainable only through an exit from philosophy. In *David Hume on Faith* he attempted a philosophical justification of this awareness through a theory of perception as immediate certainty.

The influence of Kant's philosophy, of which the first signs had appeared in the Hume essay, became dominant in the "Appendix on Transcendental Idealism." It introduced yet a new stage in Jacobi's thinking about faith. What impressed him in Kant's thought was the principle that all reliable cognition originates in sense perception. For Kant, however, that did not imply that we thereby know the *reality* of the object. Jacobi now agreed with Kant that "any assertion of the existence of a *thing in itself, outside my representation,* can never . . . carry absolute certainty with it." But he drew a quite different conclusion from this theoretical uncertainty. Whereas for Kant, the thing in itself is not only unprovable, but unknowable; for Jacobi, it is unprovable, and in that limited sense an object of faith, but no less therefore an object of immediate certainty.

Yet another distinction in Kant's critique allowed Jacobi to bring the notion of faith back into philosophy, namely, the one between *Verstand* (understanding) and *Vernunft* (reason). *Verstand* consists of an ordering, synthesizing reflection on the phenomena of sense perception. *Vernunft* opens the mind to the ideas of God, immortality, and freedom, which lie beyond the grasp of the understanding. Here also Jacobi's interpretation deviates from Kant's intention. Kant had denied that the reality of those ideas was accessible to theoretical confirmation, but he had admitted the existence of God, the immortality of the soul, and the freedom of the will as postulates of the moral act. The reality of those ideas ultimately remained an object of faith.

Kant's use of the term "faith" alerted Jacobi to the problems inherent in his own former usage of it. He adopts Kant's concept but, again, moves beyond and against its original meaning. Jacobi seeks to confirm the object of faith by grounding it in a direct intuition (which Kant had explicitly ruled out). This intuition is conveyed through *feeling,* the primary still undifferentiated root of all mental activity.[75] In this immediate mode of consciousness the mind, according to Jacobi, becomes aware of itself as spirit. He refers to this early mode of consciousness as "der in sich gewisse Geist" (the Spirit certain of itself). Since *spirit* constitutes the very core of mindfulness, Jacobi places the certainty of God's presence at this most intimate layer of consciousness.

God is "more present to [the person] through his heart than nature is to him through his external senses." We become intuitively aware of this presence in the ideas we have of the true, the good, and the beautiful, which constitute the principal content of the idea of God. "We believe in God, because we see him; though he cannot be seen with the eye of the body, he appears nevertheless to us in every upright man."[76] Although the appearance itself is not God, the feeling it evokes unmistakably *reveals* Him. Either the mind possesses an immediate awareness of God or none at all. That awareness "not only needs no proof, but excludes all proofs absolutely, and is simply and solely the *representation itself* agreeing with the thing being *represented.*"[77]

Combining Kant's view concerning the ideas of reason with Hume's notion of belief as a necessary complement to perception, Jacobi concludes that our entire knowledge of reality rests on an act of faith. Faith, then, was not the *salto mortale* outside philosophy that Kant had so severely criticized in Jacobi's writing on Spinoza. It was an essential part of philosophy itself, though its immediate certainty could not be justified by a philosophical argument. In the later "Vorrede" to his works Jacobi writes: "We took our stand on the assumption of two different faculties of perception in man, one by means of visible and tangible, hence corporeal, instruments; and the other by means of an invisible organ that in no way manifests itself to the external sense, but whose existence is made known to us through feelings alone. This organ, this spiritual eye for spiritual objects, has been called 'reason' (*Vernunft*) by men (practically by all)."[78]

Central to Jacobi's polemics with idealism and rationalism is the principle that philosophy can only reflect upon what is first *given* to the mind—either through sense experience or through reason's experience of itself. In the latter experience, the mind becomes indirectly acquainted with its founding principle in its manifestations (truth, goodness, and beauty). This immediate, though indirect, experience of God is conditioned by a moral attitude. In his *Spinoza Letters* Jacobi had already linked the quality of one's thinking to one's moral disposition, as Fichte was to do a few years later. To improve the thinking of an age, he wrote, its mode of living needs to be corrected first.[79] That philosophers resented Jacobi's frontal attack on their method and responded in kind ought not to surprise us. Even those who shared his aversion of Enlightenment rationalism reacted in a hostile way. Hegel wrote the most thorough, but also the most severe, assessment of Jacobi's theory in his early *Faith and Knowledge* (*Glauben und Wissen*, 1802). He agreed that the Enlightenment's exclusion of faith from philosophy restricted the content of philosophy to the finite, while it reduced the infinite, essential to philosophical thought, to an empty aspiration for "an unknowable God who remains beyond the limits of reason."[80] But Jacobi restricted the consciousness of the infinite to feeling and never properly integrated it with philosophy. He thereby left the problem of the Enlightenment as he found it: faith and reason remained two opposite functions of the mind that had not been reconciled.[81]

Jacobi never solved the problems he addressed. His significance lies more in his critique of rationalism and later of idealism than in his own philosophical achievement. He expressed his aversion of idealism most forcefully in his famous "Letter to Fichte" (March 3, 1799). A philosophy, whether rationalist or romantic, that asserts the self-sufficiency of the human mind in the quest of truth dissolves *being* into knowledge and reduces reality to an immanent state "where nothing is outside the I."[82] In this view, the *I*, whether it be called transcendental ego, subject, or unity of apperception, is the sole source of truth. For Jacobi as for Malebranche, truth pre-exists the knowledge that partakes of it. The knowledge of God, which he considered the central issue in philosophy, must return to Augustine's position: "In order to seek God and what is pleasing to God, one must already have Him and what is pleasing to Him in one's heart and spirit, for what is not in some way already known to us we cannot seek, not search after."[83] As Jacobi saw it, only faith enables the mind to maintain the necessary distance between itself and reality.

His simplistic view of the relation between faith and reason fully deserved Kant's and Hegel's critique. One cannot simply juxtapose one to the other or replace one by the other without destroying philosophy itself. Yet that is what Jacobi proposed in various ways at each of the stages of his development. The significance of his work is mainly negative. He effectively denounced the self-enclosedness of modern thought. The absence of genuine *otherness* is indeed a most problematic side of Enlightenment philosophy.[84] It is also the one that contemporary critics (in the first place, Emmanuel Levinas), have pounded with their heaviest artillery.

The principle of subjectivity as formulated in modern thought, namely, as sole source of meaning, obstructed the restoration of a genuinely religious philosophy. The three thinkers discussed in this section were undoubtedly right in their critique of it. Yet none of them, I think, succeeded in removing the obstacle. Indeed, all three deprived the finite of its autonomy. Malebranche did so by denying that the finite mind plays any active part in the constitution of ideas; Berkeley by denying that the physical world exists in any but an ideal way; and Jacobi by denying philosophy's independent authority over thought. But their failures drew attention to the core of the problem and thus stimulated the new reflection on the idea of subjectivity in the nineteenth century performed by Schleiermacher and Kierkegaard.

IO

Spiritual Continuity and Renewal

The ideas discussed in this chapter differ considerably from the ones we have come to consider characteristic of the Enlightenment. Not only do they fall outside the rationalist trends of the age, but they contrast just as much with those that opposed that rationalism. Some of the most prominent and influential thinkers of the time appear to have bypassed the dominant controversies altogether. Unlike the so-called anti-Enlightenment thinkers, the ones presented here do not seek, or do not seek in the first place, alternatives to the prevailing ideologies. They mostly ignore them. Their ideas remain largely continuous with those of a premodern past. That may not be immediately apparent since they often phrase them in the language of their contemporaries in whose company they seem to have felt quite at home. The controversial Johann Georg Hamann, the only one who explicitly rejected the principles of the Enlightenment, took pride in his friendship with such luminaries of the movement as Kant, Herder, and Jacobi. It was through his translation that Kant became acquainted with Hume. Bishop François de Salignac de La Mothe-Fénelon was the tutor of Louis XIV's grandson. Emanuel Swedenborg was a famous Swedish metallurgist and a respected member of parliament.

But, whether apologists or spiritual writers, they reformulated age-old doctrines. They stirred up plenty of controversy: Fénelon was condemned for Quietism; the Pietists Spener and Francke provoked the ire and contempt of the Lutheran Orthodox; Swedenborg was held by many to be a madman. Yet the former three drew upon ancient Christian sources while Swedenborg, the founder of a new sect within the Reformation, spread a spiritual message rooted in much older theosophical traditions. Contrary to what, according to Hans Blumenberg, had been typical of early modern writers, namely, that they poured new wine in old skins, these men served very old wine in new skins.

What united these theologians and separated them from their contemporaries as well as from their predecessors is the symbolic nature of their thought. In some way or other they all stressed that knowledge of God can be expressed only in *analogy* with ordinary language: theological concepts and representations symbolize transcendence more than they define it. Butler consistently speaks of *analogies* (of language); Swedenborg of *concordances;* Hamann mostly uses the term *symbols*. But all three share a common approach, sanctioned by ancient tradition.

The Search for a Symbolic Theology: Johann G. Hamann

A discussion of Johann Georg Hamann (1730–87) may seem inappropriate for introducing a chapter on spiritual trends. The paradoxical controversialist definitely does not belong in the same class with Quietists, Pietists, and Swedenborgians. Still his symbolic interpretation of the Bible and its extension to the entire human history dominates the often acrid polemics in which he was constantly involved. Hamann was essentially a spiritual man who expressed his traditional religious thought in the language of his contemporaries. A native of Königsberg, he attended the same university and audited some of the same lecturers (including Martin Knutzen) as his famous fellow citizen Immanuel Kant. As a young man he enthusiastically embraced the Enlightenment. But during a commercial mission to London, at the end of a profound spiritual crisis, he converted to an orthodox form of Christianity. He reread the Bible and wrote his observations down in *Biblical Reflections (Biblische Betrachtungen)*, which forms the major part of his *Diary of a Christian (Tagebuch eines Christen,* 1758). During the following five years of leisure he read voraciously. Surprisingly, he found Hume's *Dialogues Concerning Natural Religion* much to his taste and later translated them into German. Through this unpublished translation Kant became acquainted with the work. What attracted Hamann to Hume's philosophy was the central place of *belief* in existential judgments. For Hamann, as for Jacobi, not arguments but belief provided a natural foundation for religious faith. The fideist Hamann preferred the agnostic Hume to the believing rationalist Christian Wolff.

In a letter to Herder, Hamann wrote: "Hume is the man for me, for he at least honors the principle of belief, and includes it in his system, while our countryman [i.e., Kant] keeps on chewing the cud of his causal whirligig, without a thought for belief. I don't call that honest."[1] This letter was written before Hamann had read the *Critique of Pure Reason* in which Kant himself declared, quite possibly under Hamann's influence: "I have found it necessary to deny *knowledge*, in order to make room for *faith* (Glaube)" Still, Hamann's later critique of Kant in his own *Metakritik* (1784), though more civil, is hardly less severe. Indeed, as one commentator has noted, "It does to Kant's project the one thing it cannot tolerate: it relativizes the critical philosophy by placing it within a more basic context of interpretation."[2] Hamann objected to what he calls Kant's "purism of reason, that is, a reason detached from belief and tradition as well as from language" (*Metakritik*, p. 284; English, p. 155). Kant's separation of reason from experience, and of understanding from sensibility, "as if they were two branches of human cognition growing out of a common root" tears the concrete experience apart into mental abstractions and blind data (*Metakritik*, p. 286; English, p. 157). Countering this dualism, Hamann quotes Hume's statement that one of the most valuable discoveries of his time was Berkeley's principle that universal abstract ideas are nothing other than particular ones tied to universal names.[3] Without this insight Hume would never have become the great philosopher he was.

Hamann, even as Butler, attempted to construe a new, symbolic theology on the basis of analogy. He adopted Kant's description of analogy in the *Critique of Pure Reason* as his starting point. The philosopher had argued that in philosophy, contrary to mathematics, from the proportion of two given terms the mind may learn the relation of a third term to the fourth, but not the nature of the fourth term itself. Philosophical analogy, he concluded, merely gives us "a rule for seeking the fourth member in experience and a mark whereby it can be detected" (*Critique of Pure Reason*, A 179; Norman K. Smith, trans.). If the unknown term lies beyond experience, as the nature of a transcendent Being does, we may still refer to it by an analogy drawn form the actual experience of persons, or nature, or events that, however imperfectly, evoke the thought of such a Being. Such an "anthropomorphic" analogy, he had added elsewhere, yields symbols of God's nature but no real knowledge of it.[4] Hamann, though critical of the *Critique of Pure Reason*, recognized this as an accurate description of that unique kind of analogy between God and creation, from which the mind draws its religious symbols.

Yet in a short essay on the origin of language, Hamann showed how the biblical revelation enables us to draw more from this anthropomorphic analogy than Kant had done. Revelation conveys a concrete meaning to the obscure analogy between nature and history, on one side, and God's nature, on the other.[5] In a short fragment added to the London *Diary* Hamann wrote: "All appearances of nature are dreams, visions, enigmas, that have a meaning, a secret sense. The book of nature and of history consists of nothing but ciphers, hidden tokens that require the key of Holy Scripture to explain it all, which is the very purpose of its inspiration." (*Fragments* [*Brocken*], in *Werke,* I, 308). Obviously this reading comes close to Butler's. Time and again Hamann insists that "Scripture ought to be our dictionary and grammar" for interpreting these "natural" revelations (*Biblical Reflections,* in *Werke* I, 243).

But how could texts written for the needs of one particular nation respond to the needs and aspirations of all people at all times? Hamann responds that God's revelation originally was addressed to all mankind and only later came to be interpreted as a particular one addressed to the Jews. The first chapters of Genesis describe the beginning of the entire human race. Not until after the confusion of tongues in Babel did the revelation become restricted to the language spoken by one nation. A further restriction occurred when scribes after Moses narrowed the content down to the founding and preserving of Israel's theocracy. God's covenant with Israel had originated in the promise made to Abraham. In the Pentateuch, Moses (its reputed author) had restricted that divine promise to the laws, institutions, and rituals of a people recently freed from slavery. The scribes subordinated the promise to the law, thereby making the Bible into a Jewish document.

Through this far-fetched interpretation Hamann hoped to reconcile the idea of a universal revelation with the notion of a document pertaining only to the particular history of one people. Any revelation is by nature particular, even if it is intended for all. In a polemical tract, *Golgotha and Scheblimini* (1784; in *Werke,* III, 291–320), Hamann passionately argued this thesis against Moses Mendelssohn's rationalist *Jerusalem* (1783). Mendelssohn had claimed that Judaism coincided with the religion of reason (*Vernunftreligion*) of the Enlightenment and that the law revealed at Mount Sinai consisted merely of the moral law with some ceremonial and dietary instructions added for practical, hygienic, or political purposes. Hamann detected in this ahistorical interpretation of the Old Testament a direct threat to the obviously historical revelation of Christ, which had to be continuous with the biblical revelation on which it depended. Even Israel's "illegitimate" shift from promise to law did not change the fact that "salvation had to come from the Jews." Jesus himself remained within the Jewish tradition—in body and mind—when he restored the original promise and widened the meaning of the Covenant. On that ground, Paul and the writers of the four Gospels had interpreted events and persons of the Old Testament as figuratively anticipating the message of the New Testament.

In a number of elusive short writings that earned him his unique place in German literature, Hamann extended the relation between biblical *type* and Christian *antitype* to nonbiblical figures and events, especially to those that preceded the Christian Scriptures. His favorite Gentile prophet was Socrates, whom rationalists venerated as the patron saint of free investigation. In his *Socratic Memorabilia (Sokratische Denkwürdigkeiten,* 1760)[6] (complemented in *Clouds: A Sequel to the Socratic Memorabilia* [*Wolken: Ein Nachspiel zu Sokratische Denkwürdigkeiten*], 1761), and in the late *Golgotha and Scheblimini: By a Preacher in the Wilderness (Golgotha und Scheblimini: Von einem Prediger in der Wüste,* 1784), Hamann reclaimed the Greek sage for the Christian tradition. Had he not declared to owe his insight to divine sources: the oracle of Delphi and his personal *daemon*? The paradox of the Delphic god proclaiming Socrates wisest among men, while he himself felt that he knew nothing, confirms the difference between autonomous human cognition and knowledge derived from a transcendent source. Socrates expressed more truth than he understood. Even as Peter or as Caiphas who prophesized and proclaimed divine truths without understanding them, he occasionally served as a mouthpiece of divine wisdom (*Fragments* [*Brocken*], § 3, in *Werke,* I, 304).

Hamann claims to find a biblical precedent for extending typology beyond the biblical context. Paul repeatedly refers to extra-scriptural sources as having prophetic significance (as in Acts 17:28 where he quotes the Greek poet Aratos's words as prophetic of the Gospel). The term Hamann uses for this procedure, *metaschematism,* even appears in 2 Corinthians 4:6, where it means transferring a secular meaning to a religious one on the ground of a fundamental analogy between sacred and profane history. Still, the choice of Socrates as a Christian "type" seems surprising in view of his later objections (in *Golgotha and Scheblimini*) to "Atticism," which, he claimed, had been the source of eighteenth-century "atheism." He considered the significance the Enlightenment attached to Greek philosophy dangerous and unwarranted.

There were other thinkers of antiquity whom Hamann considered prophets of Christ: "The pagans have been great prophets. I have concluded the old year with the letters and philosophical writings of Cicero. An economy, a yeast runs through all the aeons until their completion" (letter, January 13, 1773). Hamann refers to them as "the subterranean truth that godly men did exist among the heathen and that we should not despise the cloud of these witnesses, that heaven has anointed them as its messengers and interpreters and consecrated them to precisely that vocation among their people which the prophets had among the Jews" (*Memorabilia,* p. 149; *Werke,* II, 64). Not only representative figures of the past, but all of history had a prophetic meaning for Hamann. Even modern historiography, however secular, conceals a symbolic design that appears to those who read it in the light of the spirit. "Perhaps all history is more mythology than [Bolingbroke] thinks and is, like nature, a book that is sealed, a hidden witness, a riddle which cannot be solved unless we plow with another heifer than reason" (*Memorabilia*, p. 151; *Werke*, II, 65).

Hamann's analogies often appear artificial and his reading of Scripture remains narrowly literalist. Thus he claims that Socrates, whose spiritual beauty was masked by a Silenic appearance, prefigured Christ whose divine reality was likewise hidden in the form of a servant. His typological interpretation of later historical figures appears even more far-fetched, as when he compares Peter the Great working in the shipyards of Zaandam to Jesus, the carpenter of Nazareth. But Hamann's theological significance consists not in the appropriateness of his analogies, nor in the correctness of his biblical exegesis, but in his insight that all religious language is by its very nature symbolic. This was the point that rationalist theology had missed altogether. To the believer, the stories, prophecies, and proverbs of the Bible possess, next to their natural meaning, a transcendent reference. Hamann extended this biblical symbolism to all poetic expression.

Metaphoric language for him is by nature poetic. For what is poetry in essence if not, as Goethe, an early admirer of Hamann, suggested, natural words that symbolize a spiritual reality? From this insight Hamann concluded that art and poetry possess a revelatory character and are potentially religious. "True poetry is a natural form of prophecy" (*Bibl. Refl.*, in *Werke*, I, 229). In his short tract on aesthetics, *Aesthetica in nuce* (*Werke*, II, 195–217), Hamann highlights this religious quality of poetry. "Nature and Scripture are the materials of the beautiful, creative, and imitative spirit" (ibid., 210). But to the religious mind, they also contain the substance of all poetry. Even the classical poets understood this: they imitated nature and in their mythological interpretations, endowed her with religious meaning. Modern poets have ceased to follow their example. They no longer draw genuine inspiration from mythology, Bible, or theology. As a result, poetry has lost its former depth, according to Hamann.

In his critique of the Enlightenment, Hamann strikes out at so many trends and thinkers that one cannot but wonder what his real target was. He attacks rationalism but also fideism, naturalism but also supernaturalism, classicism but also Biblicism. Nonetheless, a single, coherent vision inspires this scattered critique. He consistently defended the autonomy of the particular against universalizing ideologies of the age and attempted to restore a symbolic concept of theology that modern thought had lost.

A Subdued Piety

As theology became increasingly rationalistic in the late seventeenth and eighteenth centuries, it lost its experiential "spiritual" character. Piety became isolated from theology. The latter stressed doctrine, the former experience. Thus in France the term "mystique," previously an adjective referring to a common quality of religious life, became a noun identifying a group of devout believers favored with strong religious experiences. Religious men and women attempted to compensate for the withdrawal of religion from public life and even from theology by establishing spiritual conventicles of like-minded, linked by a common vocabulary. As Michel de Certeau has shown in his insightful *La fable mystique,* their esoteric language converted into necessary principles what once had been random reports of actual experiences.[7] It came to fulfill a "performative" function. Spiritual life was assumed to follow a predictable order of stages with standard divisions and subdivisions. I know no better example of this rigidified system than Dom Claude Martin's hagiography of his own mother, who had left him as a child in order to join the Ursuline Congregation and sail to Quebec as a missionary. The faithful son fitted each fragment of Marie de l'Incarnation's spiritual diaries neatly into pre-existing niches of purification, illumination, and union.

This isolation of spiritual life, perhaps needed for its survival in an increasingly secular society, gave spiritual life a new intensity in small devotional groups. They released an unprecedented flood of pious writings upon the Christian world. Nor did their spiritual seclusion prevent the "devout" from moving in the highest circles. In France several had infiltrated the Court. Mme. de Maintenon, Louis XIV's morganatic wife, was herself a *dévote*. Still, as some of these spiritual movements maintained a certain secrecy and kept a distance from the official Church, they sooner or later came under suspicion either of the state or the Church, if not of both. This occurred with the Jansenists and Quietists in France, the spiritual dissenters in England and the Netherlands, the early Pietists in Germany.

The spiritual movements of the Enlightenment never became part of the main culture. Alienated by its increasing secularism, they constituted a sort of spiritual counterculture. In this regard they differed from the religious humanism of the Baroque period, which had still succeeded in integrating traditional religion with modern culture. The spiritual movements of the Enlightenment, far from restoring the cultural synthesis of the past, widened the gap between culture and faith. This trend continued and even intensified during the two centuries following the Enlightenment. In the eighteenth century, the new spiritual movements, however controversial, still considered their theories rooted in ancient Christian traditions. Later mystical movements tended to become independent of institutional religion, if they did not openly collide with it. I shall discuss three types of eighteenth-century spirituality: the Quietism of Mme. Guyon and Fénelon; Lutheran Pietism as represented by Angelus Silesius, Spener, and Tersteegen; the theories of religious affection and mystical symbolism proposed by Swedenborg and Jonathan Edwards.

Quietism and Fénelon

I doubt whether any other spiritual movement has suffered more from misrepresentation and unfair polemics than the one that has come to be known by the derogatory name "Quietism." Historians commonly trace its beginnings to a text by the Italian Jesuit Achille Gagliardi, written under the inspiration of his spiritual daughter Isabella Bellinzaga. But much of the doctrine already appears in Teresa of Avila's discussion of the "quiet" state of contemplation. The theory did not become controversial until the strange condemnation of Miguel de Molinos (1685). After enormous popular success as a spiritual director in Rome (whose influence reached even the pope and several cardinals), this Spanish priest was accused of immorality in his relations with penitents and of heterodoxy in his teachings. He was charged with having taught that the person who has abandoned his will to God ought not resist temptations. Next to this moral allegation was a theoretical one concerning the question of whether passive contemplation can be acquired by human effort (as he was alleged to have taught), or whether it is exclusively infused by a special grace of God. Serious doubts remain about the validity of both accusations. One of the theses surprisingly condemned in Molinos's *Spiritual Guide* explicitly distinguished *infused* from *acquired* contemplation "wherein one must persist one's entire life as long as God does not draw the soul to infused contemplation" (Article 23 of the bulla of condemnation). Molinos unambiguously states that passive contemplation can only be infused. Barely escaping capital punishment, he was sentenced to lifelong incarceration in Rome. True to Quietist principles, he denied none of the charges — even those of which he was patently innocent — and spent the last nine years of his life in prison, where he died with the reputation of a saint. Whatever secrets this mysterious affair may hide remain buried in some twelve thousand letters kept under seal in the Vatican.

That appeared to have settled matters — at least in Rome. But in the meantime a well-to-do young widow of an ancient French family, Jeanne-Marie Guyon (1648–1717) (born Bouvières de la Mothe and distantly related to François de Salignac de La Mothe-Fénelon, her future follower, as well as to the Jansenist Arnaulds, her future enemies), began to spread theories that in some respects came remarkably close to Molinos's doctrine, though she claimed not to have read him. Her *Spiritual Torrents* (1682), written in a single stretch and not reread before publication, contains a rather traditional description of spiritual recollection. After an initial active stage, replete with consolations, the spiritually initiated are supposed to pass through a condition of spiritual death. During it, the soul is taught to be indifferent with regard to her future state—whether she will be saved or rejected. If capable of accepting this spiritual annihilation, she will enter a new life. "She only takes a new life in order to lose it in God; or rather she only lives with the life of God."[8] Like Molinos, Jeanne Guyon stressed the need for total passivity in spiritual life. What ought the soul do? "Nothing, and less than nothing. It must simply suffer itself to be possessed, acted upon, and moved without resistance . . . letting itself go naturally into all things, without considering what would be best or most plausible" (*Spiritual Torrents,* pp. 112–13). Once again, the censors charged Jeanne Guyon with attributing to human effort what belongs exclusively to divine grace. She claimed that some form of passive contemplation could be acquired, as Saint Teresa had taught. Apparently the censors based their judgments on the nominalist position that nature and the supernatural are and must remain totally separated, in their cause as well as in their effects. As the blind French mystic François Malaval wrote about his critics, they denied that grace can operate through the ordinary ways of prayer and they confused ordinary forms of contemplation with the extraordinary "infused" ones.[9]

Instructive in this affair was that Jansenists and Jesuits, traditional adversaries, conspired in attacking Quietism. For the Jansenists and their sympathizers (most prominently Bishop Bossuet), grace belongs entirely to the "supernatural" order and hence an "acquired" (i.e., natural) passivity in prayer is a priori suspect. The Jesuits accused Guyon of the opposite error: raising passivity in prayer to an ideal induces the person to neglect active moral cooperation. Still, the positions of the hostile parties show at times a remarkable similarity with the ones they opposed. The influence of François de Sales upon many Jansenists (particularly upon the nuns of Port Royal) softened their opposition to passive contemplation. The same holds true for many Jesuits, whom a subtler reading of their own founder's writings had convinced that all prayer, indeed apostolic action itself, moves toward contemplative prayer. Both the first "Quietist" text and the last famous treatise on divine abandon were written by Jesuits: Gagliardi and de Caussade.

In her subsequent *Short Method of Prayer* (*Moyen court de faire oraison,* 1685), Jeanne Guyon completed her spiritual system with the concept of pure love. She may have found it described in François de Sales's *Treatise of the Love of God* as the degree of love that induces a person to care more about God than about his or her own well-being. The idea had been implicit in Guyon's earlier work without attracting controversy. Yet in the wake of Molinos's condemnation, it became the spark that set off the anti-Quietist witch-hunt of the years 1687–88. Mme. Guyon was confined to the Convent of the Visitation in Paris, but after an investigation she received a clean bill of orthodoxy. Even after her two books had been condemned in 1695, Bossuet himself, who had initiated all the problems and was to become her worst adversary, granted her a certificate of good conduct (that also had come under question!) and of orthodoxy. During the years following her release from the convent, her theories encountered an enormous success within aristocratic circles. Mme. de Maintenon introduced her to the teachers and pupils of Saint Cyr, the school she had established for girls of the French nobility. It was probably there that she met Fénelon, who had a hand in the direction of the school.

François de Salignac de La Mothe-Fénelon (1651–1715) admired Jeanne Guyon's direct spiritual experience of which he, by his own testimony, remained deprived. In the correspondence that followed their acquaintance, he placed himself under her direction more than she under his. The most elegant French writer of the eighteenth century, culturally refined and intellectually brilliant, Fénelon had been charged with the education of the king's grandson, the duke of Burgundy, and was later consecrated archbishop of Cambrai. Among the career ecclesiastics of the time he stood out by his humility, scrupulous morality, and spiritual courage. These virtues became even more apparent after he fell into disgrace at the Court. While still in his days of glory, he performed one of the most courageous acts of the ancien régime. He, the teacher of Louis XIV's grandson, wrote a letter to the king criticizing his disastrous foreign policy. By plunging France into twenty years of almost unintermittent war he had brought its people to the verge of famine and made the country a pariah among its neighbors. All of this for the sake of bringing one of his descendants upon the throne of Spain, of extending his territory beyond its ancient borders, and of pursuing the (mostly frustrated) vainglory of winning battles. Since he was legally entitled to none of the places he had conquered, Fénelon suggested that, as an act of elementary justice, Louis XIV restore them to their rightful owners. The king had so thoroughly alienated his subjects that a revolution appeared imminent.[10] Fénelon did not send the letter directly to the king but, most likely, to Madame de Maintenon, whose full confidence he enjoyed at the time. The gesture appears all the more remarkable in that earlier in the same year, 1693, at the occasion of his reception at the Académie Française, in the habitual eulogy of his predecessor, Fénelon himself had indulged in the very flattery of the king's grandeur he was to denounce so shortly afterwards.[11]

Unquestionably, the archbishop was a complex person and, at least until the time of his disgrace, worldly and self-centered despite his genuine piety. Even his early protestation of loyalty to his consecrating bishop Bossuet and the humility with which he later submitted to Rome's censorship seem overly self-conscious.[12] Certainly Fénelon appears morally superior to the bishop of Meaux who, with the full weight of his eloquence, his rival influence at the Court, and the persistent efforts of a sleazy nephew whom he had sent to the Papal Court for the purpose of having his brother bishop condemned, mightily strove to crush ideas too subtle for his robust mind. Still, the Quietist attitude, which Fénelon preached and usually practiced, did not prevent him from accusing his adversary of bad faith, insincerity, and a malevolent intention to harm his reputation. The archbishop's "Réponse à la Relation sur le Quiétisme" permanently, though perhaps not undeservedly, damaged Bossuet's ecclesiastical standing. When learning that Bossuet was preparing a refutation of his theory, Fénelon made every effort to head off the attack before it was launched. His *Explication sur les Maximes des Saints* refuted in advance all the errors he expected to be charged with. Bossuet felt angry at seeing the wind thus taken out of his sails. In Ronald Knox's witty assessment: "Bossuet had saved the State—his favorite accomplishment, and the *Maxims* appeared to insinuate that it had not needed saving" (p. 343). The theological antagonism between the two bishops seems surprising. Both appealed to Augustine and regarded Francis de Sales as their spiritual master. Both opposed the widely held belief that the virtuous Christian was entitled to eternal beatitude. Fénelon even repeats Pascal's statement, "God never owes us anything" (*Maximes,* X). God's grace entails no obligations on his part.

What, then, was at the heart of the dispute? The etherial issue was whether the love of God, to be pure, ought to exclude all thought of personal happiness, even to the point of rendering a person indifferent with respect to eternal salvation. Today's readers may find the question too subtle to be meaningful. They are, of course, right and that subtlety discloses the fundamental weakness in the spirituality of the late seventeenth and eighteenth centuries: it was extremely self-conscious, typical of a religious attitude that, having been exiled from the culture at large, took refuge in the shelter of an introverted piety. Quietists formed a small group of initiates, almost like a gnostic cenacle. Father Lacombe, Jeanne Guyon's early, controversial director and onetime companion in her apostolic travels, referred to their followers as *les enfants de la petite Eglise,* a statement paralleled by Spener's reference to the early groups of Pietists as *ecclesiolae in Ecclesia* ("little churches within the Church"). For all its qualities, Quietism was a movement of withdrawal after the Church had lost center stage in the public arena.

In his *Explication sur les Maximes des Saints* (1697) Fénelon attempted to steer a middle course between the Quietist movement threatened with censorship and the position of his adversaries who defended a more hierarchical and less mystical form of piety. He showed that pure love, abandon, and passive contemplation were not new-fangled ideas but concepts solidly rooted in the Church's oldest tradition. The stated aim of the *Maximes* was to preserve the movement from heterodox tendencies, but its more immediate one was to blunt Bossuet's anticipated attacks. Despite the spiritual perceptiveness of the author, the *Maximes* is not Fénelon's best work. This master of epistolary exchange found it hard to condense a way of life into forty-four terse articles, scholastically divided into *vrai* and *faux*. Even his beautifully phrased letters and short tracts display a self-conscious quality that renders the disciple inferior to the masters to whom he constantly appeals — Bernard of Clairvaux and Francis de Sales. They lack the common sense of the latter as well as the lyrical enthusiasm of the former. Instead of experience Fénelon offers discourse honed to perfection. He himself, perceptive to an extreme, did not remain unaware of his problem. Reflecting upon himself he wrote: "I do not find myself in the multitude of my ideas and yet these ideas are all I find of myself. They prevent me from seeing the one, the true who will liberate me from the numbers, syntaxes, etc." His insurmountable ambivalence renders even his purest intentions suspect to himself. He confesses that he always wants to be approved of, loved, honored, and that he is idolizing his reputation.

Others also felt the ambivalence. Nicolas Malebranche, himself a onetime advocate of pure love, had no use for the archbishop's doctrine. To him the idea of pure love rested on a theological misconception, a *désintéressement imaginaire*. In his short polemical treatise *Traité de l'Amour de Dieu* (1697), he dismissed the pursuit of love without the desire of satisfaction as psychologically impossible. "If we pretend that we love God without his pleasing us, without tasting his goodness, or at least without firm hope that one day we shall possess God with pleasure, namely, through the lively and sweet perceptions his substance will produce in our soul, we pretend the impossible."[13] Would a total indifference with respect to the union with the beloved not mean that one does not love at all? Certainly in such an attitude the desire of God ceases to be desire.

But this argument does not entirely refute the pure love thesis. One may not be able to love God without implicitly desiring one's own fulfillment in this love, but one may still be motivated more by the God one loves than by the pleasure that love induces. To Malebranche's rhetorical question: "Can one ever love something by another principle than that of being happy?" the advocates of pure love would reply that, even if we cannot love God *without* the implied desire of finding fulfillment in that love, we must not love Him *because* of it. Malebranche himself had written: "God is not loved purely when loved only because of his pleasure" (*Lettres* I, *O.C.,* XIV, 55). Moreover, Fénelon leaves no doubt that pure love remains an ideal that can never be reached: we remain attached to our private interest.

Was Quietism a child of the Enlightenment or was it a reaction against it? On the surface it may appear to have been no more than an attempt to overcome the secularism of the period by a return to spiritual doctrines of the past. It undoubtedly was continuous with a premodern tradition. Fénelon constantly refers to Augustine, Bernard, and François de Sales. But a closer look at the movement also discloses the presence of decidedly modern elements that had already been at work in the Reformation and were becoming fully manifest in Pietism. It made spiritual life accessible to all believers without the mediating authority of clergy and magisterium. Instead of devotional practices, sacraments, and communal prayers, it stressed an unmediated, interior piety. This, more than specific doctrines, aroused the Catholic Church's suspicion. Those who chose the way of perfection became members of a distinct group — *les spirituels* — less submissive to authority than to the inspiration of the Spirit. In this respect at least, Quietism's self-conscious piety was fully in tune with those aspects of modernity that it doctrinally so strongly opposed.

Fénelon lost the battle for his spiritual movement. He withdrew to his diocese, seldom leaving it and observing a respectful silence. But his influence continued to grow, not only among French Catholics but also among English, German, and Dutch Protestants. Wesley included the *Maxims* in his Christian Library. In *The Spirit of Love,* William Law (1686–1761), a saintly, nonjuring Anglican clergyman, followed Fénelon's ideal of spiritual life and withdrew to solitude. Philipp Jacob Spener and August Herman Francke, the founders of the Pietist movement in Germany, recommended Fénelon, and their own writings are suffused with Quietist piety. The Protestant Pierre Poiret republished Fénelon. Thus after having been censored by Rome and exiled from Versailles, the archbishop became a leading spiritual master of Western Christians, Protestants and Catholics alike. Quietism ceased to be a Catholic sect: it became an *état d'âme* that, besides Lutherans and Calvinists, affected even deists such as Rousseau.[14]

German Pietism

By the middle of the seventeenth century, Lutheranism had ceased to be a protest movement. It had settled down as an alternate Church with distinct doctrines and rituals. Luther's vision had become framed within an orthodox scholasticism of which Melancthon's *Loci communes* was the authoritative text. Orthodoxy attempted to present Christian faith in a logically coherent system. But that system itself was inconsistently built on Luther's critique of reason in matters of faith. Lessing was to attack this inconsistency in dogma as well as in logic. Devout Lutherans, disaffected by this intellectualist theology, wistfully remembered Luther's stress on the experience of God in prayer and good works. Their aversion of the doctrine of Orthodoxy led to the movement that later came to be known as "Pietism," a name no less derogatory than that of "Quietism." Its origins go back to the theologian Johann Arndt (1555–1621), whose *True Christianity* (originally published as *Vier Bücher vom wahren Christentum* [1606] — later two more books were added) was to transform the face of Lutheranism in the second half of the seventeenth century. Arndt intended to restore Lutheran piety through a revival of its original mystical inspiration.[15] He republished Luther's edition of the late medieval *Theologia Deutsch*, as well as Johannes Tauler's *Sermons* and *The Imitation of Christ*, sources of Luther's inspiration. Arndt's own *True Christianity* was deeply steeped in medieval piety. The third book consists entirely of a commentary on Tauler's theory of mystical union with virtually no "Protestant" reinterpretation at all.[16]

Arndt had been an early forerunner. Pietism became a religious movement only after Philipp Jacob Spener's (1635–1705) republication of Arndt's work with a long introduction, later published separately under the title *Pia desideria* (1676). In it Spener complains about the sterility of Orthodox theology and advocates a mystical piety. In his commentary on the Epistle to the Romans, he writes: "Perfection in this life consists in being so united with God that the entire soul with all her powers be directed at, drawn to, and absorbed by God, so that she becomes one spirit with God, thinks of nothing but God, experiences and comprehends nothing outside God. . . . The entire foundation of such a great glory of the faithful lies in the *inhabitation of, and communion with the Lord Christ* in them."[17]

Spener, though antagonistic to Orthodox theology, nevertheless attempted to avoid causing a schism in the Church. He constantly insisted on the Lutheran origin of his ideas and missed no occasion for attacking "Papism," even while drawing upon Catholic sources. The dual strategy did not quite succeed.

His work stimulated spiritual aspirations that, despite his warnings, escaped ecclesiastical control. He himself started small groups (*ecclesiolae in Ecclesia*) that submitted only to the inner witness of the Holy Spirit. August Hermann Francke (1663–1727), Spener's favorite disciple, wrote: "To find Christ in Scripture is precious, but to find Him in one's heart is even more so. . . . One might say that one will not find Christ in Scripture if one does not discover him in one's heart."[18] Despite official resistance, Spener's views spread, particularly after Francke was appointed at the newly founded university of Halle. The enemies of Pietism proved to be right. The more the movement turned mystical, the more it deviated from Lutheran Orthodoxy. Radical Pietists such as Gottfried Arnold (1666–1714) ceased to justify their theories by referring to Orthodox sources. Instead they appealed to the Greek Fathers' doctrine about the inhabitation of God in the soul.

One cannot but notice the affinity with Quietism. Both Spener and Francke recommended the reading of Fénelon. The mystical Gerhard Tersteegen (1697–1769), raised in the Dutch Reformed tradition, stands closer to Mme. Guyon, whose work he translated, than to Calvin. For him, as for the Quietists, religion consisted entirely in a passive surrender to God's will. His ideal was "to live retired, be emptied of everything, to be alone with God in the Spirit, and separated from the world, at rest and in silence, giving place to God and things divine."[19] His followers included German Lutherans as well as Dutch Calvinists (with whom he entertained an intense correspondence in their own language).

Their enemies — as recent as Albrecht Ritschl in his learned *History of Pietism* (3 vols., 1880–86) — accused Pietists of the same vices with which Quietists had been charged: subjectivism, separatism, and a lack of serious concern for doctrine. They did indeed have much in common. During the second half of the eighteenth century, Pietism, no longer able to defend its weak theology against rationalist attacks, gradually returned to Orthodoxy. Yet even those who abandoned the movement persisted in a search for inner experience. The so-called Sturm und Drang (storm and stress) current in late eighteenth-century German literature continued to be inspired by the spirit of Pietism. Klopstock's *Messias* retains some of the trappings of popular Pietist hymns: angels everywhere, apostles in golden chairs, Jesus overseeing everything, and Satan plotting and scheming against the human race. The imagery of the epic appears contrived and much of its poetry maudlin. But Klopstock introduced the grand religious themes that, in the pen of greater poets such as Hölderlin, were to create a new poetic idiom. Indeed, Hölderlin himself wrote some Pietist songs in his early youth.[20]

Angelus Silesius's *Cherubinic Wanderer* (1657) also deserves mention, even though its publication actually preceded the Pietist movement. Yet the first two books of this work, which the author, Johann Scheffler, wrote before his conversion to Catholicism, present a more radical form of Pietism than the later one.[21] In them the soul's union with God is grounded in the creature's eternal inexistence as an idea in God.

> The rose which here on earth is now perceived by me,
> Has blossomed thus in God from all eternity. (I, 108)[22]

Once the creature begins its existence in time, its essential being continues in God and hence, as Eckhart had written, it possesses no real being of its own. "All creatures have no being, for their being consists in the presence of God."[23] But if creatures possess no being except in God, God becomes "being" only in and trough his creatures. If, as Angelus Silesius assumes, God *must* express Himself in a finite creation, the Creator depends on creation for his very being. Creation on its side, being nothing in itself, entirely depends on God.

> *Ich weiss, dass ohne mich Gott nicht ein Nu kann leben,*
> *Werd ich zu nicht, er muss von Not den Geist aufgeben.* (I, 8)
>
> (I know that without me God cannot live a "now" [moment],
> Were I reduced to naught, He also would expire.)

There are various ways of interpreting Silesius's paradoxes. Undoubtedly, some passages suggest that the soul actually loses its identity in God. But the vision underlying the *Wanderer* is pan-entheistic rather than pantheistic. All things exist in God, yet the creature's finitude irreducibly distinguishes it from God. To an all-inclusive infinite, nothing can be opposed as *other*. *Otherness* consists entirely in the *partial* character of the finite's expression of the infinite. Hence the creature relates to God as the other relates to what Nicolas of Cusa had called the "Non-other." The dialectic between the Non-other and the other in Silesius's poem assumes a particular significance when compared with the rationalist theology of the Enlightenment, which conceived the relation between God and creation as an extrinsic one between two "other" beings. For Silesius (as for Spinoza), a juxtaposition of the infinite with the finite would limit the infinite. Infinity leaves no metaphysical space beyond itself: all "other" reality must somehow exist *within* God.

Religious Affections in Edwards and in Swedenborg

As the quest for a more intimate, personal religion increased, the ancient notion of religious affections became prominent once again. According to the great New England divine Jonathan Edwards (1703–58), religious affections belong to the essence of faith. "True religion, in great part, consists in holy affections."[24] An affective awareness of God's presence, for him as for Calvin, was a sign of divine election. What did Edwards understand by the vague term "affection"? Obviously more than feeling or emotion. Affections move the will as well as the heart. They instigate the mind toward acting in a particular way. Moreover, for Edwards, the term has a cognitive no less than an emotional denotation. John E. Smith in his introduction to Edward's *Treatise concerning Religious Affections* describes them as "signposts indicating the *direction* of the soul, whether it is toward God in love or away from God and toward the world."[25] Edwards distinguishes religious affections from ordinary inclinations by the strength of their impulses. They are the vigorous spring to action that moves will, emotions, and understanding all toward the same goal.

Religious affections also possess an aesthetic quality. Though God's nature surpasses human perception, in some way the affective awareness of a divine presence impresses the soul as beautiful. "God's nature, or the divinity, is infinitely excellent; yea 'tis infinite beauty, brightness, and glory itself" (242). The concept of glory, central in Calvin's theology, refers to a quality that renders God both attractive and distant. Edwards describes it as "infinite highness and infinite condescension."[26] The light of glory illuminates the mind and arouses a selfless love that in some way corresponds to Jeanne Guyon's and Bishop Fénelon's pure love. Yet for the Puritan divine, the infinite distance between God and the created mind can never be bridged in union. The object of love is near, yet never to be possessed. Edwards speaks of an infused cognitive sense, not a new faculty, but an ability granted "the same faculty of understanding" (206) that renders the mind capable of savoring God's revelation (273, 282) and apprehending its beauty.

What induced Edwards to call this an infused *sense* rather than an infused understanding? Writing in Locke's tradition he traced any source of new knowledge to *sensation*. Reason, restricted to comparing and assessing ideas received from the senses, possesses no affective qualities, as sensation does. Hence any spiritual perception had to originate in some kind of sensation.[27] Moreover, for the Cambridge Platonists, John Smith and Henry More, who influenced Edwards, the empiricist term "spiritual sensation" disguised a Platonic intuition that had nothing in common with sensationalism. For them as for Edwards, this "spiritual sensation" could convey a necessary and eternal truth, rather than being a transient impression the truth of which was still to be established by reason. Still, Edwards emphatically distinguishes spiritual insight from notional understanding. His "sense of the heart," unlike Pascal's knowledge of the heart, yields not the kind of knowledge by which a person "knows what a triangle is, and what a square is" (272). In fact, religious affections, though originating in a cognitive sense, do not primarily grant a "seeing" of truth, but a new tasting of divine life.

Edwards attributes this affective knowledge to the Spirit of God, who dwells in the saints as in "his temple" and instills "a principle of new nature and life" (200). Suggesting a participation in God's life (392), Edwards strains the principles of reformed Christianity to the limits. He also insists on the necessity of active cooperation. Holy affections, he maintains, are rooted in the practice of Christian virtues, and they lead to a more consistent practice. It is sheer hypocrisy "to cry up faith in opposition to works" (318).[28] Even for this Puritan firebrand, doctrinal Calvinist positions lose much of their significance. For Edwards, as well as for Quietists and Pietists, the immanent presence of God forms the core of spiritual religion.

In the eighteenth century, the term "affection" had yet another meaning than the one Edwards knew. It referred to the way people or things influence (affect) one another, or, as Swedenborg wrote, "correspond" to one another. That more objective meaning defines the structure of Emanuel Swedenborg's (1688–1772) thought. This son of the bishop of Skara grew up to be one of Sweden's most distinguished scientists. As a member of the Royal Mining Commission, he wrote a much-respected study on metallurgy and made various discoveries in the fields of physiology and astronomy. In his fifty-fourth year he experienced a prolonged spiritual crisis in the course of which he allegedly began to receive visions that continued trough the rest of his life. They all related to the correspondence between physical, spiritual, and what he calls "divine" reality. He spent most of the last thirty years of his life discussing the connections and affinities between the three realms.

The twelve-volume *Arcana Coelestia* (1749–56), Swedenborg's first and most comprehensive work, consists of a Latin commentary on the two first books of the Bible. Having completed this gigantic opus, Swedenborg understandably abandoned the project of writing a commentary on the remaining books. Reading the *Arcana* (or part of it) is a unique experience that oscillates between admiration and aversion. The Polish poet Czeslaw Milosz compares the experience to wandering through a hall of mirrors that arouses a range of conflicting emotions, where mockery abruptly turns to awe and curiosity to boredom.[29] In thousands of pages the Swedish visionary describes a spiritual universe that forms the inner core and immanent cause of the physical one we know. Within it lies an even more inward, divine realm unknowable in itself but manifest in its effects. The outer or lower realities symbolize the interior, higher ones. "Whatever is seen anywhere in the universe is symbolic [others translate: representative] of the Lord's kingdom, to the point that nothing whatever occurs in the atmosphere or in space, in the world and its three kingdoms, that is not in its own way symbolic [or: representative]. . . . From the divine came heavenly realities whose essence is the good. From the heavenly realities came spiritual ones whose essence is the true. And from those two come natural realities."[30]

The two concepts of *correspondence* and *representation* play a crucial part in Swedenborg's doctrine. "Correspondence . . . [exists] between the phenomena of the inner or spiritual person and phenomena of the outer or natural person. A representation occurs *in* things proper to the world's light (that is, something in the outer or natural person) that relates to phenomena proper to heaven's light (that is, that come from the inner or spiritual person)" (*Arcana*, # 3225). Swedenborg's concordances may be compared to Bishop Butler's theological analogies. Both symbolically link the natural universe to a spiritual realm. In different ways they counter the naturalist ideologies of their time by suggesting the existence of another dimension of the real than the one of the natural sciences.

Swedenborg finds the key to this symbolism in the spiritual interpretation of the Bible. Yet rather than superimposing a spiritual sense upon the literal, he presents the spiritual as hidden within the literal. "The spiritual sense is not apparent in the sense of the letter; it is *within* it as the soul is in the body" (*The True Christian Religion* [1771], # 194). In this spiritual literalism "*each* and *every* element is [intrinsically] symbolic of spiritual and heavenly matters" (*Arcana*, # 3472).[31] Beyond the spiritual meaning Swedenborg still admits a celestial one to be grasped only indirectly "through the affection of the will" (*Doctrine of Sacred Scripture* [1764], # 19). Swedenborg justifies his symbolic perspective on the natural world by means of an immanent divine presence that moves nature from within rather than leaving it entirely to the blind force of mechanical causality. "The natural [world] has its whole source in the spiritual kingdom. Anything lacking a prior source is nothing, nothing occurs that is not connected to a cause" (*Arcana*, # 2758). Reality depends on God *from within,* not through the extrinsic causality of a product on its maker. For him, God does not create "out of nothing." The universe, the natural as well as the spiritual, "could not have been created except *in* God and *from* God"; God himself "is, in fact, its actual reality" (*Divine Love and Wisdom* [1763], # 55).

Swedenborg aims his argument at Isaac Newton, according to whom God needs an empty receptacle of infinite space and time — a physical "nothingness" — in which to create. Such a zone of emptiness contradicts the very idea of God as infinite being. "The Divine fills all space of the universe without being bound by space" (*Divine Love and Wisdom,* # 69). It must be said, however, that the promises of this theory of concordance remain mostly unfulfilled. Many of Swedenborg's "deeper" readings amount to little more than far-fetched allegories of a kind that had long been discredited. Instead of disclosing the symbolic meaning of a text, they consist of line-by-line allegorical interpretations that run parallel with the literal meaning without intimately linking one to the other.

Although the basic structure of Swedenborg's system is Neoplatonic, some Gnostic elements appear in it. Where traditional Jewish and Christian theology draws a decisive line in the structure of reality between Creator and creation, the Swedish theosophist, following the Gnostic distinction between a material, a psychic, and a spiritual level, distinguishes *two* divisions: one between the natural and the spiritual realm, the other between the spiritual and the divine. Moreover, as in the Gnostic *pleroma,* the "heavenly" sphere houses a plurality of divine beings. Most controversially, Swedenborg equates the Creator with Gnosticism's aboriginal Divine Man. The following passage appears in *Heaven and Hell* (1758), an early work that inspired William Blake: "The only form in which any angel in heaven can perceive the divine is the human form; and remarkable as it may seem, in the higher heavens, they cannot even think about the divine in any other way" (*Heaven and Hell,* # 79). Since God can exist only as God-Man, major parts of the *Arcana* are devoted to a detailed description of the concordance between human physiology and the celestial kingdom.

Czeslaw Milosz has perceived the significance of this position in the rationalist atmosphere of the time. "The Christian faith, always strongly anthropocentric, searched for a new vision to compete with the new atheistic idea of the Man-God who was to be his own redeemer. In the eighteenth century an extraordinary concept makes its appearance, one possibly related to the Adam Kadmon, the primordial, pre-cosmic man of the Cabala. For Swedenborg, God in heaven has a human form; Christ's humanity is thus a perfect fulfillment of the Godhead."[32] Indeed, even the Incarnation is an intrinsically necessary event within God. "God came into the world . . . that He might become visible" (*True Christian Religion,* # 786).

The idea of a Primal Man appears in several Gnostic myths. Yet they rarely identify this precosmic perfect Adam with the Godhead. Swedenborg here deviates from common Gnostic theory as well as from Christian orthodoxy. He reinterprets the doctrine of the Trinity in a similar sense. The Trinity did not exist before God became incarnate "in the Lord God, the Redeemer and Savior, Jesus Christ" (ibid., # 170). God, then, became fully divine only in Christ. The theosophist is convinced that Christianity is about to enter its final phase and the prophecy of the New Jerusalem to be fulfilled. In fact, the Last Judgment has already occurred in the spiritual world, yet the glorified Christ remains invisible except to those whose spiritual sight has been opened (*True*

Christian Religion, # 777). He will become manifest in a new Church, of which Swedenborg declares himself to be the divinely appointed minister. This and a few similar visions have discredited Swedenborg's mystical theology to most Christian believers.

Before dismissing his theology, we ought to establish what role the "visions" play in the whole of his work. Over a period of nearly thirty years Swedenborg alleges to have experienced visions. In them he moves easily between this world and the spiritual realm, where he engages in conversations with spirits. What renders these visions disconcerting is their ordinary, not to say pedestrian, character. They are neither awesome as those of Jeremiah or Ezechiel, nor ecstatic as the ones of Julian of Norwich or Teresa of Avila. In his reports of them Swedenborg casually chats with the spirits of the dead as with chance encounters in the street. Was he a schizophrenic genius like Strindberg and Van Gogh, as Karl Jaspers contends? The visionary message that equates Christ's Second Coming with Swedenborg's new religion (*True Christian Religion,* # 779) seems particularly strange.

Still, he impressed others as a stable person of mature judgment. Up to his final years he continued to revise and publish scientific papers and to serve as a respected member of the Swedish parliament. Some think that he may not have had any visions at all and that the "reports" merely served to illustrate his spiritual insight. Thus the French-Polish poet Oscar Milosz wonders: "Did the *memorabilia* [the passages in which he reported his visionary encounters] come before or after the system? Was the work born of a vision or an idea? Because these 'memorabilia' have the look of inventions designed as an *allegorical proof.*" Czeslaw Milosz, Oscar's distant cousin, adds that eighteenth-century literary conventions required such authenticating devices as a pseudo-memoir or a pseudo-diary, or a manuscript found in a tree trunk.[33]

It is hard to decide between the pathological and the "allegorical" hypothesis. But a realistic interpretation of the visions seems excluded. What, for instance, are we to make of Swedenborg's report of his visit to the "frigid zones" of the spiritual universe "where the northern spirits dwell" who have their heads covered with lion skins, their bodies with leopard skins, and their feet with bear skins as they ride in sledges to a Sunday service (*True Christian Religion,* # 185)? The strange transference of the present world to a spiritual universe appears almost intended to discourage the reader from taking the vision literally. Fantasy complements prejudice in the Supplement to *The True Christian Religion,* probably a late addition, where he passes in review the founders and representatives of various Western religions as he encounters them in the spiritual world. His description resembles Dante's picture of hell and purgatory. Luther is expected to move up to heaven after Swedenborg converts him from his doctrine of justification by faith alone. Calvin meets a worse fate as he persists in the "execrable doctrine of predestination" (*True Christian Religion,* # 798). Among Christians the "Papists" are the lowest and they remain unreformed.

In the end the nature of Swedenborg's visions — whether inventions, delusions, or illustrations — may not be decisive for the merit of his theology. They sharply differ from the theory in content as well as in tone and discredit neither the insight nor the religious sensitivity displayed in the theoretical parts. Swedenborg's religious and cultural impact was profound and long lasting. In the eighteenth century his doctrine influenced Goethe as well as the Würtenberg Pietists.[34] Emerson gave him a place among his *Representative Men;* Balzac admired him and so did Borges; he marked the education of William and Henry James; Blake's theosophical writings bear the stamp of Swedenborg on every page; Baudelaire used the concordances as a literary device; symbolist painters Odilon Redon and Pierre Bonnard learned from them to view physical appearance as transparent of spiritual reality. Swedenborg's symbolic vision of the physical universe may be seen as an attempt to achieve a new synthesis, if not between traditional religion and culture as a whole, at least between religion and the scientific worldview of his time. A fantastic supernaturalism compensating for a narrow literalism clouded his theological insight and conflicted with the symbolic direction of his work.

Conclusion

The ideas of the Enlightenment continue to influence our present culture. The ideal of human emancipation still occupies a central place among them, though it has since passed through a number of changes. Marxism, which until recently played a leading role in European life, may serve as an example both of the continuity with and the transformation of the original ideal. It derived its goal of social liberation from the eighteenth-century ideal of emancipation. Yet the kind of social liberation Marx had in mind obviously differs from the emancipation pursued by the Enlightenment. Eighteenth-century thought had at least in principle continued to maintain the traditional primacy of theoretical reason. Marx replaced this primacy with that of instrumental reason. Human emancipation was to result from changes in the social process of production.

In the West, Marxism now appears to belong to a perfect past and most of us consider ourselves more legitimate heirs of the Enlightenment legacy. Still, the Enlightenment itself contained a less overt but no less consequential pragmatism. The eighteenth-century notion of rationality included a universal pattern of order to be imposed upon nature and society. The idea of an enforced rationality inspired and motivated the French Revolution. Albrecht Wellmer has described the dangers implied in this project: "Enlightenment became a world-historical project of the human species, in which the species simultaneously creates itself and threatens its own destruction; its ultimate aim is social freedom, happiness, and the independence of the individual, but its secret logic aims at the extinction of the self-liberating subjects and the self-elevation of social bondage and constraint."[1]

Jürgen Habermas has made a vigorous effort to disconnect at least the Enlightenment's idea of emancipation from a narrowly practical interpretation and to restore some of the metaphysical content that practical reason, at least for its major thinkers, possessed. Deprived of all metaphysical and religious content, he claims, practical reason tends to degenerate to a utilitarian calculus, "rationality in the service of self-preservation gone wild."[2] He seeks to return to what he considers the original emancipatory project of the Enlightenment. The modern concept of reason is indeed linked to emancipatory action, as Kant had shown. But that call for action does not imply that theoretical reason must ever yield its primacy to practical intelligence. When subordinate to practice, theoretical reason forfeits the authority to raise critical questions of legitimacy. Both Nazism and Communism have shown the catastrophic consequences to which this leads.

Other contemporary thinkers have recently criticized the Enlightenment for the opposite reason. According to them, it intensified a one-sided intellectualism that had been inherent in Western thought since its Greek beginnings. In particular, they object to the typically modern concern with absolute foundations. That concern, according to Richard Rorty, originated in the early seventeenth century.[3] Western thought did not always require the support of ultimate foundations, even though it has always insisted on the necessity to justify the real. Plato's philosophy began with "nonfoundational" conversations. His dialogues remain wide open to all viewpoints, as long as the speakers do not contradict themselves. To make sense, an argument must remain consistent, but nothing should or can prevent it from admitting unproven assumptions. Premodern thinkers have never felt the need to prove all of the presuppositions of their thought. Yet, as I understand them, the concerns of Rorty and some other postmodern thinkers move beyond the intellectualism of the Enlightenment. Their critique of modernity forms part of a more comprehensive attack on a logocentrism that allegedly has obsessed Western thought from the beginning. Modern rationalism, then, would be merely a distinct, more self-conscious stage of that ancient rationalism.[4]

In my opinion, that critique of the Enlightenment continues to rely on principles inherent in the Enlightenment itself. Its summons to uninhibited critical thinking—*sapere aude*—challenges any principles that stand in the way of such a critique, including the Enlightenment's own. Formerly few dared to turn the power of their critique on the rule of reason itself. Today's critics are prepared to do so, though the source of the critical impulse lies in the very movement they criticize. Michel Foucault's thought presents an amazing example of opposition to Enlightenment in the name of Enlightenment principles. In his view, the fact that the human subject *imposes* meaning transforms the meaning-giving act itself into an exercise of power. Structures of meaning that appear as determinations of reason express in fact an underlying will to power.[5] So, he rejects the primacy of reason, essential to Enlightenment project, altogether. Here also, however, it must be said that antecedents of this critique may be found in the Enlightenment itself. Rousseau continuously attacked the rationalism on which his political critique was based. In others, such as Diderot, the inconsistency is less obvious. Yet their personal and fictional writings substantially differ from the rationalist principles that lie at the ground of their critique. It has been said with some justification that the so-called Age of Reason was reason's worst enemy.[6]

In the course of this book I have repeatedly indicated that one of the main problems of the Enlightenment stems from the assumption that the mind alone is the source of meaning. This often led to an unwarranted intellectual confidence. Many appeared insufficiently aware of the limitations of the historically conditioned individual mind and tended to identify it with the universal, *transcendental reason*. Kant, who coined the term "transcendental ego," warned against equating it with the empirical self. Others did not adequately distinguish them and ended up with an idea of reason that badly needed to be desublimated. One effect of it was that they tended to overestimate the realistic chances of their projects. Utopian treatises on perpetual peace, on a permanent international brotherhood, on the unification of all sciences, and on the future extinction of crime, bear the sign of a naive presumptuousness. For a brief period many intellectuals, especially but not exclusively in France, expected that the French Revolution, the ultimate utopia, was about to realize all the Enlightenment's hopes.

Contrary to the religious utopias of earlier ages, those of the Enlightenment appeared realistic because their supporters intended to realize them by scientific means and methods. But, as Karl Mannheim remarks, that did not make them any less utopian. "Nothing is more removed from actual events than the closed rational system. Under certain circumstances, nothing contains more irrational drive than a fully self-contained, intellectualistic world-view."[7] In fact, religious utopias, believed to be long suppressed, continued to inspire the allegedly scientific projects of the Enlightenment. Behind the rationalist outlines of the stages of world history we still detect traces of apocalyptic speculations that began with Joachim of Fiore. Lessing's essay on "The Education of the Human Race," directly influenced by Pietist sources, shows how easily a religious view of history could be transferred to a secular one. In France, the young Turgot initiated a similar transition in his "Discours sur les progrès successifs de l'esprit humain," which his admirer Condorcet developed into a fail-proof, scientific utopia. His certainty of the future as that of other utopians rested entirely on an unrestricted trust in the compelling force of reason. Having reached full intellectual maturity, humans, they assumed, would have no choice but freely to obey the voice of reason and thereby to realize the ideal state of humanity. Since then we have learned what Voltaire knew: how little reason directs human conduct.

Finally, I return to the question raised at the beginning of this book concerning the Enlightenment's relation to early and late modernity. From the preceding chapters it should appear that in the Enlightenment the original thesis of modern thought, namely, that the mind plays a creative role in the constitution of the real, found its strongest expression. That does not imply, however, that the Enlightenment's intellectual position can be derived from early modern premises. In many respects it deviated from them. Early modern thought had none of the abstract universalism characteristic of the later period. The Enlightenment *reinterpreted* the humanist idea of human creativity. The characteristic inclination of Enlightenment thought to universalize its concepts deprived the Renaissance notion of human creativity of the tragic limitations restricting each individual's potential to realize it, of which precisely the most creative men of genius — Michelangelo, Galileo, Leonardo — had remained so acutely conscious. We rarely perceive those limitations in the Enlightenment. For the later thinkers, no meaning is given with reality itself. This belief constitutes the basis of what we consider to be the Enlightenment's rationalism taken in the comprehensive sense that includes empiricist as well as philosophically "rationalist" thought.

Within that rationalism, the principle of universality, crucial in our intellectual tradition since its Greek beginnings, turned into an abstract, logical principle of reasoning. On a practical level, it became a tool of instrumental reason that enabled the West to develop a technical superiority, which allowed it to impose its views and politics on most of the world. Through colonization, technical advances, and economic power, it has attempted and mostly succeeded in restructuring other societies on a Western pattern. These developments were not accidental: they were direct consequences of the new concept of reason. That concept was isolated from the historical context in which it had previously been embedded. In premodern thought reason was never taken to be free of presuppositions. To overcome the skepticism created by the nominalist crisis, however, Descartes considered it necessary for reason to be its own foundation and not to rely on anything outside itself. That abstraction by now has shown its limitations, both the theoretical and practical. With many others, Alasdair MacIntyre has called for a return to a way of thinking that recognizes its link to a particular tradition. "What Enlightenment made us for the most part blind to and we now need to recover is . . . a conception according to which the standards of rational justification themselves emerge from and are part of a history."[8]

Since the Enlightenment has now come under such a severe revision, many have begun to wonder whether it was more than an unfortunate cultural interlude, a deviation from the course of our intellectual development. Against this position I have argued that the Enlightenment, though flawed and one-sided, accomplished an indispensable task in the development of Western thought. With admirable persistency it pursued the principle that has dominated our intellectual tradition since its beginning, namely, that things ought to be justified rather than blindly accepted from habit and custom. In its single-minded attempt to make that principle into the guiding rule of thought, the Enlightenment achieved a veritable breakthrough on the way toward consistent rationality and even provided the tools for correcting its own one-sidedness. Though the eighteenth century rarely made those corrections, its intellectual achievement remains unsurpassed.

The Enlightenment has given us some of our most important ideas: an expressive conception of art, a nonauthoritarian view of morality, political theories that build freedom and democracy within the very structures of society. These were rationally sound positions, even when the arguments that supported them often rested on questionable grounds. A theory of human rights conceived in a judicial vacuum may be hard to defend juridically, yet the very concept of such rights expresses the profoundly rational insight that human beings are *by nature* entitled to rights. The same applies to the doubtful arguments by which political philosophers legitimated the idea of a social contract. They were right in believing that political structures must serve people's needs rather than being self-justifying structures. If today we feel that the undesirable conditions in which many humans have to live impose a universal obligation on the conscience of the more fortunate ones, we may find it hard to justify that insight, but we nevertheless *know* it to be true. Time and again the rational insights of the Enlightenment surpass the arguments invoked to justify them.

Even in its attitude toward religion, which has most severely been criticized, the Enlightenment deserves considerable credit. Religious tolerance; the separation between cult and public life; the protection of the individual conscience against religious compulsion, social pressure, or cultural prejudice—all of these have become nonnegotiable positions to Western believers. The sad events mentioned at the beginning of this book show the evil a religion may do when it refuses to accept those positions. The critique of the so-called arguments for the existence of God, themselves a modern, rationalist invention, forced theology at last to abandon a long surpassed pre-Copernican conception of the world. The idea of creation conceived as a divine imparting of motion, held over from an Aristotelian cosmology, lost its meaning after Newton's theory and Diderot's attacks. The critique of religion proved painful, particularly in the irreverent form in which it was often administered; yet it was necessary and overdue. In the end religion benefited from it. It forced the religious community to seek the proper domain of religion in symbols of transcendence rather than in science, and compelled it to begin a search for the kind of spiritual depth needed to live in accordance with this insight. Paradoxically, it was the critique of the Enlightenment, however one-sided and intolerant of alternative views, that opened the eyes of Western believers to the truth and value of religions other than their own. Even deism, rationalism's own defective product, was capable of inspiring genuine piety as the example of the deeply religious Moses Mendelssohn showed and as Lessing's play based on that example proved. However we assess the Enlightenment's achievements, we could commit no greater error than to deny or reject them. They have become an essential part of what we are.

Notes

Introduction

1. Quoted in Charles Augustin de Sainte-Beuve, *Causeries du lundi* (1851–70), vol. VII, p. 325.

Chapter 1. A Definition and a Provisional Justification

1. Franco Venturi, *Italy and the Enlightenment,* ed. Stuart Woolf, trans. Susan Corsi (New York University Press, 1972), p. 33.

2. Henry Steele Commager, *The Empire of Reason: How Europe Imagined and America Realized the Enlightenment* (New York: Doubleday, 1977), pp. 242–45.

3. Peter Gay, *Voltaire's Politics: The Poet as Realist* (New Haven: Yale University Press, 1988), p. xv.

4. R. G. Collingwood, "The Historical Imagination," in his *The Idea of History* (Oxford: Clarendon Press, 1946), 231.

5. Ernest Cassirer, *An Essay on Man* (New Haven: Yale University Press, 1944), p. 222.

6. Louis Dumont, "Are Cultures Living Beings?" *Man* (1986): 587.

7. Paul Ricoeur, *Hermeneutics and Human Sciences,* trans. John B. Thompson (New York: Cambridge University Press, 1981), p. 121.

8. Georg Simmel, *The Condition of Modern Culture and Other Essays,* trans. K. Peter Etzkorn (New York: Teachers College Press, 1968), pp. 27–28.

9. Louis Dupré, *Metaphysics and Culture* (Milwaukee, Wis.: Marquette University Press, 1994) and "Is the History of Philosophy Philosophy?" *Review of Metaphysics* 42 (March 1989): 463–82.

10. Martin Heidegger, *Being and Time,* trans. John Macquarrie and Edward Robinson (New York: Harper and Row, 1962), p. 486.

11. Immanuel Kant, "Was ist Aufklärung," in *Kants Gesammelte Schriften* (Berlin: Preussische Akademie, 1902–42), vol. VII; trans. as "What Is Enlightenment?" by Lewis White Beck in *Kant on History* (Indianapolis: Bobbs-Merrill, 1963), p. 3.

12. Denis Diderot, *Essai sur les règnes de Claude et de Néron* in *Oeuvres Complètes,* ed. H. Dieckmann and J. Varloot (Paris: Hermann, 1986), vol. XXV.

13. Rüdiger Bittner, "What Is Enlightenment?" in *What Is Enlightenment?* ed. James Schmidt (Berkeley: University of California Press, 1996), pp. 345–58. We know how one-sided specialists can be in their practical judgment. Why should that judgment overrule common sense?

14. Moses Mendelssohn, "On the Question: What Is Enlightenment?" trans. James Schmidt, in *What Is Enlightenment?* pp. 53–57. The selection, the quality of the transla-tions, and the expert commentary make Schmidt's collection of essays an invaluable source of information on the German Enlightenment.

15. Destutt de Tracy, *Eléments d'Idéologie. Première partie: Idéologie proprement dite,* ed. Henri Gouhier (Paris: Vrin, 1971). Cf. Emmet Kennedy, *A Philosophe in the Age of Revolution: Destutt de Tracy and the Origins of "Ideology"* (Philadelphia: American Philosophical Society, 1978).

16. Louis Althusser, *For Marx,* trans. Ben Brewster (New York: Pantheon Books, 1969), pp. 231–32. See also Fernand Dumont, *Les Idéologies* (Paris: P.U.F., 1976), and Louis Dupré, *Marx's Social Critique of Culture* (New Haven: Yale University Press, 1983), chap. 5, "The Use of Ideology."

17. Edmund Burke, *Reflections on the Revolution in France* (1970; repr. New York: Doubleday, 1973), p. 100.

18. Hans-Georg Gadamer, *Wahrheit and Methode,* 2d ed. (Tübingen: J. C. B. Mohr, 1960), pp. 250–61.

19. Frederic Antal, *Classicism and Romanticism* (New York: Harper and Row, 1973), p. 4.

20. Edmund Husserl, "Philosophy and the Crisis of Modern Man," trans. Quentin Lauer, in *Phenomenology and the Crisis of Philosophy* (New York: Harper and Row, 1965), pp. 149–92. The quoted text appears on p. 157.

21. Edmund Husserl, "Philosophy as a Rigorous Science" (1910–11), trans. Quentin Lauer, in *Phenomenology and the Crisis of Philosophy,* pp. 71–147.

22. G. W. F. Hegel, *Phänomenologie des Geistes,* ed. Johannes Hoffmeister (Hamburg: Felix Meiner, 1952); *Phenomenology of Spirit,* trans. J. B. Baillie (New York: Harper, 1964), p. 457.

23. Paul Hazard, *La crise de la conscience européenne,* trans. J. Lewis May as *The European Mind, 1680–1715* (New York: World, 1952).

24. Cf. Peter Gay, *The Enlightenment: An Interpretation* (New York: Random House, 1967); Michael J. Buckley, *At the Origin of Modern Atheism* (New Haven: Yale Univer-sity Press, 1987).

25. Cf. Pierre-Jean Labarrière, *Le discours de l'altérité* (Paris: Presses Universitaires de France, 1982), p. 49.

26. Max Horkheimer, *Eclipse of Reason* (1947; repr. New York: Seabury Press, 1974), pp. 14, 17.

Chapter 2. A Different Cosmos

1. Gilles Deleuze, *Spinoza et le problème de l'expression* (Paris: Editions de Minuit, 1968).

2. M. J. Petry, "Hegel's Criticism of Newton" in *Clio* 13, no. 4 (1984): 334–35.

3. Hans Blumenberg, "Selbsterhaltung und Beharrung: Zur Konstitution der neuzeitlichen Rationalität," in *Subjektivität und Selbsterhaltung*, ed. Hans Ebeling (Frankfurt: Suhrkamp Verlag, 1976), pp. 144–207, esp. p. 181.

4. Isaac Newton, *The Mathematical Principles of Natural Philosophy*, bk. III, rule 3 (New York: Philosophical Library, 1964), p. 324.

5. *Mathematical Principles*, bk. I (Third Definition), p. 13.

6. Isaac Newton, *Opticks*, 4th ed. (New York: Dover Publications, 1952), Question 31, p. 397.

7. Cf. Newton's two letters to Bentley written in 1693. On this confused issue and Newton's persisting hesitation, cf. Ernan McMullin, *Newton on Matter and Activity* (South Bend, Ind.: Notre Dame University Press, 1978), esp. chaps. 1–2.

8. In answering a query by Cotes, the author of the preface to a later edition of the *Principia*, he even refers to the third law of mechanics — the equality of action and reaction — the very one of which he had elsewhere declared that it could not prevent the decrease of motion in the universe. Cf. McMullin, *Newton on Matter*, pp. 52–54.

9. On the impact of alchemy on Newton's thought, cf. R. W. Westfall, "Alchemy in Newton's Career" in M. Righini Bonelli and W. Shea, eds. *Reason, Experiment, and Mysticism in the Scientific Revolution* (New York: 1975).

10. *Mathematical Principles*, bk.I, Scholium following Definitions, p. 20.

11. *Mathematical Principles*, bk.I, Scholium following Definition VIII, pp. 18–19.

12. Immanuel Kant, *Metaphysische Anfangsgrunde der Naturwissenschaft*, in *Kants Gesammelte Schriften* (Berlin: Preussische Akademie, 1902–42), vol. IV, p. 560; *Metaphysical Foundations of Natural Science*, trans. James Ellington (Indianapolis: Bobbs-Merrill, 1970), p. 127. In a letter to Bentley of December 10, 1692, Newton argues that without an infinite (real) space the force of gravity would pull all celestial bodies together into a single mass. Only an immense space (but why infinite?) would make it possible for them to remain separate bodies. Without it, a continuous divine intervention would be needed to keep bodies from collapsing into one another. Cf. Michael Buckley, *Motion and Motion's God* (Princeton: Princeton University Press, 1971), chap. 17.

13. Newton, *Opticks*, p. 370.

14. Aristotle, *De coelo*, I, 9, 279a.

15. Thomas Bradwardine (1290–1349), *De causa Dei contra Pelagium*, ed. Henry Savile (London, 1618) and the commentary of Edward Grant, "Medieval and Seventeenth Century Conceptions of an Infinite Void Space beyond the Cosmos," in *Isis* 60, pt. 1, no. 201 (spring 1969): 39–60; Alexandre Koyré, "Le vide et l'espace infini

au XIVe siecle," *Archives d'histoire doctrinale et littéraire du moyen-âge* 24 (1949): 45–91.

16. Samuel Clarke in André Robinet, eds., *Collection of Papers which passed between the late Learned Mr. Leibniz and Dr. Clarke in the years 1715 and 1716, relating to the Principles of Natural Philosophy and Religion* (Paris: Presses Universitaires de France, 1957). Clarke's fourth reply.

17. *A Treatise Concerning the Principles of Human Knowledge,* in *The Works of George Berkeley, Bishop of Cloyne,* ed. A. A. Luce and T. E. Jessop (Edinburgh, 1948–57), no. 117, p. 94.

18. Avihu Zakai, "Jonathan Edwards and the Language of Nature: The Re-Enchantment of the World in the Age of Scientific Reasoning," *Journal of Religious History* 26 (2002): 15–41, and *Jonathan Edwards's Philosophy of History* (Princeton: Princeton University Press, 2003), chap. 3. Cf. J. E. McGuire, "Boyle's Conception of Nature," *Journal of the History of Ideas* 33 (1972): 533.

19. Jonathan Edwards, *Miscellany,* in *Works of Jonathan Edwards,* vol. XIX (New Haven: Yale University Press, 2001), pp. 565–94.

20. Melvin Woody, *Freedom's Embrace* (University Park: Pennsylvania State University, 1998), p. 220.

21. Hoxie Neale Fairchild, *Religious Trends in English Poetry,* vol. I: 1700–1740 (New York: Columbia University Press, 1939), pp. 152–53 (Reynolds), p. 40 (Prior).

22. Julien Offray de La Mettrie, *L'homme machine: Man a Machine* (1912; La Salle, Ill.: Open Court, 1993), p. 148.

23. Thomas Hobbes, *De Corpore,* IV, chap. 25, 2, in *The Latin Works,* vol. I, ed. Molesworth (London, 1839).

24. Thomas Hobbes, *Of Human Nature,* chap. 2, in *The English Works,* vol. IV.

25. Diderot, *Lettre sur les aveugles,* in *Oeuvres,* ed. Laurent Versini (Paris: Robert Lafont, 1994), vol. VII, p. 167; trans. Derek Coltman in *Diderot's Selected Writings,* ed. Lester G. Crocker (New York: Macmillan, 1966), p. 21.

26. Diderot, *Lettre,* p. 169; *Diderot's Selected Writings,* p. 23.

27. Lucretius, *De rerum natura,* I, 10/6–10/24; *The Way Things Are,* trans. Rolfe Humphries (Bloomington: Indiana University Press, 1968), p. 49.

28. Diderot, *Pensées sur l'interprétation de la nature* (# 50), in *Oeuvres,* vol. I, p. 588; *Diderot's Selected Writings,* p. 79. In a letter to Charles Pineau Duclos, dated September 10, 1765, Diderot stated quite openly: "Sensibility is a universal property of matter, an inert property in inorganic or senseless bodies . . . , a property rendered active in the same bodies by their assimilation into an animal substance, one that is living." Quoted in Michael Buckley, *At the Origins of Modern Atheism* (New Haven: Yale University Press, 1987), p. 232.

29. Diderot, *Pensées* (# 58), in *Oeuvres,* vol. I, p. 597; *Diderot's Selected Writings,* p. 86.

30. Diderot, *Pensées* (# 12), in *Oeuvres,* vol. I, p. 565; *Diderot's Selected Writings,* p. 73.

31. Diderot, *Le rêve de d'Alembert* (1769, pub. 1830), in *Oeuvres,* vol. I, p. 618; "D'Alembert's Dream," in *Diderot's Selected Writings,* p. 188.

32. Diderot, *Le rêve,* p. 636; *Diderot's Selected Writings,* p. 199.

33. Jean le Rond d'Alembert, *Essai sur les élémens de philosophie* (1759) in *Mélanges de littérature, d'histoire et de philosophie* (Amsterdam, 1763–70), vol. IV; repr. in *Corpus des Oeuvres de Philosophie en Langue Française* (Paris: Arthème Fayard, 1986), p. 27.

34. Ernst Cassirer, *Das Erkenntnisproblem* (1922; repr. Hildesheim: Georg Olms Verlag, 1971–73), vol. II, p. 411ff.

35. *Eclaircissement* (addition to the *Elémens de philosophie*) in *Mélanges,* vol. V, p. 253.

36. Ernst Cassirer, *The Philosophy of the Enlightenment* (Princeton: Princeton University Press, 1968), p. 56.

37. Marie Jean Antoine Nicolas, Marquis de Condorcet, *Eloge de d'Alembert,* in *Oeuvres de d'Alembert* (Paris: A. Belin, 1821), vol. I, p. xiv.

38. Paul-Henri, baron d'Holbach, *Système de la Nature ou des loix du monde physique et du monde moral* (Amsterdam, 1770); trans. as *The System of Nature,* by H. D. Robinson (New York: G. W. and A. J. Matsell, 1835; repr. by Burt Franklin in 1868 and in 1970), I, 2, 22. I refer to the 1970 edition by book, chapter, and page.

39. Echoes also of Pascal's "Through space the universe grasps me and swallows me up like a speck." Blaise Pascal, *Pensées,* ed. Lafuma, # 194; trans. A. J. Krailsheimer (Baltimore: Penguin Books, 1966), p. 87. Pascal was not alone in feeling lost. The skeptic Fontenelle describes the reaction of the marquise whom he has just informed that all fixed stars are centers of different solar systems, each one of which may be inhabited. "That confuses, disturbs, frightens me." Fontenelle answers: "Quite the contrary with me. I feel liberated by this endless space." Bernard Le Bovier de Fontenelle, *Entretiens sur la pluralité des mondes* (1686; Paris: Marcel Didier, 1968), p. 135.

40. Bernard Williams, *Ethics and the Limits of Philosophy* (Cambridge: Harvard University Press, 1985), pp. 136–37.

41. George Louis Leclerc, Comte de Buffon, "Discours," in *Oeuvres Complètes* (Paris, 1778), vol. I, p. 11.

42. Georges Gusdorf, *Dieu, la nature, l'homme au siècle des lumières* (Paris: Payot, 1972), pp. 270–73. Gusdorf's assessment of Buffon's significance deserves to be read in its entirety (pp. 251–81).

43. "Le boeuf," in *Histoire Naturelle,* vol. IV.

44. "Première vue de la nature," in *Oeuvres Philosophiques de Buffon* (Paris: Presses Universitaires de France, 1954), p. 34.

45. *Les Epoques de la Nature* (1778). This work appears as vols. XIV–XXIV of the *Oeuvres Complètes.* The introduction to it appears separately in *Oeuvres Philosophiques de Buffon,* p. 118. (Henceforth *Epoques.*)

46. On the history of *form,* one may consult my *Passage to Modernity* (New Haven: Yale University Press, 1993), chaps. 1 and 2.

47. "Système nouveau de la nature et de la communication des substances," orig. pub. in *Journal des Savans,* June 27, 1695, in *Die philosophischen Schriften von G. W. Leibniz,* ed. C. I. Gerhardt (Berlin 1875–90) (henceforth *Schriften*), vol. IV, p. 478; "New System of Nature," trans. in *Leibniz Selections,* ed. Philip Wiener (New York: Scribner, 1951), pp. 107–8.

48. *Discours de métaphysique,* in *Schriften,* vol. IV, p. 434; *Discourse on Metaphysics,* in *Leibniz Selections,* pp. 302–3.

49. In an article in the *Journal des Savans* (June 18, 1691), Leibniz shows how extension cannot possibly account for the resistance to motion (the natural inertia) of bodies: "If there were nothing more in bodies than extension or position, that is to say, what geometers know about it, combined with the sole notion of change, this extension would be entirely indifferent with respect to this change, and the results of the impact of the bodies would be explained solely by the geometric composition of the motions. That is, the body after the impact would continue with a motion composed of the impulsion it had before the impact and the one it would receive from the colliding body in failing to stop its motion; that is to say, in this case of collision, it would travel with the difference of the velocities and in the resultant direction." *Schriften*, vol. IV, pp. 464–65; *Leibniz Selections*, p. 101.

50. "Third Letter to Clarke," # 4, in *Schriften*, vol. VII, p. 363; *Leibniz Selections*, p. 223.

51. "Fifth Letter to Clarke," # 29, in *Schriften*, vol. VII, p. 395; *Leibniz Selections*, p. 246.

52. Ibid., # 52, in *Schriften*, vol. VII, p. 403; *Leibniz Selections*, p. 256. Also: "Absolutely speaking it appears that God can make the material universe finite in extension; but the opposite appears more agreeable to his wisdom" (# 30).

53. Ibid., # 106, in *Schriften*, vol. VII, p. 415; *Leibniz Selections*, p. 273.

54. Ibid., # 49, in *Schriften*, vol. VII, p. 402; *Leibniz Selections*, p. 255.

55. Ibid., # 55 in *Schriften*, vol. VII, p. 405; *Leibniz Selections*, p. 258.

56. Ibid., # 74, in *Schriften*, vol. VII, p. 408; *Leibniz Selections*, p. 263.

57. *Nouveaux Essais sur l'Entendement Humain*, in *Schriften*, vol. V, pp. 138 and 116; *New Essays Concerning Human Understanding*, trans. A. G. Langley (Lasalle: Open Court, 1949).

58. Newton, *Opticks*, Question 31, p. 402.

59. Leibniz, "First Letter to Clarke," in *Schriften*, vol. VII, p. 358; *Leibniz Selections*, p. 216.

60. In his *Rules for the Direction of the Mind* Descartes had argued that a rational investigation requires that we break the data of knowledge down into simple elements. In so doing the mind attains principles that are intuitively certain and from which reliable propositions may immediately be deduced. This analysis enables the mind to know the *simple natures,* the ultimate, ideal elements of the real. René Descartes, *Regulae ad directionem ingenii* (Rules for the direction of the mind), in *Oeuvres de Descartes,* ed. C. Adam and P. Tannery (Paris, 1897–1913), vol. X, p. 370 (rule 3) and p. 418 (rule 12).

61. *Monadologie*, # 8, in *Schriften*, vol. VI, p. 608; *Leibniz Selections*, p. 534. The notion of monad as Leibniz conceived of it may have come from the physiologist and theosophist J. B. Van Helmont (Brussels, 1577–1644), who assumed the existence of a neutral element in the cells that acted as a conductor of all the others.

62. "Système nouveau de la nature et de la communication des substances," in *Schriften*, vol. IV, p. 483; "New System of Nature," *Leibniz Selections*, pp. 112–13.

63. *Discours de Métaphysique*, in *Schriften*, vol. IV, # XV, p. 440; *Discourse on Metaphysics*, in *Leibniz Selections*, pp. 311–12.

64. *Nouveaux Essais*, preface, in *Schriften*, vol. V, p. 46; *New Essays Concerning Human Understanding*, trans. A. G. Langley, in *Leibniz Selections*, p. 390. See also Letter

to De Volder (January 21, 1704), in *Schriften,* vol. II, p. 262; and the clear assertion to Bayle, "Without that force [of acting] it would not be a substance" (vol. III, p. 58; *Leibniz Selections,* p. 181).

65. Letter to De Volder (March 24/April 3, 1699), in *Schriften,* vol. II, p. 169; *Leibniz Selections,* p. 158.

66. "Principes de la nature et de la grâce," # 1, in *Schriften,* vol. VI, p. 598; "Principles of Nature and Grace," in *Philosophical Works of Leibniz* (New Haven: Tuttle, Morehouse, and Taylor, 1890), p. 209 (corrected).

67. Immanuel Kant, *Prolegomena zu einer jedigen künftigen Metaphysik,* in *Kants Gesammelte Schriften,* vol. IV, §§ 14, 16, pp. 294–95; *Prolegomena to Any Future Metaphysics,* trans. Paul Carus, rev. by James W. Ellington (Indianapolis: Hacket, 1976), pp. 38–39.

68. Immanuel Kant, *De mundi sensibilis atque intelligibilis forma et principiis,* in *Kants Gesammelte Schriften,* vol. II, § 22 Scholion.

69. Immanuel Kant, *Die metaphysischen Anfangsgründe der Naturwissenschaft,* in *Kants Gesammelte Schriften,* vol. IV, p. 468; *Metaphysical Foundations of Natural Science,* trans. James Ellington (Indianapolis: Bobbs-Merrill, 1970), p. 4.

Chapter 3. A New Sense of Selfhood

1. David Hume, *A Treatise of Human Nature,* ed. L. A. Selby-Bigge (Oxford University Press, [1896] 1951), p. 253.

2. Immanuel Kant, *Kritik der reinen Vernunft,* in *Kants Gesammelte Schriften* (Berlin: Preussische Akademie, 1902–42), vol. IV, A 804–5/B 832–33; *Critique of Pure Reason,* trans. Norman Kemp Smith (London: Macmillan, 1929; New York: St. Martin's Press, 1965), p. 635.

3. Kant, *Logik,* in *Kants Gesammelte Schriften,* vol. IX, p. 25.

4. On the complicated question of the terminology of *subject* and *substance,* cf. Rudolf Boehm, *Kritik der Grundlagen des Zeitalters* (The Hague: Martinus Nijhoff, 1974), # 26. Also Edward Pols, *Mind Regained* (Ithaca: Cornell University Press, 1998), pp. 105–10.

5. How radically the term "subject" came to vary from "substance" in the course of modern thought appears in Hegel's famous statement in the preface to the *Phenomenology of Spirit:* "That Substance is essentially Subject, is expressed in the representation of the Absolute as Spirit, the most sublime Notion and the one which belongs to the modern age and its religion." G. W. F. Hegel, *Phänomenologie des Geistes* (Hamburg: Felix Meiner, 1952), p. 24.; *Phenomenology of Spirit,* trans. A. V. Miller (New York: Oxford University Press, 1977), p. 14.

6. Michel Foucault, *Les mots et les choses* (Paris: Gallimard, 1966), trans. as *The Order of Things* (New York: Random House, 1970), p. 14.

7. Paul Ricoeur, *Soi-même comme un autre* (Paris: Editions du Seuil, 1990); *Oneself as Another,* trans. Kathleen Blamey (Chicago: University of Chicago Press, 1992).

8. Kant, *Kritik der reinen Vernunft,* in *Kants Gesammelte Schriften,* vol. IV, A 349–50 (henceforth abridged in the text as *KRV*); *Critique of Pure Reason,* trans. Smith, pp. 333–34. I have used this translation throughout my work; it refers to the pages in the German edition, both the first (A) and the second (B). Cf. Carlo Frigerio, "Kant's Metaphysics of

the Subject and Modern Society," in *South-African Journal of Philosophy* 8 (November 1989): 176–81.

9. Hume, *Treatise of Human Nature,* p. 253.

10. Leslie Stephen, "English Literature and Society in the Eighteenth Century," in *Selected Writings in British Intellectual History,* ed. Noel Annan (Chicago: University of Chicago Press, 1979), p. 126.

11. George Berkeley, *A Treatise Concerning the Principles of Human Knowledge,* in *The Works of George Berkeley,* ed. A. A. Luce and T. E. Jessop (London: Nelson, 1948), vol. II, p. 84.

12. Berkeley, *Commonplace Book* (notes published in 1871), G. A. Johnston edition (London: Faber and Faber, 1930), # 660. See Risieri Frondizi, *The Nature of the Self* (Carbondale: Southern Illinois University Press, 1953), pp. 55–77.

13. When the Puritan theologian Samuel Johnson asked him, How could there be consciousness after death if perception ceases with death? Berkeley responded that the soul could continue to perceive independently of the body. An odd answer for an empiricist! Letter to Samuel Johnson of November 25, 1729 in *Works of George Berkeley,* vol. II, p. 282.

14. Hume, *Treatise of Human Nature,* bk. I, 4, 6.

15. P. Butcharov, "The Self and Perceptions: A Study of Humean Philosophy," *Philosopical Quarterly* 9 (1959): 97–115.

16. Ibid., p. 115.

17. In Marxist philosophy the priority of a socially determined *praxis* so far eclipsed the individual moral agent that it all but eliminated the notion of moral subject. Cf. Louis Dupré, *Marx's Social Critique of Culture* (New Haven: Yale University Press, 1983), esp. pp. 1–14.

18. Baron d'Holbach, *Système de la nature* (Amsterdam, 1770); *The System of Nature: With Notes by Diderot,* trans. H. D. Robinson (New York: Burt Franklin, 1868; repr. 1970), p. 11.

19. Mechanism made further inroads upon anthropology as the physiology of the brain progressed. A major step in that direction was Prochaska's and Galvani's theory of the *vis nervosa.* Cf. Daniel Robinson, *The Enlightened Machine* (New York: Columbia University Press, 1980), esp. pp. 13–17.

20. Julien Offray de la Mettrie, *L'homme machine: Man a Machine.* Original French text of 1748 and trans. by Gertrude Bussey and M. W. Calkins (La Salle, Ill.: Open Court, 1993; orig. pub. 1912), p. 135.

21. Diderot, *Le rêve de d'Alembert,* in *Oeuvres,* ed. Laurent Versini (Paris: Robert Lafont, 1994–66), vol. I, p. 617–18; *Diderot's Selected Writings,* trans. Lester Crocker (New York: Macmillan, 1966), p. 186.

22. Buffon, *Histoire Naturelle,* bk. II (1749).

23. Cf. Leopold Damrosch, *God's Plot and Man's Stories: Studies in the Fictional Imagination from Milton to Fielding* (Chicago: Chicago University Press, 1985). See also Ian Watt, *The Rise of the Novel* (Berkeley: University of California Press, 1960), pp. 75–77.

24. Georges Gusdorf, *Dieu, la nature, l'homme au siècle des lumières* (Paris: Payot, 1972), p. 80.

25. Shaftesbury, *Miscellaneous,* chap. 1, in *Characteristics of Men, Manners, Opinions,* ed. John M. Robertson (Gloucester, Mass.: Peter Smith, 1963), vol. II, p. 275.

26. Nivelle de la Chaussée, *Mélanide,* I, 4.

27. Cf. Jean Mesnard, "Le classicisme français et l'expression de la sensibilité," in *Expression, Communication, and Experience in Literature and Language,* ed. Ronald G. Popperwell (Modern Humanities Research Association, 1973), pp. 28–37. Also Rainer Baasner, *Der Begriff Sensibilité im 18. Jahrhundert: Aufsteig und Niedergang eines Ideals* (Heidelberg: C. Winters, 1988).

28. Descartes, *Traité des passions* (Article 50), in *Oeuvres de Descartes,* ed. C. Adam and P. Tannery (Paris, 1897–1913) (henceforth abridged to AT), vol. XI; pp. 368–70; *The Passions of the Soul,* trans. Elizabeth Haldane and G. R. T. Ross in *The Philosophical Works of Descartes* (New York: Cambridge University Press, 1970; orig. pub. 1911), vol. I, p. 348.

29. Descartes, Letter to Mesland, AT, vol. IV, p. 119; also Letter to Princess Elisabeth (September 1, 1645), AT, 286–87. On the difference between Descartes's theory of passions and the Stoic one, cf. Charles Taylor, *Sources of the Self* (Cambridge: Harvard University Press, 1989), pp. 148–52.

30. Spinoza held that all passions could be converted into actions (*Ethica,* V, 3).

31. Pierre Corneille, *Examen du Cid* (1660), in *Oeuvres Complètes de Corneille* (Paris: Macmillan, 1963), p. 219.

32. Ian Donaldson, "Cato in Tears: Social Guises of the Man of Feeling," in *Studies in the Eighteenth Century,* ed. R. F. Brissenden (Canberra: Australian National University Press, 1973), vol. II, pp. 377–95. See also R. S. Crane, "Suggestions Towards a Genealogy of the Man of Feeling," *ELH: A Journal of English Literary History* 1 (1934): 205–30.

33. David Hume, "The Stoic," in *Essays — Moral, Political, and Literary* (1777; Indianapolis: Liberty Classics, 1985), p. 151.

34. Abbé Prévost, *Manon Lescaut,* in *Oeuvres de Prévost* (Paris: Boulland-Tardieu, 1823), vol. III, p. 335.

35. Prévost, *Mémoires et avantures d'un homme de qualité,* in *Oeuvres de Prévost,* vol. I, p. 281. Cf. the chapter on emotions in Abraham Keller and Geoffrey Atkinson, *Prelude to the Enlightenment: French Literature, 1690–1740* (Seattle: University of Washington Press, 1970), pp. 25–81.

36. Jean-Jacques Rousseau, *Confessions,* in *Oeuvres Complètes,* ed. Bernard Gagnebin and Marcel Raymond (Paris: Ed. de la Pléiade), vol. I; trans. J. M. Cohen, p. 103.

37. Samuel Johnson, "The Life of Pope," *Lives of the Poets* (1779–81), in *The Works of Samuel Johnson* (London, 1787), vol. IV, p. 97. One of the enticements of the epistolary novel is that each statement made by the correspondent must remain open to the reader's probing.

38. Lytton Strachey, "Two Frenchmen," originally published in *Characters and Commentaries* (1933), republished in *Literary Essays* (New York: Harcourt Brace, n.d.), p. 104.

39. Alphonse De Waelhens, *Le Duc de Saint-Simon* (Brussels: Facultés Universitaires Saint-Louis, 1981).

40. Duc de Saint-Simon, *Historical Memoirs,* ed. and trans. Lucy Norton, 2 vols. (New York: McGraw-Hill, 1967), vol. I (1691–1709), p. 410.

41. Thomas Carlyle, "Boswell's Life of Johnson," in *Fraser's Magazine* (1820), republished in *Carlyle's Works* (Boston: Dana Estes, 1895), vol. II, p. 408.

42. Johnson, "Life of Pope."

43. James Boswell, *Life of Samuel Johnson* (1791; Oxford: Clarendon Press, 1887), vol. III, p. 332.

44. Carlyle, "Boswell's Life of Johnson," p. 415.

45. Thomas B. Macaulay, "Samuel Johnson," *Edinburgh Review,* 1831, republished in *The Pocket University* (New York: Doubleday, 1925), vol. II, pp. 30–34.

46. *Discours de la Méthode,* in AT, vol. VI, p. 4; *The Philosophical Writings of Descartes,* trans. John Cottingham, Robert Stoothoff, and Dugald Murdoch (Cambridge University Press, 1984), vol. I, p. 112.

47. *The Autobiography of Giambattista Vico,* trans. Max Harold Fisch and Thomas Goddard Bergin (Ithaca: Cornell University Press, 1944), p. 111.

48. Donald Verene, *Vico's Autobiography* (Oxford: Clarendon Press, 1991), chap. 5. In this excellent study of Vico's autobiography, Donald Verene compares the stages of Vico's life to the cycles of history in *The New Science* (*La scienze nuova,* 1744).

49. Giuseppe Mazzotta, *The New Map of the World: The Poetic Philosophy of Giambattista Vico* (Princeton: Princeton University Press, 1999), pp. 20–21.

50. *Autobiography of Giambattista Vico,* p. 111.

51. Andrea Battistini, *Lo Specchio di Dedalo: Autobiografia e Biografia* (Bologna: Il Mulino, 1990), pp. 83–84.

52. Jean-Jacques Rousseau, *Confessions,* in *Oeuvres Complètes* (Paris: Ed. de la Pléiade, 1957), vol. V, p. 5; trans. J. M. Cohen (Baltimore: Penguin Books, n.d.), p. 17. Henceforth abridged to O.C. and Cohen.

53. "I had always been amused at Montaigne's false ingenuousness, and at his pretence of confessing his faults while taking good care only to admit the likeable ones; whereas I, who believe, and always have believed, that I am on the whole the best of men, felt that there is no human heart, however pure, that does not conceal some odious vice." *Confessions,* bk. X, in O.C., I, 516; Cohen, p. 479.

54. Abbé Prévost, *Manon Lescaut* in *Oeuvres de Prévost,* vol. III, p. 480.

55. Jean Starobinski, *Rousseau: La transparence et l'obstacle* (Paris: Gallimard, 1971), pp. 237–38.

56. Starobinski, *Rousseau,* esp. chap. 8, "Les problemes de l'autobiographie," pp. 216–39.

57. Jean-Jacques Rousseau, *Les rêveries du promeneur solitaire,* in O.C., I, 1024.

58. From another autobiographical fragment first published in *Annales J. J. Rousseau* IV (1908), in O.C., I, 1149.

59. Charles Augustin Sainte-Beuve, "Les Confessions de Jean Jacques Rousseau," in *Causeries du lundi* (November 4, 1850) (Paris: Garnier, 1919), vol. III, pp. 78–79; *Sainte-Beuve Selected Essays,* trans. Francis Steegmuller and Norbert Guterman (New York: Doubleday, 1963), pp. 207–8.

60. Augustine, *De Trinitate,* 15, 12, 22.

61. Cf. Werner Beierwaltes, "Zu Augustins Metaphysik der Sprache" *Augustinian Studies* 2 (1971): 181–82.

62. Leibniz, "Towards a Universal Characteristic," in *Die philosophischen Schriften von G. W. Leibniz,* ed. C. I. Gerhardt (Berlin, 1875–90), vol. VII, pp. 184–89; *Leibniz Selections,* ed. Philip Wiener (New York: Scribner, 1951), pp. 17–25. Cf. Ernst Cassirer, *The Philosophy of Symbolic Forms,* trans. Ralph Manheim (New Haven: Yale University Press, 1953), vol. I, *Language,* pp. 129–32.

63. *Logique ou l'art de penser* (1662), ed. L. Martin (Paris, 1970), p. 64.

64. George Berkeley, *A Treatise Concerning the Principles of Human Knowledge,* in *Works of George Berkeley,* vol. II, p. 32.

65. János Kelemen, "Locke's Theory of Language and Semiotics," *Language Sciences* 38 (April 1976): 16–24. The quoted text appears on p. 21.

66. Shaftesbury, "Soliloquy or Advice to an Author," in *Characteristics,* ed. Robertson, I, 135.

67. James Harris, *Hermes, or a Philosophical Inquiry Concerning Language and Universal Grammar* (London, 1751), p. 335. Henceforth referred to by page numbers of this edition.

68. Vico still maintains that humans originally expressed themselves through gestures and hieroglyphs that were "naturally" (that is imitatively) related to the objects they signified. Hieroglyphic script statically imitated what gestures dynamically suggested. Giambattista Vico, *The New Science of Giambattista Vico,* trans. Thomas Goddard Bergin and Marx Harold Fish (Ithaca: Cornell University Press, 1984), # 429.

69. Diderot, *Lettre sur les sourds et muets,* in *Oeuvres,* vol. IV, pp. 26–34.

70. Jean-Jacques Rousseau, *Essai sur l'origine des langues,* intro. and notes by Catherine Kintzler (Paris: Flammarion, 1993), p. 58; *On the Origin of Languages,* trans. John H. Moran (Chicago: University of Chicago Press (1966) 1986), p. 9.

71. Starobinski, *Rousseau,* p. 171. See all of chap. 6 (pp. 149–215).

72. Johann Gottfried Herder, *Ueber den Ursprung der Sprache* (1770), in *Herders Sämtliche Werke,* ed. Bernard Suphan (Berlin, 1891), vol. V; trans. Alexander Gode as *Essay on the Origin of Language* (Chicago: University of Chicago Press, 1986; orig. pub. 1966), p. 87. Henceforth referred to by page numbers of the English translation.

73. Johann Georg Hamann, *Golgotha und Scheblimini,* in *Sämtliche Werke,* ed. Joseph Nadler (Vienna: Herder, 1949–57), vol. III, pp. 291–320. See also *Brocken* in *Sämtliche Werke,* vol. III, p. 303, and *Konxompas* in *Sämtliche Werke,* vol. III, p. 227.

74. George Steiner, *After Babel: Aspects of Language and Translation* (Oxford: Oxford University Press, 1975; repr. 1981), p. 72. Steiner rightly refers to the "mystical" nature of Hamann's method.

75. Mikhail Bakhtin, *Esthétique et théorie du roman,* trans. Daria Olivier (Paris: Gallimard, 1978).

Chapter 4. Toward a New Conception of Art

1. Hyppolite Taine, *History of English Literature,* trans. H. Van Laun (Edinburgh: Edmonston and Douglas, 1873), vol. II, p. 307.

2. Louis Martz, *Milton: Poet of Exile* (New Haven: Yale University Press, 1980), chap. 12.

3. For the difference between Virgil's "primary" epic and Milton's secondary one, cf. C. S. Lewis, *A Preface to Paradise Lost* (New York: Oxford University Press, 1961), chaps. 6 and 7.

4. Ian Watt, *The Rise of the Novel; Studies in Defoe, Richardson, and Fielding* (Berkeley: University of California Press, 1960), pp. 13–16, 274–76. Watt distinguishes the more universal (but not idealized!) traits of human nature, which Fielding emphasizes, from the more strictly individualized ones described by Defoe and Richardson.

5. Cf. Hans Frei, *The Eclipse of Biblical Narrative* (New Haven: Yale University Press, 1974), p. 148.

6. Watt, *Rise of the Novel*, p. 128.

7. Maynard Mack in his introduction to the Holt Rinehart and Winston edition of *Joseph Andrews*.

8. Christoph Martin Wieland, *Agathon*, in *Gesammelte Schriften* (Berlin: Weidmann, 1909–54; after 1954, Akademie Verlag), vol. VI (1937). I learned much from Ellis Shookman, *Noble Lies, Slant Truths, Necessary Angels: Aspects of Fictionality in the Novels of C. M. Wieland* (Chapel Hill: University of North Carolina Press, 1997).

9. Christian von Blanckenburg, *Versuch uber den Roman* (1774). Wieland did so again in the satirical *Geschichte der Abderiten* where, however, the weight of the truth question was much lighter and became absorbed within the comprehensive irony of the work.

10. Arnold Hauser, *The Social History of Art*, trans. Stanley Godman (New York: Vintage Books, 1957), vol. II, p. 179.

11. Sainte-Beuve notes the distinction between the earlier definition of a classic in *Le Dictionnaire de l'Académie* (1694): "auteur ancien fort approuvé et qui fait autorité dans la matière qu'il traite," from the one in the later (1835) edition: "ceux qui sont devenus modèles dans une langue." *Causeries du Lundi*, vol. III (Paris: Garnier, n.d.), p. 41. Some literary works became instant "classics" without any link with the ancients. Today a "classic" refers to a work of lasting significance that resists a definitive interpretation and discloses ever-new truth and value. Cf. David Tracy's insightful discussion in *The Analogical Imagination* (New York: Crossroad, 1981), chap. 3.

12. Samuel Johnson, *The Rambler*, # 125.

13. Of course, before the seventeenth century, plastic arts had not even been formally distinct from crafts, even though everyone knew the difference between a great painter and an ordinary craftsman. A similar union had existed between scientific literature written in the vernacular and belles lettres. Galileo, Bacon, Descartes, and Huygens were fine writers as well as great scientists. A number of scientific studies published during the period here considered still reflect some of the former union with art. Buffon, Fontenelle, and Hume belong as much to the history of science as of literature. They continued to write in a literary language. Scientific studies for the most part avoided the dry style, the technical jargon typical of specialized studies in our own time. The *Encyclopédie* constituted in intent as well as in execution the final attempt to unify the various fields of consciousness.

14. Anthony Ashley Cooper, Lord Shaftesbury, *An Essay on the Freedom of Wit and Humor* (IV, 3), in *Characteristics of Men, Manners, Opinions*, ed. John M. Robertson (Gloucester, Mass.: Peter Smith, 1963), vol. I, p. 90. (Henceforth abridged to title, chapter, section, and page in Robertson's edition of *Characteristics*.)

15. Ibid., IV, 3, p. 91.

16. Ibid., IV, 3, p. 94.

17. Shaftesbury, *Advice to an Author*, I, 3, in *Characteristics*, I, 136.

18. Shaftesbury, *The Moralists*, III, 2, in *Characteristics*, II, 131.

19. Shaftesbury, *The Moralists*, II, 2, in *Characteristics*, II, 132.

20. Shaftesbury, *Advice to an Author*, III, in *Characteristics*, I, 217.

21. Francis Hutcheson, *An Inquiry Concerning Beauty, Order, Harmony, Design*. This was the first of the two essays published under the title *Inquiry into the Original of Our Ideas of Beauty and Virtue* (London, 1725). I cite from the separate edition of the first essay by Peter Kivy, in the *Archives of the History of Ideas* (The Hague: Martinus Nijhoff, 1973). I refer to it by section (roman numeral) and subsection (arabic number).

22. David Hume, *A Treatise of Human Nature* (1739), ed. L. A. Selby-Bigge (Oxford: Oxford University Press, 1928; repr. 1955), p. 299.

23. "Art" in *Encyclopédie ou Dictionnaire raisonné des Sciences, des Arts et des Métiers*, vol. I (Paris, 1751); trans. of this and some other articles in *Encyclopedia Selections*, ed. Nelly Hoyt and Thomas Cassirer (Indianapolis: Bobbs-Merrill, 1965), p. 4.

24. Denis Diderot, *Traité du beau*, in *Oeuvres*, ed. Laurent Versini (Paris: Robert Lafont, 1996), IV, 99; *Diderot's Selected Writings*, trans. Lester Crocker (New York: Macmillan, 1966), p. 54.

25. Charles Batteux, *Les Beaux-Arts réduits a un meme principe* (1746) (Paris, 1773), p. 45. Diderot's response: *Lettre sur les sourds et muets*, in *Oeuvres*, IV, 11–50; partial translation in *Diderot's Selected Writings*, pp. 31–39.

26. Johann Joachim Winckelmann, *Gedanken über die Nachahmung der Griechischen Werke in der Malerei und Bildhauerkunst* (Thoughts about the imitation of the Greek works in painting and sculpture) (1755) in *Winckelmanns Werke* (Berlin-Weimar: Aufbau Verlag, 1982), pp. 1–46, esp. 11–14.

27. Tzvetan Todorov, *Theories of the Symbol,* trans. Catherine Porter (Ithaca: Cornell University Press, 1977), p. 113. All of chaps. 4 and 5 is relevant.

28. Diderot weakens his thesis by an ill-directed attempt to translate a poetic composition into a musical one on the inadequate ground that language and music are both temporal arts. Such a translation of one set of symbols into another is possible only in vocal music or in music that *accompanies* moving images, such as Prokovief's masterly accompaniment to Eisenstein's film *Alexander Nevsky* (1938).

29. Arthur M. Wilson, *Diderot* (New York: Oxford University Press, 1972), p. 530.

30. Herbert Dieckman, *Cinq Leçons sur Diderot* (Geneva: E. Droz, 1959), p. 116.

31. Jules Barbey d'Aurevilly, *Goethe et Diderot* (Paris, 1880), p. 176.

32. *Laocoön: An Essay on the Limits of Painting and Poetry* (1766), trans. Edward Allen McCormick (Indianapolis: Bobbs-Merrill, 1962).

33. Although the originality of Lessing with respect to Winckelmann is well established, the relation to Diderot is more complex. In his *Essais sur la peinture*, published the same year as Lessing's *Laocoön* (1766), Diderot writes about the famous statue: "Le Laocoon souffre, il ne grimace pas" (*Oeuvres*, IV, 489). A remark made a few pages later suggests that the reason for avoiding intense expressions in painting may be closely related to the one Lessing invoked. "The painter has only one moment. He can no more cover two moments than two actions" (ibid., p. 496). Elsewhere he condemns La Mettrie

for having himself portrayed while laughing. A person who freezes his epression in a permanent laughter lacks nobility and character, and often truth; hence it is absurd. "Laughter is always passing" (*Essais, Oeuvres,* IV, 507). In the *Pensées détachées sur la peinture* (*Oeuvres,* IV, 1018), Diderot brings up the question of priority between Virgil and the sculptor. Winckelmann had already raised this question. According to Paul Vernière, at that time Diderot knew neither Winckelmann's nor Lessing's writings on the subject (Diderot, *Oeuvres Esthétiques* [Paris: Garnier, 1968], pp. 744, 761).

34. Sir Joshua Reynolds, *Discourses on Art,* ed. and intro. Stephen O. Mitchell (Indianapolis: Bobbs-Merrill, 1964). *Discourse,* III, p. 27. Henceforth abridged to roman numeral for the *Discourse* and arabic for the page number.

35. In fact, the presence of the sublime in land- and seascapes was not fully recognized in England until the time of Cozens and Turner, even though such influential Dutch painters as Ruysdael, Rembrandt, and Van Goyen had intimated it much earlier.

36. "Goût" (Taste), in *Encyclopedia Selections,* ed. Hoyt and Cassirer, p. 337. Henceforth "Goût."

37. Shaftesbury, *Advice to an Author,* III, 3, in *Characteristics,* I, 218.

38. Shaftesbury, *The Moralists,* III, 2, in *Characteristics,* II, 125.

39. Hume, *Treatise of Human Nature,* II, 95.

40. David Hume, "Of the Standard of Taste," in *Essays Moral, Political, and Literary* (Indianapolis: Liberty Classics, 1985), p. 235.

41. Alexander Gottlieb Baumgarten, *Aesthetica* (Hildesheim: Georg Olms Verlag, 1970), § 14. This edition is a reproduction of the original one published in Frankfurt a/d. Oder in 1750. I shall refer to the numbers of the sections, which appear in all editions.

42. This was, of course, the position against which Heidegger reacted. Karsten Harries has discussed the opposition between aesthetic and ontological theories of art in a number of writings, among them *The Meaning of Modern Art* (Chicago: Northwestern University Press, 1968), and "Metaphor and Transcendence," in *On Metaphor,* ed. Seldon Sacks (Chicago: University of Chicago Press, 1979), pp. 71–88.

43. Immanuel Kant, *Kritik der Urteilskraft,* in *Kants Gesammelte Schriften* (Berlin: Preussische Akademie, 1902–42), vol. V. I refer to it by *KUK* and section number. For the first part of the *Critique of Judgment* (§§ 1–21), I quote from Walter Cerf's translation, *Analytic of the Beautiful* (Indianapolis: Bobbs-Merrill, 1963), referred to as *AB,* with Kant's paragraph number and Cerf's page number. Later parts of the *Critique* are from J. H. Bernard's translation (1892; New York: Hafner Press, 1951).

44. Kant, *Prolegomena to Any Future Metaphysics,* § 58; in *Kants Gesammelte Schriften,* vol. IV, p. 357.

45. The same idea is found in Edward Young, *Conjectures on Original Composition* (1759).

46. Joseph Addison, *The Spectator,* # 421 (London: William Tegg, 1867), p. 485.

47. M. de Saint-Lambert and Diderot, "Génie," in *Encyclopédie,* vol. VII, repr. in Diderot, *Oeuvres Esthétiques* (Paris: Garnier, 1968), p. 14. This article does not appear in the Versini edition I have used for Diderot.

48. Alexander Gerard repeated Pope's description in his 1758 and 1759 lectures in Aberdeen and in his *Essay on Taste* (1759) — both of which form the basis of his influential *Essay on Genius* (1774). Cf. Bernhard Fabian, "An Early Theory of Genius: Alex-

ander Gerard's Unpublished Aberdeen Lectures," in *Studies in the Eighteenth Century*, ed. R. F. Brissenden (Canberra: Australian National University Press, 1973), vol. II, pp. 113–41.

49. Gerard, *Aberdeen Lectures*, as quoted by Fabian in "Early Theory of Genius," p. 137.

50. Cf. Hans-Georg Gadamer, *Wahrheit und Methode* (Tübingen: J. C. B. Mohr, 1965), pp. 46–52. See also Pierre Fruchon's insightful commentary in *L'herméneutique de Gadamer: Platonisme et modernité* (Paris: Ed. du Cerf, 1994), pp. 28–38 on taste, and chap. 2 (pp. 39–53) on genius.

51. Longinus, *On Great Writing (On the Sublime)*, trans. G. M. Grube (Indianapolis: Bobbs-Merrill, 1957).

52. Samuel Monk, *The Sublime: A Study of Critical Theories in Eighteenth Century England* (1935; Ann Arbor: University of Michigan Press, 1960). On the literary history of the idea of the sublime in England this remains the primary text.

53. *The Spectator,* # 412 (1712).

54. Cf. Andrew Wilton, *Turner and the Sublime* (New Haven: British Museum Publications, Yale Center for British Art, 1981).

55. These ideas appear both in Diderot's *Pensées philosophiques* and in his *Salons* of 1765. As he often did in writing on aesthetics, Diderot followed the British model but added some perceptive analyses of his own.

56. This is the title of the translation of *Betrachtungen über das Gefühl des Schönen und Erhabenen* made by John T. Goldtwait (Berkeley: University of California Press, 1960).

57. Cf. Paul Crowther, *The Kantian Sublime* (Oxford: Clarendon Press, 1989), pp. 20–21.

58. Paul Guyer, *Kant and the Claims of Taste* (Cambridge: Harvard University Press, 1979), esp. chap. 7, and "Kant's Distinction Between the Beautiful and the Sublime," *Review of Metaphysics* 35, 4, # 140 (June 1982): 753–83.

59. Johann Winckelmann, *Sämtliche Werke,* ed. J. Eiselein (1825), vol. I, p. 207. Johann Wolfgang von Goethe, *Schriften zur Kunst* (Zurich: Artemis, 1949), vol. XIII, p. 417. All texts are cited from the same Artemis edition.

60. Goethe, *Dichtung und Wahrheit*, bk. IV, vol. X, p. 735.

61. Goethe, *Italienische Reise* (September 6, 1787), vol. XI, p. 436.

62. Goethe, *Maximen und Reflectionen*, vol. IX, # 199, p. 518.

63. Ibid., # 1113, p. 639.

Chapter 5. The Moral Crisis

1. Bernard Williams, *Ethics and the Limits of Philosophy* (Cambridge: Harvard University Press, 1985), pp. 148–49.

2. *Ethica ordine geometrico demonstrata*, bk. III, def. 3, in *Spinoza Opera,* ed. Carl Gebhart (Heidelberg: Carl Winters, 1925), vol. II, p. 146. Trans. R. H. M. Elwes in *The Works of Benedict de Spinoza* (London, 1883; New York, 1951). Henceforth abridged to E, followed by book and definition or proposition. All translations taken from Elwes.

3. On the emotions (*affectus*), one may consult Herman De Dijn, "Inleiding tot de

affectleer van Spinoza," *Tijdschrift voor Filosofie* 39 (1977) and Michael Della Rocca's essay "Spinoza's Metaphysical Psychology" in *The Cambridge Companion to Spinoza,* ed. Don Garrett (New York: Cambridge University Press, 1996) pp. 192–266. Also Errol Harris, *Spinoza's Philosophy: An Outline* (Atlantic Highlands, N.J.: Humanities Press, 1992), chap. 9, pp. 399–408.

4. John Locke, *An Essay on Human Understanding,* ed. A. C. Fraser, 2 vols. (Oxford: Oxford University Press, 1894), bk. I, chaps. 2, 3. I shall refer to it as *Essay* followed by book, chapter, and section, which are identical in all editions.

5. Voltaire, Letter to Crown Prince Frederick, quoted in Ernst Cassirer, *The Philosophy of the Enlightenment* (Princeton: Princeton University Press, 1968), pp. 244–45.

6. *Supplément au voyage de Bougainville,* in *Oeuvres Complètes,* ed. Laurent Versini (Paris: Robert Lafont, 1994), II, 552; *Diderot's Selected Writings,* p. 231.

7. In the critical reflection that follows the stories (*Suite du Dialogue*), the question of procreation is omitted altogether.

8. Denis Diderot, *Supplément,* in *Oeuvres,* II, 577; *Diderot's Selected Writings,* p. 250.

9. Diderot, *Supplément,* in *Oeuvres,* II, 547; *Diderot's Selected Writings,* p. 227.

10. Diderot, Letter to Paul Landois, June 29, 1756, in *Oeuvres,* VIII, 8.

11. Jean le Rond d'Alembert, *Essai sur les Elémens de Philosophie* (Paris: Fayard, 1986) p. 66.

12. Paul-Henri, Baron d'Holbach, *The System of Nature* (1770), trans. H. D. Robinson (New York: Burt Franklin, 1970), p. 98.

13. John Locke, *An Essay Concerning Human Understanding,* bk. II, chap. 20.

14. Shaftesbury, Letter to General Stanhope (November 7, 1709), in *The Life, Unpublished Letters and Philosophical Regimen of Anthony, Earl of Shaftesbury,* ed. Benjamin Rand (London: Swan, Sonnenschein, 1900) p. 416.

15. Ibid.

16. Stanley Greane, *Shaftesbury's Philosophy of Religion and Ethics* (Athens: Ohio University Press, 1967), p. 148.

17. *Life, Unpublished Letters . . . of Shaftesbury,* p. 158.

18. Charles Taylor, *Sources of the Self* (Cambridge: Harvard University Press, 1989) p. 257.

19. Ralph Cudworth, *A Treatise Concerning Eternal and Immutable Morality* (Andover, Mass.: Gould and Newman, 1838), bk. I, chap. 2, p. 14.

20. In *The Moralists,* pt. I, 3, in *Characteristics,* II, 22, Shaftesbury reintroduces the spider and fly and admits that only in humans a universal harmony requires disinterested affection for others.

21. Cf. Georges Gusdorf, *Naissance de la conscience romantique au Siècle des Lumières* (Paris: Payot, 1976), pp. 227–28. The entire chapter on Shaftesbury (pp. 219–43) is excellent.

22. Jean-Jacques Rousseau, *Discours sur l'origine de l'inégalité* (1755), in *Oeuvres Complètes* (Paris: Gallimard, La Pléiade, 1964), vol. III; *The Origin of Inequality,* trans. G. D. H. Cole, in *The Social Contract and Discourses* (London: J. M. Dent and Sons, n.d.), p. 199.

23. *Boswell's Life of Johnson,* ed. George Birkbeck Hill (Oxford: Clarendon Press, 1887).

24. Jean-Jacques Rousseau, *Julie, ou la nouvelle Héloïse,* bk. III, letter 15, in *Oeuvres Complètes,* vol. II, p. 335. Henceforth *Julie,* followed by the number of the letter (L).

25. Surprisingly, Rousseau uses this unconventional decision as an occasion for justifying the very conventional custom of prearranged marriages. He dismisses the idea that a good marriage requires passionate love as an illusion. In fact, erotic love is a constant source of unrest, jealousy, and privation, all of which hardly agree with the joy and peace that distinguishes a successful union (*Julie,* bk. III, L20, in *Oeuvres Complètes,* II, 373).

26. Alessandro Ferrara, *Modernity and Authenticity. A Study in the Social and Ethical Thought of Jean-Jacques Rousseau* (Albany: SUNY Press, 1993). Also "Authenticity: A Moral Notion or a Philosophical Horizon?" in *Amsterdam School for Cultural Analysis Yearbook* (Amsterdam: ASCA Press, 1999), pp. 49–68.

27. In an elegant and erudite study, *The Beautiful Soul* (Ithaca: Cornell University Press, 1955), Robert Norton compares Wieland's use of the term *die schöne Seele* in *Agathon* with Rousseau's *belle âme* in *Julie* and shows how the German and the French meanings merge in Romanticism. On Rousseau's morality of the beautiful soul as a substitute for grace, cf. Irving Babbitt, *Rousseau and Romanticism* (1919; Austin: University of Texas Press, 1976), chap. 4 (esp. p. 113).

28. Johann Christoph Friedrich Schiller, *Ueber Anmut und Würde* (On grace and dignity), in *Schillers Werke: Nationalausgabe* (Weimar: H. Böhlaus, 1943ff.), vol. XX, p. 287.

29. Rousseau, Letter to Madame de Francueil on April 20, 1751. Cf. Babbitt, *Rousseau and Romanticism,* p. 129.

30. G. W. F. Hegel, *Phänomenologie des Geistes* (1807; Hamburg: Felix Meiner Verlag, 1955), pp. 461–70; *Phenomenology of Mind,* trans. J. B. Baillie (London: Macmillan, 1931; New York: Harper and Row, 1967), chap. 6, C, pp. 664–75 (the cited words appear on p. 665).

31. Francis Hutcheson, *An Inquiry into the Original of Our Ideas of Beauty and Virtue in Two Treaties: II Concerning Moral Good and Evil* (Glasgow: Robert and Andrew Foulis, 1772), II, 3, and III, 5. I refer to chapter and section.

32. Francis Hutcheson, *A System of Moral Philosophy* (1755) (in two volumes), I, 4, 13 (book, chapter, section), in *Collected Works* (Hildesheim: Olms), vol. V, p. 78. Pleasure taken as a motive can induce only self-interested actions. In the *Essay on the Nature and Conduct of the Passions and Affections with Illustrations on the Moral Sense* (1728), I, 4, 1 (*Collected Works,* vol. V, p. 53), he insists that moral approbation does not coincide with the experience of pleasure that accompanies it.

33. Bernard Mandeville, *Fable of the Bees* (London: J. Roberts, 1729); repr. with commentary by F. B. Kaye (Oxford: Clarendon Press, 1924), pt. II, pp. 356–57.

34. William Law, *A Serious Call to a Devout and Holy Life* (1728), (New York: Paulist Press, 1978), passim. See also his *Remarks upon a Late Book, entitled, The Fable of the Bees* (1724), p. 23.

35. Louis Dumont, *From Mandeville to Marx* (Chicago: University of Chicago Press, 1977), p. 81.

36. Cf. Terence Penelhum, "Hume's Moral Psychology," in *The Cambridge Companion to Hume,* ed. David Fate Norton (Cambridge University Press, 1993), pp. 136–37.

37. David Hume, *A Treatise of Human Nature* (1739), ed. L. A. Selby-Bigge (Oxford: Clarendon Press, 1896), p. 478. Henceforth referred to by book, part, section, and page.

38. David Hume, *An Inquiry Concerning the Principles of Morals,* ed. and intro. Charles Hendel (Indianapolis: Bobbs-Merrill, 1957), appendix I, p. 106.

39. Bernard Wand, "Hume's Account of Obligation," in *Hume, A Collection of Critical Essays,* ed. V. C. Chappell (Garden City, N.Y.: Doubleday, 1966), pp. 308–36.

40. Taylor, *Sources of the Self,* p. 337–40.

41. Immanuel Kant, *Religion innerhalb der Grenzen der blossen Vernunft,* in *Kants Gesammelte Schriften* (Berlin: Preussische Akademie, 1902–42), vol. VI, p. 335. *Religion Within the Limits of Reason Alone,* trans. Theodore M. Greene and Hoyt H. Hudson (New York: Harper and Row, 1960), p. 28.

42. Goethe to Chancellor von Müller, as quoted in Ernst Cassirer, *Kant's Life and Thought,* trans. James Haden (New Haven: Yale University Press, 1981), p. 270.

43. Kant, *Vorlesungen, 1765–66* in *Kants Gesammelte Schriften,* vol. II, p. 311.

44. Kant, *Kritik der praktischen Vernunft,* in *Kants Gesammelte Schriften,* vol. V, p. 38; *Critique of Practical Reason,* trans. Lewis W. Beck (Indianapolis: Bobbs-Merrill, 1956), p. 40. Henceforth referred to as *C.Pr.R.* (English) and Ak (German).

45. Kant, *Kritik der reinen Vernunft,* A 318/B 375, in *Kants Gesammelte Schriften,* vol. III, p. 249; *Critique of Pure Reason,* trans. Norman Kemp Smith (London: Macmillan, 1929), p. 313.

46. *Kritik der reinen Vernunft,* A 548/B 576; *Critique of Pure Reason,* trans. Smith, p. 473.

47. Ibid. A 547/B 575, pp. 472–73.

48. Kant, *Religion innerhalb,* in *Kants Gesammelte Schriften,* vol. VI, p. 26; *Religion Within the Limits,* p. 21.

49. John R. Silber, "Procedural Formalism in Kant's Ethics," *Review of Metaphysics* 28, 2, # 110 (December 1974): 212.

50. Peter Winch, *Ethics and Action* (London: Routledge and Kegan Paul, 1972).

51. G. W. F. Hegel, *Ueber die wissenschaftlichen Behandlungsarten des Naturrechts,* in *Schriften zur Politik und Rechtsphilosophie, Sämtliche Werke,* ed. G. Lasson (Leipzig: Felix Meiner, 1913), VII, 354–61.

52. Christine Korsgaard, "Kant's Formula of Universal Law," *Kant-Studien* 77, 2 (1986): 20.

53. Rousseau, *Emile,* bk. IV. A similar passage, possibly written under the influence of Kant, appears in the second part of Novalis's *Heinrich von Oefterdingen:* "Conscience fills the place of God on earth and is thus the highest and the last. . . . It is the innermost essence of the person in full clarity, the aboriginal, celestial man."

54. Cf. Paul Guyer's brilliant *Kant and the Experience of Freedom: Essays on Aesthetics and Morality* (New York: Cambridge University Press, 1993), pp. 21–30.

55. Kant, *Metaphysische Anfangsgründe der Tugendlehre,* in *Kants Gesammelte Schriften,* vol. VI, p. 443; *The Metaphysical Principles of Virtue,* trans. James Ellington (Indianapolis: Bobbs-Merrill, 1964), p. 106. Henceforth abridged as *Virtue* with number and page of the English translation, followed by the Akademie edition volume and page number.

56. Kant, *Kritik der Urteilskraft,* in *Kants Gesammelte Schriften,* vol. V, p. 60; *Critique of Judgment,* trans. J. H. Bernard (New York: Hafner Press, 1951), § 60. Henceforth referred to as *C.J.* followed by the paragraph number (identical in all editions and transla-

tions). Today we have the more acccurate translations of Kant's *Critique* by Paul Guyer and Allen Wood. This text was completed before their appearances.

57. Kant, *Foundations of the Metaphysics of Morals,* trans. Lewis White Beck (Indianapolis: Bobbs-Merrill, 1969).

58. Kant, "An Old Question Raised Again," in *Kant on History,* ed. Lewis White Beck (Indiapolis: Bobbs-Merrill, 1963), p. 140; *Kants Gesammelte Schriften,* vol. VIII, p. 82. Here, as in other instances, we notice how strongly Kant's later views on ethics were influenced by his concept of history. His anthropology had, of course, marked his ethical writings early and late. Cf. Allen Wood, *Kant's Ethical Thought* (New York: Cambridge University Press, 1999).

59. Michel Foucault, *The Order of Things,* trans. of *Les mots et les choses* (New York: Random House, 1973), p. 328.

60. Emmanuel Levinas, "Philosophy and the Idea of the Infinite," trans. Alfonso Lingis, in *Levinas's Collected Papers. Phaenomenologica,* vol. C (Dordrecht: Nijhoff, 1987). See Adriaan Peperzak's excellent commentary in *To the Other: An Introduction to the Philosophy of Emmanuel Levinas* (West Lafayette, Ind.: Purdue University Press, 1993) pp. 94–95.

61. Lucien Goldmann, *Le Dieu caché: Etude sur la vision tragique dans les Pensées de Pascal et dans le théâtre de Racine* (Paris: Gallimard, 1959).

62. George Steiner, *The Death of Tragedy* (London, 1961), p. 53.

63. *Andromaque,* V, 5, in *The Complete Plays of Jean Racine,* trans. Samuel Solomon (New York: Random House, 1967), vol. I, p. 316.

64. Leslie Stephen, "English Literature and Society in the Eighteenth Century," in *Selected Writings in British Intellectual History,* ed. Noel Annan (Chicago: University of Chicago Press, 1979) pp. 146–47.

65. Friedrich Melchior, Baron de Grimm, *Correspondance littéraire, philosophique et critique* (Paris: Longchamps, 1812–13), 16 vols., vol. XII, p. 49.

66. Cf. Gustave Lanson, *Nivelle de la Chaussée et la comédie larmoyante* (Paris: Hachette, 1887). Nivelle may count as the most successful but one of the least memorable among many undistinguished practitioners of the genre.

67. Diderot, *De la poésie dramatique,* in *Oeuvres,* IV, 1283.

68. The passage is quoted in Herder's *Briefe zu Beförderung der Humanität,* # 72. I have not succeeded in locating it in Diderot's *Oeuvres Complètes,* but both the message and the wording allow no doubt about its authenticity.

69. Edward Young, preface to *Love of Fame,* quoted in Thomas Maresca, *Pope's Horatian Poems* (Columbus: Ohio State University Press, 1966), p. 9. The first two chapters of Maresca's study sketch a useful development of satire.

70. Northrop Frye, *The Anatomy of Criticism* (Princeton: Princeton University Press, 1957), p. 223.

Chapter 6. The Origin of Modern Social Theories

1. Terence Marshall, "Leo Strauss et la question des Anciens et des Modernes," *Cahiers de Philosophie Politique et Juridique* 23 (1993): 68–69. Cf. also Leo Strauss, *Natural Right and History* (Chicago: University of Chicago Press, 1953), esp. chaps. 3 and 4.

2. John Finnis, *Natural Law and Natural Rights* (New York: Oxford University Press, 1980), pp. 375–76.

3. A. P. d'Entrèves, *Natural Law: An Historical Survey* (1951; New York: Harper and Row, 1965), pp. 30–31. Emphasis mine. See also James B. Murphy, "Nature, Custom, and Stipulation in Law and Jurisprudence," *Review of Metaphysics* 43 (June 1990): 751–90.

4. Marcus Tulius Cicero, *De republica,* III, 22.

5. Thomas Aquinas, *Summa Theologiae,* trans. Dominican Fathers of the English Dominican Province (London: Burns, Oates, and Washbourne, 1920). Multiple editions with revisions.

6. Otto Gierke, *Natural Law and the Theory of Society, 1500 to 1800* (1913), trans. and intro. Ernest Barker (Cambridge: Cambridge University Press, 1934; repr. Boston: Beacon Press, 1951), p. 97.

7. John Locke, *An Essay Concerning the True Original, Extent and End of Civil Government,* II, § 6. I have used Sir Ernest Barker's edition in *Social Contract* (New York: Oxford University Press, 1960). Henceforth referred to by chapter (roman numeral) and paragraph.

8. John Dunn, *The Political Thought of John Locke* (Cambridge: Cambridge University Press, 1969), p. 97.

9. Jeremy Waldron, *The Dignity of Legislation* (New York: Cambridge University Press, 1997, chap. 5.

10. David Walsh, *The Growth of the Liberal Soul* (Columbia: University of Missouri Press, 1997), pp. 128–29; I have followed Walsh's and Dunn's interpretation of the state of nature.

11. Brian Tierney, *The Idea of Natural Rights: Studies on Natural Rights, Natural Law and Church Law, 1150–1625.* (Atlanta: Scholars Press, 1997; Grand Rapids: Wm. B. Eerdmans, 2001). On the significance of the dispute on poverty, see also Richard Tuck, *Natural Rights Theories: Their Origin and Development* (Cambridge: Cambridge University Press, 1979), pp. 18–23.

12. James B. Murphy, "Nature, Custom, and Stipulation," *Review of Metaphysics* 43 (1990): 751–90. The same idea underlies much of his *The Moral Economy of Labor: Aristotelian Themes in Economic Theory* (New Haven: Yale University Press, 1993).

13. "What Is Fair" is John Finnis's translation in *Natural Law and Natural Rights,* p. 206. I do not think, however, as Finnis does, that Aquinas's concept of *jus* corresponds in all respects to the Roman interpretation of it.

14. Alasdair MacIntyre, "Community Law, and the Idiom and Rhetoric of Rights," *Listening* 26, no. 2 (spring 1991): 96–110 (quote on p. 105). Also *After Virtue,* chap. 6.

15. Frans De Wachter, "Ethiek en mensenrechten," *Tijdschrift voor Filosofie* 49, no. 4 (1987): 586.

16. Thomas Hobbes, *Leviathan* (1651; Baltimore: Penguin Books, 1968), chap. 14, p. 189.

17. Benedict de Spinoza, *Tractatus Politicus,* chap. 2, § 3, in *Spinoza Opera,* ed. Carl Gebhardt (Heidelberg: Carl Winters, 1925), vol. III, pp. 276–77.

18. Spinoza, *Tractatus,* chap. 2, § 15, in *Opera,* p. 281.

19. Karl Marx, *Grundrisse* (Berlin: Dietz Verlag, 1953), pp. 391 and 384; trans. Martin Nicolaus (Baltimore: Pelican Books, 1973), pp. 491 and 485.

20. Jeffrie Murphy, *Kant: The Philosophy of Right* (London: Macmillan, 1970), p. 125.

21. Gierke, *Natural Law and the Theory of Society,* p. 113.

22. Bentham, who had supported the revolutions in America and France, criticized the declarations of inalienable rights proclaimed in Virginia and Carolina as rendering penal laws invalid since such "inalienable" rights would prevent them from executing or incarcerating criminals and even from depriving them of property. Elie Halévy, *The Growth of Political Radicalism,* trans. Mary Morris (New York: Augustus M. Kelley, 1972), p. 174.

23. Edmund Burke, *Reflections on the Revolution in France* (1790; New York: Doubleday-Anchor Books, 1973), p. 72.

24. Gierke, *Natural Law and the Theory of Society,* p. 101.

25. Donald W. Hanson, *From Kingdom to Commonwealth* (Cambridge: Harvard University Press, 1970), p. 318.

26. Charles-Louis de Secondat, Baron de Montesquieu, *Lettres persanes,* in *Oeuvres Complètes* (Paris: La Pléiade, 1949), vol. I, p. 269.

27. Jean-Jacques Rousseau, *Discours sur l'origine et les fondemens de l'inégalité parmi les hommes,* in *Oeuvres Complètes* (Paris: La Pléiade, 1964), vol. III, *Ecrits Politiques,* p. 152; *A Discourse on the Origins of Inequality Among Men,* trans. G. D. H. Cole (London: J. M. Dent, n.d.), p. 195.

28. Rousseau, *Discours,* p. 164; Cole, p. 207. Rousseau's view may have been influenced by Montesquieu's claim that as soon as humans enter society equality ceases and the state of war sets in. Charles-Louis de Secondat, Baron de Montesquieu, *L'esprit des lois,* bk. I, chap. 3 in *Oeuvres Complètes* (Paris: La Pléiade, 1951), vol. II, p. 236. The link between the beginning of social life and the origin of inequality was not universally accepted. Helvetius rejected it.

29. Jean-Jacques Rousseau, *Du contrat social* (I, 4), in *Oeuvres Complètes,* vol. III, p. 356; *Social Contract,* trans. Ernest Barker (New York: Oxford University Press, 1960), p. 174. Henceforth abridged as *SC* followed by chapter and section; they are identical in all editions.

30. Montesquieu, *L'esprit des lois,* in bk. XV, 2 and bk. VIII, 3, in *Oeuvres Complètes* (Paris: NRF, La Pléiade, 1949), vol. II, pp. 491–92 and p. 352.

31. Robert Derathé, *Jean-Jacques Rousseau et la science politique de son temps* (Paris: Presses Universitaires de France, 1950), p. 168.

32. Marsiglio of Padua, *Defensor minor,* 12, 5. In *Writings on the Empire,* ed. Cary Nederman (New York: Cambridge University Press, 1993).

33. Jean-Jacques Rousseau, *Discours sur l'économie politique* (1755), in *Oeuvres Complètes,* vol. III, p. 277; "A Discourse on Political Economy," in *The Social Contract and Discourses by Jean-Jacques Rousseau* (London: J. M. Dent, n.d; New York: E. P. Dutton), p. 278.

34. Robert Derathé, "Introduction to *Contrat Social,*" in Rousseau, *Oeuvres Complètes,* vol. III, p. xcviii. It is worth noting how far Rousseau's position stands from modern liberalism, which he in other respects influenced. While the liberal idea implies that the choice of values be left to the individuals, for Rousseau the primary task of education is to instill values conducive to the state's well-being.

35. Rousseau, Letter written to Johann Martin Usteri in 1763, as quoted in Lucio Colletti, *From Rousseau to Lenin* (New York: Monthly Review Press, 1972), p. 177.

36. Cf. Niklas Luhman, "Grundwerte als Zivilreligion," in Heinz Kleger and Alois Müller, eds., *Religion der Bürger: Zivilreligion in Amerika und Europa* (Munich: C. Kaiser, 1986), pp. 175–94. An excellent analysis of the relation between religion and civil society is Inigo Bocken, "Bij gratie van de burger: Religie en burgerlijke maatschappij," in Jaap Grappelaar, ed., *Burgers en hun bindingen* (Budel: Damon, 2000), pp. 75–128.

37. On "civil society," cf. Manfred Riedel, "Der Begriff der 'Bürgerlichen Gesellschaft' und das Problem seines geschichtlichen Ursprungs" in *Studien in Hegels Rechtsphilosophie* (Frankfurt: Suhrkamp, 1969).

38. Henri Denis, "Deux collaborateurs de l'Encyclopédie: Quesnay et Rousseau," *La Pensée* 38 (1951): 44–45.

39. Michael Halberstam, *Liberalism, Totalitarianism, and the Aesthetic* (New Haven: Yale University Press, 2000), p. 133. Also, Hannah Arendt, "On the Nature of Totalitarianism," in *Essays in Understanding* (New York: Harcourt, Brace, 1994), pp. 328ff.

40. Barker, Introduction to *Social Contract*, p. xxxix.

41. Montesquieu, *De l'esprit des lois,* in *Oeuvres Complètes de Montesquieu,* annotated by Roger Caillois (Paris: La Pléiade, 1949 and 1951), 2 vols.; *The Spirit of Laws,* trans. Thomas Nugent and rev. J. V. Prichard (London: G. Bell and Sons, 1873; repr. Chicago: University of Chicago Press, 1952). I shall use this translation throughout and refer to passages by book (roman numeral) and chapter (arabic). Because of the many editions of *L'esprit des lois* available in French and English, page numbers are neither practical nor needed; most chapters are short and many do not exceed one paragraph.

42. Gian Vincenzo Gravina, *Origines juris civilis* (1717). This pioneering work influenced both Vico and Montesquieu.

43. Montesquieu, "Essai d'observations sur l'histoire naturelle" (1719–21), in *Oeuvres Complètes,* vol. I, p. 39. In *The Spirit of Laws* he appears less certain. "Whether brutes be governed by the general laws of motion, or by a particular movement I cannot determine" (*SL,* I, 1).

44. Montesquieu, *Considérations sur les causes de la grandeur des Romains et de leur décadence,* chap. 18. Our remarks concern only secular history, because in chaps. 16 and 22 of the *Considérations* (1734) he appears to admit a direct providential intervention in the establishment and maintenance of the Christian faith. But one may question the sincerity of this distinction. Cf. Robert Shackleton, *Montesquieu: A Critical Biography* (Oxford: Oxford University Press, 1961), pp. 162–63.

45. Cf. Sharon Krause, "The Spirit of Separate Powers in Montesquieu," *Review of Politics* 62, no. 2 (spring 2000): 231–65.

46. Gustave Lanson, *Histoire de la littérature française* (Paris: Hachette, 1894; numerous reprints), p. 706. See also Henri Auguste Barckhausen's manful yet not altogether successful attempt to show the presence of a consistent order in *L'esprit des lois,* in the chapter entitled, "Le désordre de l'Esprit des Lois," in *Montesquieu, ses idées et ses oevres* (Paris 1907).

47. Shackleton, *Montesquieu,* p. 318.

48. How much significance Montesquieu attached to this chapter appears from the effort he put into it. "For three months I thought I was going to kill myself in the writing of a book on *The Origins and Evolutions of Our Civil Laws.* It will take three hours to

read it, but I assure you that under the amount of work my hair has turned white" (Letter to Msgr. Cerate, March 28, 1748).

49. Adam Smith, *An Inquiry into the Nature and Causes of the Wealth of Nations* (1776; Chicago: University of Chicago Press, 1952), bk. I, chap. 2, p. 7.

50. Adam Smith, *The Theory of Moral Sentiments* (1757), Aalen reprint, p. 101.

51. Smith, *Moral Sentiments,* p. 555.

52. Mandeville, *The Fable of the Bees* (Oxford: Clarendon Press, 1924), vol. I, p. 194.

53. Mandeville, *Fable,* vol. II, p. 352. On the relation between Mandeville and Smith, cf. Louis Dumont, *From Mandeville to Marx* (Chicago: University of Chicago Press, 1977).

54. Jeremy Bentham, *Introduction to the Principles of Morals and Legislation* (1780, printed; 1789, published), ed. H. L. A. Hart (London: Methuen, 1978).

55. H. L. A. Hart, Introduction to *Principles,* p. li.

56. Peter Stanlis, *Edmund Burke and the Natural Law* (Ann Arbor: University of Michigan Press, 1958). Cf. also André Van de Putte, "De natuurwet bij Edmund Burke," *Tijdschrift voor Filosofie* 54, no. 3 (September 1992): 393–423, esp. pp. 404–5.

57. Edmund Burke, *Reflections on the Revolution in France* (1790; New York: Doubleday, 1973), p. 100. Abridged as *Reflections.*

58. Letter to William Smith in 1795, as quoted in Russell Kirk, *Edmund Burke: A Genius Reconsidered* (Wilmington, Del.: Intercollegiate Studies Institute, 1997), pp. 201–2.

59. Edmund Burke, *Letters on a Regicide Peace* (1796–97), in *Select Works of Edmund Burke* (based on the Oxford: Clarendon Press edition of 1874–78), (Indianapolis: Liberty Fund, 1999), pp. 180ff.

60. Thomas Paine, *The Rights of Man* (1781), bound with Burke, *Reflections on the Revolution in France* (New York: Doubleday, 1973), p. 278.

61. Michael Sandel, *Liberalism and the Limits of Justice* (New York: Cambridge University Press, 1982), p. 179.

Chapter 7. The New Science of History

1. Hannah Arendt, "The Concept of History," in *Between Past and Future* (1954; New York: Penguin Books, 1977), pp. 66–67.

2. Johann Christoph Gatterer, *Vom historischen Plan . . .* (1767), cf. Rudolf Vierhaus in "Historisches Interesse im 18. Jahrhundert" in *Aufklärung und Geschichte,* ed. H. E. Bödeker et al. (Göttingen: Vandenhoeck and Ruprecht, 1986), p. 271. On Jonathan Edwards's comprehensive theology of history, cf. Aviha Zakai's excellent *Jonathan Edwards's Philosophy of History: The Reenchantment of the World in the Age of Enlightenment* (Princeton: Princeton University Press, 2003).

3. On the difficult balance between the universal and the particular, cf. Albert Cook, "History Writing as a Separate Genre," in *Clio* 15, no. 2 (1986): 171–89.

4. Cf. Carl Hempel, "The Function of General Laws in History," *Journal of Philosophy* 39 (1942), repr. in Herbert Feigl and Wilfrid Sellars, *Readings in Philosophical Analysis* (New York: Appleton Century Crofts, 1949); and Alan Donagan, "Explanation in History," *Mind* 66, no. 262 (1957): 145–64.

5. Benedetto Croce, *La filosofia di Giambattista Vico* (1911; Bari: Laterza, 1973), p. 46.

6. Giambattista Vico, *Vita di Giambattista Vico da lui stesso descritta,* ed. Benedetto Croce and Fausto Nicolini (Bari: Laterza, 1929); *Autobiography,* trans. Max Harold Fisch and Thomas Goddard Bergin (Ithaca: Cornell University Press, 1944), p. 125.

7. A critique of Descartes's principles appears in Giambattista Vico, *Principi di Scienza nuova d'intorno alla comune natura delle nazioni* (3d ed., 1744), ed. Fausto Nicolini (Bari: Laterza, 1928), § 1212; *The New Science of Giambattista Vico,* trans. Thomas Goddard Bergin and Max Harold Fisch (Ithaca: Cornell University Press, 1984; repr. 1994). (I refer to these editions by paragraph number and, unless otherwise indicated, I have followed the Bergin-Fisch translation. Yet § 1212, part of an appendix taken from the second edition (1730), does not appear in the Bergin-Fisch translation.)

8. In his early *De nostri temporis studiorum ratione* (1709) Vico questioned the norm of indubitability as a criterion of truth, and even of certainty.

9. Croce, *La filosofia di Giambattista Vico,* p. 33. David Lachterman, "Vico and Marx: A Precursory Reading," in *Vico and Marx,* ed. Giorgio Tagliacozzo (New York: Humanities Press, 1983), pp. 38–61, and H. S. Harris, "Philosophy and Poetry: The War Renewed" in *Clio,* 23, no. 4 (summer 1994): 395–408, esp. 404–6, have also argued the presence of a strong Cartesian strand.

10. Aristotle, *Physics,* II, 8, 199.

11. I have corrected "institutions" to "things" (*cose*) and added emphasis to stress the plural. "Natura di cose altro non è che nascimento di esse in certi tempi e con certe guise, le quali sempre che sono tali, indi tali e non altre nascon le cose." Bk. I, *Degnità.*

12. Vico, *Scienza nuova prima* (1752), in *Opere,* ed. A. Battistini (Milan: Mondadori, 1990), p. 88. My translation.

13. On the imaginative universal, cf. Donald Verene, *Vico's Science of the Imagination* (Ithaca: Cornell University, 1981), esp. chaps. 3 and 5.

14. Giuseppe Mazzotta, *The New Map of the World: The Poetic Philosophy of Giambattista Vico* (Princeton: Princeton University Press, 1999), p. 130.

15. Ibid., p. 148.

16. Hayden White, "The Value of Narrativity in the Representation of Reality," *Critical Inquiry* 7 (1980): 9.

17. This point has been elegantly argued by Donald Verene in *The New Art of Autobiography: An Essay on the Life of Giambattista Vico, Written by Himself* (Oxford: Clarendon Press, 1991). Also *Vico's Science of the Imagination.*

18. On Vico's persistent exposure of this misconception, cf. Jeffrey Barnouw, "The Critique of Classical Republicanism and the Understanding of Modern Forms of Polity in Vico's *New Science,*" *Clio* 9, no. 3 (spring 1980): 393–41.

19. Fred Dallmayr, "Natural History and Social Evolution: Reflections on Vico's *Corsi e recorsi,*" in *Vico and Contemporary Thought,* ed. Giorgio Tagliacozzo, Michael Mooney, and Donald P. Verene (Atlantic Highlands, N.J.: Humanities Press, 1979), pt. 2, pp. 199–215.

20. Max Horkheimer and Theodor W. Adorno, *Dialectic of Enlightenment,* trans. John Cumming (New York: Herder and Herder, 1972), p. 36.

21. Massimo Lollini, *Le Muse, le maschere e il sublime: G. B. Vico e la poesia nel età della 'ragione spiegata'* (Naples: Guida, 1994), p. 126.

22. Francis Bacon, *Novum Organum,* trans. R. L. Ellis in *The of Works of Francis Baco,* ed. James Spelling et al. (London, 1858–74), vol. VIII, aphorism 64.

23. This total immanence of God in history was, of course, Hegel's fundamental thesis and before him that of Herder and Hölderlin.

24. Giovanni Gentile, in "Dal concetto della grazia a quello della Providenza" in *Studi Vichiani* (Florence: Sansoni, 1969), pp. 145–61.

25. Cf. P. S., Dreyer, "Doel als geskiedkundige kategorie" (Purpose as historical category), *Suid-Afrikaanse Tydskrif vir Wysbegeerte — South African Journal of Philosophy* 8, nos. 3–4 (November 1989): 182–86 (double-columned). I have followed the basic argument on teleology in ancient and modern Western thought presented in this article.

26. Cf. Karl Loewith, *Meaning in History* (Chicago: University of Chicago Press, 1949).

27. Hans Blumenberg, *The Legitimacy of the Modern Age,* trans. Robert Wallace (Cambridge: MIT Press, 1976), p. 30.

28. Ludwig Edelstein, *The Idea of Progress in Classical Antiquity* (Baltimore: Johns Hopkins University Press, 1967). The myth of progress was balanced by one of decline.

29. Hannah Arendt, *The Life of the Mind* (New York: Harcourt Brace, 1978), p. 55. The title of Joseph Glanvill's work is *Plus Ultra: The Progress and Advancement of Knowledge Since the Days of Aristotle* (1668). I have written on Bacon and the early discussion in *Passage to Modernity.*

30. In his *Digression sur les Anciens et les Modernes,* Fontenelle argued that the human potential always remains identical: nature does not change. Yet endowed with memory, individuals, even entire nations, retain what they have learned from one generation to another. In arts and letters, however, memory is of little service: the creative process starts ever anew. *Parallèle des Anciens et des Modernes* (1688–96). Later Condorcet was to defend progress on the basis of the opposite view of nature. Human nature, far from being unchangeable, was endowed with an intrinsic capacity for growth.

31. British writers were less inclined to abandon the classical tradition. Boswell quotes Dr. Johnson as saying long after the matter had been settled in France: "Modern writers are the moon of literature; they shine with reflected light, with light borrowed from the ancients." Dryden and Pope continued to write well in classical forms.

32. Jean Le Rond d'Alembert, *Essai sur les élémens de philosophie* (Paris: Fayard, Corpus des Oeuvres de Philosophie en Langue Française, 1986), p. 20. His "Preliminary Discourse" to the *Encyclopédie* has been translated by R. Schwab (Indianapolis and New York: Bobbs Merrill, Library of Liberal Arts, 1963).

33. "Art" in Diderot, d'Alembert, *Encyclopedia Selections,* trans. Nelly S. Hoyt and Thomas Cassirer (Indianapolis, New York: Bobbs Merrill, Library of Liberal Arts, 1965), p. 5. See also, the article "Encyclopédie."

34. Denis Diderot, *Essai sur les règnes de Claude et de Néron,* in *Oeuvres Complètes,* ed. H. Dieckmann and J. Varloot (Paris: Hermann, 1986), vol. XXV, pt. 2, p. 5.

35. Baron d'Holbach, *The System of Nature,* trans. H. D. Robinson (New York: Burt Franklin, 1868, 1970), p. 115.

36. Letter to Damilaville, March, 19, 1766 in Voltaire, *Correspondance* in *Oeuvres* (Paris: La Pléiade), vol. VIII, § 9356, pp. 409–10.

37. Voltaire, *Essai sur les moeurs et l'esprit des nations* (1756). This work went

through numerous variations and editions. Publication started with seven articles in *Mercure de France* in 1745–46. A pirated edition was followed by Voltaire's own in 1756. He added sixteen chapters to the 1761 editions and, to the "final" edition of 1769, a long *Discours préliminaire,* previously published under the title *Philosophie de l'histoire* (1765). After that date marginalia still kept appearing until 1778. I have used the edition René Pomeau published in the Classiques Garnier (Paris, 1963), referring in roman numerals to the sections of the *Discours préliminaire* and to the chapters of the main text. The discussions of India and China appear in the *Discours,* sections XVII and XVIII. The ones on the Islam, in the main text, chaps. VI and VII.

38. Cf. Voltaire, *Dictionnaire philosophique,* s.v. Grégoire VII.

39. On the universalism of Voltaire's history, cf. Georg G. Iggers, "The European Context of German Enlightenment Historiography," in *Aufklärung und Geschichte,* ed. Hans E. Bödeker, Georg G. Iggers, Jonathan Knudsen, and Peter H. Reill (Göttingen: Vandenhoeck und Ruprecht, 1986), esp. pp. 230–32.

On the literary quality, cf. Hayden White, "The Historical Text as Literary Artifact," in *The Writing of History: Literary Form and Historical Understanding,* ed. Robert M. Canary and Henry Kozicki (Madison: University of Wisconsin Press, 1978), pp. 41–62. Also, Robert Anchor, "Narrativity and the Transformation of Historical Consciousness," *Clio* 16, no. 2 (1987): 121–37.

40. Anne-Robert-Jacques Turgot, "Discours sur les progres successifs de l'esprit humain," in *Oeuvres de Turgot,* 2 vols., ed. Eugène Daire and Hyppolite Dussard (Paris, 1844), p. 599. All references are to vol. II. The numbers of the "Discourses" are in roman numerals.

41. Du Pont de Nemours, Turgot's admiring disciple, notes that Turgot did not want to humiliate Bossuet. "Il préférait de recomposer ce livre, de lui donner l'étendue qu'il y aurait désirée, et d'y consigner les principes que l'illustre évêque de Meaux avait passés sous silence, n'avait peut-être pas conçus, n'aurait peut-être pas adoptés" (II Discourse, p. 627 note).

42. He died, probably by his own hand, the night before the police came to arrest him.

43. Jean Antoine Nicolas Caritat, Marquis de Condorcet, *Esquisse d'un tableau historique des progrès de l'esprit humain,* in *Oeuvres Complètes* (Brunswick and Paris, 1804), vol. VIII, p. 370.

44. The same idea was to play a central role in Marx's theory concerning the social conditions for the use of technology. Thus, the steam engine did not assume practical usefulness until society was economically enough evolved to use it. *Capital I,* trans. Samuel Moore and Edward Aveling (New York: International Publishers, 1967), p. 375.

45. Cf. Condorcet's marginal notes "Fragments de l'histoire de la première époque" that appear in the 1847–49 edition. My attention was drawn to this by Frank Manuel's beautiful essay on Condorcet in *The Prophets of Paris* (Cambridge: Harvard University Press, 1962; New York: Harper Torchbooks, 1965), pp. 53–102.

46. On this issue, cf. Hiram Caton, *The Politics of Progress: The Origins and Development of the Commercial Republic, 1600–1835* (Gainesville: University Presses of Florida, 1988), esp. pp. 334–36.

47. Friedrich Meinecke, *Die Enstehung des Historismus,* 4th ed., in *Friedrich Mein-*

ecke Werke, ed. H. Herzfeld, O. Hinrichs, and W. Hofer, vol. II (Munich: Oldenbourg Verlag, 1765), p. 230.

48. Edward Gibbon, *Memoirs of My Life and Writings* (1796), ed. J. B. Bury (1935), p. 160. For *The History of the Decline and Fall of the Roman Empire,* I have used the most accessible edition published by the University of Chicago Press, 1952. I refer to it by chapter, page, and column (a or b).

49. Cf. Christopher Dawson, *The Historic Reality of Christian Culture* (London: Routledge and Keegan Paul, 1960).

50. Glen W. Bowersock, "The Vanishing Paradigm of the Fall of Rome," *Bulletin. The American Academy of Arts and Sciences* 40, no. 8 (1996). On the many interpretations of the "fall," see Alexander Demandt, *Der Fall Roms: Die Auflösung des römischen Reiches im Urteil der Nachwelt* (Munich: C. H. Beck, 1984).

51. Several historians have stressed the economic basis of the decline, among them Michael Rostovtzeff, Eduard Meyer, W. L. Westermann, and A. E. R. Boak.

52. J. B. Bury, *History of the Later Roman Empire, 395–565* (London: Macmillan, 1923), vol. I, p. 311.

53. Samuel Coleridge, *Lectures 1795: On Politics and Religion,* ed. Lewis Patton and Peter Mann (Princeton: Princeton University Press, 1970), p. 182.

54. In other instances when there is no "story" to tell, the condensation of a development protracted over centuries into a single chapter makes excellent sense, as in the admirable survey of Roman jurisprudence over the centuries in chap. 44. On the impact of the novel on the moral nature of Gibbon's narrative history, see Leo Braudy, *Narrative Form in History and Fiction: Hume, Fielding, Gibbon* (Princeton: Princeton University Press, 1970).

55. Friedrich Meinecke, *Die Entstehung des Historismus.*

56. I refer to Bernhard Suphan's edition of Herder's *Sämtliche Werke* (Berlin; Weidmannsche Buchhandlung, 1877–99). *Auch eine Philosophie der Geschichte* is vol. V; *Ideen zur Philosophie der Geschichte der Menschheit,* vols. XIII and XIV; *Briefe zur Beförderung der Humanität,* vols. XVII and XVIII. An English translation of the *Ideen* by T. O. Churchill appeared in 1800 in London (to my knowledge still the only one) as *Reflections on the Philosophy of the History of Mankind.* It was reprinted in abridged form by Frank Manuel in the series Classic European Historians, edited by Leonard Krieger (Chicago: University of Chicago Press, 1968). Since this edition is by far the easiest available I refer to it whenever possible. Other translations are my own. I refer to the *Reflections* by book, chapter, and, whenever available, by page in Manuel's edition; to the *Letters* by collection, number, and page.

57. Isaiah Berlin, *The Crooked Timber of Humanity,* ed. Henry Hardy (New York: Vintage Books, 1992); also, "Herder and the Enlightenment," in *Vico and Herder* (New York: Viking Press, 1976). See the pertinent critique in Damon Linker, "The Reluctant Pluralism of J. G. Herder," *Review of Politics* 62, no. 2 (spring 2000): 267–94.

58. Wolfgang Förster, "Johann Gottfried Herder: Weltgeschichte und Humanität" in *Aufklärung und Geschichte,* ed. Hans Bödeker et al. (Göttingen: Vandenhoeck and Ruprecht, 1986), pp. 363–87, particularly p. 371.

59. Linker, "Reluctant Pluralism of J. G. Herder," p. 293.

60. *Kants Gesammelte Schriften* (Akademie edition), vol. VII, p. 53; trans. as "Review

of Herder's *Ideas for a Philosophy of the History of Mankind"* by Robert E. Anchor in *Kant on History,* ed. Lewis White Beck, (Indianapolis: Bobbs-Merrill, 1963), p. 37.

61. Kant, "Beantwortung der Frage: Was ist Aufklärung?" in *Kants Gesammelte Schriften,* vol. VII, pp. 35–42; trans. as "What Is Enlightenment?" by Lewis Beck White in *Kant on History,* pp. 3–10.

62. "Eine alte Frage . . ." in *Kants Gesammelte Schriften,* vol. VII, p. 88; trans. as "An Old Question Raised Again: Is the Human Race Constantly Progressing?" by Robert E. Anchor in *Kant on History,* p. 147.

63. Kant, "Vom ewigen Frieden" in *Kants Gesammelte Schriften,* vol. VIII, pp. 343–86; trans. as "Perpetual Peace" by Lewis Beck White in *Kant on History,* pp. 85–135.

Chapter 8. The Religious Crisis

1. Eric Voegelin, *From Enlightenment to Revolution,* ed. John Hallowell (Durham: Duke University Press, 1975), pp. 18–23.

2. There are, of course, reports of ancient floods in various lands, including China. Martin Martini, S.J., a missionary in China, attempted to find support in them for the historical character of the biblical story. In his *Sinicae Historiae* (1658) he suggests that the Chinese chronicles may have been inaccurate in dating the flood, or even that the legendary emperor Yaüs was in fact Noah himself. David Wetsel, " '*Histoire de la Chine*': Pascal and the Challenge to Biblical Time," *Journal of Religion* 69, no. 2 (April 1989): 199–219.

3. Benedict de Spinoza, *Tractatus Theologico-Politicus,* in *Spinoza Opera,* ed. Carl Gebhardt (Heidelberg: Carl Winters, Universitäts Buchhandlung, 1926), vol. III, pp. 28, 100; trans. R. H. M. Elwes (New York: Dover Publications, 1951), p. 101. (See also p. 93.) Abridged as *TTP* and Elwes for the English translation.

4. Hans Frei, *The Eclipse of Biblical Narrative* (New Haven: Yale University Press, 1973), pp. 151–56.

5. Such was the thesis of Leo Strauss's *Die Religionskritik Spinozas als Grundlage seiner Bibelwissenschaft* (1930). Much of that position is still accepted by Y. Yovel, *Spinoza and Other Heretics* (Princeton: Princeton University Press, 1989). Spinoza's contemporary Lambert van Velthuysen had already accused him of such a devious strategy.

6. This appears to be Herman De Dijn's position, expressed in a number of writings but most clearly in "Spinoza and Revealed Religion" in *Studia Spinozana* 11 (1997).

7. In *Vroomheid, vrede, vrijheid: Een interpretatie van Spinoza's Tractatus Theologico-Politicus* (Assen: Van Gorcum, 1996), Angela Roothaan has drawn full attention to the significance of this meeting.

8. Spinoza, *Correspondence,* Letter 43.

9. On the salvational power of a specific faith through the universal religion of Christ in the *Tractatus,* cf. A. Matheron, *Le Christ et le salut des ignorants* (Paris, 1971). Unfortunately this work is written from a rather narrowly Marxist point of view. More balanced is Herman De Dijn, "Spinoza and Revealed Religion."

10. "By tradition Simon understands not a *diadoche* that, through the apostolic succession attests to the continuity of a chain that ends in Christ, the Word of God, even less a *paradosis* that would guarantee an incorrupt transmission and preservation of the re-

vealed text throughout the centuries." F. Saverio Mirri, *Richard Simon e il metodo storico-critico di B. Spinoza* (Florence: Le Monnier, 1972), p. 77.

11. This change in scriptural interpretation during the eighteenth century has been well analyzed by Hans Frei in *Eclipse of Biblical Narrative,* chap. 3, pp. 51–65.

12. Frei, *Eclipse,* chap. 6, pp. 105–14.

13. Gotthold Ephraim Lessing, Letter of March 20, 1777, in *Sämtliche Schriften,* ed. Karl Lachmann and Franz Muncker (Leipzig: Göschen, 1886–1924), 23 vols. (Henceforth abridged as L-M and volume.) This letter appears in vol. XVIII, p. 227, trans. Henry Chadwick in *Lessing's Theological Writings* (Stanford: Stanford University Press, 1957), p. 13. I take all translations from this work, wherever available.

14. "On the Origin of Revealed Religion," thesis II, in L-M, XIV, 313; Chadwick, p. 105.

15. "On the Toleration of Deists," L-M, XII, 268–70.

16. L-M, XIII, 127; Chadwick, pp. 17–18.

17. In the early fragment "The Christianity of Reason" (1752–53), Lessing expresses this idea and there explicitly defines the role of the Spirit as the harmony between Father and Son (L-M, XIII, 43; Chadwick, p. 94).

18. There exists an early translation of *Axiomata* by H. H. Bernard in his *Cambridge Free Thoughts and Letters on Bibliolatry* (London, 1862).

19. The ultimate authority of the Bible in Church doctrine had already been a major source of controversy between Luther and the Catholic Church. Some of his followers and most Calvinist churches stressed the *uniqueness* of this authority even more strongly calling themselves "reformed in accordance with the word of God" to indicate that God's Spirit is entirely bound to the word. Cf. the chapter "The Word and the Will of God" in Jaroslav Pelikan, *The Christian Tradition: A History of the Development of Doctrine,* vol. IV, chap. 4 (Chicago: University of Chicago Press, 1984), pp. 183–244.

20. Samuel Clarke, *Discourse Concerning the Being and Attributes of God, the Natural Obligations of the Natural Religion, and Truth and Certainty of the Christian Revelation* (London, 1704–5), pt. II, pp. 12–23.

21. John Locke, *A Second Vindication of the Reasonableness of Christianity* in *The Works of John Locke,* 10 vols. (London 1823; reissued Aalen: Scientia, 1963), VII, 188.

22. Peter Gay, *The Enlightenment: An Interpretation* (New York: Random House, 1966), vol. I, pp. 303–4.

23. Bernard Mandeville, *The Fable of the Bees* (London, 1729; reissued by Clarendon Press, Oxford, 1924), vol. II, p. 243.

24. Nathaniel Culverwell, *An Elegant and Learned Discourse on the Light of Nature,* ed. Robert A. Greene and Hugh MacCallum (Toronto: University of Toronto Press, 1931), p. 6. Both Culverwell and Whichcote, though influenced by Stoicism, were sincere Christians and indeed Calvinists, albeit of slightly Arminian leanings. Culverwell describes as the purpose of his *Elegant and Learned Discourse of the Light of Nature* (1652) "to vindicate the use of reason in matters of religion," yet at the same time "to chastise the sauciness of Socinus and his followers." Later members of the Cambridge School were to ground their position in Neoplatonic philosophy, but in the seventeenth century it still rested primarily on the Stoa and on Scholastic Aristotelianism.

25. From a letter to Bolingbroke.

26. Robert Shackleton, "Pope's *Essay on Man* and the French Enlightenment," in *Studies in the Eighteenth Century,* vol. II, ed. R. F. Brissenden (Canberra: Australian National University Press, 1973), pp. 1–16. If the two French translators had not retracted the ideas it expressed, the Sorbonne would have placed the *Essay* on its list of condemned books.

27. Cf. Arthur Friedman, "Pope and Deism," in *Pope and His Contemporaries,* ed. James C. Clifford and Lewis A. Landa (Oxford: Clarendon Press, 1949) pp. 89–95.

28. Hoxie N. Fairchild, *Religious Trends in English Poetry,* vol. I: 1700–1740 (New York: Columbia University Press, 1939), p. 521.

29. Such was the interpretation of Herbert Schöffler in *Protestantismus und Literatur: Neue Wege zur Englischen Literatur des achtzehnten Jahrhunderts* (Leipzig, 1922).

30. Fairchild, *Religious Trends,* p. 553. The final two chapters of this now neglected work are rich in insights on sentimental religion.

31. *An Essay Concerning Human Understanding* (1690), Fraser edition (Oxford University Press, 1894). I refer to it by book, chapter, and section.

32. Cf. Nicholas Wolterstorff, "The Assurance of Faith," *Faith and Philosophy* 2, no. 4 (October 1990): 396–417.

33. John Locke, *The Reasonableness of Christianity* (1695), # 238. I refer to the (standard) numbers of the sections.

34. John Edwards, *Some Thoughts concerning the Several Causes and Occasions of Atheism, especially in the Present Age, with some Brief Reflections on Socinianism and on a Late Book entitled: "The Reasonableness of Christianity as Delivered in the Scriptures"* (London: J. Robinson and J. Wyat, 1695).

35. Locke, *A Second Vindication of the Reasonableness of Christianity* in *Complete Works of John Locke,* vol. VIII, p. 188.

36. Matthew Tindal, *Christianity as Old as the Creation* (London, 1730), p. 199.

37. Others attacked the reasonableness of Locke's scriptural argument. Thus Anthony Collins in *A Discourse of the Grounds and Reasons of the Christian Religion* (1724) criticized the validity of the argument that Jesus had fulfilled the biblical prophecies as being so vague that any religious teacher could have claimed the same. Thomas Woolston completed this critique by denying the credibility of the miracles that were supposed to support the fulfillment. Once the bond that had linked scriptural revelation to reason was broken, the theory of rational religion entered into conflict with revelation (*Discourses on the Miracles of Our Saviour* [1727–29]). On a more general level, Collins distinguished the reports of historical facts which, being empirical, carry no guarantee of absolute certainty, from the universal and necessary truths of reason. On the development of Lockean thought into deism, see Gay, *Enlightenment,* vol. I, pp. 374–80.

38. Henry Duméry, *Le problème de Dieu* (Paris: Desclée De Brouwer, 1975), p. 15.

39. Cf. Louis Dupré, *A Dubious Heritage: Philosophy of Religion after Kant* (New York: Paulist Press, 1977), pt. III, pp. 129–77.

40. Carl Becker, *The Heavenly City of the Eighteenth Century Philosophers* (New Haven: Yale University Press, 1932), p. 56.

41. Etienne Gilson, *God and Philosophy* (New Haven: Yale University Press, 1941), p. 106.

42. Voltaire, *Elémens de philosophie de Newton* (1738), in *Oeuvres* (1785), vol. LXIII, pt. 1, chap. 6.

43. Jean le Rond d'Alembert, "Discours préliminaire," *Encyclopédie,* ed. Picaret, p. xv.

44. Ernst Cassirer, *The Philosophy of the Enlightenment* (Princeton: Princeton University Press, 1968), p. 164.

45. John Locke, *A Letter Concerning Toleration* (1689), ed. and intro. James H. Tully (Indianapolis: Hacket, 1983). The introduction contains a useful survey of Locke's positions over a thirty-year period.

46. This theocracy had culminated in Pope Boniface VIII's bulla *Unam Sanctam* (1302), in which he declared that both the spiritual and the temporal swords had been divinely entrusted to the Roman Pontiff. *Enchiridion Symbolorum,* ed. Henricus Denzinger (Barcelona: Herder, 1948), # 469.

47. Cf. Stanley Greane, *Shaftesbury's Philosophy of Religion and Ethics* (Athens: Ohio State University Press, 1967).

48. Anthony Ashley Cooper, Third Earl of Shaftesbury, "Miscellaneous Reflections," II, 3, in *Characteristics of Men, Manners, Opinions, Times, etc.,* ed. John Robertson, 2 vols. (Gloucester, Mass.: Peter Smith, 1963), II, 220.

49. He made this statement in an address to the Academy of Bordeaux delivered in 1716. "La politique des Romains dans la religion" anticipates what he was to write on the subject in the later *Grandeur et décadence des Romains* (1734).

50. Voltaire, *L'examen inportant de Milord Bolingbroke* (1767), chaps. 13, 15, in *Oeuvres Complètes de Voltaire* (Paris: Hachette, 1859), vol. XXI; *An Important Study by Lord Bolingbroke,* in *Voltaire on Religion,* trans. Kenneth Appelgate (New York: Frederick Ungar, 1979), pp. 135–41 and 144–46.

51. Cited from the so-called Homilies, which Voltaire ironically credited himself with having delivered in a London chapel in 1765. Trans. Kenneth W. Appelgate in *Voltaire on Religion,* p. 80. Peter Gay's important *Voltaire's Politics: The Poet as Realist* (New Haven: Yale University Press, 1988), though primarily focused on Voltaire's multiple political involvements, is also a richly documented source on the writer's complex position on religious issues.

52. *Essai sur les moeurs et l'esprit des nations et sur les principaux faits de l'histoire depuis Charlemagne jusqu'à Louis XIII* (1756; Paris: Editions Garnier, 1963), 2 vols., introduction, vol. I, p. 95.

53. Even Gustave Lanson, who admires Voltaire's literary and historical talents, takes exception at his allegedly historical critique of religion: "There is nothing dirtier, more hateful and more undignified in Voltaire's work than what he wrote about the Jews and the origin of Christianity. Renan has pronounced the definitive condemnation of all that. Neither science nor the taste of our time allows us to reverse this condemnation." Gustave Lanson, *Voltaire* (Paris: Hachette, 1906), p. 171.

54. Diderot called it "a rehash of all the old naughtiness the author has uttered against Moses and Jesus Christ, the prophets and the apostles, the Church, the popes, the cardinals, priests, and monks."

55. Jean-Jacques Rousseau, *Emile* (1762), bk. IV, in *Oeuvres Complètes* (Paris: La Pléiade, 1969), vol. IV, p. 541.

56. *Julie ou la nouvelle Héloïse* (Paris: La Pléiade, 1964), pt. VI, letter 8.

57. Rousseau, *Du Contrat Social* (1762) in *Oeuvres Complètes* (Paris: La Pléiade, 1964), vol. III, p. 467; *The Social Contract,* ed. Sir Ernest Barker, in *Social Contract* (Oxford University Press (1947/1960) p. 304.

58. Christian Wolff had discussed it in his inaugural lecture as philosophy professor in Halle, "Oratio de Sinarium Philosophia practica" (1721). Christian Wolff, *Gesammelte Werke* (Hildesheim and New York, 1974), vol. XXXV, pp. 25–126. Cf. Hermann Lübbe, *Religion nach der Aufklärung* (Graz: Styria, 1986), pp. 306–27.

59. Edmund Burke, *Reflections on the Revolution in France* (1790; New York: Doubleday-Anchor Books, 1973), p. 106.

60. Robert N. Bellah, "Civil Religion in America," *Daedalus* 96, no. 1 (1967), repr. in *Beyond Belief* (New York, Harper and Row, 1970), pp. 168–89. This essay touched off a lively debate, some of which appeared in Russell E. Richey and Donald G. Jones, eds. *American Civil Religion* (New York: Harper and Row, 1974). See also Richard John Neuhaus, *Time Toward Home: The American Experiment as Revelation* (New York: Seabury, 1975), esp. chaps. 19, and 20, and John F. Wilson, "The Status of Civil Region in America" in *The Religion of the Republic,* ed. Elwyn A. Smith (Philadelphia: Fortress Press, 1971).

61. As Michael Buckley, S.J., has shown in *At the Origins of Modern Atheism* (New Haven: Yale University Press, 1987), deism does not imply atheism. See esp. pp. 37–38.

62. David Hume, *Dialogues Concerning Natural Religion,* ed. Richard Popkin (Indianapolis: Hacket, 1980), II, 14. I shall refer to this edition, the most easily available, by section and page. Since the sections are short, the quoted passages may easily be found in other editions.

63. For a popular presentation, cf. Ilya Prigogine and Isabelle Stengers, *Order Out of Chaos, Man's New Dialogue with Nature* (New York: Bantam, 1986).

64. For an elaboration of this critique, see Louis Dupré, "The Teleological Argument," in *Dubious Heritage,* pp. 152–65.

65. A great deal has been written on the question which one of the characters represents Hume's own views. From the beginning most commentators have identified the skeptical Philo as the one. Yet others, including Nicholas Wolterstorff, consider the dialogues an exchange between an empiricist skepticism (represented by Philo) and an empiricist defense of religion (represented by Cleanthes) as both present in Hume's mind. The fact is that Hume himself in a letter to Gilbert Elliot (March 10, 1751) requests Elliot's assistance for making Cleanthes's argument "formal and regular." Apparently he had a personal stake in Cleanthes's position. For alternatives and for an excellent assessment of Hume's agnosticism, cf. James Noxon, "Hume's Agnosticism," in *Hume: A Collection of Critical Essays,* ed. V. C. Chappell (New York: Doubleday, 1966), pp. 360–83.

66. David Hume, *An Enquiry Concerning Human Understanding,* 2d ed., ed. L. A. Selby-Bigge (Oxford: Clarendon Press, 1902), X, 131.

67. Antony Flew, *God and Philosophy* (New York: Harcourt, Brace, and World, 1966), pp. 150–52. See also, his *Hume's Philosophy of Belief* (London: Routledge and Kegan Paul, 1961).

68. Cf. James Collins, *The Emergence of the Philosophy of Religion* (New Haven: Yale

University Press, 1967), pp. 32–33. Phenomenologists of religion, such as Joachim Wach, Rudolf Otto, and Mircea Eliade, have strongly reacted against the tendency to derive religion from other categories — be they concepts or emotions. They consider religion a constitutive element in the mind's structure, not a former stage in the history of consciousness.

69. David Hume, *The Natural History of Religion,* ed. H. E. Root (Stanford: Stanford University Press, 1957), introduction, p. 21. I refer to this work by section and page number.

70. Cf. Frank Manuel, *The Eighteenth Century Confronts the Gods* (Cambridge: Harvard University Press, 1959), p. 177.

71. An excellent report on Diderot's development toward atheism may be found in Buckley, *At the Origins of Modern Atheism,* pp. 194–250.

72. Baron Paul d'Holbach, *Système de la Nature* (Amsterdam, 1770), bk. II, chap. 5; trans. as *The System of Nature* by H. D. Robinson (New York: Burt Franklin, 1868; repr. 1970). I shall refer to this translation by book, chapter, and page.

73. Arthur M. Wilson, *Diderot* (New York: Oxford University Press, 1972), p. 176.

74. Pierre Bayle, *Dictionnaire historique et critique,* ed. A. J. Q. Beuchot, 16 vols. (Paris, 1820–24). See also the articles "Caligula," "Lucrèce," "Hobbes." On the basis of *Pensées diverses* (CXIII and LXXI) and other texts, Gabriel Vahanian concludes that Bayle is primarily an "iconoclast," a destroyer of idols: "Par delà la Theodicée: L'héritage de Pierre Bayle," in *Teodicea Oggi* (*Archivo di Filosofia* 56 [1988]), pp. 29–36.

75. Friedrich Nietzsche, *The Birth of Tragedy,* trans. Walter Kaufman (New York: Random House, 1967), # 5, p. 52.

76. Unlike Sartre, Maurice Merleau-Ponty refused to call himself an atheist because of the religious connotation of the term. On the dialectical character of modern atheism, cf. Buckley, *At the Origins of Modern Atheism,* chap. 6, and Louis Dupré, "On the Intellectual Sources of Modern Atheism" *International Journal for Philosophy of Religion* 45 (1999): 1–11.

77. Wallace Stevens, *Opus Posthumous* (New York: Alfred A. Knopf, 1977), p. 158.

Chapter 9. The Faith of the Philosophers

1. Cf. Yves M. J. Congar, O.P., *A History of Theology,* trans. Hunter Guthrie, S.J. (Garden City, N.Y.: Doubleday, 1968), and esp. chap. 3.

2. Cf. Konrad Feiereis, *Die Umprägung der natürlichen Theologie in Religionsphilosophie* (Leipzig: St. Benno-Verlag, 1965). This study contains an excellent history of natural theology.

3. Cf. Walter Van Herck, "De taak van de godsdienstfilosofie," *Bijdragen. Tijdschrift voor filosofie en theologie* 59 (1998): 428–52.

4. As I have tried to show in *A Dubious Heritage: Philosophy of Religion after Kant* (New York: Paulist Press, 1977), pt. 3.

5. Bertrand Russell, *A History of Western Philosophy* (New York: Simon and Schuster, 1945), p. 595. For the complete argument, Bertrand Russell, *A Critical Exposition of the Philosophy of Leibniz* (London, 1937), pp. 59ff.

6. Gottfried Wilhelm Leibniz, *Discours de Métaphysique,* # 14, in *Die philosophischen*

Schriften von Gottfried Wilhelm Leibniz, ed. C. I. Gerhard, 7 vols. (Berlin: Weidmann, 1875–90), vol. IV, p. 438 (henceforth abridged as *Schriften*); trans. George R. Montgomery, rev. by Albert R. Chandler in *The Rationalists* (New York: Doubleday, n.d.), p. 424.

7. "On the Philosophy of Descartes" (1679–1680), in *Schriften,* IV, 274, also 289; *The Philosophical Works of Leibnitz,* trans. George Martin Duncan (New Haven, Conn.: Tuttle, Morehouse and Taylor, 1908), p. 1.

8. *Philosophical Works of Leibnitz,* trans. Duncan, p. 3.

9. "The Principles of Nature and Grace, Founded on Reason" (1714), # 11, in *Schriften,* VI, 603, trans. in *Leibniz, Theology and Philosophy,* ed. C. R. Morris, trans. R. Latta (New York: Doubleday, 1934).

10. Letter to Arnauld in *The Leibniz-Arnauld Corespondence,* trans. H. T. Mason (Manchester: Manchester University Press, 1967), pp. 147–48.

11. Philip Clayton, *The Problem of God in Modern Thought* (Grand Rapids: Wm. B. Eerdmans, 2001), pp. 197–98. This important work draws attention to Leibniz's casual interest in mysticism and to the impact of Henry More's work on Leibniz.

12. "The Principles of Nature and Grace" (1714), # 9, in *Schriften,* VI, 602.

13. *Theodicy,* # 173, in *Schriften,* VI, 217; trans. E. M. Huggard (London: Routledge and Kegan Paul, 1951), my emphasis.

14. *Leibniz: Textes inédits,* ed. Gaston Grua (Paris: Presses Universitaires de France, 1948), p. 302.

15. In a collection of letters and fragments published in 1931 the critical distinction between indifference and freedom of choice appears: "It is not indifference of equilibrium, so to speak that constitutes freedom, but the faculty of choosing among several possibles, even though they are not all equally feasible or convenient for the one who acts." Paul Schrecker, *Gottfried Wilhem Leibniz: Lettres et fragments inédits sur les problèmes philosophiques, théologiques, politiques de la réconciliation des doctrines protestantes* (1669–1704) (Paris: Felix Alcan, 1931), p. 97. I owe this citation to Robert Merrihew Adams, *Leibniz: Determinist, Theist, Idealist* (New York: Oxford University Press, 1994), a careful analysis of the theories of contingency as well as of the notion of *Ens perfectissimum.*

16. There is, however, the Spinozistic expression in an early text. "That all things are distinguished not as substances, but as modes." Yet, Leibniz here is concerned to show that things are not *isolated* from each other as substances, but *distinct* through certain qualities of their substantial being. If they were wholly different in their substantial being, no universal harmony could exist.

17. Cf. Letter to Bourguet in *Schriften,* III, 575.

18. Robert Sleigh, "Leibniz on Divine Foreknowledge," *Faith and Philosophy* 11, no. 4 (1994): 547–71.

19. This distinction had already been criticized by Spinoza: "The intellect of God, insofar as it is conceived to constitute God's essence, is, in reality, the cause of things, both of their essence and of their existence" (*Ethics,* bk. I, prop. 17). Kolakowski shows why the distinction does not hold. "In God Himself essence and existence converge and this implies that His will is identical with His essence. God neither obeys rules which are valid regardless of His will nor produces these rules according to His whims or as the result of

deliberating various options; He is those rules." Leszek Kolakowski, *Religion* (New York: Oxford University Press, 1982), p. 25.

20. *Discours de Métaphysique,* #32, in *Schriften,* IV, 456. The phrase "determines them from without" is to be understood in a relative sense; God is the only "other" reality that directly influences the creature. The expression says nothing about the nature of the divine causality, whether it is intrinsic or extrinsic.

21. As Robert M. Adams calls it in "Must God Create the Best?" in *The Virtue of Faith and Other Essays in Philosophical Theology* (New York: Oxford University Press, 1987). For a theological development of this idea, cf. Kenneth L. Schmitz, *The Gift: Creation* (Milwaukee: Marquette University Press, 1982).

22. Hermann Lübbe, *Religion nach der Aufklärung* (Graz-Vienna: Verlag Styria, 1986), p. 195 (my translation). Cf. also Gabriel Marcel, *Journal Métaphysique* (Paris: Gallimard, 1935), p. 65, and Jan Sperna Weiland, "La théodicée c'est l'athéisme" in *Teodicea Oggi,* ed. Marco Olivetti (Padua: CEDAM, 1988), pp. 37–50.

23. I have discussed the terms of that problem in *Religious Mystery and Rational Reflection,* chap. 4 (Grand Rapids: Wm. B. Eerdmans, 1998), pp. 41–64.

24. Leibniz, *A System of Theology,* trans. Charles William Russell (London: Burns and Lambert, 1850), p. 11. Robert M. Adams assumes that this text may not entirely reflect Leibniz's personal position, but perhaps the maximum he would be willing to subscribe to, if it were acceptable to the Catholic Church. Robert Adams, "Leibniz's Examination of the Christian Religion, *Faith and Philosophy* 11, no. 4 (October 1994): 517–46.

25. "Principles of Nature and Grace, Founded on Reason" (1714), # 15–16, in *Schriften,* VI, 609.

26. In a letter written toward the end of his life he admitted the Platonic inspiration of his work: "I have ever since my youth been greatly satisfied with the ethics of Plato, and also, in a way with his metaphysics." *Schriften,* III, 637.

27. Leslie Stephen, *History of English Thought in the Eighteenth Century* (1876; New York: Harcourt, Brace and World, 1962), vol. I, p. 100.

28. Samuel Clarke, *Discourse Concerning the Being and Attributes of God, the Natural Obligations of Natural Religion, and the Truth and Certainty of the Christian Revelation.* Henceforth abridged as *Discourse.* This work unites the Boyle lectures of 1704, originally published as *A Demonstration of the Being and Attributes of God,* with the second series, delivered in 1705, and first published as *A Discourse Concerning the Unchangeable Obligations* . . . . I have used the tenth, corrected edition of 1749 and refer to it by volume (I or II), proposition, and page.

29. Samuel Clarke, *A Collection of Papers which passed between the late Learned Mr. Leibniz and Dr. Clarke in the years 1715 and 1716, relating to the Principles of Natural Philosophy and Religion,* ed. and intro. André Robinet (Paris: Presses Universitaires de France, 1957). Abridged as *L,* for *Letters* from I to V.

30. Clarke's argument has been the subject of a number of contemporary studies, among them William Rowe, *The Cosmological Argument* (Princeton: Princeton University Press, 1975); Richard M. Gale, *On the Nature and Existence of God* (New York: Cambridge University Press, 1981), chap. 7; and Michael J. Buckley, S.J., *At the Origins of Modern Atheism* (New Haven: Yale University Press, 1987), chap. 3.

31. John Henry Newman, in a letter to Edward Hawkins (December 5, 1852).

32. Joseph Butler, *The Analogy of Religion, Natural and Revealed* ((1736), (London: Macmillan, 1900), pt. II, chaps. 1 and 5. Because of numerous editions of this work, I shall refer only to Butler's own divisions: roman numeral for the part, arabic number for the chapter, followed by the number of the section.

33. *Jerusalem* (1783), in *Moses Mendelssohns gesammelte Schriften,* ed. G. B. Mendelssohn (Leipzig, 1843–45), vol. III.

34. Immanuel Kant, *Religion innerhalb der Grenzen der bloszen Vernunft,* in *Kants Gesammelte Schriften* (Berlin: Preussische Akademie, 1902–42) (henceforth referred to as Ak), vol. VI, p. 21; *Religion Within the Limits of Reason Alone,* trans. Theodore M. Greene and Hoyt Hudson (LaSalle, Ind.: Open Court, 1934; reissued New York: Harper and Brothers, 1960), bk. I, introduction, p. 17. I shall refer to this translation as *Religion,* followed by book, section, and page.

35. Letter to Wolke in *Kants Gesammelte Schriften,* vol. X, p. 178, trans. in *Kant's Life and Thought* by Ernst Cassirer (New Haven: Yale University Press, 1981), p. 19.

36. "Ueber das Miszlingen aller philosophischen Versuche in der Theodicee" in *Kants Gesammelte Schriften,* vol. VIII, pp. 255–71.

37. Ibid., p. 267. On Kant's critique of traditional theodicy, cf. Michael Stoeber, *Evil and the Mystics' God* (Toronto: University of Toronto Press, 1992), chap. 5. For a positive view of Kant's discussion of evil, cf. David McKenzie, "A Kantian Theodicy," *Faith and Philosophy* 1, no. 2 (April 1984): 236–47.

38. Nicolas Malebranche, *De la Recherche de la Vérité* (1674–75), in *Oeuvres Complètes de Malebranche,* gen. ed. André Robinet (Paris: Vrin, 1958), vol. I, ed. by Genevieve Rodis-Lewis, preface, p. 8. Future references to this work will be indicated as follows: RV roman numeral for the book (and, if needed, for part of the book), arabic number for the chapter; followed by the volume of this edition of the *Oeuvres Complètes* (hereafter *O.C.*) (bks. I–III in vol. I; bks. IV–VI in vol. II). I shall cite from the translation of Thomas M. Lennon and Paul J. Olscam, *The Search after Truth* (Columbus: Ohio State University Press, 1980), and from other translations that appear in *Malebranche Philosophical Selections,* ed. Steven Nadler (Indianapolis: Hacket, 1992), whenever available. The present text appears on p. 3.

39. Cf. Malebranche, *Conversations chrétiennes* (1677), II, *O.C.,* II, 50–52. Henri Gouhier, *La philosophie de Malebranche et son expérience religieuse* (Paris: Bloud et Gay, 1926), p. 27. Gouhier, who edited some of Malebranche's works, may well be his most perceptive interpreter.

40. Malebranche, *Première lettre touchant la défense de M. Arnauld* (1685), ed. André Robinet in *O.C.,* VI, 194. The voice of Augustine's *De magistro* is heard here as throughout the *Recherche de la Vérité.*

41. Victor Delbos, *Etude de la philosophie de Malebranche* (Paris: Bloud et Gay, 1924), p. 22.

42. *Méditations chrétiennes et métaphysiques* (1683), IV, 1, ed. Henri Gouhier and André Robinet, *O.C.,* X (1959), 36. Abridged as *Méditations.* Cf. also Armand Cuvillier, *Essai sur la mystique de Malebranche* (Paris: Vrin, 1954), pp. 38–41.

43. *Traité de la Nature et de la Grâce* (1680), ed. by Ginette Dreyfus, *O.C.,* V, 36 (henceforth abridged as *TNG*).

44. *Entretiens sur la Métaphysique et sur la Religion* (1688), ed. André Robinet, O.C., XII, 29–48; *Phil. Sel.*, pp. 147–58.

45. Antoine Arnauld, *Des vraies et des fausses idées* (1684) in *Oeuvres de Messire Arnauld* (Lausanne: d'Arnay, 1780), vol. XXXVIII, pp. 204–5.

46. Malebranche, *Réponse au livre des Vraies et Fausses Idées* (1684), ed. André Robinet, O.C., VI (1966), chap. 22, p. 153. (Some modern Cartesians have agreed with Malebranche, including that crypto-Cartesian, Jean-Paul Sartre.)

47. Victor Cousin, *Fragments philosophiques cartésiens*, p. 345.

48. *The Fragments* published by Victor Cousin contain an anonymous report according to which Malebranche explicitly denied the Cartesian thesis that truth is constituted by divine *fiat*. "I asked him [Malebranche] if it was conceivable that God could see that 2 + 2 = 4 before having willed it to be so. He answered yes, because this truth is God himself." Victor Cousin, *Fragments philosophiques* (1866), vol. III, p. 139. Henri Gouhier hereby refers to a statement made by Malebranche himself in one of the numerous "Eclaircissements" he kept adding to his text: "God who makes everything did not make it [truth], though He engenders it permanently through the necessity of His being" (RV, "Eclairissement" 8; granted in Gouhier, *La philosophie de Malebranche*, p. 41).

49. *Traité de morale* (1683), ed. Michel Adam, O.C., XI, chap. 2.

50. God grants the *grâce de sentiment* in accordance with the thoughts and desires through which Christ foresaw and preordained the destiny of all future generations. Arnauld dismissed this hypothesis as absurd. How could the fate of billions depend on the knowledge or ignorance of one human, and hence finite, consciousness! Fénelon, for once in agreement with his antagonist, reacted sharply and to the point. "In this little book [*Traité de la Nature et de la Grâce*] Malebranche justifies the inefficacy of God's will with respect to the salvation of all men entirely by an impotence derived from the simplicity of God's ways and from the limits of Jesus Christ's brain. This is new in the Church, remote from any theology, and unworthy of God." At the instigation of Bossuet (then still his friend), Fénelon also wrote a *Réfutation du Traité de la Nature et de la Grâce* (1687) which, however, remained unprinted until 1820. Fénelon, *Lettres sur la grâce et la predestination*, in *Oeuvres Choisies de Fénelon* (Paris: Hachette, 1862), vol. III, p. 181.

51. Malebranche, *Réponse a une Dissertation de Mr. Arnauld contre un Eclaircissement du Traité de la Nature et de la Grâce* (1685), ed. André Robinet, O.C., VII, 485.

52. The eminent historian of science Pierre Duhem praises both his insights and his command of scientific methods in *La Loi du Choc des Corps d'après Malebranche* (Paris: Vrin, 1924) and *La Physique des successeurs de Descartes* (Paris: Vrin, 1934).

53. Berkeley, *Philosophical Commentaries*, ed. A. A. Luce (London: T. Nelson and Sons, 1944), p. 548.

54. Berkeley, *Dialogues*, II, in *The Works of George Berkeley, Bishop of Cloyne*, ed. A. A. Luce and T. E. Jessup, 9 vols. (London: T. Nelson, 1948), vol. II, p. 214.

55. Charles Peirce, *Collected Papers*, ed. Charles Hartshorne and Paul Weiss (Cambridge: Belknap Press, 1931–58), vol. VIII, p. 10.

56. Douglas Anderson and Peter S. Groff, "Peirce on Berkeley's Nominalistic Platonism," *American Catholic Philosophical Quarterly* 72, no. 2 (spring 1998): 165–78.

57. For Berkeley, there are no universal ideas but particular ones may constitute a universal meaning in and through their relations to other ideas. Berkeley, *A Treatise Concerning the Principles of Human Knowledge,* in *Works of George Berkeley,* vol. II, # 15, p. 32.

58. Berkeley, *Alciphron,* IV, 10, in *Works of George Berkeley,* vol. III, p. 154. Roman numeral refers to the dialogue, number to the section.

59. George Berkeley, *Principles of Human Knowledge,* ## 30–32, in *Works of George Berkeley,* vol. II, pp. 53–54.

60. Berkeley, *Three Dialogues,* in *Works of George Berkeley,* vol. II, p. 232

61. Berkeley, *Principles,* introduction, ## 20–21, in *Works of George Berkeley,* vol. II, pp. 37–38.

62. Berkeley, *Siris,* # 225, in *Works of George Berkeley,* vol. V, p. 107. Henceforth indicated by number.

63. Cf. Nicholas Everitt, "Quasi-Berkeleyan Idealism as Perspicuous Theism," *Faith and Philosophy* 14, no. 3 (July 1997): 353–77.

64. Lucien Lévy-Brühl, *La philosophie de Jacobi* (Paris, 1894), p. 23.

65. Friedrich Heinrich Jacobi, *Werke,* ed. Friedrich Roth and Friedrich Köppen (Leipzig: Gerhard Fleischer, 1815; reproduced by Wissenschaftliche Buchgesellschaft, Darmstadt, 1980), 6 vols. Henceforth abridged to *Werke* and volume. Trans. with introduction by George di Giovanni as *Edward Allwill's Collection of Letters* in Friedrich Heinrich Jacobi, *The Main Philosophical Writings and the Novel Allwill* (Montreal: McGill University Press, 1994), pp. 468, 476.

66. Jacobi, *Main Phil. Writings,* p. 187.

67. Jacobi, "Vorrede" (preface) in *Werke,* II, 50; *Main Phil. Writings,* pp. 558–59.

68. *Kant's Gesammelte Schriften,* vol. VIII, pp. 133–47.

69. George di Giovanni, Introduction to *Main Phil. Writings,* p. 85. This introduction is, in fact, the best monograph on Jacobi available in English.

70. Jacobi, *Allwill,* in *Main Phil. Writings,* p. 437.

71. Jacobi, *Werke,* III, 44; *Main Phil. Writings,* p. 519.

72. Jacobi, *Werke,* III, 44; *Main Phil. Writings,* p. 513. Cf. also di Giovanni, Introduction, pp. 114–15.

73. *David Hume,* in *Werke,* II, 27; *Main Phil. Writings,* p. 266.

74. *David Hume,* in *Werke,* II, vi; *Main Phil. Writings,* p. 256.

75. Feeling, the undifferentiated ground of consciousness, is not specified to any particular object. In it consciousness still remains in a state of pure immanence. How much all mental activity proceeds from it was brilliantly argued in Suzanne Langer's psychological study, *Mind: An Essay on Human Feeling,* vol. I (Baltimore: Johns Hopkins Press, 1967), and more recently in the neurophysiological study of Antonio Damasio, *The Feeling of What Happens* (New York: Harcourt, 1999).

76. Jacobi, "Vorrede," in *Werke,* II, 119–20; *Main Phil. Writings,* p. 588.

77. Jacobi, "Beylage" to *Spinoza Letters,* in *Werke,* IV/1, 210; *Main Phil. Writings,* p. 230.

78. Jacobi, "Vorrede," in *Werke,* II, 74; *Main Phil. Writings,* p. 56

79. Jacobi, *Werke,* IV/1, 237–28.

80. Georg Wilhelm Friederich Hegel, *Glauben und Wissen,* in *Werke,* Jubiläumausgabe, ed. H. Glockner (Stuttgart, 1927–39), vol. I, p. 286.

81. This point has been well argued by Peter Jonkers in "God or Nothing," in *Hegel-Jahrbuch 2002,* pp. 272–78.

82. Jacobi, *Werke,* III, 23; *Main Phil. Writings,* p. 509.

83. Jacobi, *Werke,* III, 48; *Main Phil. Writings,* p. 522.

84. Jacobi, *Werke,* III, 43; *Main Phil. Writings,* p. 519.

Chapter 10. Spiritual Continuity and Renewal

1. Letter of May 10, 1781, in *J. G. Hamanns Briefwechsel,* ed. W. Ziesemer (Wiesbaden: Insel Verlag, 1952).

2. Johann Georg Hamann, "Metakritik," in *Sämtliche Werke,* ed. Nadler in 6 vols. (Vienna, 1949–57), vol. III, pp. 281–89; "*Metakritik* on the Purism of Reason," trans. Kenneth Haynes in *What Is Enlightenment?* ed. James Schmidt (Berkeley: University of California Press, 1996), pp. 154–67. In that collection appears also Garrett Green's essay, "Modern Culture Comes of Age: Hamann versus Kant on the Root Metaphor of Enlightenment," pp. 291–305, The quote appears on p. 299.

3. David Hume, *Treatise of Human Nature,* bk. I, sec. 7.

4. The justification of symbols of the divine does not appear in the *Critique of Pure Reason* but in the *Prolegomena to Any Future Metaphysics* (1783) published two years later. Cf. *Kants Gesammelte Schriften* (Berlin: Akademie, 1902–1942), vol. IV, p. 358; trans. James W. Ellington (Indianapolis: Hacket, 1977), p. 98. In the *Critique of Judgment* Kant defined a symbol as an indirect presentation of a concept by means of an analogy between a sensible intuition and an object known intellectually. Thus he justified the link between analogy and symbol, which Butler and Hamann grasped intuitively.

5. *Ritter von Rosenkreuz letzte Willensmeinung über göttlichen und menschlichen Ursprung der Sprache* (1772), in *Werke,* III, 27.

6. Hamann, *Sokratische Denkwürdigkeiten,* in *Werke,* II, 57–82; trans. James C. O'Flaherty, *Hamann's Socratic Memorabilia* (Baltimore: Johns Hopkins University Press, 1967).

7. Michel de Certeau, *La fable mystique* (Paris: Gallimard, 1982).

8. Jeanne Guyon, *Spiritual Torrents,* in *A Short Method of Prayer and Spiritual Torrents,* trans. A. W. Marston (Sampson Low, 1875), chap. 9.

9. In a letter quoted by Jean-Robert Armogathe, *Le Quiétisme* (Paris: Presses Universitaires de France, 1973), p. 31.

10. François de Salignac de La Mothe-Fénelon, "Lettre à Louis XIV," in *Oeuvres* (Paris: Gallimard, La Pléiade, 1983), vol. I, p. 544.

11. Cf. his "Discours à l'Académie Française," in *Oeuvres,* I, p. 537.

12. Ronald Knox calls them "almost hysterical." Ronald Knox, *Enthusiasm: A Chapter in the History of Religion* (Oxford: Oxford University Press, 1950), p. 340.

13. Nicolas Malebranche, *Traité de l'Amour de Dieu et Lettres au P. Lamy* (1697), ed. André Robinet, O.C., XIV (1963), 23.

14. Cf. P. M. Masson, *La religion de Jean-Jacques Rousseau,* vol. II, *La "Profession de*

foi de Jean-Jacques" (Paris: Hachette, 1916); Max Wieser, *Der sentimentale Mensch gesehen aus der Welt holländischer und deutscher Mystiker im 18en Jahrhundert* (Gotha-Stuttgart: F. A. Perthes, 1924); Emilienne Naert, *Leibniz et la querelle du Pur Amour* (Paris: Vrin, 1959).

15. Heiko Oberman, preface, in Johann Arndt, *True Christianity,* trans. and intro. by Peter Erb (New York: Paulist Press, 1979), p. xi.

16. Cf. Wilhelm Koepp, *Johann Arndt: Eine Untersuchung über die Mystik im Luthertum* (Berlin, 1912). Peter Erb's introduction to his translation of *True Christianity* is excellent. Unfortunately that edition contains only bk. I and summaries of the other, more mystical ones.

17. Philipp Jacob Spener, *Die Heilige Schrift: Altes und Neues Testament,* vol. VI (*Romerbrief*), p. 155. On the inhabitation of Christ in Pietist theology, cf. Hans-Jürgen Schrader, "Le Christ dans le coeur de ses fidèles," in *Le Christ entre Orthodoxie et Lumières,* ed. Maria-Cristina Pitassi (Geneva: Droz, 1994).

18. August Hermann Francke, *Christus der Kern der Heiligen Schrift* (Halle, 1702), p. 428.

19. *Life and Character of Gerhard Tersteegen,* trans. Samuel Jackson (London: Black, Young and Young, 1834), entry November 4, 1742.

20. On the religious sources of Hölderlin's poetry, cf. Hans Urs von Balthasar, *Herrlichkeit,* vol. III/1, *Im Raum der Metaphysik* (Ensiedeln: Johannes Verlag, 1965) pp. 644–89; *The Glory of the Lord,* vol. V, trans. Oliver Davies, Andrew Louth et al. (San Franscisco: Ignatius Press, 1991) pp. 298–338.

21. I omit books III and IV written after his conversion to Catholicism in the style of the Counter-Reformation. In book V, added in later editions, Silesius resumes his earlier views. Had he written it earlier or did he consider his radical views compatible with Catholic doctrine? Cf. Leszek Kolakowski, *Chrétiens sans Eglise,* chap. 9, pp. 567–639.

22. Wherever available I have used Maria Shrady's elegant partial translation of Angelus Silesius, *The Cherubinic Wanderer* (New York: Paulist Press, 1986). In other cases I give my own prose translation or that of Maria Böhm, *Angelus Silesius' Cherubinischer Wandersmann: A Modern Reading with Selected Translations* (New York: Peter Lang, 1997).

23. Meister Eckhart, *Die deutschen Werke,* ed. Joseph Quint et al. (Stuttgart: Kohlhammer, 1938ff.), vol. I, pp. 69–70; Meister Eckhart, *Sermons and Treatises,* trans. M. O'C. Walshe (London: Watkins, 1979), vol. I, p. 284.

24. Jonathan Edwards, *A Treatise Concerning Religious Affections,* ed. John E. Smith, vol. 2 of *The Works of Jonathan Edwards* (New Haven: Yale University Press, 1959), p. 95.

25. John E. Smith, Introduction to *Religious Affections,* in *Works of Jonathan Edwards,* vol. II, p. 12.

26. Jonathan Edwards, "The Excellency of Christ," in *Works of Jonathan Edwards,* vol. XIX, *Sermons and Discources* (New Haven: Yale University Press, 2000).

27. On this epistemological issue I follow William Wainwright's essay, "Jonathan Edwards and the Sense of the Heart," *Faith and Philosophy* 7, no. 1 (January 1990): 43–62.

28. Smith, Introduction to *Religious Affections,* p. 42.

29. Czeslaw Milosz, *The Land of Ulro,* trans. Louis Iribarne (New York: Farrar Straus Giroux, 1984), p. 139.

30. Emanuel Swedenborg, *Arcana Coelestia* (# 3483), in 12 vols. (1749–56). All works have been translated (from Latin) into English. Two selections taken from the *Arcana* have recently been retranslated by George F. Dole, under the titles *Emanuel Swedenborg, The Universal Human and Soul-Body Interaction* (New York: Paulist Press, 1984), and *A Thoughtful Soul: Reflections from Swedenborg* (Westchester, Pa.: Chrysalis Books, 1995). The latter contains texts, topically arranged and selected from various works. I have followed Dole's modern translation wherever it was available and have preserved the standard numbering of the sections.

31. Signe Toksvig in her intellectual biography of Swedenborg traces the method of this spiritual exegesis to the sixteenth-century Calvinist Sebastian Castillio. Castillio writes: "Only the person who has in himself the illumination of the same spirit that gave the original revelation can see through the garment of the letter to the external message, the ever-living word hidden within." Signe Toksvig, *Emanuel Swedenborg: Scientist and Mystic* (New Haven: Yale University Press, 1948), p. 151.

32. Milosz, *Land of Ulro*, p. 139.

33. Ibid., p. 53.

34. Even Kant who parodied Swedenborg's visions in his *Dreams of a Ghost-Seeer* had three years earlier expressed his respect for the visionary's clairvoyant powers, which he did not question.

Conclusion

1. Albrecht Wellmer, *Critical Theory of Society* (New York: Seabury Press, 1974), p. 132.

2. Jürgen Habermas, *The Philosophical Discourse of Modernity* (Cambridge: MIT Press, 1987), p. 112.

3. Richard Rorty, *Essays on Heidegger and Others* (New York: Cambridge University Press, 1996), p. 171.

4. Rorty, *Essays on Heidegger*, p. 174. Cf. my essays, "Alternatives to the Cogito," *Review of Metaphysics* 40 (June 1987): 687–716, and "Postmodernity or Late Modernity? Ambiguities in Richard Rorty's Thought," *Review of Metaphysics* 47 (December 1993): 277–95.

5. Michel Foucault, *The Archeology of Knowledge,* trans. M. Sheridan Smith (New York: Harper and Row, 1976).

6. Emmet Kennedy, "Anticipations of Postmodernist Enlightenment Epistemology," in *The Postmodernist Critique of the Project of Enlightenment*, ed. Sven-Eric Liedman, in *Poznan Studies in the Philosophy of the Sciences and the Humanities,* vol. LVIII (1997), pp. 105–21. Peter Gay wrote that the Enlightenment was not an Age of Reason but a revolt against rationalism. *The Enlightenment: An Interpretation* (New York: Random House, 1967), vol. I, p. 141.

7. Karl Mannheim, *Ideology and Utopia* (1936), trans. Louis Wirth and Edward Shils (New York: Harcourt, Brace, and World, 1955), p. 219.

8. Alasdair MacIntyre, *Whose Justice? Which Rationality?* (South Bend, Ind.: Notre Dame University Press, 1988), p. 7.

Index